CRIMINAL LAW

CRIMINAL LAW

Fifth Edition

Timothy H. Jones, LLB, M Phil, PhD
Professor of Public Law, Swansea University

and

Michael G.A. Christie, MA, LLB
Former Lecturer in Private Law, University of Aberdeen

W. GREEN

THOMSON REUTERS

Published in 2012 by
W. Green, 21 Alva Street,Edinburgh EH2 4PS
Part of Thomson Reuters (Professional) UK Limited
(Registered in England & Wales,
Company No 1679046. Registered Office and
address for service: Aldgate House,
33 Aldgate High Street, London EC3N 1DL)

www.wgreen.co.uk

Typeset by LBJ Typesetting Ltd, Kingsclere
Printed and bound in Great Britain by CPI Group (UK) Ltd, Croydon

No natural forests were destroyed to make this product;
Only farmed timber was used and replanted

A CIP catalogue record for this book is available from the British Library

ISBN 978-0-414-01834-1

Thomson Reuters and the Thomson Reuters logo are
trademarks of Thomson Reuters.

PREFACE TO FIFTH EDITION

The present edition seeks to provide coverage of the changes in both statutory and common law over the past four years. It will be noticed that many more statutory offences have been dealt with than was the case in previous editions — this since the Scottish Parliament has been far from idle over the period. As before, statutes have been treated as if they were presently in force (no matter the de facto position). One exception to this "rule" has been made, however, since the abolition of common law offences under the Sexual Offences (Scotland) Act 2009 has been delayed, and it has been thought proper to retain coverage of such offences (as well as their statutory replacements) meantime. But it should not be thought that such offences will provide any guide to the interpretation of the 2009 statutory regime.

As ever we should wish to express our thanks to the whole editorial team at Greens — especially to Kirsty Price and Rebecca Standing – for their unfailing patience and encouragement.

An attempt has been made to state the law as of June 1, 2012.

CONTENTS

TABLE OF CASES

Table of Cases

Table of Cases

Table of Cases

Table of Cases

Table of Cases

Table of Cases

Table of Cases

Table of Cases

Table of Cases

TABLE OF UNITED KINGDOM STATUTES

TABLE OF STATUTES OF THE SCOTTISH PARLIAMENT

TABLE OF UNITED KINGDOM STATUTORY INSTRUMENTS

TABLE OF STATUTORY INSTRUMENTS OF THE SCOTTISH PARLIAMENT

TABLE OF CONVENTIONS AND TREATIES

CHAPTER 1

INTRODUCTION TO CRIMINAL LAW

WHAT IS CRIMINAL LAW?

The criminal law consists of a series of rules. These rules define what is not **1–01** permissible in social conduct according to certain moral principles or political policies. An example of a moral principle is that "injuring others in their persons or property is wrong". Accordingly, the criminal law includes such well-known crimes as theft, assault and rape. An example of a political policy which forms the basis of a criminal offence is that a licence must be purchased for a television receiver.

Public law

It is important to appreciate from the outset that criminal law forms part of **1–02** "public law", rather than "private law".[1] Private law (sometimes referred to as "civil law"[2]) is concerned with regulating disputes which do not directly involve the state. This is not to say that the state does not take an active interest in areas such as company law or family law. What it does mean is that governmental agencies are not directly on the side of one of the litigants: the state does not claim a direct interest in the outcome of a particular court case.

The same cannot be said of public law, which relates directly to the state in a **1–03** political and sovereign role. In a broad sense, public law is concerned with the structure of government, and the powers, duties and obligations of public officials and private citizens. Criminal law has a public law character. A crime constitutes an offence not just against an individual, but also against the state. The state must take a direct interest in protecting persons within its territory from conduct which has been declared to be, or accepted as, criminal. This feature is reflected in the fact that crimes are generally prosecuted in the name of the Crown on behalf of the community, rather than by privately retained lawyers, let alone aggrieved individuals (see below, para.2–58). Private prosecution indeed is highly exceptional in Scotland (see below, para.2–59). Thus it is that reports of serious criminal cases are cited as *"Her Majesty's Advocate v [name of the accused]"*. Her Majesty's Advocate refers to the chief Scottish law officer of the Crown (more commonly known as the "Lord Advocate"). In less serious cases, the prosecution will be recorded in the name of the local procurator fiscal, holding office under the Lord Advocate. It is these public officials and their deputes who are charged with the

---

[1] Erskine, *Institute*, IV, iv, 1, refers to "that part of our public law which relates to crimes".
[2] See, generally, P.H. Robinson, "The Criminal—Civil Distinction and the Utility of Desert" (1996) 76 B. U. L. Rev. 201.

task of conducting criminal prosecutions on behalf of the state. Unlike private law litigation, furthermore, where the aggrieved party (the "pursuer" in Scottish terminology) must instigate legal action against the "defender", the Crown, through its appointed representatives, can undertake the prosecution of a person accused of committing a crime, even if this is against the wishes of the victim (or "complainer").

THE PROPER SCOPE OF THE CRIMINAL LAW

1–04 A question which has long been the subject of debate among both criminal lawyers and philosophers is that of the proper scope of the criminal law. In particular, this debate has been concerned with the extent to which the criminal law should be used to enforce moral standards. A number of scholars have argued that society is permitted, and sometimes obliged, to enforce morality by means of the criminal law. The legal philosopher H.L.A. Hart identified two versions of this argument: the "conservative thesis" and the "disintegration thesis".[3] According to Hart, the conservative thesis stands for

> "the claim that society has the right to enforce its morality by law because the majority have the right to follow their own moral convictions that their moral environment is a thing of value to be defended from change."[4]

Proponents of the disintegration thesis value morality as, "the cement of society, the bond, or one of the bonds, without which men would not cohere in society."[5] It must be upheld in order to prevent social disintegration. In his book, *The Enforcement of Morals,* the principal advocate of the disintegration thesis, Lord Devlin, argued that

> "the law must protect . . . the institutions and the community of ideas, political and moral, without which people cannot live together. Society cannot ignore the morality of the individual any more than it can his loyalty; it flourishes on both and without either it dies."[6]

Writing more than two centuries earlier, the institutional writer Erskine had similarly argued that crimes should be penalised because they threatened to "loosen the bonds of society".[7]

1–05 In common parlance, the criminal law tends to be discussed in terms of serious crimes against the person (such as murder, rape and assault), and serious crimes against property (including theft, fire-raising and malicious mischief). Questions as to the proper scope of the criminal law do arise, even in relation to such long-recognised crimes. Recent issues before the Scottish courts have included the form of intention required for a murder resulting from fire-raising,[8] the applicability of

---

[3] H.L.A. Hart, "Social Solidarity and the Enforcement of Morality" (1967) 35 U. Chi. L. Rev. 1, drawing upon R. Dworkin, "Lord Devlin and the Enforcement of Morals" (1966) 75 Yale L.J. 986.
[4] Hart, "Social Solidarity and the Enforcement of Morality" (1967) 35 U. Chi. L. Rev. 1, 2.
[5] Hart, "Social Solidarity and the Enforcement of Morality" (1967) 35 U. Chi. L. Rev. 1.
[6] Lord Devlin, *The Enforcement of Morals* (London: Oxford University Press, 1965), p.22.
[7] Erskine, IV, iv, 2.
[8] *Petto v HM Advocate* [2011] HCJAC 80; 2011 S.L.T. 1043.

the crime of breach of the peace to domestic disputes[9] and whether it is competent to charge a company with culpable homicide.[10] However, the main focus of the "criminalisation" debate has tended to be elsewhere, involving those crimes intended to protect public morality, for example, "public indecency" (see below, Ch.12).[11]

Scotland would generally be regarded as having a highly moralistic criminal **1–06** law (at least in its origin[12]) but there are types of behaviour which, although generally regarded as immoral, have never been within its scope: for example, breach of contract. Thus, to say that the task of the criminal law is to uphold moral standards is not a sufficient answer to the question as to the proper scope of the criminal law. It merely raises the further issues of how much morality, and whose, the law should uphold. Lord Devlin appeared to concede as much, since he recognised the impossibility of setting theoretical limits on the power of the law to enforce morality. His solution was to apply the standard of the "reasonable" or "right-minded" person, "the man in the jury box", because "the moral judgment of society must be something about which any 12 [presumably 15 in Scotland] men or women drawn at random might after discussion be expected to be unanimous."[13]

The harm principle

A very different approach from that of Lord Devlin can be found in the philos- **1–07** ophy of liberalism. The most famous statement of the liberal approach to the role of the law in the maintenance of morality is that of the nineteenth-century philosopher, John Stuart Mill. He maintained

> "the only purpose for which power can be rightfully exercised over any member of a civilized community, against his will, is to prevent harm to others. His own good, either physical or moral, is not a sufficient warrant."[14]

An individual is only answerable to society for conduct "which concerns others".[15] Under the harm principle, therefore, the individual should be granted the maximum degree of liberty consistent with the rights of others. Thus one might say that an individual should be permitted to behave in a shamelessly indecent fashion, perhaps by showing an obscene film to a number of willing viewers, if no "harm" is caused.[16]

The harm principle has been developed further by Feinberg, who, as a further **1–08** justification for criminalisation, puts forward an "offense principle". This is based upon the necessity "to prevent serious offense to persons other than the actor".[17] His preferred version of the harm principle is:

---

[9] *Hatcher v Harrower* [2010] HCJAC 92; 2010 S.C.C.R. 903.

[10] *Transco Plc v HM Advocate (No.1),* 2004 J.C. 29.

[11] See *Webster v Dominick,* 2003 S.L.T. 975; 2003 S.C.C.R. 525.

[12] See, further, L. Farmer, "Narratives of Guilt and Innocence in Scottish Criminal Trials" (2000) J. R. 285, 294.

[13] Devlin, *The Enforcement of Morals* (1965), p.15.

[14] J.S. Mill, *On Liberty* (London: John W. Parker and Son, 1859), Ch.1, para.9.

[15] Mill, *On Liberty* (1859), Ch.1, para.9.

[16] See *Webster v Dominick,* 2003 S.C.C.R. 525, overruling *Watt v Annan,* 1978 J.C. 84; 1978 S.L.T. 198.

[17] J. Feinberg, *Harm to Others* (New York: Oxford University Press, 1985), p.26.

"It is always a good reason in support of penal legislation that it would probably be effective in preventing (eliminating, reducing) harm to persons other
than the actor (the one prohibited from acting) *and* there is probably no other
means that is equally effective at no greater cost to other values."

This reformulation emphasises a concern with the efficacy of utilising the criminal law.

1–09   The harm principle has been very influential among writers on the criminal law.
It captures the common feeling that the interests of the state should make accom-
modation for individual freedom. It also reflects the view that a primary function
of the criminal law is the prevention of harm.[18] This approach is very different
from that of the disintegration thesis, which asserts that the role of the law is to
protect the moral and political institutions of society, and the "community of
ideas" necessary for society to cohere (see above, para.1–04). From this perspective, it would be legitimate to criminalise indecent behaviour, even though no
"harm" has been caused to anyone, because someone who acts in that fashion (for
example, encouraging the patrons of a nightclub to expose their private parts in
return for free drinks[19]) could be regarded by the members of a jury as posing a
threat to society's moral fabric.

PUNISHMENT

1–10 The rules of the criminal law define crimes and can be distinguished from those
found in other branches of the law by the way in which it is sought to make them
effective. As is well understood, those who contravene the criminal law make
themselves liable to *punishment*. Indeed, so varied are the moral principles and
political policies (which inspire what is not permitted) that it is sometimes
suggested that punishment is *the* distinctive characteristic which all crimes share.
This, however, leads to the question: "What is punishment?" In times past, the
answer would not have proved too difficult—at least in practical terms. When
those found to be contraveners of the criminal law were regularly hanged,
beheaded, mutilated, branded, whipped or otherwise corporally abused, then
punishment clearly entailed the infliction of some kind of physical suffering.[20]
But from the nineteenth century onwards, such physical suffering has increasingly
come to be regarded as unsuitable in a developed western society. Today, therefore, the principal sanctions for criminal behaviour are expressed as terms of
imprisonment or monetary penalties (fines). There are more anodyne alternatives
available too—which include community payback orders[21] and awards of
compensation to victims. Since awards of compensation (damages) can also be
made under quite different branches of the law (for example, for failing to honour
an agreement under the law of contract, or injuring someone by carelessness
under the law of delict), and civil penalties are not unknown either (see below,

---

[18] See, more generally, P.H. Robinson, "A Theory of Justification: Societal Harm as a Prerequisite for
Criminal Liability" (1975) 23 U.C.L.A. L. Rev. 266.
[19] Compare the facts at issue in *Geddes v Dickson,* 2001 J.C. 69; 2000 S.C.C.R. 1007, noting the
impact of *Webster v Dominick,* 2003 S.C.C.R. 525.
[20] See D. Hume, *Commentaries,* ii, p.488.
[21] See the Criminal Procedure (Scotland) Act 1995 ss.227A–227ZN as inserted by the Criminal
Justice and Licensing (Scotland) Act 2010 (asp 13) s.14(1).

para.2–18), one must endeavour to be much more precise in order to appreciate why punishment is so closely associated with the criminal law.

This point was taken up by the American scholar, Henry M. Hart. In a famous **1–11** article,[22] he stated that the differentiating feature of the criminal law is that only criminal sanctions (that is, punishments) are both accompanied and justified by the condemnation of the community (that is, by a finding of guilt, which is referred to as "conviction"). Accordingly, one could say that it is this feature of the criminal law which distinguishes it from the civil law of contract and delict. The essential quality of punishment for a crime is to be found in the criminal conviction itself. In practice, a requirement to pay damages for breach of contract, or for the consequences of a negligent act, could have a punitive impact as great as the imposition of a fine in a criminal court. The distinctive character of the judgment of a criminal court is to be found in its informational and symbolic function: the formal declaration that the accused has done wrong.[23] Indeed, Hart's preferred definition of a crime was

> "conduct which, if duly shown to have taken place, will incur a formal and solemn pronouncement of the moral condemnation of the community."[24]

This definition, however, is only really persuasive in relation to the more serious **1–12** crimes long recognised by the common law. In modern times, the ambit of the criminal law has expanded enormously. Of course, Henry M. Hart was aware of this development. He remarked upon the unfortunate tendency of modern criminal statutes to punish individuals whose conduct is "morally neutral". Hart considered this to be an abuse, because "a criminal conviction carries with it an ineradicable connotation of moral condemnation and personal guilt."[25] Nevertheless, the problem with Hart's definition remains that it is difficult to maintain that public condemnation always inheres in a criminal conviction. For example, it would be unrealistic to suggest that every individual convicted of careless driving is subject to denunciation by his community. However, this problem is as much one of the adequacy or suitability of a particular sanction, or of the appropriateness of bringing the conduct in question within the scope of the criminal law.[26] The notion of punishment remains central to any plausible and self-contained account of the criminal law; and punishment cannot be imposed ithout conviction by a competent court.

PRINCIPLES OF CRIMINAL RESPONSIBILITY

Conviction certainly entails more than a mere finding that, e.g. "A killed B". This **1–13** in itself is a legally neutral statement. To justify punishment, the stage has to be attained where it is possible to conclude, e.g. that "A is guilty of murdering B".

---

[22] H.M. Hart, "The Aims of the Criminal Law" (1958) 23 Law and Contemp. Prob. 401.

[23] See A.P. Simester, J.R. Spencer, G.R. Sullivan and G.J. Virgo, *Simester and Sullivan's Criminal Law: Theory and Doctrine,* 4th edn (Oxford: Hart, 2010), pp.4–5.

[24] Hart, "The Aims of the Criminal Law" (1958) 23 Law and Contemp. Prob. 401, 405.

[25] Hart, "The Aims of the Criminal Law" (1958) 23 Law and Contemp. Prob. 401, 424.

[26] There have been suggestions that minor violations of the criminal law should be dealt with separately; see, e.g. K. Mann, "Punitive Civil Sanctions: The Middle Ground Between Civil and Criminal Law" (1992) 101 Yale L. J. 1795.

Clearly that stage could not be reached in law if A was an armed police officer who had killed B, a suicide bomber, about to detonate the explosives he was carrying. The prime function of the criminal law is that of articulating the circumstances under which it is justifiable to hold a person punishable for his conduct. This is a two-stage process.

1–14 First, there must be examination of what in general will have to be shown for conviction to be justified, no matter which particular crime is involved. This concerns what are known as the principles of criminal responsibility. Some basic principles of that sort are considered as part of Ch.2, while the better known and more traditional ones are dealt with in Ch.3 (actus reus and mens rea), Ch.4 (voluntariness) and Ch.5 (causation). These principles are regarded as essential moral and legal safeguards to ensure that only those who deserve it are in fact convicted and made liable to punishment. If occasionally adherence to these allows a few, possibly "guilty" persons to escape condemnation, this tends to be regarded as an acceptable price to pay. Different legal systems, however, display varied approaches to the acceptability of allowing such escapes from justice. Scottish criminal law, in particular, is currently in a phase of viewing with suspicion the suggestion that such principles should be weighted in favour of accused persons—as readers will doubtless conclude for themselves from their own studies and observations. But where derogations from, or adjustments to, these principles seem to have occurred, it will clearly be necessary to assert some cogent, countervailing justifications. That having been stated, it is also necessary to declare that some of the principles espoused by academic writers and others are controversial—in terms of their interpretation and scope, as well as their applicability (see, in particular, the discussion of the concept of voluntariness in Ch.4). A fair amount of space, therefore, has been reserved for their discussion. As has been aptly written: "We must not be naive about the subtlety with which the law is capable of reflecting fine moral judgments and distinctions."[27]

1–15 Secondly, there must be an examination of what precisely has been made or declared punishable under Scots law. The principles referred to in the previous paragraph do not provide any guide to the individual acts and omissions that are not permitted under a particular system of law. Although there may be a basic core of crimes (nominally, at least) common to most legal systems, the totality of criminal acts and omissions is usually unique to a particular country or society. Chapters 9 to 12 are, therefore, devoted to a detailed study of selected acts and omissions proscribed under the law of Scotland. Unless plainly stated to the contrary, what is discussed there has no necessary application to the United Kingdom as a whole, or to any other jurisdiction.

AIMS OF THE CRIMINAL LAW

1–16 The aims of the criminal law are very much those of its central characteristic—namely, punishment. The prevailing theoretical approaches to the justification of punishment are retributivism and utilitarianism. Retributivism is founded on the idea that the criminal, because of the wrongdoing, deserves punishment. It is an approach which looks back in time to the commission of the crime in question.

---

[27] N. Lacey, *State Punishment: Political Principles and Community Values* (London: Routledge, 1988), p.71.

Utilitarianism, on the other hand, looks forward to the consequences of imposing punishment. The infliction of punishment upon the wrongdoer is justified because it serves a useful purpose: its imposition will result in benefits to society. In practice, the legal system tends to reflect aspects of both approaches. Criteria derived from both theories are to be found in the most commonly articulated reasons for the imposition of punishment.

Deterrence

The aim of punishment most closely associated with utilitarianism is deter- **1–17** rence. Unlike the branches of the civil law, which are expressed in terms of conditional causes and effects (for example, if one does not make a will, then one's property on death will devolve in certain predetermined ways), the intention of the criminal law is to *prevent* persons acting (or, sometimes, omitting to act) in particular ways. One could envisage this being promoted by a system of incentives and rewards, such as lower insurance premiums for drivers who avoid committing motoring offences. However, this would be regarded as too fragile a method of preventing harmful, injurious, destructive or antisocial behaviour; and, in practice, criminal justice systems rely on punishment. It would be naive indeed to imagine that the mere threat of punishment could entirely eradicate the sorts of behaviour which have been proscribed by the criminal law. The most that can be hoped for is that the threat will exercise sufficient psychological restraint over the *majority* of the population. The threat itself should be sufficient to deter. For those who were not in fact deterred, punishment within the parameters imposed by the law must actually be imposed with the object of personal deterrence for the future. Publicity for the punishments imposed might also be important in helping to restrain those still wavering on the brink of criminal conduct.

Retribution

Of course, if deterrence were the only aim, then the maximum possible penal- **1–18** ties would always seem justified, whenever there was an opportunity to impose punishment in fact.[28] This might well be effective in preventing the individuals who were sentenced from committing further crimes, particularly if life imprisonment or capital punishment were to be meted out to them. However, this policy would be counter-productive as far as the rest of society was concerned, if that punishment was not seen to be proportionate to what the individual had actually done. Not only, therefore, should a sentence after conviction aim to deter (both personally and generally); it should also aim to be "just desserts"[29] for what has been done, after all the circumstances have been taken into consideration. This principle of just desserts should not be confused with the biblical enjoinment of

---

[28] Indeed, it is a familiar criticism of utilitarianism that the punishment of the innocent could be justified in the interests of deterrence. The retributivist has to recognise, however, that any system of criminal justice runs the risk of convicting the innocent. This is why appeals are allowed and there is the opportunity for reconsideration afforded by the Scottish Criminal Cases Review Commission. History shows that no system is foolproof.

[29] The classic account remains A. von Hirsch, *Doing Justice* (Boston: North Eastern University Press, 1976). The approach is developed in A. von Hirsch, *Past or Future Crimes. Deservedness and Dangerousness in the Sentencing of Criminals* (New Brunswick, N.J.: Rutgers University Press, 1985) and *Censure and Sanctions* (New York: Oxford University Press, 1991).

an eye for an eye and a tooth for a tooth. Although its advocates do sometimes use it to argue that more punishment than is applied currently can be justified, modern Scots law has departed from corporal punishments. Further, it is clearly impossible to order the rape of a convicted rapist, or take property from a convicted, but destitute thief.[30] Judges are simply required to do the best they can in the way of proportionality, given the circumstances of the offender, the nature of the crime, and what the law will allow. One might think that a victim's views would be relevant to consideration of sentence under this heading, but Scots law has not in the past favoured such an approach.[31]

Reformation

1–19   The modern criminal law may also aim to reform or rehabilitate. It is unlikely that the primary punishments (prison or fines) will have any such effect. In particular, an enlightened prison regime is currently the exception rather than the rule in Scotland. However, alternative "punishments" (depending on the significance one cares to give to that term), such as community payback orders, do seem to contemplate more than deterrence or retribution (often, one might add, to the dismay of the victims of the crimes in question).

Public protection

1–20   The notion of deterrence implies that an offender, or a potential offender, will be capable of exercising rational judgment and can be deterred by the threat of punishment from infringing the criminal law. Where this is clearly not so, then measures may have to be taken to protect others from the future conduct of that sort of convicted person—which may entail incarceration, or other restraint, far beyond the requirements of simple deterrence or retribution. When mental disorder is involved, then the same principle applies—although one might not wish (or indeed have) to register a conviction in such a case. Scots law certainly appears to adhere to these particular views (see Ch.4, following).

CRIMINAL PROCEDURE

1–21 The criminal law would be quite ineffective in pursuing its aims unless there were police to detect and deter the commission of crimes, prosecutors to conduct cases against suspected persons, courts to assess the evidence for and against such suspects, the whole panoply of prisons, social work agencies (for community payback orders) and so on. In brief, criminal law requires complementary procedural devices. The law of criminal procedure is, however, generally beyond the scope of this book.[32]

---

[30] This was an issue which taxed I. Kant, *The Philosophy of Law. An Exposition of the Fundamental Principles of Jurisprudence as the Science of Right,* translation by W. Hastie (Edinburgh: T. and T. Clark, 1887), pp.243–244.

[31] *HM Advocate v McKenzie*, 1990 J.C. 62; 1990 S.L.T. 28 but note the impact of the Criminal Justice (Scotland) Act 2003, which makes provision for the use of "victim statements" in the sentencing process.

[32] See *Renton and Brown's Criminal Procedure According to the Law of Scotland*, 6th edn (Edinburgh: W. Green).

CRIMINAL EVIDENCE

The success of criminal prosecutions (on which the efficiency of the law is often **1–22** seen to depend) and the procurement of fair dealing for suspected persons are predicated on the sort of evidence that can be led before a court of law. Again, there are detailed rules, and principles, which operate here; but the law of criminal evidence is generally also beyond the scope of this book.[33]

---

[33] See F. Raitt, *Evidence—Principles, Policy and Practice,* 4th edn (Edinburgh: W. Green, 2008); F. Davidson, *Evidence* (Edinburgh: W. Green, 2007).

CHAPTER 2

NATURE AND SOURCES OF SCOTS CRIMINAL LAW

General

2–01   Unlike many European countries, e.g. France, Germany, and the United States of America (both at federal and individual state levels), there is no criminal code in Scotland.[1] This means that there is no convenient place where any *official* list or description of Scottish crimes can be found. Equally there is no authorised account of the principles which govern the operation of the criminal law. It follows that this area of the law is less certain (but more flexible) in Scotland than may be the case elsewhere. Whether this is an advantageous situation will often depend on the perspective—i.e. whether one views the matter from the point of view of the accused or the prosecutor.

2–02   Of course, the absence of a code does not make it impossible to give a perfectly intelligible and pragmatic account of Scots criminal law.[2] Both principles and crime descriptions appear, for example, in modern textbooks (such as this one) and have been compiled from authoritative sources. As textbooks themselves are not normally recognised as being in any way authoritative, it is necessary to appreciate what are the true legal sources on which their authors have relied. These sources must invariably be checked too before any legal opinion based on textbook or periodical literature is ventured. Although legal sources may be described as a constant, interpretation of what they are found to contain is a very real variable of which careful account must be taken.

---

[1] Dissatisfaction with this state of affairs has led a group of Scottish law professors to draft an unofficial code. The text of that code ("A Draft Criminal Code for Scotland") together with commentary was published under the auspices of the Scottish Law Commission in September 2003. For an account by one of the code's authors of some of the deficiencies she perceives in the existing Scots "common law" (see below, paras 2–03 to 2–09), see Pamela R. Ferguson, "Codifying Criminal Law (1): A Critique of Scots Common Law" [2004] Crim. L.R. 49: the same author also compares the Draft Criminal Code for Scotland with its English counterpart in "Codifying Criminal Law (2): The Scots and English Draft Codes Compared" [2004] Crim. L.R. 105. For some critical analysis of a specific part of the Scots Draft Criminal Code, see Jennifer Temkin, "A New Law on Sexual Offences for Scotland: A Comment on the Draft Criminal Code" (2006) J.R. 29; and for some acknowledgment of the usefulness of the draft code, see Scottish Law Commission, *Report on Rape and Other Sexual Offences* (The Stationery Office, 2007), Scot. Law Com. No.209, para.1.9, and see also the opinion of Lord Justice Clerk (Gill) in *Petto v HM Advocate* [2011] HCJAC 80; 2011 S.L.T. 1043, para.21.

[2] See below, Ch.14.

SOURCES—THE COMMON LAW

Traditionally, rules pertaining to the "common law" are said to be those of such **2–03** long standing that their origins cannot be traced. Such rules are often described as "consuetudinary", i.e. customary. Alternatively, if a rule does in fact have a clear origin, it is still reckoned as a common law one if it has no *legislative* foundation. More practically, however, it is the criminal law expounded by judges of the superior criminal courts in actual proceedings before them which lawyers are wont to refer to as "common law." The superior criminal courts in Scotland for this purpose are the High Court of Justiciary as a trial court and the High Court of Justiciary as an appeal court (in the widest sense).[3] Since 1999, decisions of the Judicial Committee of the Privy Council,[4] and, since 2009, decisions of the Supreme Court of the United Kingdom[5] on "compatability or devolution issues"[6] referred or appealed to them[7] must be included[8] where such issues are concerned with matters affecting the common law—as, for example, where claims should be made that the Lord Advocate has undertaken (or proposes to undertake) the prosecution of a common law crime which allegedly does not conform to applicable rights under the European Convention on Human Rights.[9]

The High Court of Justiciary was altered to more or less its modern form in **2–04** 1672,[10] but its authenticated history can be traced for many centuries prior to that. To establish any part of the common law through judicial decisions from earliest times down to the present would thus be a mammoth task involving (inter alia) painstaking research in the records of the Court as these are preserved in the National Records of Scotland in Edinburgh. In practice then, a simpler route has evolved.

Professor (sometimes "Baron") David Hume made a study of what might be **2–05** gleaned from High Court decisions down to 1797. With some (minor) additions of his own, he was thus able to deduce and publish an account of the common law of

---

[3] See *Jessop v Stevenson*, 1988 J.C. 17 at 20, final para.; *Elliott v HM Advocate*, 1995 S.L.T. 612, Lord Justice-Clerk Ross at 615K–L.

[4] See the Scotland Act 1998 s.98 Sch.6 Pt II in its un-amended form.

[5] See the Constitutional Reform Act 2005 Pt 3 (especially ss.23 and 40(4)(b), as also Sch.9 Pt 2 (especially paras 93, 103 and 106). These provisions transfer the appropriate jurisdiction from the Judicial Committee of the Privy Council to the Supreme Court of the United Kingdom, and came into force on October 1, 2009: see The Constitutional Reform Act 2005 (Commencement No. 11) Order 2009 (SI 2009/1604) art.2(a),(d).

[6] See below, para.2–13.

[7] See the Scotland Act 1998 s.98 para. 1 (as amended by the Scotland Act 2012 s.36(4)), and Sch.6 paras 9, 11, 13, 33 and 34—noting that these paras (other than 9) were amended by the Constitutional Reform Act 2005 Sch.9 paras 103(5), (8) and 106(4), (5) such that a reference to the "Supreme Court" was in each case substituted for that of the "Judicial Committee".

[8] A past determination made by the Supreme Court of the United Kingdom on such an issue is not binding on that Court itself when it considers a similar issue in the future, but is binding in all other legal proceedings: see the Constitutional Reform Act 2005 s.41(3) and (4)(b). (For the law previously pertaining to the Judicial Committee of the Privy Council, see the Scotland Act 1998 s.103(1); s.103 was repealed by the Constitutional Reform Act 2005 Sch.18 Pt 5.)

[9] Cf. *Smith v Donnelly*, 2002 J.C. 65; 2001 S.L.T. 1007, where a devolution (now a compability issue was raised on the basis that the common law offence of breach of the peace was too vaguely defined to conform with art.7 of the European Convention on Human Rights: an appeal against the decision of the Scottish Appeal Court to the Judicial Committee of the Privy Council does not seem to have been attempted—although such an appeal would have been competent, with the appropriate leave.

[10] See the Scots Act c.40 in A.P.S., VIII, 80 at 87–88.

Scotland pertaining to criminal matters. Two new editions were produced by him which updated the common law to 1819 and 1829. He died in 1838, but a prominent advocate (Benjamin R. Bell) republished the 1829 edition together with updating notes of his own (drawn from High Court decisions) in 1844. This is invariably, though not quite accurately, referred to as the fourth edition of Hume's *Commentaries*. This work has for many decades been accorded authoritative status. Whenever a question relating to the common law of crimes is at issue, the starting point for Scottish lawyers (and sometimes the end point too) is any statement Hume might have made on the matter. Occasionally, judges of the High Court have disagreed with his pronouncements,[11] but more often than not, they have treated his writings with the utmost deference.[12] Hume's *Commentaries* are, therefore, much more than a mere textbook. They are regarded as an important *source* of the common law of crimes at the time they were written, and indeed as the initial point for subsequent research into the present state of that common law.

2–06   It is necessary to establish an initial point for research since the common law is constantly being developed by High Court judges in actual criminal proceedings before them. So long as there is a common law of crimes in Scotland, this evolutionary process will continue. That process applies to the definitions of existing crimes, defences to those crimes, evidential and procedural matters, and even to principles. The notion of flexible development is simply inseparable from the notion of common law, in so far as Scots criminal law is concerned. Nor is such development of the law necessarily incompatible with the European Convention on Human Rights (in so far as the Convention rights have been incorporated within domestic law by virtue of the Human Rights Act 1998) provided that that development remains within reasonable and foreseeable bounds.[13]

2–07   There are some other text-writings which judges of the High Court have looked upon with something of the same favour accorded to Hume. Foremost among these is Archibald Alison's *Principles of the Criminal Law of Scotland*, published in 1832. Although this work relies heavily on Hume's earlier text, it nevertheless

> "draws freely on [Alison's] own experience as an advocate-depute [*i.e.* criminal prosecutor] and quotes over 1,000 cases in which he was personally engaged and of which there was and is no other published report."[14]

It is also possible that J. H. A. Macdonald's *Practical Treatise on the Criminal Law of Scotland* (latest edition 1948) may continue to enjoy some particular

---

[11] See e.g. *John Smith* (1838) 2 Swin. 28; *S v HM Advocate*, 1989 S.L.T. 469; *Lord Advocate's Reference (No.1 of 2001)*, 2002 S.L.T. 466; 2002 S.C.C.R 435.

[12] See, e.g. *Thomson v HM Advocate*, 1983 J.C. 69; 1983 S.L.T. 682; *Khaliq v HM Advocate*, 1984 J.C. 23; 1984 S.L.T. 137; *Drury v HM Advocate*, 2001 S.L.T. 1013; 2001 S.C.C.R. 583.

[13] See, e.g. *SW v United Kingdom; CR v United Kingdom* (1996) 21 E.H.R.R. 363, especially at 398–399, paras 35/33 and 36/34; see also *HM Advocate v H*, 2002 S.L.T. 1380, per Lord Maclean at 1381, para.5, and *Lucas v United Kingdom* (2003) 37 E.H.R.R. (CD) 86—the judgment in which being conveniently set out at 2004 S.C.C.R. at 377F–383C. Reference should also be made to Ch.14.

[14] Sheriff J. Irvine Smith at p.vii of his introduction to the 1989 reprint of A. Alison, *Alison's Principles of the Criminal Law of Scotland* (London: Butterworth, 1989).

authority over and above its status as an important text-book of the nineteenth and twentieth centuries.[15]

No text-writings, other than those mentioned above, have been regarded as **2–08** sources of criminal common law. For example, the outstanding work of scholarship written in the twentieth century on Scots criminal law, Gordon's *Criminal Law*,[16] contains much lucid, influential and persuasive writing on the subject; but the author's opinions and deductions have very rarely been preferred to those of Hume, Alison and Macdonald.[17]

The present common law, then, consists of the deductions, conclusions and **2–09** opinions of Hume, Alison and Macdonald together with such alterations, additions and amendments as have been made to date by appropriate courts[18] in particular criminal proceedings before them. Since the early nineteenth century, such proceedings have been published in a variety of different law reports (see below, Appendix B), and these provide the most important modern source of the common law.

Sources—Legislation

Legislation refers to technically written rules promulgated in a predefined way at **2–10** a particular point in time by a person or body recognised as having the authority to do so. Such rules differ from those of the common law in that they are not subject to similar development—i.e. they cannot be added to or altered by judges in actual criminal proceedings before them. They may only be enlarged or amended by subsequent acts of legislation. Of course, judges can interpret the words of such rules. Indeed they must do this if the arid generalisations of legislation are to be made applicable to (and thus decisive of) actual criminal cases. If such interpretations are made by judges of the High Court of Justiciary, then such decisions make law in a very real sense. The interpretations then become part of the legislative rule itself. But it is not the case that such interpretations would ever be spoken of as forming part of the common law. Common law and legislation thus remain separate sources of the criminal law; but, although the common law can have no effect on existing legislation, the converse is not true. Legislative rules can radically alter portions of the common law—as can be illustrated by reference to the Sexual Offences (Scotland) Act 2009 (asp 9) which contains provisions replacing many (if not most) of the relevant common law rules.[19]

---

[15] Cf. the opinion of Lord Cameron in *Watt v Annan*, 1978 J.C. 84 at 88 to 89, and that of Lord Justice-Clerk Gill in *Webster v Dominick*, 2005 1 J.C. 65 at 78, para.44. Cf. also *Drury v HM Advocate*, 2001 S.L.T. 1013, where Macdonald's account of murder was considered to be incomplete, if not erroneous.

[16] G.H. Gordon, *Criminal Law* (Edinburgh: W. Green, 1968). The current edition is the third, Vol.1 (2000), Vol.2 (2001), to which there is a supplement (2005); a new fourth edition, by James Chalmers and Fiona Leverick is now in preparation and should be published in 2014.

[17] See, e.g. *Smart v HM Advocate*, 1975 J.C. 30; *Roberts v Hamilton*, 1989 J.C. 91; *Scott v HM Advocate*, 1995 S.C.C.R. 760. Although the trial judge, Lord Osborne, referred to academic writings as part of the reason for the directions he gave the jury in *Jamieson v HM Advocate*, 1994 S.L.T. 537 at 539H, those writings were entirely ignored by the Appeal Court in deciding that what he had said amounted to a misdirection in law.

[18] See above, para.2–03.

[19] See, e.g. below, paras 9–24, 9–79 and 9–91.

Parliamentary legislation

2–11   The supreme source of criminal legislation in Scotland is Parliament. Today, there are two parliaments to consider—the United Kingdom Parliament in London (hereafter referred to as "Parliament", for convenience), and the Scottish Parliament in Edinburgh[20]: the former of these enjoys absolute sovereignty over the whole of the United Kingdom, whilst the latter is able to legislate only for Scotland and within parameters set for it by Parliament under the Scotland Act 1998 and the Scotland Act 2012.[21]

Parliament may enact what it pleases; and a great deal of criminal law for the United Kingdom, and for Scotland in particular, has been produced in this way.[22] Primary legislation[23] enacted by Parliament is referred to as an "Act of Parliament" or a "Statute". So absolute is Parliament's sovereignty that it is possible (although unlikely) for it to enact legislation which is not compatible with the rights and fundamental freedoms of the European Convention on Human Rights, as these rights and freedoms (known as "Convention rights") have been brought within the law of the United Kingdom by the Human Rights Act 1998[24]: should this happen, and the legislation cannot be interpreted so as to conform with Convention rights, the validity and enforceability of that legislation is unaffected—and the most which can be done by courts is to issue a "declaration of incompatibility".[25] The position of the Scottish Parliament is, however, somewhat different, in that its powers have been devolved from the sovereign United Kingdom Parliament.

The Scottish Parliament

2–12   The Scottish Parliament, which met for the first time in 1999, has the authority to make laws known as "Acts of the Scottish Parliament".[26] Such Acts must, however, conform to the "legislative competence" set for it under the 1998 Act: in particular, it must not enact laws which would apply outwith Scotland,[27] relate to reserved matters,[28] or be incompatible with any of the Convention rights (as set

---

[20] The Scottish Parliament must not be confused with the old Scots Parliament which legislated for Scotland until disbanded under the terms of the Union with England Treaty in 1707: see A.P.S., XI, 406 et seq. Legislation of the old Scots Parliament was not set aside in 1707; but that legislation has gradually been removed or radically altered by various "Statute Law Revision" or "Statute Law Repeals" Acts of Parliament. Enactments of the old Scots Parliament are now of little importance to the criminal law.

[21] Hereafter, in this Chapter, referred to as the "1998 Act".

[22] Thus, e.g. all the law on offences relating to road traffic matters and prohibited drugs has hitherto been enacted by or under the authority of Parliament.

[23] As opposed to "delegated or subordinate" legislation: see below, para.2–14.

[24] See s.1 and Sch.1 (both as amended by art.2 of the Human Rights Act 1998 (Amendment) Order 2004 (SI 2004/1574)) of the Human Rights Act 1998.

[25] See the Human Rights Act 1998 ss.3 and 4: not all courts have this power—see s.4(5) and *Smith v Scott* [2007] CSIH 9; 2007 S.L.T. 137 (a decision by three judges, of the Court of Session, constituting the Registration Appeal Court). See also s.10 of that 1998 Act. (It should be noted that s.4(5) is amended by the Mental Capacity Act 2005 Sch.6 para.43, by the Constitutional Reform Act 2005 Sch.9 para.66, and by the Armed Forces Act 2006 Sch.16 para.156.)

[26] See the 1998 Act s.28(1). For matters of interpretation, and technical issues, relating to Acts of the Scottish Parliament, see the Interpretation and Legislative Reform (Scotland) Act 2010 (asp 10).

[27] As defined in s.126(1) of the 1998 Act; and see s.29(2)(a).

[28] As set out in Sch.5 of the 1998 Act—which include matters and offences relating to misuse of drugs, firearms (as amended relative to air weapons by the Scotland Act 2012 s.10), official secrets, road traffic, and abortion (see Sch.5 Pt II ss.B1, B4 and B8, E1and J1: and see s.29(2)(b)). See also amendments made by the Scotland Act 2012 ss.19–22.

out in the Human Rights Act 1998) or with EU law.[29] Any Act which exceeds the Scottish Parliament's legislative competence is simply not law.[30] Even where matters do fall within the legislative competence of the Scottish Parliament, the United Kingdom Parliament retains over-all power of enactment, thus maintaining its absolute sovereignty.[31] Scottish criminal law is, however, devolved to the Scottish Parliament, and it may thus legislate for Scotland relative to criminal offences, jurisdiction, evidence, procedure, penalties and the treatment of offenders.[32] The offices of the chief Scottish prosecutors—i.e. the offices of the Lord Advocate (sometimes referred to as "Her Majesty's Advocate") and Solicitor General for Scotland—are now offices within the "Scottish Government"; and all members of the Scottish Government are collectively known as the "Scottish Ministers".[33] It follows, therefore, that most functions to be performed in Scotland by Ministers of the Crown under United Kingdom Parliamentary legislation (i.e. legislation enacted prior to the commencement of the 1998 Act) will now be performed in Scotland by the Scottish Ministers.[34]

Compatibility and devolution issues

Issues relating to the competence of the Scottish Parliament to enact particular **2–13** laws, or to the way in which members of the Scottish Government (in particular, the chief prosecutors or law officers) carry out or propose to carry out their functions, may arise before or be referred to the courts. These are generally known as "compatibility or devolution issues". For the purposes of this book, the most important of these issues concern the following: whether an Act of the Scottish Parliament falls within that Parliament's legislative competence[35]; whether the purported or proposed exercise of a function by a member of the Scottish Government (in particular by the Lord Advocate[36] in undertaking criminal proceedings against a person for a particular crime) is incompatible with any of the relevant rights and fundamental freedoms of the European Convention on Human Rights[37]; and, whether the failure by a member of the Scottish Government

---

[29] See s.29(2)(d) of the 1998 Act, as modified by the Treaty of Lisbon (Changes in Terminology) Order 2011 (SI 2011/1043) art.6(2).

[30] 1998 Act s.29(1); e.g. *Cameron v Cottam* [2012] HCJAC 19; 2012 S.L.T. 173.

[31] See s.28(7) of the 1998 Act.

[32] See s.126(5) of the 1998 Act: Sch.5 must be consulted, however, for specific matters which are reserved to Parliament.

[33] See s.44 (1), (2) of the 1998 Act, as amended by the Scotland Act 2012 s.12.

[34] See s.53 of the 1998 Act.

[35] This is important since if any provision of an Act is not within the Scottish Parliament's legislative competence, that Act cannot be treated as law: s.29(1) of the 1998 Act. See, e.g. *Cameron v Cottam* [2012] HCJAC 19; 2012 S.L.T. 173.

[36] This reference includes any person (such as a procurator fiscal) deriving authority from the Lord Advocate, but not (unusually) if such a person is at the relevant time performing a statutory duty ex officio where he neither acts on behalf nor comes within the responsibility of the Lord Advocate: see *Goatley v HM Advocate* [2006] HCJAC 55; 2007 S.L.T. 14, Opinion of the Court, para.15, at 19J–L (relative to the Crown Agent).

[37] This refers to those rights and freedoms (the Convention rights) brought into United Kingdom law by the Human Rights Act 1998. It should also be noted that under s.57(2) of the Scotland Act 1998, members of the Scottish Government (including, of course, the Lord Advocate and Solicitor General for Scotland) have no power to do any act in so far as that act is incompatible with any Convention right or with EU law: see, e.g. *Stevens v HM Advocate*, 2002 S.L.T. 1249, Lady Paton at 1252K to 1253B, paras 18-20; see also *HM Advocate v H*, 2002 S.L.T. 1380, and cf. *Dickson v HM Advocate* [2007] HCJAC 65; 2008 S.L.T. 12 (court of five judges).

(in particular the Lord Advocate) to act is incompatible with any of these rights and freedoms.[38] Such issues may arise, of course, before any Scottish criminal court; but JP courts, Sheriff Courts and Trial Courts of the High Court[39] may refer such issues to the High Court of Justiciary (sitting as a non-trial court)[40] for resolution there: and, indeed, if such an issue arises in proceedings before a bench of two or more judges of the High Court, that Court may choose to refer the determination of the issue to the Supreme Court of the United Kingdom, which normally sits in London. The intention appears to be that disputes over compatibility and devolution issues should be debated and settled at a high level of the court hierarchy; and, further, provision is made for appeals (with leave) from the decision on such an issue by a bench of two or more judges of the High Court to the Supreme Court of the United Kingdom.[41] Provision is also made for the Lord Advocate or the Advocate General[42] to require a Scottish court to refer such an issue which has arisen before it to the Supreme Court of the United Kingdom, provided that the Lord Advocate or Advocate General is a party to these proceedings.[43] Despite the fact, however, that many constitutional matters may fall to be decided ultimately by the Supreme Court (because of that court's role in the determination of such issues), that Court is not as such a Constitutional court[44]; and constitutional matters which are not also compatibility or devolution issues cannot be heard by it.[45]

SUBORDINATE (OR DELEGATED) LEGISLATION

2–14 The United Kingdom Parliament, and now the Scottish Parliament, may permit other persons or bodies to create legislation. Thus, Acts of Parliament or Acts of the Scottish Parliament may delegate the power to legislate—always making clear, of course, the parameters within which the person (typically a secretary of state) or body (e.g. the Scottish Ministers) in question must operate. As far as

---

[38] See Sch.6 Pt I para.1(a)–(f) of the 1998 Act, as amended and extended by the Scotland Act 2012 s.36(4).

[39] See below, Appendix D. "High Court" is an abbreviation for the "High Court of Justiciary".

[40] 1998 Act Sch.6 Pt II para.9; the Criminal Procedure (Scotland) Act 1995 s.288ZB(1) (as inserted by the Scotland Act 2012 s.35). It is assumed that such a High Court will consist of a bench of at least three judges: but cf. *Stevens v HM Advocate*, 2002 S.L.T. 1249, where Lady Paton opined that it was not necessary under the terms of s.4 of the Human Rights Act 1998 for more than one judge of the High Court to determine the compatibility with Convention rights of a particular provision of a statute passed by the United Kingdom Parliament.

[41] 1998 Act Sch.6 Pt II paras 11 and 13 (as amended by the Constitutional Reform Act 2005 Sch.9 para.103); the Criminal Procedure (Scotland) Act 1995 ss.288ZB(4) and 288AA (as inserted by the Scotland Act 2012 ss.35 and 36(6) respectively). See, e.g. *HM Advocate v R.*, 2003 S.L.T. 4.

[42] The Advocate General for Scotland is the law officer who advises the United Kingdom Government on Scottish legal matters: see s.87 of the 1998 Act.

[43] 1998 Act Sch.6 Pt V para.33 (as amended by the Constitutional Reform Act 2005 Sch.9 paras 93 and 106); see, e.g. *Spiers v Ruddy* [2007] UKPC D2; 2008 S.C.C.R. 131; *McGowan v B* [[2011] UKSC 54; 2012 S.C.C.R. 109. See also the Criminal Procedure (Scotland) Act 1995 ss.288A and 288B (as inserted by the 1998 Act Sch.8 para.32(2) and amended by Scotland Act 2012 ss.34(2), (5)–(8) and 36(7)–(9)), 288ZA, 288ZB(2), (3), (5), and 288AA (as inserted by the Scotland Act 2012 s.34(3) and (6)).

[44] Cf. the role of the Supreme Court in the United States of America.

[45] See *Hoekstra v HM Advocate (No.5)*, 2001 S.C. (P.C.) 37; cf. *Mills v HM Advocate (No.2)*, 2001 S.L.T. 1359, at 1365B–C, where the court actually refers to the Judicial Committee of the Privy Council's role as "a constitutional court", in the context of the constitutional settlement effected by the Scotland Act 1998. (The Judicial Committee of the Privy Council's jurisdiction here was transferred to the Supreme Court of the United Kingdom in 2009: see above, para.2–03.)

Scottish delegated (or subordinate) legislation is concerned, what is enacted will not be law if it would have been outwith the legislative competence of the Scottish Parliament were it to have been included in a statute[46]; and a member of the Scottish Government has no power to make any subordinate legislation which would be incompatible with any of the Convention rights[47] or with EU law.[48]

A great deal of the criminal law is now to be found in such delegated (or subordinate) legislation, especially, for example, much of the road traffic law; and many criminal procedure rules are to be found in law-making which has been delegated to the judges of the High Court of Justiciary.[49]

Types of subordinate legislation

Legislation, made by a Secretary of State, the Scottish Ministers, or the High **2–15** Court of Justiciary under the authority of a Parliamentary Act, always has the title and form of a "Statutory Instrument" or "Scottish Statutory Instrument",[50] and may be found in any well-stocked law library or by calling up the appropriate web site.[51]

"Byelaws", however, make up a separate form of delegated legislation. In particular, Scottish local authorities may make these, their powers to do so being apparently very wide:

> "A local authority may make byelaws for the good rule and government of the whole or any part of their area, and for the prevention and suppression of nuisances therein."[52]

Their discretion here, however, is restricted by the requirement that any proposed byelaw should first have been confirmed by the Scottish Ministers[53] before it acquires the force of law. Byelaws certainly form a source (although admittedly a minor source) of criminal law.[54]

In addition to byelaws, a Scottish local authority or National Park Authority can make "Management Rules" relating to the conduct of persons on property which the authority owns or manages. Whilst it is not a crime to contravene such rules, it is an offence to refuse to leave such property when an authorised officer requires

---

[46] 1998 Act s.54. See above, para.2–12.
[47] i.e. those parts of the European Convention on Human Rights taken into United Kingdom law by virtue of the Human Rights Act 1998.
[48] See s.57(2) of the 1998 Act.
[49] See the Criminal Procedure (Scotland) Act 1995 s.305. Rules of procedure enacted by the High Court are called "Acts of Adjournal".
[50] The standard abbreviation for a statutory instrument is "SI"; for a Scottish Statutory Instrument the abbreviation is "SSI". For definitions and more technical issues relative to SSIs specific to functions of the Scottish Ministers (etc.), see in particular Pt 2 of the Interpretation and Legislative Reform (Scotland) Act 2010 (asp 10); s.27(2)(d) of that Act now confirms that Acts of Adjournal made by the High Court of Justiciary are included as SSIs.
[51] For all UK and Scottish primary and secondary legislation, the appropriate official web site is invoked by utilising the address http://www.legislation.gov.uk [Accessed June 1, 2012]; thereafter, select "United Kingdom" or "Scotland" (as the case may be), and then select the appropriate "Browse UK Legislation" or "Browse Scotland Legislation" link—which will in turn present menus from which to choose.
[52] Local Government (Scotland) Act 1973 s.201(1) and (2), as amended by the Local Government etc. (Scotland) Act 1994 s.180(1) Sch.13 para.92(61).
[53] See s.53 of the Scotland Act 1998.
[54] See, e.g. *McCallum v Brown*, 2000 J.C. 6. See also Gordon Junor, "Byelaws—By Law" (2002) S.L.T. (News) 131.

one to do so on the grounds that a breach of the rules has taken place or is likely to happen.[55]

Extra-national legislation

2–16   Since the accession of the United Kingdom (and thus Scotland) to the European Community (known as the European Economic Community prior to the coming into force of the Treaty on European Union in November 1993),[56] certain Community legislation (in particular regulations) promulgated by the Council or the Commission is of direct effect within Scotland, and automatically supersedes any existing (and contrary) national law. Other Community legislation (e.g. directives) requires express implementation in this country before the expiry of predetermined calendar dates.[57] Where implementation is required, however, this can be achieved by (for example) mere ministerial regulations or orders in council—although no really serious crimes can be created in Scotland in such ways.[58] Nevertheless, the importance of EU law as a source of criminal law is constantly increasing, especially in the areas of road traffic law and environmental protection. Where EU law is of relevance to the criminal law, questions of interpretation are bound to arise. Under art.234 of the Treaty Establishing the European Community,[59] national courts may request preliminary rulings from the European Court of Justice as to the interpretation and validity of Community laws, and Scottish courts have made such requests on several occasions.[60] If the meaning of a particular piece of Community legislation is plain, however, Scottish courts may give it that meaning without resort to the European Court.[61] Equally, where there are previous rulings of the European Court which are applicable to the case on hand, Scottish courts are bound to take account of those rulings.[62]

---

[55] See the Civic Government (Scotland) Act 1982 ss.112–118, as extended and modified by the National Parks (Scotland) Act 2000 (asp 10) Sch.2 para.10.

[56] See the European Communities Act 1972, as amended. See also the European Union Act 2011, especially s.18, and the Treaty of Lisbon (Changes in Terminology) Order 2011 (SI 2011/1043) art.6(2).

[57] See the consolidated version of the Treaty Establishing the European Community 1957 (as amended) art. 249 (originally art.189); European Communities Act 1972 s.2, as amended in particular by the Legislative and Regulatory Reform Act 2006 s.27(1), and by the European Union (Amendment) Act 2008 Sch. Pt 1.

[58] See the European Communities Act 1972 s.2(2)(a) [amended as in fn.57, above, and as varied *quoad* the Scottish Ministers by art.3 of the Scotland Act 1998 (Transfer of Functions to the Scottish Ministers etc.) Order 2005 (SI 2005/849)] and Sch.2 para.1(1)(d), as amended by the Scotland Act 1998 Sch.8 para.15.

[59] Consolidated version: the Article was originally numbered 177.

[60] See, e.g. *Wither v Cowie*, 1994 S.L.T. 363 (where, inter alia, a Council regulation required member states to notify the Commission of any change to their existing sea-fishing laws, and a sheriff court requested a preliminary ruling on the validity of UK fishing laws which had been implemented without such prior notification), and *Walkingshaw v Marshall*, 1992 S.L.T. 1167 (where certain UK legislation, prohibiting the carriage of particular types of nets by British registered fishing vessels in Scottish inshore waters, having been attacked as both discriminatory and contrary to the principle of proportionality and thus contrary to Community law, was referred by the High Court of Justiciary to the European Court for a preliminary ruling as to its validity).

[61] See, e.g. *Westwater v Thomson*, 1993 S.L.T. 703— although it was emphasised there that the principles to be employed in interpreting Community law are those of the European Community and not those of the domestic law of Scotland.

[62] See, e.g. *Baron Meats Ltd v Lockhart*, 1991 J.C. 129, where the High Court of Justiciary followed a prior decision of the European Court on the meaning of "door to door selling" as applicable to vehicles fitted out as mobile shops.

Jurisprudence of the European Court of Human Rights

Under the provisions of the Human Rights Act 1998, parts of the European **2–17** Convention on Human Rights have been incorporated within Scots (and United Kingdom) law. Thus, persons charged with, and/or proceeded against, for offences have the benefit of the applicable rights and fundamental freedoms (the "Convention rights") set out in Sch.1 to the Act[63]; and the jurisprudence of the European Court of Human Rights (and other judicial organs at one time established under the terms of the Convention) must be taken into account by any court in Scotland (or indeed elsewhere in the United Kingdom) in determining any issue relative to Convention rights which has arisen in proceedings before it.[64] The Human Rights Act also makes it unlawful[65] for a public authority (which includes expressly any court and impliedly any public prosecutor[66]) to act (or fail to act) in any way which is incompatible with applicable Convention rights—as, presumably, these rights are understood in the jurisprudence of the European Court of Human Rights.[67] If a court finds that an act (or omission) by a public authority is thus unlawful, that court may grant such relief (within its powers) as it considers "just and appropriate".[68] In addition, the same Act preserves the right of an individual to petition the European Court of Human Rights directly—once all available avenues of relief under Scots law have been explored without success.[69]

THE DEFINITION OF CRIME

Among other things, the sources of the criminal law referred to above should **2–18** reveal the current catalogue of crimes. A comprehensive yet succinct definition of what makes any particular act or omission or situation criminal rather than not is probably an impossibility, given the enormous range of matters which are definitely criminal.[70] There seems little to connect (morally or otherwise), for example, the deliberate killing of another human being (intentional murder at common law) and trading as a window cleaner without having obtained a licence.[71] It is possible, of course, to refer to the threat of punishment which is often said uniquely to underlie any truly criminal proscription (see above, Ch.1). But this raises the

---

[63] See the Human Rights Act 1998 s.7(1).
[64] See the Human Rights Act 1998 s.7(1). Notice that the courts are not bound by such jurisprudence, but are simply required to take it into account. It is anticipated, however, that courts will be slow to depart from opinions cast by the European Court of Human Rights itself: cf. *Ambrose v Harris* [2011] UKSC 43; 2011 S.L.T. 1005 (especially the opinion of Lord Hope at paras 14–20).
[65] This does not mean that a criminal offence is thereby committed: see the Human Rights Act 1998 s.7(8), "Nothing in this Act creates a criminal offence."
[66] Under s.6(3) of the Human Rights Act 1998, a public authority includes a court and any person whose functions include functions of a public nature.
[67] See the Human Rights Act 1998 s.6(1), (3), (6): under subs. (2), there is no unlawfulness if the public authority could not have acted differently due to the terms of applicable primary (and sometimes subordinate) legislation.
[68] See s.8 of the Human Rights Act 1998. Cf. s.9.
[69] See s.11 of the Human Rights Act 1998.
[70] See Gordon, *Criminal Law*, 3rd edn (2000/2001), Ch.1; *Smith and Hogan Criminal Law*, edited by David Ormerod, 12th edn (Oxford: Oxford University Press, 2008), Ch.2.
[71] Civic Government (Scotland) Act 1982 ss.7 and 43.

problem of what content should be given to the term "punishment." Under the Local Government Finance Act 1992,[72] for example, a failure to supply particular information to a local authority in connection with council tax results in the imposition of a penalty of £50 (rising in some cases to £200 for subsequent failures). The imposition of such penalties might well be taken as punishment of a very real sort; but it is abundantly clear that no crime is intended or involved. It is equally possible to stress that crimes are uniquely the objects of a particular type of procedure—involving prosecutors, courts and proceedings which are very definitely different from anything encountered in the civil law field.[73] But such attempts at definition are problematic, often circular and perhaps unnecessary. Modern statutes invariably identify clearly what is intended to be criminal by employing the word "offence" (virtually a legal synonym for "crime") in the context of "summary" or "indictment" (i.e. plainly criminal) procedure. The maximum fine or period of imprisonment will also clearly be stated. The identification of what is criminal under legislative provisions is, therefore, unlikely to present difficulties.

2–19   In the common law field, where inevitably matters are rather more fluid, identification of particular acts or omissions as criminal or not may indeed pose occasional problems. But even here, resort is not had to any standard definition of the essence of "crime." Such issues of identification are resolved by the "inherent" power of the High Court of Justiciary to declare the common law, which it does from time to time in particular cases according to ad hoc criteria of its own choosing.

The Declaratory Power of the High Court

2–20   In "declaring the common law," the High Court may simply be declaring the ambit of a known crime (a function usually accepted as necessary under any common law system[74]), or (more specifically) correcting errors into which previous courts had fallen[75]; or it might be purporting to exercise a distinct power to criminalise behaviour which was not previously known to be criminal. Any exercise of such a distinct power (usually referred to as the "Declaratory Power") would now be contrary to the principles of clarity, accessibility and non-retroactivity of criminal provisions—principles which are expressed in, or implied

---

[72] See s.97(4) and Sch.3 of the Local Government Finance Act 1992. The Treasury has the authority (under Sch.3 para.5) to alter the value of the penalties set out in the text.

[73] Gordon, *Criminal* Law, 3rd edn (2000/2001), para.1.04.

[74] See below, Ch.14, especially paras 14–08 to 14–14, for a discussion of the High Court's ability to develop the law in this way.

[75] See, e.g. *Brennan v HM Advocate*, 1977 J.C. 38, overruling *Kennedy v HM Advocate*, 1944 J.C. 171, in which the High Court had erroneously followed English law; *Galbraith v HM Advocate*, 2001 S.C.C.R. 551, overruling *Connelly v HM Advocate*, 1990 S.C.C.R. 504, in which the High Court had interpreted the defence of diminished responsibility too restrictively; *Lord Advocate's Reference (No.1 of 2001)*, 2002 S.L.T. 466, overruling *HM Advocate v Sweenie* (1858) 3 Irv. 109, in which the High Court had misinterpreted the essential elements of common law rape; and *Webster v Dominick*, 2005 J.C. 65, overruling *Watt v Annan*, 1978 J.C. 84, in which the High Court had erroneously confirmed as criminal at common law conduct described as "shamelessly indecent".

by art.7(1) of the European Convention on Human Rights.[76] In more detail, the main principle here (sometimes expressed in Latin as *nullum crimen sine lege*) enjoins that no one should be convicted for an act or omission which was not clearly and knowably criminal at the time it was done. A corollary may also be stated—namely that no one should be denied a defence which was clearly relevant and available in law at the time of commission of some act or omission. In so far, therefore, as it might purport to recognise a power of the courts to make new common law crimes or cancel common law defences in actual cases, Scots criminal law would breach these principles.[77]

During the time when a "Declaratory Power" was believed to be possessed lawfully by the courts, however, the writers who espoused it and the judges who operated it might be thought to have given some useful guidance relative to the circumstances in which a new crime could legitimately be created—i.e. some useful guidance on what identifies particular behaviour as criminal. This matter is briefly considered in the paragraphs which follow.

Historical authority for the existence of the power

It appears that the first written notice of such a power was given by Hume in the **2–21** 1797 edition of the *Commentaries*[78] although he gives few examples of its actual use. That might give rise to the charge that the declaratory power was something of a novelty—if not a product of the author's own imagination—but Alison[79] also refers to it, independently of any reference to Hume, and apparently quotes 16 different instances of its application. The judges of the High Court also endorsed the existence of the power in many cases.[80] There is also clear confirmation of this situation in Macdonald,[81] although his primary (footnote) authority is given as Hume. There can be little doubt, therefore, that the authoritative text-writers and the judges themselves asserted the right of the High Court of Justiciary to enlarge the contents of the common law; but what principles would have to be satisfied before particular behaviour could be criminalised and how would the High Court

---

[76] See above, para.2–17. See also *Jacobs, White and Ovey, The European Convention on Human Rights,* edited by R. White and C. Ovey, 5th edn (New York: Oxford University Press, 2010), pp.296–304.

[77] Adherence to such principles, and Convention rights generally in the matter of legislation is, of course, the responsibility of Parliament, although all criminal courts are obliged to interpret legislation so as to conform with Convention rights: see the Scotland Act 1998 s.101; the Human Rights Act 1998 s.3. In respect of the Scottish Parliament, any enactment which is not in conformity with Convention rights is not within its legislative competence, and, therefore, would not be law: Scotland Act 1998 s.29.

[78] Hume, *Commentaries,*Vol.i, p.52; 1844 edn, Vol.i, p.12.

[79] Alison, *Principles of the Criminal Law of Scotland* (1989), Vol.i, pp.624–644.

[80] See *Taylor*, October 19, 1808, Burnett, App. No. X, per Lords Craig, Armadale, Meadowbank (by implication) and Lord Justice-Clerk Hope; *Bernard Greenhuff* (1838) 2 Swin. 236, per Lords Moncreiff (at 265) and Mackenzie (at 268–69), and Lord Justice-Clerk Boyle (at 259), who all make reference to Hume, and Lord Medwyn (at 270) who favoured Alison's analysis; *Sugden v HM Advocate*, 1934 J.C. 103, per Lord Justice-Clerk Aitchison (at 109) who refers to it as a "prerogative of the Justiciary derived from its history, and coming down from the days of the Justiciar"; and *Grant v Allan*, 1987 J.C. 71, per Lord Justice-Clerk Ross at 77 where he asserts that "there are circumstances where it will be appropriate for the court to exercise this power", whilst conceding that great care requires to be taken in its exercise.

[81] J.H.A. Macdonald, *A Practical Treatise on the Criminal Law of Scotland*, 5th edn (Edinburgh: W. Green, 1948), p.193.

have had to be constituted in order to make criminal what was not known to have been criminal before? Attempting to answer these questions posed certain difficulties.

Meaning of the "High Court" in the context of the power

2–22   It seems agreed that the declaratory power was only possessed by the High Court of Justiciary[82] and not by any lesser court (see below, Appendix D). What is unclear, however, is what was here meant by the "High Court." According to the court itself in *Jessop v Stevenson*[83]: "A decision of a judge of the High Court of Justiciary is a decision of the High Court of Justiciary." That does not mean, however, that a single High Court judge could (or can[84]) necessarily exercise all the powers of that institution as a "Collegiate Court."[85] Gordon opined in 1978 that a "quorum" of the court had to be present,[86] but it is hard to know what that meant in the context of the declaratory power. Prior to the reforms of the late nineteenth century, when all judges of the Court of Session also became members of the supreme criminal court,[87] it was feasible, and not uncommon, for the whole court of six or seven judges—depending on whether the Lord Justice-General was present—to sit in relation to decisions on inter alia the exercise of the power.[88] A possible de facto exercise of the power by two judges on circuit at Aberdeen was clearly unusual and required explanation.[89] But the whole court now consists of at least 38[90] judges; and in modern times, therefore, it would not have been unreasonable to conclude that a minimum of three judges would have formed a "quorum" for the purposes of the declaratory power. That represents the minimum number for appeal proceedings,[91] and for matters certified to the High Court under the Criminal Procedure (Scotland) Act 1995 s.103(4); and it is by appeal or certification that issues concerning the exercise of the power would have come before that court.

---

[82] See Gordon, *Criminal Law*, 2nd edn (Edinburgh: W.Green, 1978), para.1–43.
[83] *Jessop v Stevenson,* 1988 J.C. 17 at 20.
[84] Cf. *Stevens v HM Advocate*, 2002 S.L.T. 1249.
[85] See "Courts", *Stair Memorial Encyclopaedia* (London: Lexis Nexis/Butterworth), Vol.6, pp.859 and 904.
[86] Gordon, *Criminal Law*, 2nd edn (1978), para.1–43; see also *Khaliq v HM Advocate*, 1984 J.C. 23, per Lord Avonside at 24.
[87] Criminal Procedure (Scotland) Act 1887 s.44.
[88] See *Wright* (1809) Burnett 134, App. No.vii; *Greenhuff* (1838) 2 Swin. 236; *Fraser* (1847) Ark. 280; *Ballantyne* (1859) 3 Irv. 352. In *Lord Advocate's Reference (No. 1 of 2001)*, 2002 S.L.T. 466, the majority of the court took the view that a six judge court did not qualify as "the whole court", and that thus a six judge court, in *Sweenie* (1858) 3 Irv. 109, could be overruled by a modern court of seven.
[89] *Irvine*, September 1784, Burnett 133, commented on in *Wright* (1809) Burnett 134, App. No.vii, per Lords Craig, Armadale, Meadowbank and Lord Justice-Clerk Hope.
[90] This number does not include temporary judges, nor those who have retired but sit in terms of s.22 (as amended by the Constitutional Reform Act 2005 Sch. 9 para.43, and the Judiciary and Courts (Scotland) Act 2008 (asp 6) ss.23 and 64(3)) of the Law Reform (Miscellaneous Provisions) (Scotland) Act 1985.
[91] Criminal Procedure (Scotland) Act 1995 ss.103(2) and 173(1); but note that for appeals against (generally) sentence alone, the quorum of the court falls to two (unless the two are unable to agree)—see ss.103(3) (as amended by the Crime and Punishment (Scotland) Act 1997 Sch.1 para.21(13)(a)) and 173(2) (as amended by the Criminal Justice and Licensing (Scotland) Act 2010 (asp 13) Sch.2 para.11).

Rationale for the power

Both Hume[92] and Alison[93] assume that it will always be necessary to create new **2–23** crimes; and in fact few would dispute that assumption. They further assume, however, that both Parliaments *and* the High Court are competent to create such new crimes. But the rationale behind the court's entitlement to do so is simply not revealed. Since Parliaments are constitutionally recognised as having legislative functions, it is hardly surprising that they may from time to time increase the stock of available crimes. Courts in the modern world, however, are not generally recognised as having legislative powers co-extensive with those of legislatures, and some explanation for the High Court's one time ability to declare acts (or omissions) to be criminal would seem to be called for. The best explanation which the judiciary themselves have suggested is that the High Court simply occupied a unique constitutional position within the United Kingdom;

> "I hold it to be law, that the right of enquiring into all injuries to individuals by criminal acts, as well as of defining in such cases the nature and extent of the punishment, is constitutionally entrusted to this Court."[94]

It seems, therefore, not particularly clear why the High Court ever had, or claimed **2–24** to have, such a power—there having been competent legislatures for Scotland at all times during the existence of that Court; nor is it always clear what size of court was necessary to operate the power: but that the power was used in the 19th and 20th centuries seems beyond doubt, and this would seem to hold out the prospect of providing some answer to the troublesome question—"What are the essential characteristics of behaviour deemed to be criminal?" If the court declared some act or omission to be criminal, one would expect to obtain useful information as to why it had done so.

Criteria for the power's exercise

Hume's somewhat unhelpful view[95] was that the power might be exercised **2–25** where the act (or omission) in question was "obviously of a criminal nature." In the case of *John Ballantyne*[96] Lord Justice-Clerk Inglis ventured the view that Hume meant by that acts which were *mala in se*, i.e. evils in themselves. This, if correct, connotes the criterion of "immorality," with all the vagueness that that implies. Nevertheless, some judges have clearly opined that the perceived (public) immorality of an act (or omission) will suffice to exercise the crime-making power,[97] especially if likely to corrupt the young,[98] or pose "danger" to society.[99] In more modern times, however, the High Court appears to have rejected such a

---

[92] Hume, *Commentaries,* i, 12.
[93] Alison, *Principles*, i, 624.
[94] *Wright* (1809) Burnett, App. No.vii, per Lord Meadowbank; see also *Sugden v HM Advocate*, 1934 J.C. 103 at 109 where Lord Justice-Clerk Alness asserted the power to be a "prerogative right of the Justiciary derived from its history".
[95] Hume, *Commentaries,* i, 12.
[96] *Ballantyne* (1859) 3 Irv. 352 at 359.
[97] See *Greenhuff* (1838) 2 Swin. 236, per Lord Justice-Clerk Boyle at 258; Lord Meadowbank at 264.
[98] *Greenhuff* (1838) 2 Swin. 236, per Lord Justice-Clerk Boyle at 258.
[99] *Greenhuff* (1838) 2 Swin. 236, per Lord Moncreiff at 266; *Barr* (1839) 2 Swin. 282, per Lord Mackenzie at 310.

criterion. More had to be shown than that the act (or omission) was "reprehensible and immoral"[100]; in particular, it might suffice if "injurious consequences to persons or property" could be demonstrated[101]—which itself shows a tendency towards the acceptance of Alison's less vague criterion (see below, para.2–26). The major problem with any appeal to immorality is, of course, that few people can be found to agree as to what is or is not immoral. And this problem is merely re-phrased by opining that an act (or omission) must be "so grossly immoral and mischievous on the face of it that no man can fairly be ignorant of its nature" before the court could exercise its crime-making power.[102]

2–26   The other most-often-quoted criterion is that proffered by Alison.[103] His view was that the power might be exercised in respect of an act (or omission) which was both in itself wrong (*malum in se*) and hurtful to the persons or property of others. There is a pragmatic flavour to this which almost anticipates the development of the "harm" principle by John Stuart Mill and others[104]; and there was some judicial acceptance of it.[105] It also may underlie the decisions in *Strathern v Seaforth*[106] —a decision which definitely involved use of the power, according to *Sugden v HM Advocate*[107] —and *Khaliq v HM Advocate*,[108] where use of the power was less certain.

2–27   There are various other criteria which have been judicially mentioned as justifying the exercise of the power—for example, that the act was criminal under English common law,[109] that it would be absurd to take any other view,[110] and that there must be something akin to a "public nuisance."[111] None of these, however, really provided any sensible or practical test.

Lord Cockburn's views

2–28   Of the six judicial opinions cast in the case of *Bernard Greenhuff*,[112] the only dissenting voice was that of Lord Cockburn. He rejected flatly any suggestion that the court might declare an act (or omission) to be criminal simply on the grounds of its immorality. If immoral acts were to be criminalised, then that was a matter for Parliament and not for the court.[113] But the High Court might, he thought, legitimately develop the common law in certain ways since

---

[100] *Grant v Allan*, 1987 J.C. 71, per Lord Justice-Clerk Ross at 77; *HM Advocate v Semple*, 1937 J.C. 41, per Lord Justice-Clerk Aitchison at 45–46 and Lord Fleming at 47.

[101] *Ballantyne* (1859) 3 Irv. 352, per Lord Justice-Clerk Inglis at 359–60.

[102] *Greenhuff* (1838) 2 Swin. 236, per Lord Mackenzie at 268, approved in *Ballantyne* (1959) 3 Irv. 352, by Lord Justice-Clerk Inglis at 360.

[103] Alison, *Principles*, i, 624.

[104] Mill, *On Liberty* (1859), Chs I and IV. See above, paras 1–07 to 1–09.

[105] See *Kerr v Hill*, 1936 J.C. 71, per Lord Justice-General Normand at 75; *Ballantyne* (1859) 3 Irv. 352, per Lord Justice-Clerk Inglis at 359–60; *HM Advocate v Semple*, 1937 J.C. 41, per Lord Justice-Clerk Aitchison at 45–46 and Lord Moncrieff at 48; *Barr* (1839) 2 Swin. 282, per Lord Medwyn at 315.

[106] *Strathern v Seaforth*, 1926 J.C. 100.

[107] *Sugden v HM Advocate*,1934 J.C. 103, per Lord Justice-Clerk Alness at 109.

[108] *Khaliq v HM Advocate*, 1984 J.C. 23.

[109] See *Greenhuff* (1838) 2 Swin. 236, per Lord Justice-Clerk Boyle at 258, Lord Moncreiff at 266 and Lord Mackenzie at 269; *Barr* (1839) 2 Swin. 282, per Lord Moncreiff at 314.

[110] See *Strathern v Seaforth*, 1926 J.C. 100, per Lord Justice-Clerk Alness at 102.

[111] *Greenhuff* (1838) 2 Swin. 236, per Lord Medwyn at 270.

[112] *Greenhuff* (1838) 2 Swin. 236.

[113] *Greenhuff* (1838) 2 Swin. 236 at 272.

"[a]n old crime may certainly be committed in a new way; and a case, though never occurring before in its facts, may fall within the *spirit* of a previous decision, or within an established *general principle* . . . There is no . . . exercise of any extraordinary power needed, in the Court's merely determining that an act that has never presented itself before, *comes within the range of a known term, case or principle*."[114]

Clearly, a crime can be committed in a new way.[115] Hume would no doubt have **2–29** been surprised to learn that a person could be killed by exposure to a radioactive source; but the method employed is hardly of the essence of criminal forms of killing, and death occasioned by deliberate irradiation would hardly excite comment as an example of murder (all other things being equal).

Equally, it is always possible to argue that some act (or omission) falls within **2–30** the spirit of a previous decision (meaning, no doubt, that one may extend by analogy the definition, as previously understood by the courts, of any common law crime) and that it ought, therefore, to be considered as an example of that crime. Lord Cockburn himself gave colour to such argument in the case of *John Barr*,[116] where falsely swearing that one was qualified to vote in an election was considered by him to be a species of fraud or of perjury,[117] since it shared the essential characteristics of those crimes. With respect to any common law crime, however, it can be a somewhat arbitrary process to identify what are its essential characteristics—as was amply demonstrated in the case of *William Fraser*.[118] There the accused had intercourse with a married woman by pretending to be her husband. He thus obtained her consent by a trick. Surely the essence of common law rape was thus satisfied, there being no true consent? Yet the majority of the court (including Lord Cockburn) held that consent had been obtained, and that, therefore, rape must be ruled out. It could not thus be extended. Quite apart from the arbitrary way in which these two cases (*Barr* and *Fraser*) were determined, it should be noted that extending crimes to novel situations by means of analogy is as much a breach of the principle *nullum crimen sine lege* (see above, para.2–20) and of art.7 of the European Convention on Human Rights as declaring acts to be criminal simply because they offend against some supposed rule of morality or whatever.[119]

Lord Cockburn's third suggestion that a novel act, in so far as the criminal law **2–31** is concerned, may nevertheless fall within an established general principle is no less perplexing, since he did not explain what was meant by such a principle nor how such principles were to be established. As Gordon[120] has surely correctly pointed out, principles may be deduced, from existing known crimes, of such generality as to be capable of encompassing many different forms of behaviour.

---

[114] *Greenhuff* (1838) 2 Swin. 236 at 274 (italics as in the original report).
[115] See, e.g. Lord McCluskey's acknowledgement of this in *HM Advocate v Harris*, 1993 J.C. 150 at 159F.
[116] *Barr* (1839) 2 Swin. 282.
[117] *Barr* (1839) 2 Swin. 282 at 316–317.
[118] *William Fraser* (1847) Ark. 280.
[119] See *Kokkinakis v Greece* (1993) 17 E.H.R.R. 397 at 423, para.52, which was affirmed in *SW v United Kingdom; CR v United Kingdom* (1996) 21 E.H.R.R. 363, at 398–399, paras 35/33 and 36/34.
[120] Gordon, *Criminal Law*, 3rd edn (2000/2001), para.1.22.

Thus, for example, from the known crimes of theft, fraud and embezzlement, it may be deduced that "dishonest conduct is criminal." If that deduction were then considered as some general principle supporting those known crimes, there could be no limit, on Cockburn's thesis, to the proscription of, say, many supposedly legitimate business activities simply on the basis that they smacked of "dishonesty." This would appear to be a highly questionable process, since it seems perfectly capable of upholding the declaratory power (so heavily criticised by Cockburn) in all but name.

2–32   Nevertheless, since Cockburn was apparently offering an alternative to the declaratory power, an alternative which was, therefore, not subject to the rules for the power's operation, e.g. only exercisable by a quorum of the High Court (see above, para.2–22), it became acceptable for even single judges of the court to "find" general principles in order to justify decisions which otherwise might have entailed the declaration of new crimes. Thus in *HM Advocate v Martin*[121] Lord Cameron was able to invoke the "principle" that conduct which violated the order and course of justice was criminal. That then enabled him (at least in part) to find that helping a prisoner to escape from an extramural working party was indeed a crime, without any resort to the declaratory power. Similarly, in *Khaliq v HM Advocate*,[122] it was possible to determine that the supply of harmful substances to others was criminal, since it fell under the broad criminalising "principle" of "that which was capable of causing real injury." Again, in *Watt v Annan*,[123] showing an obscene or indecent film to consenting adults was found criminal since it lay within the general "principle" that "all shamelessly indecent conduct is criminal." Where it suited the High Court to do so, however, an "obvious" general "principle" (e.g. that dishonest conduct is criminal) was ignored, and the alternative exercise of the declaratory power deliberately avoided.[124]

2–33   It is, therefore, uncertain whether Lord Cockburn was simply describing a legitimate developmental facility possessed (relative to the common law) by the High Court, or whether he was drawing attention to another *form* of the declaratory power he had been at such pains to discredit. Fortunately, the power is now relegated to the realm of "historical curiosity"; but unfortunately, it seems plain that former attempts by the High Court to formulate new types of criminal behaviour by exercise of the power do little to answer the general question why certain conduct deserves to be stigmatised as criminal at all.

---

[121] *HM Advocate v* Martin, 1956 J.C. 1 at 3.

[122] *Khaliq v HM* Advocate, 1984 J.C. 23.

[123] *Watt v* Annan, 1978 J.C. 84. This case was overruled by a court of five judges in *Webster v Dominick*, 2005 1 J.C., 65, where Lord Justice-Clerk Gill said at 75, para.28: "The decision in *Watt v Annan* was a direct consequence of *McLaughlan v Boyd* [1934 J.C. 19]. The excessive statement of Lord Justice General Clyde in *McLaughlan v Boyd* [at 23, lines 4–7] set no limit to the ambit of shameless indecency. The effect of the statement was to enable the court, by characterising any form of conduct as shamelessly indecent, *to exercise the declaratory power*. The result was the creation of a crime that had no basis in principle and was unconstrained by any clear or logical boundaries [emphasis added]."

[124] See *Grant v Allan*, 1987 J.C. 71. See also *HM Advocate v Forbes*, 1994 S.L.T. 861, where the Crown's argument, that "housebreaking with intent to commit any crime" was a general principle (see 863F), was rejected by the court (see 864J).

CLASSIFICATIONS OF CRIMES

Scots law does not formally group crimes into classes. Thus, the classifying of **2–34** crimes as "felonies, misdemeanours, or petty misdemeanours" as favoured in the American Law Institute's Model Penal Code,[125] is unknown in this country. Nor is any particular distinction made here between the terms "crime" and "offence." It thus makes equal legal sense in Scotland to speak of the "crime" or the "offence" of murder.

Of course, there are two distinct types of criminal procedure in this country. **2–35** "Summary" procedure is (supposedly, if not in fact) flexible, quick and relatively informal; involves a non-jury type trial (if a trial is held); and is normally reserved for the less serious type of crime. On the other hand, "solemn" procedure (or procedure "on indictment") is more lengthy and rule-bound, involves a judge and jury trial (if a trial is held), and is supposedly reserved for the more serious type of offence. It might appear, therefore, that a classification by way of procedure would be appropriate—crimes being divided into those which were "summary" and those which were "indictable." This is not possible, however. Most common law crimes may be processed by either form of procedure—depending upon the discretion of the prosecutor and the seriousness of the individual case. It is thus generally not the type of crime that is more or less serious, but individual examples of it. Whilst it is true that some statutory offences are designated as attracting only summary procedure, or triable only on indictment, it is equally true that many such offences may be processed in either way, thus equating them with common law offences, from the procedural point of view. There is no satisfactory way, therefore, of classifying crimes in Scotland according to the procedural regime which they attract.

It is traditional, however, and very convenient, particularly for the purposes of **2–36** textbook writing, to group crimes together according to some significant feature that they possess (or, more accurately, appear to possess) in common. Thus, later chapters in this book are headed "Crimes Against the Person," "Crimes of Dishonesty," "Crimes Against Property," and so on: but these groupings have no official basis whatsoever. Gordon has stressed a similar (though more general) theme in his useful thesis that there are both conduct and result crimes.[126] His view is that in relation to some crimes, what is forbidden consists primarily of the "result" of conduct, the precise form of conduct employed to achieve that result being of minimal interest to the law. Murder is his stock example here. (One must pause, however, to observe that conduct is still involved in murder—and crucially so, if anyone is to be convicted of such a crime.) The alternative is a "conduct" crime, where the result, if any, of human conduct is in no sense required for conviction.[127] Although it is plain that not all offences can be neatly classified in such a way (see, for example, the offence of being "drunk and incapable of taking care" of oneself in a public place,[128] which seems to involve neither conduct nor result, and which Smith and Hogan[129] would refer to as a "state of affairs" crime),

---

[125] American Law Institute, Model Penal Code, Official Draft (1985), s.1.04(1).

[126] Gordon, *Criminal Law*, 3rd edn (2000/2001), para.3.05.

[127] Gordon's initial example being that of perjury—on which see *Lord Advocate's Reference (No.1 of 1985)*, 1986 J.C. 137.

[128] Civic Government (Scotland) Act 1982 s.50(1).

[129] *Smith and Hogan Criminal Law*, 12th edn (2010), pp.58–60.

the identification of those crimes which require a result does highlight that area of the criminal law where issues of causation are at a premium (see below, Ch.5).

2–37 There is some judicial support for a classification of crimes based upon the Latin tags *mala in se* and *mala prohibita*. *Mala in se* refer to those crimes which are morally reprehensible—evils in themselves; and clearly murder, rape, assault and some other traditional common law crimes would answer to that sort of description. At the opposite end of the scale, *mala prohibita* are "mere regulatory offences" or "not criminal in any real sense"[130]—offences which have no perceptible moral content, and which may be described as administrative rules given the added efficacy that only criminal sanctions can command. Examples may be seen in the offences of installing or using a television receiver where the installation and use are not authorised by a licence,[131] and failing to exhibit in the prescribed manner a vehicle licence on a vehicle which is used or kept on a public road (and in respect of which excise duty is chargeable).[132] This sort of classification is often resorted to in relation to statutory offences—where criteria are being sought to identify offences of strict liability, i.e. those not requiring proof or inference of mens rea (see below Chs 3 and 13). But there are many offences (even common law ones) where it cannot affirmatively be said that moral reprehensibility is always involved. Abortion, culpable homicide, carrying an offensive weapon, incest, brothel keeping, and so on may or may not involve moral obloquy, depending upon the circumstances; but it is difficult to envisage any of them being described as a mere regulatory offence. Opinions on issues of morality are in any event so hopelessly diverse that this sort of classification is of very limited utility.

BASIC PRINCIPLES OF THE CRIMINAL JUSTICE SYSTEM[133]

Jurisdiction

2–38 No proceedings against a person for a crime can competently be commenced before a Scottish court (see below, Appendix D) unless that crime and the person alleged to have committed it are subject to the jurisdiction of that court. Diplomatic immunity apart, each "prosecutable person" (see below, paras 2–43 to 2–52), whatever his nationality, can be prosecuted before a court within whose territorial area he is alleged to have committed a crime. It is clearly important, therefore, to establish where an alleged crime was committed. If the place of the crime (usually referred to as the "locus") is outwith the United Kingdom, then generally there

---

[130] See *Sweet v Parsley* [1970] A.C. 132, per Lord Reid at 149F, quoting from Wright J. in *Sherras v De Rutzen* [1895] 1 Q.B. 918 at 922.

[131] See the Communications Act 2003 s.363.

[132] See the Vehicle Excise and Registration Act 1994 s.33 (as amended by the Finance Act 1996 Sch.2 para.10; the Finance Act 1997 Sch.3 para.4; the Finance Act 2002 Sch.5 para.10; and the Finance Act 2008 s. 147). See also *Strowger v John* [1974] R.T.R. 124.

[133] The paragraphs which follow are intended to provide no more than a basic sketch of the main features of the Scottish criminal justice system. For detailed discussion and commentary, the reader is referred to the standard works on procedure, e.g. *Renton & Brown: Criminal Procedure*, 6th edn (London: Sweet & Maxwell) looseleaf with regular updating service, and evidence, e.g. F.P. Davidson, *Evidence* (Edinburgh: W. Green, 2007). For a modern guide to the European Convention on Human Rights, see *Jacobs, White and Ovey, The European Convention on Human Rights*, edited by R. White and C. Ovey, 5th edn (New York: Oxford University Press, 2010).

will be no jurisdiction possessed by any Scottish court in respect of that crime. But there are many exceptions, mostly statutory. Under s.11(1) of the Criminal Procedure (Scotland) Act 1995, for example, a British citizen or subject, who commits murder or culpable homicide (as these are understood in Scotland) in a country outwith the United Kingdom, may be prosecuted for what he did before a Scottish court.[134] Other exceptions, such as piracy, may be within the jurisdiction of Scottish courts as a matter of international comity. If the locus is completely or partly outwith Scotland but within the United Kingdom, the issue of jurisdiction may depend on the nature of the crime itself and also whether that crime is of statutory or common law origin. In *Clements v HM Advocate*,[135] for example, the Scottish courts assumed jurisdiction over persons who were based in London and who had furnished their criminal activities only in that city. But the statutory crime in question[136] was one where criminal activities in one location vitally contributed to the end-result of the crime in another—and that other location was Edinburgh. Where, therefore, a crime is of such a nature that chains of inter-locking activities in different parts of the United Kingdom are involved in its commission, the Scottish courts may have jurisdiction over persons who never visited Scotland at all (except to be prosecuted) and who were unaware that the end-locus was Scotland. The crime in that case was, however, of unusually wide scope.[137] As far as common law crimes are concerned, it seems that a similar rule will pertain where the crime in question involves a scheme of cross-border activities and where a material part of those activities takes place in Scotland.[138] In addition, of course, to a particular court having territorial jurisdiction in respect of the locus, it must also be competent to deal with the type of crime involved. Thus, e.g. only a High Court can competently try a person accused of murder or rape—even though the crime in question occurred within the territorial area of a sheriff or JP court.[139]

Prescription

A prosecution will be barred as incompetent if the time limit laid down by the **2–39** law has prescribed before commencement of proceedings. There are two main aspects to this. First, in relation to common law crimes, there is no period of prescription at all.[140] Whatever may have been the position under Roman law or in Scotland during the eighteenth century, there is now no time bar on the prosecution of any common law offence (although the lack of availability of witnesses,

---

[134] See also the Criminal Procedure (Scotland) Act 1995 s.11A (as inserted by the Criminal Justice (Terrorism and Conspiracy) Act 1998 s.7, and as amended by the Criminal Justice and Licensing (Scotland) Act 2010 (asp 13) s.50) relative to conspiracy to commit any offence outwith Scotland: for "conspiracy" see below, paras 7–37 to 7–56.
[135] *Clements v HM Advocate*, 1991 J.C. 62.
[136] A contravention of s.4(3)(b) of the Misuse of Drugs Act 1971, i.e. being concerned in the supplying of a controlled drug to another.
[137] See *Kerr v HM Advocate*, 1986 J.C. 41.
[138] See *Laird v HM Advocate*, 1985 J.C. 37. See also the provisions of the Criminal Procedure (Scotland) Act 1995 s.11(4) pertaining to theft and reset.
[139] For further details, discussion and authorities, see *Renton and Brown: Criminal Procedure*, 6th edn under the title "Jurisdiction"; Gordon, *Criminal Law*, 3rd edn (2000/2001), paras 3.41 to 3.47. For an account of the Scottish criminal courts, see below, Appendix D.
[140] *Sugden v HM Advocate*, 1934 J.C. 103.

and diminished powers of recollection by them may detrimentally affect proposed prosecutions relating to crimes allegedly committed many years in the past).

2–40   Second, in relation to statutory offences, each piece of relevant legislation must be consulted in order to determine if a specific time limit exists, and, if so, when the prescriptive period begins to run. The Road Traffic Offenders Act 1988 Sch.1, for example, identifies those offences to which the specific time limits contained in s.6 of that Act apply; and, as a more specific example, under s.44 of the Animal Health and Welfare (Scotland) Act 2006 (asp 11), proceedings for an offence under s.23 of that Act (e.g. causing or arranging an animal fight) cannot be brought more than three years after the commission of the offence (or, in the case of a continuous contravention, after the last date on which the offence was committed)—whereas the offence of abandoning an animal for which one is responsible (under s.29) appears to have no prescriptive period applied to it. Section 29 of that Act, however, furnishes a series of offences; and if no specific time limit is set in relation to a statutory offence which is triable summarily, then a general prescriptive period of six months (from the date of the alleged offence) applies.[141]

DELAY IN PROGRESSING PROCEEDINGS

2–41 There are statutory time limits applicable to prosecutions under either sort of procedure (i.e. summary or on indictment)[142] which are designed to ensure that accused persons will not remain in custody for too long before being brought to trial, or, in the case of solemn prosecutions alone, to ensure that accused persons who are not in custody will be brought to trial within a reasonable space of time.[143]

2–42   In addition, delay in the progress of prosecutions is subject to art.6(1) of the European Convention on Human Rights,[144] which, in so far as relevant, states:

> "In the determination . . . of any criminal charge against him,[145] everyone is entitled to a fair and public hearing within a reasonable time by an independent and impartial tribunal[146] established by law."

---

[141] Criminal Procedure (Scotland) Act 1995 s.136. The rule is a general one only, however, and may be excluded or varied by particular statutory provisions: for example, under the Architects Act 1997 s.21(4)(c), and relative to an offence under s.20 of that Act, s.136 of the 1995 Act is to be read as if "two years" was substituted for the "six months" which generally applies. See also s.292 (as amended by the Criminal Proceedings etc. (Reform) (Scotland) Act 2007 (asp 6) Sch.1 para.24) of the 1995 Act for the meaning of an offence "triable only summarily".

[142] See above, para.2–35.

[143] Criminal Procedure (Scotland) Act 1995 s.65 (as amended by the Criminal Procedure and Investigations Act 1996 s.73(3); the Crime and Punishment (Scotland) Act 1997 Sch.1 para.21(9); the Criminal Procedure (Amendment) (Scotland) Act 2004 (asp 5) s.6; and the Criminal Proceedings etc. (Reform) (Scotland) Act 2007 (asp 6) Sch.1 para.12(1)) and s.147 (as amended by the said 2007 Act (asp 6) s.11).

[144] See the Human Rights Act 1998 Sch.1.

[145] For an account of the stage in criminal proceedings at which art 6(1) may be engaged, see *Jacobs, White and Ovey, The European Convention on Human Rights,* edited by R. White and C. Ovey, 5th edn (2010), pp.246–247. See also, e.g. *Dyer v Watson,* 2002 S.C.(P.C.) 89, and, *Untershutz v HM Advocate,* 2003 S.C.C.R. 287.

[146] Cf. *Starrs v Ruxton; Ruxton v Starrs,* 1999 S.C.C.R. 1052; see also *Dickson v HM Advocate* [2007] HCJAC 65; 2008 S.L.T. 12 (court of five judges).

What amounts to a "reasonable time" depends on the facts and circumstances of each case[147]; but the Convention right here extends to the whole proceedings, including any appeal.[148] If the delay is due to an act (or failure) of the Lord Advocate (or a prosecutor for whom he or she is responsible), then the matter will be a "compatibility or devolution issue".[149]

PROSECUTABLE PERSONS

The range of persons who can successfully be prosecuted for an alleged crime is **2–43** not confined to human beings, but, on the other hand, does not extend to all human beings. In particular in Scotland, a "child" under the age of eight years cannot "be guilty of any offence" by virtue of conclusive statutory presumption.[150] This presumption is probably based on an assumed lack of capacity of young children for any true criminal appetite, or on some general notion that young children cannot be expected to exercise adult restraints. A majority of the Inner House (Second Division) of the Court of Session has held, however, that the basis of the presumption is that a child under eight years of age is incapable of having mens rea (or "dole").[151] But there the court was dealing with two alleged common law offences where mens rea is always an essential element; and, in any event, such a basis would require rewriting of the statutory presumption by addition of words such as "which requires *mens rea*"—thus producing a possibly undesirable limitation on the operation of the rule.[152] Whatever its true basis, the presumption entails that no child under the age of eight years can be prosecuted before any Scottish court for what he has apparently done or for the consequences of what he has failed to do; any purported prosecution would be met by the plea of "non-age" in bar of trial.[153]

Older children

The presumption previously mentioned[154] does not apply to children above the **2–44** age of eight years; but under a fairly recent amendment to the law,[155] a child under the age of 12 years may not be prosecuted for an offence—which means that a child of or over that age may indeed face prosecution save "for an offence which was committed at a time when the [he or she] was under the age of 12 years."[156] There is also a further rule; a child of or over the age of 12 but under the age of 16 years cannot be prosecuted except by or on the instructions of the Lord

---

[147] There are a considerable number of case decisions involving this aspect of art.6, but see in particular *Gibson v HM Advocate*, 2001 S.L.T. 591.

[148] See, e.g. *Mills v HM Advocate (No.2)* 2001 S.L.T. 1359; *Gillespie v HM Advocate*, 2003 S.C.C.R. 82.

[149] See above, para.2–13, and *Mills v HM Advocate (No.2)*, 2001 S.L.T. 1359.

[150] See the Criminal Procedure (Scotland) Act 1995 s.41.

[151] See *Merrin v S*, 1987 S.L.T. 193.

[152] Cf. J. Chalmers and F. Leverick, *Criminal Defences and Pleas in Bar of Trial (Edinburgh: W. Green, 2006)*, p.193, para.9.01.

[153] For this and other pleas in bar of trial, see Chalmers and Leverick, *Criminal Defences and Pleas in Bar of Trial* (2006), Chs 9 and 14 to 19; cf. Ch.20.

[154] See above, para.2–43.

[155] See the Criminal Procedure (Scotland) Act 1995 (hereafter referred to as "the 1995 Act") s.41A(1), as inserted by the Criminal Justice and Licensing (Scotland) Act 2010 (asp 13) s.52(2).

[156] See the 1995 Act s.41A(2), inserted as indicated above in the immediately preceding note.

31

Advocate—and then only before a High Court or a Sheriff Court.[157] In summary, the effect of these rules is that children who are aged eight years or over (but under 12) can commit offences[158] although they cannot be prosecuted for them; children who are aged 12 years or over (but under 16) may be prosecuted for offences they are alleged to have committed (although there are limitations to this); and persons aged 16 or above may be prosecuted in the "normal" manner. Where a child is competently prosecuted, steps have to be taken to render the proceedings rather less public and awe inspiring than would be the case where adult offenders alone are involved.[159]

Children's hearings

2–45   It is for consideration how children below the age of 12 (who cannot be prosecuted), or those aged 12 to 16 years (who in fact have not been prosecuted) are "dealt with" for any offences they are alleged to have committed. Since 1971,[160] most such children are referred to a "children's hearing" which is not concerned (as a criminal court would be) with fact-finding or punishment at all, but rather with the need to safeguard and promote children's welfare—usually as a paramount consideration.[161] This process begins when such a child is referred to an official called the "Principal Reporter".[162] Such references can occur on a wide variety of grounds—of which that "the child has committed an offence" is but one.[163] If the principal reporter considers that the ground or grounds upon which the reference was made may have merit, he or she must then consider whether a "compulsory supervision order"[164] may be necessary in respect of the child in question: if such an order may be so necessary, then the principal reporter must arrange for a "children's hearing" to be held. Such a hearing consists of three persons drawn from a pool of those appointed to be members of the "Children's Panel",[165] and its primary function is to ascertain from the child in question (and each "relevant person"[166]) whether the referral grounds are accepted. If they are, then the hearing must decide whether to make a compulsory supervision order.[167] If they are not, or if they are not understood by the child (or any relevant person), the hearing will in most cases then ask the principal reporter to apply to a sheriff

---

[157] See the 1995 Act s.42(1), as amended by the Criminal Justice and Licensing (Scotland) Act 2010 (asp 13) s.52(3).

[158] This is implicit from the statutory wording: see the reference above in fn.156. Children under the age of eight years are also non-prosecutable, of course, but apparently on the more fundamental basis that they are deemed incapable of committing crimes.

[159] Criminal Procedure (Scotland) Act 1995 ss.42, 142. For the meaning of "child" relative to s.142, see s.307(1)—which refers to the Children (Scotland) Act 1995 s.93(2)(b), as now replaced by the Children's Hearings (Scotland) Act 2011 (asp 1) Sch.5 para.2(11)(ii).

[160] This was the year when the relevant parts of the Social Work (Scotland) Act 1968 came into force. The relevant law is now to be found in the Children's Hearings (Scotland) Act 2011 (asp 11)—hereafter referred to as "the 2011 Act".

[161] See the 2011 Act ss.25 and 26.

[162] See the 2011 Act s.14 and Sch.3.

[163] See the 2011 Act s.67(2)(a)–(o): the ground relevant to the present discussion will be found at s.67(2)(j).

[164] This is a "term of art" given meaning in the 2011 Act s.83: it consists of an order which contains any of the measures set out in s.83(2)—none of which amounting in any way to punishment.

[165] For "children's panel" and "children's hearings", see (initially, at least) the 2011 Act ss.4 and 5.

[166] See the 2011 Act s.200.

[167] See above, fn.164.

for a determination whether the grounds in question are established.[168] The sheriff, to whom application is made, must then make such a determination after hearing appropriate evidence[169]—which, in the case of the ground that "the child has committed an offence", must reach the high standard of proof[170] which applies in criminal proceedings.[171] Any appeal from the decision of a children's hearing or from the determination of a sheriff (as appropriate) is heard by the Sheriff Principal or (ultimately) the Court of Session—which distances this whole process from any involvement with criminal courts or the criminal justice system: it is truly a process sui generis (of its own kind).

Non-human persons

A non-human, "legal" person can be prosecuted for an alleged crime.[172] In **2–46** Scotland, certain business organisations—in particular companies formed and registered under the Companies Acts[173]—are treated in law as if they had an existence (a *persona*) separate from the human beings who direct them or are employed by them. But that existence, being the creation of statute law and thus a pure abstraction, is a peculiar one in that a company (or other relevant business "organisation") cannot itself perform acts (or fail to perform them) and cannot itself possess any particular state of mind—although acts (or omissions) and states of mind are very generally required as essential components of criminal liability.[174] If, therefore, such an abstract "person" is to be prosecuted, convicted and punished for crime, some rule will have to be formed which attributes the acts (or omissions) and mental states of human beings occupying positions within (say) a

---

[168] See the 2011 Act ss.93 and 94.

[169] This is not done in open court: see the 2011 Act s.101(3).

[170] See below, para.2–55.

[171] See the 2011 Act s.102(3). Under s.102(2), the sheriff who makes the determination must be one who would have had jurisdiction if the child were being prosecuted for the offence in question; almost certainly, in the case of children under eight years of age, there would be no sheriff who could meet that criterion—see *Merrin v S,* 1987 S.L.T. 193. In that case, decided by the Court of Session under previous "children's hearing" legislation, a majority of the second division decided that a sheriff had been correct to dismiss an application to determine whether a child had "committed" two common law offences—since the child in question had been under the age of eight years at the material time. The effect of that decision was to remove such a child from the "children's hearing" system altogether—unless some ground of referral, other than that he had committed an offence, could be found. Under the present legislation (the 2011 Act), it is uncertain whether the principle of *Merrin v S* can extend to children aged eight years or over but under 12 years; the intention probably is that it should not so extend (especially given that the 2011 Act accepts that such children can commit offences although they are not prosecutable for them, and given also the definition of "child" promulgated in the 2011 Act s.199).

[172] *Transco Plc v HM Advocate,* 2004 J.C. 29.

[173] I.e. the Companies Act 2006, and its predecessors: see the 2006 Act s.1. Partnerships in Scotland also have a *persona* separate from the individual partners who compose them: Partnership Act 1890 s.4(2); see also the Criminal Procedure (Scotland) Act 1995 ss.70 and 143 as amended respectively by the Criminal Proceedings etc. (Reform) (Scotland) Act 2007 (asp 6) ss.28, 17 and by the Criminal Justice and Licensing (Scotland) Act 2010 (asp 13) ss.66 and 67—noting that partnerships, incorporated companies and others are now referred to in the 1995 Act as "organisations" (see the 1995 Act s.307, as amended by the Criminal Justice and Licensing (Scotland) Act 2010 (asp 13) s.65) and, as such, prosecutable. See also Scottish Law Commission, *Report on Criminal Liability of Partnerships* (The Stationery Office, 2011) Scot. Law Com. No. 224.

[174] See below, Ch.3. It now seems accepted that common law crimes in general require proof of mens rea for conviction: *Transco Plc v HM Advocate,* 2004 J.C. 29, per Lord Hamilton (with whom Lord MacLean agreed) at 50–51, paras 2–43.

company to that company itself: thus, such a human being who can be proved to have performed a criminal act (with the requisite state of mind) will himself bear criminal responsibility for it, and can be prosecuted accordingly—but so too will the company itself, by application of an accepted rule of attribution. Both "persons" will thus have liability.

Until the decision in the case of *Transco Plc v HM Advocate*,[175] it was not clear if Scots law had such a rule of attribution or whether companies (or other relevant business "organisations") in Scotland might be prosecuted for all offences, irrespective of whether they were common law or statutory.[176] In *Transco Plc*,[177] however, an indictment was brought against a company for (inter alia) culpable homicide, in that the company had allegedly failed to obtemper its duties in providing safe regimes for the supply of gas to domestic premises and thus, in full knowledge of the risks, caused the deaths of four persons when an explosion occurred. The company, of course, was incapable itself of such failure or such knowledge; but the indictment alleged that the failure and knowledge had been attributed to the company over many years via committees and posts established within that company's organisation. The Appeal Court reviewed the authorities, and concluded that there was an accepted rule of attribution for corporate liability in English law,[178] that that rule was accepted also in Scots law,[179] and that the application of that rule was decisive of the company's objections to the competency and relevancy[180] of the charge of culpable homicide. The substance of the rule was (and is) that the company would itself be liable criminally if a named person (or group of persons acting collectively)[181] of sufficient status within that company[182] could be proved to have done a criminal act (or omission) with the required state of mind: in brief, the criminal responsibility of such a person (or group) would thus be attributed to the company itself. It is essential for the operation of the rule that some such person, or group, should be precisely identified[183]: and it was precisely because the Crown in *Transco Plc*[184] could not produce such identification that the charge of culpable homicide was held to be competent (since a company or other relevant business organisation *can* be prosecuted for a

---

[175] *Transco Plc v HM Advocate*, 2004 J.C. 29.

[176] Under the Criminal Procedure (Scotland) Act 1995 ss.70 and 143, it was (and is) simply assumed that prosecution of relevant business "organisations" was (and is) generally possible: and many specific statutes made (and make) the assumption that prosecution of such organisations is to be expected: see the Adoption and Children (Scotland) Act 2007 (asp 4) s.115, and the Sexual Offences (Scotland) Act 2009 (asp 9) s.57 for typically worded modern examples. Most of the existing case law, however, concerns the liability of companies.

[177] *Transco Plc v HM Advocate*, 2004 J.C. 29.

[178] Reference was made in particular to the opinions of Lord Reid, in *Tesco Supermarkets Ltd v Nattrass* [1972] A.C. 153 (HL) at 170E–G, and Lord Hoffmann, in *Meridian Global Funds Management Asia Ltd v Securities Commission* [1995] 2 A.C. 500 (P.C.) at 506–509.

[179] The court referred in particular to the opinion of the court in *Purcell Meats (Scotland) Ltd v McLeod*, 1987 S.L.T. 528.

[180] For an explanation of the significance of these objections, see the opinion of Lord Hamilton in *Transco Plc v HM Advocate*, 2004 J.C. 29, at 46, para.31.

[181] See *Transco Plc v HM Advocate*, 2004 J.C. 29, opinion of Lord Hamilton (with whom Lord MacLean agreed) at 58, para.62.

[182] I.e. sufficient status to be regarded, relative to the matter in question, as the directing (or controlling) mind and will of the company. In view of this, the rule is often referred to as the "directing mind and will" rule.

[183] Thus the rule is sometimes also referred to as the "identification" rule.

[184] *Transco Plc v HM Advocate*, 2004 J.C. 29.

common law crime[185]) but irrelevant (since the Crown were unable to show that the accepted rule of attribution could be satisfied in this case.[186]

Crimes committed by others

A person may be validly prosecuted for a crime he did not personally commit. **2–47** He may be liable for its commission "art and part" (i.e. as an accessory, see below, Ch.7) or vicariously (usually by being the employer of the person actually responsible). Vicarious liability[187] seems to be confined, however, to statutory offences which make specific provision for it[188] and statutory offences where the courts have decided that it is appropriate.[189]

Persons unfit for trial

A prosecutable person must not be "unfit for trial". To be considered as falling **2–48** within that category, it must be established on the balance of probabilities (rather than beyond reasonable doubt) that the person in question is incapable, by means of mental or physical condition, of participating effectively in the trial. That must be established to the satisfaction of the High Court of Justiciary or the Sheriff Court (as the case may be), and the relevant court is required to have regard to (inter alia) the ability of that person to understand the nature of the charge, the requirement of tendering an informed plea, the purpose of the trial, and the evidence which may be given against him—as well as his ability to instruct legal representatives; such a court may also have regard to any other factor which it considers to be relevant. It is not sufficient, however, if the person in question is found simply to be unable to remember whether the alleged events occurred as they are described in the charge.[190]

---

[185] This is in general true; but it may be a practical impossibility to indict a company for murder, since the only punishment available for a person convicted of that crime is life in prison: see the Criminal Procedure (Scotland) Act 1995 s.205.

[186] See *Transco Plc v HM Advocate*, 2004 J.C. 29, opinion of Lord Hamilton at 58–59, para.63. The Crown had argued that the failures manifest, and knowledge of risks possessed, by many committees and (unnamed) persons within the company over many years might be attributed to the company on a cumulative basis; but the court rejected this contention, as resting on the application of a differently formed rule based on the principle of aggregation which was not accepted in either English or Scots law. (This case demonstrates the great difficulty of actually proving that the rule of attribution is satisfied, and thus that a corporate body such as a company is criminally liable for a common law offence: for that reason, the United Kingdom Government has created a discrete statutory offence known in Scotland as "corporate homicide". Briefly, this offence is committed by an organisation (which includes a corporation) if the way in which its activities are managed or organised causes a person's death and amounts to a gross breach of a relevant duty of care owed to that person: see the Corporate Manslaughter and Corporate Homicide Act 2007 s.1 and below, para.9–78, for a more detailed description of the offence.)

[187] See below, para.13–23.

[188] This is now very rare. For example, the express provision for such liability in the Licensing (Scotland) Act 1976 (see s.67(1), (2) and Sch.5 Table col.3) is not reflected in the Act which replaces it—viz. the Licensing (Scotland) Act 2005 (asp 16), where the general approach to licensing offences is in any event different from that of its predecessor.

[189] It is now well accepted that vicarious liability does not apply to common law offences: see below, para.13–24, and *Transco Plc v HM Advocate*, 2004 J.C. 29, per Lord Hamilton (with whom Lord MacLean agreed) at 54, para.53.

[190] See the Criminal Procedure (Scotland) Act 1995 s.53F, as inserted by the Criminal Justice and Licensing (Scotland) Act 2010 (asp 13) s.170(1).

The common law rule

2–49   At common law, there was a rule that once a person had been prosecuted for an offence and a verdict had been reached of either guilt or acquittal, it was (and is) not lawful for him to be re-prosecuted for that same offence; a good plea "in bar of trial" would lie if such a re-prosecution were to have been attempted—such a plea being known as res judicata or "tholed assize" (though no jury—assize—need have been involved at all). To that common law rule, there was created a statutory exception, in that the Appeal Court could (and still may) give authority for a new prosecution after hearing an appropriate appeal from the convicted person against his conviction[191] or from the prosecutor against acquittal.[192]

Statutory re-formulations

2–50   That common law rule has recently, and in accordance with a report by the Scottish Law Commission,[193] been re-stated in statutory form; it has also been officially re-titled as the rule against "Double Jeopardy".[194] Under that rule, it is not competent to charge a person, who had been convicted or acquitted of an offence either on indictment or complaint, with the same offence or with any other offence (with which he could have been convicted on that indictment or complaint) or with an offence arising

> "out of the same, or largely the same, acts or omissions as gave rise to the original indictment or complaint and [which] is an aggravated way of committing the original offence."

Along with this rule is a re-stated account of the relative plea in bar of trial, which applies where a person is charged with an offence (again on indictment or complaint) and pleads in bar of his trial for that offence that it

> "arises out of the same, or largely the same, acts or omissions as have already given rise to [his] being tried for, and convicted or acquitted of, an offence"[195];

the trial court must sustain such a plea if it is satisfied (on the "balance of probabilities" standard) of the truth of what has been pled—although this is subject to that court's being persuaded by the prosecutor that the case should nevertheless,

---

[191] See e.g. the Criminal Procedure (Scotland) Act 1995 ss.118(1)(c), 119 (as amended by the Criminal Procedure (Amendment) (Scotland) Act 2004 (asp 5) Sch.1 para.32, the Criminal Proceedings etc. (Reform) (Scotland) Act 2007 (asp 6) Sch. para.16(6), and the Criminal Justice and Licensing (Scotland) Act 2010 (asp 13) ss.76(4)), 183(1)(d), and 185.

[192] See e.g. the Criminal Procedure (Scotland) Act 1995 ss.175(3)(a), 176(1), 183(1)(d) and 185, as also ss. 97A, 97B, 97D and 107A— all as inserted by the Criminal Justice and Licensing (Scotland) Act 2010 (asp 13) ss.73 and 74.

[193] Scottish Law Commission, "Report on Double Jeopardy" (Stationery Office, 2009), Scot. Law Com. No.218.

[194] See the Double Jeopardy (Scotland) Act 2011 (asp 16) s.1; it is to be noted that, by virtue of s.14, s.1 has retrospective effect.

[195] See the Double Jeopardy (Scotland) Act 2011 (asp 16) s.7, and in particular s.7(1), (2).

for some special reason,[196] proceed to trial, provided that that court also considers that it is in the interests of justice to do so.[197]

Statutory exceptions[198] to the Double Jeopardy rule

The first exception to the Double Jeopardy rule occurs where a person has been **2–51** acquitted of an offence under previous summary or solemn proceedings, and where subsequently he (or indeed some other person acting alone or along with the acquitted person) has been convicted of "an offence against the course of justice in connection with those former proceedings". This also applies where the relevant court[199] has concluded on the balance of probabilities that such an offence must have been committed by the acquitted person and/or some other person.[200] In such circumstances, on an appropriate application to the High Court of Justiciary by the Lord Advocate that Court will (always bearing in mind the strictness of the relevant statutory provisions) set aside the original acquittal, and grant authority for a new prosecution.[201] A second exception also involves an acquitted person (as mentioned above)—but who subsequently is found to have admitted committing the offence of which he had been acquitted.[202] Finally, a person who has been acquitted of an offence taken on indictment before the High Court of Justiciary (and not before any court of lower status) may find himself excepted from the Double Jeopardy rule, and thus subject to a new prosecution contrary to that rule, if new evidence becomes available that he committed the original offence or a "relevant offence".[203]

Specific exceptions to, or clarifications of, the statutory re-formulations

The re-formulations of the Double Jeopardy rule and relative plea in bar or trial **2–52** envisage that a person cannot lawfully be charged with an offence "broadly similar" to, or based on largely the same acts or omissions as, one of which he has already been convicted or acquitted.[204] Section 8 of the Double Jeopardy

---

[196] "Special reason" is not defined at this point in the Double Jeopardy (Scotland) Act 2011 (asp 16); cf.,however, s.9(1)(b) of that Act, where an assertion that the original trial had been a nullity is stated to be a "special reason".

[197] See the Double Jeopardy (Scotland) Act 2011 (asp 16) s.7(3) and (4).

[198] Each of these exceptions applies retrospectively: see the Double Jeopardy (Scotland) Act 2011 (asp 16) s.14.

[199] The relevant court here is a bench of three High Court of Justiciary judges, although provision is made for a differently constituted bench "as for example . . . the whole [High Court of Justiciary] sitting together" however impractical, it seems, that might be: see the Double Jeopardy (Scotland) Act 2011 (asp 16) s.5(3)–(6).

[200] See the Double Jeopardy (Scotland) Act 2011 (asp 16) s.2(1), (3); offences against the course of justice include those of interfering with the trial judge or a juror (s.2(4)), the withholding of evidence or the giving of false evidence (s.2(7)), and generally "perverting, or . . . attempting to pervert the course of justice" which does not itself include (s.2(8)) perjury or an offence contrary to s.44(1) of the Criminal Law (Consolidation) (Scotland) Act 1995.

[201] See the Double Jeopardy (Scotland) Act 2011 (asp 16) s.2(2), (4)–(6).

[202] See the Double Jeopardy (Scotland) Act 2011 (asp 16) s.3; notice must be taken, however, of the specific provisions (of that section) which must be obtempered before the original acquittal can be set aside and authority granted for a new prosecution. See also the 2011 Act ss.5 and 6.

[203] "Relevant" offences are defined in the Double Jeopardy (Scotland) Act 2011 (asp 16) s.4(2); s.4 must be read in its entirety, however, along with ss.5 and 6, in order to understand fully this particular exception.

[204] See above, para.2–50.

(Scotland) Act 2011 (asp 16) specifically provides for the possibility of a person's being tried for murder after he has been convicted or acquitted (on indictment or complaint) of an offence other than murder—notwithstanding that the acts or omissions involved are the same or largely the same. If the detailed provisions of that section are satisfied, then a quorum of three judges of the High Court of Justiciary can determine that such a person's plea in bar of trial (on the basis of double jeopardy) is to be repelled. To reach that stage, however, the prosecutor must assert a special reason why the plea should not succeed—namely, that there is new evidence that that person committed the murder now charged, or that the person has admitted committing it.[205] More generally, whatever the charge in respect of which the person in question makes a plea in bar of trial under s.7 of the said Act, where the prosecutor argues as a special reason for repelling the plea that the original trial was a nullity, the High Court of Justiciary may be persuaded that it should allow the trial to continue.[206] In addition the said Act makes special provision for relevant pleas in bar of trial which involve foreign proceedings.[207] It also makes special provision for the situation in which a person has been convicted or acquitted of (for example) the assault and injury of another person who subsequently dies; if the provisions relative to that sort of situation are satisfied, then the person in question may competently be charged with the murder, the culpable homicide, or any other offence of causing the death of that other person.[208]

CHARGE MUST RELATE TO A KNOWN CRIME

2-53 The charging document in a solemn procedure case is known as an indictment. The equivalent in a summary procedure case is known as a complaint. These documents must allege that the accused committed a known crime. If they do not, then they may be attacked and disposed of as "irrelevant." There is really no problem in relation to statutory offences, since clearly an existing enactment either is or is not validly referred to. But common law offences do pose difficulties. Some of these offences are "innominate" (i.e. having no short, recognisable name—or *nomen juris*—as opposed to the better known crimes with instantly recognisable titles, such as murder, theft and rape), and consequently must be charged by a more or less lengthy description.[209] It will often be a moot point whether the description given is adequate or whether it relates to something entirely novel.[210] It must also be borne in mind that conviction is possible in

---

[205] See the Double Jeopardy (Scotland) Act 2011 (asp 16) s.8 (1)–(6).

[206] See the Double Jeopardy (Scotland) Act 2011 (asp 16) s.9. Under s.9(2), it should be noted that if such a plea is raised before the Sheriff or Justice of the Peace court, the case must then be remitted to the High Court of Justiciary for a decision whether to sustain or repel the plea; also, in terms of s.9(4), the ultimate reason for repelling such a plea must be that it is in the interests of justice to do so. See further on the question of the alleged nullity of previous proceedings in respect of which (a) a person has been convicted or acquitted, and (b) the prosecutor wishes to mount a new prosecution, s.12 of that Act.

[207] See the Double Jeopardy (Scotland) Act 2011 (asp 16) s.10.

[208] See the Double Jeopardy (Scotland) Act 2011 (asp 16) s.11. For the avoidance of doubt, all provisions of that Act are made retrospective quoad convictions and/or acquittals which occurred before the Act came into force, save for ss.5,6 and 13–17: see s.14.

[209] See, for example, charge (1) in *Khaliq v HM Advocate*, 1984 J.C. 23 at 24.

[210] But compare the Criminal Procedure (Scotland) Act 1995 Sch.3 para.2, which requires only that the appropriate document sets forth facts relevant and sufficient to constitute a crime.

respect of any part of a charge, provided that part itself constitutes an identifiable crime,[211] and that specific statutes do allow "hidden" alternative charges to be considered by a judge (summary cases) or a jury (solemn cases).[212]

There is probably no de minimis principle[213] operated in Scots criminal law. It **2–54** is thus not a competent objection to any criminal charge that the matter is too trivial for consideration by a court. Scottish public prosecutors (see below, para.2–58) are deemed to have considered fully the matter of triviality at a stage prior to the drawing of a complaint or indictment.

ACCUSATORIAL FORM OF PROCEDURE

The principle followed by Scots criminal law is that the prosecutor, public or **2–55** private, must not only make the accusation against the person in question, but also prove the matter to the satisfaction of the judge (summary case) or jury (solemn case). On a charge being made by way of complaint or indictment, it is not for the accused to satisfy the judge or jury as to his innocence. To that extent at least, there is compliance with art.6(2) of the European Convention on Human Rights[214]) which states that "Everyone charged with a criminal offence shall be presumed innocent until proved guilty according to law." The prosecutor must, therefore, provide the court with evidence. In Scotland, that generally entails the provision of two independent pieces of evidence in respect of every material issue in the case against the accused. (Such provision is generally referred to as the requirement for corroboration; but under the "Carloway Review"[215] of November 17, 2011, it has been recommended that the need for corroboration should be dispensed with in Scots criminal law.) The "evidential burden", therefore, lies on the prosecutor. But he also carries the "persuasive burden". He must persuade the judge (or the jury) that the case against the accused is true beyond reasonable doubt. If he fails on either of these burdens, the case will be lost (possibly at an early stage, on a plea from the accused that there is "no case to answer").[216]) Precisely what the prosecutor must establish by way of evidence and persuasion depends upon the

---

[211] Criminal Procedure (Scotland) Act 1995 Sch.3 para.9(2).

[212] See, e.g. the Criminal Procedure (Scotland) Act 1995 Sch.3 para.8(2)–(4) (certain crimes of dishonesty— noting that paras 8(3A),(3B) were added by the Criminal Justice and Licensing (Scotland) Act 2010 (asp 13) s.48) as also the general provision in para.14—where a statutory charge may contain a hidden common law one in respect of which conviction may follow (as, e.g. in *Horsburgh v Russell*, 1994 S.L.T. 942, *Anderson v Griffiths*, 2005 1 J.C. 169, and *Robertson v Klos* [2005] HCJAC 136; 2006 S.C.C.R. 52). See also, e.g. the Sexual Offences (Scotland) Act 2009 (asp 9) Sch.3.

[213] The complete Latin tag is *de minimis non curat lex*, i.e. the law does not concern itself with trivial matters.

[214] See the Human Rights Act 1998 Sch.1.

[215] The "Carloway Review" is available electronically at http://www.scotland.gov.uk/About/ CarlowayReview [Accessed June 1, 2010].

[216] See the Criminal Procedure (Scotland) Act 1995 ss.97 and 160 which relate to such a plea's being made at the close of the prosecution case. With respect to indictment cases only, however, it is possible for an accused to make a later plea (that the evidence is insufficient in law to justify his being convicted of an offence charged, or impliedly contained, in the indictment and/or that there is no evidence to support "some part of the circumstances set out in the indictment") either at the close of the whole evidence or after the prosecutor's address to the jury: see the Criminal Procedure (Scotland) Act 1995 ss.97A to 97C, as inserted by the Criminal Justice and Licensing (Scotland) Act 2010 (asp 13) s.73.

particular crime charged and its actus reus and mens rea requirements (see below, Ch.3). In a result crime (see above, para.2–36), the issue of causation (see below, Ch.5) will also have to be addressed.[217])

2–56 The Scottish prosecutor is regarded as being "the master of the instance." That means he has entire discretion as to whether the case should be prosecuted at all,[218]) as to the way in which the case will be prosecuted (the accused, for example, having no right to demand jury trial), and as to the conduct of the case in court before a judge or a judge and jury.[219]) He may in particular abandon the case, "desert the diet", either temporarily, *pro loco et tempore*, subject to any prescriptive time periods which apply (see above, paras 2–39 and 2–40) or permanently, *simpliciter*, or cause the proceedings to be adjourned, or even decline after a verdict of "guilty" to "move", i.e. ask, for sentence, in which event (or certainly in an indictment case) no sentence can be passed by the presiding judge.[220])

ADVERSARIAL FORM OF PROCEDURE

2–57 In Scotland, as in the Anglo-American family of legal systems, a trial is conducted by the opposing parties (i.e. the prosecutor and the accused—or more commonly, his lawyer or advocate)[221]) before a largely silent judge, or judge and jury. It is not

---

[217] For detailed information on evidential matters, see Davidson, *Evidence* (2007).

[218] Thus he may ignore the complainer's wish that the offender should not be prosecuted, see, e.g. *Sze v Wilson*, 1992 S.L.T. 569.

[219] Thus the Lord Advocate cannot be required to give reasons for any decisions taken which are entirely within the province of the Crown, see, e.g. *HM Advocate v O'Neill*, 1992 J.C. 22.

[220] For observations on the current practice, see *HM Advocate v McGee*, 2006 S.L.T. 818, Lord Hardie at 82E–L, para.9.

[221] Under the Criminal Procedure (Scotland) Act 1995 s.288C (as inserted by the Sexual Offences (Procedure and Evidence) (Scotland) Act 2002 (asp 9) s.1; and as amended by the Criminal Justice (Scotland) Act 2003 (asp 7) s.15(2), the Criminal Procedure (Amendment) (Scotland) Act 2004 (asp 5) s.4(1) and Sch. para.55(a),(b), the Mental Health (Care and Treatment) (Scotland) Act 2003 (Modification of Enactments) Order 2005 (SSI 2005/465) Sch.1 para.27(5), the Sexual Offences (Scotland) Act 2009 (asp 9) Sch.5 para.2(7), and the Criminal Justice and Licensing (Scotland) Act 2010 (asp 13) s.69(2)), an accused is prohibited from conducting his case in person at a relevant hearing (as defined in s.288C(1A), as inserted by the 2010 Act (asp13) s.69(2)(a)) which includes a trial, for a listed sexual offence; this also applies in the case of a non-listed offence where a court makes an order that it is satisfied that there is such a substantial sexual element in the alleged commission of the offence that that offence ought to be treated in the same way as one that is listed (s.288C (3), (4)). Reference may also be made to the Vulnerable Witnesses (Scotland) Act 2004 (asp 3) s.6—which adds ss.288E and 288F (as amended by the 2010 Act (asp 13) s.69(4) and (5) respectively) to the 1995 Act, and applies a similar restriction on the accused's conduct of his own case at any hearing relative to listed offences (see s.288E(3)) or other specified offences at the discretion of the court (s.288F) where a child under the age of 12 or a "vulnerable witness" (see s.271 of the 1995 Act, as substituted by the Vulnerable Witnesses (Scotland) Act 2004 (asp 3) s.1(1), modified by the above mentioned (SSI 2005/465) Sch.1 para.27(3), and amended by the 2010 Act (asp 13) ss.87 and 88) is to give evidence. When the accused is not permitted to conduct his own case, he may engage a lawyer to act for him—which failing, the court will appoint one to so act: see s.288D (as inserted by the Sexual Offences (Procedure and Evidence) (Scotland) Act 2002 (asp 9) s.2(1), and as amended by the Criminal Justice (Scotland) Act 2003 (asp 7) s.15(3), the Criminal Procedure (Amendment) (Scotland) Act 2004 (asp 5) s.4(2) and Sch. para.56, the Criminal Proceedings etc. (Reform) (Scotland) Act 2007 (asp 6) s.35(6), and the 2010 Act (asp 13) s.69(3)) of the 1995 Act. It remains to be seen whether these provisions are entirely compatible with art.6(3)(c) of the European Convention on Human Rights (see the Human Rights Act 1998 Sch.1).

for the judge (or the jury, if present) to question the witnesses. The judge (or jury) must simply follow the questioning and cross-questioning conducted by the two sides, then give a verdict according to what has been heard. It is also of the essence of this "adversarial" procedure that the accused (or his lawyer) is entitled to question the prosecutor's witnesses and introduce evidence of his own by way of defence.[222]) General and special defences (see below, Ch.8) are regarded as the accused's responsibility—in the first instance, at least. He will have the "evidential burden" of placing some evidence favouring them before the court—but without assuming any responsibility for persuading the court of their truth. Mental disorder (formerly known as "insanity") and Diminished Responsibility are well known exceptions to that principle, both of these defences requiring that the accused carries not only the usual evidential burden but also the persuasive burden since there is a presumption, which must be overcome, that he was not mentally disordered (or not suffering from diminished responsibility) at the time of the offence. The standard of proof required of him in such situations is "on the balance of probabilities", i.e. that it is more probable than not that he was mentally disordered or suffering from diminished responsibility at the material time.[223]) It is never for the accused to prove anything on the prosecutorial standard of "beyond reasonable doubt".

PUBLIC PROSECUTION

The norm, in Scotland, is for criminal prosecutions to be instituted and conducted **2–58** by the public prosecution service consisting of the Lord Advocate, the Solicitor General for Scotland, advocates-depute, and area and district procurators fiscal. The service operates from the Crown Office in Edinburgh and from area and district fiscals' offices throughout the country. Procurators fiscal normally deal with cases set for proceedings before sheriff and JP courts. In High Courts (as also before the Appeal Court), advocates-depute (or the Lord Advocate or the Solicitor General in person) normally present cases on behalf of the public.[224]) It has become customary to designate public prosecutors as "the Crown".

Private prosecutors

Since considerable confidence is reposed in the public prosecution service, **2–59** demand for private prosecution is low. It appears that a private party, wishing to prosecute under solemn procedure, must use the rather archaic and long-winded form of document called "criminal letters" rather than the more modern "indictment", and must apply (by "bill") to the High Court for the issue of such "letters". That court will not normally issue these unless the application for them is supported by the Lord Advocate, although it is possible in exceptional

---

[222] See art.6(3)(d) of the European Convention on Human Rights, as set out in the Human Rights Act 1998 Sch.1.

[223] See the Criminal Procedure (Scotland) Act 1995 ss.51A and 51B (as inserted by the Criminal Justice and Licensing (Scotland) Act 2010 (asp 13) s.168).

[224] Although solicitor-advocates may be permitted to do so, see the Criminal Procedure (Scotland) Act 1995 s.301.

circumstances for the court to permit their issue without his concurrence.[225] It is essential, however, for the prospective private prosecutor to show that he has been personally wronged by the alleged offence. It is not possible in Scotland to prosecute in respect of a crime that is no more than a general public wrong.[226] It appears, too, that there are crimes which are always to be regarded as primarily public wrongs, in respect of which only public prosecutors can be permitted to take action.[227] Private prosecution under summary procedure is generally not competent.[228]

PUBLIC PROCEEDINGS

2–60 It is a principle of Scots criminal law (which thus far accords with art.6 of the European Convention on Human Rights by which public authorities are now bound[229]) that criminal trials, though not necessarily preliminary proceedings, should take place in the presence of the accused[230] (so that he may participate, or, if legally represented, instruct his lawyer) and in public (presumably so that justice can be seen to be done). To this principle, there are some exceptions. In particular, a summary trial may take place in the accused's absence if he fails to appear and the court is satisfied that it is in the interests of justice to do so[231]; also, the accused may be removed if he "misconducts himself"[232]; and, further, the public may be excluded when evidence is being tendered in a solemn trial for rape "or the like".[233] That justice must not only be done, but be seen to be done, is both proverbial and a ground of appeal. The test is not whether, for example, the trial judge was *in fact* impartial or in good faith, but whether any suspicion might linger in the mind of a reasonable person that there might have been a lack of impartial justice.[234] Curiously, there have been more reported cases on this matter since it was stated in *Bradford v McLeod* that the paucity of recorded examples was a tribute to Scots law.[235] Thus, imposing sentence without giving an opportunity for a plea in mitigation,[236] congratulating the mother of a young complainer

[225] See *J & P Coats Ltd v Brown* (1909) 6 Adam 19; X v Sweeney, 1982 J.C. 70.
[226] See *McBain v Crichton*, 1961 J.C. 25.
[227] See, e.g. *Meehan v Inglis*, 1975 J.C. 9.
[228] See s.138 of the Criminal Procedure (Scotland) Act 1995, and the now repealed s.63 of the Criminal Justice (Scotland) Act 1995.
[229] See above, para.2–17.
[230] Criminal Procedure (Scotland) Act 1995 s.92(1) (as amended by the Criminal Procedure (Amendment) (Scotland) Act 2004 (asp 5) s.10(1)) and s.153(1) (as amended by the Criminal Proceedings etc. (Reform) (Scotland) Act 2007 (asp 6) s.14(5)).
[231] See the Criminal Procedure (Scotland) Act 1995 s.150A, as inserted by the Criminal Proceedings etc. (Reform) (Scotland) Act 2007 (asp 6) s.14(4): note that this rule also applies to diets other than those of trial, and is subject to safeguards mentioned in s.150A.
[232] Criminal Procedure (Scotland) Act 1995 s.92(2)–(2F),(4) (as amended and/or inserted by the Criminal Procedure (Amendment) (Scotland) Act 2004 (asp 5) s.10(2)–(4)), and s.153(2).
[233] Criminal Procedure (Scotland) Act 1995 s.92(3): cf. art.6(1) of the European Convention on Human Rights (see the Human Rights Act 1998 Sch.1).
[234] See *Hogg v Normand*, 1992 S.L.T. 736; *Starrs v Ruxton; Ruxton v Starrs*, 1999 S.C.C.R. 1052; *Rimmer, Petitioner*, 2002 S.C.C.R. 1.
[235] *Bradford v McLeod*, 1986 S.L.T. 244, at 248G.
[236] *Bassi v Normand*, 1992 S.L.T. 341.

who had just given evidence in court,[237] using intemperate language in court,[238] and falling asleep on the bench[239] have all fallen foul of the general principle.[240]

PROCEEDINGS CONDUCTED FAIRLY

It is axiomatic that all stages of criminal proceedings should be conducted fairly **2–61** and impartially according to predetermined rules of evidence and procedure. In particular, proceedings must not be conducted according to arbitrary and ad hoc rules. Scots law is also bound by art.6 ("Right to a fair trial") of the European Convention on Human Rights,[241] whereunder not only does an accused person have the right "to a fair and public hearing within a reasonable time by an independent and impartial tribunal established by law"[242] but also the following "minimum rights"[243]

> "(*a*) to be informed promptly, in a language which he understands and in detail, of the nature and cause of the accusation against him;
> (*b*) to have adequate time and facilities for the preparation of his defence;
> (*c*) to defend himself in person or through legal assistance of his own choosing or, if he has not sufficient means to pay for legal assistance, to be given it free when the interests of justice so require;
> (*d*) to examine or have examined witnesses against him and to obtain the attendance and examination of witnesses on his behalf under the same conditions as witnesses against him;
> (*e*) to have the free assistance of an interpreter if he cannot understand or speak the language used in court."

In addition to these rights, under Scots law the accused or his legal representative always has the right to speak last in a criminal trial.[244]

NO RIGHT TO JURY TRIAL

Unlike the law of England and many States in the United States of America, Scots **2–62** law does not permit accused persons to elect for a jury rather than a bench (i.e. judge alone) trial. They must simply accept what the prosecutor or, unusually, the law (e.g. in murder and rape cases) dictates. Scottish prosecutors' discretion is absolute in this matter, which explains why jury trials are much less common in this country than elsewhere. If jury trial is considered proper, the accused's case

---

[237] *Hogg v Normand*, 1992 S.L.T. 736.
[238] *Sneddon v Lees*, 1996 S.L.T. 294.
[239] *Frew v Brown*, 1996 S.L.T. 282. See also the following examples, *Faroux v Brown*, 1996 S.C.C.R. 891; *Lorimer v Normand*, 1997 S.C.C.R. 582 (and *Walls v Heywood*, 2000 S.C.C.R. 21); *Milton v McLeod*, 1999 S.C.C.R. 210; *Murray v Watt*, 2002 S.C.C.R. 122; *McDonald v Craigen*, 2002 S.C.C.R. 405.
[240] By way of contrast, what was alleged to have taken place in the privacy of the jury room was not considered to be covered by the principle—*Russell v HM Advocate*, 1991 J.C. 194.
[241] See the Human Rights Act 1998 Sch.1.
[242] See above, para.2–60.
[243] European Convention on Human Rights art.6(3).
[244] Criminal Procedure (Scotland) Act 1995 ss.98 and 161.

will be determined (unless foreclosed by, for example, a plea of guilty) by a jury of 15 persons, rather than the more usual six to 12 persons favoured elsewhere in the Anglo-American family of legal systems.[245] Scottish juries are selected almost totally at random[246] with no recourse to the extensive voir dire processes found in so many American States.[247]

VERDICTS

2–63 In Scottish criminal trials, both judges (in bench trials) and juries may consider three possible verdicts—guilty, not guilty, and not-proven. Although it is not easy to state or understand the circumstances under which a not-proven verdict will be appropriate,[248] there is no doubt that such a verdict effectively acts as one of acquittal.[249] It is also generally a misdirection in law for a judge to discourage a jury from returning a verdict of not-proven[250]; yet the view taken is that Scottish juries are so familiar with that "third verdict" that it is not generally a misdirection *not* to draw it specifically to their attention.[251] On the other hand, judges have been advised by the Appeal Court not to attempt to distinguish not-proven from not guilty.[252] Recent attempts to rid Scots law of the not-proven verdict have, however, been met by spirited professional opposition: and the latest legislative reforms have left all three verdicts intact. Juries in Scotland do not, of course, give reasons for the verdicts at which they arrive after due (in private) deliberation; the absence of such reasons does not, however, imply any necessary unfairness to the accused, and the European Court of Human Rights has recently affirmed that this is so—provided that jury verdicts are understandable (both by the accused and the public) and given in a procedural framework (from clear indictments through to the existence of appeals) which provides sufficient safeguard to avoid the risk of arbitrariness.[253]

FAIR SENTENCING

2–64 It is also axiomatic that a person who pleads guilty to, or is found guilty of, an offence should be sentenced fairly and impartially within the limits imposed by

---

[245] But it is possible to proceed with a trial where a jury has been reduced to 12, although even then (as with a full jury) a guilty verdict can only be returned where a majority of 8 favours it—Criminal Procedure (Scotland) Act 1995 s.90. Indeed, juries smaller than 15 are not unknown in Scotland. During the Second World War, and for a short time thereafter, trials were undertaken before juries of seven persons—see, e.g. *MacDermid v HM Advocate*, 1948 J.C. 12.

[246] Cf. *B v HM Advocate*, 2006 S.L.T. 143; sub nom. *Brown v HM Advocate*, 2006 S.C.C.R. 80.

[247] All challenges to persons being sworn as jurors in Scotland require cause to be shown (unless both parties at the trial agree that a particular person should be "excused")—Criminal Procedure (Scotland) Act 1995 s.86. For an example of a case where undisclosed prior knowledge by a juror, as to the accused's criminal past, led to a conviction being quashed on the basis that the court had not been seen to be impartial (as is required under art.6(1) of the European Convention on Human Rights), see *McLean v HM Advocate*, 2001 S.C.C.R. 526.

[248] Cf. *McNicol v HM Advocate*, 1964 J.C. 25, observations of Lord Justice-General Clyde at 26–27.

[249] *McDonald v HM Advocate*, 1989 S.L.T. 298.

[250] *McNicol v HM Advocate*, 1964 J.C. 25.

[251] *Harkin v HM Advocate*, 1992 S.L.T. 785, following *MacDermid v HM Advocate*, 1948 J.C. 12.

[252] *Fay v HM Advocate*, 1989 J.C. 129; *Cussick v HM Advocate*, 2001 S.C.C.R. 683.

[253] See *Judge v United Kingdom (App. No. 35863/10)*, 2011 S.C.C.R. 241.

law. This implies that, in law, the penalty for a particular offence will always be expressed in the abstract as a maximum fine or maximum period of detention available for that offence, such that a judge will be free to choose any appropriate sentence not exceeding that maximum—always bearing in mind the particular circumstances of the offence and the offender. In this way, individual sentencing should escape criticism on the grounds of arbitrariness, and thus ensure conformity with the requirements of art.5 of the European Convention on Human Rights.[254] Exceptionally, however, sentences for some crimes have been expressed in terms of a minimum penalty which a judge must impose following conviction[255]; but these too will escape from the charge of arbitrariness provided a judge is also permitted in law to impose a shorter or different sentence where there are "exceptional circumstances".[256] Criticisms of particular sentences as either too lenient or too severe are certainly as common in Scotland as elsewhere; but it is inevitable in any system which generally allows wide discretion to judges (the present norm in the United Kingdom) that not all sentencing exercises will meet with universal approval. Several provisions assist, however, in the attainment of greater consistency and fairness in sentencing. First, in the course of deciding appeals against sentence (in a broad sense), the Appeal Court may pronounce an opinion on the sentence or other disposal or order which is appropriate in any similar case[257]; and trial courts thereafter must consider any such opinion in the course of deciding upon appropriate sentences, or other disposals or orders, in individual cases.[258] Secondly, the "Scottish Sentencing Council"[259] (established inter alia to promote consistency in sentencing practice) is required to prepare from time to time "sentencing guidelines" which must be taken into account by criminal courts, either at first instance or on appeal; such guidelines are of no effect, however, until they have been approved by the High Court of Justiciary[260] Thirdly, not only may the prosecutor appeal on a point of law against a sentence passed but he may also

---

[254] Article 5 states: "(1) Everyone has the right to liberty and security of person. No one should be deprived of his liberty save in the following cases and in accordance with a procedure prescribed by law: (a) the lawful detention of a person after conviction by a competent court." The European Court of Human Rights has consistently taken the view that "lawful detention" here involves the fundamental principle that detention must not be arbitrary; see, e.g. *Saadi v United Kingdom (App. No.13229/03)* (2008) 47 E.H.R.R. 427, paras 7–71.

[255] Certain offences under the Firearms Act 1968 are of this nature: see, e.g. s.51A (as inserted by the Criminal Justice Act 2003 s.287, and as amended by the Violent Crime Reduction Act 2006 s.30).

[256] See, e.g. *Cochrane v HM Advocate* [2010] HCJAC 117; 2011 S.C.C.R. 63, which involved an offence (of the sort referred to in the fn. immediately above) under the Firearms Act 1968; this sentencing appeal was heard by a bench of three judges after the two judges normally involved in such an appeal failed to agree on whether there had been "exceptional circumstances" in the case.

[257] Criminal Procedure (Scotland) Act 1995 ss.118(7) and 189(7), as these provisions are amended by the Protection of Children (Scotland) Act 2003 (asp 5) s.16(4)(b) and (10)(b) respectively, and re-amended (to restore them to much their original forms) by the Protection of Vulnerable Groups (Scotland) Act 2007 (asp 14) Sch.4 paras18(c) and 25. Such opinions may lead to the preparation of (or review of existing) "sentencing guidelines" by the "Scottish Sentencing Council": see the Criminal Justice and Licensing (Scotland) Act 2010 (asp 13) s.8, as also s.9 (which obliges that Council to "publish" such opinions).

[258] Criminal Procedure (Scotland) Act 1995 s.197.

[259] See the Criminal Justice and Licensing (Scotland) Act 2010 (asp 13) s.1(1) and Sch.1: note that this Council is established as "a body corporate".

[260] See the Criminal Justice and Licensing (Scotland) Act 2010 (asp 13) ss.2–8.

appeal on the ground that a sentence passed was unduly lenient.[261] There have been many reported decisions relative to sentences alleged to have been unduly lenient, and it has emerged that the proper test in such matters is not whether the Appeal Court itself would have imposed a heavier sentence but whether the trial judge's sentence was outwith the range of sentences which a judge at first instance, applying his mind to all the relevant factors, could reasonably have considered appropriate.[262] "Relevant factors" will obviously vary from case to case; but the gravity of the offence itself, the past criminal record of the accused, the effect of the crime on the victim (psychological as well as physical), and society's need for retribution and/or deterrence have all figured prominently in the Appeal Court's deliberations.[263]

RIGHT OF APPEAL

2–65 Scots law adheres to the principle that a convicted person should have a right of appeal against his conviction, his sentence or both.[264] The single, broad ground is that there has been a miscarriage of justice. But leave of a single judge of the High Court of Justiciary is required.[265] Prosecutors in a summary case may appeal by stated case on a point of law against an acquittal, or against the sentence

---

[261] Criminal Procedure (Scotland) Act 1995 s.108 and s.175 (4), (4A), both as substituted (or, in the case of s.175 (4A) inserted) by the Crime and Punishment (Scotland) Act 1997 s.21(1), and as amended by (a) the Crime and Disorder Act 1998 Sch.6 paras 6 and 7; (b) the Proceeds of Crime Act 2002 s.115; and (c) the Criminal Justice and Licensing (Scotland) Act 2010 (asp 13) s.6(7),(8), as also Sch.2 paras 8 and 12. Notice, however, that in terms of s.175(4), which relates to summary procedure, the prosecutor is restricted to such classes of case as may be specified by the Secretary of State. No such restriction applies to the Lord Advocate in solemn procedure cases.

[262] *HM Advocate v Bell*, 1995 S.L.T. 350.

[263] See, e.g. *HM Advocate v Callaghan*, 1996 S.C.C.R. 709; *HM Advocate v McC*, 1996 S.C.C.R. 842; *HM Advocate v Carpenter*, 1998 S.C.C.R. 706; *HM Advocate v. Heron*, 1998 S.C.C.R. 449; *HM Advocate v Carnall*, 1999 S.C.C.R. 904; *HM Advocate v Allan*, 2000 S.C.C.R. 219; *HM Advocate v Paterson*, 2000 S.C.C.R. 309; *HM Advocate v Millbank*, 2002 S.C.C.R. 771; *HM Advocate v Hegarty* 2002 S.C.C.R. 1022; *HM Advocate v M(IWK)*, 2003 S.C.C.R. 499; *HM Advocate v Shearer*, 2003 S.C.C.R. 657; *HM Advocate v Stalker*, 2003 S.C.C.R. 734; *HM Advocate v Gilmour*, 2004 S.C.C.R. 117; *HM Advocate v Hercus*, 2004 S.C.C.R. 140; *Bott v Morton*, 2005 S.C.C.R. 311; *HM Advocate v Norris*, 2005 S.C.C.R. 482; *HM Advocate v Thomson*, 2006 S.C.C.R. 265; *HM Advocate v Kirk*, 2007 S.C.C.R. 44; *HM Advocate v Mullen*, 2007 S.C.C.R. 330; *Lord Advocate v Harrison*, 2008 S.L.T. 112; *HM Advocate v Williamson* [[2011] HCJAC 87; 2011 S.C.C.R. 563.

[264] Criminal Procedure (Scotland) Act 1995 ss.106 (as altered by (a) the Crime and Punishment (Scotland) Act 1997 ss.17(1),18(1) and 23(b); (b) the Protection of Children (Scotland) Act 2003 (asp 5) s.16(2); (c) the Crime and Disorder Act 1998 Sch.8 para.119; and (d) the Protection of Vulnerable Groups (Scotland) Act 2007 (asp 14) Sch.4 para.14) and 175 (as altered by (a) the 1997 Act ss.17(2), 21(2) and 23(c); (b) the 1998 Act Sch. 8 para.123; (c) the Proceeds of Crime Act 2002 s.115(6)–(8); (d) the 2003 Act (asp 5) s.16(7); and (e) the 2007 Act (asp 14) Sch.4 para.21).

[265] Criminal Procedure (Scotland) Act 1995 s.107 (solemn case), as amended by the Crime and Punishment (Scotland) Act 1997 Sch.1 para.21(15), the Criminal Justice (Scotland) Act 2003 (asp 7) s.62, the Criminal Proceedings etc. (Reform) (Scotland) Act 2007 (asp 6) Sch. para.16(1), and the Double Jeopardy (Scotland) Act 2011 (asp 16) Sch. para.8; and also (summary case) ss.180 (as amended by the Bail, Judicial Appointments etc. (Scotland) Act 2000 (asp 9) Sch. para.7(4), and the said 2007 Act (asp 6) s.25(1) and Sch. para.18(2)), and 187 (as amended by the Protection of Children (Scotland) Act 2003 (asp 5) s.16(9); the Criminal Proceedings (Reform) (Scotland) Act 2007 (asp 6) s.25(3) and Sch. para.18(3); the Protection of Vulnerable Groups (Scotland) Act 2007 (asp 14) Sch.4 para.24; and the Criminal Justice and Licensing (Scotland) Act 2010 (asp 13) Sch.2 para.14).

passed[266]—in addition to appealing against what they consider to have been an unduly lenient sentence.[267] The inviolability of jury acquittals, however, is jealously guarded, since prosecutors are not permitted to appeal against findings of "not guilty" (or "not proven"[268]) in solemn procedure cases. But it is possible for prosecutors to seek clarification of the law as pronounced by the judge in such a case where the accused has been acquitted (or convicted) by referring the legal issues involved to the Appeal Court for a ruling. This is known as a "Lord Advocate's Reference".[269] The outcome of such a reference has no effect on the original acquittal (or conviction).

LEGAL ASSISTANCE FOR THE ACCUSED

Given the ever-growing complexity of the criminal law and the relative imbalance **2–66** in resources between the state, in bringing prosecutions through its prosecution service, and the accused, in having to defend them, it is imperative that legal assistance should be provided for those who cannot afford to employ a lawyer.[270] Scots law prides itself in having made provision for legal aid since the early fifteenth century,[271] though it is doubtful that criminal cases were then catered for. Certainly the early, simple schemes have given way to much more complicated rules.[272]

PROVISION FOR EXTRAORDINARY CIRCUMSTANCES

The Nobile Officium

It is inevitable in any legal system that situations will arise which have not been **2–67** foreseen and in respect of which the existing law consequently provides no answer or remedy. It would be possible, of course, for such matters to be resolved eventually by Parliament or the Scottish Parliament through legislation; but Scots law provides a quicker solution. Persons aggrieved by some issue, for which the law provides no relief, may apply by petition for the exercise of the *nobile officium* of the High Court of Justiciary. This refers to a broad, equitable power which that court traditionally possesses to effect relief in suitable cases, the suitability of a case being wholly within the discretion of the court. For example, under the extradition legislation in force in the 1970s, it was discovered that Parliament had provided only one way of challenging a person's detention where his extradition had been requested by a foreign state—namely by application for the English prerogative writ of habeas corpus. Since that writ was (and remains) unknown in

---

[266] Criminal Procedure (Scotland) Act 1995 s.175(3).
[267] Criminal Procedure (Scotland) Act 1995 s.175(4), as amended by the Criminal Justice and Licensing (Scotland) Act 2010 (asp 13) Sch.2 para.12(b).: see above, para.2–64.
[268] See above, para.2–63.
[269] Criminal Procedure (Scotland) Act 1995 s.123.
[270] And indeed this is a requirement under art.6(3)(c) of the European Convention on Human Rights: see above, para.2–61, and *Vickers v Buchanan*, 2002 S.C.C.R. 637.
[271] A.P.S., II, 1424, c.24, 8.
[272] See *The Parliament House Book* (Edinburgh: W. Green), Vol. 3, Division G "Legal Aid", for a detailed account of the relevant legislative rules.

Scotland, a person detained in this country successfully sought a Scottish way of challenging that detention by appropriately petitioning the High Court.[273]

2–68 Since the *nobile officium* power clearly represents an equitable jurisdiction, it would be wrong to regard cases where it had been exercised or denied as necessarily forming precedents for the future in like cases. But equitable decisions have always had a habit of crystallising into "hard" law, and it has become clear that the *nobile officium* power will not be exercised unless the matter in question is truly unforeseeable and extraordinary,[274] there is no other remedy available in law,[275] the petitioner is in good faith,[276] and there will be no conflict with statutory provisions to the contrary.[277] The decided cases certainly suggest that the High Court is reluctant to use this power save in the clearest instances of oppression or injustice.[278]

The Scottish Criminal Cases Review Commission

2–69 Since 1999, the Scottish Criminal Cases Review Commission has been able to refer the case of any person convicted before a Scottish criminal court to the High Court, so that the case can be determined by that Court as an appeal (in connection with conviction or sentence) under the Criminal Procedure (Scotland) Act 1995.[279] It does not matter whether that person in respect of that case had previously brought any appeal before the High Court or not; and it is within the Commission's discretion to refer such a case to the High Court on the simple grounds that "a miscarriage of justice may have occurred" and "that it is in the interests of justice that a reference should be made".[280] The Commission has wide powers of

---

[273] *Wan Ping Nam v Federal German Republic*, 1972 J.C. 43 (noting that the main legislative provisions relating to extradition are now to be found in the Extradition Act 2003, as amended). Resort to the *nobile officium* may be made by the Lord Advocate, as well as by some aggrieved private individual: see, e.g. *Lord Advocate, Petitioner*, 1998 J.C. 209 (noting that there is now no such offence as "shamelessly indecent conduct"— see *Webster v Dominick*, 2005 1 J.C. 65).

[274] Alison, *Principles*, ii, 23, para.13; cf. *La Torre v Lord Advocate* [2006] HCJAC 81; 2007 S.L.T. 51.

[275] See, e.g. *Wilson, Petitioner*, 1992 S.L.T. 145: cf. *Anderson v HM Advocate*, 1974 S.L.T. 239 (a person lodging a stated case is deemed to have abandoned any other mode of appeal: see now s.184 of the Criminal Procedure (Scotland) Act 1995).

[276] *Woods, Petitioner*, 1994 S.L.T. 197.

[277] See, e.g. *Young, Petitioner*, 1994 S.L.T. 269 (noting that the statutory provisions are now ss.116(1), 124(2) (as amended by the Scotland Act 2012 s.36(11)) of the Criminal Procedure (Scotland) Act 1995); *McWilliam, Petitioner*, 2002 S.C.C.R. 656 (see also below, para.2–69).

[278] As, e.g. where the Appeal Court per incuriam exceeded its powers—*Allan, Petitioner*, 1993 J.C. 181 (noting that the statutory provision referred to is now s.189 (as amended) of the Criminal Procedure (Scotland) Act 1995). See also *Arthur, Petitioner*, 2003 S.C.C.R. 6, where the petitioner had been sentenced for murder prior to the prosecutor's having "moved for sentence", and the unusual case of *Cochrane, Petitioner* [2006] HCJAC 27; 2006 S.L.T. 349. Cf. *Granger, Petitioner*, 2001 S.C.C.R. 337.

[279] See ss.194B,194E of the Criminal Procedure (Scotland) Act 1995, as inserted by the Crime and Punishment (Scotland) Act 1997 s.25: it should be noted that s.194B is amended by the Criminal Procedure (Legal Assistance, Detention and Appeals) (Scotland) Act 2010 (asp 15) s.7(2), and that s.194DA (inserted by the said 2010 Act (asp 15) s.7(4)) permits the High Court to reject any such reference made to them.

[280] Criminal Procedure (Scotland) Act 1995 s.194C, inserted by the Crime and Punishment (Scotland) Act 1997 s.25, and as amended by the Criminal Procedure (Legal Assistance, Detention and Appeals) (Scotland) Act 2010 (asp 15) s.7(3). Cf. *Raza v Scottish Criminal Cases Review Commission* [2007] CSOH 152; 2007 S.C.C.R. 403 (petition to the Court of Session for judicial review of a decision by the Commission).

investigation relating to their functions,[281] and can seek the High Court's opinion on any matter germane to their task of "considering whether to make a reference".[282] Since no criminal justice system can ever guarantee the complete absence of miscarriages of justice, and since the *nobile officium* power of the High Court is in practice one of somewhat limited application,[283] the establishment of this Commission is a matter of considerable importance.[284]

---

[281] See Criminal Procedure (Scotland) Act 1995 ss.194F to 194I, inserted by the Crime and Punishment (Scotland) Act 1997 s.25; see also s.194IA, as inserted by the Criminal Justice and Licensing (Scotland) Act 2010 (asp 13) s.105.

[282] Criminal Procedure (Scotland) Act 1995 s.194D(3), inserted as above: see, e.g. *Scottish Criminal Cases Review Commission, Petitioners*, 2001 S.C.C.R. 775.

[283] See above, para.2–68.

[284] Cf., however, the unusual case of *Cochrane, Petitioner* [2006] HCJAC 27; 2006 S.L.T. 349.

CHAPTER 3

ACTUS REUS AND MENS REA

BASIC CONCEPTS AND DEFINITIONS

3–01 The purpose of this chapter is to provide an introduction to the fundamental principles of criminal liability. The basic rule is commonly expressed in a Latin maxim: *actus non facit reum nisi mens sit rea*—conduct does not make a man guilty unless his mind is also guilty. Generally speaking, a crime will have these two features: the actus reus, the physical or external component; and mens rea, which is the mental element. Actus reus and mens rea constitute the essential ingredients of criminal liability at common law. There are, however, a large number of statutory offences which do not require proof of mens rea. These are the so-called crimes of "strict liability". Crimes of this type are discussed in Ch.13. For the time being, the focus will be on more traditional crimes which do require proof of both mens rea and actus reus.

3–02 An understanding of the terminology of actus reus and mens rea is essential to the student of criminal law. They constitute the fundamentals of the criminal lawyer's vocabulary. These terms do not, however, have a fixed meaning. The specific forms that actus reus and mens rea take differ from one crime to another. This point can be demonstrated in a straightforward way. The actus reus of assault is an attack by one person upon another. In contrast, the actus reus of theft is the taking or appropriating, without lawful authority, of property which belongs to someone else. Similarly, the mens rea involved in murder is different from that involved in culpable homicide. In both crimes someone has been killed, but it is only by examining the accused's mental state that one can determine whether he is a murderer or not.

ACTUS REUS

CONDUCT REQUIRED

3–03 The actus reus of a crime is simply the harmful or blameworthy conduct which the law seeks to prevent. It is the "doing something wrong" ingredient of criminal liability. All crimes require conduct, or an overt act. Thought crimes are unknown in the Scottish legal system: "No one can be punished for merely what goes on in his own head."[1] The criminal law imposes punishment only for the

---

[1] *Morton v Henderson,* 1956 J.C. 55, per Lord Justice-General Clyde at 57.

actions which result from thoughts, not for "unfulfilled intents".[2] As Lord Justice-Clerk MacDonald emphasised in *HM Advocate v Mackenzie,*[3] a "mere expression of willingness" to do something "morally reprehensible" is insufficient. If the prosecution cannot prove the actus reus required by the definition of the crime charged, there cannot be a conviction for that crime. An accused has to have performed an, "act which falls within the category either of accomplished or attempted crime."[4] As is explained in detail in Ch.6, if the accused has advanced sufficiently far in his preparations, he can be convicted of an attempt to commit a crime.

It is also axiomatic that the accused must have actually done something to bring **3–04** about what the criminal law seeks to forbid. In *Hogg v Macpherson*[5] the appellant was the driver of a horse-drawn furniture van. While he was driving the van along a street on a very windy day, a "furious" gust of wind blew the van over. The van struck and broke a street lamp. Under legislation then in force, the appellant was liable to make recompense for the damage, whether it was caused by negligence or by accident. The offence of which the appellant had been convicted was that of failing to pay the sum demanded by the local authority.[6] It was accepted that the appellant could have done nothing to avoid causing the damage. Lord Justice-General Clyde observed:

> "All I can say is that it seems to me as plain as can be from the circumstances of the case that the breaking of the lamp was not the appellant's act at all, either negligent or accidental, and that, accordingly, upon the facts found proved, there was no justification for the award made."[7]

Consequently, the conviction could not stand.

CONDUCT CRIMES AND RESULT CRIMES

A distinction is sometimes drawn between "conduct crimes" and "result crimes" **3–05** (see above, para.2–36). On occasion, the law simply forbids a certain form of conduct. A straightforward example would be the possession of a controlled drug under the Misuse of Drugs Act 1971. It is simply the act of possessing the drug which constitutes the actus reus. More generally, however, the law requires some forbidden consequence to result from the conduct. Many common law crimes contain within their definition a requirement of resultant harm. The result of the crime of murder is obviously that someone is killed, but it is not really significant *how* the victim dies. The criminal law is concerned here only with penalising the result of the conduct. There are no separate laws governing, for example, murder by stabbing or murder by strangulation.

---

[2] *HM Advocate v Mackenzie,* 1913 S.C. (J.) 107, per Lord Justice-Clerk MacDonald at 111.

[3] *HM Advocate v Mackenzie,* 1913 S.C. (J.) 107 at 112.

[4] *HM Advocate v Mackenzie,* 1915 S.C. (J.) 107 at 112.

[5] *Hogg v Macpherson,* 1928 J.C. 15.

[6] General Police and Improvement (Scotland) Act 1862 s.128, as incorporated in the Edinburgh Municipal and Police Act 1879 s.93.

[7] *Hogg v Macpherson,* 1928 J.C. 15 at 17.

CAUSATION

3–06 In a result crime, it is necessary to prove as part of the actus reus both conduct and consequences. The prosecution will also need to establish the existence of a sufficient causal link between the conduct of the accused and the result. In *Kimmins v Normand*,[8] the appellant had been convicted of the reckless injury of a police officer. Prior to commencing a search for controlled drugs, the officer had asked the appellant whether he was in possession of any needles. He denied that he was. In fact, there was an unguarded needle in the appellant's pocket, and an injury was caused to the police officer's hand. The Appeal Court held that there was a sufficient causal connection between the appellant's denial and the resulting injury. The reasoning was that it must have been obvious to the appellant that the explanation for the officer's question was that he was about to place his hand into the appellant's pocket. It was a reasonable inference that the denial would lead to the officer's doing so. The court's conclusion was that "there was a causal connection between the denial and the end result."[9] The issue of causation is examined in detail in Ch.5.

TYPES OF ACTUS REUS

3–07 Regardless of whether a particular offence is classified as a conduct crime or a result crime, the actus reus will be one of three possible types: (1) an overt (or positive) act; (2) an omission—a failure to act where there is a legal duty to act; or (3) a state of affairs.

1. Overt acts

3–08 What is meant by an "act" is simply a movement of a part of the body. The criminal law excludes consideration of the relevant thought processes from the definition of the actus reus of a crime. What the actor thought or intended will invariably be dealt with under the head of mens rea. Generally the relevant act will have a physical or external manifestation, but this need not necessarily involve actual movement of the limbs. Merely speaking to another person could constitute the actus reus of a crime (most notably incitement and breach of the peace).

2. Omissions

3–09 The general rule of the common law is that there can be no criminal liability for an omission, unless at the time of the failure to act there was a legal duty to act. It is only in limited circumstances that the criminal law extends to acts of omission, as well as acts of commission. There is, for example, no legal duty to prevent the commission of a crime. But if the law *does* impose a duty to act, then a failure to

---

[8] *Kimmins v Normand*, 1993 S.L.T. 1260; distinguished in *Mallin v Clark*, 2002 S.L.T. 1202. For detailed discussion of the crime of reckless injury, see below, para.9–34.

[9] *Kimmins v Normand*, 1993 S.L.T. 1260 at 1261H. In the absence of injury, the appellant could have been charged with reckless endangerment; see *Normand v Morrison*, 1993 S.C.C.R. 207; *Donaldson v Normand*, 1997 S.L.T. 1303. In *Normand v Robinson*, 1994 S.L.T. 558, there was held to be a sufficient causal link between the organisation of a "rave" on derelict premises and the reckless endangerment of those in attendance.

comply with that requirement can constitute sufficient conduct for the actus reus of the crime.[10] There is no exception for the accused who did not know that he was under a legal duty. This legal duty to act can derive from a number of sources. The obligation to act may be created by statute: there are a number of statutory offences which are specifically defined in terms of an omission to act. One straightforward example is failing to provide a specimen of breath under the breathalyser legislation.[11] As well as conduct crimes of this kind deriving from statute, it is possible to commit a result crime by means of omission. To starve a child to death could be the result of an omission.[12] This might be described as committing a crime of commission by omission (assuming the presence of the requisite mens rea for either culpable homicide or murder).

A duty to act?

There are also instances where the common law would probably impose a duty **3–10** to act. This will be the case where, for example, an individual has undertaken to do something upon which the health and safety of others depends. Examples of this are the cases of *William Hardie,*[13] where a charge of culpable homicide brought against an Inspector of Poor who had ignored the deceased's application for poor relief was held to be relevant; and an English case, *R. v Instan,*[14] where a fatal omission by a niece to provide food and medical attention for her invalid aunt resulted in a manslaughter (equivalent to culpable homicide) conviction. The crimes in these two examples were committed by failing to fulfil a legal duty. In *William Hardie* the legal duty was derived from a contract. The failure to act was not just a breach of contract with his employer, however, but provided the possible basis for a conviction[15]: the duty of care also extended to members of the public he was paid to protect. In *Instan* the duty had been assumed voluntarily. This would seem to imply that if someone agreed to look after a neighbour's child and the child drowned in the bath while that child-minder was watching television, then a conviction for culpable homicide could ensue. This scenario could be analysed either in terms of a voluntary assumption of a duty of care, or of a contractual obligation.[16]

The duty to limit the harm caused by a dangerous act

There may also be occasions where the accused has created a dangerous situa- **3–11** tion and is therefore under a legal duty to do what he can to remedy the situation. If he omits to do so, then this can constitute the actus reus of a crime. The accused in *HM Advocate v McPhee*[17] was charged with murder. He had committed a serious assault on a woman, and had left her injured and unconscious in an open

---

[10] See *Buchmann v Normand,* 1994 S.C.C.R. 929.

[11] Road Traffic Act 1988 s.8(9).

[12] See *George Fay* (1847) Ark. 397. For a rare modern example of homicide by omission, see *Bone v HM Advocate,* 2005 S.C.C.R. 829.

[13] *William Hardie* (1847) Ark. 247.

[14] *R. v Instan* [1893] 1 Q.B. 450.

[15] Although the charge was held to be a relevant one, it was not proceeded with.

[16] Failure to provide for a child in one's care also constitutes an offence in its own right: see the Children and Young Persons (Scotland) Act 1937.

[17] *HM Advocate v McPhee,* 1935 J.C. 46. See also *Miller and Denovan v HM Advocate,* 1960, noted at 1991 S.L.T. 211.

field. Lord Mackay, the trial judge, upheld the relevancy of the indictment, stating that there could be a murder conviction,

> "if he is proved to have wickedly and feloniously exposed the unconscious woman regardless of consequences to the inclemency of the weather, and if she died in consequence . . . both of the beating and the exposure . . ."[18]

3–12 In *MacPhail v Clark,*[19] the accused was a farmer who was charged with culpable and reckless endangerment. He had set fire to some straw in a field near a public road, but neglected to ensure that no danger was caused. The fire spread to vegetation on the verge of the road with the result that there was a collision on the road. This resulted in injuries to people driving there at the time.[20] At no time did the accused make any attempt to remedy the dangerous situation which he had caused. The sheriff held that the accused, as a farmer, was aware of the dangers of straw burning and knew of the presence of the road. He had allowed the fire to spread and had thereby demonstrated a reckless indifference to the consequences of his actions. He was convicted. Where the farmer was at fault was in his omitting to take sufficient precautions to safeguard against the fire spreading. A somewhat different approach was taken in the more recent case of *McCue v Currie,*[21] where the court seemed reluctant to endorse the general proposition that there is a legal duty to act in a situation where a danger has been created. In this case, the accused had entered a caravan for the purpose of theft and was using a cigarette lighter to see his way around. He accidentally dropped the lighter. A fire was started. He was aware that this was the case, but did nothing to extinguish it or summon assistance. The caravan was destroyed. It was held that this could not amount to the crime of culpable and reckless fire-raising, since guilt must be determined by reference to the act of starting the fire (which was accidental) and not subsequent events (however reprehensible). What is surprising about this decision, perhaps, is the absence of recognition of a general proposition that an omission to do what there is a legal duty to do is the equivalent of an act. It may be that the "accidental" nature of the fire-raising had a particular influence on the decision of the court,

> "fire raising which is merely accidental . . . is not a crime, and cannot become so on account of subsequent behaviour on the part of the person concerned."[22]

No general duties to act

3–13 It has been stressed that, absent a legal duty to act, an omission cannot constitute the actus reus of a crime. The corollary of this is that, if a court determines that the actus reus of a crime can be committed by omission, this is to impose a legal duty to act upon all citizens who find themselves in the same position. Naturally enough, the courts are somewhat reluctant to create new legal obligations of this kind, preferring to leave this activity to the legislature. This

---

[18] *HM Advocate v McPhee,* 1935 J.C. 46 at 50. The accused was convicted of culpable homicide.
[19] *MacPhail v Clark,* 1983 S.L.T. (Sh. Ct.) 37.
[20] Since the crime charged seems to have been reckless endangerment, the injuries were not necessary to conviction, but acted by way of aggravation; see below, para.9–35.
[21] *McCue v Currie,* 2004 S.C.C.R. 200.
[22] *McCue v Currie,* 2004 S.C.C.R. 200 at 207, para.25.

disinclination on the part of the judiciary can be seen clearly in the decision of the Appeal Court in *Paterson v Lees*.[23]

The charge here was of shameless indecency. The appellant had been acting as a babysitter, when one of the children put on a video containing indecent material. The appellant allowed the children to continue watching. In other words, he *omitted* to stop the children viewing the material in question. The Appeal Court was unanimous in deciding that the crime of shameless indecency could not be committed in this way: it was not a crime to permit children to view indecent material. Lord Justice-General Rodger stated[24]:

> "By holding that it was criminal for the appellant to do nothing and so to permit the children to view the film, the sheriff was in effect affirming that our criminal law imposes upon a person in the appellant's position a positive duty to act to prevent children from seeing obscene and indecent material."

His Lordship regarded this as "one giant leap for the law".[25] The decision as to whether this should be done was one for the legislature, and not for the court.

The criminal law has never imposed a general duty to assist another person who **3–14** is in peril. The law does not maintain that everyone is obliged to be his brother's keeper.[26] There may be a moral duty to act, but this will not necessarily constitute a legal duty. The man who stands by and watches a small child drown in a swimming pool does not commit a crime, even though he might have saved the child with ease and at no risk to himself. The situation would, of course, be very different if the man was the child's father. There would then be a legal duty to act.[27] Similarly, a duty to intervene would arise if the bystander were an attendant employed to ensure the safety of swimmers. In some other jurisdictions, however, there exist specific offences of failing to assist a person who is in peril.[28] This is sometimes described as a duty of "easy rescue". It will be subject to some kind of proviso that the assistance can be rendered without danger. Although there may be strong moral arguments supporting the desirability of such an offence, the common law dictates otherwise.

3. A state of affairs

There are a number of statutory offences which are defined in such a way that **3–15** they can be committed when a certain state of affairs exists, or where the accused

---

[23] *Paterson v Lees*, 1999 J.C. 159 (noting that the crime of shameless indecency no longer exists as a result of the decision in *Webster v Dominick*, 2003 S.L.T. 975). In *McCue v Currie*, 2004 S.C.C.R. 200 also it is stated that if there is a case for enacting a new crime of culpably failing to take appropriate steps after a situation of danger to persons or property has arisen as a result of a person's actions, that is a matter for legislative, rather than judicial, activity.

[24] *Paterson v Lees*, 1999 J.C. 159 at 161F.

[25] *Paterson v Lees*, 1999 J.C. 159 at 161F.

[26] See J. Hall, *General Principles of Criminal Law*, 2nd edn (Indianapolis: Bobbs-Merrill Co Inc, 1960), p.210.

[27] See the Australian case of *R. v Russell* [1933] V.L.R. 59. There is a possible analogy here with nineteenth century cases in which it was held to be homicide where a new-born baby died as a result of the mother's failure to summon help at the time of birth; see *Isabella Martin* (1877) 3 Coup. 379; *HM Advocate v Scott* (1892) 3 White 240. See also *Bone v HM Advocate*, 2005 S.C.C.R. 829, where the allegation against the appellant was that she had wilfully failed to protect and ensure the wellbeing of her child in the face of her co-accused's assaults, as a consequence of which the child had died.

[28] See, e.g. French Penal Code art.63(2).

is in a particular situation. There is no express requirement of conduct. An example of this type of offence is s.4(1) of the Road Traffic Act 1988, which makes it an offence for a person to be unfit to drive through drink or drugs while in charge of a mechanically propelled vehicle on the road. The offence is a state of affairs: being in charge of a vehicle while unfit.[29]

MENS REA

THE MENTAL ELEMENT

3–16 As a general rule, the criminal law does not apply to an individual who has acted without mental fault. The common law draws a general distinction between conduct which is meant and conduct which is not deliberate. This precondition for the establishment of criminal liability has long been part of the Scottish criminal legal heritage. The explanation for this requirement of a blameworthy state of mind is that it serves to justify the imposition of punishment. This mental element is generally referred to as the mens rea. It is a presumption of the common law that crimes require mens rea.[30] Statutory offences which impose strict liability are by way of an exception to the common law principle.

Mens rea and dole

3–17 Mens rea is not the easiest concept to grasp. In the simplest of terms, it refers to the mental element required by the definition of a particular crime, as distinct from the actus reus. That is, the mens rea is the individual's state of mind at the time that the forbidden conduct took place. (Perversely and confusingly, some authorities refer to the actus reus as containing a form of mens rea. What is meant there is that the conduct, amounting to the actus reus of a particular crime, should be "voluntary" as a minimum requirement of liability. "True" mens rea would still have to be established over and above.) One can identify two distinct meanings attached to the concept of mens rea (treated quite separately from the actus reus*)*. The first of these is that mens rea connotes a general notion of moral blameworthiness. This conception of mens rea correlates to the traditional Scottish term for the mental element of "dole", derived from the Latin *dolus* (the definition of which includes "evil intent, wrongdoing with a view to the consequences").[31] It is the term dole which is to be found in many of the older cases. Hume defined dole as "that corrupt and evil intention, which is essential . . . to the guilt of any crime."[32] He stated that the requirement of dole did not mean that there had to be an intention to do the particular crime. Rather, the actus reus "must be attended with such circumstances as indicate a corrupt and malignant disposition, a heart

---

[29] The question of whether an accused assumed charge of the vehicle is one of fact; see *Kelso v Brown,* 1998 S.L.T. 921.

[30] *Blane v HM Advocate,* 1991 S.C.C.R. 576, per Lord Justice-General Hope at 581D; *Paterson v Lees,* 1999 J.C. 159, per Lord Sutherland at 163E.

[31] C.T. Lewis and C. Short, *A Latin Dictionary* (Oxford: Clarendon Press (1993 printing), 1879), p.607.

[32] Hume, *Commentaries,* i, 21.

contemptuous of order and social duty."[33] This conception of the mental element indicating an evil character might be appropriate to the most serious offences, such as murder or an aggravated assault, but it is plainly not applicable to the majority of crimes (which are far less serious). For most crimes, especially those created by statute, it is more helpful to think in terms of mens rea as a mental state specific to a particular crime.

This is the second meaning of mens rea, and is the conception which has gained **3–18** prominence.[34] Nevertheless, the traditional approach to mens rea does persist. Although the term dole is not in common use today, the moralistic approach reflected in Hume still provides the background to the modern criminal law.[35] The concept of "wicked recklessness" has long been a significant aspect of the law of murder. More recently, there has been judicial discussion of whether—and under which circumstances—the epithet "wicked" should be applied to the intention to kill in murder.[36] The significance of this remains a matter for detailed discussion within the account of murder presented in Ch.9. In the context of intention, it may be that "wicked" is used as shorthand to refer to the absence of any applicable defence (for example, self-defence, provocation or diminished responsibility).

"Evil intent" features in the crime of assault. Again, it remains unclear whether **3–19** the adjective "evil" has any particular legal significance. In the *Lord Advocates Reference (No.2 of 1992)*,[37] Lord Justice-Clerk Ross suggested that it means only "that assault cannot be committed accidentally or recklessly or negligently". If this is correct, the intention behind an assault would not have to accord with the dictionary definition of the word "evil" to attract criminal liability.[38] The desirability of a modern criminal law relying upon concepts of "evilness" and "wickedness", with the definition of crimes dependent upon the significance attributable to such notions, would no doubt be questioned by some. Certainly it reflects a perspective on the mental element in crime rather different from the more technical approach prevailing in Anglo-American criminal law. The debate between the two approaches is no doubt an interesting one, but rather misses the point. The Scottish approach is reflective of the historical background of the criminal law in the jurisdiction. The common law continues to rely upon moralistic concepts to describe the necessary mental element of crimes.[39]

There may indeed be some advantage to the "pre-modern" approach prevailing in Scots law. Some would see merit in its recognition

---

[33] Hume, *Commentaries*, i, 22. The "character theory" of criminal responsibility is not, of course, unique to Hume. See, more generally, G. Mousourakis, "Character, Choice and Criminal Responsibility" (1998) 39 *Cashiers de Droit* 51.

[34] See, e.g. *Byrne v HM Advocate (No.2)*, 2000 S.L.T. 233.

[35] See *Transco Plc v HM Advocate (No.1)*, 2004 J.C. 29.

[36] See *Drury v HM Advocate*, 2001 S.L.T. 1013 and *Elsherkisi v HM Advocate* [2011] HCJAC 100; 2011 S.C.C.R. 735.

[37] *Lord Advocate's Reference (No.2 of 1992)*, 1993 J.C. 43 at 48, relying upon Gordon, *Criminal Law*, 2nd edn (1978), para.29.30; applied in *Quinn v Lees*, 1994 S.C.C.R. 159. For a fuller discussion of this issue, see below, paras 9–15 and 9–16.

[38] Support for this interpretation comes from the *Lord Advocates Reference (No.1 of 2000)*, 2001 J.C. 143 at 154D, where the opinion of the court was that the "malice" element of the common law crime of malicious mischief did "not require proof of spite or any other form of motive".

[39] See *Transco Plc v HM Advocate (No.1)*, 2004 J.C. 29.

"that what is ultimately in issue is the community's moral judgment on the accused's behaviour, and not the satisfaction of a legal formula."[40]

Subjectivity and objectivity

3–20   Criminal lawyers often refer to mens rea as being assessed either subjectively or objectively. A subjective approach to mens rea requires that the accused had actually foreseen the consequences of his actions. Did he know that the particular result would ensue from his conduct? In contrast, if an objective approach to mens rea is adopted, the accused will be judged according to the standard of what he should have foreseen, or of what was foreseeable.[41] It will be permissible to conclude that he had the necessary mens rea because he really should have known what was going to happen. There will be less emphasis upon triers of fact putting themselves in the position of the accused and deciding what he actually thought at the time of the actus reus. It is easier for a prosecutor to prove beyond reasonable doubt the existence of mens rea if it is assessed objectively, rather than subjectively; and in Scotland it is assessed objectively.[42]

Mens rea and motive

3–21   It is important at the outset to distinguish mens rea from motive, since the two are not infrequently confused. Motive (sometimes called the ulterior intention) is concerned with the reason why an individual acted as he did. What caused him to act in the way in which the prosecution alleges? The substantive criminal law is generally unconcerned with motive in this sense. Lord Justice-Clerk Inglis observed in the case of *Alexander Milne*[43]: "The motive may remain a mystery, while the murder is an accomplished fact." That said, motive could be very significant in evidential terms.

3–22   Thus the criminal law is generally unconcerned with the reasons why the accused acted as is alleged. He may be a protester who believes himself to be acting for the best of reasons when breaking the law. This was the position in the *Lord Advocate's Reference (No.1 of 2000)*,[44], where protesters against nuclear weapons committed malicious mischief against property of the Royal Navy. The fact that they had not acted out of "spite" was regarded as irrelevant by the Appeal Court.[45] To similar effect is *Ralston v HM Advocate*,[46], which concerned a prisoner who had taken part in rooftop protest. He was convicted of committing a breach of the peace. He claimed that he had acted in order to protest against prison conditions. On appeal, the High Court upheld the sheriff's direction to the jury that, even if Ralston's motives had been blameless, they were irrelevant to determining whether his conduct constituted a breach of the peace. In the

---

[40] G.H. Gordon, "Subjective and Objective *Mens Rea*" (1975) 17 *Crim. L.Q.* 355, 390. The point is made of the role of wicked recklessness in murder.

[41] See, e.g. *Sutherland v HM Advocate*, 1994 S.C.C.R. 80, per Lord Justice-General Hope at 92C–D.

[42] Modern authorities for this proposition include *Jamieson v HM Advocate*, 1987 S.C.C.R. 484; *Blane v HM Advocate*, 1991 S.C.C.R. 576; *McIntosh v HM Advocate*, 1993 S.C.C.R. 464; *HM Advocate v Purcell* [2007] HCJAC 13; [2008] J.C. 131; *Transco Plc v HM Advocate (No.1)*, 2004 J.C. 29.

[43] *Alexander Milne* (1863) 4 Irv. 301 at 345.

[44] *Lord Advocate's Reference (No.1 of 2000)*, 2001 J.C. 143.

[45] *Lord Advocate's Reference (No.1 of 2000)*, 2001 J.C. 143 at 154D–E.

[46] *Ralston v HM Advocate*, 1989 S.L.T. 474; followed in *HM Advocate v Forbes*, 1994 S.L.T. 861.

Lord Advocates Reference (No.2 of 1992),[47], the accused contended that he had pointed a gun at the owner of a shop during an apparent armed robbery as part of a joke. It was held that this was a claim as to the motive or ulterior intention. This was irrelevant if he had been acting deliberately.

THE CATEGORIES OF MENS REA

The concept of mens rea embraces those who have made a decision and chosen to **3–23** break the law. An example would be the person who drives his car towards another with the specific purpose of striking and killing him. Mens rea, however, is not limited to this one mental state. The criminal law distinguishes among a number of analytically distinct levels of mens rea. This reflects a recognition that some law-breakers act with a greater degree of "evil intent" or "wickedness" than others do, and can properly be held to a higher degree of culpability. Thus the individual who drives his car at such a speed that any reasonable person would foresee that someone might be killed, but does not aim the vehicle at anyone, would be held to be less culpable (subject to a less severe penalty) than the driver in the previous example.

This second example also illustrates the point that the mens rea of some crimes **3–24** can extend to those who do not anticipate causing any harm, but really ought to have realised the risks involved in their actions. Mens rea does not refer to any one mental state. It cannot be equated with intent. There are degrees of mens rea. In *Quinn v Cunningham*,[48] Lord Justice-General Clyde observed

> "it is an essential element in the constitution of a crime at common law that there should be either an intention to commit a wrong or an utter disregard of what the consequences of the act in question may be . . .".

In relation to common law (and statutory) crimes, therefore, there are two core states of mind: (1) intention; and (2) recklessness. That said, Scottish practice recognises a wide variety of terms to indicate mens rea in common law crimes. These include, inter alia, knowledge, malice and wilfulness.

1. Intention

Some crimes, most notably assault,[49] theft[50] and wilful fire-raising,[51] can only **3–25** be committed intentionally.[52] This does not mean that there has to have been advance planning or prolonged deliberation. Intention involves no more than a resolve or purposive decision to act in a particular way. The Scottish courts have not progressed very far towards defining the concept of intention. Three reasons for this can be suggested. The first is that the generally objective approach to mens rea in Scots law makes it unnecessary to measure with precision the degree

---

[47] *Lord Advocate's Reference (No.2 of 1992)*, 1993 J.C. 43.
[48] *Quinn v Cunningham*, 1956 J.C. 22 at 24.
[49] *Lord Advocates Reference (No.2 of 1992)*, 1993 J.C. 43; *HM Advocate v Harris*, 1993 J.C. 150.
[50] Hume, *Commentaries*, i, 73 ("felonious purpose" required).
[51] *Byrne v HM Advocate (No.2)*, 2000 S.L.T. 233.
[52] The common law presumption would be that intention is the requisite mental element, unless there is authority suggesting otherwise.

of intention present at the time of the actus reus. Whilst conceding that intention is a subjective state of mind,[53] it is accepted in Scots law that there can be objective proof (see below, paras 3–27 and 3–28).[54] The second reason is that there may have been a desire to avoid the difficulties in which the English courts have found themselves as the result of a series of cases on the concept of intention.[55] These problems have arisen as the result of judges attempting to give juries detailed guidance on how intention can be proved. Scottish courts have been more prepared to treat the concept of intention as an ordinary word, the meaning of which will be apparent to juries. A third reason is that the English cases are concerned with intention in the law of murder. Since Scots law recognises the alternative mens rea of wicked recklessness, this means that intention is not necessarily the central issue in such cases.[56]

3–26   One useful definition of intention is that adopted by Lord Ross in his charge to the jury in *Sayers v HM Advocate*[57]:

> "An 'intention' to my mind connotes a state of affairs which the party 'intending' . . . does more than merely contemplate; it connotes a state of affairs which, on the contrary, he decides, so far as in him lies, to bring about, and which . . . he has a reasonable prospect of being able to bring about, by his act of volition."

Although helpful, this definition has to be read in the context of a conspiracy case. It is concerned with an intention to perform a future action.[58] The criminal law is generally concerned with determining what constitutes an intention to effect a result which has actually been brought about. Not all intended actions are preceded by an opportunity for reflection and conscious decision-making. This intuition sits well with the Scottish approach to mens rea, which tends not to see mens rea as a mental process which can be investigated separately from what the accused has actually done. As Lord Justice-Clerk Grant observed in *HM Advocate v Wilson*,

---

[53] See, e.g. *Boyle v Ritchie*, 1999 S.C.C.R. 278, per Lord Prosser at 281E–F.

[54] *Boyle v Ritchie*, 1999 S.C.C.R. 278; see also *Byrne v HM Advocate (No.2)*, 2000 S.L.T. 233 at 238G.

[55] See the decisions of the House of Lords in *Hyam v DPP* [1975] A.C. 55; *R. v Moloney* [1985] A.C. 905; *R. v Hancock and Shankland* [1986] A.C. 455; and *R. v Woollin* [1999] 1 A.C. 82. In *Petto v HM Advocate* [2011] HCJAC 80; 2011 S.L.T. 1043 at 1045E–F, para.13, however, the English terminology of "virtual certainty" is used in the context of a major fire started on the ground floor of a tenement block and the grave risk of death or serious injury created to those in the building at the time: "While there may be no desiderative element in the mind of such a person, his appreciation of the virtual certainty that such a risk will eventuate . . . should . . . be rightly equiperated with an intention that such consequences should occur." It remains to be seen whether the High Court will wish in the future to explore further the meaning of intention, or whether that case will remain exceptional.

[56] See *Cawthorne v HM Advocate*, 1968 J.C. 32. Noting that the wickedly reckless accused must at least have intended to do physical injury to the deceased (see *HM Advocate v Purcell* [2007] HCJAC 13; 2008 J.C. 131 and below para.9–52). This explains why in a case of fire-raising (*Petto v HM Advocate* [2011] HCJAC 80; 2011 S.L.T. 1043) it was necessary to libel the accused as having intended the death of the victim to uphold the murder conviction.

[57] *Sayers v HM Advocate*, 1981 S.C.C.R. 312 at 318. The source of this quotation is *Cunliffe v Goodman* [1950] 2 K.B. 237, per Lord Justice Asquith at 253. And see now *Petto v HM Advocate* [2011] HCJAC 80; 2011 S.L.T. 1043.

[58] For discussion of this issue, see R.A. Duff, *Intention, Agency and Criminal Responsibility* (Oxford: Basil Blackwell, 1990), pp.17 and 44–47.

Latta and Rooney[59]: "It is by their acts, as frequently happens in other spheres of life, that we know them."

Proving intention

Unless the accused has confessed to his state of mind, intention will have to be **3–27** proved by inference from the evidence: "His intention must, in the absence of any admissions by him, be derived from the circumstances surrounding the incident."[60] In *Cawthorne v HM Advocate*,[61] Lord Avonside pointed out:

> "It is impossible . . . to look into the mind of the man, and when, therefore, you are seeking to evaluate the effect of the evidence in regard to the nature and purposes of the act you can only do so by drawing an *inference* from what that man did in the background of all the facts of the case which you accept as proved."

This evidence will consist of the words and conduct of the accused, and the **3–28** circumstances surrounding the crime. Lord Justice-General Hope explained in *Hughes v Crowe*[62] that the actions of the accused have

> "to be of a sufficient quality to enable the inference to be drawn of *mens rea*. That is an inference to be drawn from the nature and quality of the acts complained of . . .".

In a case of assault, for example, the necessary intention could be inferred from the fact that a punch was thrown. The prosecution would not have to offer specific proof of the accused's intention. In an example such as this, the accused will need to raise a reasonable doubt about the presence of an intention to assault in order to secure an acquittal. He will bear the tactical burden of overcoming the inference that the assault was committed intentionally.[63] Sometimes, however, the conduct of the accused will be consistent with entirely innocent behaviour, and a simple inference of intention will be impossible. If this is the case, then some additional evidence will be required from the prosecution for the purpose of proving the presence of a criminal intent. An example might be a charge of theft by shoplifting, since it is possible to mistakenly leave a shop without paying. An intention to steal would also have to be shown to be present (see below, para.10–28). The prosecution might do so by producing evidence that the accused had acted furtively.[64]

---

[59] *HM Advocate v Wilson, Latta and Rooney* Unreported, 1968, but see C.H.W. Gane and C.N. Stoddart, *Casebook on Scottish Criminal Law*, 2nd edn (Edinburgh: W. Green, 1988), p.204.

[60] *Carr v HM Advocate*, 1995 S.L.T. 800 at 804B–C. See also Erskine, IV, 4, 8: "dole . . . can only be discovered from the outward circumstances from which it is presumed."

[61] *Cawthorne v Lord Advocate*, 1968 J.C. 32 at 33.

[62] *Hughes v Crowe*, 1993 S.C.C.R. 320 at 323. See also *MacDonald v Cardle*, 1985 S.C.C.R. 195 (a rather unusual case); *Mason v Jessop*, 1990 S.C.C.R. 387; *Carney v HM Advocate*, 1995 S.L.T. 1208; *McGill v HM Advocate*, 2000 S.C.C.R. 28.

[63] See F. Raitt, *Evidence Principles, Policy and Practice*, 4th edn (Edinburgh: W. Green, 2008), para.2.04.

[64] See Erskine, IV, 4, 8: "And in actions which are either innocent or criminal, according to the good or bad intention of the agent, dole must also in that case be presumed or not, from the circumstances previous to or concomitant with the crime." *Barr v O'Brien*, 1991 S.C.C.R. 67, provides an example of an intent to steal by shoplifting being proved by inference from the conduct of the accused; for an example of where intention to steal could not be inferred, see *Wilson v Barbour* [2009] HCJAC 30; 2009 S.L.T. 437.

3–29 Scottish criminal law recognises a distinction between an individual who has acted recklessly and one who has purposely brought about a particular result.[65] In practical terms, it is important to draw a boundary between recklessness and intention, because some crimes can only be committed intentionally. This point is emphasised in the opinion of the Appeal Court in *Byrne v HM Advocate (No.2)*.[66] This decision concerned the common law crime of wilful fire-raising, for which the requisite mental element is intention. The opinion emphasises that it is

> "vital for a judge to keep the concepts of intention and recklessness distinct
> ... nor can any form of recklessness be treated as equivalent to intent."[67]

It was therefore a misdirection to tell a jury that intention "could be implied from conduct indicating an utter disregard of the likelihood of the fire spreading to the subjects in question."[68] The court overruled (in part) an earlier decision, *Blane v HM Advocate*,[69] where it appeared to have been suggested that wilful fire-raising could be committed recklessly. In *Blane*, Lord Justice-General Hope had observed[70]

> "since the matter must be approached objectively I think it is open to infer-
> ence, where the accused is shown to have acted with a reckless disregard for
> the likely consequences of what he does, that he intended those consequences
> to occur."

This was to blur the distinction between the concepts of intention and reckless-ness. It is not possible to conclude that an individual intended a consequence as to which he was reckless. It was emphasised in *Byrne v HM Advocate*[71] that what a jury has to decide is whether the evidence is sufficient to permit an inference of intention to be drawn; this cannot be done "[i]f all that they infer from the evidence is that the accused was reckless, even to a very high degree". However reckless an actor may have been as to the consequence of an action, this is quite different from having intended to bring it about. In *Petto v HM Advocate*[72] it was suggested that an "appreciation of the virtual certainty" that a risk will ensue could "be rightly equiperated with an intention that such consequences should occur." The accused had raised a fire on the ground floor of a tenement block; the resident of a second floor flat was killed. He had therefore acted

> "in the certain knowledge that those who are in the building, and especially
> those who are on the upper floors, will be at grave risk of being killed or seri-
> ously injured in the consequence of the fire."[73]

---

[65] *HM Advocate v Harris*, 1993 J.C. 150, per Lord Justice-Clerk Ross at 154E, founding upon *HM Advocate v Phipps* (1905) 4 Adam 616.
[66] *Byrne v HM Advocate (No.2)*, 2000 S.L.T. 233.
[67] *Byrne v HM Advocate (No.2)*, 2000 S.L.T. 233 at 238L and 239G.
[68] *Byrne v HM Advocate (No.2)*, 2000 S.L.T. 233 at 238J.
[69] *Blane v HM Advocate*, 1991 S.C.C.R. 576 at 582E. See below, para.11–32.
[70] *Blane v HM Advocate*, 1991 S.C.C.R. 576 at 582E.
[71] *Byrne v HM Advocate (No.2)*, 2000 S.L.T. 233 at 238L.
[72] *Petto v HM Advocate* [2011] HCJAC 80; 2011 S.L.T. 1043 at 1045, para.12.
[73] *Petto v HM Advocate* [2011] HCJAC 80; 2011 S.L.T. 1043 at 1045, para.12.

These observations were made in the context of distinguishing an outcome that could be said to have been intended from one about which the accused has been reckless. It seems unlikely that the court intended to suggest that any form of recklessness could amount to intention.

2. Recklessness

The criminal law has long regarded the reckless law-breaker as culpable and **3–30** deserving of punishment. What constitutes criminal recklessness is "a total indifference to and disregard for the safety of the public".[74] The standard applicable at common law is that articulated by Lord Justice-General Clyde in *Quinn v Cunningham*.[75] His opinion contains two definitions of recklessness as a mental element in crime: (i) "an utter disregard of what the consequences of the act in question may be so far as the public are concerned"[76]; and (ii) "recklessness so high as to involve an indifference to the consequences for the public generally".[77] Although the wording is different, the legal principle is the same. The key notion is "disregard" or "indifference" to the risks attending the conduct in question. Examples of actions held to permit the requisite inference of criminal recklessness include:

1. test firing a high calibre rifle from the front of a house, in the vicinity of other properties and of areas to which the public had access[78];

2. chasing bullocks from a field, causing them to escape on to a railway line and then on to a public road[79];

3. driving at 156 mph on a road where the speed limit was 70 mph.[80]

The standard is an objective one. In none of these three examples had the accused given thought to the risk or danger involved in their actions. It was this very indifference which gave rise to culpability. The individual who chased the bullocks appears to have thought that he was involved in some kind of "game", being unaware of the seriousness of his actions.[81] The gentleman who was found to have discharged his firearm recklessly claimed to have thought that he was acting in a safe manner.[82] In respect of the speeding motorist, the risk to other road users was said to be obviously foreseeable and to drive at such an excessive speed could not be described as anything other than culpable and reckless.[83]

The decision in *Allan v Patterson*[84] concerned the interpretation of the concept **3–31** of recklessness in the context of the repealed statutory offence of reckless driving.

---

[74] *RHW v HM Advocate*, 1982 S.L.T. 420 at 420.
[75] *Quinn v Cunningham*, 1956 J.C. 22; applied in *Cameron v Maguire*, 1999 J.C. 63.
[76] *Quinn v Cunningham*, 1956 J.C. 22 at 24.
[77] *Quinn v Cunningham*, 1956 J.C. 22 at 25.
[78] *Cameron v Maguire*, 1999 J.C. 63.
[79] *Robson v Spiers*, 1999 S.L.T. 1141.
[80] *Robertson v Klos*, 2006 S.C.C.R. 52.
[81] *Robson v Spiers*, 1999 S.L.T. 1141 at 1143C.
[82] *Cameron v Maguire*, 1999 J.C. 63 at 64H, although he did concede: "On looking at it again now, I wouldn't do it again, no."
[83] *Robertson v Klos*, 2006 S.C.C.R. 52 at 60, para.22. For contrasting academic views on the concept of recklessness, see J. Barton, "Recklessness in Scots Criminal Law: Subjective or Objective?" (2011) *Juridical Review* 143 and F. Stark, "Rethinking Recklessness" (2011) *Juridical Review* 163.
[84] *Allan v Patterson*, 1980 J.C. 57; see also *Black v Allan*, 1985 S.C.C.R. 11, discussed below in para.11–26.

Lord Justice-General Emslie stated that inquiry into the state of knowledge of the individual driver at the time of the offence was not required. In order to be able to "apply the adverb recklessly to the driving in question",[85] it had to be established

> "that it fell far below the standard of driving expected of the competent and careful driver and that it occurred either in the face of obvious and material dangers which were or should have been observed, appreciated and guarded against, or in circumstances which showed a complete disregard for any potential dangers which might result from the way in which the vehicle was being driven."

This suggests that recklessness is a description of behaviour as much as a state of mind, although Lord Emslie did accept that

> "in reaching a decision upon the critical issue a Judge or jury will be entitled to have regard to any explanation offered by the accused driver designed to show that his driving in the particular circumstances did not possess the quality of recklessness at the material time."[86]

It is important, however, to read Lord Emslie's opinion in the context of a statute which made it an offence to drive recklessly. The offence was targeted at performing an otherwise lawful activity, but doing so in a way which could be described as reckless. But, as Lord Justice-General Hope explained in *Carr v HM Advocate*,[87] in relation to a common law crime (fire-raising in this instance)

> "it is not the manner of doing an act which would otherwise be lawful which is in issue but the question whether the accused had the *mens rea* necessary for the commission of a crime."

The issue is "whether the accused's actions showed a complete disregard for any dangers which might result from what he was doing ... ". The decision in *Cameron v Maguire*[88] makes it clear that, at least in relation to common law crimes, the correct standard to apply is that laid down in *Quinn v Cunningham*,[89] and not that propounded in *Allan v Patterson*.

Objectivity and recklessness

3–32   As has been emphasised, the test for establishing recklessness is essentially an objective one. Scots law does not require that the accused has actually and subjectively realised the risk attendant upon his conduct before it can be

---

[85] *Allan v Patterson*, 1980 J.C. 57 at 60.
[86] *Allan v Patterson*, 1980 J.C. 57 at 60.
[87] *Carr v HM Advocate*, 1995 S.L.T. 800 at 803K–L; applied in *Thomson v HM Advocate*, 1995 S.L.T. 827.
[88] *Cameron v Maguire*, 1999 J.C. 63, doubting *Gizzi v Tudhope*, 1983 S.L.T. 214, which had applied the *Allan v Paterson* test in the context of the common law crime of recklessly discharging a firearm. The approach in *Cameron v Maguire* was endorsed in *Transco Plc v HM Advocate (No.1)*, 2004 J.C. 29.
[89] *Quinn v Cunningham*, 1956 J.C. 22; see above, para.3–30.

categorised as criminally reckless. An individual who has given no thought to a risk may be reckless. The argument would be that this very "thoughtlessness" is blameworthy: the accused really *ought* to have given thought to the risks. The two appellants in *Miller and Denovan v HM Advocate*[90] had been convicted of a murder in the course of a robbery. The deceased had been struck on the head with a large piece of wood. The intention of the appellants seems to have been to rob, not kill, and they were convicted on the basis of the alternative mens rea for murder of wicked recklessness. Lord Justice General Clyde observed[91]:

> "Both appellants displayed a callous disregard of whatever injuries they may have done him. They centred their whole attention upon snatching all they could from his pockets, rolling his body over . . . in order to get easier access to them. Once their purpose was achieved they fled into the night and left him to die."

The question which arises is how the appellants could be said to be reckless of their victim's life. They were so intent upon robbery that they did not notice the risk to life which their actions had brought about. Applying a subjective approach to recklessness, one would have to say that they had not been reckless as to the risk of death. Even though the appellants had perpetrated a vicious assault, there was no subjective appreciation or awareness of endangering life. In contrast, the objective approach taken in Scots law focuses upon the indifference to the victim's life demonstrated by the nature of the assault. Miller and Denovan's wicked recklessness was exhibited by what they did. The fact that they failed to appreciate the risk to the victim demonstrated their callous disregard for his life.

One issue which can arise is the position of the accused who would not have **3–33** appreciated the risk attendant upon his action, even had he applied his mind to the issue. The "reasonable man" would have appreciated the risk, but the accused, perhaps because of immaturity or lack of understanding, could not. His action may have been the result of inadequacy (for which he cannot be blamed), rather than any sort of indifference or disregard on his part. In one unreported case, it appears that the accused's age and mental capacity were held to be relevant.[92] In the context of intention, in *Petrovich v Jessop*,[93] the Appeal Court accepted that transient factors such as lack of sleep and stress could lead to a reasonable doubt as to the normal inference of mens rea. It may also be that such considerations could also refute an inference of recklessness.

Negligence

Negligence is similar to recklessness in that it also requires an individual to **3–34** have engaged in risk-creating conduct that deviates from the standards of the reasonably careful man. The difference lies in the degree of carelessness exhibited. The common law does not generally regard negligent conduct as sufficiently

---

[90] *Miller and Denovan v HM Advocate*, 1960, noted in *Parr v HM Advocate*, 1991 S.L.T. 211. The ensuing discussion of this case has been influenced by Duff, *Intention, Agency and Criminal Liability* (1990), pp.157–167.

[91] *Parr v HM Advocate*, 1991 S.L.T. 208 at 211K–L.

[92] *HM Advocate v S* Unreported, October 15, 1999.

[93] *Petrovich v Jessop*, 1990 S.L.T. 594.

blameworthy to attract the sanction of the criminal law (rather than the law of delict). Although the notion of "gross negligence" has sometimes been used as an alternative for recklessness,[94] there is the potential for confusion with the civil law if the word "negligence" is used in this context.[95] There are many statutory offences which rely upon negligence.

CONCURRENCE OF ACTUS REUS AND MENS REA

3–35 If the definition of a crime requires both actus reus and mens rea, then there will need to be a concurrence or coincidence of these two elements in order for criminal liability to be established. If there is a mens rea without an actus reus or an actus reus without mens rea (unless the offence is one of strict liability), there is again no crime. This requirement of concurrence does not mean, however, that in a result crime the mens rea must continue until the result occurs. In a case of murder, for example, an error as to the method or time of death will not affect criminal liability. All that is necessary is that the mens rea actuates the conduct which causes the death. This point is illustrated by the decision of the Privy Council in *Thabo-Meli v R*.[96] The appellants had been convicted of murder before the High Court of Basutoland. They had struck the victim over the head and, believing him to be dead had thrown the "body" over a cliff. The evidence was that the victim in fact died from exposure from being left at the bottom of the cliff. The appellants argued that the elements of the crime were not satisfied as mens rea and actus reus did not coincide in time. At the time when the blow had been inflicted death had not occurred, even though mens rea was present, and at the time of death the appellants did not have mens rea. The Privy Council held that it was not possible to divide up what was in reality one series of acts in the way that the appellants had argued. Lord Reid observed that it would be

> "too refined a ground of judgment to say that, because they were under a misapprehension at one stage and thought that their guilty purpose had been achieved before, in fact, it had been achieved, therefore they are to escape the penalties of the law."[97]

3–36 Generally the requirement of concurrence will mean that the mens rea must either precede the forbidden conduct or exist contemporaneously with the actus reus, but it is possible that in an exceptional case mens rea could be superimposed upon it. A decision to this effect is the English one of *Fagan v Metropolitan Police Commissioner*.[98] The accused had driven his car on to a police officer's foot. The officer asked him to drive off his foot, but for a time the accused refused to do so. It could not be proved that the original driving on to the foot had been accompanied by the requisite mens rea for the crime of battery. Nevertheless, the majority

---

[94] *Paton v HM Advocate*, 1936 J.C. 19 at 22; see *McDowall v HM Advocate*, 1998 J.C. 194 at 198E–G, where Lord Justice-General Rodger applied to culpable homicide the common law test of recklessness described above.

[95] This point was made by Lord Osborne in *Transco Plc v HM Advocate (No.1)*, 2004 J.C. 29, para.4.

[96] *Thabo-Meli v R.* [1954] 1 W.L.R. 228. See also *R. v Le Brun* [1992] 1 Q.B. 61.

[97] *Thabo-Meli v R.* [1954] 1 W.L.R. 228 at 230.

[98] *Fagan v Metropolitan Police Commissioner* [1969] 1 Q.B. 439.

of the Divisional Court took the view that the accused's conduct did constitute a battery. The reasoning was that the driving of the car on to the complainer's foot and allowing it to remain there could be treated as one continuing act of the application of force. On this analysis, the accused's act was not complete by the time his mens rea began (which would have been the case if the driving on to the complainer's foot had been treated as a single complete act). The accused's mens rea could therefore be superimposed on the existing continuing actus reus which he had caused. *Fagan* is thus persuasive authority for the view that, where an actus reus can be regarded as a continuing one, it is sufficient if mens rea is present at some stage during its continuance.

Transferred intent

The issue of concurrence can also arise where an individual acts intending to harm or to kill one person, but in fact harms or kills someone other than the intended victim. The actus reus of assault or murder has been brought about, but in an unexpected way. This was the situation in *Roberts v Hamilton*.[99] A had aimed a blow at B, but struck C instead. One view would be that such an eventuality is irrelevant to the definition of the crime, and should have no effect upon the culpability of the accused.[100] In Anglo-American criminal law, this type of case is covered by the doctrine of transferred intent.[101] This operates to make the accused's criminal responsibility exactly the same as if the blow had landed upon the intended victim, rather than a bystander.[102] In *Roberts v Hamilton*, the accused was convicted of assault and this was upheld on appeal. One explanation offered for the decision was that the intention to assault the intended victim could be transferred to the actual victim.[103] Although Hume is supportive of the notion of transferred intent,[104] *Roberts v Hamilton* is rare as a Scottish authority recognising the doctrine.[105] Indeed, whatever may be the position in Anglo-American criminal law, it is clear that there is no place in Scots law for a generalised doctrine of transferred intent, applicable to all crimes of intention. In relation to wilful fire-raising, the High Court has set its face against the doctrine. In *Blane v HM Advocate*,[106]. it was held that an intention to set fire to moveable property could not be transferred to the heritable property destroyed by the resulting fire.

3–37

---

[99] *Roberts v Hamilton*, 1989 J.C. 91.

[100] A.P. Simester, J.R. Spencer, G.R. Sullivan and G.J. Virgo, *Simester and Sullivan's Criminal Law: Theory and Doctrine*, 4th edn (Oxford: Hart, 2010), pp.164–165.

[101] See, e.g. *People v Scott*, 14 Cal. 4th 544 (1996).

[102] For the doctrine of transferred intent to operate, the accused must have the requisite mens rea of the crime for which he is being prosecuted. That is, the doctrine will not operate where the accused has the mens rea for one crime, but in fact perpetrates the actus reus of a crime which requires a different mens rea.

[103] The additional explanation proffered was that what had happened was so unlikely under the circumstances that criminal liability could not be avoided (founding upon *Connor v Jessop*, 1988 S.C.C.R. 624, which followed Macdonald, p.2).

[104] Hume, *Commentaries*, I, 22–25; see also Erskine, IV, 4, 43. In *Roberts v Hamilton*, the Appeal Court rejected the appellant's contention that Hume's account of transferred intent was confined to murder.

[105] In *Petto v HM Advocate* [2011] HCJAC 80; 2011 S.L.T. 1043 at 1047, para.27, Lord Eassie offers (obiter) support to the doctrine's applicability to murder.

[106] *Blane v HM Advocate*, 1991 S.C.C.R. 576; applied in *McKelvie v HM Advocate*, 1997 S.L.T. 758.

This approach was endorsed in the full bench decision of *Byrne v HM Advocate*.[107] The explanation for the reluctance to transfer the intention in cases of wilful fire-raising is that the effect would be to penalise the accused for unintended consequences, in a crime where intention is required. Unlike the straightforward assault case, perhaps, the outcome of intentionally raising a fire is all too unpredictable. The intention may be to set fire to some old packing cases, but the warehouse can be destroyed. The appropriate charge in such a case is that of culpable and reckless fire-raising.[108]

---

[107] *Byrne v HM Advocate (No.2)*, 2000 S.L.T. 233 at 239D.
[108] On fire-raising generally, see below, paras 11–28 to 11–37. It could equally be argued that the accused in *Roberts v Hamilton* could have been convicted of causing reckless injury. This crime is described in detail in Ch.9.

CHAPTER 4

VOLUNTARY ACTS AND AUTOMATISM

THE ACADEMIC VIEW

TEXTBOOKS AND OTHERS

"The foundation of criminal liability is conduct, for without an act there can **4–01** be no liability. But not any act will do. There are qualifications that an act must meet, and the first is that it be *voluntary*."[1]

This statement by an academic writer is echoed in major textbooks around the world. Thus, in Smith and Hogan's *Criminal Law*,[2] it is asserted that

"[w]hat is clear is that the voluntariness of an act is a more fundamental element of criminal liability than what we normally think of as *mens rea*."

Again, in Burchell and Milton's *Principles of Criminal Law* (South Africa), it is stated that

"[t]o qualify as conduct of which the criminal law will take cognisance the conduct must be (*a*) that of a human being which was (*b*) voluntary."[3]

Gordon appears to take the same view, as the following quotation indicates: "the term 'act' is usually restricted to 'voluntary' acts, so that a man is responsible only for his voluntary acts."[4] Nor is that view confined to textbook writings. Many criminal codes in the United States, for example, have adopted the provision in the Model Penal Code[5] that:

---

[1] H. Gross, *A Theory of Criminal Justice* (New York: Oxford University Press, 1979), p.67.
[2] *Smith and Hogan Criminal Law*, edited by David Ormerod, 12th edn (Oxford: Oxford University Press, 2008), para. 4.2.1.2, p.55.
[3] J.M. Burchell and J.R.L. Milton, *Principles of Criminal law*, 3rd edn (Cape Town: Juta, 2005), p.178. See also P.R. Ferguson and C. McDiarmid, *Scots Criminal Law: A Critical Analysis* (Dundee: Dundee University Press, 2009), para.6.4.1, p.129; Finbarr McAuley and J. Paul McCutcheon, *Criminal Liability* (Dublin: Round Hall, 2000), p.122; and A.P. Simester and G.R. Sullivan, *Criminal Law: Theory and Doctrine*, 3rd edn (Oxford: Hart, 2007), p.103.
[4] Gordon, *Criminal Law*, 3rd edn (Edinburgh: W.Green, 2000/2001), para.3.08.
[5] American Law Institute, *Model Penal Code Official Draft* (1985), s.2.01.

"A person is not guilty of an offense unless his liability is based on conduct that includes a voluntary act or the omission to perform an act of which he is physically capable."[6]

In the United Kingdom, however, the proposed criminal code for England and Wales[7] makes no mention of the "voluntariness" of an act as an element (essential or otherwise) of criminal liability[8]; and the following judicial opinion is rather *un*-typical:

"The requirement that [there] should be a voluntary act is essential, not only in a murder case, but also in every criminal case."[9]

Regrettably, it is not at all immediately apparent what is meant by these various views; and an illustration may help to clarify the issues involved.

Illustration

4–02   Suppose that John is seen at the wheel of his car, as it travels from Glasgow to Renfrew. On a perfectly straight piece of road, in good daylight conditions of visibility and weather, his vehicle is observed to swerve suddenly to the "wrong" side of the road and collide with an oncoming motor-cycle. The motor-cyclist is thrown into the air and his bike crushed. John's vehicle pauses for less than two seconds before speeding away from the scene of the incident. Some minutes later, his vehicle knocks down a police officer who had stepped into the road in order to signal him to stop. The police officer is seriously injured. On the face of things, John would seem to have committed a number of offences—since cars (at the time of writing, at least) are incapable of directing their own movements. The offences in question might include dangerous driving under s.2 of the Road Traffic Act 1988 (as substituted by s.1 of the Road Traffic Act 1991), or perhaps the lesser offence of careless or inconsiderate driving under s.3 of the Road Traffic Act 1988 (as substituted by s.2 of the Road Traffic Act 1991), and almost certainly failing to stop after an accident under s.170 of the Road Traffic Act 1988. Were the motor-cyclist to die of his injuries, then even more serious charges might possibly apply (e.g. culpable homicide at common law; the offence of causing death by dangerous driving under s.1 of the Road Traffic Act 1988, as substituted by s.1 of the Road Traffic Act 1991; or the offence of causing death by careless, or inconsiderate, driving under s.2B of the Road Traffic Act 1988, as inserted by s.20(1) of the Road Safety Act 2006).[10] *A propos* the unfortunate police officer, charges of assault or even attempted murder at common law might easily be envisaged.

---

[6] See, e.g. Joshua Dressler, *Understanding Criminal Law*, 2nd edn (New York: Matthew Bender, 1995), p.71.

[7] Law Commission, *Criminal Law: A Criminal Code* (The Stationery Office, 1989), Law Com. No.177.

[8] The "Draft Criminal Code for Scotland with Commentary" (published under the auspices of the Scottish Law Commission, 2003) also makes no mention of "voluntariness": see above, para.2–01 at fn.1.

[9] *Bratty v Attorney General for Northern Ireland* [1963] A.C. 386, per Lord Denning at 409. What Lord Denning then went on to say is, however, quoted with apparent approval by the court in *Finegan v Heywood*, 2000 S.C.C.R. 460, at 463D-E, para.6; see also 464A, para.7.

[10] For "culpable homicide", see below, paras 9–59 to 9–76; for the statutory meaning of "dangerous driving", see s.2A of the Road Traffic Act 1988, as inserted by s.1 of the Road Traffic Act 1991; and for the statutory meaning of "careless or inconsiderate driving", see s.3ZA of the 1988 Act, as inserted by the Road Safety Act 2006 s.30. See also the new offence of causing serious injury by dangerous driving: the 1988 Act s.1A, as inserted by the Legal Aid, Sentencing and Punishment of Offenders Act 2012 s.143(2).

ACTS OF AN INNOCENT AGENT OR EVENTS
BEYOND HUMAN CONTROL

If in the preceding example, John had been alert and apparently in full control of **4–03** his vehicle "at the relevant time," then one might assume that he had simply been travelling too fast for his own capabilities or the mechanical tolerances of his car (or that he had been paying scandalously little attention to his driving)—and that he had panicked when the "accidents" occurred. One would have little sympathy for his plight. But suppose that he had been driving competently enough at a wholly reasonable speed just before the first "accident", and that events thereafter were directed by a passenger who seized the steering wheel without prior warning and deliberately aimed the vehicle at the passing motor-cyclist. The passenger also, one may conjecture (with some suspension of disbelief), caused the car to move off after the initial collision, and thereafter knock down the police officer, by physically forcing John's hands and feet to execute the required movements. If John had no reason to anticipate such behaviour on the part of his passenger, one would probably conclude that he had simply been an innocent agent (see below, para.7–33) in the execution of the real culprit's plan—no more responsible for the act or its result than a broken glass in the hands of a violent man.[11] John could not reasonably have been said to be "driving" or doing anything at all during the crucial time periods. If the question were to be posed: "Who was driving at the relevant moments?"—one would surely not answer that it was John. No part of the conduct or acts making up the actus reus of any of the crimes involved (see above, para.4–02) could be said to have been his; and the same conclusion would follow, at least in respect of the initial collision, if the car swerved because a sudden defect manifested itself in the steering, or a tyre burst without warning— assuming that either event placed the car beyond any reasonable human control.[12]

ACTING UNCONSCIOUSLY OR SEMI-CONSCIOUSLY

One might further suppose, however, again in relation to the above example (in **4–04** para.4–02), that the car collided with the unfortunate victims because John was "unconscious" at the time, or, was "semi-conscious" or in a state of "impaired consciousness." Perhaps he had had an epileptic fit or a "heart attack" whilst at the wheel and was thus unaware of what he was doing for a particular period of time; or he might have become comatose or semi-conscious because he suffered from a condition (such as diabetes) where full consciousness depended upon a very fine balance being struck between the ingestion of prescribed drugs (such as insulin)

---

[11] See, for instance, the contribution of Mr. Smith to Mrs. Craft's death in *R. v Mitchell* [1983] 2 W.L.R. 938.

[12] Cf. *Attorney General's Reference (No. 4 of 2000)* [2001] 2 Cr. App. R. 417 (CA), where the error of a driver in pressing the accelerator instead of the brake (which was proved against him) was contrasted with the situation where the engine of his vehicle might have suddenly surged due to mechanical defect (which he had claimed but was unable to establish). It might be noted here that "dangerous driving" extends to the case where "it would be obvious to a competent and careful driver that driving the vehicle in its current state would be dangerous": see s.2A of the Road Traffic Act 1988, as inserted by s.1 of the Road Traffic Act 1991. The situation postulated would be different, therefore, had John known of the defect, or the poor state of his tyres, prior to the commencement of his journey.

and normal foodstuffs—and that balance had ceased to be maintained. Perhaps, again, he might have slept badly or not at all the night before and succumbed to tiredness whilst at the wheel (which might at least explain the initial collision under the postulated non-adverse road and weather conditions). Yet again John might have been drinking alcohol prior to setting out on his journey: he might have been plainly drunk. In all of these possible scenarios, John might nevertheless appear to be driving. It might appear that he was manipulating the controls and directing the movements of the vehicle—which is what "driving" amounts to in Scots law.[13] If one was now to ask: "Who was driving at the relevant moments?" it would be difficult to say it was anyone other than John himself—particularly since the vehicle was (apparently) purposefully driven off after the initial collision.

The problem

4–05 Where the only person (in retrospect, at least) who could have influenced the course of events apparently did things which had a major causal influence over that course of events (as in the illustration set out above, at para.4–02), then a problem relating to his responsibility for the outcome exists if he "did" those things whilst he was unconscious or only semi-conscious (as in the various scenarios described above, in para.4–04). If he apparently did those things, then it is very difficult to conclude that he did not do them at all. That does not lead to the conclusion, however, that he is necessarily criminally responsible for them. The first component of criminal liability, it will be remembered, is not just an "act" (i.e. "doing something") but an actus reus. It can, therefore, be postulated that it is a "responsible" human act (and not a "bare" act) which the criminal law seeks. The law thus attempts, or should attempt, to give effect to the intuitive feeling that there is a significant difference in responsibility between a driver who collides with another vehicle because he has been wantonly driving too fast and one who (in fact) causes a similar "accident" because he has temporarily, through no fault of his own, lost the ability to comply with the dictates of the criminal law by making, or refraining from making, particular bodily movements. Of course, in many instances that difference in responsibility can be accounted for by the law's taking note that a person so incapacitated lacks mens rea. He may have "acted" after a fashion, but not so as to give rise to any inference that he intended the outcome, had knowledge of the criminative circumstances, or foresaw (objectively or subjectively) the risks, such was his lack of awareness of what was happening. To that extent, then, it would hardly be necessary to attempt to distinguish a "bare" act from a "responsible" one. The matter would simply be settled in terms of whether there was or was not mens rea—given his personal circumstances at the time.[14]

---

[13] See *Ames v MacLeod*, 1969 J.C. 1, *McArthur v Valentine*, 1990 J.C. 146, *Hoy v McFadyen*, 2000 S.C.C.R. 875; cf. *DPP v Alderton* [2004] R.T.R. 367 (an English case, the test for "driving" being slightly different there).

[14] Of the crimes possibly committed in the scenario depicted above in para.4–02 failing to stop after an accident (see *Harding v Price* [1948] 1 K.B. 695), assault (see *Smart v HM Advocate*, 1975 J.C. 30), culpable homicide (see *Transco Plc v HM Advocate*, 2004 J.C. 29; also see paras 9–59 to 9–76, below), and attempted murder (see *Cawthorne v HM Advocate*, 1968 J.C. 32) all require some form of mens rea.

The need to distinguish different sorts of act

There are, however, some crimes (some statutory ones—see below, Ch.13) **4–06** where liability is said to be "strict." That means in effect that there is no requirement that the prosecutor should show mens rea on the part of the accused, or bring forward evidence from which it might be inferred.[15] In bald terms, proof that the accused brought about the forbidden result or performed the forbidden conduct is quite sufficient for conviction.[16] To take effective cognizance of incapacitating defects (mental or physical) accompanying human conduct, it would be necessary, therefore, in such cases to distinguish between conduct amounting to a "bare" act and that amounting to an actus reus.[17] Similarly, with respect to any criminal justice system which pursues an objective method of proving mens rea (as is believed to be the case in Scotland—see above, Ch.3), it may be necessary to distinguish "responsible" human conduct from "mere" human conduct, since proof of the actus reus will very often imply the existence of the required mens rea. In the illustration above (see para.4–02), for example, if John's car was apparently driven *at* the unfortunate policeman, it would be simple to infer from the facts that the driver intended to kill the officer, or was completely indifferent whether he lived or died—either (generally) sufficing for the crime of attempted murder.[18] There is thus a case to be made for marking off "bare" human conduct from the "responsible" sort.

What distinctions can be made?

With reference once again to the illustration (see above, paras 4–02 to 4–04), **4–07** there is plainly a distinction to be made between John's conduct where he willingly courts the risks of an "accident" by wantonly driving too fast, and his conduct where he "drives" in the throes of an epileptic fit or a heart attack. There is also perhaps a further distinction to be made, for example, between his "driving" whilst experiencing such a fit or attack, and his doing so whilst intoxicated— depending to a large extent on the way in which he came to be intoxicated (though other factors are also involved—e.g. the type and known effects of the intoxicant). These distinctions, however, are exceedingly difficult to generalise. It is tempting to conclude, for example, that the issue depends on whether or not the apparent actor was conscious (in the sense of "being aware") of what he was doing at the relevant time. But this is not an infallible guide. A person afflicted by cerebral palsy will (usually) be fully conscious of the random movements of his limbs; but it does not follow that one should wish to label such movements as "responsible" acts, even though they might result in prima facie assaults upon others unfortunate enough to be within range. The same might be said of so called

---

[15] Cf. J. Chalmers and F. Leverick, *Criminal Defences and Pleas in Bar of Trial (Edinburgh: W. Green, 2006)*, p.140, para.7.06; Smith and Hogan, *Criminal Law* (2008), pp.54–55.

[16] Of the crimes possibly committed in the scenario depicted above in para.4–02, dangerous driving, careless (or inconsiderate) driving, and causing death by dangerous or careless (or inconsiderate) driving are probably all of this type.

[17] Cf. A. Ashworth, *Principles of Criminal Law*, 6th edn (Oxford: Oxford University Press, 2009), pp.87–88.

[18] *Cawthorne v HM Advocate*, 1968 J.C. 32: cf. *Drury v HM Advocate*, 2001 S.L.T. 1013.

"reflex" movements where a human physiological response is triggered automatically by the application of external stimulus.[19]

4–08 It has become customary, at least in academic writings, to refer to the primary distinction as that between a voluntary (i.e. responsible) act and an involuntary (i.e. bare) one. This, however, only produces a terminological shift. Meaning must still be given to the replacement terms. Equally, it has become customary to speak of a "voluntary" act as a "willed" bodily movement, or as conduct which flows from an exercise of "will"[20]—which suggests that the presence or absence of some mental process is the issue at stake. If this is correct, then a mental element must be involved in conduct truly amounting to an actus reus—although this disturbs the neat symmetry of criminal law theory, namely that the mental element of mens rea is separate from the actus reus.[21] It is, however, rather uncertain what can be meant by the "will" in such an analysis. Clearly it must be different from "wanting" or "desiring" what one does, since these terms normally connote the seeking of goals well beyond the actions themselves; nor can it be squared with more limited conceptions of "wanting" or "desiring", since one may in fact do something (for example, visit a dentist) which is opposed to one's short term desires or wants (c.f. the long term desire to have attractive and effectively-functioning teeth). The term "will", therefore, seems to be no less obscure than the terms "responsible" or "voluntary".

Legal effect of involuntariness

4–09 It is also uncertain what should be the result of making a distinction between "bare" acts and "responsible" ones. For the authors of the American Model Penal Code, a person is to be held "not guilty of an offense" unless his conduct includes a voluntary act (see above, para.4–01). Fletcher,[22] on the other hand, remarks that "we intuitively recoil at the notion of punishing" persons in respect of acts where the "will" was not operative; and LaFave and Scott also suggest that it is punishment which cannot be justified for "involuntary" acts.[23] Obviously, punishment cannot be imposed unless there is a finding of guilt; but the converse is not necessarily true. A person may be convicted of an offence, but may thereafter be discharged without punishment at all (unless, of course, conviction itself is taken to be a form of punishment). As far as current Scots law is concerned, the criminal law does not always sanction acquittal in cases where there were "involuntary" acts[24]; but provided there are sound reasons for convicting in particular types of involuntariness (e.g. in cases of self-induced intoxication) and provided also that (save where there is a clear rule to the contrary[25]) the involuntariness of the

---

[19] See *Jessop v Johnstone*, 1991 S.C.C.R. 238. For a more sophisticated analysis, see H. Gross, *A Theory of Criminal Justice* (Oxford: Oxford University Press, 1979), pp.67–73.

[20] See, for example, Smith and Hogan, *Criminal Law*, 12th edn (2008), p.52; cf. Ashworth, *Principles of Criminal Law*, 6th edn (2009), p.88.

[21] See G. Williams, *Criminal Law: The General Part*, 2nd edn (London: Stevens & Sons, 1961), p. 12; G. Williams, *Textbook of Criminal Law*, 2nd edn (London: Stevens and Sons, 1983), p.147, para.7–2.

[22] G.P. Fletcher, *Rethinking Criminal Law* (Boston, Little, Brown, 1978), p.426.

[23] W.R. La Fave and W.A. Scott, *Criminal Law*, 2nd edn (St. Paul, Minnesota: West, 1986) pp.197–198.

[24] See below, para.4–35.

[25] As there is, e.g. in relation to self-induced intoxication.

acts is not to be totally disregarded at the point when an appropriate disposal of the case comes to be considered by the court, the law can still be regarded as both principled and fair.

Voluntariness as an essential element of liability

Regrettably, it is further uncertain whether the "voluntariness" of an act is **4–10** indeed to be taken as an essential element of criminal liability. If it were to be accepted as an essential element[26] then one would expect "voluntariness" to be something which prosecutors were duty bound to establish at criminal trials. Neither academic writings nor judicial dicta, however, support such a proposition. At best, those who favour a requirement of "voluntariness" take the view that an act will be presumed to be "voluntary" until some evidence to the contrary is presented.[27] This has had the effect of highlighting the issue as one of "*in*voluntariness" and of shifting the emphasis from that of "fundamental element" to that of "defence." Smith and Hogan, for example, remark[28] that

"[i]t is a defence known as 'automatism' that this element [that an act was voluntary] has not been proved by the Crown."

Some text writers, therefore, deal with the whole issue here under the heading of "Defences,"[29] others tackle it almost exclusively under the title of "*Actus Reus*,"[30] whilst others present it under both such headings.[31]

Involuntariness as a defence—automatism

In English and Scots criminal law, it is now clear that the whole issue has **4–11** become one for the defence in the first instance. The accused must somehow place some evidence before the court or jury which will tend to displace the tacit presumption that his proven conduct was "voluntary." He must, therefore, discharge the initial evidential burden required by the defence of "automatism." He must show that his acts could be construed as "involuntary." If that construction finds favour, it may be that the reason for his involuntariness falls within the

---

[26] See above, para.4–01, "a more fundamental element than ... *mens rea*." See also Ashworth, *Principles of Criminal Law*, 6th edn (2009), p.87.

[27] See *Bratty v Attorney General for Northern Ireland* [1963] A.C. 386, per Lord Denning at 413; *Ryan v The Queen* (1967) 40 A.L.J.R. 488 per Barwick C.J. at 492, followed in *R. v Falconer* (1991) 65 A.L.J.R. 20; and Ashworth, *Principles of Criminal Law*, 6th edn (2009), pp.87–88.

[28] Somewhat oddly in its context at Smith and Hogan, *Criminal Law*, 10th edn (London: Lexis Nexis UK, 2002), p.39.

[29] See Chalmers and Leverick, *Criminal Defences and Pleas in Bar of Trial* (2006), Ch.7 (where the appropriate "defence" is examined along with "insanity"—these two defences being convincingly said there to be "two sides of the same coin": see in particular paras 7.01, and 7.26 to 7.45); see also G. Williams, *Textbook of Criminal Law*, 2nd edn (London: Stevens & Sons, 1983), Pt 4—Defences, Ch.29, pp.662–684.

[30] See Smith and Hogan, *Criminal Law*, 10th edn (2002), pp.37–41, where it was nevertheless also treated as the defence of "Automatism."

[31] See, e.g. A.W. Mewett and M. Manning, *Criminal Law*, 2nd edn (Toronto: Butterworths,1985), Ch.3, pp.73–78; Ch.9, pp.279–289.

legal meaning of mental disorder,[32] and thus within the special defence of that name. In that event, it would seem possible to invoke the statutory provisions which allow that special defence to negative the criminal responsibility of the mentally disordered; it should be borne in mind, however, that these provisions define "mental disorder" in a way which many recognised automatism situations might find difficult to satisfy, and that they require the person in question to establish such disorder on the balance of probabilities—a burden which exceeds a mere evidential one, and which may be more difficult to discharge.[33] In English law, the scope of the independent defence has been narrowed to that of "non-insane automatism"; and that, as has repeatedly been said by English judges, is itself of very narrow scope.[34] The English judiciary, therefore, has taken every opportunity to make the defence difficult to establish; and in practice, pleas of non-insane automatism are there seldom successful. The strange practice has also arisen in English law of permitting an accused to withdraw his defence of automatism in favour of a guilty plea where the trial judge has ruled that the defence truly amounts to one of "insanity".[35] This seems to confound both principle and policy notions of public safety.

The scope of a legally relevant act

4–12 An added difficulty for those who favour an "involuntary act" defence is that the judiciary has proved more than willing to enlarge the scope of the "acts" in question. In the illustration concerning John (see above, para.4–02), the incidents (possibly attracting criminal liability) are of fairly short duration. His car was "driven" into the path of a motor-cycle, collided with that cycle, and then was "driven" away—all within the space of a few seconds, no doubt. Similarly, the knocking down of the police officer will have occupied a very short interval of time. If it was established that, during the relevant time periods, John was truly "unconscious" (i.e. unaware of his surroundings and his obligations as a driver—even though his eyes may have been open and his behaviour apparently normal), and if his legally relevant acts were to be confined to only those narrow periods of time, then it is certainly possible to conclude that his actions were not "responsible" ones (with whatever effect that is deemed to have in law). He would not be responsible for what he did during those few seconds. It should not then matter

---

[32] In England, it has been said that that would amount to "insane" automatism: see, e.g. *R. v Burgess* [1991] 2 W.L.R. 1206, per Lord Lane C.J. at 1208E. In Scotland, however, the term "insanity" has been deleted from forensic language: see, in particular, the effect of Pt 7 of the Criminal Justice and Licensing (Scotland) Act 2010 (asp 13), on the relevant provisions of the Criminal Procedure (Scotland) Act 1995. (Part 7 of the 2010 Act was founded on recommendations of the Scottish Law Commission: see *Report on Insanity and Diminished Responsibility* (The Stationery Office, 2004) Scot. Law Com. No.195.) It is to be noted that all common law rules relating to a special defence of insanity have been abolished: Criminal Justice and Licensing (Scotland) Act 2010 (asp 13) s.171.

[33] See the Criminal Procedure (Scotland) Act 1995 s.307(1)—s.v. "mental disorder"— which refers the reader to the definition given by the Mental Health (Care and Treatment) (Scotland) Act 2003 (asp 13) s.328(1) and Sch.4 para.8(16)(d). In particular, "mental disorder" means any mental illness, personality disorder or learning disability; the special defence of "mental disorder" excludes, however, psychopathic personality disorder—see s.51A(2) of the 1995 Act, as inserted by the Criminal Justice and Licensing (Scotland) Act 2010 (asp 13) s.168.

[34] See *Bratty v Attorney General for Northern Ireland* [1963] A.C. 386; *R. v Quick* [1973] Q.B. 910; *R. v Sullivan* [1984] A.C. 156; *R. v Hennessy* [1989] 1 W.L.R. 287.

[35] See, e.g. *R. v Sullivan* [1984] A.C. 156; *R. v Hennessy* [1989] 1 W.L.R. 287.

what the reason for his unconsciousness was. In any event, if the reason was connected with something which was not his fault and which he could not have anticipated (a stroke or heart-attack, for example), one would not wish to enlarge the field of view. But, if John (say) had known himself to be diabetic and had further known that failure to take insulin would lead to the rapid onset of unconsciousness in his case due to hyperglycaemia,[36] then one feels the need to inquire whether he had taken his medication at all that day. If he had not, then his "acts" may be seen as including the fault-ridden ones of failing to take insulin *and* then driving, all in the knowledge that unconsciousness might well intervene before his destination was reached. One would perhaps not then view the incidents as "involuntary" on his part at all—provided that a wide-angled view of his "actings" can legitimately be taken. Truly, he might have been unaware of what he was doing during an incident and its immediate aftermath; but he was certainly not unaware when he began to drive that his actions might pass beyond his control. This may be enough, therefore, to mark his acts as responsible ones after all (for the purposes of at least some crimes); but this will depend on how widely the law is prepared to look for relevant actings, and how concerned it is whether he should have been able to anticipate precisely what eventually happened. Enlarging the field of view, therefore, can turn unconscious or uncontrolled actions into responsible ones.[37]

Ryan v The Queen

A well known illustration here can be found in the Australian case of *Ryan v The Queen*[38] where the accused set out to rob a petrol filling-station. He carried a loaded, sawn-off rifle with him, and used it as a threat to subdue the person in charge of the cash-box there. The accused ordered that person to face a wall and hold his hands out behind him—so that these could then be tied securely with a piece of rope the accused thought he had in his pocket. Whilst he searched his pocket for that rope, two things happened. The person being coerced in that way suddenly crouched down and half turned round; and the accused "shot" him in the neck—killing him. The accused claimed that he had been holding the rifle (which did not have its safety catch set) with one hand, and that the act of pulling the trigger had been "involuntary." It was, he said, a reflex action "triggered" by the sudden movement on the part of the victim. Subsequent police tests suggested that there might be some basis for that possibility—which might have been decisive in the later proceedings for criminal homicide. In fact, he was convicted of murder; and his subsequent appeal was dismissed partly on the view that

> "the jury, having concluded that the discharge of the gun was involuntary could have concluded that the act causing death was the presentation of the cocked, loaded gun with a safety catch unapplied and that its involuntary discharge was a likelihood which ought to have been in the contemplation of the applicant when presenting the gun in the circumstances."[39]

---

[36] See *R. v Hennessy* [1989] 1 W.L.R. 287 and below para.4–27. Cf. *MacLeod v Mathieson*, 1993 S.C.C.R. 488 Sh.Ct.

[37] Cf. *Finegan v Heywood*, 2000 S.C.C.R. 460, where the appellant's condition of parasomnia—brought on (as he should have anticipated) by drinking some six pints of beer—was treated by the Appeal Court as one within the *ratio* of *Brennan v HM Advocate*, 1977 J.C. 38.

[38] *Ryan v The Queen* (1967) 40 A.L.J.R. 488.

[39] *Ryan v The Queen* (1967) 40 A.L.J.R. 488, per Barwick C.J. at 494.

Where the focus was widened slightly beyond the mere pulling of the trigger, there was thus produced a voluntary act which the court could have accepted as *the* cause of the death in all the circumstances there.

CONCLUSION

4–14 It is *theoretically* satisfying to conclude that a person can only be criminally liable for his "voluntary acts". But it is very difficult to give content to the word "voluntary"; and it is not always easy to identify what is *the* "act" for the purposes of a particular crime. It seems in general agreed, however, that a person should not be punished for his involuntary acts. Punishment after all cannot deter a person from repeating his conduct if he did not know or could not help what he was doing at the time.[40] Nor can it deter third parties successfully, since the imposition of punishment will be viewed as simply unfair in the circumstances. Still less would punishment be seen to be merited in such a case; and, therefore, its imposition could not be retributively justified.

THE POSITION UNDER SCOTS LAW

ACTS OF AN INNOCENT AGENT OR
EVENTS BEYOND HUMAN CONTROL

4–15 Under Scots law, a person who is physically compelled by another to be the innocent agent of a criminal act is not responsible for that act. Criminal liability clearly remains with the other person—since the act is truly his. It would be absurd and unjust to take any other view (see above, para.4–03), and the case of *Hugh Mitchell*[41] provides ample authority. There, Mitchell attacked his wife, kicking and punching her whilst she was holding their four-month old baby in her arms. In terms of the indictment, it was alleged that *he* caused his wife, by the assault he made upon her, to compress or squeeze the child so as to obstruct its respiration in some way—by all which, or part thereof, the child was mortally injured and thus culpably killed by *him*. This part of the charge was found relevant by the three-judge High Court; and the jury eventually convicted him of the culpable homicide of the child on the stated basis. There was no question of his wife's having had any liability at all for the child's death. Her contribution to the fatality was recognised as no greater than that of some inanimate object in the hands of her husband. It is equally apparent that Scots law would not hold a person criminally liable for an event which was beyond his power to control (although normally this would be treated as an event he had not *caused*). Reference may be made here to the decision in *Hogg v MacPherson*,[42] which is considered above at para.3–04. It will be seen that Lord Justice-General Clyde held there that "the breaking of the lamp was not the appellant's act at all, either negligent or accidental."[43] It seems

---

[40] See, e.g. *Finegan v Heywood*, 2000 S.C.C.R. 460, where that part of the appropriate sentence which related to disqualification from driving was quashed on appeal.
[41] *Hugh Mitchell* (1856) 2 Irv. 488.
[42] *Hogg v Macpherson*,1928 J.C. 15.
[43] *Hogg v Macpherson*, 1928 J.C. 15 at 17.

78

that the same view could be taken of genuine reflex actions; but these are difficult to define, and there are few, reported Scottish cases which have featured them. In *Jessop v Johnstone*[44] Lord Justice-Clerk Ross did say:

"We appreciate that there may be cases where a person instinctively reacts to violence in a reflex way, such as if a person is suddenly and without warning struck and turns round sharply so that he comes in contact with his assailant."

The appeal court held, however, that the facts of the case did not support a finding of "reflex response." Had the facts done so, presumably the court would have endorsed the sheriff's original decision to acquit—although that had been based by him on a consequent lack of mens rea.

Hypnotic or Similar Influences

If a person is forcibly or unwittingly hypnotised by another (assuming forcible **4–16** or unwitting hypnotism of a person to be possible) and thus made to do that other's bidding, then that person surely becomes an innocent agent—just as much as if he had been physically compelled; and the same conclusion would seem to follow if drugs were to be administered to him by stealth or force, in order to make him comply with the administrator's criminal designs.[45]

ACTING UNCONSCIOUSLY OR SEMI-CONSCIOUSLY

Where a person has apparently acted purposively, and there was no question of **4–17** physical compulsion by another or from natural phenomena (see above, para.4–15) and no question of hypnotic influence (see above, para.4–16) then it may be that he did so whilst unconscious, or whilst not fully conscious. He may have been observed in the act of assaulting another, driving a car, or taking things away from a store without paying for them; but it may also be the case that due to some mental dysfunction (going beyond mere inattention) he was not aware (or not fully aware) of what he was doing. His mental condition, then, may have been less than normal at the relevant time. Scots law does not ignore such a mental condition, but appears to inquire into the cause producing it.

Causal factor—mental disorder

If that cause is capable of being proved on the balance of probabilities to be a **4–18** mental disorder which rendered the person in question unable to appreciate the nature or wrongfulness of his conduct (act or omission) at the material time, that person may be acquitted of the assault, the driving offence, the theft, or whatever. Of course, such an acquittal will then be on the ground of mental disorder; but that does not commit the court, in either a solemn or a summary case, to order the acquitted person's detention in a hospital. The court instead may, for example, make a guardianship order, a supervision and treatment order, or make no order at

---

[44] *Jessop v Johnstone*, 1991 S.C.C.R. 238 at 240E.
[45] See *HM Advocate v Raiker*, 1989 S.C.C.R. 149, per Lord McCluskey's charge to the jury at 154C—although his approach stressed the consequent lack of mens rea of the "innocent agent."

all.[46] The often expressed view, therefore, that such an acquittal holds severe consequences for an accused person,[47] is no longer as compelling as once was the case—especially since the more neutral "mental disorder" replaced the former "insanity" as the appropriate term to use in such cases. It should be noted, however, that such an acquittal is nowadays dependent upon the accused's having raised a plea of mental disorder as a special defence; it seems no longer possible for the prosecutor or the court to initiate the matter.[48]

Causal factor—external to the accused—automatism

4–19   In *Ross v HM Advocate*[49] a full bench of five appeal court judges decided, for the first time authoritatively,[50] that a straightforward acquittal was competent where an accused person behaved in an apparently criminal fashion after drugs had been administered to him without his knowledge or consent. Ross had been at a party where a can of lager from which he had been drinking was surreptitiously "laced" by others with LSD (lysergic acid diethylamide) and five or six "jellies" of temazepam. Unwitting as to its contents, Ross continued to imbibe from the same can, with the result that his conduct became uncharacteristically bizarre and exceptionally violent. Amongst other things, he then stabbed several persons, inflicting upon them serious, life-threatening injuries. The case was, therefore, concerned with the criminal responsibility of one who knowingly consumes some alcohol whilst unknowingly ingesting hallucinogenic drugs (i.e. LSD—temazepam generally, and on its own at least, having a tranquillising effect). The appeal court, however, ignored the fact that Ross had knowingly taken drink, and instead was content to emphasise that proof of mens rea is essential for conviction,[51] that the burden of proving mens rea lies on the Crown throughout a trial,[52] and that some evidence introduced during the trial of an "external factor" operating on the accused's mental condition at the relevant time may prevent the Crown establishing that he had (or must have had) the necessary mens rea.[53] On the face

---

[46] Criminal Procedure (Scotland) Act 1995 s.57 (as amended by the Adults with Incapacity (Scotland) Act 2000 (asp 4) Sch.5 para.26(1); the Criminal Justice (Scotland) Act 2003 (asp 7) s.2; the Mental Health (Care and Treatment) (Scotland) 2003 (asp 13) Sch.4 para.8(3); and the Criminal Justice and Licensing (Scotland) Act 2010 (asp 13) Sch.7 paras 38 and 39); see also ss.57A–D (as inserted by the 2003 Act (asp 13) s.133, and the Criminal Justice and Licensing (Scotland) Act 2010 (asp 13) Sch.2 para.5), 58–61 (as amended by the 2003 Act (asp 13) Sch.4 para.8(4),(5),(6),(7),(10), the Adult Support and Protection (Scotland) Act 2007 (asp 10) Sch.1 para.4, and the Criminal Justice and Licensing (Scotland) Act 2010 (asp 13) Sch.2 para.6, and Sch.7 paras 40 and 41), 62–63 (as amended by the Criminal Justice and Licensing (Scotland) Act 2010 (asp 13) Sch.7, paras 42 and 43), and Sch.4 (as amended by the Mental Health (Care and Treatment) (Scotland) Act 2003 (Modification of Enactments) Order 2005 (SSI 2005/465) Sch.1 para.27).

[47] See, e.g. *Ross v HM Advocate*, 1991 J.C. 210 per Lord Justice-General Hope at 213.

[48] See Pt 7 of the Criminal Justice and Licensing (Scotland) Act 2010 (asp 13), especially s.168 (which adds inter alia s.51A to the Criminal Procedure (Scotland) Act 1995) and s.171 (which abolishes the former common law rules).

[49] *Ross v HM Advocate*, 1991 J.C. 210.

[50] See Lord Murray's direction to the jury in *HM Advocate v Ritchie*, 1926 J.C. 45, which was approved in *Ross*.

[51] *Ross v HM Advocate*, 1991 J.C. 210, per Lord Justice-General Hope at 217; per Lord McCluskey at 227–228.

[52] *Ross v HM Advocate*, per Lord Justice-General Hope at 219; Lord Allanbridge at 223; Lord McCluskey at 228; and Lord Brand at 232.

[53] *Ross v HM Advocate*, 1991 J.C. 210, per Lord Justice-General Hope at 221; Lord McCluskey at 230.

of things then, the court treated the issue as one involving "lack of *mens rea*" rather than lack of voluntariness (or responsibility) in relation to the conduct itself. This approach leaves the issue of "strict liability" offences in limbo (see above, para.4–06); and indeed only Lord McCluskey[54] obliquely acknowledged that such offences might exist. Clearly if the only effect of an "external factor" is to negative mens rea, then persons (such as Ross) would have to be convicted of any strict liability offences of which they stood accused. Of course, the majority of the charges in Ross's case were common law ones; and the one statutory accusation (police assault under s.41(1)(a) of the Police (Scotland) Act 1967) did not involve strict liability and had, in any event, dropped from the picture at appellate level. It may well be, therefore, that the court did not address itself to the problem of "strict" statutory offences at all since these were simply not germane to the case on hand; and it remains just possible to read parts of the opinions as if something more fundamental than "lack of *mens rea*" was involved—in other words, as if a fundamental element was missing in a case such as that of *Ross* which rendered the actus not reus and which also had the effect of negativing mens rea where that was an essential requirement of the particular crime in question. This, however, is somewhat speculative,[55] and is not a view encouraged by later cases where reference is made to the "defence" of "automatism" consisting of an inability to form mens rea.[56] What is clear then is that an external factor affecting the normal mental condition of the accused can lead to an acquittal if certain qualifying conditions are met.

Automatism—qualifying conditions

As is so often the case with landmark decisions, the defence of automatism **4–20** created in *Ross v HM Advocate*[57] has been clarified in subsequent appeal court rulings. Perhaps the most important of these is *Sorley v HM Advocate*.[58] It is worth reproducing what was said by the Lord Justice-General there[59] in relation to the defence:

---

[54] *Ross v HM Advocate*, 1991 J.C. 210, 228.

[55] But see, for example, Lord Justice-General Hope's view at 222 that the external factor "must be one which resulted in a total loss of control of his actions in regard to the crime with which he is charged"; Lord Allanbridge's view at 223 that "an accused will not have the necessary *mens rea* if his mind is so affected by [an external] factor that the result is a total loss of control over his actions which have led to the alleged crime charged being committed"; and Lord Weir's opinion at 232 that "the accused must have been suffering from a total alienation of reason rendering him incapable of controlling or appreciating what he was doing."

[56] See, e.g. *Sorley v HM Advocate* 1992 J.C. 102, the opinion of the court at105; *HM Advocate v Bennett*, 1996 S.C.C.R. 331, Lord Justice-General Hope at 336G–337A. See also the Criminal Procedure (Scotland) Act 1995 s.78(2) (as amended by the Criminal Justice and Licensing (Scotland) Act 2010 (asp 13) Sch.7 para.46), where "automatism" is treated as if it were a special defence. Chalmers and Leverick, *Criminal Defences and Pleas in Bar of Trial* (2006), p.140, para.7.06) consider the problem in more detail and conclude either that it is incorrect to regard strict liability offences as being devoid of any element of mens rea or that automatism might "be regarded as a freestanding excuse defence so far as offences of strict liability are concerned."

[57] *Ross v HM Advocate*,1991 J.C. 210.

[58] *Sorley v HM Advocate*,1992 J.C. 102.

[59] *Sorley v HM Advocate*, 1992 J.C. 102 at 105.

"As the law now stands on this matter, automatism consisting of an inability to form *mens rea*[60] which is due to an external factor,[61] and not to some disorder of the mind itself which is liable to recur,[62] is a defence so long as there is evidence that three requirements are satisfied. These are that the external factor must not be self-induced, that it must be one which the accused was not bound to foresee[63] and that it must have resulted in a total alienation of reason amounting to a total loss of control of his actions in regard to the crime with which he is charged . . . ".

The first of these requirements seems to disqualify an accused person from availing himself of the defence if, for example, he voluntarily pours alcohol down his throat[64] or voluntarily ingests some other substance which has the effect of producing a total alienation of his reason.[65] It has been shown, however, that it is not the voluntariness or deliberateness of the pouring or ingesting which is crucial. In *Ebsworth v HM Advocate*,[66] the accused had broken a bone in his leg. Since the fracture refused to heal, the injury was extremely painful, and the accused's remedy was to take large quantities of proprietary analgesics (on this occasion, 50 tablets of paracetamol) combined with prohibited drugs (on this occasion, 10 tablets of diamorphine). He took these quite deliberately. He then suffered "a total alienation of reason", and committed various offences (including assault to severe injury and permanent disfigurement) whilst in that mental state. The trial sheriff withdrew Ebsworth's defence of automatism from the jury, on the basis that his condition was self induced and his motive irrelevant. The appeal court, however, ruled that the first two of the qualifying conditions for the defence should be seen as together reaching out to meet the same goal. As Lord Justice-General Hope put it:

---

[60] At least two of the charges in *Cardle v Mulrainey*, 1992 S.L.T. 1152 (driving without insurance, contrary to s.143(1)(a), (2), and, as the holder of a provisional driving licence, driving without a supervisor being present, contrary to s.97(3),(7) of the Road Traffic Act 1988) were probably of strict liability—a fact noted by the sheriff (see 1158I) but entirely ignored by the appeal court. The sheriff considered that, notwithstanding that mens rea did not have to be established by the Crown in respect of these offences, it would still on principle have to be shown that the accused's conduct was voluntary. Also, in *MacLeod v Mathieson*, 1993 S.C.C.R. 488 Sh.Ct., the sheriff assumed (but merely for the sake of dealing with and rejecting the defence arguments) that automatism applied to careless driving under s.3 of the Road Traffic Act 1988, although such an offence is not normally thought of as requiring mens rea.

[61] See below, paras 4–24 to 4–32.

[62] See below, paras 4–33 to 4–46.

[63] In *MacLeod v Mathieson*, 1993 S.C.C.R. 488 Sh.Ct., the sheriff decided that this requirement had not been met in relation to a charge under s.3 of the Road Traffic Act 1988: the subsequent statutory definition of "careless, or inconsiderate driving" under s.3ZA of the 1988 Act (as inserted by the Road Safety Act 2006 s.30) would support his decision as also the conventional view that a s.3 offence is of strict liability: cf. Peter W. Ferguson, "Road Traffic Law Reform" (2007) S.L.T. (News) 27, 28 (where, it seems, "2ZA" should be read as "3ZA").

[64] In accordance with *Brennan v HM Advocate*, 1977 J.C. 38. See in this context, *Finegan v Heywood*, 2000 S.C.C.R. 460.

[65] If the accused's claim is that his drink was laced with drugs (of which he was unaware and had no reason to suspect) by a third party, there must be evidence to support that claim: see, e.g. *HM Advocate v Bennett*, 1996 S.C.C.R. 331.

[66] *Ebsworth v HM Advocate*, 1992 S.L.T. 1161.

"The element of guilt or moral turpitude lies in the taking of drink or drugs voluntarily and reckless of their possible consequences."[67]

It is not so much, therefore, that the external factor itself must not be self induced; rather it is the "alienation of reason" produced by that factor which must not have been deliberately or recklessly effected by the accused. In *Ebsworth*, therefore, it was the grossly excessive consumption of drugs—the purpose itself being not perhaps an illegitimate one—which ruled out the defence. Such excess simply courted totally unpredictable mental dysfunction (with concomitant effect on behaviour), and thus showed clear recklessness as to the consequences.

The third qualifying requirement insists that the external factor should be **4–21** shown to have caused the total alienation of reason, which should itself be characterised by a total loss of control over what one does.[68] If the alienation or loss of control is not total, this will rule out the defence and prevent acquittal on that ground[69] —although mitigation of punishment after conviction would remain possible. It is also highly desirable that medical evidence should be available to confirm that the alleged causal link between the external factor and the accused's state of mind (at the time of the offence) was a plausible one, and that that state of mind would reasonably have been describable in the circumstances as one of total alienation of reason.[70] For this purpose it seems that medical expert witnesses are permitted to sit in court during the leading of evidence[71] so that they may comment appropriately during their own evidence on what they have heard.[72]

EFFECT OF ROSS v HM ADVOCATE ON SCOTS LAW

Prior to the decision in *Ross*, the authoritative dictum in Scotland was that of Lord **4–22** Justice-General Clyde in his opinion in the certified case of *HM Advocate v Cunningham*[73] where he said that:

"Any mental or pathological condition short of insanity—any question of diminished responsibility owing to any cause, *which does not involve insanity*—is relevant only to the question of mitigating circumstances and sentence."[74]

---

[67] *Ebsworth v HM Advocate*, 1992 S.L.T. 1161 at 1166F. See *Finegan v Heywood*, 2000 S.C.C.R. 460.

[68] In English law too, it has been held that the loss of control should be total—see, e.g. *Attorney General's Reference (No. 2 of 1992)* [1994] Q.B. 91 CA, Lord Taylor of Gosforth, C.J., at 105C.

[69] See *Cardle v Mulrainey* 1992 S.L.T. 1152, where the suggestion that this was too strict a standard was rejected. See also *HM Advocate v Bennett*, 1996 S.C.C.R. 331, Lord Justice-General Hope (opinion of the court) at 338A.

[70] *Sorley v HM Advocate*, 1992 J.C. 102. In *MacLeod v Napier*, 1993 S.C.C.R. 303, Lord Justice-Clerk Ross at 307C indicated that it might be possible to succeed without expert evidence, but considerable detailed evidence would then be essential to convince the court that there was a satisfactory basis for the defence. (According to *Sorley*, if there is no such satisfactory basis, the trial judge should withdraw the defence from the jury, in a solemn case.)

[71] I.e. evidence given by eye-witnesses who saw the accused's behaviour and can provide information sufficient to satisfy all the essential elements of the defence: *Sorley v HM Advocate*, 1992 J.C. 102, Lord Justice-General Hope at 107.

[72] See, e.g. *Cardle v Mulrainey*, 1992 S.L.T. 1152; *MacLeod v Mathieson*, 1993 S.C.C.R. 488 Sh.Ct.

[73] *HM Advocate v Cunningham*, 1963 J.C. 80 at 84.

[74] The phrase in italics reads "short of insanity" in the version given at 1963 S.L.T. 345 at 347.

Those, and there were many, who would then have liked Scots law to recognise acquittals in at least some cases of mental dysfunction not related to mental illness, suggested that Lord Clyde's opinion should be seen as advocating extension of the concept of "legal insanity".[75] That would at least have secured an acquittal—although the then consequences (mandatory incarceration in a mental hospital, for an indictment case at least) were not to their liking and often absurd (e.g. that a person suffering from diabetic hypoglycaemia (see below, para.4–27) should be so incarcerated for wholly pointless psychiatric "treatment").[76] But contrary views (i.e. that *Cunningham* really required conviction in non mental illness cases) existed,[77] and prior to *Ross v HM Advocate* (see above, para.4–19), it seemed certain from cases subsequent to *Cunningham* that these contrary views prevailed. Whatever may have been the case in English law, where a very wide view was favoured, Scots law was not, it seems, prepared to extend its then notion of legal insanity to mental dysfunctions not clearly related to recognised mental illnesses[78] (and now that in Scotland the term "insanity" has been replaced by "mental disorder", it is unthinkable that is should do so[79]). Prior to *Ross*, therefore, where an accused person was not fully aware of what he was doing owing to a mental dysfunction, the only question to be answered was whether that mental condition was due to genuine mental illness or not. If it was, then the test for legal insanity (as it was then referred to) would probably have been met, and the accused would have been dealt with according to the law relating to offenders who committed their offences whilst in that state. If it was not, then conviction seemed inevitable (in the absence of any other line of defence); but the disposal of the convicted person would then have been at large—attracting such mitigation as the merits of the case seemed to require.

4–23   The full bench in *Ross v HM Advocate*,[80] however, decided that Lord Clyde's opinion, offering only an "insanity" disposal or conviction with mitigation of penalty in all cases of mental dysfunction, was over concerned with public policy or safety, and too little concerned with basic principle.[81] Lord Clyde's opinion was thus overruled to the extent that

> "it held that *any* mental or pathological condition short of insanity is relevant only to the question of mitigating circumstances and sentence."[82]

[75] See Gordon, *Criminal Law,* 2nd edn (1978), para.3–18; W. M. Reid, "Three Steps Back" (1963) S.L.T. (News) 166. In modern law, of course, the term "insanity" should now be rendered as the less stigmatic "mental disorder": see Pt 7 of the Criminal Justice and Licensing (Scotland) Act 2010 (asp 13), and the Scottish Law Commission, *Report on Insanity and Diminished Responsibility* (The Stationery Office, 2004), Scot. Law Com. No.195 on which Pt 7 is based.
[76] Acquittal of an accused person on the ground of mental disorder no longer, of course, necessitates such incarceration: see para.4–18, above.
[77] See, for example, J.W.R. Gray, "A Purely Temporary Disturbance" (1974) J.R. 227.
[78] See *Brennan v HM Advocate*, 1977 J.C. 38, opinion of the court at 46, where the charge to the jury in *HM Advocate v Aitken*, 1975 S.L.T. (Notes) 86, is strongly disapproved.
[79] See Pt 7 of the Criminal Justice and Licensing (Scotland) Act 2010 (asp 13), as also the definition of "mental disorder" set out in the Criminal Procedure (Scotland) Act 1995 s.307(1) (as inserted by the Mental Health (Care and Treatment) (Scotland) Act 2003 (asp 13) Sch.4 para.8(1) and (16)) which refers to s.328(1) of the 2003 Act (asp 13).
[80] *Ross v HM Advocate*, 1991 J.C. 210, and see above, para.4–19.
[81] See, e.g. *Ross v HM Advocate*, 1991 J.C. 210, Lord Justice-General Hope at 217–218.
[82] See *Ross v HM Advocate*, 1991 J.C. 210, Lord Justice-General Hope at 222.

Straightforward acquittal *was* possible if the accused's mental dysfunction was not due to mental illness, but rather to the effect of an "external factor"—provided certain safeguards were met (see above, paras 4–20 to 4–21).

External factors

The court in *Ross v HM Advocate* did not find it necessary to explain what was **4–24** meant by "external factor"; nor did it seek to provide illustrations of the concept. Lord Justice-General Hope did,[83] however, refer to the English case of *R v Sullivan*[84] and, with apparent approval, to that part of Lord Diplock's opinion there where he said:

> "I do not regard that learned judge [Devlin J. in *R v Kemp* [1957] 1 Q.B. 399 at p. 407] as excluding the possibility of non-insane automatism (for which the proper verdict would be a verdict of 'not guilty') in cases where temporary impairment (not being self-induced by consuming drink or drugs) results from some external physical factor such as a blow on the head causing concussion or the administration of an anaesthetic for therapeutic purposes."

It would appear, therefore, that the Scottish court had in mind external *physical* factors, such as those considered in the paragraphs which follow.

(1) Alcohol and non-prescribed drugs

Whether the effects on the mind of the voluntary ingestion or, as the case may **4–25** be, inhalation or injection, of alcohol or non-prescribed drugs can be taken into account for the purposes of criminal liability would seem to depend on the "knowledge" of the person concerned.[85] If he knew he was taking the substance in question, and willingly did so, and knew, or ought to have known, the effects it might have on him, then it has been recognised for some time that criminal liability is neither excluded nor diminished.[86] If the consumption or ingestion was not voluntary, then *Ross v HM Advocate* clearly allows acquittal—at least in respect of an offence requiring mens rea.[87]

(2A) Prescribed drugs—general

Where medically prescribed drugs are taken by the person for whom they were **4–26** intended (in accordance with medical advice as to dose, contra-indications and circumstances), and have an unforeseen effect on that person's mental condition

---

[83] *Ross v HM Advocate,* 1991 J.C. 210 at 216.
[84] *R. v Sullivan* [1984] A.C. 156 at 172G–H.
[85] Cf. the English case of *R. v Hardie* [1985] 1 W.L.R. 64.
[86] See *Brennan v HM Advocate,* 1977 J.C. 38, which dealt with gross, self-induced intoxication with alcohol and LSD—both substances popularly associated with violent and irrational behaviour. See also *Finegan v Heywood,* 2000 S.C.C.R. 460. It has now been made clear that a person who has been convicted of an offence committed whilst he was under the influence of "voluntarily consumed alcohol" cannot have such intoxication taken into account by way of mitigation of sentence: see Criminal Justice and Licensing (Scotland) Act 2010 (asp 13) s.26.
[87] *Ross v HM Advocate,* 1991 J.C. 210, per Lord McCluskey at 225 to 226; and see above, para.4–19. See also *Sorley v HM Advocate,* 1992 J.C. 102 (LSD and sleeping pills); *Cardle v Mulrainey,* 1992 S.L.T. 1152 (amphetamines); and *MacLeod v Napier,* 1993 S.C.C.R. 303 ("speed").

leading to the alleged commission of a criminal act, then this ought to result in his acquittal.[88] Anaesthetics administered as part of some proper surgical, medical or dental treatment must follow the same rule—as hinted at by Lord Fraser in his charge to the jury in *McGregor v HM Advocate*[89] —a charge approved of generally by Lord Justice-General Hope in *Ross v HM Advocate.*[90]

(2B) Prescribed drugs—diabetes—hypoglycaemia

4–27   Normally functioning bodily processes effect the production of glucose which then enters the bloodstream. The pancreas detects the rising levels of glucose in the blood and produces insulin—thus enabling the cells of the human body to take up the glucose which they require to perform their proper functions. In this way glucose is consumed, the rising blood-glucose level is checked and reversed and the production of insulin falls off—until the bodily processes referred to above repeat themselves— in an automatic fashion. The result is that blood-glucose concentrations are kept within normal parameters. In simple terms, diabetes is an illness in which the sufferer either produces no insulin (type 1 diabetes) or produces insulin which is ineffective (type 2 diabetes). If that illness is untreated, a very high blood-glucose level (sometimes referred to as hyperglycaemia) can occur, and can result in drowsiness, inability to concentrate, and perhaps even coma.[91] Treatment of type 1 diabetes generally involves the taking of insulin by the patient; type 2 diabetes can be treated by diet or by appropriate drugs. It must be obvious that effective treatment by insulin or drugs requires care, so that normal blood-glucose levels can be maintained at any particular time. In partic-ular, if too much insulin (or too much of the relevant drug) is injected or ingested, especially in the absence of adequate foodstuffs, blood-glucose levels may fall too rapidly for normal bodily processes to respond; the result may be a condition known as hypoglycaemia. Such a condition may occur very rapidly, and is characterised by drowsiness, inability to concentrate, growing unawareness of actions, and (finally) coma—if unchecked. Diabetics are, or should be, aware of the possibility of hypoglycaemia occurring during the management of their illness, and should, therefore, take appropriate precautions since persons experiencing such a condition have been known to act aggressively,[92] and will almost certainly be unable safely to operate machinery or drive motor vehicles.[93] A hypoglycaemic condition can, therefore, be of interest to the criminal law; and if such a condition occurs and appears to result in criminal conduct, it is of some importance to establish whether that condition was caused by the taking of medication (a plain external factor) or by the illness itself (a matter considered further below at para.4–42).

4–28   Where, for example, a crime is apparently committed by a person experiencing an "attack" of hypoglycaemia due to his intake of prescribed medication, then he should be acquitted if a criminal charge is brought. He would clearly have been

---

[88] See *Ebsworth v HM Advocate*, 1992 S.L.T. 1161, Lord Justice-General Hope at 1166H-J. Cf. *Carrington v HM Advocate*, 1994 S.C.C.R. 567.
[89] *McGregor v HM Advocate* (1973) S.C.C.R. Supp. 54 at 57.
[90] *Ross v HM Advocate,* 1991 J.C. 210, at 217.
[91] See, e.g. *R. v Hennessy* [1989] 1 W.L.R. 287.
[92] See, e.g. *R. v Bailey* [1983] 1 W.L.R. 760.
[93] See, e.g. *MacLeod v Mathieson*, 1993 S.C.C.R. 488 Sh.Ct.

suffering from a sufficient mental dysfunction at the relevant time—a mental dysfunction due to an external factor. It does not matter here that the medication was voluntarily taken by that person. It is the mental dysfunction (and its sufficiency) which counts; and surely no diabetic could be assumed to have taken medication in order to induce a condition of hypoglycaemia. Of course, the other qualifying conditions for a "defence" based on an external factor still apply (see above, paras 4–20 to 4–21). In particular, the mental dysfunction and its effects must not be ones the accused had any reason to anticipate. If, for example, the accused had injected himself with the correct dose of insulin, but then neglected to eat food (contrary to medical advice), then normally he should be able to foresee that his motor skills might be adversely affected. It should be plain to him that he ought to avoid driving or operating machinery. If he does not refrain from such activities, then he should not be immune from criminal liability for the consequences.[94] On the other hand, if the accused is alleged to have committed crimes of violence in the course of (for example) an insulin-induced, hypoglycaemic episode, then the question arises whether it is common knowledge (and if so, whether apparent to the particular accused person) that failure to take food can have such violent repercussions.[95] If it is common knowledge, and particularly where it was known to the accused, then he surely was bound to anticipate that violence would ensue. The opposite conclusion will obviously be reached if there was no such knowledge. From this point of view, the conviction ordered by the appeal court in the case of *Carmichael v Boyle*[96] must now be doubted.

Carmichael v Boyle. Boyle was charged with breach of the peace, assault and **4–29** statutory assault under the Police (Scotland) Act 1967 s.41(1)(a). He was a doubly unfortunate individual, in that he suffered from both an abnormally low level of intelligence and an unstable form of diabetes. His form of that disease was particularly difficult to manage, the balance between intake of insulin and food being an extremely critical one. Boyle, in view of his limited intellect, found it very difficult to follow his medically prescribed regime. He frequently omitted to have regular meals, and thus had often become hypoglycaemic. He had also been violent when in such a condition. It was claimed on his behalf, nevertheless, that he should be acquitted of the charges brought against him since he had taken his prescribed insulin on the day in question, but, thereafter, having failed to take sufficient food, had exhibited the classic signs of hypoglycaemia at the time of the alleged offences. It was argued, therefore, that he would probably have been unaware of what he had been doing at the relevant times. There was no question of his mental condition at those relevant times being treated as mental disorder, of course. Medical evidence simply confirmed that there was no underlying mental illness. The sheriff, who dealt with this case, frankly admitted that he had no sympathy with the then Scots law rule (see above, para.4–22), and, therefore, sought to avoid it. He did so by holding (in terms which now seem wholly proper) that the charges against Boyle entailed crimes which required mens rea to be established. Since the accused had been seen kicking and punching other people by several witnesses, there was no doubt that there was sufficient evidence from

---

[94] See, e.g. *Moses v Winder* [1981] R.T.R. 37.
[95] See, e.g. *R. v Bailey* [1983] 1 W.L.R. 760, per Griffiths L.J. at 764H–765B.
[96] *Carmichael v Boyle*, 1985 S.L.T. 399.

which the mens rea of assault could be inferred. Persons who kick and punch can usually be taken to have intended those actions. But the sheriff also considered that the evidence of hypoglycaemia meant that the accused could not in fact have been capable of intending the actions which amounted to the assaults charged. He, therefore, acquitted him on that basis. On appeal by the prosecutor, the appeal court simply affirmed that the then existing rule had to be applied—namely, since Boyle had not been suffering from mental illness at the times in question, he had to be convicted. Standing the more modern decision in *Ross v HM Advocate*[97] Boyle was probably entitled to an acquittal. His condition was brought about by the insulin he had legitimately taken—by an external factor. It was true, of course, that he had failed to take sufficient food and had been drinking; but such were his intellectual failings that it could hardly be said that he should have anticipated the consequent mental dysfunction and its violent effects.[98]

(3) Toxic fumes

4–30   Exposure to toxic fumes, which have a sufficient effect on the mental condition of an accused person at the material time, must surely result in an acquittal on any relevant criminal charge—provided that the qualifying conditions set out in *Ross v HM Advocate*[99] are satisfied: toxic fumes in such a situation would clearly form an external factor. Such exposure was argued in *HM Advocate v Murray*[100] by way of defence to certain driving offences; but the decision in that case was made many years prior to the handing down of the opinions in *Ross*. If an identical case were to present today, however, it is doubtful if the qualifying conditions referred to above could be satisfied. In *Murray*, the accused was charged with serious offences—causing the death of three passengers in the car he was driving (when it collided with a parked van), and driving with more than the permitted level of alcohol in his blood (both statutory offences now contained in ss.1 and 5(1) of the Road Traffic Act 1988, as amended). At the trial, Murray attempted to lead evidence that just before he had left his work at a dry-cleaning establishment to drive home on the evening in question, he had been exposed to the toxic fumes of tetrachlorethylene (a chemical used in the dry-cleaning process). He had apparently hoped thereby to convince the jury that he had not been aware of what he was doing and that he was thus entitled to an acquittal. The trial judge ruled, however, that although the evidence could be heard, it could not lead to an acquittal on the first charge. At best, it could simply lead the jury to make a recommendation for leniency. Of course, the evidence of intoxication by a substance other than alcohol would have gone to the merits of the second charge since it clearly required the intoxicant to be alcohol—but that is a separate issue. The trial judge was no doubt influenced by the now-discredited rule laid down in *HM Advocate v Cunningham*.[101] But, as the accused worked in an establishment where toxic chemicals were admittedly used, should he not have been aware of the possibility of exposure to the fumes from those chemicals and of the likely

---

[97] *Ross v HM Advocate,* 1991 J.C. 210 and para.4–19 above.
[98] Cf. *R v Quick* [1973] Q.B. 910, per Lawton L.J. at 922E–G.
[99] *Ross v HM Advocate,* 1991 J.C. 210: see above, paras 4–20 to 4–21, above, for "qualifying conditions".
[100] *HM Advocate v Murray,* 1969 S.L.T. (Notes) 85.
[101] *HM Advocate v Cunningham,* 1963 J.C. 80; see above, paras 4–22 and 4–23.

effect on his driving skills? Was what happened not something he was bound to foresee? Such matters would perforce require to be investigated before an acquittal under the post-*Ross* law could be sustained.

(4) Blows producing concussion

If a person were to be the victim of an assault which left him dazed and **4–31** concussed, or if he were to be struck on the head in some accidental way which left him similarly (but temporarily) incapacitated, then an external factor would be present to avoid conviction for any crime apparently committed by him when he was so dazed and concussed. This must follow from the decision in *Ross v HM Advocate*.[102]

(5) Stress, anxiety and depression

An attempt was apparently made in the English case of *R v Hennessy*[103] to argue **4–32** that stress, anxiety and depression could be external factors if they resulted in some relevant mental dysfunction at the time the defendant was alleged to have committed a crime. It was claimed that the defendant in the case was diabetic, and that psychological stress on such a person could lead to a state of hyperglycaemia (see above, para.4–27). The defendant, however, had neglected to take any insulin for some days prior to his "committing" the alleged offences; and the Court of Appeal[104] pointed out that

> "stress, anxiety and depression can no doubt be the result of the operation of external factors, but they are not, it seems to us, in themselves separately or together external factors of the kind capable in law of causing or contributing to a state of automatism."

Indeed, the Court of Appeal also pointed out that the accused's line of defence, if successful, would have amounted to legal insanity, as that concept was then defined in England. Despite what is hinted at in *Hennessy*, it is suggested that Scots law would not and should not accept a stressful situation as a sufficient "external factor" since it lacks the direct quality of (apparently required) "physical contact" with the accused, and, in any event is hardly an unforeseeable occurrence with unforeseeable effects. Stress is a common human experience for which no particular provision should be made by the criminal law unless, of course, that sort of experience is so serious as to amount to mental disorder.

Causal factor—internal

If the position of external factors which produce total alienation of reason is **4–33** reasonably clear, the same cannot be said of non-external (i.e. "internal") factors. Lord Justice-General Hope in *Ross*[105] stressed that the court was

---

[102] *Ross v HM Advocate*, 1991 J.C. 210; see above, para.4–19; cf. *Stevenson v Beatson*, 1965 S.L.T. (Sh.Ct.) 11, noting that the sheriff there erroneously held that an "onus" lay on the accused; and cf. also the English case of *R. v Stripp* (1978) 69 Cr. App. R. 318.

[103] *R. v Hennessy* [1989] 1 W.L.R. 287.

[104] *R v Hennessy* [1989] 1 W.L.R. 287, per Lord Lane C.J. at 294C.

[105] *Ross v HM Advocate*, 1991 J.C. 210 at 217.

"not concerned in this case with a pathological condition such as epilepsy or with the questions of public policy which may affect how such cases should be approached."

Accordingly, the opinions cast in that case provide no guidance as to the treatment of non-external factor situations, other than to indicate that a problem exists in respect of them. Lord McCluskey made this plain when he said[106]:

"The policy of the law in relation to the criminal responsibility of persons who act under the influence of a continuing or recurrent mental or pathological condition short of insanity which derives from some disease or physical morbidity might have to be different."

But how different? If external factors, leading to temporary but total loss of control via total alienation of reason, can lead to straightforward acquittals where certain qualifying conditions are met (see above, paras 4–20 to 4–21), presumably internal factors leading to a similar loss of control may justifiably have a different outcome—and especially so if there was a risk of recurrence and a consequent issue of public safety. If, for example, such an internal factor was capable of amounting to mental disorder which at the time of the alleged conduct (act or omission) rendered the accused unable to appreciate the nature or wrongfulness of that conduct, then a successful special defence on that ground should lead to acquittal (see above, para.4–18). This was certainly the favoured approach of Lord Denning in *Bratty v Attorney General for Northern Ireland*[107] where he said

"any mental disorder [including epilepsy or cerebral tumour] which has manifested itself in violence and is prone to recur is a disease of the mind. At any rate it is the sort of disease for which a person should be detained in hospital rather than be given an unqualified acquittal."[108]

With the modification that genuine external causes of mental dysfunction are to be excluded from that dictum,[109] Lord Denning's formulation has repeatedly been endorsed in England.[110] The standard English approach, therefore, is to treat internal causes of mental dysfunction leading to total loss of control as examples of "legal insanity", and especially so if such mental dysfunction is associated with violence and is likely to recur.[111] Was this ever, or can it now be, the standard approach in Scotland?

4–34   It is suggested that this was not, and that (especially as a result of fairly recent legislation) this cannot now be, the case in Scotland. The English definition of

---

[106] *Ross v HM Advocate,* 1991 J.C. 210 at 231.

[107] *Bratty v Attorney General for Northern Ireland* [1963] A.C. 386 at 412.

[108] Echoes of this occur in *Ross v HM Advocate,* 1991 J.C. 210, opinion of Lord Justice-General Hope at 213: "We are concerned here only with a mental condition of a temporary nature which was the result of an external factor and not of some disorder of the mind itself which was liable to recur."

[109] See *R. v Quick* [1973] Q.B. 910, per Lawton L.J. at 917F–918G and 922E–923C.

[110] See, e.g. *R. v Burgess* [1991] 2 W.L.R. 1206, per Lord Lane C.J. at 1211G to 1212A.

[111] See Smith and Hogan, *Criminal Law,* 12th edn (2008), p.57.

insanity is very wide (or at least is very wide for the purposes of the defence of automatism)[112]—much wider, indeed, than was ever the case in Scotland. The basis of the Scottish approach was that "insanity" (when that term was in use) should relate to mental illness, as understood by suitably qualified medical practitioners; and from that basis, it would be exceedingly odd to have to regard persons suffering from the effects of a disease such as diabetes or epilepsy as being mentally ill for some legal purposes. In any event, it appears to have been agreed in *Ross v HM Advocate*[113] that Lord Clyde's original dictum in *HM Advocate v Cunningham*[114] was defective rather because of its width than anything else. As Lord Justice-General Hope said[115]:

> "The conclusion which I invite your Lordships to reach in this case is that *Cunningham* was wrongly decided in so far as it held that *any* [Lord Hope's own emphasis] mental or pathological condition short of insanity [as it was then described] is relevant only to the question of mitigating circumstances and sentence."

That conclusion (with which the remaining members of the appeal court agreed) suggests that there may be a class of mental dysfunction, caused by an internal factor not amounting to mental illness, where a special approach is called for. Although the court in *Ross* did not go on to specify what that special approach should be,[116] it must be plain that two considerations influence the solution. The first of these is that there may be a need to cater for future public safety where an internal factor produces a mental condition whereunder the accused is unable to prevent himself acting violently (or perhaps just "criminally"), and especially so where such a mental condition may occur again. Indeed, there is a feeling that internally generated mental dysfunctions are very likely to recur since there may be no obvious and understandable external cause for them: thus, the perceived need to consider future public safety in relation to "internal" rather than "external" factors. The second consideration concerns the frequent references in *Ross* and elsewhere to such mental conditions being "short of" or "not amounting to" insanity (as the terminology of the time put it). These references emphasised clearly that acquittal on the ground of insanity (as it then was) could not be a legitimate option in such cases unless resort was had to the grossest of fictions; and now, in the modern law, the matter seems beyond doubt.

The position in modern scots law

Recent reforms[117] in Scotland seem to have removed any lingering doubts that **4–35** there might be a concept of "legal insanity" which could justifiably differ from

---

[112] See, e.g. *R v Hennessy* [1989] 1 W.L.R. 287, per Lord Lane C.J. at 291C–293H; and *R v Sullivan* [1984] A.C. 156, per Lord Diplock at 170–173.

[113] *Ross v HM Advocate*, 1991 J.C. 210.

[114] *HM Advocate v Cunningham*, 1963 J.C. 80 at 84; see above, para.4–22.

[115] *Ross v HM Advocate*, 1991 J.C. 210.

[116] See, e.g. *Ross v HM Advocate*, 1991 J.C. 210, Lord McCluskey's opinion at 231, quoted above at para.4–33.

[117] See Pt 7 of the Criminal Justice and Licensing (Scotland) Act 2010 (asp 13), which abolishes common law notions of a "special defence of insanity" and a plea of "insanity in bar of trial", and substitutes a new statutory defence (and plea) based squarely on "mental disorder", as that is defined in s.328(1) of the Mental Health (Care and Treatment) (Scotland) Act 2003 (asp 13).

medically assessed mental illness; it now seems wholly unlikely, therefore, that relevant "internal" causal factors (as these have hitherto been understood within the topic of automatism) could per se be consistent with any acquittal based on the mental illness of the accused. It remains for consideration, however, whether such "internal" causal factors are consistent with acquittal at all. Indeed, decided cases from the late nineteenth century to the present day suggest that the preferred approach may involve conviction of such persons in respect of crimes factually proved against them, coupled to disposals which cater inter alia, and so far as possible, for future public safety. The emphasis, in other words, lies not so much on punishment, since in many such cases consideration of penalty would be quite unjust, but rather on a disposal which gives due consideration to the need to limit future danger to others. This approach can be seen in most of the Scottish cases considered in the paragraphs which follow. Whilst it is true that the persons concerned in many of these cases may have been more deserving of sympathy than prosecution and criminal conviction, public policy surely required a realistic solution to a difficult problem. After conviction, of course, a court will usually be able to consider a wider range of criteria as to the future dangerousness of such a person than would have been possible under the rules of evidence which pertain during a trial.[118] Conviction also opens up the widest possible range of disposals as the law presently stands.[119]

Internal factors

(1) "Naturally" induced sleep

4–36   Whilst it is unusual for "criminal" acts to be performed during natural sleep, it is not entirely unknown. In the case of *Simon Fraser*[120] the accused was asleep in bed together with his wife and 18 month old son (apparently a not-uncommon domestic arrangement in the nineteenth century). According to his own declaration,[121] he dreamt that a white beast flew through the floor and round the back of the bed where the child was lying. He further dreamt that he tried to catch it, and indeed caught something which he dashed against the floor and door of the room. He then came to his senses and found that it was his son he had caught and so treated. The child died shortly afterwards of its injuries. Fraser never denied that he had caused his son's death. In reply to a murder charge brought against him, however, he pled "not guilty" and advanced the defence that he was asleep at the time. At his trial, three medical experts testified that he was *not* "insane" (in the Scottish forensic language of the time) but that he did suffer from an abnormal mental condition. According, again, to his own declaration, Fraser had strange dreams every night—usually between midnight and 1 a.m.—but was rarely "outrageous" except every six months or so. By being "outrageous", he apparently meant "violent", since about 18 months prior to the killing of his child, he dreamt that his wife was being attacked by a dog which led him to throw some

---

[118] Cf., however, the provision for risk assessment and lifelong restriction orders under ss.210B–210F of the Criminal Procedure (Scotland) Act 1995, as inserted by the Criminal Justice (Scotland) Act 2003 (asp 7) s.1, noting that s.210EA is added by the Management of Offenders etc. (Scotland) Act 2005 (asp 14) s.19, and that s.210F is amended by the 2005 Act (asp 14) s.14.

[119] Cf. a straightforward acquittal, to which no conditions whatsoever can be attached.

[120] *Simon Fraser* (1878) 4 Coup. 70.

[121] N.R.S., J.C. 26/1269.

pieces of furniture at it. In consequence, his wife had received bruising to her arm and eye. The trial judge, Lord Justice-Clerk Moncreiff, told the jury[122] that he supposed they would agree that Fraser was totally unconscious of what he had done to his son and he suggested that they return a finding

> "that the pannel [a Scots law term for the accused] killed his child, but that he was in a state in which he was unconscious of the act which he was committing by reason of the condition of somnambulism, and that he was not responsible."

The jury did so.

Opinions as to what that verdict meant have varied.[123] However, the preponder- **4–37** ance of the evidence points to conviction.[124] The Solicitor-General, for example, who was prosecuting the case in person, successfully requested an adjournment of two days following the jury's verdict—the pannel to be kept in custody during that time. The original court records[125] narrate the fact of the adjournment as follows:

> "The court delayed pronouncing sentence in the meantime: Continued the diet against the pannel till Wednesday first the seventeenth current at three o'clock, and ordained him in the meantime to be detained in the prison of Edinburgh."

At the resumed diet, the Solicitor-General deliberately refrained from "moving for sentence" a privilege he has where a person has been found guilty of a crime. The reason in this case why the prosecutor so refrained was that the pannel and his father had signed an agreement as follows[126]:

> "I, Simon Fraser, having in view the nature of the attacks to which I am occasionally subject at night, do hereby solemnly promise and undertake that I shall always sleep alone; and I, Simon Fraser, Senior, father of the said Simon Fraser, do hereby solemnly promise and undertake, so far as in my power, to see and take care that my son fulfils the promise before written made by him."

---

[122] *Simon Fraser* (1878) 4 Coup. 70 at 75.

[123] See, e.g. G. Williams, *Criminal Law: The General Part*, 2nd edn (1961), p.173—"he . . . was not convicted of murder, nor indeed of anything"; cf. N. Walker, *Crime and Insanity in England* (Edinburgh: Edinburgh University Press, 1968–1973), Vol.1. p.170, where he questions the "assumption which one finds in later writers, that the result of Fraser's case was an acquittal." James Chalmers and Fiona Leverick, in *Criminal Defences and Pleas in Bar of Trial* (2006), para.7.31, correctly point out that J.H.A. Macdonald (who, as Solicitor General, prosecuted in *Simon Fraser*) referred in his book to the case as having resulted in an acquittal (See J.H.A. Macdonald, *A Practical Treatise on the Criminal Law of Scotland,* revised by the author and N.D. Macdonald, Advocate, 3rd edn (Edinburgh: W. Green, 1894), p.510; edited by R. MacGregor Mitchell, 4th edn (Edinburgh: W. Green, 1929), p.569; edited by James Walker and D.J. Stevenson, 5th edn (Edinburgh: W. Green, 1948), pp.347–348): but Chalmers and Leverick eventually conclude that the case is "authority for very little, if anything."

[124] As Lord Justice-General Hope concluded in *Ross v HM Advocate*, 1991 J.C. 210 at 217.

[125] N.R.S., J.C. 4/77.

[126] N.R.S., AD14/78/166.

Prevention of harm to others in the future was thus thought to have been secured; and the ultimate mitigation of punishment was achieved by the prosecutor's declining to move for sentence at all. It is true, of course, that the court attached no sanction if the undertaking were to be breached by Fraser in the future. But the trial was widely reported in the press[127] and the public thus placed on its guard. In *Ross v HM Advocate*[128] Lord Justice-General Hope opined that the approach taken in *Simon Fraser* was "a very special one."[129] Special approaches may well, however, be justified in such unusual situations.

4–38 *R. v Burgess.* The outcome in *Simon Fraser* can be contrasted with the attitude of the Court of Appeal in the English case of *R. v Burgess*.[130] There the accused attacked a woman, hitting her over the head with a bottle and a video-recorder. He submitted a defence of non-insane automatism (in terms of the then English forensic language), in that he had been asleep and sleep-walking at the time. The trial judge ruled that his defence amounted to insanity, since there was no external cause for his mental dysfunction at the time of the attack. The jury, therefore, acquitted him on the ground of insanity—thus (as the law then was) automatically securing his detention in a mental hospital. It is difficult to feel completely comfortable with such a decision; but the Court of Appeal endorsed it fully.

4–39 *Finegan v Heywood.* Nowadays, it seems reasonably clear that *Simon Fraser*[131] (since the charge had been one of murder) would be regarded as a case to which diminished responsibility was probably applicable[132]; Fraser would thus have been convicted of culpable homicide—although the problem of an adequate disposal would remain. A more modern case of parasomnia (as sleep walking tends now to be referred to) arose in *Finegan v Heywood*.[133] The accused was charged in the sheriff court with a variety of driving offences contrary to the Road Traffic Act 1988.[134] These offences were probably all of "strict liability"[135]; but there was a further charge of theft, in respect of which proof of mens rea would, of course, have been a necessary element. He was acquitted of that common law charge, however, and his plea of automatism on the basis of somnambulism was rejected. He appealed against conviction of the driving offences on the basis that his plea of automatism should not have been rejected. The Appeal Court, however, upheld the convictions on the grounds that although he probably had been in a state of somnambulism at the time of the offences, it had been found by the sheriff that that state had been triggered by the appellant's voluntary consumption of at

---

[127] See, e.g. *The Scotsman*, July 16 and 18, 1878.

[128] *Ross v HM Advocate*, 1991 J.C. 210 at 217.

[129] A similar view was expressed by the court in *Finegan v Heywood*, 2000 S.C.C.R. 460, at 463B, para.4. See below, para.4–39.

[130] *R v Burgess* [1991] 2 W.L.R. 1206.

[131] See above, paras 4–36 to 4–37.

[132] See *Galbraith v HM Advocate*, 2002 J.C. 1. The common law position set out in that case has now become broadly crystallised in statute: see the Criminal Justice and Licensing (Scotland) Act 2010 (asp 13) s.168; see also below, paras 4–49 to 4–50.

[133] *Finegan v Heywood*, 2000 S.C.C.R. 460.

[134] Driving with more than the permitted level of alcohol in his breath; taking and driving away a motor vehicle without the consent of the owner or other lawful authority; and, using a motor vehicle without insurance: contrary to ss.5(1)(a), 178(1)(a) and 143(1) and (2), respectively.

[135] See above, para.4–06, and below, Ch.13.

least six pints of beer; that the appellant had been aware that such consumption of alcohol acted as such a trigger; and that, therefore, the case was to be treated as similar to one where there had been self-induced intoxication by voluntary consumption of alcohol.[136] As the Court said[137]:

> "[T]he defence of automatism cannot . . . be established upon proof that the appellant was in a transitory state of parasomnia which was the result of, and indeed induced by, deliberate and self-induced intoxication."

It does not necessarily follow, of course, that, had there been no element of "fault" on the appellant's part in his lapsing into a state of parasomnia, the Court in *Finegan v Heywood* would have been prepared to accept that automatism had been made out; but if the facts had revealed that a soft drink had been spiked with alcohol by a third party without Finegan's knowledge at all, then the effect of his imbibing that might have created a situation which prima facie involved automatism—unless his susceptability to parasomnia were to be used to distinguish that situation from the legal position established in *Ross*.[138]

(2) Disease—certain types of epilepsy

Violent, unpredictable behaviour can follow certain types of epileptic fit, **4–40** although the sufferer will probably be totally unaware of what he does. In *HM Advocate v Mitchell*,[139] for example, the accused had savagely killed a woman with blows from a knife and a meat-chopper. His defence was "psychic epilepsy"— that he had experienced the sort of epileptic fit which is not accompanied by the usual outward signs of a grand mal seizure (e.g. convulsions, tongue-biting, and foam evident at the mouth). As this, therefore, was a wholly "internal" fit and seemed consistent with a wholly mental condition, he submitted a defence of (in the terminology of the time) "legal insanity". This was accepted as such by both the judge and the jury. Of course, it does not follow from that case that all types of epilepsy are to be (or ever can be) regarded as mental illnesses for the purposes of the criminal law in Scotland[140] and if particular types do not square with the definition of mental disorder,[141] then the result should be conviction accompanied by whatever disposal seems appropriate in the circumstances to secure public safety. This was made quite plain in *HM Advocate v Cunningham*.[142] That case concerned not crimes of violence, but taking and driving away a van without the permission of the owner, causing death by dangerous driving—the van had mounted the pavement and knocked down four pedestrians—and being unfit to drive owing to the consumption of drink or drugs.[143] The accused had tendered a

---

[136] Thus following the *ratio* of *Brennan v HM Advocate*, 1977 J.C. 38.

[137] *Finegan v Heywood,* 2000 S.C.C.R. 460 at 464F, para.10.

[138] *Ross v HM Advocate*, 1991 J.C. 210.

[139] *HM Advocate v Mitchell*, 1951 J.C. 53.

[140] Cf. the approach taken by the English courts in *R. v Sullivan* [1984] A.C. 156.

[141] See the Mental Health (Care and Treatment) (Scotland) Act 2003 (asp 13) s.328(1), which now replaces any former reference to "insanity" in the law: see further Pt 7 of the Criminal Justice and Licensing (Scotland) Act 2010 (asp 13).

[142] *HM Advocate v Cunningham*, 1963 J.C. 80, as modified by *Ross v HM Advocate*, 1991 J.C. 210; see above, paras 4–22 and 4–23.

[143] All statutory offences, now to be found in ss.178, 1 and 4(1) respectively of the Road Traffic Act 1988, as amended where appropriate by the Road Traffic Act 1991.

defence of "temporary dissociation" (i.e. that he had not been aware of what he had been doing at the critical times) owing to "an epileptic fugue or other pathological condition." Since this had been tendered as a defence which, if established, would lead to the unconditional acquittal of the accused, the prosecutor sought a ruling from the trial judge that acquittal could not follow from it unless the mental condition it referred to was consistent with "legal insanity" (as was then the appropriate terminology). The trial judge, Lord Wheatley, certified this point to a larger court of three High Court judges who confirmed that the prosecutor's contention was correct. If an epileptic or similar mental condition was not such as to amount to "legal insanity", then the result would be conviction (assuming that the Crown's case was otherwise established) tempered by such mitigation of the "normal" sentence as seemed appropriate. There was no suggestion in the court's decision that such an accused person would have to be punished in any usual sense of that word.

4–41   It had sometimes been hinted at[144] that the pre-*Ross*[145] decision in *Cunningham*[146] was in any event inconsistent with the result of the full bench ruling in *HM Advocate v Hayes*,[147] but this was and is not really so. Andrew Hayes had been driving a bus when he had some sort of epileptic seizure. The result was that the bus ceased to be under his complete control, collided with two parked lorries and overturned. Several persons were injured (including the drivers of the two parked vehicles) and four passengers in the bus lost their lives. The charge brought against Hayes was one of culpable homicide at common law together with, as an alternative, the less serious statutory offence of dangerous driving. He submitted a defence of "temporary dissociation" (see above, para.4–40) due to "masked epilepsy" or other pathological condition. After trial, the jury found him guilty of culpable homicide but also found his defence of "temporary dissociation" proved. There can be little doubt, therefore, that he had been found guilty of the more serious crime; but his counsel asked the trial judge, Lord Carmont, to inquire if the jury meant by this that they would have found him guilty "if he had been a normal man." When the question was put, it appeared that the jury might have meant just that—and Lord Carmont went on to inquire if they therefore wished to reconsider their verdict. This resulted in the jury's apparently wishing to find him "not guilty", and some confusion as to what was then the proper verdict. The court records[148] clearly reveal that Lord Carmont reinstated the jury's original verdict—such that the accused stood convicted of culpable homicide. Of course, this left the problem of disposal since the conviction had been accompanied by a finding that the defence had also been established. His Lordship, therefore, certified the question of disposal to a full bench of the High Court at Edinburgh (the court consisting of Lord Justice-General Cooper, Lord Justice-Clerk Thomson, and Lords Mackay, Carmont, Jamieson, Russell and Keith). It is highly significant that Hayes had his bail continued during the intervening period. It is also highly

---

[144] See Gane and Stoddart, *A Casebook on Scottish Criminal Law*, 1st edn, p.216; Gordon, *Criminal Law,* 2nd edn (1978), para.3–20.

[145] *Ross v HM Advocate*, 1991 J.C. 210.

[146] See above, para.4–40.

[147] *HM Advocate v Hayes* Unreported November 1, 1949, High Court at Edinburgh, but noted in H.W. Gane, C.N. Stoddart and J. Chalmers, *A Casebook on Scottish Criminal Law*, 4th edn (Edinburgh: W. Green, 2009), pp.242–243, note 2.

[148] N.R.S., J.C. 5/28, Appendix No.40.

significant that the Solicitor-General (who was appearing in person for the Crown) opened the proceedings at Edinburgh by "moving for sentence." These things would have been impossible had Hayes not been convicted. The outcome was that he was not to be punished in any conventional way. Instead, he was to be discharged provided he agreed to surrender his driving licences and promised never to drive vehicles again—undertakings which he found it prudent to make. The seven judges of the High Court seemed keen to stress that this was not to be taken as a precedent—suggesting that all such cases (as indeed all sentencing decisions) should be treated on an individual basis. No formal agreement (as in *Simon Fraser's* case, see above, para.4–37) was necessary since the licences were presumably at once handed to the court. The licensing authorities were also to be notified accordingly.

(3) Disease—diabetes

A brief description of diabetes has already been given (see above, para.4–27). **4–42** It is clearly not a mental illness. It would be absurd to attempt to treat it by psychiatric means. Where the disease itself (as opposed to some drug or similar preparation taken for its treatment) creates a mental dysfunction leading to total lack of control, then it seems plain in England that the resulting condition amounts to legal insanity.[149] In Scotland, it is thought that the result of disease-induced hypoglycaemia (see above, para.4–27) leading to total loss of control at the time of an alleged offence should be conviction together with such disposal as will take into account the likelihood of future public danger from the person concerned. If this is correct, then the correctness of the decision in *Farrell v Stirling*[150] must be doubted. There the sheriff had fully accepted[151] that the accused "carried out his normal regime as a diabetic so far as injection of insulin and diet were concerned", yet acquitted him of a statutory driving charge where the evidence suggested total lack of control at the time. Where the disease itself randomly creates a situation of total lack of control despite the best endeavours of medicine to stabilise the sufferer's condition, a clear concern for future public safety exists to which neither straightforward acquittal nor acquittal on the ground of mental disorder provides an adequate or realistic response.[152]

(4) Disease—spontaneous hypoglycaemia

What pertains to diabetes should also follow in relation to other diseases which **4–43** produce (of their own accord) similar effects. Thus, in *Stirling v Annan*[153] the accused was said to suffer from a condition known as "spontaneous hypogly- caemia." That illness caused the sufferer to experience sudden and unexpected diminutions in the level of sugar in his blood from time to time. During such

---

[149] See, e.g. *R. v Quick* [1973] Q.B. 910, per Lawton L.J. at 922H to 923A; *R. v Hennessy* [1989] 1 W.L.R. 287, per Lord Lane C.J. at 293G.
[150] *Farrell v Stirling*, 1975 S.L.T. (Sh.Ct.) 71.
[151] *Farrell v Stirling*, 1975 S.L.T. (Sh.Ct.) 71 at 73, col.2.
[152] In *MacLeod v Mathieson*, 1993 S.C.C.R. 488 Sh.Ct., the sheriff was prepared for the sake of argu- ment to accept that hypoglycaemia was an external factor—possibly because of doubts as to whether it was caused by insulin or the disease. In rejecting the accused's defence of automatism, he distinguished *Farrell v Stirling*, 1975 S.L.T. (Sh.Ct.) 71, on the ground that there, the accused had had no prior warning that he was subject to such attacks.
[153] *Stirling v Annan*, 1984 S.L.T. 88.

hypoglycaemic episodes, he was reckoned to be totally unaware of what he might in fact be doing—such as (in the case itself) removing and pocketing various items from the shelves of a self-service store, and thereafter walking from the store without attempting to pay for them. Stirling was in fact convicted of theft in respect of the items he had taken—a decision which, it is suggested, was probably correct. On appeal, however, the advocate-depute conceded that a miscarriage of justice might have occurred. The conviction was thus quashed. To date, it remains unclear why such a concession was made. There was certainly no suggestion that any external factor was involved which might have brought the case (prospectively, of course) within the ambit of *Ross v HM Advocate*.[154]

(5) Disease in general—HM Advocate v Ritchie

4-44   Many diseases, or sudden illnesses for that matter, can lead to total unconsciousness or to mental conditions where the patient is totally unable to control his actions. Heart attacks, strokes,[155] arteriosclerosis,[156] and brain tumours[157] may obviously all have such effects. A related situation appears to have occurred in *HM Advocate v Ritchie*,[158] as that case is now properly to be understood.[159] The accused was charged with culpable homicide in that he, whilst driving a motor vehicle, had knocked down and killed a pedestrian; his defence (tendered as a "special defence") amounted to this —that

> "by the incidence of temporary mental dissociation due to toxic exhaustive factors he was unaware of the presence of the deceased on the highway and of his injuries and death, and was incapable of appreciating his immediately previous and subsequent actions."

It appears that the phrase "toxic exhaustive factors" referred to the absorption of toxins into the accused's blood from lung abscesses, from which he had suffered since being wounded during the "war". Thus, in post-*Ross*[160] terminology, his state of unawareness was actually due to disease—a non-external factor[161]—but fell "short of insanity [i.e. (now) mental disorder]". The case is reported in terms of Lord Murray's charge to the jury. His Lordship did not distinguish between internal and external factors; nor did he consider (it seems) "insanity" (i.e. now mental disorder) as a possible interpretation of the accused's "special defence". In fact, he presented the jury with a stark choice between (a) the accused's having overestimated his strength and capabilities in view of recent illness (this probably amounting to a "fault" element in itself) and thus having driven recklessly, and (b) his having become, while ordinarily quite justified in driving,

---

[154] *Ross v HM Advocate,* 1991 J.C. 210; see above, para.4–19.

[155] See, e.g. the English civil case of *Roberts v Ramsbottom* [1980] 1 W.L.R. 823.

[156] See, e.g. the English case of *R. v Kemp* [1957] 1 Q.B. 399.

[157] See, e.g. the English case of *R. v Charlson* [1955] 1 W.L.R. 317.

[158] *HM Advocate v Ritchie,* 1926 J.C. 45.

[159] See Chalmers and Leverick, *Criminal Defences and Pleas in Bar of Trial* (2006), para.7.34 (which draws upon the researches of Jenifer Ross in the N.R.S.).

[160] *Ross v HM Advocate,* 1991 J.C. 210.

[161] Unless the wound suffered in the war could be counted as "external"; but the application of ordinary principles of causation would surely end any such argument: see below, Ch.5 generally, and para.5–07 in particular.

"—owing to a cause which he was not bound to foresee, and which was outwith his control—either gradually or suddenly not the master of his own action"

such that "a question as to his responsibility or irresponsibility for the consequences of his action" arose "and may form the ground of a good special defence."[162] The jury returned a verdict of not guilty on the grounds that Ritchie was, at the relevant time, "suffering from abnormality, and was therefore not culpable . . .".[163]

The soundness of Lord Murray's direction to the jury was attacked by the court in *Cunningham v HM Advocate*[164]; but *Cunningham* was overruled by the larger court in *Ross v HM Advocate*[165]—and the impression gained from the opinions cast in *Ross* is that Lord Murray was generally correct to advise the jury in the way that he had. Where he had been wrong was to direct them that the *onus* to prove a defence of "mental dissociation" lay on the accused. But he might also, of course, have been wrong to direct the jury that they might return an unqualified verdict of acquittal—depending on what verdict *should* follow on automatism consequent upon a non-external factor. It has been suggested above that conviction, with its myriad disposal possibilities, might be justified in such circumstances—actual disposal depending particularly on the possibility of recurrence and the issue of public safety. Other commentators tend, however, to favour a verdict of acquittal on the simple ground of automatism.[166] The problem may be capable of resolution, however, if "external factor" were to include the results of physical disease[167]; but until the Appeal Court has the opportunity of clarifying the terms used in *Ross*'s case,[168] the problem will remain.[169]

(6) Weak intellect

In *Clark v HM Advocate*[170] a married couple was charged with the wilful neglect **4–45** of a young child in a manner likely to cause it unnecessary suffering and injury—

---

[162] *HM Advocate v Ritchie*, 1926 J.C. 45, Lord Murray's charge to the jury at 49. The Crown's contention in the case was that the accused had caused the death by grossly negligent driving, and that any state of "mental dissociation" arose subsequently, and in direct response to, the accused's discovery of the "accident". The accused's contention was that he had been in a state of dissociation prior to the "accident"; accordingly no *culpa* or blame attached to him, and he was thus entitled to a verdict of not guilty. The Crown suggested that if the jury accepted the accused's version of the facts, the trial judge should advise them to return a special verdict similar to that in *Simon Fraser*'s case [(1878) 4 Coup. 70; see above, paras 4–36 to 4–37]: this Lord Murray declined to do.

[163] *HM Advocate v Ritchie*, 1926 J.C. 45 at 51.

[164] *HM Advocate v Cunningham*, 1963 J.C. 80, Lord Justice General Clyde at 83.

[165] *Ross v HM Advocate*, 1991 J.C. 210 (court of five judges).

[166] See, e.g. Chalmers and Leverick, *Criminal Defences and Pleas in Bar of Trial* (2006), Ch.7, esp. paras 7.28–7.36, where (at para.7.34) the authors eventually conclude that, were a case similar to that of *Ritchie* to occur today, an unqualified acquittal on the ground of automatism would be justified on policy grounds.

[167] As opposed, perhaps, to "mental disease"; but that would present its own problems in relation to mental abnormalities consequent upon epilepsy or diabetes: cf. Chalmers and Leverick, *Criminal Defences and Pleas in Bar of Trial* (2006), para.7.35.

[168] *Ross v HM Advocate*, 1991 J.C. 210.

[169] For a short critical appraisal of the "external factor doctrine", see R.D. MacKay and B.J. Mitchell, "Sleepwalking, Automatism and Insanity" [2006] Crim. L.R. 901, 903.

[170] *Clark v HM Advocate*, 1968 J.C. 53.

contrary to the Children and Young Persons (Scotland) Act 1937 s.12(1).[171] The defence attempted at the trial to lead psychiatric evidence that both of the accused were

> "so feckless and incompetent that they did not appreciate what the result of their failure [to provide adequate food and medical aid for the child] would be."[172]

In brief, the argument was that they were well aware of what they did or refrained from doing for the child, but were totally unaware of the effects which their conduct or omissions would have because of some congenital weakness of intellect from which they suffered. Whilst it is true that such weakness of intellect is an internal factor, it is also true that such weakness had no effect on the ability of the two accused to control their conduct. It is suggested, therefore, that there was no relevant internal factor in the case, and that the "normal" convictions affirmed by the appeal court were correct. Weakness of intellect has, therefore, little relevance in this part of the criminal law, unless (in a murder case only) it substantially impairs the ability of the accused to determine and control his actions, when it may amount to diminished responsibility.[173]

(7) Hysterical amnesia

4–46   Loss of memory (amnesia) is also a condition which should have no bearing whatever on criminal liability—assuming that it occurred after the critical event(s) and is not symptomatic of some graver and more long-lasting mental condition. On that assumption, it can have no effect on a person's ability to control his conduct at the time of an alleged offence. There is a suggestion, however, that "hysterical amnesia" at the time of the alleged offence might be pled as at least a mitigatory matter in an appropriate case. In *Russell v HM Advocate*[174] a defence of that description (of which few further details are revealed) was not considered improper except in so far as it paralleled a plea in bar of trial which had already been rejected.[175]

CONCLUSION

4–47 If the approach of Scots law to the problem of internal factors has been properly set out above in para.4–35, then Scotland deals with cases of total loss of control (following from total alienation of reason) in relation to proven criminal conduct according to the following categories: (1) where that total loss of control is caused by mental illness, then the accused may be acquitted on the ground of mental disorder (should he successfully raise the appropriate special defence), with the

---

[171] The Children and Young Persons (Scotland) Act 1937 s.12(1) is currently to be read as amended by the Children Act 1975 Sch.4 Pt III, the Children (Scotland) Act 1995 Sch.4 para.7(2)(a), and the Criminal Justice (Scotland) Act 2003 (asp 7) s.51(5)(a).

[172] *Clark v HM Advocate*, 1968 J.C. 53, per Lord Justice-Clerk Grant at 56.

[173] See below, paras 4–49 and 4–50. See also *John McLean* (1876) 3 Couper 334, per Lord Deas at 337–340.

[174] *Russell v HM Advocate*, 1946 J.C. 37, per Lord Justice-Clerk Cooper at 45.

[175] See also the English case of *R. v Isitt* [1978] R.T.R. 211.

consequences which such a verdict has (see above, para.4–18); (2) where that total loss of control is caused by an external factor which meets the qualifying conditions, then the accused will be acquitted unconditionally on the ground of automatism; and (3) where that total loss of control is due to disease or illness not amounting to mental disorder and especially where it is likely to recur, then the accused should probably be convicted in order that measures of treatment or restraint may be considered for the purpose of future public safety, there being no such thing as "acquittal with conditions" in Scots law. Difficult issues appear to be raised, of course, where there are two or more causal factors at work. In diabetic automatism cases, for example, the effect of insulin (external) on the accused's mental state may have to be weighed against the causal factor of the disease itself (internal): and in the "lager can" type of case, where drugs are allegedly pushed into the accused's chosen alcoholic drink,[176] the effect of drink knowingly ingested (external, but generally not relevant to the defence of automatism) should strictly be weighed against the effect of the drugs (external, and possibly within the defence) on the accused's mental state. These are, however, issues of fact and degree—and will have to be solved in a common-sense way.

In the case of crimes which require mens rea, the method of dealing with **4–48** accused persons who fall within category (3) above may seem unjustifiable— since such accused clearly possess no more subjective mens rea than those who fall within category (2). But unless *HM Advocate v Cunningham*[177] and leading decisions which followed it[178] are overturned completely,[179] the preferring of convictions is possibly the best way of reconciling the prior case-law with what was said by the appeal court in *Ross*. Of course, the opinions in *Ross* do not rule out straightforward acquittals for at least some persons who fall within category (3)—perhaps, for example, for those who suffer a wholly unforeseeable stroke or heart attack whilst driving a mechanically propelled vehicle. And it may be that Scots law will eventually categorise such persons according to a more sophisticated classification. But it is certainly to be hoped, in accordance with a general approach which Scots law has long favoured, that all those—especially police, prosecutors and judges—who influence the practice of the law (and thus the law itself) will approach difficult cases in this area bearing in mind "in a common sense way their sense of fairness."[180]

A Note on Diminished Responsibility

It has been suggested above[181] that Scots criminal law envisages the conviction of **4–49** those who were at the material time unconscious or semi-conscious due to "internal factors", but that their mental abnormalities (not amounting perhaps to

---

[176] See, e.g. *Ross v HM Advocate*, 1991 J.C. 210; *Sorley v HM Advocate*, 1992 J.C. 102; *Cardle v Mulrainey*, 1992 S.L.T. 1152.

[177] *HM Advocate v Cunningham*, 1963 J.C. 80.

[178] In particular *Clark v HM Advocate*, 1968 J.C. 53 and *Carmichael v Boyle*, 1985 S.L.T. 399.

[179] *Ross v HM Advocate*, 1991 J.C. 210 did not go that far—see Lord Justice-General Hope's opinion at 222.

[180] *R. v Quick* [1973] 1 Q.B. 910, per Lawton L.J. at 922C.

[181] See above, para.4–47.

medically recognised mental illnesses[182]) might be taken into account in mitigation of, or by way of substitution for, punishment; appropriate disposal of such cases after conviction might thus achieve some form of functional justice. It has further been suggested above[183] that *Simon Fraser's* case might best have been dealt with by invoking the plea of diminished responsibility, for its mitigating effect; it might thus be thought that such a plea would be appropriate in all cases of "involuntariness" due to internal factors. This, however, is not so. Fairly recent legislation has confined the plea of diminished responsibility to cases where murder has been charged.

4–50   Whatever may have been the scope of diminished responsibility at common law,[184] that concept is now solely shaped by statute.[185] Diminished responsibility is expressly confined to "a person who would otherwise be convicted of murder", and requires such a person to establish on the balance of probabilities that his

> "ability to determine or control conduct for which [he] would otherwise be [so convicted] was, at the time of the conduct, substantially impaired by reason of abnormality of mind."

If diminished responsibility is so established, then the person in question will be convicted of culpable homicide—which enables a wide variety of disposal options to be considered. "Abnormality of mind" is not defined by the relevant legislation—which does, however, declare that such a mental condition "includes mental disorder"[186]; and "mental disorder" means any mental illness, personality disorder or learning disability "however caused or manifested", excluding (*quoad* relevant) "dependence on, or use of alcohol or drugs" and "acting as no prudent person would act".[187]

---

[182] Even if such abnormality is capable of recognition as a mental illness, the accused may, in modern law, choose not to tender a special defence of mental disorder or may be debarred from doing so (see the Criminal Procedure (Scotland) Act 1995 s.51A (and especially subss. (2) and (4)) as inserted by the Criminal Justice and Licensing (Scotland) Act 2010 (asp 13) s.168).

[183] See above, para.4–39.

[184] Cf., e.g. the opinion of the court in *Galbraith v HM Advocate*, 2002 J.C. 1.

[185] See the Criminal Procedure (Scotland) Act 1995 s.51B (as inserted by the Criminal Law and Licensing (Scotland) Act 2010 (asp 13) s.168; s.171 of that Act abolishes inter alia "any rule of law providing for . . . (b) the plea of diminished responsibility").

[186] See the Criminal Procedure (Scotland) Act 1995 s.51B(2), as inserted by the Criminal Justice and Licensing (Scotland) Act 2010 (asp 13) s.168. Under s.307(1) of the said 1995 Act, "mental disorder" is given the meaning which it has in the Mental Health (Care and Treatment) (Scotland) Act 2003 (asp 13) s.328(1): see the said 2003 Act Sch.4 para.8(16)(d).

[187] See the Mental Health (Care and Treatment) (Scotland) Act 2003 (asp 13) s.328(1), (2). See also the Criminal Procedure (Scotland) Act 1995 s.51(b)(3) (as inserted by the Criminal Justice and Licensing (Scotland) Act 2010 (asp 13) s.168) for further provisions relative to the "influence of alcohol, drugs or other substances" on diminished responsibility.

CHAPTER 5

CAUSATION

Introduction

The issue of causation is raised by the legal definitions of many different **5–01** crimes. For example, as is described in Ch.10, it is a requirement of the crime of fraud that there be a causal connection between the false pretence and the actions of the dupe. There are also many crimes which contain in their definitions an element of resultant harm. These include crimes against property, such as malicious mischief or fire-raising, and also crimes against the person. An example of the latter is the crime of aggravated assault. This might result in, for example, severe injury or permanent disfigurement to the victim of the attack. As previously noted, liability for a result crime, such as an aggravated assault, can only be imposed upon an individual if it was his conduct which *caused* the harm to the complainer (see above, para.3–06). If the prosecution cannot establish a causal link between the accused's conduct and the consequences of the assault, then liability for the aggravating features of the crime will not be imposed upon him.

In many cases causation can be determined without any great difficulty. If A **5–02** attacks B with a hatchet, there is no problem in attributing the resultant severe injury to the conduct of A. The facts speak for themselves. This is not to say, of course, that difficult factual issues cannot arise.[1] In particular, problems can arise when there are a number of factors contributing to the result and/or when other events intervene between the conduct of the accused and the consequential harm. Without doubt the most complex and difficult problems arise in the law relating to homicide. Most of the important authorities on causation concern either murder or culpable homicide. There may have been a considerable length of time elapsing between the infliction of the original injury and the death. The explanation for the importance attached to causation in the law of homicide is that the law strives to determine when a death is attributable to the conduct of the accused.[2]

CAUSATION IN FACT

THE "BUT FOR" TEST

The first issue to be considered in a result crime, such as homicide, is whether the **5–03** accused did *in fact* cause the victim's death. The issue is frequently resolved by the application of the "but for", or sine qua non, test: but for the conduct of the

---

[1] See, e.g. the facts at issue in *Garden v HM Advocate*, 1999 S.L.T. 1352.
[2] G.P. Fletcher, *Rethinking Criminal Law* (New York: Oxford University Press, 2000), p.358.

accused, would the victim have died? It is not necessary that the conduct of the accused has been the only cause of the harm. Nor is it necessary that his conduct be a substantial cause, provided that it is a material, and more than a minimal, cause.[3]

NECESSITY FOR CAUSAL LINK

5–04 In most cases, proof of causation in fact will not present any major problem to the prosecution. As in the aggravated assault example outlined above, the issue will be self-evident. But the existence of a causal link will always need to be established: it should not be taken for granted.[4] On occasion, the evidential issues to be considered may be complex, perhaps with conflicting medical evidence.[5] In *Hendry v HM Advocate*,[6] a conviction for culpable homicide was upheld on appeal. The appellant had assaulted a 67 year old man, who died as a result of a heart attack a short while thereafter. Only minor injuries had been caused to the deceased, but he had a pre-existing heart condition which could have led to death after any degree of exertion or distress. There were further complicating factors, in that the deceased had angina, he had consumed a large amount of alcohol, he had eaten a large meal, and he had climbed a flight of stairs. All of these were stress factors which could have additionally contributed to the heart attack. The key issue for the prosecution was to prove beyond reasonable doubt the existence of a causal link between the assault and the heart attack.

5–05 In *Lourie v HM Advocate*,[7] the appellants' convictions for culpable homicide were quashed by the Appeal Court. Lourie and another youth had been charged on the basis that they had entered the house of an elderly woman uninvited and stolen a handbag in her presence. The appeal was allowed because there was insufficient evidence that the deceased had observed the theft and it was unclear whether or not the appellants had entered the house uninvited. The prosecution maintained that the woman had been put in a state of fear and alarm by the appellants' actions. It was argued that the deceased's fatal heart attack had been a direct consequence. The death had ensued soon after the visit by the appellants. An expert medical witness called by the prosecution testified that a heart attack could have been the result of an increase in strain. The defence argued either that the death could have been a complete coincidence, or that she had died as the result of exertion which may have accompanied the events which took place. It was argued that if the latter was indeed the case, the death was not the result of the illegal act in the sense that the act had caused the woman's death. The first point to note about a set of facts such as these is that any doubt would have to be resolved in favour of an accused. If a jury thought that the woman's death might have been coincidental, then there would have to be an acquittal. The defence's second argument is more problematic. Assuming that there had been sufficient evidence to support the prosecution case, the woman had only been required to exert herself because of the unlawful

---

[3] See *Watson v HM Advocate*, (1978) S.C.C.R. Supp. 192.

[4] See *Malone v HM Advocate*, 1988 S.C.C.R. 498.

[5] See, e.g. *Karling v HM Advocate*, 1999 S.C.C.R. 359.

[6] *Hendry v HM Advocate*, 1987 J.C. 63.

[7] *Lourie v HM Advocate*, 1988 S.C.C.R. 634.

actions of the appellants. But for their actions, the woman would have lived longer. To anticipate the discussion in the rest of this chapter somewhat, there would not then appear to be any difficulty in establishing the necessary causal link between the conduct of the accused and the consequential death of the victim.

CAUSATION IN LAW

CAUSES AND CONDITIONS

Causation is not, however, simply a question of fact. It is necessary, but not suffi- **5–06** cient, that the accused's conduct be a factual cause of the death or other type of harm. Not every factor which meets the "but for" standard is sufficient for the imposition of criminal liability.[8] If a reckless motorist drives the wrong way down a motorway and collides with another vehicle, killing the occupant, the presence of the other vehicle is a "but for" cause of the crash. Common sense suggests that the presence of the victim on the road should not be regarded by the criminal law as the cause of his death. This could be described instead as a *condition*, rather than a cause, of the fatality. A condition is a normal event or circumstance which is necessary for the result to occur, but cannot be said positively to have caused it.

PROXIMITY REQUIREMENT

There must be causation *in law*. The law requires that a cause be "proximate". **5–07** This requirement of proximity reflects the law's concern only with those causal factors that are closely connected to the result. In relation to homicide, the rules of law relating to proximate cause are intended to provide a safeguard against liability attaching to an individual whose acts are remote from the victim's death, or where his conduct contributes only minimally. Similar considerations apply in relation to those other crimes in which the issue of causation is implicit.

THE LEGAL PRINCIPLES OF CAUSATION

The legal principles governing causation in law take the form of guidelines rather **5–08** than strict legal rules. The most significant of these are examined in the following sections. What follows is not a description of rules which will consistently determine questions of causation. Causal analysis relies much upon common sense and moral intuition.

The characteristics of the victim

It is commonly stated that the accused must "take his victim as he finds him".[9] **5–09** This is sometimes referred to as the "thin skull" rule. The rule means that the accused will be criminally liable if death results from some pre-existing weakness in the victim. As Lord Jamieson said in *Bird v HM Advocate*,[10] it is not a

---

[8] See *McDonald v HM Advocate* [2006] HCJAC 89; 2007 S.C.C.R. 10, at 16, para.11.
[9] See, e.g. *HM Advocate v Rutherford*, 1947 J.C. 1.
[10] *Bird v HM Advocate*, 1952 J.C. 23 at 25.

"defence that the victim was an old person, an infirm person, or a person that suffered from a bad heart, and that if he had been young and healthy the consequences would not have happened."

The type of situation covered by the rule is where A strikes B on the head in a way that would normally cause only bruising, but, because B has an unusually thin skull, the blow fractures B's skull and he dies. A cannot then claim that B's unusual physique breaks the chain of causation between his conduct and the death. The basis for this rule is a consideration of public policy: the accused should not have injured the victim in the first place. On a strict analysis, however, it could not really be said that the accused had "voluntarily" caused the death of the victim, since he believed, perhaps quite reasonably, that the victim had a normal skull. It could even be argued that the death was accidental. Nevertheless, the criminal law obliges him to take responsibility for the consequences of his actions.

Psychological characteristics

5–10   This rule operates reasonably enough (if harshly on occasion) in relation to the physical characteristics of the victim, but how far can it be taken? Should it extend to the psychological characteristics or religious beliefs of the victim? The English case of *R. v Blaue*[11] indicates that the courts would be unlikely to make any distinction between physical and psychological characteristics. The appellant in this case had stabbed the victim numerous times and pierced her lung, after she had rejected his sexual advances. The victim was a Jehovah's Witness. At the hospital to which she had been taken, the victim refused the immediate blood transfusion necessary to save her life. The refusal was based on her religious belief that it would be a sin to accept the transfusion. She died from her wounds shortly afterwards. The appellant contended that the deceased's refusal to have the blood transfusion was unreasonable and, as such, had broken the chain of causation. The Court of Appeal rejected this argument. Lord Justice Lawton stated:

> "[T]hose who use violence on other people must take their victims as they find them. This in our judgment means the whole man, not just the physical man. It does not lie in the mouth of the assailant to say that his victim's religious beliefs . . . were unreasonable. The question for decision is what caused her death. The answer is the stab wound. The fact that the victim refused to stop this end coming about did not break the causal connection between the act and the death."[12]

Blaue is a persuasive authority for the view that an assailant must take his victim as he finds him, both physically and psychologically. One view would be that there are dangers in expressing the principle too widely. It would be asked whether psychological characteristics (including religious beliefs, however far removed from the mainstream) should be treated in the same way as the physical weaknesses of a victim. An alternative approach could be to focus less upon the

---

[11] *R. v Blaue* [1975] 1 W.L.R. 1411.
[12] *R. v Blaue* [1975] 1 W.L.R. 1411 at 1415.

reasonableness or otherwise of the victim's beliefs, and more upon the unreasonableness of expecting a person in a life-threatening situation to abandon her religious conviction.[13]

The conduct of the victim

It thus appears that even an "unreasonable" refusal of medical treatment by a **5–11** victim will not break the chain of causation. There are, however, a number of different ways in which a victim could contribute to his own demise. The question then arises: are there any circumstances in which the conduct of the victim will be held to have broken the causal link? In the case of *Joseph and Mary Norris*[14] the original wound inflicted by the accused was trivial. The victim went drinking, removed his bandages and went out late at night in poor weather. He contracted tetanus and died. Lord Craighill directed the jury that the question for them to answer was whether the tetanus would have developed whether or not the victim had acted in the way he did. If the tetanus was the consequence of the conduct of the accused, then they were liable for the result. If, however, the disease had been brought on by the imprudence of the victim, then there should be a verdict of not guilty.

No duty on complainer to mitigate harm

This charge to the jury is unusual in that, perhaps because of the trivial nature **5–12** of the original wound,[15] considerable emphasis was placed on the conduct of the deceased. The more commonly expressed view is that a victim is not under any legal duty to mitigate the effects of the injuries inflicted upon him. The central issue is whether the injuries inflicted by the assailant are an operating and substantial cause of death. It would appear that the victim is quite at liberty to neglect his own well being and the assailant must take the consequences of his actions. This basic principle is restated in many of the relevant authorities.[16] For example, in *James Williamson*,[17] Lord Justice-Clerk Inglis said that the fact that a victim

> "is weaker than his neighbours, either from natural constitution or bad habit, can never make the slightest difference in the question of guilt or innocence."

Similarly, the accused has to take responsibility for any harm occurring to the **5–13** victim during an escape. If he causes so much fear in the victim that he dies in the course of a desperate escape attempt, then the accused will be held to have caused the death of the victim. In *McDonald v HM Advocate*[18] the appellant and another were charged with culpable homicide by assaulting the deceased in his third-floor flat and causing him to fall from a window. His death had occurred after he had

---

[13] See H.L.A. Hart and T. Honoré, *Causation in the Law*, 2nd edn (Oxford: Oxford University Press, 1985), p.361.

[14] *Joseph and Mary Norris* (1886) 1 White 292.

[15] See also Hume, *Commentaries*, i, 182.

[16] See, e.g. *R. v Dear* [1996] Crim. L.R. 595.

[17] *James Williamson* (1866) 5 Irv. 326 at 328.

[18] *McDonald v HM Advocate* [2006] HCJAC 89; 2007 S.C.C.R. 10. See also the case of *Patrick Slaven* (1885) 5 Coup. 694, where the accused had assaulted a woman with intent to ravish her. They pursued her as she tried to escape, and she fell over a cliff and died. It was held that the conduct of the accused had caused the death.

fallen to the ground while trying to escape shortly after the attack. Under these circumstances, the High Court took the view that a causal relationship between the assault and the subsequent death could be established.

The daft complainer?

5–14   In the English case of *R. v Roberts*,[19] the complainer was a young lady to whom the appellant had given a lift. During the journey he made a number of improper suggestions to her and touched her breasts. The complainer jumped from the car, which was travelling at a speed between 20 and 40 mph, suffering grazing and concussion in the escape. The appellant claimed that the complainer's action in jumping out of the car had broken the chain of causation and thereby relieved him of liability for her injuries. The Court of Appeal was not impressed by this argument. Lord Justice Stephenson was of the opinion that only if the actions of the complainer had been "daft" would the chain of causation have been broken. In *R. v Williams and Davis*,[20] the deceased was a hitchhiker who had jumped from a moving car in order to escape an attempted robbery. The Court of Appeal set out two questions which should be addressed in such a case,

> "first, whether it was reasonably foreseeable that some harm . . . was likely to result from the threat itself; and, secondly, whether the deceased's reaction . . . was within the range of responses which might be expected from a victim placed in the situation which he was."[21]

What had to be considered was

> "whether the deceased's conduct was proportionate to the threat; that is to say that it was within the ambit of reasonableness and not so daft as to make it his own voluntary act which amounted to a *novus actus interveniens* and consequently broke the chain of causation."[22]

5–15 These two English decisions lend support to the view that, if the victim acts unreasonably, the accused should not be held liable for the harm. The unreasonable behaviour becomes the cause. There is also a suggestion to this effect in *McDonald v HM Advocate*,[23] where it is said that if the victim of an assault

> "reacted in a wholly unforeseeable or unreasonable way that would mean that the attack would cease to be a direct cause of the death and thus the requisite causal link would not be established."

Induced suicide

5–16   A not unrealistic scenario would have a rapist infecting his victim with AIDS. She decides to commit suicide rather than suffer a lingering death. Should the

---

[19] *R. v Roberts* (1971) 56 Cr. App. R. 95.
[20] *R. v Williams and Davis* [1992] 1 W.L.R. 380.
[21] *R. v Williams and Davis* [1992] 1 W.L.R. 380 at 389D.
[22] *R. v Williams and Davis* [1992] 1 W.L.R. 380 at 388H.
[23] *McDonald v HM Advocate* [2006] HCJAC 89; 2007 S.C.C.R. 10 at 16, para.11, endorsing the approach of the trial judge.

rapist be held to have caused the death? There are American cases, such as *People v Lewis*,[24] and *Commonwealth v Wright*,[25] which suggest that where the victim has, as a result of the egregious conduct of the accused, become so disturbed as to commit suicide, the accused will be held to have caused the death of the victim. The point has yet to be resolved in a Scottish case. In *John Robertson*,[26] Lord Handyside reserved his opinion on the question of whether an induced suicide would break the chain of causation:

> "If the act of suicide was the immediate consequence of the violence, I am not prepared to say what such a state of facts might warrant. I do not say that it would amount to culpable homicide, although it would certainly come very near to it."

Whether as a matter of principle, or through an application of the "thin skull" rule, it is possible that a court would determine that the rapist should be held to have caused the death of the victim.

The concept of a novus actus interveniens

It is a fundamental requirement of causation in law that the conduct of the **5–17** accused be a sufficiently direct cause of the consequential harm to the victim. It is quite possible that a number of other "but for" causes will contribute to the eventual result. Some will be more significant than others, but very few will be of sufficient significance to break the causal chain. The legal term for an event which does break the chain of causation is a novus actus interveniens. The example which is frequently given is that of an assault victim left in a field who is subsequently struck by lightning and dies. The initial assault would not then be seen as the proximate cause of that result. In order to break the chain of causation between the assailant and the consequential harm in this way, the novus actus must supersede the original conduct. The law takes a very restrictive view of what can constitute a superseding cause significant enough to break the causal link. An individual can even be held responsible for the harms which result from the intervening conduct of his victim (see above, paras 5–12 and 5–13).

An informative authority in this regard is *Khaliq v HM Advocate*,[27] the cele- **5–18** brated decision concerning "glue sniffing kits". Here the High Court held that the subsequent voluntary acts of the purchaser of such a kit could not constitute a novus actus interveniens relieving the sellers of responsibility for the "real injury" caused. The causal link was not broken merely because a voluntary act on the part of the recipient of the intoxicant was required in order to bring about the harmful consequences. In the *Lord Advocate's Reference (No.1 of 1994)*,[28] this principle was applied in the context of culpable homicide. The fact that the deceased had

---

[24] *People v Lewis*, 124 Cal. 551 (1899).

[25] *Commonwealth v Wright*, 455 Pa. 480 (1974).

[26] *John Robertson* (1854) 1 Irv. 469 at 470.

[27] *Khaliq v HM Advocate*, 1984 J.C. 23; applied in *Ulhaq v HM Advocate*, 1991 S.L.T. 614; *Borwick v Urquhart*, 2003 S.C.C.R. 243.

[28] *Lord Advocate's Reference (No.1 of 1994)*, 1995 S.L.T. 248. See also *MacAngus v HM Advocate; Kane v HM Advocate* [2009] HCJAC 8; 2009 S.L.T. 137 at 151, para.46: "a deliberate decision by the victim of the reckless conduct to ingest the drug will not necessarily break the chain of causation."

voluntarily ingested the amphetamine supplied by the accused did not relieve him of criminal responsibility for the death.

Assault and subsequent infection

5–19   It is not difficult to envisage many natural events which could intervene between the conduct of the accused and a resulting harm. A straightforward example would be the non-fatal wound which becomes infected and the victim dies as a result of the infection. There is no difficulty in saying that the individual who inflicted the wound is liable for the death. The immediate cause of death may have been the infection, but the original wound will be cognised by the law to be the proximate cause of death. This situation can be distinguished from that where the victim is exposed to some other, entirely unpredictable, cause of death. It is possible that the victim of an assault might coincidentally contract a fatal disease while lying in hospital. In the American case of *Bush v Commonwealth*,[29] the victim caught a fatal dose of scarlet fever from the hospital physician who treated him. It was held that it was the disease, not the original assault, which had caused the death.

5–20   In the case of *James Wilson*,[30] a wound inflicted on the victim developed into erysipelas while he was being treated in hospital. There was a dispute as to whether another patient had infected the victim, or whether it was a direct complication of the original injury. Lord Cockburn charged the jury that the original wound should be regarded as the cause of death provided that the disease was "not altogether new, but a natural consequence of the injury."[31] If, on the other hand, "the disease was ... entirely new—not produced by the wounds, but by infection, or some other external cause" death was caused by the coincidental infection and not by the wound. The *caveat* entered to this principle by Lord Cockburn is most important:

> "Suppose a man to die of apoplexy, but that apoplexy to have been caused by a blow. It will not ... do for the prisoner to say ... I gave you a blow, but I did not give you apoplexy. He must stand the peril of the consequences of his act."[32]

This passage reiterates the basic principle of causation already referred to. It is clear that in order for a subsequent infection to constitute a novus actus interveniens it will need to be quite independent of the original wound. As it was put by the Courts Martial Appeal Court in *R. v Smith*,[33]

> "only if the second cause is so overwhelming as to make the original wound merely part of the history can it be said that the death does not flow from the wound."

In a homicide case, the focus will be placed on the original wound. The subsequent aggravation will generally be disregarded, unless it has clearly arisen from an independent cause.

---

[29] *Bush v Commonwealth*, 78 Ky. 268 (1880).
[30] *James Wilson* (1838) 2 Swin. 16.
[31] *James Wilson* (1838) 2 Swin. 16 at 19.
[32] *James Wilson* (1838) 2 Swin. 16 at 18. Cf. *J. Campbell* (1819) Alison, *Principles* i, 147.
[33] *R. v Smith* [1959] 2 Q.B. 35 at 43.

Medical treatment

In fact, *Smith* concerned poor medical treatment rather than a subsequent **5–21** infection. The general principle in relation to *malregimen*, as it is sometimes called, is that negligent medical treatment is irrelevant since the accused must stand the consequences of his unlawful conduct. As was stated in the case of *James Williamson*[34]

> "it will never do . . . if a wound calculated to prove mortal in itself is afterwards followed by death, to say that every criticism that can be made of the treatment of the patient after the wound is received is to furnish a ground for acquitting the person who inflicted the wound of either murder or culpable homicide."

The situation is essentially the same as when the victim unreasonably refuses medical treatment. The conduct of the accused will still be held to be the proximate cause of death. The only distinction which might be drawn is between negligent medical treatment which merely serves to aggravate the original wound and treatment which is so grossly negligent as to constitute an independent cause of death. "Ordinary" negligence would not appear to be sufficient. There would need to be something approaching criminal recklessness on the part of the doctor. As a matter of policy, a court would be most unwilling to regard anything done by a doctor in the ordinary course of medical treatment as constituting a novus actus interveniens,

> "it will only be in the most extraordinary and unusual case that [medical] treatment can be said to be so independent of the acts of the defendant that it could be regarded in law as the cause of the victim's death to the exclusion of the defendant's acts."[35]

In *R. v Smith*[36] the appellant had been convicted of the murder of a fellow soldier. **5–22** The two had been involved in a fight, during the course of which the victim was stabbed a number of times with a bayonet. On the way to a medical station the victim was twice dropped from a stretcher and there was a considerable delay before he received treatment. The appellant contended that these subsequent events had broken the chain of causation. The court rejected this argument. It held that his conduct would be regarded as the cause in law, since it had been shown that it was the operating and substantial cause of death. In this case the victim had clearly died because of the stab wounds. Only if the original wounds could be said to have merely provided the setting in which some other causes of death operated would the court have been prepared to say that the chain of causation had been broken.

Discontinuing life support

In *Finlayson v HM Advocate*[37] it was held that switching off a life support **5–23** machine did not break the chain of causation. Here an injection of a controlled drug had caused brain death in the victim. The High Court determined that the

---

[34] *James Williamson* (1866) 5 Irv. 326 at 328.
[35] *R. v Cheshire* [1991] 1 W.L.R. 844, per Beldam L.J. at 851G.
[36] *R. v Smith* [1959] 2 Q.B. 35.
[37] *Finlayson v HM Advocate*, 1979 J.C. 33.

effects of the injection constituted the substantial and continuing cause of death. This causative link had not been affected by the decision to switch off the life support machine, which was a reasonable one in the circumstances. The court decided, in effect, that the life support machine had merely held the consequences of the injection in abeyance. When the machine was switched off, the injection continued to be the cause of death. The court adopted the dictum of Lord Wright in *The Oropesa*[38]:

> "To break the chain of causation it must be shown that there is something which I will call ultroneous, something unwarrantable, a new cause which disturbs the sequence of events, something which can be described as either unreasonable or extraneous or extrinsic."

The finding of the court was that switching off the life support machine did not pass this test. A further observation made by the court was that switching off the machine was *foreseeable*.

The test of foreseeability

5–24   This concept of foreseeability is prayed in aid in many of the authorities concerning causation. For example, in *R. v Roberts*[39] the Court of Appeal relied upon the fact that the complainer's attempt to escape was a reasonably foreseeable consequence of what the appellant had done. The basic notion is that whether or not an intervening cause will be held to have broken the chain of causation depends upon its foreseeability. The test is whether the harm was due to an intervening event that a reasonable person could have foreseen. If not, then the superseding cause will be regarded in law as the proximate one. For example, A assaults B and leaves him unconscious on the seashore, below the high-water mark. B drowns when the tide comes in. It is plain that A cannot escape liability on the basis that he did not cause the death, but the sea did. The likelihood of B drowning was eminently foreseeable.[40] A possible limit to the test is that identified by Lord Reid in the civil case of *McKew v Holland and Hannen and Cubitts (Scotland) Ltd*[41]:

> "it does not follow that [an accused] is liable for every consequence which a reasonable man could foresee. What can be foreseen depends almost entirely on the facts of the case, and it is often easy to foresee [a] *novus actus interveniens* as being quite likely."

This is why the test is better seen as one of *reasonable* foreseeability, rather than one of foreseeability per se. The test is an objective one.

Foreseeability and malregimen

5–25   The foreseeability test could be applied to the *malregimen* cases. One application of the test would be that if the original assault is foreseeably fatal, then subsequent medical maltreatment could not break the chain of causation. An alternative

---

[38] *The Oropesa* [1943] P. 32 at 39.
[39] *R. v Roberts* (1972) 56 Cr. App. R. 95; see above, para.5–14.
[40] Compare the facts at issue in the New Zealand case of *R. v Hart* [1986] 2 N.Z.L.R. 408.
[41] *McKew v Holland and Hannen and Cubitts (Scotland) Ltd*, 1970 S.C.(HL) 20 at 25.

application might be to say that "ordinary" negligence on the part of a doctor is foreseeable: everyone knows that doctors make mistakes.[42] The implication would be that grossly negligent or reckless treatment could break the chain of causation, since that would be unforeseeable.

In the English case of *R. v Jordan*[43] it was held that "palpably wrong" medical **5–26** treatment had broken the chain of causation. As stressed earlier, however, it would be the truly exceptional case where such a conclusion could be reached. In *Jordan* the original wound inflicted on the victim had nearly healed at the time of death. The proximate cause of death was the injection of a drug to which the victim was allergic. The court held that the original injury was merely the setting within which another cause of death operated. In this case the court reached the conclusion described by Lord Justice-Clerk Inglis in the case of *James Williamson*[44]:

> "If a person receives a wound . . . which is not fatal in itself . . . and then afterwards by unskilful and injudicious treatment this wound assumes a more serious aspect, and finally terminates in death, it is possible to say . . . that the wound inflicted by the prisoner is not the cause of death, because it would not by itself have produced death but for the bad treatment which followed on it."

This passage needs to be treated with considerable caution. The deceased only received the poor medical treatment because he had been the victim of a life-threatening assault. Why should the assailant not be regarded as having caused the death?

Fatality and foreseeability

The argument is sometimes made that it is possible to draw a distinction **5–27** between an injury which is foreseeably fatal and one which is not. There is no guarantee, however, that a court would consider the foreseeability test as applicable in such a case. It may prefer a simple application of the "but for" or "thin skull" rules. Much may come to depend on the nature of the original assault. Which test a court decides to apply may well depend upon an assessment of the accused's "blameworthiness" (see below, para.5–33). In *R. v Blaue*[45] the English Court of Appeal did not apply the principle of foreseeability to the rule that the victim had to be taken as she was found. It will be recalled that there was a refusal to draw any distinction between physical characteristics which, even if unusual, can be argued to be foreseeable, and unusual psychological characteristics. It is surely not reasonably foreseeable that a victim will hold religious beliefs which preclude her accepting life-saving medical treatment (see above, para.5–10).

FACT, LAW AND POLICY

THE PROBLEM OF CAUSATION

The task which confronts the criminal lawyer in relation to causation is that of **5–28** defining the necessary circumstances for its establishment. Causation is important

---

[42] *R. v Cheshire* [1991] 1 W.L.R. 844, per Beldam L.J. at 849D–F.
[43] *R. v Jordan* (1956) 40 Cr. App. R. 152.
[44] *James Williamson* (1866) 5 Irv. 326 at 328; see above, para.5–15.
[45] *R. v Blaue* [1975] 1 W.L.R. 1411.

because, without this requirement, an individual with a negligible or non-existent connection to a crime could be punished. The criminal law does not engage in a wide-ranging philosophical inquiry about the concept of causation. The practical aim of the law is to identify those causes for which the accused can be held responsible. This involves a normative, as well as a factual judgment. In the simplest of terms, these causes will be those that make some noteworthy contribution to the circumstances surrounding the forbidden harm. Every cause must meet the "but for" test. A helpful definition of what constitutes a cause is that of Fletcher:

> "Among all the necessary conditions for a particular event, the 'causes' are those conditions that make the difference under the circumstances."[46]

It should be recognised that the criminal law does adopt an individualist ideology in matters of causation.[47] The law does tend to locate responsibility in individuals for their actions, in isolation from societal factors. It is almost trite to say the legal analysis of causation will be different from the psychological or sociological. The criminal law does not, for example, accept unemployment or upbringing as causal factors. The focus is necessarily much narrower than this.

The legal context

5–29   The principle of proximate cause requires that the conduct of the accused must have been the legal cause, as well as the factual cause, of the actus reus in order for him to be criminally liable. This concept of a proximate cause is a somewhat obscure one. There is no precise method for identifying whether a cause is proximate or not. A court will not discover the proximate cause purely by applying a method derived from logic. It will be faced with two major legal issues of causation to resolve. First, under what circumstances can one say that there is a causal link between the accused's conduct and the consequent harm? Secondly, what can constitute a novus actus interveniens breaking the chain of causation? A number of the different tests employed by the courts to resolve these questions have been outlined in this chapter. These tend to take the form of guidelines, rather than strict rules.

The factual context

5–30   It should also be emphasised that, because causation is a mixed question of law and fact, it is dangerous to reach dogmatic conclusions independently of the facts of a case. The particular constellation of facts confronting a court may be of primary significance. A judge will be very wary of trespassing on the territory of the jury.[48] In *Finlayson v HM Advocate*, Lord Justice-General Emslie said that

---

[46] Fletcher, *Rethinking Criminal Law* (2000), p.595.
[47] For a critical account, see A. Norrie, *Crime, Reason and History*, 2nd edn (London: Butterworths, 2001), Ch.7.
[48] This concern also finds reflection in the treatment of expert (medical) evidence. It is not necessary for there to be such evidence expressed in a particular way before the jury is entitled to conclude that the causal link has been proved. It is for the jury, and not any expert witness, to determine whether a cause of death has been established beyond reasonable doubt. See *Hendry v HM Advocate*, 1987 J.C. 63; *Fyfe v HM Advocate*, 1998 S.L.T. 195; *Paxton v HM Advocate*, 2000 S.L.T. 771.

"it was not in any event a matter for the Judge to determine *ab ante* whether, as a matter of fact, it could be said that the chain of causation had been broken. That was a matter inextricably bound up with the other facts in the case which were for determination by the jury."[49]

It would, of course, be quite legitimate for a judge to point out that a subsequent **5–31** event could not in law constitute a novus actus interveniens. This might be the case if the victim had refused medical treatment because of his religious beliefs.[50] A judge would be at liberty to direct a jury that the refusal was, as a matter of law, not to be regarded as a superseding cause which had broken the chain of causation.

The policy context

One view of the issue of causation is that the courts do not in fact rely upon **5–32** generally applicable principles of the kind described in this chapter. Gordon's view is that:

"What often happens in practice is that courts discuss causal theories learn-edly and at length, and purport to reach a conclusion by reference to a logical appraisal of these theories; but in fact the causal criterion applied to the case is chosen, not because of its intrinsic logic and correctness, but because it is the one which leads most easily to the same answer as would be given the question: 'Should A bear the blame for this?'"[51]

The argument seems to be that courts resort to considerations of policy when determining whether the accused has caused a particular harm. (A more limited version of this argument is that a court will utilise a moral judgment in deciding whether or not causation is established.) There are difficulties with this interpreta-tion. It is always dangerous to claim that a court is doing something other than what it says it is. Perhaps a better view would be that the principles in this area of law are both flexible and overlapping. As a consequence, a court will have a choice over which principle or test to apply. For example, the doctrine of reason-able foreseeability can lead to a different conclusion from an application of the "thin skull" rule (see above, para.5–27). A further problem with the policy approach is that, even as a purported explanation of what the courts do in practice, it offers precious little guidance for future cases.

Causation and responsibility

Causation cannot simply be judged objectively in terms of physical acts. As **5–33** Gordon recognises in the passage quoted above, some element of responsibility or blameworthiness must come into the equation. The legal analysis of causation is closely linked to the process of allocating responsibility for the criminal act. Indeed, one influential view is that an analysis of causation is dependent upon the

---

[49] *Finlayson v HM Advocate*, 1979 J.C. 33 at 36. See also the observations in *Johnston v HM Advocate* [2009] HCJAC 38; 2009 J.C. 227.

[50] See *R. v Blaue* [1975] 1 W.L.R. 1411; see above, para.5–10.

[51] Gordon, *Criminal Law*, 3rd edn (2000/2001), para.4.01. Having made this statement, Gordon does proceed to discuss the legal principles in detail. The law, it seems, is not so easily escaped.

criterion of blameworthiness.[52] The principle informing this approach is that if blame can be attributed to an accused, the result is proximate and the causal link will be established. This means that if an accused has mens rea, one can conclude that he expected, or should have expected, the harm resulting from his unlawful conduct. He is blameworthy and causation will be established. (This is not to say that the presence of mens rea can create a causal link which is not already there. Causation in fact would have to be established.) In contrast to the pure policy approach, there is here at least some guidance for resolving future cases. If the accused had the necessary mens rea, and contributed causally to bringing about the actus reus, he should be held responsible. On this analysis, it is defensible to maintain that the person who recklessly supplied unlawful drugs to the deceased is responsible for the result.[53] The voluntary action of the victim in taking the drugs is also a cause, but does not prevent the supply of the drugs also being regarded by the criminal law as a cause (rather than a condition) of the actus reus. As noted in *MacAngus v HM Advocate; Kane v HM Advocate*, the approach in Scotland has been

"that the actions (including in some cases deliberate actions) of victims . . . do not necessarily break the chain of causation between the actings of the accused and the victim's death."[54]

---

[52] H. Gross, *A Theory of Criminal Justice* (Oxford: Oxford University press, 1979), pp.232–254.

[53] See *MacAngus v HM Advocate; Kane v HM Advocate* [2009] HCJAC 8; 2009 S.L.T. 137 at 150, para.42; contrast *R. v Kennedy (No.2)* [2007] UKHL 38; [2008] 1 A.C. 269.

[54] *MacAngus v HM Advocate; Kane v HM Advocate* [2009] HCJAC 8; 2009 S.L.T. 137. For critical discussion of this decision, see L. Farmer, "Practical, but nonetheless principled"? *MacAngus and Kane*" (2009) 13 *Edinburgh Law Review* 502.

CHAPTER 6

ATTEMPT

Introduction

The question to be addressed in this chapter can be stated quite simply: under **6–01** what circumstances does the criminal law impose responsibility for an endeavour to commit a crime? The key to understanding the law in this area is to appreciate that conduct prior to the successful completion of a criminal end can itself constitute a crime. Conduct which is criminalised at this preliminary stage is known as an "inchoate", or incomplete, crime. There are three principal inchoate crimes recognised in Scots law: *attempt; conspiracy;* and *incitement* (sometimes known as *instigation*). Conspiracy and incitement are discussed in the next Chapter. This Chapter is concerned solely with the law of attempt.

Attempted crimes fall into two common categories. The first is where there has **6–02** been an act designed to bring about a substantive crime, and which would have brought it about under normal circumstances. The expected chain of events is then interrupted by an unforeseen event. For example, a fire is raised in order to destroy a building, but is extinguished before it takes hold. A charge of attempted wilful fire-raising, with the building as its object, would be appropriate. The second type of attempted crime occurs where there has also been an act designed to bring about a substantive crime, but the expected result does not occur because of a misjudgment or mistake on the part of the perpetrator. Thus one could expect a charge of attempted murder in the typical examples where a weapon has misfired, or the bullet missed its target.

An attempt to commit any crime is criminal.[1] As the preceding examples **6–03** demonstrate, the basic notion of an attempted crime is easy to grasp. The difficulty is that the legal definition of attempt tends towards vagueness; different interpretations of the relevant principles are to be found in the authorities. It is also true to say that some of the concepts underlying the crime of attempt are somewhat elusive and even counter-intuitive; this is particularly true in relation to so-called "impossible" attempts.

Why attempts are penalised

The clearest rationale for punishing attempts is that summarised by Hart: "The **6–04** criminal had gone so far as to do his best to execute a wicked intention."[2] In particular, the individual who has attempted to commit a crime may well be equally as dangerous as the one who has succeeded in his criminal enterprise. The difference between the two attempts in terms of success or failure could

---

[1] Criminal Procedure (Scotland) Act 1995 s.294.
[2] H.L.A. Hart, *Punishment and Responsibility* (Oxford: Clarendon Press, 1968), p.128.

simply be attributable to chance or luck. A further argument is that the individual who attempts to commit a crime causes harm worthy of punishment through the creation of public anxiety.

6–05 There is also the issue of deterrence to consider. Hart makes the point that

> "the accused has manifested a dangerous disposition to do all he can to commit a crime, and the experience of punishment may check him in the future, since it may cause him to attach more weight to the law's threats."[3]

As far as more general deterrence is concerned, the same considerations which apply to a completed crime would appear to apply equally in the case of an attempt.

6–06 The criminalisation of attempts is also justifiable as a preventive measure. Without the recognition of inchoate crimes, the police would have no legal basis for intervening at a preliminary stage. After all, one fundamental aim of the criminal law must be to try to prevent would-be criminals from succeeding in their aims. This would become much more difficult if the criminal law was concerned only with completed crimes.

Disguised attempts

6–07 There are a number of substantive crimes which can be seen as "disguised" attempts. There exists a range of statutory offences which are targeted at preventing crimes, and which prohibit preparations to commit crimes. For example, the law restricts the carrying of weapons[4] and, in certain circumstances, equipment which could be of use in committing theft.[5] There are also common law crimes which serve a preventive purpose. Housebreaking with intent to steal[6] functions as an inchoate offence which penalises conduct in a similar way to the law of attempt, but at an even earlier stage in the criminal endeavour. An example should help to clarify the point: A breaks into a house in order to steal an item of property. He may not, however, have proceeded sufficiently far to be guilty of attempting to commit the intended crime (theft). As Lord Justice-General Normand observed in *Coventry v Douglas*:[7]

> "The mere presence of a person in a particular place may be only preparatory to the execution of the criminal intent, and not itself an overt criminal act."

The independent crime of housebreaking with intent to steal allows A to be apprehended at the time of gaining entry (or even attempted entry[8]). There is no need to wait on A beginning to perpetrate whatever crime he has in mind.

---

[3] Hart, *Punishment and Responsibility* (1968), p.129. See also W. Ullmann, "The Reasons for Punishing Attempted Crimes" (1939) 51 J.R. 353; R.A. Duff, *Criminal Attempts* (Oxford: Clarendon Press, 1996), Ch.5.

[4] See, e.g. the Carrying of Knives etc. (Scotland) Act 1993.

[5] Civic Government (Scotland) Act 1982 s.58 (applicable where the accused has two or more convictions for theft).

[6] See *Charles Macqueen and Alex Baillie* (1810) Hume, *Commentaries*, i, 102.

[7] *Coventry v Douglas*, 1944 J.C. 13 at 20. In *HM Advocate v Forbes*, 1994 S.L.T. 861, the Appeal Court left open the question of whether it constituted attempted assault and rape to enter premises, strip down and prowl around with intent to assault and rape.

[8] See *Burns v Allan*, 1987 S.C.C.R. 449; *Heywood v Reid*, 1996 S.L.T. 378. For an account of the elements of this crime, see below, para.10–35.

Assault itself is a crime which can encompass an incomplete result. As is **6–08** described in greater detail in Ch.9, although the attack on the complainer must be physical in character to constitute an assault, there need not be a physical result.[9] In *Stewart v Procurator Fiscal of Forfarshire*,[10] the accused was convicted of assault after he had aimed a blow at the complainer, but had missed; and in *Gilmour v McGlennan*,[11] it was held that to point a toy gun at someone could constitute assault. Thus the definition of assault appears to include within its definition an attempt. It might be thought that the charge of attempted assault is redundant, since it could involve libelling that an accused had attempted to attempt to attack the complainer. The charge of attempted assault does, however, sometimes occur in practice.[12]

MENS REA

Just as in relation to a completed crime, the two elements of mens rea and actus **6–09** reus are present in an attempted crime. As far as mens rea is concerned, the basic rule appears to be quite simple: the mens rea of an attempted crime is the same as that of the relevant substantive crime. Where the crime is one of intention, few problems are caused. For example, the requisite mens rea for the crime of attempted theft is the same as that for the substantive crime: the "essence" is "an intention to commit the crime of theft."[13]

RECKLESSNESS

The conceptual problems arise in relation to those crimes which can be **6–10** perpetrated recklessly. If the mens rea of an attempted crime is the same as that of the substantive crime, does this mean that one can attempt to commit a crime of recklessness? Does the law recognise the possibility of a reckless attempt? The difficulty raised by this question is whether it should be possible to "blunder" into an attempt.[14] In other jurisdictions,[15] and perhaps in earlier times in Scotland,[16] the answer to these two questions would have been in the negative. It is a commonly expressed view that there must be an intention to commit the crime of which an attempt is libelled.[17] That is, an essential element of an attempt is that

---

[9] See below, paras 9–05 to 9–12.

[10] *Stewart v Procurator Fiscal of Forfarshire* (1829) 2 S.J. 32.

[11] *Gilmour v McGlennan*, 1993 S.C.C.R. 837.

[12] See below, para.9–12. It also has distinguished academic support; see R.M. Perkins, "An Analysis of Assault and Attempts to Assault" (1962) 47 Minn. L. Rev. 71, 81.

[13] *Coventry v Douglas*, 1944 J.C. 13, per Lord Fleming at 19. See also *Johnstone v Lees*, 1995 S.L.T. 1174 (conviction for attempting to pervert the course of justice dependent upon intention).

[14] F. Sayre, "Criminal Attempts" (1928) 41 Harv. L. Rev. 821, 843; T. Arnold, "Criminal Attempts— The Rise and Fall of an Abstraction" (1930) 40 Yale L. J. 53, 68.

[15] See *Knight v The Queen* (1992) 175 C.L.R. 496 (Australia); *R. v Ancio* (1984) 6 D.L.R. (4th) 577 (Canada); Criminal Attempts Act 1981 s.1(1); and *R. v Whybrow* (1951) 35 Cr. App. R. 141 (England and Wales).

[16] See the references in Hume, *Commentaries*, i, 27–28, to "criminal purpose" and "criminal resolution".

[17] See R.M. Perkins, "Criminal Attempt and Related Problems" (1955) 2 U.C.L.A. L. Rev. 319, 340.

the result required by the definition of the substantive crime should have been intended. The very notion of an attempt appears to necessitate that the accused has "tried" to do something, and that there is an intended consequence. In murder, for example, this would be the death of the intended victim.

6–11   Scots law appears to take a rather different approach to the mens rea of an attempted crime. There is an objective focus upon what the accused actually did, rather than what he intended at the time. Particular regard must be paid to the decision in *Cawthorne v HM Advocate*.[18] This case determined that the mens rea for attempted murder is the same as that for murder[19]; the only difference being that in attempted murder the victim does not actually die. As Lord Brand explained in the course of his charge to jury in *HM Advocate v Blake*[20]:

> "'Attempt to murder' is the charge brought against a man who is alleged to have made an attack on another in circumstances in which, had his victim died as a result of his attack, the crime would have been murder."

Murder can be committed "unintentionally", in the sense that the accused need not foresee the death of the victim as a consequence of his conduct if he demonstrates wicked recklessness.[21] Following *Cawthorne,* one can say that wicked recklessness is sufficient mens rea for attempted murder; there need not be an actual intention to kill. An illustration of this approach to the mens rea of attempted murder is provided by Lord Keith's charge to the jury in *McGregor v HM Advocate*[22]:

> "If you go out and recklessly fire off a firearm or wave a knife or dagger about and kill somebody, that may be murder. The test of attempted murder is whether, if the actions of the accused had resulted in the death of one of the [victims] you would have said that was murder or not. If a man drives along with a policeman on his bonnet in such a way that the policeman falls off and is killed . . . —if you would have said that was murder, then you would be entitled to convict him [of attempted murder]."

6–12   The approach outlined above, which recognises that one can attempt to commit a crime of recklessness, is at variance with the ordinary concept of an attempt. It is an unnatural use of language to say that A, who is reckless as to the result of his assault upon B, and without intending to kill him, attempts to murder B.[23] The

---

[18] *Cawthorne v HM Advocate*, 1968 J.C. 32; applied in *HM Advocate v Kerr* [2011] HCJAC 17; 2011 S.L.T. 430 at 432, para.7 ("it is clear that the *mens rea* for the crime of murder and attempted murder is identical"). Alison, *Principles*, i, 163, appears to endorse this approach, but this is because wicked recklessness is there treated as equivalent to an intention to kill. There is no authoritative judicial decision clarifying to which crimes of recklessness, other than murder, the *Cawthorne* principle applies.

[19] Lord Justice-Clerk Ross described this principle as "well settled" in *Brady v HM Advocate*, 1986 J.C. 68 at 76. See also *Strachan v HM Advocate*, 1994 S.C.C.R. 341.

[20] *HM Advocate v Blake*, 1986 S.L.T. 661 at 662H.

[21] See, e.g. *Miller and Denovan v HM Advocate*, 1960, noted in *Parr v HM Advocate*, 1991 S.L.T. 208 at 211 (discussed above in para.3–32).

[22] *McGregor v HM Advocate* (1973) S.C.C.R. Supp. 54 at 56.

[23] Not that this alone can be dispositive of the issue; see, further, T.H. Jones, "Attempted Murder" (1992) S.L.T. (News) 341.

Cawthorne approach can, however, be seen as consistent with the prevailing objective approach to the establishment of criminal liability. In Scotland, the accused is to be sanctioned because he nearly committed a crime, that is, came close to perpetrating the actus reus. His blameworthy mental state is reflected in this fact.[24]

ACTUS REUS

POLICY ISSUES

The greater difficulties in the law of attempt relate to the actus reus. The primary **6–13** issue is that of determining the point at which it can be said that the accused's conduct has proceeded sufficiently far towards the commission of a completed crime, so that it can be classified as a criminal attempt. Where can the line be drawn between a criminal attempt and a non-criminal preparation? There are two fundamental policy concerns which weigh upon this issue. The first is that of facilitating the police in the tasks of crime prevention and law enforcement. The test adopted for establishing the actus reus must offer a reasonable chance for intervention before the criminal endeavour reaches its proposed end. One decision which appears to conflict with this requirement is *Guthrie v Friel*.[25] The Appeal Court held that an appellant who had been apprehended sitting in his car, with the seat belt fastened, having started the engine, and with the headlights turned on, could not be said to be attempting to drive. It was stated that the position might have been different had the handbrake been released.

Of equal significance, perhaps, should be a concern for civil liberties and the **6–14** rights of the individual. The criminal law should not seek to penalise conduct which is extremely preparatory to the commission of a crime. The law must avoid punishing an individual merely for having undesirable thoughts.[26] Given the inevitable tension between these two concerns, it is not surprising that Scots law does not provide a clear guide to the actus reus of attempted crimes. Although it is clear which is the prevailing test, no single approach to the question has received unequivocal support. The relevant authorities are inconsistent as to what actus reus is necessary before preparatory actions by an accused constitute an attempt to commit a crime. It is only on rare occasions that the courts have articulated explicitly a test or theory to identify when a criminal attempt occurs. Nevertheless, it is possible to identify three significant theories by inference from the facts of different cases and the observations of judges. The three theories or tests are (1) irrevocability, (2) last act and (3) perpetration. A further problem is that these tests have a tendency to overlap one another; nor have the courts always sought to clarify which approach is being adopted.

---

[24] The Scottish approach appears consistent with that of O.W. Holmes, *The Common Law* (Boston: Little Brown and Co, 1881), p.66: "It may be true that in the region of attempts . . . the law began with cases of actual intent, as those cases are the most obvious ones. But it cannot stop with them, unless it attaches more importance to the etymological meaning of the word *attempt* than to the general principles of punishment."

[25] *Guthrie v Friel*, 1993 S.L.T. 899.

[26] *Morton v Henderson*, 1956 J.C. 55, per Lord Justice-General Clyde at 57.

IRREVOCABILITY THEORY

6–15 There are authorities which appear to suggest that a criminal attempt cannot be committed at a stage before the final chain of events is irrecoverable by the actions of the accused. In *HM Advocate v Mackenzie*,[27] Lord Justice-Clerk Macdonald referred to the

> "well-established and most just rule of law, which does not allow of punishment for unfulfilled intents and preparations which have not culminated in an irrevocable act of commission or attempt."

In *HM Advocate v Tannahill and Neilson*,[28] Lord Wark stated that in order to constitute a criminal attempt there had to be, "some overt act, the consequences of which cannot be recalled by the accused." This approach to the actus reus was endorsed by Lord Justice-General Clyde in *Morton v Henderson*.[29] In neither of these latter two cases, however, was there evidence of anything more than a mere suggestion that a crime (fraud in both instances) might be perpetrated. The judicial opinions expressed on both occasions went beyond what was immediately necessary to dispose of the cases, and are inconsistent with the views expressed elsewhere. That said, Lord Justice-Clerk Ross appeared to accept the applicability of the irrevocability test in *McKenzie v HM Advocate*.[30]

6–16 What appears to lie behind this approach to criminal attempts is a feeling of disquiet about the very notion of criminalising behaviour prior to the commission of a crime. This general attitude is well summarised in the reported observations of the defence counsel in the case of *Samuel Tumbleson*[31]:

> "Attempts to commit crimes want that character of completeness, of finality, which would make it proper to prosecute them criminally. In many such cases it can hardly be said that the individual has proceeded beyond intention,— that he has done anything partaking, in strictness, of the character of an overt act; and it is of overt acts alone that the law can take cognizance."

One continues to find echoes of this language, even in modern decisions.[32]

LAST ACT THEORY

6–17 There are authorities which suggest that a criminal attempt occurs when an accused has done all that he believes is necessary to commit the proposed crime. In the case of *Janet Ramage*,[33] the accused had placed some poison in a teapot

---

[27] *HM Advocate v Mackenzie*, 1913 S.C.(J.) 107 at 111. In *Burns v Allan*, 1987 S.C.C.R. 449, this case was cited as authority for the perpetration test (see below, para.6–19). The judgments in *Mackenzie* do say that the accused must have moved beyond the stage of preparation, but this is in the context of his having performed an irrevocable act.

[28] *HM Advocate v Tannahill and Neilson*, 1943 J.C. 150 at 153.

[29] *Morton v Henderson*, 1956 J.C. 55.

[30] *McKenzie v HM Advocate*, 1988 S.L.T. 487.

[31] *Samuel v Tumbleson* (1863) 4 Irv. 426 at 428.

[32] See, e.g. *McKenzie v HM Advocate*, 1988 S.L.T. 487; *Guthrie v Friel*,1993 S.L.T. 899.

[33] *Janet Ramage*, Hume, *Commentaries*, i, 28.

from which the intended victim was expected to take a drink. A charge of attempted murder was held to be relevant. Similarly, it was emphasised in *Samuel Tumbleson*[34] that, in order to constitute attempted murder by poisoning, it was not necessary that the intended victim should actually take the poison. An application of what has been described as the "irrevocability" test could not support these conclusions. In *Janet Ramage*, for example, the consequences of the accused's act were not incapable of recall: she could have removed the teapot before the victim drank any of the tea. What the accused had performed was the *last act* required to bring about the murder.

There is little to commend either the "last act" or "irrevocability" theories of criminal attempts. The conduct of an accused will commonly provide an adequate foundation for an inference of mens rea at a stage prior to the reaching of an irrevocable, or the last, act. There is also the practical point that an application of either test would severely hamper the police in seeking to prevent crime. It would become well nigh impossible to effect an arrest during an attempt in order to prevent the commission of the proposed crime. **6–18**

PERPETRATION THEORY

It is for these reasons that a more flexible approach to the actus reus is generally thought to be preferable. An application of the "perpetration" theory simply involves asking whether or not the accused has committed an act which is sufficiently proximate to the commission of the completed crime. That is, an attempt involves perpetration rather than preparation. This is the prevailing approach to the actus reus of attempts in Scots law, "before a charge of attempting to do something can be established, the individual must have passed from mere preparation to perpetration."[35] The leading authority for this flexible approach to the actus reus of criminal attempts is *HM Advocate v Camerons*,[36] where Lord Justice-General Dunedin charged the jury that the fundamental issue was "to discover where preparation ends and where perpetration begins ... [I]t is a question of degree, and ... it is a jury question." **6–19**

In this case the accused were convicted of attempting to defraud an insurance company. The evidence produced at the trial was that the accused had staged a fake robbery, but that no formal insurance claim had been submitted. Clearly, therefore, the accused had not performed the last act necessary for the commission of the fraud. It would also have been possible for the accused to change their minds and to decide to proceed no further with the proposed fraudulent scheme. This case serves to illustrate the weaknesses of both the last act and irrevocability tests. Their application to the facts in this case could not have led to a conviction. **6–20**

---

[34] *Samuel Tumbleson* (1863) 4 Irv. 426.
[35] *Guthrie v Friel*, 1993 S.L.T. 899, per Lord Justice-Clerk Ross at 901C. The judicial support is distinguished: *HM Advocate v Innes* (1915) 7 Adam 596, per Lord Justice-General Strathclyde at 601; *Docherty v Brown*, 1996 J.C. 48, per Lord Justice-General Hope at 50, and Lord Justice-Clerk Ross at 57 and 60.
[36] *HM Advocate v Camerons* (1911) 6 Adam 456 at 485. The Lord Justice-General was adopting this language from Hume, *Commentaries*, i, 29 (although Hume, *Commentaries*, i, 27, supports the last act doctrine).

6–21   Examples of conduct which have been held to be more than merely preparatory include:

1. Joining a queue at a turnstile: statutory offence of attempting to enter a football ground while drunk[37];

2. Menacing a police officer with a machete, without striking him, at the same time as threatening to kill him: attempted murder[38];

3. Disconnecting an external burglar alarm: attempted house-breaking with intent to steal[39];

4. Inserting a hand into a till: attempted theft[40];

5. Throwing a spade through the window of a post office: attempted robbery.[41]

6–22   One possible criticism of the perpetration theory is its vagueness. Not all of the examples listed above appear equally proximate to the perpetration of the substantive crime in question. The great difficulty is that of identifying the point at which an accused has moved from mere preparation towards the commission of a crime.[42] Is it the case that, as one trial judge observed,[43] "the answer to that question can only be intuitive and a matter of impression and degree"? It would be difficult for a workable law of criminal attempts to be very precise. Hume recognised that there is

> "a great variety of ambiguous cases, with respect to which it is very difficult to say where preparation ends and perpetration begins."[44]

In *Coventry v Douglas,*[45] Lord Justice-General Clyde likewise accepted that, "the line of demarcation between preparation and perpetration cannot be defined in any general proposition".

6–23   The perpetration theory approach does, nevertheless, possess the inestimable advantages of practicality and workability. Nor should it be thought that Scots law is alone in applying a flexible approach in determining what constitutes a criminal attempt. English law defines the actus reus of an attempt as "an act which is more than merely preparatory to the commission of the offence."[46] Other jurisdictions appear to apply equally vague tests.

---

[37] *Barrett v Allan*, 1986 S.C.C.R. 479 (the statutory offence is now contained in the Criminal Law (Consolidation) (Scotland) Act 1995 s.20(7)(b)).

[38] *Strachan v HM Advocate*, 1994 S.C.C.R. 341.

[39] *Burns v Allan*, 1987 S.C.C.R. 449. See also *Heywood v Reid*, 1996 S.L.T. 378: smashing a security light sufficiently proximate to constitute attempted house-breaking with intent to steal.

[40] *Coventry v Douglas*, 1944 J.C. 13.

[41] *Andrew v HM Advocate*, 2000 S.L.T. 402.

[42] A court in the United States referred to it as "a murky 'twilight zone' ": *United States v Williamson*, 42 M.J. 613 (1995) at 617, fn.2.

[43] *Barrett v Allan*, 1986 S.C.C.R. 479, per Sheriff Hyslop at 480.

[44] Hume, *Commentaries*, i, 29.

[45] *Coventry v Douglas*, 1944 J.C. 13 at 20. See also Lord Walker, "The Growth of the Criminal Law" (1958) J.R. 230, 237: "it is needless to say the point when preparation ends and perpetration begins raises a problem of some nicety."

[46] Criminal Attempts Act 1981 s.1(1). It should not be thought that the application of this test in English law has been without difficulty. For discussion, see A.P. Simester, J.R. Spencer, G.R. Sullivan and G.J. Virgo, *Simester and Sullivan's Criminal Law: Theory and Doctrine,* 4th edn (Oxford: Hart, 2010), pp.329–332.

IMPOSSIBILITY

It would be fair to suggest that no aspect of the criminal law has generated **6–24** more confusion than the law relating to impossible attempts. Throughout the common law world much academic and judicial energy has been expended in efforts to determine in what circumstances an accused can be convicted for an impossible attempt: that is, for an attempt to commit a crime which cannot for some reason succeed. The kind of situation at issue is where the accused has the requisite mens rea for the proposed crime and has moved from the stage of preparation to that of perpetration. The only defensive avenue open to him is that of the impossibility of perpetrating the intended crime. The classic question in this context is whether it could constitute attempted murder to shoot at a corpse, thinking that it was a live body.[47] More likely examples would be where the pocket which the accused intends to pick is empty, or where goods which the accused intends to reset are not in fact stolen. In *Docherty v Brown*,[48] Lord Justice-Clerk Ross suggested that the writing on this topic was out of proportion to its practical significance. It is not proposed to add greatly to that body of literature here.

In any event, the position in Scots law is clear. Following the full-bench **6–25** decision in *Docherty v Brown*,[49] it is settled as a general principle that the impossibility of completing the intended result does not act as a general defence VITAL to a charge of an attempted crime. It was recognised there that it is a basic characteristic of any attempted crime that the result has not been brought about. The reason for this lack of success would not appear to possess any legal significance. In *Docherty v Brown,* the accused had been charged with attempting to possess drugs with intention to supply, contrary to the Misuse of Drugs Act 1971.[50] The appellant had taken possession of some tablets in the mistaken belief that they contained a controlled drug, when they did not in fact do so. It was held that in such circumstances an attempt charge was relevant. All five judges were satisfied on this point. Lord Justice-Clerk Ross stated:

> "The fact that something is physically impossible will prevent an accused from being convicted of the complete crime, but it does not prevent him being relevantly charged with attempt to commit that crime provided that he has the necessary *mens rea,* and does some positive step towards executing his purpose."[51]

An older authority is *Lamont v Strathern.*[52] In this case, the High Court held it was attempted theft where the accused had placed his hand in an empty pocket with the intent to steal. Lord Sands stated that he was unimpressed

---

[47] This situation arose on the facts of *Collins v HM Advocate*, 1991 S.C.C.R. 898, but did not fall to be determined by the court.

[48] *Docherty v Brown*, 1996 J.C. 48 at 50.

[49] *Docherty v Brown*, 1996 J.C. 48. For analysis of this decision, see D. Sheldon, "Impossible Attempts and Other Oxymorons: *Docherty v Brown*" (1997) 1 Edin. L.R. 250.

[50] Misuse of Drugs Act 1971 ss.5(3) and 19.

[51] *Docherty v Brown*, 1996 J.C. 48 at 57.

[52] *Lamont v Strathern*, 1933 J.C. 33. *Lamont v Strathern*, 1933 J.C. 33.

"by the metaphysical argument that, whereas one cannot take what is not there, therefore one cannot attempt to take what is not there."[53]

6–26 In *Docherty v Brown,*[54] the Appeal Court disapproved two earlier cases which had suggested that where there was an attempt to procure a criminal abortion, but the prosecution was unable to prove that the woman was pregnant, no criminal liability attached to the attempt. The principal authority for this rule was *HM Advocate v Anderson,*[55] a decision which was followed in *HM Advocate v Semple.*[56] This rule had long appeared to be anomalous and inconsistent with the decision in *Lamont v Strathern.*[57] There had been attempts to reconcile the two, most recently in *Maxwell v HM Advocate,*[58] but these had not been convincing. It is unrealistic to try and differentiate a case of attempted abortion from one of attempted theft. In *Lamont v Strathern,* Lord Sands distinguished the rule in *Anderson* by stating that in the case of an attempted abortion "a pregnant woman is the condition of the offence", whereas, in the case of an attempted theft from the complainer's pocket, "a pocket which may contain something of value is the only condition."[59] This attempted distinction was ingenious, but unconvincing. The presence in the pocket of property to steal could equally be regarded as a condition of an attempted theft, something which the law does not require.[60]

6–27 The feature which is common to all these cases is that, had the facts been as the accused believed them to be, he would have perpetrated the intended crime. The conduct falls squarely within attempted crime. The accused had gone well beyond the stage of preparation. The requisite inference of mens rea could be drawn. The accused failed to perpetrate a crime because of a circumstance which was unknown to him and outwith his control. There is no convincing reason why there should be a defence available to the accused simply because he did not utilise the proper means to accomplish the crime, or because he was for some reason unable to commit the crime on the instant occasion. The lack of success is not related in any way to his intention to perpetrate the crime. The apparent "impossibility" of the result is irrelevant.[61]

6–28 Nevertheless, there will no doubt continue to be disquiet about attributing criminal liability to an accused who has attempted to do the impossible. There are two principal concerns. The first is that the conduct in impossible attempts cannot always be said to demonstrate criminality as serious as that which a prosecution for an attempted crime might suggest. For example, A is under the misapprehension that B has a weak heart and that, if subjected to a violent shock, will die. He is desirous of causing B's death. To this end, he suddenly jumps out in front of B, shouting loudly. When viewed objectively, this incident could not be described as an attempt to murder B. In subjective terms, of course, A has the mens rea of murder and he has clearly tried at least to begin to perpetrate the intended crime.

---

[53] *Lamont v Strathern*, 1933 J.C. 33 at 36.
[54] *Docherty v Brown*, 1996 J.C. 48.
[55] *HM Advocate v Anderson*, 1928 J.C. 1.
[56] *HM Advocate v Semple*, 1937 J.C. 41.
[57] *Lamont v Strathern*, 1933 J.C. 33.
[58] *Maxwell v HM Advocate*, 1980 J.C. 40.
[59] *Lamont v Strathern*, 1933 J.C. 33 at 38.
[60] See *Docherty v Brown*, 1996 J.C. 48, per Lord Sutherland at 63.
[61] *Docherty v Brown*, 1996 J.C. 48, per Lord Justice-Clerk Ross at 60.

The reason why the accused failed to commit the intended murder was due to a circumstance for which he was not responsible (that is, the fact that B has a strong constitution). There is, however, an alternative interpretation: A's criminal liability should relate to what he actually did. Adopting this perspective, his conduct would appear to constitute a simple assault or a breach of the peace. There was no outward manifestation of a criminal intention to kill B. A could be punished for attempted murder only on the basis of his thoughts.

The second concern is that many impossible attempts involve conduct which **6–29** appears innocuous when viewed objectively. In a case of attempted reset, for example, the retention of property which has not been stolen is objectively innocent. This may increase the risk of convicting those who are innocent. Where the conduct of an accused is objectively innocent, it is much more difficult to infer the presence of the necessary mens rea. The prosecution case will be based primarily on evidence of the accused's internal thought processes and subjective purpose. In endeavouring to prove the accused's guilt, the prosecution will be unusually dependent upon whether there has been a confession.[62] There may also be reliance upon hearsay testimony as to what the defendant said about his purpose to others, and upon other circumstantial evidence. This could mean that there would be a heightened danger of convicting an innocent person, or of attributing too much criminal liability to an accused. As in the scenario described in the previous paragraph, this could lead to a conviction for attempting a serious offence (murder), when a conviction for a completed less serious offence (assault or breach of the peace) might be more appropriate.

Inherent Impossibility

Accepting that impossibility should not ordinarily afford a defence, there remains **6–30** to be considered the accused who fails to commit the intended crime because he has chosen an "inherently" impossible or unreasonable method of attempting the crime. The example which is generally quoted is that of an attempt to murder by voodoo or witchcraft. Should the accused in such a case be held to be guilty of attempted murder, if it is proved that he believed that the invocation of a spell could kill? Should a case of this kind be treated differently from that where the accused tried to shoot the victim with an empty revolver? The difficulty is in being able to say that the accused is sufficiently dangerous to merit a conviction for attempted murder. In *Docherty v Brown*[63] Lord Justice-General Hope recognised that

> "where on the true facts the notion that a crime could have been committed was fanciful . . . no good purpose would be served in prosecuting a person who acted in this way, because his actings were so wholly misconceived as to cause no risk of harm to anyone."

---

[62] Compare the facts of *Anderton v Ryan* [1985] A.C. 560 (but note that the account of English law given there was overruled in *R. v Shivpuri* [1987] 1 A.C. 1).

[63] *Dochetry v Brown*, 1996 J. C. 48 at 51.

ABSOLUTE IMPOSSIBILITY

6–31 An issue of absolute impossibility would arise in a case where the crime which the accused thinks he is perpetrating is not recognised as such by the criminal law. The accused may think it a crime to hunt rabbits, but the criminal law prohibits neither the conduct of the accused nor the result which he intends to bring about. The accused cannot be prosecuted because he believed his conduct to be criminal. Regardless of his intention, an accused cannot be convicted of attempting to commit a non-existent crime. This doctrine of absolute impossibility can be seen as one aspect of the principle of prospectivity (see below, para.14–09). The conduct in question is not a crime either at common law or under statute; it cannot be criminalised retrospectively as a result of the accused's blameworthy mental state. If the intention of the accused does not correlate to a recognised crime, his desire to do something criminal is not sufficient for the imposition of criminal liability. It is not for the accused to extend the boundaries of criminal liability in this manner.

CHAPTER 7

COMPLICITY AND CONSPIRACY

Introduction

This Chapter is concerned with criminal acts that involve more than one indi- **7–01**
vidual. It describes both the characteristics of multi-party criminal conduct and
"the doctrine of law which ascribes to associates in crime in certain cases responsibility for the criminal acts of their associate."[1] There is an account of how the
accused who associates himself with a criminal actor can be held liable, even
though he does not personally bring about (that is to say, *cause)* the actus reus.
The Scottish courts traditionally have adopted a rather robust attitude towards the
collectivisation of criminal responsibility.[2]

In the ensuing discussion three types of criminal liability are described. First, **7–02**
the law of complicity penalises all those who participate in the commission of a
crime. Liability of this character is known in Scots law as *art and part* guilt.
Secondly, there is the crime of *conspiracy,* which penalises all those who merely
agree to commit a crime. Conspiracy is a crime in its own right, but can also form
the basis of art and part guilt. That is, where the conspiracy is put into effect and
the crime committed, liability for complicity can be founded on the accused's
conspiratorial relationship with others. Thirdly, there is the crime of *incitement*
(sometimes known as *instigation*), which is committed where the accused solicits
another to perpetrate a crime.

ART AND PART GUILT

The basic principle

Art and part guilt, sometimes described as "acting in concert", has long formed **7–03**
part of the common law. The fundamental principle is that where two or more
people engage together in committing a crime, each actor is equally guilty of the
whole crime irrespective of the particular role played by each individual. The law
recognises that, to be found guilty of a crime, the accused need not have participated in every act necessary to constitute that crime. The example that is commonly
given by way of illustration is that the man who keeps watch during a robbery by
standing at the door of a bank is as guilty of the crime of robbery as the man who
actually takes the money from the safe.

---

[1] *Docherty v HM Advocate*, 1945 J.C. 89, per Lord Moncrieff at 94.
[2] See *McKinnon v HM Advocate (No.2)*, 2003 S.L.T. 281; *Vogan v HM Advocate*, 2003 S.C.C.R. 564;
Cameron v HM Advocate [2008] HCJAC 10; 2008 S.C.C.R. 669; *Johnston v HM Advocate* [2009]
HCJAC 38; 2009 J.C. 227.

naturally, there are certain restrictions to the broad principle of art and part guilt. More is required than proof that two or more people were involved.[3] The law does not recognise guilt by association.[4] The accused must have been aware of what the others involved in the criminal enterprise were doing. Further, in that knowledge, he must have assisted the others to some extent. That is, he must have participated in some way in the acts involved. Both of these requirements are described in this chapter.

PARTIES TO CRIME

7–05 There is not, in Scots law, a separate offence of "aiding and abetting" someone in the commission of a crime. The general rule is that no distinction is drawn between the different parties involved on the basis of their degree of involvement. This means that anyone who involves himself in even a minor way in a criminal enterprise may be unsure when he is criminally liable and when he is not. This uncertainty is the price to be paid for his immoral actions.[5] It can, nevertheless, sometimes be helpful to visualise a number of different roles where several individuals participate in the commission of a crime: (1) the *instigator,* who intends that the crime be committed and persuades someone else to do so; (2) the *aider,* who assists in the commission of the crime; and (3) the *principal,* who is the "actual" perpetrator of the crime.

DIRECT AND DERIVATIVE LIABILITY

7–06 In art and part guilt these different degrees of participation merge into joint liability for the commission of the crime, but it is only the principal who is directly liable; it is only he who is guilty of the whole crime in his own right. The art and part guilt of the instigator and the aider must derive from the commission of the crime (and be dependent upon it), since they only participate in the circumstances surrounding the criminal enterprise. In terms of the example above, one can say that the lookout derives his criminal liability from the commission of the robbery. He is guilty art and part because he has assisted in the commission of the crime, not because he directly stole anything from the bank.

7–07 It is important to appreciate that art and part guilt does not impose criminal liability for the actions of another simply because of a relationship between the parties. As will be more fully described in succeeding paragraphs, there must be some behaviour on the part of the instigator or aider designed to persuade or assist before the law imposes liability on him for the actions of the actual offender. What this notion of derivative liability does signify is that the art and part guilt of the instigator or aider (but not that of a joint principal) is dependent upon the crime having been perpetrated.[6] If the crime is not committed, or if the accused cannot properly be said to have participated in its commission, the question of art and

---

[3] See *Hobbins v HM Advocate*, 1997 S.L.T. 428, per Lord Justice-General Hope at 431B–C; *Rooney v HM Advocate* [2007] HCJAC 1; 2007 S.C.C.R. 49.

[4] See *Khalid v HM Advocate*, 1990 J.C. 37.

[5] L. Katz, *Bad Acts and Guilty Minds* (Chicago: University of Chicago Press, 1987), p.260.

[6] See, further, S. Kadish, "Complicity, Cause and Blame: A Study in the Interpretation of Doctrine" (1985) 73 Cal. Law Rev. 323, 337.

part guilt does not arise, although that of conspiracy or incitement may do. Art and part guilt is not a form of inchoate liability.

COMMON PURPOSE

The starting place for any discussion of the concept of art and part guilt must be to **7–08** consider how an individual who is not directly engaged in the conduct that constitutes the actus reus of the crime can be held liable for the actions of others. The criminal law generally recognises only personal liability: the derivative liability inherent in art and part guilt appears to be inconsistent with this fundamental principle. An individual may become art and part guilty of the crime as the result of personal conduct, but once he is subsumed into the legal category of art and part guilt his criminal liability becomes dependent upon the actions of another person. The justification for this type of derivative liability is that the person involved art and part intends to assist, or participate in, the commission of the crime. In the terminology of art and part guilt, there must be a "common purpose". The nature and scope of this common criminal purpose is discerned on an objective basis. It is not confined to what was in the actual knowledge or appreciation of an accused. The question to be answered is what was foreseeable as likely to happen and what was or was not obvious.[7] That said, a common purpose cannot be established by evidence that the accused "*may* have known what the other . . . *might* have been doing".[8] If the common purpose or plan cannot be established, then the principle of art and part guilt cannot be invoked. Each accused would have to be judged on the basis of his own actions, and not those of his co-accused or of anyone else.

If there is a common purpose, the particular accused, by providing voluntary **7–09** and intentional or reckless assistance, identifies himself with the conduct of the co-accused whom he has assisted (and who may be the "actual" perpetrator of the actus reus). He thereby becomes art and part guilty of the crime. The criminal actions of the co-accused can then be imputed to him. The mens rea required for the crime in question will be inferred upon proof of the intentional or reckless assistance in the commission of the crime. It would, of course, be open to an accused to rebut this inference by pointing to evidence suggestive of a reasonable doubt. Art and part guilt is not based on innocent assistance.

DEGREES OF INVOLVEMENT

Art and part guilt covers a wide range of degrees of involvement in the commis- **7–10** sion of crimes. It can extend from the offering of relatively minor assistance or advice, to full participation in the actus reus of the crime. The criminal law regards all conduct within these extremes as constituting art and part guilt. In terms of the example outlined above (see above, para.7–03), art and part guilt would include the individual who, with knowledge of the plan, supplied the robber with some piece of information or equipment which was utilised to facilitate entry to the

---

[7] *Cameron v HM Advocate* [2008] HCJAC 10; 2008 S.C.C.R. 669. In *Docherty v HM Advocate*, 1945 J.C. 89 at 96, Lord Moncrieff used the phrase "reasonable expectation"; see also *Hobbins v HM Advocate*, 1997 S.L.T. 428, per Lord Justice-General Hope at 431B. The test is thus an objective one; see *McKinnon v HM Advocate (No.2)*, 2003 S.L.T. 281 at 286F.

[8] Disapproving Sheriff's charge: *Khalid v HM Advocate*, 1990 J.C. 37, per Lord Justice-General Hope at 39.

bank. This would still be the case even if the counsellor or supplier were nowhere near the bank at the time of the robbery. Indeed, his physical presence or absence is irrelevant to the question of art and part guilt. The person who supplies a necessary piece of equipment may in fact be of more assistance to the actual perpetrator of the crime than the lookout.

7–11   It is possible, of course, to draw a distinction between the individual who provides some minor assistance or counsel and the individual who fully participates in the commission of the crime itself. Indeed, the criminal law would tend to see the latter as simply a joint criminal enterprise, with more than one primary or principal offender, rather than as an example of art and part guilt. In terms of the bank robbery example: if two or more people were involved in entering and stealing from the safe in the bank, it would not be strictly necessary to analyse the situation in terms of art and part guilt. Both can be regarded as joint principal offenders. Nevertheless, it is clear that the principle of art and part guilt extends to this situation just as much as when there has been something less than full participation in the crime by an aider or instigator. In practice, however, the criminal law would draw a distinction between these two situations—if only in terms of sentencing.

Assistance and participation

7–12   It bears repeating that, before art and part guilt can be established, the prosecution have to prove that the accused assisted the principal offender to commit the crime. Once assistance has been established, however, the precise extent of it is not really significant. Depending upon the precise facts at issue, almost any type of assistance can suffice. This requirement of assistance is generally described as one of participation. This does not mean, of course, that the accused has to have participated in the perpetration of the actus reus of the crime before art and part guilt can be attributed to him. Rather, what is meant is participation in the criminal enterprise which results in the commission of the crime.

7–13   Further, it is not necessary for the prosecution to prove that the crime would not have been committed without the accused's participation. In art and part guilt there is no "but for" requirement: an accused will still be regarded as guilty art and part even if his participation was causally unnecessary to the commission of the crime. That is, it is no defence for the lookout and the supplier of the getaway vehicle to state that the principal offender would have perpetrated the bank robbery regardless of their assistance. This absence of a causation requirement is reflected in the fact that any degree of assistance or participation suffices.

Psychological assistance

7–14   The requisite assistance or participation required to establish art and part guilt could come in the form of psychological influence. This would occur when the accused has counselled or instigated the commission of the crime. The legal terminology for this state of affairs is "antecedent (or prior) concert". If the accused cannot be proven to have actually participated in the actus reus of the crime, he can only be guilty art and part if there is evidence of prior concert.[9]

---

[9] *Spiers v HM Advocate*, 1980 J.C. 36. See *Little v HM Advocate*, 1983 J.C. 16, for an example of instigation as the basis for art and part guilt.

In a case where antecedent concert is libelled, it is necessary for the prosecution **7–15** to establish that the commission of the crime was a likely result of the psychological assistance rendered by the accused. The instigation would have to be such as to induce the criminal conduct. Advice of a very general character would not be sufficient to establish guilt.[10] There would have to be a connection between the instigation and a specific crime. *HM Advocate v Johnstone and Stewart*[11] illustrates this requirement. The alleged crime here was that of being art and part guilty in an illegal abortion. The first accused had given the name of an abortionist (the second accused) to another woman. The accused had no connection with the abortionist, whom she knew only by name. Because of this tenuous link, she was acquitted. Lord Moncrieff charged the jury that the mere giving of a name in these circumstances could not constitute participation in the subsequent crime. In order to establish antecedent concert there would have had to be some communication between the two accused.

Physical assistance

Physical assistance can take a variety of forms. For example, it could entail **7–16** supplying a weapon to be utilised during a bank robbery. As such, it would constitute antecedent concert. Alternatively, art and part guilt could involve participating more directly in the crime by acting as the lookout or by driving the getaway vehicle.

Prior agreement

Art and part guilt can most easily be proved where there is actual participation **7–17** in the crime itself. In many such cases there will have been a prior agreement to participate in the commission of the crime. A straightforward example is provided by the facts in the case of *HM Advocate v Fraser and Rollins*.[12] In accordance with a pre-arranged plan, a woman lured the victim to a park where two men were waiting to rob him. The victim was assaulted and died of his injuries. All three were equally liable for the man's death and equally guilty of murder.

Spontaneous assistance

The concert necessary to art and part guilt can also arise from a spontaneous **7–18** coming together at the time of the offence. The traditional approach can be seen in the case of *HM Advocate v Gallacher*.[13] This case arose out of a feud between the members of a travelling circus and some of the inhabitants of Hamilton. As is often the case the precise facts are not too clear, but it appears that one of the local men started a fight with the deceased victim, who had been mistaken for one of the circus staff. A number of other men joined in and stood around the victim who was kicked to death. Three members of the crowd were convicted of murder.

---

[10] Hume, *Commentaries*, i, 278–279.
[11] *HM Advocate v Johnstone*, 1926 J.C. 89.
[12] *HM Advocate v Fraser and Rollins*, 1920 J.C. 60.
[13] *HM Advocate v Gallacher*, 1951 J.C. 38, unreported on this point; discussed by Gordon, *Criminal Law*, 3rd edn (2000/2001), para.5–55. The more common situation would be that where the murderous scope of spontaneous concert is inferred from the nature of the weapons used: *Donnelly v HM Advocate* [2007] HCJAC 59; 2007 S.C.C.R. 577 (including, in that case, a knife, a baseball bat and a spring cosh).

There was no evidence of antecedent concert. The conviction was based on the fact that they "were in a kicking crowd animated by a common purpose, joining in the attack, assisting and encouraging". It is important to recognise, however, that the accused who joins in an assault which has already commenced does not in any way become responsible by adoption for what has gone on before his intervention.[14] Accession after the fact is not a doctrine which is recognised in Scots law.[15] Equally, it is possible for there to be an initial common purpose (perhaps to assault the victim), which changes (perhaps to a murderous one).[16] In order to establish art and part guilt, it would have to be proved that the accused was still a participant at this later stage. Even in the circumstances of a group assault, the modern tendency is to recognise the desirability of discriminating among the accused by reference to the degree of participation and mens rea.[17] The prosecution has to prove that an accused was a participant rather than a bystander.

Participation by omission?

7–19   The first principle to note is that, "mere presence at the scene of a crime is insufficient of itself to constitute art and part guilt."[18] Evidence of active encouragement or assistance is required.[19] In *HM Advocate v Kerr*[20] the three accused were charged with assault with intent to ravish. One of the accused did not actually participate in the attack, but had stood nearby watching. He did not speak to either his co-accused or to the complainer during the attack. His conduct was held not to attract art and part guilt. In such a case, however, the outcome would be different if there was sufficient evidence that the accused had been present as part of a common plan and in order to assist the actual perpetrator(s).[21]

7–20   The corollary of this principle is that neither does failure to prevent the commission of a crime impose art and part guilt. The fact that this makes the commission of the crime easier would appear to be irrelevant. However, if it could be established that the reason for the "omission" was a desire to assist or encourage the commission of the crime, there would not then appear to be any barrier to art and part guilt. There would then be the necessary common purpose. Similarly, if there is a legal duty to intervene, art and part guilt can arise out of a failure to act. In *Bonar and Hogg v McLeod*[22] a senior police officer was held to be guilty art and part in an assault on a prisoner by a junior officer which he had done nothing to

---

[14] *McLaughlan v HM Advocate*, 1991 S.L.T. 660; *Kabalu v HM Advocate (No.1)*, 1999 S.C.C.R. 348.

[15] Hume, *Commentaries*, i, 281; *Collins v HM Advocate*, 1991 S.C.C.R. 898, per Lord Allanbridge at 903E (although noting that, "a jury in Scotland can consider anything which an accused does after the victim dies to see if such evidence assists them as a jury to determine whether or not that accused was acting in previous concert with the killer or killers as the time of the death"). See also *Martin v Hamilton*, 1989 J.C. 101.

[16] See *Mowat v HM Advocate*, 1999 S.C.C.R. 688.

[17] The same approach has been applied to the issue of an individual's liability for specific crimes alleged to have been committed by a mob; see *Coleman v HM Advocate*, 1999 S.L.T. 1261. The crime of mobbing is discussed in Ch.12.

[18] *Quinn v HM Advocate*, 1990 S.C.C.R. 254, per Lord Justice-Clerk Ross at 260G. See also *Lawler v Neizer*, 1993 S.C.C.R. 299; *Mowat v HM Advocate*, 1999 S.C.C.R. 688.

[19] *Jamieson v Guild*, 1989 S.C.C.R. 583.

[20] *HM Advocate v Kerr* (1871) 2 Coup. 334; see also *Mowat v HM Advocate*, 1999 S.L.T. 688.

[21] *Stillie v HM Advocate*, 1992 S.L.T. 279. See also *White v MacPhail*, 1990 S.C.C.R. 578.

[22] *Bonar and Hogg v McLeod*, 1983 S.C.C.R. 161.

prevent and from which he had failed to disassociate himself. The position of the senior officer was stated to have been that of an official standing by and allowing a breach of the law.

LIABILITY FOR THE OUTCOME

The essence of art and part guilt is that the accused either execute a common plan, **7–21** or demonstrate a spontaneous common purpose. It is necessary to establish the presence of concert, either prior to the commission of the crime, or through a coming together at the time of the actus reus. If the prosecution cannot prove concert, then each individual will be liable only to the extent that his own actions can be proved to the satisfaction of the court.[23] This may even result in the acquittal of both. As Lord Justice-General Emslie observed in *Morton v HM Advocate*[24]:

> "It is undoubtedly true that where two people are charged with a crime and there is no concert and there is no evidence as to which of the two committed the critical act then neither can be convicted."

HM Advocate v Welsh and McLachlan[25] provides an example. The two accused were alleged to have broken into a house where one of them (it was not known which) had killed the owner. There was no evidence of a common plan between the accused to use violence, and the violence was both sudden and unexpected. Lord Young charged the jury that each accused could only be held culpable for his own actions. Since it was not known who had killed the victim, both accused were acquitted of homicide.

The basic problem facing the prosecution in a case such as *Welsh and McLachlan* **7–22** is an evidential one. There are difficulties when the circumstances are suggestive of death as the result of a single blow.[26] Can it be proved that the accused was at least complicit in the death, rather than a bystander? The result in *Welsh and McLachlan* would have been very different had the prosecution been able to prove a common purpose or plan. In that case one could then apply the basic doctrine of art and part guilt that all the accused are regarded as equally liable for the outcome of the criminal conduct. The particular outcome does not have to be intended by the accused before he can be found guilty art and part. Rather, he will be held responsible for any *foreseeable* consequence. For example, if during the course of an armed robbery of a bank one accused shot and killed an assistant for refusing to hand over any money, on a strict application of art and part guilt the co-accused would be equally guilty of murder. Although the specific killing may not have been planned, it is a foreseeable consequence of an armed robbery. This rule can operate harshly on occasion. The accused can still be convicted as guilty art and part even though he lacks the mens rea of the specific crime of murder. This would particularly be the case if he had played only a small part in the criminal enterprise.

---

[23] *Humphries v HM Advocate*, 1994 S.C.C.R. 205.
[24] *Morton v HM Advocate*, 1986 S.L.T. 622 at 623C. See also *Johnston v HM Advocate* [2009] HCJAC 38; 2009 J.C. 227 at 245, para.50.
[25] *HM Advocate v Welsh and McLachlan* (1897) 5 S.L.T. 137. See also *HM Advocate v Robertson* (1896) 2 Adam 92; *Alexander v Adair*, 1938 J.C. 28; *Docherty v HM Advocate*, 1945 J.C. 89.
[26] *Docherty v HM Advocate*, 1945 J.C. 89, per Lord Carmont at 101.

Distinguishing between co-accused

7–23   Perhaps it is in order to alleviate the harshness of the doctrine that the courts are sometimes prepared to distinguish between co-accused in apportioning culpability. In fact, it is conceivable that the minor participant in the bank robbery scenario would be convicted of culpable homicide and the actual killer of murder. Both are guilty of homicide, but their culpability could be assessed separately by reference to their respective *mentes reae* at the time of the offence. *Melvin v HM Advocate*[27] provides authority for this proposition. The two accused had been charged with robbery and murder, but there was no evidence of antecedent concert. One accused was convicted of murder and the other of culpable homicide. It was held that it was legitimate to assess the degree of recklessness displayed by each of the accused in this way. In *Malone v HM Advocate*[28] this issue arose in the context of a fatal assault committed jointly by the two accused. It was stressed that only striking differences in the conduct of each assailant could justify convicting one accused of culpable homicide and the other of murder.[29] It is thus not necessary in every case where there are two or more accused of murder art and part to charge the jury that it is possible to find one accused guilty of murder and another guilty of culpable homicide.[30]

Foreseeability and the common purpose

7–24   An accused will not be held responsible for any conduct on the part of a co-accused which goes unforeseeably outwith the common plan or purpose. In *Welsh and McLachlan*[31] Lord Young made the point that an unexpected attack need not be foreseeable to anyone other than the actual assailant. Thus, if the reason for the shooting in the bank robbery example had been that the assistant was having an affair with the killer's wife, the homicide would then be unrelated to the planned crime and there would be no art and part guilt for the death.

7–25   This issue, as to whether the use of a weapon by a co-accused was foreseeable, is not uncommon in cases of alleged art and part guilt in murder.[32] Lord Justice-Clerk Wheatley identified the essential question in *Walker and Raiker v HM Advocate*[33]: did the accused know, or should he have known, that use of a weapon

---

[27] *Melvin v HM Advocate*, 1984 S.L.T. 365; distinguished in *McKinnon v HM Advocate (No.2)*, 2003 S.L.T. 281. See *Hopkinson v HM Advocate* [2009] HCJAC 9; 2009 S.L.T. 292.

[28] *Malone v HM Advocate*, 1988 S.C.C.R. 498.

[29] It is possible that one accused might be able to avail himself of a defence of provocation which would warrant a verdict of culpable homicide, despite an equal participation in the attack: *Gray v HM Advocate*, 1994 S.L.T. 1237.

[30] *Moir v HM Advocate*, 1993 S.L.T. 1191.

[31] *HM Advocate v Welsh and McLachlan* (1897) 5 S.L.T. 137; see above, para.7–22.

[32] See, for example, *Kiely v HM Advocate*, 1988 S.C.C.R. 120. There might also be an issue as to use to which a weapon was to be put: *Hopkinson v HM Advocate* [2009] HCJAC 9; 2009 S.L.T. 292. A related question which can arise is whether the weapon used by the actual perpetrator is of a similar type to that which the accused had contemplated. In *O'Connell v HM Advocate*, 1987 S.C.C.R. 459, the issue was whether a metre long piece of wood was a lethal weapon of a similar nature to a hammer. It was held that this was a question of fact for the jury to determine.

[33] *Walker and Raiker v HM Advocate*, 1985 J.C. 53; distinguished (on its factual application) in *Mathieson v HM Advocate*, 1996 S.C.C.R. 388. See also *Carrick v HM Advocate*, 1990 S.C.C.R. 286; *Robertson v HM Advocate*, 1990 S.C.C.R. 345.

was involved in the planned crime? Was it within the scope of the common purpose? If the use of a weapon by one accused is sudden and unexpected, liability for the consequences of its use will not be imposed on a co-accused.[34] In *Boyne v HM Advocate*[35] the Appeal Court reiterated the basic principle that, to be found guilty art and part, the accused would have to know or, "have reasonable cause to anticipate" that a weapon might be used on the victim. This issue had to be addressed, "from the appellant's state of knowledge about what was going on."[36] In *Brown v HM Advocate*[37] it was stated that a jury was not bound to convict of murder where two accused had been involved art and part in a knife attack on the deceased. In a case where

> "the murderous act went beyond the joint common purpose and there was no evidence to show which of the two assailants had used the knife",

one could not exclude the possibility that, "all that was in contemplation was to use weapons to inflict serious injury", and that the appropriate verdict was culpable homicide.[38] To secure a verdict of guilty of murder art and part, therefore, the prosecution would have had to prove either that the accused (wickedly)[39] intended the death of the victim or had contemplated, as part of the common purpose, an act of the necessary degree of wicked recklessness (such as that the deceased would be stabbed by plunging a knife into his heart).[40] The change in emphasis in *Brown* was that it suggested that the prosecution had to prove, not only that the accused contemplated the use of a weapon by the principal offender, but also that its use would be accompanied with the requisite mens rea of murder (either a (wicked)[41] intention to kill or, more usually in such cases, wicked recklessness). This test was rejected as too individualistic in *McKinnon v HM Advocate (No.2)*,[42] where the court took a more traditional approach. The emphasis should be placed on what was foreseeable given the nature and scope of the criminal purpose. The *Brown* approach was, of course, premised upon the idea that to associate oneself with a knife attack can give rise to an inference of something less than wicked recklessness. This is not an approach commanding universal support. Some doubt has been expressed about the appropriateness of a verdict of culpable homicide, rather than murder, in the circumstances of an assault with a murderous

---

[34] *Docherty v HM Advocate*, 1945 J.C. 89, per Lord Moncrieff at 95–96.

[35] *Boyne v HM Advocate*, 1980 S.L.T. 56. In *Docherty v HM Advocate*, 1945 J.C. 89 at 96, Lord Moncrieff alluded to "the doctrine that secondary responsibility for a criminal act arises only in cases of reasonable expectation." See also *Hobbins v HM Advocate*, 1997 S.L.T. 428, per Lord Justice-General Hope at 431B.

[36] *Boyne v HM Advocate*, 1980 S.L.T. 56, per Lord Justice-Clerk Wheatley at 59. Lord Wheatley also gave the example of an accused who, as a member of a gang, was involved in an attack on a victim. He sees another member of the gang unexpectedly take out a knife and deliver a fatal blow. If the accused then carried on with the attack on the victim that would constitute art and part guilt of murder.

[37] *Brown v HM Advocate*, 1993 S.C.C.R. 382.

[38] *Brown v HM Advocate*, 1993 S.C.C.R. 382, per Lord Justice-General Hope at 392A.

[39] See *Drury v HM Advocate*, 2001 S.L.T. 1013.

[40] *Brown v HM Advocate*, 1993 S.C.C.R. 382 at 391E–F. See also *Codona v HM Advocate*, 1996 S.L.T. 1100.

[41] See *Drury v HM Advocate*, 2001 S.L.T. 1013.

[42] *McKinnon v HM Advocate (No.2)*, 2003 S.L.T. 281; applied in *Touati and Gilfillian* [2007] HCJAC 73; 2008 J.C. 214 and *Cameron v HM Advocate* [2008] HCJAC 10; 2008 S.C.C.R. 669.

weapon, such as a knife.[43] On the other hand, it is possible for an accused not to appreciate the full significance of the attack in which he participated. As Lord Sutherland noted in his charge to the jury in *Mathieson v HM Advocate*, the accused might have thought that the knife "was only going to be used to inflict the odd cut or slash or something of that kind".[44]

Distributing liability between the parties

7–26   Thus it is possible for a co-accused to be guilty of a lesser offence than the actual perpetrator of the crime. Does this mean, conversely, that someone who assists in the commission of a crime can be guilty art and part of a more serious offence than the actual offender can, or that he can be convicted if the actual offender is acquitted? The answer to both these questions is a qualified affirmative. It is arguable whether or not there is a conceptual barrier to a conviction for a more serious offence than that of the actual offender. One difficulty can be mentioned at the outset. Art and part guilt can be derived from the commission of a crime, without "direct" involvement in its perpetration. How can it then be possible to be more guilty art and part than the "actual" offender? How can the person who merely assisted him acquire guilt beyond that of the actual perpetrator? One view would be that once it has been established that the actual offender caused the actus reus, the liability of any other particular accused should be assessed according to his own mens rea. Such an approach would appear to be in accord with the decision in *Melvin v HM Advocate*.[45]

7–27   It is debatable how far outside the law of homicide the approach should be taken—given that it does appear to represent a departure from the traditional rule of equality of liability for the outcome among the participants. Further, there are obvious limitations to the *Melvin* doctrine. If A instigates B to commit an aggravated assault on C, but B perpetrates a simple assault only, then it would not be possible to convict A of an aggravated assault. This crime has not been committed. A has the appropriate mens rea, but there is no actus reus. He can only be guilty art and part of the assault which B actually commits. (He would also be guilty of inciting B to commit an aggravated assault.) In the context of homicide, however, it is submitted that the flexible approach does make sense. If unlawful homicide is regarded as a single crime which has two levels of culpability (murder and culpable homicide), then there is no objection in principle to saying that the liability of the aider or instigator should be founded on his own mens rea. For example, the accused, assuming that he has the requisite mens rea for murder, could instigate a homicide in circumstances where the actual killer is guilty of culpable homicide only. An example would be where the instigator informs the killer that if he returns home he will find his wife committing adultery. As is detailed in Ch.9, it is likely that the husband will have available the partial defence of provocation. This could result in a conviction for culpable homicide, instead of

---

[43] See *Coleman v HM Advocate*, 1999 S.L.T. 1261, per Lord Coulsfield at 1269G–1270D; *Barrie v HM Advocate*, 2002 S.L.T. 1053 (referring the issue to a larger court). See, further, the account of murder in Ch.9.

[44] *Mathieson v HM Advocate*, 1996 S.C.C.R. 388 at 393F.

[45] *Melvin v HM Advocate*, 1984 S.L.T. 365; see above, para.7–23. The absence of antecedent consent is crucial, see *McKinnon v HM Advocate (No.2)*, 2003 S.L.T. 281 at 288F.

murder. The instigator, however, acted with deliberation and premeditation. He cannot claim to have been provoked. He would be convicted of murder.

Acquittal of the actual offender

Do the same considerations apply where the actual offender is acquitted? Does **7–28** the acquittal mean that there is no crime of which to be art and part guilty? The fact that the principal offender was acquitted does not necessarily mean that the crime in question has not been committed, or that the accused did not participate. The actual offender may have been acquitted because he was, for example, mentally disordered or coerced. In these two instances a crime would have been committed of which one could still be guilty art and part. There are cases, however, where acquittal of the actual offender would be inconsistent with the establishment of art and part guilt. If in a case of a planned rape the accused who actually had sexual intercourse with the complainer was acquitted of rape because the complainer had in fact consented, the co-accused who assisted would also be entitled to an acquittal. There would not have been a crime of which to be guilty art and part.

It appears that the mere fact that it would have been legally impossible for a **7–29** particular accused to have committed the crime in his own right is no bar to a conviction on the basis of art and part guilt. Hume gives the example of an unmarried man or woman who goes through a marriage ceremony knowing that the other party is already married. Art and part guilt would attach to this assistance to commit bigamy.[46] *Vaughan v HM Advocate*[47] illustrates the point. Vaughan had been accused of acting in concert with the mother of a small boy, in forcing the child to have intercourse with the mother contrary to the Incest Act 1567.[48] The accused was not related to either the mother or the boy. This meant, of course, that he could not himself have committed incest in this instance. The High Court held that he could still be guilty art and part for acting in concert with the co-accused mother in the commission of the offence. Similarly, in *Reid v HM Advocate*,[49] it was held that a woman could be guilty art and part of the statutory offence of living off the earnings of prostitution, even though the relevant provision applies only to a "male person".[50]

Acquittal of joint principal

The doctrine of art and part guilt is apt to cover the situation where it would **7–30** perhaps be more accurate to speak in terms of there being more than one principal offender, rather than a single principal offender and a number of lesser participants in the commission of the crime (see above, para.7–11). In such a case there is no difficulty in convicting one accused while another is acquitted.[51] The explanation might simply be that there is more probative evidence against one party to the joint enterprise than against the other.[52] *Capuano v HM Advocate*[53] illustrates

---

[46] Hume, *Commentaries,* i, 462.
[47] *Vaughan v HM Advocate*, 1979 S.L.T. 49.
[48] See now Criminal Law (Consolidation) (Scotland) Act 1995 s.1.
[49] *Reid v HM Advocate*, 1999 J.C. 54.
[50] Criminal Law (Consolidation) Scotland Act 1995 s.11(1).
[51] See *Johnston v HM Advocate*, 1998 S.L.T. 788 at 790G.
[52] *Low v HM Advocate*, 1994 S.L.T. 227.
[53] *Capuano v HM Advocate*, 1985 S.L.T. 196. See also *HM Advocate v Camerons* (1911) 6 Adam 456; *Tobin v HM Advocate*, 1934 J.C. 60.

this situation. The appellant had been charged with assault through acting along with others. His two co-accused had been acquitted. The appellant's argument was that, since he was charged with being involved as an accessory, he could not be convicted when the others were acquitted. The Appeal Court stated that there was ample evidence of the appellant's participation in the crime, and that this was not a case where the conviction depended upon that of the co-accused principal offenders.[54] Lord Justice-General Emslie gave the example of four robbers libelled to have acted in concert, three of who entered the premises and one who remained outside in order to drive them away from the location. If the only positive evidence of identification were of the driver, it would be appropriate for him alone to be convicted.[55] It has also been held that the acquittal of an alleged accomplice at an earlier trial is not a bar to a subsequent conviction of an accused libelled to have acted in concert with him.[56] An acquittal in a criminal trial does not, of course, amount to a positive finding of innocence. It indicates, rather, that the prosecution was unable to prove its case beyond a reasonable doubt.

Actual offender acquitted because mens rea absent

7–31   The more difficult case arises where the accused is alleged to have participated in some capacity other than that of a joint principal, but the actual offender is acquitted because he lacks the mens rea necessary for the crime. Since Scots law purports to draw no distinction between the parties to a crime this point might seem to be irrelevant. It is sometimes argued, however, that in cases of this nature there is no crime of which to be guilty art and part.

7–32   A case at point here is the much-discussed decision of the English Court of Appeal in *R. v Cogan and Leak*.[57] Cogan was acquitted of the rape of Leak's wife on the basis that he lacked the necessary mens rea. The "crime" had been instigated by Leak, who compelled his wife to have sexual intercourse with Cogan. Leak falsely told Cogan that his wife would agree to the intercourse. Cogan's "mistake" as to the wife's consent negated his mens rea. The question arose as to whether Leak could be convicted as an accessory. The court held that he could and offered two explanations why this was so. The first was that Cogan could perhaps be regarded as Leak's innocent agent. Since Leak caused Cogan to misunderstand the situation, he had used Cogan's "body as the instrument for the necessary physical act."[58]

7–33   The concept of innocent agency or instrumentality is an accepted principle of criminal law (see above, para.4–03). The doctrine can be invoked where the accused has, with the requisite mens rea, manipulated a mentally disordered person or a child below the age of criminal responsibility to commit a crime. It would not be necessary to have resort to the doctrine of art and part guilt. His guilt does not owe anything to the conduct of a co-accused. He will be convicted because he is regarded as directly liable for committing the crime. In crimes such as theft or housebreaking with intent to steal, the acquittal of an innocent agent does not present a barrier to establishing liability.

---

[54] Although the accused was in fact libelled to have acted in concert with unnamed others, in addition to the co-accused; see the discussion in *Howitt v HM Advocate*, 2000 J.C. 284 at 287H–I.
[55] *Capuano v HM Advocate*, 1985 S.L.T. 196 at 196.
[56] *Howitt v HM Advocate*, 2000 J.C. 284 (opinion of the full bench, overruling *McAuley v HM Advocate*, 1946 J.C. 8).
[57] *R. v Cogan and Leak* [1976] 1 Q.B. 217.
[58] *R. v Cogan and Leak* [1976] 1 Q.B. 217 at 223.

The difficulty in applying this doctrine to Leak was the then existence in English **7–34** law of the marital rape exemption.[59] Similar conceptual difficulties would arise where it was a woman who utilised an innocent agent to have non-consensual sexual intercourse with the complainer. She could not commit the crime of rape herself, so how can the existence of an innocent agent make her directly liable?

The court's second explanation was that there was no reason why Leak could **7–35** not be viewed as Cogan's accomplice. The fact that Cogan was innocent was held not to alter the fact that the complainer was raped.[60] That is, the actus reus of rape was committed when Leak's wife was forced to have non-consensual sexual intercourse. The argument would appear to be that Cogan committed the crime of rape at Leak's instigation and that this crime could then be imputed to Leak. The difficulty with this approach is in being able to say that the crime of rape was committed where the mens rea was absent. One of the constituent elements of the crime of rape was lacking. Cogan's behaviour was immoral and reprehensible, but English law did not regard it as a crime. If Cogan did not commit a crime, then how could one say that Leak was engaged in a criminal act with him? How could there be liability as an accomplice if there was no crime?

DISSOCIATION

One final issue to consider in relation to art and part guilt is whether it is ever **7–36** possible to assist in a criminal endeavour, but then escape liability through abandoning the enterprise and withdrawing. An instigator could, perhaps, avoid art and part guilt if he terminated his relationship with the other participants and communicated this fact to them.[61] More generally, if an accused can bring forward evidence of dissociation, this will go to the issue of whether he was in fact acting in concert. Lord Justice-General Emslie said in *MacNeil v HM Advocate*[62]

> "evidence of 'dissociation' by a participant in the preparation of a crime or offence in contemplation will be highly relevant in any decision as to whether he can be held to be in concert with those who proceed to commit it."

To accord some legal recognition to the existence of dissociation is only sensible. To hold otherwise might deter people from withdrawing from a criminal enterprise and be taken to indicate that there was no point in doing so.

CONSPIRACY

Legal definition

Conspiracy is "constituted by the agreement of two or more persons to further **7–37** or achieve a criminal purpose".[63] A definition which continues to have some

---

[59] Now no longer accepted in either Scotland (see *S v HM Advocate*, 1989 S.L.T. 469) or England (see *R. v R* [1992] 1 A.C. 599).

[60] Likewise, the fact that Leak himself could not rape his wife would not be a barrier to accomplice liability; see above, para.7–30.

[61] *HM Advocate v Baxter* (1908) 5 Adam 609, per Lord Macdonald at 615. It is suggested there that it might be necessary to communicate with the police.

[62] *MacNeil v HM Advocate*, 1986 J.C. 146 at 159.

[63] *Maxwell v HM Advocate*, 1980 J.C. 40, per Lord Cameron at 43; adopted in *Howitt v HM Advocate*, 2000 J.C. 284 at 287C.

attraction for the Scottish courts is that of the Lord Chancellor, Viscount Simon, in the *civil* case of *Crofter Hand-Woven Harris Tweed Co v Veitch*[64]:

> "Conspiracy, when regarded as a crime, is the agreement of two or more persons to effect any unlawful purpose, whether as their ultimate aim, or only as a means to it, and the crime is complete if there is such agreement even though nothing is done in pursuance of it."

Amendment to this definition is necessary: the word "unlawful" has to read as "criminal", to make it consistent with what Lord Cameron said in *Maxwell v HM Advocate*.[65] Lord Cameron there defined a criminal purpose as

> "one which if attempted or achieved by action on the part of an individual would itself constitute a crime by the law of Scotland."[66]

This means that, before a conspiracy can be classified as criminal, its purpose necessarily would have had to be criminal if done by one person.

7–38   It should be stressed that, unless the prosecution can prove the existence of an agreement, there cannot be a conviction for conspiracy. Under no circumstances, of course, could the mere presence of the accused be sufficient.[67] There must be *actual* agreement between the parties to a conspiracy. As is the case with instigation as a basis for art and part guilt, matters must go beyond simply putting a suggestion to someone with a view to further discussing the issue, and maybe reaching agreement in the future. That would not constitute a conspiracy, there being no "meeting of minds". Rather, it might be an attempted conspiracy or incitement (see below, para.7–57).

FORMS OF CONSPIRACY

7–39   It is possible that the members of an alleged conspiracy actually might have met together to agree their plan, but this is not essential to the establishment of conspiratorial liability. Conspiracies can take a variety of other forms. In particular, it is not necessary for every member of a conspiracy to be aware of the existence of every other member.

Chain conspiracies

7–40   A "chain" conspiracy can arise where A agrees with B who agrees with C, and so on. The fact that A is unaware of C's involvement is no bar to saying that they, along with B, are parties to the same conspiracy. The difficulty raised for the prosecution by this type of conspiracy is as to how the individuals in the chain can properly be linked together, particularly where there is a large number of links.

---

[64] *Crofter Hand-Woven Harris Tweed Co v Veitch*, 1942 S.C. (HL) 1 at 5; quoted in *Maxwell v HM Advocate*, 1980 J.C. 40, per Lord Cameron at 43; and in *HM Advocate v Megrahi (No.1)*, 2000 S.L.T. 1393, per Lord Sutherland at 1395F.

[65] *Maxwell v HM Advocate*, 1980 J.C. 40.

[66] *Maxwell v HM Advocate*, 1980 J.C. 40 at 43. This too is the import of *Cochrane v HM Advocate*, 2002 S.L.T. 1424 at 1426.

[67] *Coleman v HM Advocate*, 1999 S.L.T. 1261, per Lord Justice-Clerk Cullen at 1264L–1265A, 1269A, 1273D.

Wheel conspiracies

A conspiracy can also take the form of a wheel. This occurs where there are a **7–41** number of parties who each agree with one central ringleader, who forms the "hub" of the wheel. Each agreement between the hub and a party to the conspiracy forms a "spoke". For the wheel conspiracy fully to take shape, however, the prosecution would need to be able to establish the existence of a "rim" around the wheel. This is essential to proving the existence of one large, single conspiracy. If there is no rim, then there are simply a number of conspiracies to which the hub is a party: there are as many conspiracies as there are spokes in the wheel.

CONTROVERSIAL NATURE OF CONSPIRACY

From a prosecution perspective, conspiracy can be a useful way of dealing with **7–42** behaviour considered to be dangerous or undesirable, but which does not constitute a complete or attempted crime. Despite this apparent utility to prosecutors, the crime of conspiracy remains controversial. From a defence perspective, the crime of conspiracy is problematic. It can be used to penalise conduct which is extremely precursory to the perpetration of the actus reus of a substantive crime. Further, the crime lays stress upon the mental state of the accused, since the crucial issue is whether there was an agreement between the parties to the alleged conspiracy. There may be less emphasis upon the conduct of an accused. This heightens the danger that an accused will be penalised not for what he himself did, but for consorting with other people who are much more intimately involved in the "conspiracy". The criminal law should be scrupulous in seeking to avoid guilt by association or guilt by confusion; a zealous prosecutor could use conspiracy as a catchall charge.

PROVING THE CONSPIRATORIAL AGREEMENT

Proof of the agreement essential to a criminal conspiracy will generally be infer- **7–43** ential. Sometimes overt acts will have been committed by some or all of the accused, but this will not always be the case. But even if there have been some such overt acts, the existence of mens rea, in the form of an agreement and commitment to the criminal purpose of the conspiracy, will have to be proved by inference. For example, if a group of men is apprehended wearing masks and carrying weapons, while sitting in a car outside a bank, there is a clear inference to be drawn that there is an agreement to rob the bank. The group is unlikely to be there for any other purpose.[68]

Lord Justice-Clerk Grant pointed out to the jury in *HM Advocate v Wilson,* **7–44** *Latta and Rooney*[69]:

> "[Y]ou won't often get eye-witnesses of the agreement being made or eavesdroppers who actually heard it being made. Accordingly, in many cases it is

---

[68] Compare the facts of *West v HM Advocate*, 1985 S.C.C.R. 248; see also *Coleman v HM Advocate*, 1999 S.L.T. 1261, per Lord Justice-Clerk Cullen at 1264L–1265A.

[69] *HM Advocate v Wilson, Latta and Rooney* Unreported, 1968 but see Gane and Stoddart, *Casebook on Scottish Criminal Law*, 2nd edn, p.203.

a question of judging from the acts of the alleged conspirators whether in fact there was a conspiracy between them in pursuance of which they are acting."

The evidence derived from such a decisional process will not always be as unambiguous as the example in the previous paragraph. An individual who may appear at an early stage of the conspiracy to be involved might not be firmly committed and could have ceased to play any part before the complete crime had been committed. This problem is raised in a crucial form by the absence of any requirement of proximity, such as is to be found in the law of attempt.

A RATIONALE FOR THE CRIME OF CONSPIRACY?

7–45 It is possible to identify two main justifications for criminalising conspiracies. The first is that recognition of the crime of conspiracy can serve as an instrument to prevent the commission of crimes. Conspiracy, like attempt, is an inchoate crime. All that is required to constitute a conspiracy is an agreement. It is not necessary to have done anything in pursuance of it. This means that the law relating to conspiracy becomes operative at an earlier stage than the law of attempt. The agencies of law enforcement are thereby given the opportunity to intervene at an earlier stage than would otherwise be the case. In this sense, conspiracy is a useful adjunct to the law of attempt. The intervention of the criminal law is justified by the fact of the agreement to commit a crime. This agreement and consequent commitment to the criminal enterprise is regarded as sufficient evidence of the threat posed by the accused.

7–46 The second justification is concerned with the special dangers which are perceived to attend criminal conduct by a group. The rationale here is similar to that underlying art and part guilt. The premise is that a conspiracy poses a greater threat to law and order than a number of individuals working alone. If there is a conspiracy, it may be more likely that the proposed crime will be committed. Even if one individual reneges on the agreement, his co-conspirators can still continue. Psychological factors relating to the nature of groups may make it more likely that the criminal purpose will be achieved. The co-conspirators will provide one another with mutual support and loyalty. Most conspiracies do lead to the commission of the planned crime.

RELATIONSHIP WITH ART AND PART GUILT

7–47 In addition to constituting a crime in its own right, conspiracy can provide a method of holding one member of a criminal group accountable for the actions of his co-accused. As Lord Justice-Clerk Grant expressed it in *Wilson, Latta and Rooney*[70]:

"Normally a man is responsible only for what he himself does, but if he is involved in a conspiracy he may be responsible not only for what he himself does but for what his fellow-conspirators do."

---

[70] *HM Advocate v Wilson, Latta and Rooney* Unreported, 1968, but see Gane and Stoddart, *Casebook on Scottish Criminal Law*, 2nd edn, p.203.

That is, a conspiracy can provide the basis for establishing art and part guilt. To give an example: two accused agree together that a particular individual should be murdered. This agreement in itself makes them guilty of conspiracy. If one accused then goes on to perpetrate the killing, the conspiratorial agreement can form the basis for holding the other accused guilty art and part of the murder.

However, art and part guilt can arise without there being a conspiracy. If during **7–48** a bank robbery a customer were spontaneously to come to the assistance of the robber, there would be art and part guilt. There would not be a conspiracy, of course, because there was no agreement between the two individuals. In many instances of art and part guilt, however, there will be sufficient evidence from which to infer the existence of a conspiratorial agreement. An example would be the supplier of a weapon used in the course of the robbery.

Interesting example of Art 1 Part

CONSPIRACY IN PRACTICE

The basic legal concept underlying a criminal conspiracy is straightforward, but **7–49** this does not mean that there are no difficulties in practice. In practical terms, an obvious problem is that caused by a trial involving a potentially large number of accused, each with individual legal representation. The most significant difficulty, however, is caused by the tendency to have over-long and complex indictments. Even a cursory examination of the reported cases in this area of law will show this.

Agreement pursued by specific crimes

One category of conspiracy is where specific crimes have been carried out in **7–50** pursuance of the agreement.[71] The case of *Wilson, Latta and Rooney*[72] provides an example. The indictment contained libels of a conspiracy to pervert the course of justice and the commission of subornation and attempted subornation in pursuance of the conspiracy. The jury was informed that it was still possible to convict of subornation, even if there was an acquittal in relation to the conspiracy.

persuading someone to commit perjury.

Agreement pursued by criminal means

Conspiracy indictments sometimes do not set out any specific crime by means **7–51** of which the agreement was to be carried out. The indictment will state instead that the conspiracy was to be effected by "criminal" or "violent" means. An example is provided in the unreported case of *HM Advocate v Walsh*.[73] The charge here was of conspiring to further the purposes of the IRA, "by the unlawful use of force and violence . . . for the purpose of endangering . . . lives . . . and destroying property."

If the indictment libels a conspiracy to achieve some purpose by criminal **7–52** means, then the prosecution will have to prove the existence of these. This point was made clear in *Sayers v HM Advocate*.[74] The indictment libelled a conspiracy

---

[71] See, e.g. *HM Advocate v Megrahi (No.1)*, 2000 S.L.T. 1393.

[72] *HM Advocate v Wilson, Latta and Rooney* Unreported, 1968, but see Gane and Stoddart, *Casebook on Scottish Criminal Law*, 2nd edn, p.203.

[73] *HM Advocate v Walsh* Unreported, 1921. Discussed by Gordon, *Criminal Law*, 3rd edn (2000/2001), paras 6.64–6.65.

[74] *Sayers v HM Advocate*, 1982 J.C. 17.

to further the purposes of the Ulster Volunteer Force by criminal means. Sayers was found guilty by the jury, but under deletion of the criminal means detailed in the indictment. On appeal, it was held that there was inadequate specification and that the charge of which Sayers had been found guilty was therefore irrelevant. The crime of conspiracy could not be established in the absence of specification of the alleged criminal means.

Conspiracy and non-proximate preparations

7–53   A charge of conspiracy can be utilised as a substitute for one of attempt. There has been an agreement to commit the crime, but the accused has not moved sufficiently far towards perpetration to constitute an attempt. *West v HM Advocate*,[75] which concerned a conspiracy to assault and rob people employed in particular premises, provides an example of this type of conspiracy. The libel was that in furtherance of a conspiracy the accused

> "did loiter in the vicinity of said premises . . . and thereafter enter said premises while . . . in possession of a blade from a pair of scissors, and . . . in possession of an open razor, all with intent to assault said employees with said weapons and rob them of money."

On appeal, it was held that there was sufficient evidence from which the existence of a conspiracy could be inferred.

Impossibility

7–54   If the factory outside which the appellant in *West v HM Advocate* was apprehended had in fact been deserted, would the "impossibility" of carrying out the agreed crime have afforded a defence? This issue of impossibility in relation to inchoate crimes was addressed in detail in the previous chapter on attempt. It is not proposed to repeat in substance what was said there. The same conceptual problems which arise in relation to attempting to do the impossible appear also in conspiracy.

7–55   In conspiracy, as in attempt, it is difficult to see why mere impossibility should afford a defence. It should not be relevant to the question of conspiratorial liability that the agreement to carry out the robbery could not be fulfilled because of a mistake in the planning. This appears to have been the approach taken in *Maxwell v HM Advocate*.[76] Here Lord Cameron stressed that since a conspiracy is an agreement to achieve a criminal purpose, it is the criminality of the purpose and not the result which makes the agreement criminal.

Withdrawal as a defence?

7–56   The crime of conspiracy is committed the moment that the agreement is made. This means that there is no such thing in legal terms as "withdrawal" from a conspiracy. But if an accused had signalled his dissociation from the purpose of the conspiracy, this could serve to relieve him of art and part guilt for the subsequent commission of the completed crime by his co-conspirators (see above, para.7–36).

---

[75] *West v HM Advocate*, 1985 S.C.C.R. 248.
[76] *Maxwell v HM Advocate*, 1980 J.C. 40.

INCITEMENT

ATTEMPTED CONSPIRACY

It is a crime to attempt to form a conspiracy. The crime is known as incitement. It **7–57** is committed where the accused has approached another person and invited him to participate in the perpetration of a crime.[77] There is no requirement that the accused actually instruct the other person to commit the crime in question.[78] An example of an appropriate libel in an indictment might be that of an "attempt by A to induce B to enter the conspiracy and incite him to assist in carrying out a robbery." The crime is complete as soon as the incitement occurs. The law does not insist upon any further action towards committing the actus reus. The requisite mens rea is that of a serious intention that the party incited commit the relevant crime.[79]

RELATIONSHIP WITH ART AND PART GUILT AND CONSPIRACY

As in the case of conspiracy, incitement is not only a crime in its own right, but **7–58** can provide a foundation for art and part guilt. Incitement is one of the ways in which an individual can participate in and assist the commission of a crime. Thereafter he can be called to account for the criminal act (see above, para.7–14). To give an example: A incites B to murder C. At this stage A is guilty of the crime of incitement. If B does kill C, then A is guilty art and part of the murder. A will not be convicted of incitement, because this crime merges with his art and part guilt for murder. If the murder bid failed, then the incitement would similarly merge with the attempted murder.

In this example, of course, there is an intermediate stage of conspiracy when B **7–59** agrees to A's suggestion. Again, if the murder were perpetrated, this would be treated as a basis for establishing art and part guilt, rather than a crime in its own right. A conspiracy charge would only become appropriate if B agreed to the proposal, but failed to carry it into effect.

POLICY ARGUMENTS

The crime of incitement permits the application of criminal liability at a much **7–60** earlier stage than the law of attempt, or even the crime of conspiracy. If the accused has invited another to commit a crime, that is sufficient in itself. There is no requirement of agreement, and none of moving towards the perpetration of the proposed crime. In *Baxter v HM Advocate*,[80] for example, the accused's conviction for incitement to murder was upheld in circumstances where he had done little more than discuss with the incitee the possible ways to kill the intended victim and the fee payable. One argument would be that the crime of incitement is directed at behaviour too remote from the actual commission of the actus reus. If A incites B to commit a particular crime, he hopes that B will enter a

---

[77] See *HM Advocate v Tannahill and Neilson*, 1943 J.C. 50; *Morton v Henderson*, 1956 J.C. 55.

[78] *Baxter v HM Advocate*, 1998 J.C. 219 at 221E.

[79] *Baxter v HM Advocate*, 1998 J.C. 219 at 222B, 223A.

[80] *Baxter v HM Advocate*, 1998 J.C. 219.

conspiratorial agreement to commit the crime. Assuming that B agrees, the crime of conspiracy is committed. However, there is no requirement that the proposed conspiracy be proximate even to an attempt to commit the crime which the inciter originally had in mind. Thus one view could be that incitement is an excessively inchoate crime and penalises behaviour which is too preparatory to the commission of the intended crime.

7–61   The justification for criminalising the act of incitement is largely the same as that for a completed conspiracy. Incitement is regarded as worthy of punishment because it is an attempt to form a conspiracy. This is conduct which is regarded as sufficiently dangerous in itself to justify the intervention of the criminal law. Particular dangers are seen to flow from the agreement of a number of individuals to commit a crime (see above, para.7–46). A further rationale is that of protecting the individual who is incited from corruption.

CHAPTER 8

DEFENCES

INTRODUCTION

This chapter discusses a wide range of defences[1] which an accused can plead in a **8–01** criminal case. The accused's interest in raising a legally recognised defence is that it can serve either to elide criminal liability altogether or to diminish the seriousness of the crime for which he is convicted. The most significant of this latter category of "partial" defences are diminished responsibility and provocation, which do not lead to acquittal, but to conviction for culpable homicide rather than murder.

DEFENCES IN PRACTICE

It is possible to identify two principal ways in which defences can operate. **8–02** First, some defences represent an effort by the accused to raise a reasonable doubt concerning a material element of the prosecution's case. Examples would include the defence of mistake of fact, which negates the mens rea of the crime, and the defence of alibi, which establishes that the accused could not have perpetrated the actus reus. These can be described as "failure of proof" defences. They do not provide a ground of defence independent of the definition of the crime. A failure of proof defence is the absence of one or more of the requisite elements of the crime in question. Secondly, there are those defences (including self-defence, coercion and necessity) which result in the acquittal of the accused even though the prosecution has proved each element in the definition of the crime. This means that, as Lord Justice-General Rodger observed in *Drury v HM Advocate*,[2] "a person who intentionally kills in self-defence is not guilty of murder or indeed of any other crime."

Justifications

Some defences—notably self-defence—amount to a justification for the **8–03** accused's conduct. The essence of a justification defence is that it renders a notional infringement of the criminal law lawful. According to Hart,[3] a justified act is one that, "the law does not condemn, or even welcomes". The accused who

---

[1] See J. Chalmers and F. Leverick, *Criminal Defences and Pleas in Bar of Trial* (Edinburgh: W. Green, 2006) for a modern, analytical study of defences in Scotland.
[2] *Drury v HM Advocate*, 2001 S.L.T. 1013 at 1016I, para.10.
[3] Hart, *Punishment and Responsibility* (1968), p.13.

raises a justification defence asserts that he has done nothing wrongful for which he should be punished. For example, if A kills B in self-defence, this act is justified. A may have perpetrated the actus reus of unlawful homicide, but, because of the fact that A acted to counter unjustified and life-threatening aggression from B, his use of fatal force becomes justified. The act of killing B is permitted by the criminal law.

Excuses

8–04   An excuse defence exculpates the accused who has satisfied all the elements of a crime but who, because of some excusing condition, cannot be regarded as responsible for his actions. The basic distinction between a justification and an excuse is that the former focuses upon the conduct of the accused, whereas the latter concentrates upon his responsibility. Unlike a justification, an excuse does not render conduct lawful and proper. An excuse negates the accused's personal responsibility for violating the criminal law. Excuses are recognised by the criminal law in circumstances where an accused has perpetrated an unjustifiable act, but cannot be regarded as morally blameworthy. The accused who pleads the defence of involuntary intoxication to a charge of murder does not claim that the killing was justifiable. His contention is that he should not be regarded as morally blameworthy, and should therefore be excused from criminal responsibility.

MITIGATING CIRCUMSTANCES

Plea in mitigation

8–05   Even if an accused cannot avail himself of a legally recognised defence, he can always ask a court to take what he claims to be mitigating circumstances into account. The fact that he does not fulfil the legal requirements of a defence does not mean that the accused will not be able to persuade a court to impose a lesser punishment upon conviction than would normally be the case. As was stressed in *Falconer v Jessop*[4] "one of the rights which an accused person has is to speak in mitigation before sentence is passed."

Evidence of mitigating circumstances

8–06   Further, an accused is entitled to introduce evidence of mitigating circumstances in the course of his trial. This is the case irrespective of the irrelevance of the evidence as a defence. In *Clark v HM Advocate*[5] Lord Walker noted that

> "an accused person is entitled as of right to lay before the jury all evidence which might properly induce them to commend him to leniency in the event of his being held guilty."

Thus, an accused who wishes to argue that his conduct was not wholly voluntary, but is unable to meet the strict legal test of involuntariness, might be able to lead the self-same evidence at his trial by way of mitigation.[6] Likewise, an accused

---

[4] *Falconer v Jessop*, 1975 S.L.T. (Notes) 78.
[5] *Clark v HM Advocate*, 1968 J.C. 53 at 58.
[6] See above, paras 4–19 to 4–21; *HM Advocate v Murray*, 1969 S.L.T. (Notes) 85.

who is unable to establish a defence of coercion or necessity may be able to persuade a court that the special circumstances which led to the commission of the crime indicate that a less severe sentence would be appropriate.[7]

SPECIAL DEFENCES

Procedure

"Special defence" is a procedural term of art in Scots law. It refers to certain **8–07** defences which an accused is not allowed to state unless a written plea has been lodged at least seven clear days before the preliminary hearing (where his case is to be heard in a High Court) or at, or before, the first diet (where he is to be tried before a sheriff-and-jury court), except where he is able to satisfy the court that there was cause for his not having done so.[8] The position is similar (mutatis mutandis) in summary prosecutions.[9] There is no definitive list of special defences, but one can identify four generally accepted ones[10]:

(1) alibi;

(2) incrimination;

(3) mental disorder[11]; and

(4) self-defence.

The features common to these special defences are those described by Lord **8–08** Walker in *Adam v MacNeill*[12]:

> "Generally speaking, a special defence is one which puts in issue a fact (1) which is not referred to in the libel, and (2) which, if established, necessarily results in acquittal of the accused."

---

[7] See *Graham v Annan*, 1980 S.L.T. 28; *Morrison v Valentine*, 1990 S.C.C.R. 692; *Cochrane v HM Advocate*, 2001 S.C.C.R. 655.

[8] Criminal Procedure (Scotland) Act 1995 s.78(1), (3) (as amended by the Criminal Procedure (Amendment) (Scotland) Act 2004 (asp 5) Sch.1 para.25(a), (b)). "Preliminary hearings" apply to High Court proceedings (see the 1995 Act ss.72–72D—as substituted/inserted by the 2004 Act s.1(3)), and "first diets" are procedural steps in indictment cases before the sheriff court (see the 1995 Act s.71, as amended by the Sexual Offences (Procedure and Evidence) (Scotland) Act 2002 (asp 9) s.8(2) and Sch.1 para.5; the Vulnerable Witnesses (Scotland) Act 2004 (asp 3) ss.2(1), 7(1); the Criminal Procedure (Amendment) (Scotland) Act 2004 (asp 5) ss.14(1), 19 and Sch.1 para.20; the Criminal Procedure (Amendment) (Scotland) Act 2004 (Incidental, Supplemental and Consequential Provisions) Order 2005 (SSI 2005/40) art.4; the Criminal Proceedings etc. (Reform) (Scotland) Act 2007 (asp 6) Sch.1 para.12(2) and the Criminal Justice and Licensing (Scotland) Act 2010 (asp 13) Sch.7 para.45: see also the 1995 Act s.66(6), as amended by the Criminal Justice (Scotland) Act 2003 (asp 7) s.61(1)(b), and the 2004 Act (asp 5) s.1(1)).

[9] See the Criminal Procedure (Scotland) Act 1995 s.149B, as inserted (in substitution for original ss.149, 149A) by the Criminal Proceedings etc. (Reform) (Scotland) Act 2007 (asp 6) s.19 and as amended by the Criminal Justice and Licensing (Scotland) Act 2010 (asp 13) s.125(7).

[10] Cf. Chalmers and Leverick, *Criminal Defences and Pleas in Bar of Trial* (2006), para.2–03.

[11] Criminal Procedure (Scotland) Act 1995 s.51(A)(3), inserted by Criminal Justice and Licensing (Scotland) Act 2010 (asp 13) s.168.

[12] *Adam v MacNeill*, 1972 J.C. 1 at 5.

Notice need not be given in respect of any defence other than the four recognised special defences and the three (coercion, automatism and consent in sexual offences)[13] treated as if they were special.[14] The category of special defences is not an exclusive one; the statutory list is not exhaustive of potential defences. It is a concept of procedural, rather than substantive, law.

ALIBI

8–09 The defence of alibi is quite simply that, at the time when the crime is alleged to have been committed, the accused was not at the place libelled.[15] In order to be relevant, the special defence lodged as the foundation for the plea of alibi must be definite.[16] It must specify the place where the accused alleges that he was, and at what time.

INCRIMINATION

8–10 The defence of incrimination (otherwise known as impeachment) is that the crime was not committed by the accused, but by another person, named if known. It is not a special defence where the accused utilises a "cut-throat" defence and incriminates his co-accused, but the same statutory requirement that notice of intention to lead such evidence be lodged is applicable.

MENTAL DISORDER

8–11 If the accused was mentally disordered at the time of committing the crime charged, he is entitled to an acquittal upon that basis.[17] What was described under the common law as "insanity" is now labeled with the more neutral terminology of mental disorder.[18] The effect of this defence is that, even if the accused did

---

[13] Consent is defined to include a defence both of actual consent on the part of the complainer and of the accused's belief that such consent existed: Criminal Procedure (Scotland) Act 1995 s.78(2A) (inserted by the Sexual Offences (Procedure and Evidence) (Scotland) Act 2002 (asp 9) s.6(1)(b)), ss.149B(3)–149B having been substituted for the original ss.149 and 149A by the Criminal Proceedings etc. (Reform) (Scotland) Act 2007 (asp 6) s.19. The relevant sexual offences are listed in s.288C of the 1995 Act (inserted by s.1 of the 2002 Act, and as amended by the Mental Health (Care and Treatment) (Scotland) Act 2003 (Modification of Enactments) Order 2005 (SSI 2005/465) Sch.1 para.27(5), the Sexual Offences (Scotland) Act 2009 (asp 9) Sch.5 para.2(7), the Criminal Justice and Licensing (Scotland) 2010 (asp 13) s.69(2), and the Sexual Offences (Scotland) Act 2009 (Supplemental and Consequential Provisions) Order 2010 (SSI 2010/421) Sch. para.1).

[14] Criminal Procedure (Scotland) Act 1995 s.78(2), (2A), (2B)—as amended and/or inserted by the Sexual Offences (Procedure and Evidence) (Scotland) Act 2002 (asp 9) s.6(1)—and s.149B(2), s.149B having been substituted for the original ss.149 and 149A by the Criminal Proceedings etc. (Reform) (Scotland) Act 2007 (asp 6) s.19 and as amended by the Criminal Justice and Licensing (Scotland) Act 2010 (asp 13) s.125(7). See also s.78(1A), as inserted by the 2010 Act (asp 13) s.124(4); and note the modification (so as to include diminished responsibility) to s.78(2) of the 1995 Act effected by the 2010 Act (asp 13) Sch.7 para.46.

[15] For discussion of the scope of the defence, see *Balsillie v HM Advocate*, 1993 J.C. 233.

[16] See *HM Advocate v Laing* (1871) 2 Coup. 23.

[17] Criminal Procedure (Scotland) Act 1995 s.51(A)(1) (as inserted by the Criminal Justice and Licensing (Scotland) Act 2010 (asp 13) s.168).

[18] The common law defence of insanity was explicitly abolished by s.171(a) of the Criminal Justice and Licensing (Scotland) Act 2010 (asp 13). The legislative reforms were consequential upon recommendations made by the Scottish Law Commission; see *Report on Insanity and Diminished Responsibility* (The Stationery Office, 2004), Scot. Law Com. No.195.

commit the crime, his mental disorder relieves him of responsibility for his actions and he cannot be convicted. In effect, the actus reus is admitted, but mens rea is denied.

The fact that an accused is found not guilty by reason of mental disorder does **8–12** not mean, however, that he has to be released. An accused who pleads successfully the special defence of mental disorder will have his case disposed of in terms of statutory provisions under which (by virtue of the imposition of a compulsion order and restriction order) he can be detained in a hospital without limit of time.[19] Indeed, it is possible for an accused who has been acquitted on the grounds of insanity to lose his liberty for as long as, or even longer than, if he had been convicted and sentenced to imprisonment. In this context the special defence of mental disorder would not be operating as a defence in the traditional sense; rather, it would serve as a mechanism for activating the (potentially indefinite) confinement of a person who is considered to be a danger to society.

Attitudes to acquittal because of mental disorder tend to be ambivalent. The **8–13** Scottish legal system attaches great significance to the principle that an accused should only be regarded as criminally liable when his conduct can be regarded as that of a responsible actor. If an accused can establish that this necessary element of rationality did not characterise his conduct at the time of committing the crime, then he should not be regarded as blameworthy. On the other hand, were the defence to be raised, it could well be in a highly publicised and serious case. It is possible that the desire to punish a wrongdoer may take precedence over the view that punishment of the mentally disordered is inappropriate.

Statute now provides that an accused person should not be held **8–14**

"criminally responsible for conduct constituting an offence, and is to be acquitted of the offence, if the person was at the time of the conduct unable by reason of mental disorder to appreciate the nature or wrongfulness of the conduct."[20]

The term "conduct" includes both acts and omissions.[21] The defence can be raised only by the person charged with the offence.[22] It cannot therefore be raised by the Crown or by the court of its own accord. The standard of proof is on the balance of probabilities.[23]

There are thus two elements to the statutory test. The first is the presence of a **8–15** mental disorder on the part of the accused at the time of the conduct constituting

---

[19] Criminal Procedure (Scotland) Act 1995 s.57(1)(a), (2)(a) and (b) (as amended by the Criminal Justice (Scotland) Act 2003 (asp 7) s.2(a), and the Mental Health (Care and Treatment) (Scotland) Act 2003 (asp 13) Sch.4 para.8(3)(a)), s.57(4) (as substituted by the 2003 Act (asp 13) Sch.4 para.8(3)(d)); s.57A(7) (inserted by the 2003 Act (asp 13) s.133); and s.59 (as amended by the 2003 Act (asp 13) Sch.4 para.8(5)). Notice that under s.57(2), as amended, a court has a range of disposals which are open to it in such a case; see also s.57(3), as substituted by the Criminal Justice (Scotland) Act 2003 (asp 7) s.2, and as amended by the 2003 Act (asp 13) Sch.4 para.8(3)(b). See above, para. 4–18.

[20] Criminal Procedure (Scotland) Act 1995 s.51A(1) (as inserted by the Criminal Justice and Licensing (Scotland) Act 2010 (asp 13) s.168).

[21] Criminal Procedure (Scotland) Act 1995 s.51A(5).

[22] Criminal Procedure (Scotland) Act 1995 s.51A(4).

[23] This replicates the common law rule that for the defence of insanity: *HM Advocate v Mitchell*, 1951 J.C. 53.

the offence. The second is that the mental disorder should have a specific effect. The effect stipulated is the inability of the accused to appreciate either the "nature" or the "wrongfulness" of the conduct constituting the offence. These are alternative, not cumulative, conditions: the defence can be established by proving lack of appreciation in respect of only one of them. The concept of appreciation that is being utilised is wider than that of mere knowledge. Failure to appreciate the nature of conduct would not therefore be precluded by knowledge of the physical attributes of the conduct. Similarly, the defence may be available to an accused who knew that his conduct was in breach of legal or moral norms, but who had reasons for believing that he was nonetheless right to do what he did.

8–16   The defence is *not* available where

> "the mental disorder in question consists only of a personality disorder which is characterised solely or principally by abnormally aggressive or seriously irresponsible conduct."[24]

What is being described here, of course, is a psychopathic personality disorder. It is this which is excluded from the scope of the special defence. An accused with a different form of personality disorder (paranoid or schizotypal, for example) could avail himself of the defence, provided that the effect to which it gives rise satisfies the statutory test set out above. The defence would also be available where a psychopathic personality disorder co-existed with another mental disorder (including other personality disorders), provided also that the effect of the other mental disorder met the statutory test.

SELF-DEFENCE

8–17 If an action is done in self-defence it is not criminal. A special defence is available to an accused whose otherwise criminal use of physical force against the complainer (or deceased) is justifiable[25] because it was necessary to protect himself (or a third party) from an attack, or threat of attack, by the complainer. The defence is premised on the fact that the accused did commit the actions libelled by the prosecution. To be relevantly pled as a special defence, therefore, the accused will have to admit that he perpetrated the acts libelled, albeit that he claims to have been justified in so acting.[26]

8–18   It is possible to identify two principal situations where a plea of self-defence can arise. The first is where it is pled by an accused charged with either murder or a crime related to it (for example, attempted murder or assault to the danger of life). Secondly, the accused charged with a non-aggravated assault may claim to have been justified in utilising a lesser, non-fatal degree of force. As might be expected, most of the relevant authorities concern the application of the defence in homicide prosecutions. The ensuing discussion reflects this emphasis and is concerned principally with the use of a fatal degree of force in self-defence. The

---

[24] Criminal Procedure (Scotland) Act 1995 s.51A(2).
[25] In some cases, the person utilising self-defence will be *excusable* rather than have had his actions considered as justifiable, e.g. where he has made a reasonable, but erroneous, assumption as to the need for defensive measures of force: see below, para.8–26 and Chalmers and Leverick, *Criminal Defences and Pleas in Bar of Trial* (2006), para.3–04.
[26] See *HM Advocate v McGlone*, 1955 J.C. 14.

problem which the law has to confront is that of drawing an appropriate line between the State's obligation to protect its citizens and the individual's right to use deadly force to repel an aggressor.[27]

The rules of self-defence

Since a killing perpetrated in self-defence is not criminal, the parameters of this **8–19** special defence are severely restricted. There are three conditions which have to be met before the defence is available. The classic formulation of these requirements is to be found in Lord Keith's charge to the jury in *HM Advocate v Doherty*[28]: (i) "there must be imminent danger to the life or limb of the accused"; (ii) "the retaliation that he uses in the face of this danger must be necessary for his own safety"; and (iii) "if the person assaulted has means of escape or retreat, he is bound to use them." These three prerequisites are cumulative. If any one of the three is insupportable on the evidence, the trial judge is under a duty to withdraw the issue from the jury.[29] But if there is even slight evidence to support the accused's claim to have been acting in self-defence, the matter should be left to the jury to consider.[30]

Imminence requirement

Unless the threat is imminent, self-defence does not act as a justification.[31] This **8–20** notion of imminence connotes that, unless the accused had acted against his assailant, the assault would have occurred immediately. The conduct of the accused would not fulfil the legal requirement if the assailant had threatened to put his life at risk on some subsequent occasion.

Necessity and proportionality

The second rule of self-defence has two elements to it: the force must be both **8–21** necessary in the circumstances and proportional to the threat which is being combated. The moral basis of the common law's approach to self-defence is that human life, including that of an assailant, should not be taken unnecessarily. This means that an accused is not justified in killing an assailant where a non-fatal response would be sufficient to counter the attack. One might say, for example, that, if there were an attempt to stab the accused by an elderly and infirm assailant, it would not be justifiable for the accused to kill in self-defence, if he knows that he can avoid his own death by disarming the assailant.

This example illustrates the requirement that the degree of force used in retali- **8–22** ation by the accused must not be disproportional[32]: it must not exceed what is reasonably necessary in the circumstances. This rule is subject to the clarification

---

[27] G.P. Fletcher, *A Crime of Self-Defense* (New York: Free Press, 1988), p.18. Article 2 of the European Convention on Human Rights, which protects the right to life, allows for deprivation of life "when it results from the use of force which is no more than absolutely necessary . . . in defence of any person from unlawful violence".

[28] *HM Advocate v Doherty*, 1954 J.C. 1 at 4–5.

[29] *Pollock v HM Advocate*, 1998 S.L.T. 880 at 883B–C.

[30] *Crawford v HM Advocate*, 1950 J.C. 67 at 69; applied in *Whyte v HM Advocate*, 1997 S.L.T. 24 at 25J. See also the non-homicide case of *Croly v HM Advocate*, 2004 S.C.C.R. 389.

[31] Hume, *Commentaries*, i, 224.

[32] *Pollock v HM Advocate*, 1998 S.L.T.

which follows, since the courts do not weigh the matter too finely. In *Doherty*, Lord Keith told the jury:

"You do not need an exact proportion of injury and retaliation; it is not a matter that you weigh in too fine scales . . . Some allowance must be made for the excitement or the state of fear or the heat of blood at the moment of the man who is attacked . . .".[33]

The same point is made in Hume[34]:

"In deciding on pleas of this sort, the Judge will not insist on an exact proportion of injury and retaliation, but rather be disposed to sustain the defence unless the [accused] has been transported to acts of great cruelty or great excess."

8–23 What is necessary in any particular case is a matter for the jury to decide on the evidence, but it will be directed that the benefit of the defence is lost where the force used to counter the attack is excessive. As Lord Cameron observed in *Fenning v HM Advocate*[35]:

"[T]he protection which the law affords to the victim of an attack is not a licence to use force grossly in excess of that necessary to defend himself. . . . That is the foundation upon which the plea itself is based."

In *Doherty* Lord Keith emphasised that the jury had "to consider [the] question of proportion between the attack made and the retaliation offered."[36] The nature of the attack which is being countered is of particular relevance in determining the proportionality or otherwise of the degree of retaliatory force used by the accused. The law appears to be that an accused can never be justified in using fatal force to combat what he knows to be a non-fatal attack, even if the only means of countering the attack is to kill the assailant.[37] In *McCluskey v HM Advocate*,[38] Lord Strachan stated:

"Speaking generally, homicide will not be justified by self-defence unless it is committed of necessity in the just apprehension on the part of the killer that he cannot otherwise save his own life."

In *Doherty* Lord Keith gave the following example:

---

[33] *HM Advocate v Doherty*, 1954 J.C. 1 at 4–5. See also *Whyte v HM Advocate*, 1997 S.L.T. 24.
[34] Hume, *Commentaries*, i, 335.
[35] *Fenning v HM Advocate*, 1985 J.C. 76 at 81.
[36] *HM Advocate v Doherty*, 1954 J.C. 1 at 5.
[37] The one exception to this strict rule appears to be in the case of common law rape; see below, para.8–35.
[38] *McCluskey v HM Advocate*, 1959 J.C. 39 at 40.

"[I]f a man was struck a blow by another man with the fist, that could not justify retaliation by the use of a knife, because there is no real proportion at all between a blow with a fist and retaliation by a knife . . .".[39]

Indeed, if it were clear that the accused had acted "with an intensity and savagery which went far beyond any measures reasonably required"[40] in self-defence, the trial judge would have a duty to withdraw the issue from the jury.

In *McCluskey* the accused was charged with murder. He claimed that the killing **8–24** arose out of his defending himself from an attempt by the deceased to commit sodomy upon him. Lord Strachan, the trial judge, refused to charge the jury that, if they believed the accused's story, they could acquit on the basis of self-defence. In the event, he was convicted of culpable homicide. On appeal, danger to life was stressed as a necessary condition to a successful plea. Lord-Justice General Clyde was firmly of the opinion that there could be

"no justification at all for extending this defence to a case where there is no apprehension of danger to the accused's life . . . but merely a threat . . . of an attack on the appellant's virtue."[41]

McCluskey was followed in *Elliott v HM Advocate*,[42] where the evidence was that the accused had killed not in fear of his life, but in fear that he would be subjected to homosexual assaults. The trial judge's withdrawal of the plea of self-defence from the jury was upheld on appeal.

The duty to retreat

If reasonable means of escape from the attack are available, then there is an **8–25** obligation to use them.[43] There is a duty to retreat, rather than use fatal force against the assailant. The proviso to this rule is that it should be a safe avenue of retreat. Hume[44] points out that

"though the party ought to retire from the assault, yet this is always said under provision, that he can do so without materially increasing his own danger, or putting himself to an evident disadvantage with respect to his defence".

The rationale for this rule lies in its consistency with the general principle that, out of proper respect for the value of human life, fatal force should not be inflicted other than when absolutely necessary. Imposing a duty to withdraw does not increase the risk of harm to the victim of an attack, because, as Hume suggests,

---

[39] *HM Advocate v Doherty*, 1954 J.C. 1 at 5. See also *Moore v MacDougall*, 1989 S.C.C.R. 659.
[40] *Pollock v HM Advocate*, 1998 S.L.T. 880 at 883D.
[41] *McCluskey v HM Advocate*, 1959 J.C. 39 at 42.
[42] *Elliott v HM Advocate*, 1987 S.C.C.R. 278.
[43] See, e.g. *McBrearty v HM Advocate*, 1999 S.L.T. 1333. See also the non-homicide case of *McInally v HM Advocate*, 2006 S.C.C.R. 39; [2006] HCJAC 48: the rule also, of course, applies to such cases.
[44] Hume, *Commentaries*, i, 229.

retreat is not insisted upon where it might place the would-be self-defender in danger.

The self-defender's belief

8–26 Where there has been an apprehension of danger by an accused, a plea of self-defence is not necessarily defeated by the fact that he was in error. The availability of the special defence is based on reasonable appearances, rather than objective reality. An accused is excusable for having used fatal force in self-defence where he reasonably believes that his assailant poses an imminent danger to his life, and that fatal force is necessary to protect himself. Self-defence is permissible where the accused makes a reasonable error of fact regarding the material conditions of the defence. In *Owens v HM Advocate*[45] Lord Justice-General Normand stated:

> "[S]elf-defence is made out when it is established to the satisfaction of the jury that the [accused] believed that he was in imminent danger and that he held that belief on reasonable grounds. Grounds for such belief may exist though they are founded on a genuine mistake of fact."

This statement of law was affirmed in *Jones v HM Advocate*.[46] Lord Justice-Clerk Ross observed:

> "The question is whether the assault by the appellant was justified, and whether the evidence discloses that what he did was for his own safety in order to ward off danger actually threatened or which he reasonably apprehended was threatened."[47]

8–27 In *Crawford v HM Advocate*[48] Lord Justice-General Cooper emphasised that

> "when self-defence is supported by a mistaken belief rested on reasonable grounds, that mistaken belief must have an objective background and must not be purely subjective or of the nature of a hallucination."

This approach has been endorsed most recently in *Lieser v HM Advocate*,[49] where it was reiterated that a person who claimed to have been acting in self-defence, because he believed that he was in imminent danger, had to have reasonable grounds for that belief. It was suggested there that it was

> "for reasons essentially of policy that the law has chosen to require certain conditions to be present before an accused may said to be wholly justified in acting in self-defence, even in the case of an intentional homicide".[50]

---

[45] *Owens v HM Advocate*, 1946 J.C. 119 at 125.
[46] *Jones v HM Advocate*, 1990 J.C. 160.
[47] *Jones v HM Advocate*, 1990 J.C. 160 at 172, emphasis added.
[48] *Crawford v HM Advocate*, 1950 J.C. 67 at 71.
[49] *Lieser v HM Advocate* [2008] HCJAC 42; 2008 S.L.T. 866.
[50] *Lieser v HM Advocate* [2008] HCJAC 42; 2008 S.L.T. 866 at 869, para.10.

Defence of others

The special defence extends to the use of reasonable force to protect another **8–28** person from an unjustified attack.[51] Lord Wheatley stated in *HM Advocate v Carson*[52]: "If a man sees another man being unlawfully attacked, he is entitled to stop that unlawful attack." Where the accused has come to the assistance of a third party, the defence will be available even though he need not have become involved, and could have retreated from the situation.[53] The "duty to retreat" necessarily has a different application when the action in question was undertaken to defend another. As was noted in *Dewar v HM Advocate*,[54] to insist upon the accused taking any opportunity to avoid the attack would be "inconsistent with the idea that . . . the law entitles a person to intervene in defence of another."

Self-generated self-defence

It may be counter-intuitive to suggest that a self-generated necessity to kill **8–29** could support a claim of self-defence.[55] If A picks a fight with B, threatening to kill him, he is not justified in killing B if the latter responds to A's original threat by attacking him. One cannot say, however, that a person who starts a fight can never plead self-defence

> "in a case in which there is a struggle, the right of self-defence may be invoked by the original assailant as well as by a man who was at the outset his victim."[56]

It is possible to conceive of circumstances where A could be justified in using a fatal degree of force against B, even though he perpetrated some wrongful act which initiated the chain of events leading to the fatal outcome for which he is being prosecuted. If A perpetrated a minor assault upon B, causing the latter to become unreasonably provoked and to attempt to kill A, the original assailant would appear to be justified in killing B, even though he is not free from fault. In *HM Advocate v Robertson and Donoghue*,[57] Lord-Justice General Normand observed that if

> "the victim, in protecting himself or his property, uses violence altogether disproportionate to the need, and employs savage excess, then the assailant is in his turn entitled to defend himself against this assault by his victim."

---

[51] See *Moss v Howdle*, 1997 S.L.T. 782 at 786C–D; *Barrie v HM Advocate*, 2002 S.L.T. 1053 at 1055H, para.4.

[52] *HM Advocate v Carson*, 1964 S.L.T. 21.

[53] *Fitzpatrick v HM Advocate*, 1992 S.L.T. 796.

[54] *Dewar v HM Advocate* [2009] HCJAC 40; 2009 J.C. 260 at 261, para.9.

[55] See Hume, *Commentaries*, i, 223.

[56] *HM Advocate v Robertson and Donoghue* Unreported, 1945, per Lord-Justice General Normand, quoted in *Boyle v HM Advocate*, 1993 S.L.T. 577 at 587D.

[57] *HM Advocate v Robertson and Donoghue* Unreported, 1945, per Lord-Justice General Normand, quoted in *Boyle v HM Advocate*, 1993 S.L.T. 577 at 587D. See also *HM Advocate v Kizileviczius*, 1938 J.C. 60.

8–30   In *Boyle v HM Advocate*,[58] the accused admitted committing a breach of the peace through being part of a mob which had threatened another group of people. He had joined in the subsequent fight, armed with a knife, and had killed a member of the opposing mob. He pled self-defence, claiming that he had acted to protect a third party. The Appeal Court regarded it as

> "a misdirection for the trial judge to tell the jury that the appellant could not plead self defence if he was a willing participant in the sense that he joined in the fight willingly. Even if he was a participant in the sense that he stepped forward into the fight, it would all depend . . . upon the circumstances whether self defence could be pleaded."[59]

This approach to the issue was followed in *Burns v HM Advocate*.[60] The important issue is whether the victim's retaliation to the accused's initial assault is such that the latter is entitled to defend himself. This

> "depends upon whether the violence offered by the victim was so out of proportion to the accused's own actings as to give rise to the reasonable apprehension that he was in an immediate danger from which he had no other means of escape, and whether the violence which he then used was no more than was necessary to preserve his own life or protect himself from serious injury."[61]

Self-defence and provocation

8–31   Provocation is discussed in detail in the next chapter, but it bears stressing at this juncture that the issues of self-defence and provocation are quite different in substance and effect.[62] They are conditional upon distinct factual circumstances. It is not uncommon for an accused in a murder trial to plead both, but they are not matters of concurrent consideration: the issue of provocation only comes into play once the jury has rejected the claim of self-defence.

8–32   Self-defence is a special defence which, if successfully pled, results in an acquittal. A killing in self-defence is justified. Provocation does not lead to an acquittal. If established, it will result in a verdict of guilty of culpable homicide. It is not a justification for the killing; it is an excuse which affects the accused's culpability (culpable homicide, instead of murder).[63] The rationale is that an accused who has been provoked into losing his self-control should not be judged by the same standards as the person who kills "in cold blood".

Women and self-defence

8–33   An all too common scenario in self-defence cases is that of a woman who has killed her male partner, who has physically and sexually abused her over a long

---

[58] *Boyle v HM Advocate*, 1993 S.L.T. 577.
[59] *Boyle v HM Advocate*, 1993 S.L.T. 577 at 588A.
[60] *Burns v HM Advocate*, 1995 S.L.T. 1090.
[61] *Burns v HM Advocate*, 1995 S.L.T. 1090, per Lord Justice-General Hope at 1093I.
[62] Although, as noted in *Drury v HM Advocate*, 2001 S.L.T. 1013, both can impact upon the otherwise "evil" character of an intent to kill.
[63] *Drury v HM Advocate*, 2001 S.L.T. 1013, per Lord Justice-General Rodger at 1017I, para.16.

period of time. Many such homicides will be "confrontational".[64] These occur where the woman has killed her abusive partner when he was posing an immediate danger to her life. There is no difficulty in accommodating such a case within the rules of conventional self-defence described above. A second category of case can be described as "non-confrontational". These occur where the abuser has been killed either while asleep, or during some other lull in the violence. Can the woman be said to have acted in self-defence, when the man is not about to attack her on the occasion in question? If the homicide were a pre-emptive move on the part of the woman, it would be difficult for her to satisfy the rules of self-defence, particularly the imminence requirement. As a matter of principle, it would be difficult to justify such a killing. The abuser has not lost his right to life through being violent on other occasions. He is still entitled to the same legal protection as any other victim of a would-be self-defender. In the event that self-defence is not available, there may be the possibility of a verdict of culpable homicide rather than murder, on the basis of "cumulative" provocation.[65]

A further possibility is that the woman may misinterpret an innocent movement **8–34** on the part of the man as an attack to the danger of her life. She will want to rely upon the fact that she had been "battered" on previous occasions to support the reasonableness of her erroneous view that she was about to be attacked. This is an evidential problem.[66] The general rule is that while an accused can lead evidence concerning the victim's general character, it is not competent to lead evidence of specific acts of violence alleged to have been committed by the deceased upon the accused some time previously.[67] The difficulty posed by this evidential rule concerns how the accused can establish that the deceased was a violent person unless she is permitted to cite specific actions on the part of the man. There have been occasions, however, when courts have been prepared to depart from a strict application of this doctrine. In *HM Advocate v Kay*[68] the accused had killed her husband and pled self-defence. Lord Wheatley admitted evidence of assaults upon her by the deceased on five previous occasions as relevant to her claim that she reasonably believed her life to be in danger on the instant occasion. The basis for this decision was that the indictment libelled that the accused had herself demonstrated malice towards the deceased on previous occasions. In the interests of fairness, therefore, the accused was allowed the opportunity to prove in turn by detailed evidence that she had reason to apprehend danger from the deceased.

The one exception to the danger to life requirement for killing in self-defence is **8–35** in the case of rape. In his opinion in *McCluskey v HM Advocate,*[69] Lord Justice-General Clyde specifically makes allowance for the availability of the plea to a woman who has killed in the course of resisting an attempt to rape her. This privilege was not extended to the male victim of a homosexual attack. Lord Clyde's reasoning was based on the fact that rape, unlike sodomy, required a complete

---

[64] The terminology is adapted from H. Maguigan, "Battered Women and Self-Defense: Myths and Misconceptions in Current Reform Proposals" (1991) 140 U. Pa. L. Rev. 379 at 382 fn.2.
[65] See below, para.9–68.
[66] F. Raitt, *Evidence—Principles, Policy and Practice*, 4th edn (Edinburgh: W. Green, 2008), paras 12–27, 12–28.
[67] See *HM Advocate v Fletcher* (1846) Ark. 171; *Brady v HM Advocate*, 1986 J.C. 68.
[68] *HM Advocate v Kay*, 1970 J.C. 68; described as "a very special case" by Lord Justice-Clerk Ross in *Brady v HM Advocate*, 1986 J.C. 68 at 74.
[69] *McCluskey v HM Advocate*, 1959 J.C. 39.

absence of consent on the part of the complainer.[70] It may be doubted whether this accords with the modern view of rape, which no longer holds that there is any requirement of overcoming the complainer's will by force.[71] The equivalent offence under s.1 of the Sexual Offences (Scotland) Act 2009 (rape) likewise relies upon lack of consent rather than force as the essential element (and can be committed upon either a man or a woman). In neither instance (at common law or under statute), therefore, need there be a danger to life. This at least raises a question over the appropriateness of an exemption from the normal rules of self-defence.

OTHER DEFENCES

ACCIDENT

8–36   One can envisage many different circumstances where an accused could be responsible for accidentally bringing about the actus reus of a crime. If a result has been brought about accidentally, that would be inconsistent with the existence of mens rea. No criminal responsibility can rest upon an accused for an accident.[72] In *Mackenzie v HM Advocate*,[73] Lord Avonside pointed out that the defence of accident is always open and that

> "however tenuous the evidence may have been, 'accident' is a question of fact and must be left to the decision of a jury."

Objective test

8–37   It bears pointing out that the fact that a result was accidental from the accused's perspective does not mean that the criminal law will regard it as such. In *McGregor v HM Advocate*[74] Lord Keith gave the example of an accused who had driven his car along with a policeman on the bonnet in such a way that the policeman had fallen off and was killed. He pointed out that

> "it is a matter of more or less accident whether he is killed or not, whether he happens to land on his head or some other part of his body."

Nevertheless, the motorist would still be regarded as criminally responsible for causing this "accidental" death. It is necessarily an objective test and a court will take cognisance of the principle, outlined by Macdonald, "that where the result . . . was likely to occur, the perpetrator is answerable."[75] Likewise, the doctrine of

---

[70] *McCluskey v HM Advocate*, 1959 J.C. 39 at 42–43.

[71] See the *Lord Advocate's Reference (No.1 of 2001)*, 2002 S.L.T. 466.

[72] See *McCue v Currie*, 2004 S.C.C.R. 200, at 207D, para.25 In that case, it was held that accidentally setting fire to property did not amount to culpable and reckless fire-raising, and could not become so by the subsequent failure of the accused to attempt to extinguish the flames or summon appropriate assistance.

[73] *Mackenzie v HM Advocate*, 1983 S.L.T. 220 at 223–224.

[74] *McGregor v HM Advocate* (1973) S.C.C.R. Supp. 54 at 56.

[75] J.H.A. Macdonald, *A Practical Treatise on the Criminal Law of Scotland*, 5th edn (Edinburgh: W. Green, 1948), p.2; see also *Roberts v Hamilton*, 1989 J.C. 91.

transferred intent operates in a limited way to penalise a result of the accused's conduct which he might regard as accidental (see above, para.3–37).

Crimes of recklessness

Crimes of recklessness and negligence can function in a similar manner. The **8–38** fact that an accused has been involved in a road traffic "accident" does not mean that he will not be convicted of dangerous or careless driving. Worthy of note is *HM Advocate v Pearson,*[76] where the accused was charged with the murder of one woman and the assault of another. He claimed that he had "accidentally" stabbed the two women while swinging a knife about recklessly. In the course of his charge to the jury, Lord Cameron stated:

> "If you on the evidence came to the conclusion that . . . the accused . . . whilst recklessly swinging that knife about stabbed this unfortunate woman, that would not in law be accident entitling him to an acquittal . . .".[77]

Accident and self-defence

It is not unknown for an accused to lodge a special defence of self-defence and **8–39** then to introduce evidence supportive of a claim of accident at his trial. The relationship between these two defences is a complex one. It has been held by the Appeal Court that the two pleas will not always be mutually exclusive.[78] But, in order to succeed in the plea of self-defence, it is necessary for an accused to admit bringing about the actus reus of the alleged crime (see above, para.8–17). This will ordinarily give rise to an inference of mens rea and may be difficult to reconcile with a claim that the actus reus was brought about accidentally. This might seem to suggest that an accused should have to make a choice between the defences of accident and self-defence. However, in practice, accused persons can be inclined to make claims such as: "I was acting in self-defence when I killed him, but it was an accident anyway"; or "I killed him accidentally, but I acted in self-defence." If the accused adduces any evidence, however improbable, his claim will go to the jury. Nevertheless, it is arguable that the issues of accident and self-defence should be regarded as distinct in conceptual terms. It is submitted that the proper basis of self-defence is that the crime may have been committed with mens rea, but that the accused was justified in acting as he did. The fact that he was acting in self-defence may preclude the characterisation of his intent as "evil" or "wicked", but it does not mean that his action was unintended. If the accused lacks mens rea because it was an accident, he is not guilty, irrespective of circumstances suggestive of self-defence. That is, the defence operates even though the prosecution can prove all the elements of the crime. As Lord Morison stated in his charge to the jury in *Surman*[79]:

---

[76] *HM Advocate v Pearson* (1967) S.C.C.R. Supp. 20.
[77] *HM Advocate v Pearson* (1967) S.C.C.R. Supp. 20 at 21.
[78] See *Surman v HM Advocate*, 1988 S.L.T. 371, per Lord Justice-Clerk Ross at 374L; *HM Advocate v Woods*, 1972 S.L.T. (Notes) 77.
[79] *Surman v HM Advocate*, 1988 S.L.T. 371 at 372K (emphasis added).

"Self-defence is a *deliberate act intended by the victim of an attack* for his own protection and an act which has been reasonably committed for . . . the protection of the person who is accused."

Lord Morison went on to say that a person who kills in self-defence lacks "wicked intent."[80] In this second quotation the judge is using the notion of intent in a broad sense to indicate that there is a difference in moral terms between a "wicked" killer and one who kills in self-defence. That there is such a moral difference is unarguable, but the criminal law caters for this difference through the existence of the doctrine of self-defence. It seems to be an unnecessary complication or qualification to merge the concepts of self-defence and mens rea in the way Lord Morison indicates. It is certainly not the case that an accused's plea of self-defence will be defeated because he possessed mens rea.[81] Self-defence, unlike accident, is not a failure of proof defence. By way of contrast, reference can be made to Lord Cameron's charge to the jury in *HM Advocate v Brogan*,[82] where he simply observes that an act done in self-defence lacks a "criminal quality". That is to do no more than to restate the basic principle that otherwise criminal conduct will not be regarded as such if perpetrated in self-defence, and is consistent with the approach adopted here. If the plea of self-defence is applicable, it is difficult to see how the actus reus can have been brought about accidentally. If it was brought about accidentally, the accused lacks the requisite mens rea and should be acquitted.[83] The issue of self-defence is pre-empted by the defence of accident and, it is argued here, is superfluous, since it has no effect upon the accused's intention to bring about the actus reus (intention here being used in a narrow sense, specific to a particular crime, in contrast to Lord Morison's view in *Surman*).

ERROR

Error of law

8–40   It is not a requirement of mens rea that the accused should have been aware of the illegality of his behaviour. Subject to very limited exceptions, ignorance or error of law is no defence.[84] This doctrine is deeply embedded in Scottish criminal jurisprudence. According to Hume,[85] even though the accused

"thought that it was a lawful act, and liable to no punishment, . . . he still has no defence in this sort of imperfect and corrupt belief."

---

[80] *Surman v HM Advocate*, 1988 S.L.T. 371 at 372L. Although not referred to in *Drury v HM Advocate*, 2001 S.L.T. 1013, this is consistent with the view expressed there that murder requires a wicked intent to kill.

[81] See *Drury v HM Advocate*, 2001 S.L.T. 1013, per Lord Justice-General Rodger at 1016I, para.10.

[82] *HM Advocate v Brogan*, 1964 S.L.T. 204.

[83] See *HM Advocate v Woods*, 1972 S.L.T. (Notes) 77, per Lord Justice-Clerk Grant at 78.

[84] See, e.g. *HM Advocate v H*, 2002 S.L.T. 1380, per Lord Maclean at 1381J, para.5. Some other jurisdictions do have a less restrictive approach. In South African criminal law, in particular, error or ignorance of law can be a defence to a crime which relies upon intention. See, generally, K. Amirthalingham, "Mens Rea and Mistake of Law in Criminal Cases: A Lesson from South Africa" (1995) 18 U. N.S.W. Law Jnl 428.

[85] Hume, *Commentaries*, i, 26. In *Tennant v Gilmour*, 1923 J.C. 19, Lord Justice-General Clyde held that misconstruing a statutory regulation could not afford a defence.

In *Clark v Syme*[86] the accused was charged with malicious mischief after he had killed his neighbour's sheep. His defence was that he believed that he had a legal right to do so after giving due warning to the neighbour about sheep damaging his crops. Lord Justice-General Clyde was unequivocal in rejecting this defence of error of law:[87]

> "The mere fact that his criminal act was performed under a misconception of what legal remedies he might otherwise have had, does not make it any the less criminal."

The rationale for the rule

Various reasons have been given for the rule that error of law does not affect **8–41** criminal responsibility. Sometimes it is said that there is a powerful presumption that citizens have knowledge of the criminal law, but there can be little justification for this view. There may be a distinction to be drawn between the traditional common law of crimes and the modern statutory offences. Common law crimes tend to be in accord with widely held moral values; a claim to be ignorant of the criminal character of appropriating someone else's property may scarcely be credible.[88] On occasion, however, the common law may develop in an unexpected way.[89] It might be argued that some recognition of error of law is therefore appropriate. In Scotland, however, this would be regarded as a question of judicial restraint in the development of the law, rather than the occasion for the application of a defence. In respect of statutory offences, most people have only a vague idea of the detailed content of the modern criminal law. It contains a myriad of regulatory and technical offences. The rule that dictates the irrelevancy of error of law, however, is premised upon the notion that the law is both settled and readily comprehensible. Anyone who purports to have made an error of law is blameworthy for not having made the effort to become acquainted with the law's prohibitions.[90] Whether this is a defensible approach might be doubted. The criminal law is not always accessible to the ordinary citizen. Even to the legally trained, the law can be complex.

A pragmatic justification for the rule is that accused persons would raise fraud- **8–42** ulent claims of error of law which the prosecution would find difficult to disprove.[91] But is an error of law claim any more difficult to judge than any other matter with which the criminal courts deal on a regular basis? The more plausible justification for the general rule of law is a broader utilitarian one. It is in the interests of society for citizens to educate themselves regarding the criminal law

---

[86] *Clark v Syme*, 1957 J.C. 1.

[87] *Clark v Syme*, 1957 J.C. 1 at 5; applied in the *Lord Advocate's Reference (No.1 of 2000)*, 2001 J.C. 143 at 181F, para.109. See also below, paras 11–15 to 11–17.

[88] See *Dewar v HM Advocate*, 1945 J.C. 5; followed in *Herron v Diack*, 1973 S.L.T. (Sh. Ct.) 27.

[89] L. Hall and S.J. Seligman, "Mistake of Law and Mens Rea" (1940–41) 8 U. Chi. L. Rev. 641, 675, refer aptly to "the indefiniteness of the premises from which the common law may deduce criminality" (footnote omitted). In respect of modern Scots law, human rights law acts as an external restraint upon judicial creativity; see below, Ch.14.

[90] See H.M. Hart, "The Aims of the Criminal Law" (1958) 23 Law and Contemp. Probs 401, 412.

[91] J. Austin, *Lectures on Jurisprudence or The Philosophy of Positive Law,* abridged by R. Campbell (London: J. Murray, 1880), p.239.

so that they will obey it. The best way to achieve this end is to apply a strict rule that errors of law will not be excused.[92] There could otherwise be the risk that citizens would be encouraged to be ignorant of the standards of behaviour mandated by the criminal law.

Error of law and mens rea

8–43   The typical error of law case is that exemplified by *Clark v Syme*[93]: the accused claims that he made an error regarding the criminal law under which he is being prosecuted. The law's analysis of this situation is that if the accused, with mens rea, brings about the actus reus of a crime, he is criminally liable. It is no defence for him to say that he did not know that the actus reus was proscribed by the criminal law. A far less common alternative is that an accused will admit awareness of the criminal law for which he is being prosecuted, but will instead claim to have been in error about the civil law. It is arguable that in some circumstances a mistake regarding the civil law could operate to negative the mens rea in the definition of the crime. For example, if A is charged with malicious mischief arising out of an incident where he has intentionally damaged property belonging to B, an error of the civil law which led him to believe that the property was his own should be a defence.[94]

8–44   The limitation to this principle is that it could not apply where the criminal law sets a standard which is not the same as that by which the accused chooses to abide. The principle must be confined to the civil law, and to concepts such as the ownership of property. It was no defence for the accused in *Clark v Syme*[95] to assert that he believed the law permitted him to kill his neighbour's sheep. In *Andrew Ewart*,[96] the accused, together with his victim, had been guarding a churchyard. The accused mistook his colleague for a "body-snatcher" and shot and killed him. He was held guilty of murder, since it would have been murder to kill someone who had in fact come to remove dead bodies. His error was as to the criminal law. (The error of fact as to the victim's identity was similarly irrelevant.)

Erroneous claims of right

8–45   The defence of claim of right in crimes of dishonesty is said to be a recognised exception to the general rule as to the irrelevancy of error of law.[97] If that is so, then an error as to a belief in a legal right to appropriate will exclude the mens rea of theft, as it eliminates the requisite element of "dishonest" appropriation. If A appropriates B's property under the misconception that it is lawfully his, A's action is not theft. This conclusion would be in accord with the general principle described above, under which an error of civil law can operate as a defence by preventing the accused from having mens rea in acting as he did. Again, however, the accused's error would have had to be one which led him to believe that he had

---

[92] O.W. Holmes, *The Common Law* (Boston: Little, Brown & Co, 1881), p.48. For criticism of this thesis, see L.D. Houlgate, *"Ignorantia Juris:* A Plea for Justice" (1967) 78 *Ethics* 32, 38.
[93] *Clark v Syme*, 1957 J.C. 1.
[94] A persuasive authority to this effect is the English case of *R. v Smith* [1974] Q.B. 354.
[95] *Clark v Syme*, 1957 J.C. 1.
[96] *Andrew Ewart* (1828) Syme 315.
[97] Gordon, *Criminal Law,* 3rd edn (2000/2001), para.14.55. See, further below, para.10–17.

a right to act as he did. It could not be sufficient that he simply believed that his act of appropriation did not constitute a crime. The distinction between an error of civil law (the law of property) and criminal law (the law of theft) is fundamental. An error as to the former might give rise to the defence of claim of right; an error as to the latter never could.

Dewar v HM Advocate

Dewar, the manager of a crematorium, had been convicted of the theft of a large **8–46** quantity of coffin lids and a number of coffins.[98] His defence was that he believed that the coffin lids were his to keep or use as he saw fit: to treat as scrap. His belief was that he was merely following the general and accepted practice in crematoria. It was conceded that this belief was unfounded in fact. The jury was charged in terms of the law of erroneous claim of right. On appeal, however, the view was taken that the law of error was inapplicable. The basis for this opinion was that the accused claimed an error of law which was supported only by his belief that his actions were merely in accord with common practice. The court accepted that a defence of claim of right could succeed where it was based on an error of fact, but stressed that the error must be "founded on rational grounds", and could not be based on the "singular" idea of the accused himself.[99]

An alternative approach to that of the Appeal Court in *Dewar* would be to **8–47** concede that the accused may have been making an error about the law of property, in which case it could have constituted a relevant error of law (serving to negative the mens rea of theft). On this view, the issue would become whether Dewar had acted as he did because of a belief that it was not contrary to the criminal law to appropriate the coffin lids; or whether his behaviour had been actuated by an error as to the law of property. One imagines that it would have proved difficult for Dewar to satisfy a court that the latter had been the case. Nevertheless, it is difficult to agree with the conclusion of Lord Justice-General Normand that the answer to the question was so obvious that there was no need for Dewar's claim to be put before the jury.

Error of fact

The criminal law takes a more charitable view of errors of fact than errors of **8–48** law. There are two principal ways in which error of fact can affect criminal responsibility. First, the accused may claim to have been in error about a fact that would make his conduct justifiable or excusable. For example, A erroneously believes that he is about to be subjected to a fatal attack by B, so he kills him in self-defence (see above, paras 8–26 and 8–27). Secondly, the accused may claim to have been in error about a fact relevant to an ingredient of the definition of the crime for which he is being prosecuted. The present discussion is concerned mainly with this second category of error.

A shoots and kills B because of his mistaken belief that he is shooting at a deer. **8–49** A has perpetrated the actus reus of the crime of murder. Applying an objective test, one can draw an evidential inference of the presence of the requisite mens rea. The accused was in error about the fact that he was shooting at a human

---

[98] *Dewar v HM Advocate*, 1945 J.C. 5.
[99] See also Hume, *Commentaries*, i, 78.

being: a fundamental element of the law of murder. He is, of course, not guilty of murder. His error of fact will operate to negative the constituent of mens rea included in the crime of murder (an intention to kill, or wicked recklessness as to the death of, a human being). A will be found not guilty of murder because the prosecution will be unable to prove one of the prerequisites of the crime; the mens rea of murder cannot be satisfied by an intention to kill a deer. It should be stressed that error of fact operates as a defence in this manner only to the extent that it can be demonstrated to have affected A's mens rea.[100] Indeed, it might be thought misleading to utilise the term "defence" in this context. The issue could be interpreted as simply whether or not the accused had the mens rea required by the definition of the crime concerned.[101]

8–50   Need A's error of fact as to his target's identity be a reasonable one, in order to provide an answer to a criminal charge? By analogy from the law of erroneous self-defence, the answer would appear to be in the affirmative: the accused's erroneous belief must be subjected to a reasonableness test (see above, paras 8–26 and 8–27). Authority can also be derived from *Dewar v HM Advocate*,[102] where Lord Justice-Clerk Cooper charged the jury that the accused's error as to a claim of right had to be a "reasonable belief, based on colourable grounds."

Honest error in rape

8–51   The decisions in *Meek v HM Advocate*[103] and *Jamieson v HM Advocate*[104] represented a diversion from this consistent line of authority. It was held that an erroneous belief in the complainer's consent need not be reasonable in order to constitute a defence to a charge of rape.[105] The reasoning behind this approach seems to have been that where an error as to the complainer's consent existed, even if unreasonable, it prevented the formation of the requisite mens rea. This led to the conclusion that an accused acting under such a misconception could not be guilty.

8–52   These proved to be controversial decisions. The burden of risk of the "error" made by the male accused seemed to be placed upon the female complainer. The actus reus of rape was reviewed by a full court in the *Lord Advocate's Reference (No.1 of 2001)*.[106] There was at least a suggestion that the subjective approach to mens rea reflected in *Meek* and *Jamieson* might be revisited.[107] Subsequently, the Scottish Law Commission made a variety of recommendations,[108] legislated in the Sexual Offences (Scotland) Act 2009. The offences created under that Act are

---

[100] See *McIver v HM Advocate*, 1991 S.L.T. 81.
[101] In this case, murder; a conviction for culpable homicide, however, would not be precluded.
[102] *Dewar v HM Advocate*, 1945 J.C. 5 at 8; see above, para.8–46, and below, para.10–17.
[103] *Meek v HM Advocate*, 1983 S.L.T. 280.
[104] *Jamieson v HM Advocate (No.1)*, 1994 J.C. 88. See also *McPhelim v HM Advocate (No.1)*, 1996 S.C.C.R. 647; *Marr v HM Advocate (No.1)*, 1996 S.L.T. 1035 (applying the "honest error" doctrine to "indecent" assault).
[105] According to the *Lord Advocate's Reference (No.1 of 2001)*, 2002 S.L.T. 466, per Lord Justice-General Cullen at 476A–B, para.44, the definition of the crime of rape is intentionally or recklessly having sexual intercourse without consent. See the account of rape given in Ch.9.
[106] *Lord Advocate's Reference (No.1 of 2001)*, 2002 S.L.T. 466.
[107] *Lord Advocate's Reference (No.1 of 2001)*, 2002 S.L.T. 466, per Lord Justice-General Cullen at 473G–H, paras 28–29, 476B, para.44.
[108] Scottish Law Commission, *Report on Rape and Other Sexual Offences* (The Stationery Office, 2007), Scot. Law Com. No.209.

discussed in detail in Ch.9. Here it can be noted that the Act requires any belief in consent (for example, in respect of sexual assault by penetration under s.2) to have been reasonable; in determining whether an accused's belief is reasonable, regard is to be had "to whether [he or she] took any steps to ascertain whether there was consent . . . and, if so, what those steps were."[109] The standard being applied is an objective one.

Reliance on erroneous advice

Where a person in fact commits an offence, this may arise because she relied on **8–53** the erroneous advice of another. Does she, therefore, have a defence based on this type of error? If that advice came from a source on whom, or in which, it would have been reasonable to rely, it would seem harsh indeed to hold her criminally liable for the offence: surely there is a strong case to be made out for an acquittal in such circumstances? The fault, if any, will lie with the person tendering the advice. But if there is a defence of "reliance on erroneous advice" in Scots criminal law, it rests on two cases which are somewhat special, in that both were concerned with statutory offences. The first of these is *Roberts v The Local Authority of Burgh of Inverness*.[110] There, it was an offence under s.61 of the Contagious Diseases (Animals) Act 1878[111] to do anything, without lawful authority or excuse, in contravention of (inter alia) relevant regulations of a local authority. Under such regulations, it was permitted to move a "milch" cow from the County of Inverness to the Burgh of Inverness provided that a particular declaration and licence accompanied the beast. Roberts was accordingly charged as being a person who had moved such a cow without declaration or licence. He had, however, applied for the appropriate documents to the only person who could grant them; and that person had told Roberts that they were no longer required. This information was erroneous; but it was information on which Roberts relied. At his appeal against conviction, the question at issue was whether, in the circumstances, he had had "lawful excuse". Lord Justice-Clerk Macdonald held that he had, opining[112]:

> "It is monstrous to suppose that a man who acts on the advice of the author-ised servant of the Local Authority, who declines to give him a certificate because it is unnecessary, is to be found guilty of an offence . . . ".[113]

The other, more modern, case is that of *Dyer v Gallacher*.[114] Here the accused was **8–54** charged with having in his possession, with a view to their sale, a collection of hats and scarves which apparently bore the registered trade marks of Rangers Football Club, Plc—all contrary to s.92(1)(c) of the Trade Marks Act 1994. There was a defence to such an offence if the accused showed on reasonable grounds that he believed that no infringement of the trade marks in question had been

---

[109] Sexual Offences (Scotland) Act 2009 s.16.
[110] *Roberts v The Local Authority of Burgh of Inverness* (1889) 2 White 385.
[111] This Act was repealed (for Scotland) in 1914.
[112] *Roberts v The Local Authority of Burgh of Inverness* (1889) 2 White 385 at 392.
[113] It may be significant that the Lord Justice-Clerk also emphasised that both parties—the appellant and his adviser—had been in good faith: *Roberts v The Local Authority of Burgh of Inverness* (1889) 2 White 385 at 391.
[114] *Dyer v Gallacher* [2007] HCJAC 19; 2007 S.C.C.R. 152.

involved.[115] After trial, the sheriff acquitted the accused for reasons which the Appeal Court eventually rejected: this meant that a conviction would have to be substituted for the original verdict, unless the statutory defence could be made out. The court held that the respondent (the Crown having brought the appeal), although wrong in his view of the law, had had reasonable grounds for his erroneous belief: it seems that he had been acquitted on similar charges on a previous occasion, and that the head of the appropriate department entrusted with enforcement of the legislation had publicly described the state of the law as "muddied". The respondent thus fell to have his acquittal sustained.[116] It will be appreciated that the cases outlined in this, and the immediately preceding, paragraph are hardly conclusive as to the existence of any general defence of "reliance on erroneous advice".[117]

INTOXICATION

8–55 The ensuing discussion is concerned with examining whether, and in what circumstances, an accused can avoid the imposition of criminal liability for his wrongdoing as a result of his intoxication from either drink or drugs. The law relating to intoxication can be divided into two general categories: voluntary and involuntary. Different considerations apply according to which classification of intoxication is under discussion.

Voluntary intoxication

8–56   Intoxication can be said to be voluntary where the accused is blameworthy in becoming intoxicated. This fault element will exist where he has voluntarily consumed a substance, which he either knew, or should have known, would cause him to become intoxicated. (An exception to this rule is necessary for the circumstance where the intoxicant has been medically prescribed, or is taken for a medicinal purpose.)[118] The general rule is that voluntary intoxication is not an excuse for a criminal act. As Hume describes,[119] if Scots law

> "does not consider the man's intemperance as an aggravation, [it] at least sees very good reasons why it should not be allowed as an excuse, to save him from the ordinary pains of his transgression."

The rationale underlying this approach is one of public policy: it arises from recognition of the potential for harm which can follow from the ingestion of alcohol or drugs.[120] A further policy consideration is that alcohol is a factor in the

---

[115] See s.92(5) of the Trade Marks Act 1994.

[116] The following passage from the Appeal Court's opinion (2007 S.C.C.R. 152 at 158D, para.18) is perhaps worthy of note: "The sheriff . . . accepted that reasonable ground for belief could not be founded on error of law. Even if that is correct (as to which we reserve our opinion), it does not preclude the section 92(5) defence in the present case . . . ".

[117] For general discussion of this matter, see Chalmers and Leverick, *Criminal Defences and Pleas in Bar of Trial* (2006), paras 13–25 to 13–36.

[118] See *Ebsworth v HM Advocate*, 1992 S.C.C.R. 671, per Lord Justice-General Hope at 680B–D.

[119] Hume, *Commentaries*, i, 45.

[120] See *DPP v Majewski* [1977] A.C. 443, per Lord Elwyn-Jones at 469F.

commission of many crimes. The implications of accepting voluntary intoxication would be open-ended.[121]

Voluntary intoxication and mens rea

There have been attempts in the past to raise a defence based upon the argument **8–57** that intoxication can negative the mental element in crime. The contention has been that an accused's mind can be so affected by alcohol or drugs that he is incapable of forming the requisite mens rea. Scots law does not recognise any such defence

"where the absence or apparent absence of *mens rea* is attributable to self-induced intoxication, that cannot produce any kind of defence."[122]

As exemplified by the decision in *Brennan v HM Advocate*,[123] the High Court takes the view that a voluntarily intoxicated accused is responsible for the consequences of his actions. He can be held responsible for anything that happens while he is intoxicated. The potential consequences of becoming intoxicated are widely known; an accused can be blamed for taking the risks which everyone knows to be involved in becoming intoxicated.

In *Brennan* the court was facilitated in adopting this approach by the fact it was **8–58** a crime of recklessness which was at issue. Murder need not be committed intentionally; wicked recklessness suffices. Even if intoxication could negative the presence of an intention to kill, it was of no avail unless it could also negative wicked recklessness. The crucial question in *Brennan* was whether his conduct displayed wicked recklessness. The court's view was that voluntary intoxication was sufficiently reckless in itself:

"[I]t is extremely difficult to understand how actings may lose the quality of . . . recklessness because the actor was in an intoxicated state brought about by his own deliberate and conscious purpose."[124]

Did Brennan know what he was doing? He had ingested between 20 and 25 pints **8–59** of beer, a glass of sherry and a quantity of LSD. His claim that he did not know what he was doing when he stabbed his father to death is not implausible. It is possible to become so intoxicated as to lose appreciation of what one is doing. But this is somewhat beside the point in a crime which can be committed recklessly. The act of getting intoxicated is culpable in itself. As *Brennan* indicates, if the crime is one of recklessness the accused's attempt to use intoxication as an excuse to negative his mens rea will necessarily fail.[125]

---

[121] See Alison, *Principles,* i, 661.
[122] *Donaldson v Normand,* 1997 S.L.T. 1303 at 1304J. For the differing ways in which voluntary intoxication is treated in other jurisdictions, see Chalmers and Leverick, *Criminal Defences and Pleas in Bar of Trial* (2006), paras 8–14 and 8–15. Although Scots law adopts a robust approach, it would not be alone in refusing to admit evidence of intoxication as a defence to any crime. See M. Keiter, "Just Say No Excuse: The Rise and Fall of the Intoxication Defense" (1997) 87 J. Crim. L. & Criminology 482 (describing developments in the United States).
[123] *Brennan v HM Advocate,* 1977 J.C. 38.
[124] *Brennan v HM Advocate,* 1977 J.C. 38 at 50.
[125] See, for example, *Donaldson v Normand,* 1997 S.L.T. 1303, where the *Brennan* doctrine is applied to the crime of culpable and reckless conduct.

The extent of the no-excuse rule

8–60   The issue remains whether the rule that voluntary intoxication does not negative mens rea applies to all crimes, or only to those which can be committed recklessly. There are some crimes, including assault and theft, which can only be committed intentionally. Does this mean that it is a defence for the accused to show that he was so drunk as to be unable to form the requisite intention to assault or steal? It seems not. The no-excuse rule appears to apply to all crimes, irrespective of the particular mens rea required by any definition of the crime. In *Brennan*, the court took a robust view of the purported excuse of intoxication, concluding:

> "There is nothing unethical or unfair or contrary to the general principle of our law that self-induced intoxication is not by itself a defence to any criminal charge, including in particular the charge of murder."[126]

This approach was re-affirmed in *Ross v HM Advocate*.[127] Lord Justice-General Hope explained that

> "where the condition which has resulted in an absence of *mens rea* is self induced . . . the accused must be assumed to have intended the natural consequences of his act."[128]

This "exception" to the normal rule of criminal responsibility requiring mens rea is justified on "grounds of public policy."[129]

8–61   A possible conceptual difficulty with this no-excuse rule is that it equates the wrongful act of becoming intoxicated with the degree of culpability required by the definition of the crime. In *Brennan*[130] voluntary intoxication was equated with wicked recklessness. Getting intoxicated may be reckless, but is it "wickedly" so? The problem becomes more acute in crimes with a special degree of intention, such as theft. When the courts insist upon a particular mens rea in the definition of a common law crime, they do so because it is that particular mental element which renders the accused more blameworthy than when that element is absent. A refusal to regard as relevant any claim that the accused lacked the requisite mens rea might be seen as defeating the purpose of including the specific mental element in the definition of the crime.

A plea in mitigation?

8–62   It is clear that voluntary intoxication is not a defence to a criminal charge. It is not uncommon, however, for it to be led by way of a plea in mitigation, particularly in cases of minor breaches of the peace and similar offences. Hume himself observes[131] that intoxication might be used in mitigation of sentence in relation to crimes

---

[126] *Brennan v HM Advocate*, 1977 J.C. 38 at 51.
[127] *Ross v HM Advocate*, 1991 J.C. 210.
[128] *Ross v HM Advocate*, 1991 J.C. 210 at 214.
[129] *Ross v HM Advocate*, 1991 J.C. 210 at 214.
[130] *Brennan v HM Advocate*, 1977 J.C. 38.
[131] Hume, *Commentaries,* i, 46.

"which are neither attended with any profit to the delinquent, nor any necessary or immediate damage to one's neighbour, or to society; and which are chiefly reputed criminal, on account of the violation of order and decency, and the possible evil influence on the minds of others."

If A has been shouting and bawling in the street in a way which would otherwise satisfy the definition of breach of the peace, intoxication offers at least some explanation as to his conduct. It may allay the fear that he is a dangerous individual, rather than simply an annoying drunk. (This is not to suggest, of course, that drunks cannot sometimes be dangerous; the line between drunkenness as an explanatory or mitigating factor and as an aggravating factor is a fine one.)

Mental disorder

The law has never recognised a defence of (temporary) mental disorder resulting **8–63** from the voluntary ingestion of alcohol or drugs. In respect of the former common law defence of insanity, in *HM Advocate v McDonald*,[132] Lord Justice-Clerk Macdonald pointed out that, although

"we talk of a man being mad with drink because at the time when he has got . . . drink in him he acts like a madman . . . he is not in these circumstances a madman recognised by the law as irresponsible for his actions."

In *Brennan* it was stressed that the transitory effects of the alcohol and LSD were not sufficient in law to amount to the common law defence of insanity. Even if the accused's mental faculties had been substantially impaired, he had to be regarded as legally responsible for his actions. Similarly, in *Finegan v Heywood*,[133] it was held that the defence of automatism (parasomnia, in this instance) could not be established where it "was the result of, and indeed induced by, deliberate and self-induced intoxication." In respect of the partial defence to murder of diminished responsibility, it is provided by statute that a person who kills whilst in state of intoxication cannot found a plea of diminished responsibility on that condition,[134] but also that the presence of intoxication does not preclude diminished responsibility provided that there is a basis for the plea independently of the intoxication.

"Real" mental disorder

In *McDonald*, Lord Justice-Clerk Macdonald drew a distinction between an **8–64** isolated act of drinking, which might cause an individual to act like a "madman", and the prolonged imbibing of excessive drink which had caused actual brain disease. He regarded the latter as exculpatory. He spoke of the circumstance where a "man's reason is overthrown, either permanently or for a course of time." In such a case the accused does not know "the 'quality of what he is doing', and he is not responsible."[135]

---

[132] *HM Advocate v McDonald* (1890) 2 White 517 at 519. The language used may be anachronistic, but the legal principle remains relevant.
[133] *Finegan v Heywood*, 2000 S.L.T. 905 at 908H.
[134] Criminal Procedure (Scotland) Act 1995 s.51B(3).
[135] *HM Advocate v McDonald* (1890) 2 White 517 at 521.

8–65   As Lord Justice-Clerk Macdonald realised, habitual and excessive indulgence in alcohol or drugs can result in permanent brain damage and a mental disorder. (In *Brennan* there was no evidence of brain damage.) Provided that the statutory test[136] is met, therefore, a mental disorder caused by the long-term use of intoxicants is not inconsistent with the special defence. If the accused does meet the requirements of the defence of mental disorder, he is entitled to an acquittal upon that basis.

Involuntary intoxication

8–66   Intoxication might be said to be involuntary where the alcohol or drug has been consumed as the result of an honest error, or another person has used fraud or coercion to cause the accused to consume it (see above, paras 4–16 and 4–25). In *McGregor v HM Advocate*[137] Lord Keith's charge to the jury suggested that involuntary intoxication could result in incapacity to form the mens rea and could therefore be a defence. He drew an analogy between involuntary intoxication and somnambulism. On appeal, however, the view was expressed that this direction had been too favourable to the accused. In *HM Advocate v Raiker*[138] Lord McCluskey suggested that an accused would lack "the criminal state of mind that is a necessary ingredient of any crime" where he had acted "wholly and completely under the influence of some drug which was administered by force or by stealth without his consent." This view would appear to be correct, but for coerced intoxication to afford a defence it would be necessary to show that the acts were the product of the involuntary intoxication and that "it was a drug which like hypnosis put his will as it were under the control of another."[139]

8–67   Following the decision in *Ross v HM Advocate*,[140] it is clear that involuntary intoxication can operate as a defence where it constitutes non-insane automatism (see above, paras 4–19 to 4–23). The preconditions for the availability of the defence, as described by Lord Justice-General Hope,[141] are

> "that the external factor [the intoxication] . . . must not be self-induced, that it must be one which the accused was not bound to foresee and that it must be one which resulted in a total loss of control of his actions in regard to the crime with which he is charged."

In *Sorley v HM Advocate*[142] it was stressed that there are strict limits to the availability of the defence. There is a requirement of clear evidence of the accused's state of mind and also of the "causative link" between the involuntarily consumed intoxicant and his behaviour.[143] The presence of self-induction will be fatal to any claim of involuntariness.[144]

---

[136] Criminal Procedure (Scotland) Act 1995 s.51A.
[137] *McGregor v HM Advocate* (1973) S.C.C.R. Supp. 54.
[138] *HM Advocate v Raiker*, 1989 S.C.C.R. 149 at 154B–C.
[139] *HM Advocate v Raiker*, 1989 S.C.C.R. 149 at 154B–C.
[140] *Ross v HM Advocate*, 1991 J.C. 210.
[141] *Ross v HM Advocate*, 1991 J.C. 210 at 222.
[142] *Sorley v HM Advocate*, 1992 J.C. 102.
[143] *Sorley v HM Advocate*, 1992 J.C. 102, per Lord Justice-General Hope at 107; see also *Ebsworth v HM Advocate*, 1992 S.L.T. 1161; *MacLeod v Napier*, 1993 S.C.C.R. 303.
[144] See *Finegan v Heywood*, 2000 S.L.T. 905.

COERCION

The character of the defence

To establish the defence of coercion in relation to a serious crime, an accused **8–68** must show that he violated the criminal law in order to avoid imminent death or serious injury at the hands of a coercer.[145] A classic example for an application of the defence would be the motorist who is forced at gunpoint to transport an armed robber away from the scene of the crime. He is subsequently charged with being art and part of the robbery. In a situation such as this, the doctrine of coercion recognises that for the driver to violate the law is less serious than to adhere to the letter of the law, thereby risking death or serious injury.

If the accused has been coerced into committing a crime, he avoids the harm **8–69** which has been threatened to him, but does so at the expense of contravening the law and possibly injuring an innocent third party. Unlike the person who has acted in justifiable self-defence, he does not promote a value supported by the law.

The common law imposes strict limits upon the availability of coercion as a defence. In *HM Advocate v McCallum*[146] Lord Allanbridge pointed out to the jury:

> "When you come to consider this defence [coercion], I think it is right—as I am sure you will appreciate—that it would make life very easy for criminals and very difficult for law enforcement if, whenever a criminal was actually caught, he could turn round and say, 'I admit I committed the crime but I was coerced into doing it by someone else.' That being so, any such defence must be very carefully considered indeed."

The rationale of the defence

The basis of the defence of coercion in Scots law is that identified by Lord **8–70** Hunter in *Thomson v HM Advocate*,[147] where he said

> "that the will and the resolution of the accused must have been overborne by threats which he believed would be carried out so that he was not at the material time acting of his own free will."

Similarly, in *HM Advocate v Docherty*,[148] Lord Keith told the jury that

> "[t]he essence of the matter is that the will of the accused should be overborne by threats which he believed would be carried out."

Statements such as these can be misleading. A coerced individual retains free will in the sense that he can choose how to conduct himself. If he decides to break the criminal law in order to avoid death or serious injury, then he makes a choice. The law's emphasis on this purported lack of free will is more a reflection of the fact that the accused's opportunity to exercise his capacity to choose will have been

---

[145] See, generally, *Moss v Howdle*, 1997 J.C. 123; *Cochrane v HM Advocate*, 2001 S.C.C.R. 655.
[146] *HM Advocate v McCallum* (1977) S.C.C.R. Supp. 169.
[147] *Thomson v HM Advocate*, 1983 J.C. 69 at 74.
[148] *HM Advocate v Docherty* (1976) S.C.C.R. Supp. 146.

substantially undermined by the coercer's threats. The reason for not imposing criminal liability on the coercee is the recognition that it is unfair to punish the blameless person whose only choice was the morally unacceptable one between self-sacrifice and breaking the law.

Coercion and mens rea

8–71   It is sometimes suggested that a coerced accused should be found not guilty on the basis that he lacked mens rea at the time of committing the crime. An observation to this effect can be found in Lord McCluskey's charge to the jury in *HM Advocate v Raiker*,[149] where it is suggested that a person who acts under coercion, "lacks the criminal state of mind that is a necessary ingredient of any crime." This view of the effect of coercion can be questioned.[150] If B threatens A that he (A) will be killed unless he assaults C, A has the requisite intent for the crime of assault against C when he hits him. A may be excused for having mens rea because he was coerced, but the intention to assault is present. If A does not have the requisite mens rea, he is not guilty of assault, irrespective of whether he was subjected to coercion. Conversely, even if A does possess the requisite mens rea, his conduct can be excused by operation of the defence of coercion.[151]

The rules of coercion

8–72   The rules governing the availability of the defence of coercion are still largely those outlined by Hume.[152] He identifies four "qualifications": (1) "an immediate danger of death or great bodily harm"; (2) "an inability to resist the violence"; (3) "a backward and an inferior part in the perpetration"; and (4) "a disclosure of the fact, as well as restitution of the spoil, on the first safe and convenient occasion." According to the decision of the High Court in *Thomson v HM Advocate*,[153] it appears that the first two remain preconditions for the availability of the defence, but that the extent of participation in the crime and/or restoration of the spoils go only to the credibility of the accused's plea. As regards the nature of the coercer's threat, it is thought that something less than one of death or serious injury would be insisted upon by a court where the crime committed by the coercee was not a particularly serious one: the rule laid down in *Thomson* should be read in the context of a case of armed robbery.

Threats of present and future violence

8–73   In his initial opinion in *Thomson*, Lord Hunter states that

"all the Scottish authorities are based on the principle that a defence of coercion, in order to be successful, requires that the danger must be immediate."[154]

---

[149] *HM Advocate v Raiker*, 1989 S.C.C.R. 149 at 154B.
[150] *Lord Advocate's Reference (No.1 of 2000)*, 2001 J.C. 143, held that the closely related defence of necessity could have no impact upon mens rea.
[151] For a useful discussion of the relationship between coercion and mens rea, see the Canadian case of *Hibbert v The Queen* (1995) 99 C.C.C.3d 193.
[152] Hume, *Commentaries*, i, 53.
[153] *Thomson v HM Advocate*, 1983 J.C. 69.
[154] *Thomson v HM Advocate*, 1983 J.C. 69 at 74.

This requirement that the threat be imminent will be familiar from the discussion of self-defence (see above, para.8–20). It was explained in the following terms by Lord Justice-Clerk Wheatley in the same case:[155]

> "[I]t is only where, following threats, there is an immediate danger of violence, in whatever form it takes, that the defence of coercion can be entertained, and even then only if there is an inability to resist or avoid that immediate danger."

One question which arises is whether the defence can ever be founded on present **8–74** threats of future harm. In general terms the answer has to be in the negative, because of the immediacy requirement. In Lord Wheatley's terms, there must be an

> "immediate danger of the threat being implemented in the event of non-compliance at the point of time when the decision had to be made."[156]

Lord Allanbridge charged the jury in *HM Advocate v McCallum*[157]:

> "It is one thing to force a man to commit a crime by actually holding a pistol to his head . . . —that is an immediate threat. It is another thing to threaten a man that if he does not commit a crime he . . . can be killed or injured in the future—that is a future threat . . . [W]hen you are considering in law the question of the defence of coercion it is to immediate and not to future threats that you look."

The reason for discounting threats pertaining to the future is that the individual threatened is expected to seek the protection of the police.[158] In *Thomson*, however, Lord Wheatley does concede that

> "even in the ordinary condition of a well-regulated society there may be circumstances where a person is exposed to a threat of violence . . . from which he cannot be protected by the forces of law and order and which he is not in a position to resist."[159]

Lord Wheatley appears to be suggesting that there could be an exceptional case where threats of future danger could be admitted as evidence of coercion, if recourse to the police would be ineffective. His Lordship goes on to say that:

> "If such a situation arose it would have to be determined on its facts, and no profit can be gained from an exercise in hypothetical cases."[160]

---

[155] *Thomson v HM Advocate*, 1983 J.C. 69 at 77.
[156] *Thomson v HM Advocate*, 1983 J.C. 69 at 80.
[157] *HM Advocate v McCallum* (1977) S.C.C.R. Supp. 169.
[158] See *Trotter v HM Advocate*, 2001 S.L.T. 296.
[159] *Thomson v HM Advocate*, 1983 J.C. 69 at 78.
[160] *Thomson v HM Advocate*, 1983 J.C. 69 at 78.

Objective standard

8–75   The law applies an objective test when considering the impact of the threats upon the coercee. Only limited account is taken of the personal characteristics of the accused, even though these may have affected the way in which the accused reacted to the threats made to him. As stated in *Cochrane v HM Advocate*,[161] the jury is required to,

> "consider whether an ordinary sober person of reasonable firmness, sharing the characteristics of the accused, would have responded as the accused did."

If the accused does not possess, "reasonable firmness", the jury must disregard this fact, and take account only of his other characteristics.[162] Thus, in *Cochrane, no account could be taken of the fact that the appellant was unusually compliant (in the top 10 per cent of the population, according to expert evidence). Lord Justice-General Rodger explained that the logic of the objective test requires the jury to disregard the fact that the accused is more susceptible to threats than the norm, unless some kind of recognised psychiatric condition is involved. This is a hard rule, but is explicable in terms of the law's caution in admitting coercion as a defence. The intention is to keep the operation of the defence within strict limits.[163]

A defence to murder?

8–76   In his charge to the jury in *Collins v HM Advocate*,[164] Lord Allanbridge stated that "as a matter of law coercion is not a defence in Scotland to the crime of murder". His explanation was:

> "It is because of the supreme importance that the law affords to the protection of human life. It is repugnant that the law should recognise in any individual in any circumstances however extreme the right to choose that one innocent person should be killed rather than any other person including himself."

It should not be thought, of course, that the unavailability of the defence of coercion is likely to act as a deterrent to an individual who has to choose between death and killing an innocent. Kant made the point that the possibility of subsequent punishment could not overcome the certainty of being killed.[165]

---

[161] *Cochrane v HM Advocate*, 2001 S.C.C.R. 655, per Lord Justice-General Rodger at 670F–G, para.29; see also 667C–G, paras 21–22. (There are parallels with the law of provocation, described in Ch.9.)

[162] *Cochrane v HM Advocate*, 2001 S.C.C.R. 655 at 671A, para.29.

[163] *Cochrane v HM Advocate*, 2001 S.C.C.R. 655 at 666E–F, para.20.

[164] *Collins v HM Advocate*, 1991 S.C.C.R. 898 at 902C. See to like effect *HM Advocate v Peters* (1969) 33 J.C.L. 209. For a detailed discussion of this issue, see Chalmers and Leverick, *Criminal Defences and Pleas in Bar of Trial* (2006), paras 5–27 to 5–31.

[165] I. Kant, *The Philosophy of Law. An Exposition of the Fundamental Principles of Jurisprudence as the Science of Right,* translation by W. Hastie (Edinburgh: T. and T. Clark, 1887), p.53. The point is made of necessity, but is applicable to coercion.

Defences

NECESSITY

To the extent that Scots law recognises a defence of necessity, it is a limited and **8–77** residual one. It exculpates conduct contrary to the criminal law that the dictates of common sense and moral fairness suggest is excusable or justifiable, but which does not fall within the categories of a traditionally recognised defence (for example, self-defence or coercion). Necessity has long been problematic, partly due to Hume's evident disapproval of the plea,[166] and because of a lack of direct High Court authority. Hume appears to reject necessity even as a mitigating factor. In the case of stealing food because of hunger, for instance, he rejects a defence of, "compulsion by want".[167] Hume notes the difficulty of distinguishing genuine cases from those of, "pretended necessity". He fears that everyone could become the judge of, "his own wants and distresses". Nevertheless, the High Court in modern times had not been prepared to say that a defence of necessity did not exist, despite having had opportunities so to do.[168] It is only recently, however, that the High Court has acknowledged formally that there is a defence of necessity, if in a limited way.[169] The particular form of necessity which has been recognised as a defence is coercion by force of circumstances.[170] The theoretical basis of the defence is that coercion itself is but a "species of the genus necessity".[171] It is founded upon the notion that

> "there is so pressing a need for action that the actor has no alternative but to do what would otherwise be a criminal act under the compulsion of the circumstances in which he finds himself."[172]

This coercion or compulsion must dominate the mind of the accused at the time of the otherwise criminal act; there must be a causal relationship. If the accused has not made a choice between saving life and limb or contravening the criminal law, and has acted without thinking, the defence will not be available.[173] Immediate danger of sexual assault can trigger the defence.[174]

The facts of *Moss v Howdle*[175] appear exemplary for an examination of neces- **8–78** sity as a defence. The appellant had been convicted of a speeding offence on a

---

[166] Hume, *Commentaries,* i, 55; see also Alison, *Principles,* i, 675.

[167] Hume, *Commentaries,* i, 55.

[168] See, e.g. *Morrison v Valentine*, 1991 S.L.T. 413; *McLeod v MacDougall*, 1989 S.L.T. 151.

[169] See *Moss v Howdle*, 1997 J.C. 123 (where the opinion of the court emphasises the coercive character of the defence); *Lord Advocate's Reference (No.1 of 2000)*, 2001 J.C. 143 (where the term necessity is used); *D v Donnelly* [2009] HCJAC 37; 2009 S.L.T. 476 (which proceeds upon the basis that there is a defence of necessity).

[170] It is evident that the development in English law of a defence of duress of circumstances has had some influence upon the Scottish courts. For discussion of the English case law, see See A.P. Simester, J.R. Spencer, G.R. Sullivan and G.J. Virgo, *Simester and Sullivan's Criminal Law: Theory and Doctrine,* 4th edn (Oxford: Hart, 2010), pp.734–735, and Chalmers and Leverick, *Criminal Defences and Pleas in Bar of Trial* (2006), para.4–07.

[171] *R. v Howe* [1987] A.C. 417, per Lord Hailsham at 429C–D; adopted in *Moss v Howdle*, 1997 J.C. 123 at 127H–128B.

[172] *Lord Advocate's Reference (No.1 of 2000)*, 2001 J.C. 143 at 157G, para.39.

[173] See *Dawson v McKay*, 1999 S.L.T. 1328 at 1332B–G.

[174] *D v Donnelly* [2009] HCJAC 37; 2009 S.L.T. 476.

[175] *Moss v Howdle*, 1997 J.C. 123. For analysis of this decision, see M.G.A. Christie, "The Mother of Invention? Moss v Howdle" (1997) Edin. L.R. 479.

motorway. He had been driving, when his passenger suddenly shouted out in pain. Thinking that the passenger was severely ill, the appellant had driven at high speed to the nearest service station. In fact, the passenger was merely suffering from cramp, but it was accepted that the accused had reasonably believed him to be seriously ill. The first matter to be considered is whether there is any general defence applicable to circumstances such as these. The Appeal Court accepted that there was, drawing the parallel with coercion. The latter defence is available where the accused has committed a crime in order to escape from a threat of death or serious injury made by a third party. The court could

> "see no reason why it should be excluded simply because the immediate threat of death or great bodily harm which the accused is trying to evade arises . . . from illness, rather than from the actings of a third party."[176]

The defence recognised by the court is one of necessity, in the form of coercion by the circumstances in which the accused finds himself. It is clear that the defence can be based upon a medical emergency.[177] Other relevant circumstances could include natural disasters and the actions of third parties. The argument for the defence is at its strongest in a case such as *Moss v Howdle*, where the accused was not acting out of self-interest, but (as he thought) in order to secure the health of his passenger. Not all potential cases of necessity will be so suggestive of altruism. Reference can be made to the sheriff court decision in *Tudhope v Grubb*.[178] The accused was charged with an offence of attempting to drive with an excess of alcohol in his blood. He had attempted to drive in order to escape further injury after he had been assaulted by a number of men. The sheriff decided that in these circumstances a defence of necessity was available and the accused was acquitted.

8–79   There are a number of limitations to the availability of the defence of necessity. As summarised in the *Lord Advocate's Reference (No.1 of 2000)*[179] these include: (i) "good cause to fear that death or serious injury would result unless he acted"; (ii) "that cause for fear must have resulted from a reasonable belief as to the circumstances"; (iii) "the actor must have been impelled to act as he did by those considerations"; and (iv) "the defence will only be available if a sober person of reasonable firmness, sharing the characteristics of the actor, would have responded as he did." These requirements are familiar from coercion.[180] As in that defence, the fundamental condition is an immediate danger to life or of serious injury.[181] The court observed in *Moss v Howdle*[182] that this "requirement is apt to delimit the scope of the defence and to keep it within narrow bounds." The requirement of immediacy is a significant one. If the danger is other than immediate, there will be time to take an alternative course of action. Thus, in the *Lord Advocate's Reference*

---

[176] *Moss v Howdle*, 1997 J.C. 123 at 127H.

[177] *Moss v Howdle*, 1997 J.C. 123 at 128E–F.

[178] *Tudhope v Grubb*, 1983 S.C.C.R. 350 Sh.Ct.; apparently approved in *Moss v Howdle*, 1997 J.C. 123 at 127D–G.

[179] *Lord Advocate's Reference (No.1 of 2000)*, 2001 J.C. 143 at 158H–I, para.42.

[180] As in relation to coercion, it is most unlikely that necessity could ever afford a defence to a murder charge. See above, para.8–76; *R. v Dudley and Stephens* (1884) 14 Q.B.D. 273; cf. Chalmers and Leverick, *Criminal Defences and Pleas in Bar of Trial* (2006), paras 4–23 to 4–31.

[181] *McNab v Guild*, 1989 S.C.C.R. 138 at 141D–142A; *Moss v Howdle*, 1997 J.C. 123 at 126E; *D v Donelly* [2009] HCJAC 37; 2009 S.L.T. 476, para. 4.

[182] *Moss v Howdle*, 1997 J.C. 123.

(No.1 of 2000),[183] there was no question of a defence of necessity being available to the respondent anti-nuclear protesters, who over several months had planned their activities, which included malicious mischief against naval property. Their actions were not committed as a response to any immediate perception of danger; there was no indication that the damage done by the protesters could have had any conceivable impact upon the supposed risk posed by nuclear weapons.[184]

It is fundamental that there be no alternative means of preventing the threatened **8–80** harm. If there is a non-criminal course open, this must be taken. This is where the appellant in *Moss v Howdle*[185] fell short of qualifying for the defence. The Appeal Court adopted the sheriff's finding, which was that the appellant had not asked his passenger what was wrong with him. The correct thing for the appellant to do would have been to stop at the side of the motorway, inquire what was wrong, and then decide upon an appropriate course of action. The appellant did have a choice about what to do. The Appeal Court concluded[186]:

"Since the sheriff has found that the appellant could have prudently followed an alternative course of action which would not have involved committing the offence in question or any offence at all, we too must proceed on the basis that he had a real choice and was not constrained to commit the offence. That being so, the defence of coercion . . . is not available to him."

---

[183] *Lord Advocate's Reference (No.1 of 2000)*, 2001 J.C. 143.
[184] *Lord Advocate's Reference (No.1 of 2000)*, 2001 J.C. 143 at 178H–179D, para.100.
[185] *Moss v Howdle*, 1997 J.C. 123. See, to similar effect, *D v Donnelly* [2009] HCJAC 37; 2009 S.L.T. 476.
[186] *Moss v Howdle*, 1997 J.C. 123 at 130E–F. See also *Ruxton v Lang*, 1998 S.C.C.R. 1, which suggests that even where there is no alternative to a course of action which contravenes the criminal law, this must be brought to an end as soon as the relevant coercive circumstances have ceased.

CHAPTER 9

CRIMES AGAINST THE PERSON

General Introduction

9–01   The crimes considered in this chapter deal mainly with readily identifiable harms caused to particular victims. Most thus fall within John Stuart Mill's "harm principle" (see para.1–07, above), and require no further justification. "Harm" here generally means injury—such as physical injury (including death)—but also includes injury of a subtler or more psychological kind.

1. (A) ABDUCTION

9–02   Hume[1] discusses abduction under the description: "Of forcible abduction and marriage." This suggests that the crime might be rather limited both as to victim and purpose; but this is not the modern approach. A charge of abduction of a child of six has been received without objection,[2] as has such a charge relating to an adult male.[3] Burnett's remark would, therefore, seem to have been accepted, namely:

"When the abduction is neither with a view to marriage, nor rape, it is punishable *tanquam* [sic] *crimen in suo genere* [*i.e.* as a crime in its own right] as an unjust oppression, and restraint."[4]

It is thus thought that Sheriff Mitchell correctly stated the law when he said:

"the essence of abduction [is] to carry off a person against his or her will without lawful authority. It humbly [seems] to me that abduction for any purpose is criminal. I refer to Macdonald and to the 5th edn. at p. 124."[5]

Thus, a man wrongfully arrested by a police officer on a wholly spurious charge of breach of the peace was criminally abducted by that officer, according to the decision

---

[1] Hume, *Commentaries*, i, 310.
[2] *M v HM Advocate* (1980) S.C.C.R. Supp. 250. See also the first charge in *Anderson v HM Advocate*, 2001 S.C.C.R. 738 (abduction of nine year old boy).
[3] *Elliot v Tudhope*, 1987 S.C.C.R. 85. For a modern example of a charge of abduction see *Bashir v HM Advocate* [2006] HCJAC 16; 2006 S.C.C.R. 99.
[4] J. Burnett, *A Treatise on Various Branches of the Criminal Law of Scotland* (Edinburgh: Archibald Constable & Co, 1811), p.109.
[5] *Elliot v Tudhope*, 1987 S.C.C.R. 85 at 93.

in *Elliot v Tudhope*, where it was also accepted by Sheriff Mitchell[6] that "unlawfu. detention was a recognised crime at common law." It has been held, however, that a charge of abduction, which specified that a child below the age of puberty was confined "against his will", required the Crown to show that the child was unwilling to go with his alleged abductor, and that such a charge could not be established solely on proof that the "carrying off" had been without "parental authority".[7] The mens rea element of abduction is uncertain, but probably amounts to intention to carry off (or, possibly, just detain) a person knowing that it is against that person's will; the causing of actual fear and alarm seems to be unnecessary here.[8]

1. (B) SLAVERY

Abduction[9] is, of course, a common law offence. A recent, somewhat analogous **9–03** statutory offence[10] is committed if a person

"holds another person in slavery or servitude and the circumstances are such that [he] knows or ought to know that the [other] person is so held";

the offence is also committed if a person

"requires another person to perform forced or compulsory labour and the circumstances are such that [he] knows or ought to know that the [other] person is being required to perform such labour."

The operative terms in the offence (i.e. slavery, servitude, being required to perform forced or compulsory labour) are to be construed in accordance with art.4 of the Human Rights Convention.[11]

---

[6] *Elliot v Tudhope*, 1987 S.C.C.R. 85 at 93.

[7] *Brouillard v HM Advocate*, 2004 J.C. 176, opinion of the court at 183–184, paras. 22–23. The court observed in that case that where the victim was, e.g. too young to give a valid consent, then it had not been authoritatively settled whether, or under what circumstances, a charge of abduction could validly be brought; and that it had not been settled whether such a charge could be brought where a child was enticed or induced to go away with his alleged abductor (see 183, para.20), where reference is made to Alison's *Principles* p.630—and to his statement that the latter was "a crime at common law" (under reference to the case of *Richard Smith*, July 16, 1829, where a teacher of elocution had enticed a girl of nine years to come with him to recite poetry to an audience; cf. *Margaret Macmillan or Branaghan* (1839) Bell's Notes, 26)—and to Lord Kincraig's view, in *M v HM Advocate* (1980) S.C.C.R. Supp. 250 at 250, that evidence of a child's being led away or induced to follow "would be sufficient proof that she was taken away against her will"). Cf. the crime of "Plagium", which is dealt with below, at para.10–15.

[8] See *Brouillard v HM Advocate*, 2004 J.C. 176, opinion of the court at 181, para.15—the sheriff's view on this point being unchallenged.

[9] See above, para.9–02.

[10] See the Criminal Justice and Licensing (Scotland) Act 2010 (asp 13) s.47. The offence attracts maximum penalties of 14 years and/or a fine (on conviction on indictment), and 12 months and/or a fine of the statutory maximum (on summary conviction): see s.47(3).

[11] See the Criminal Justice and Licensing (Scotland) Act 2010 (asp 13) s.47(4), which directs attention to "the Convention for the Protection of Human Rights and Fundamental Freedoms agreed by the Council of Europe at Rome on 4 November 1950." Article 4 of that Convention offers little in the way of definition—save to exclude certain work or service from the ambit of "forced or compulsory labour". For a more detailed account of art.4, and the jurisprudence of the European

2. (A) Common Law Assault

ssault at common law covers a very wide spectrum of harmful or
producing behaviour. As was said by Lord Justice-Clerk Hope in *Kennedy
v Young*[12]: "The word assault is one of the most flexible terms." In Hume's time,
however, it seems that "assault" was just one of a number of expressions used to
denote criminal forms of "real injury." As he puts the matter[13]:

> "the law is provided with sundry . . . terms . . . such as assault, invasion,
> beating and bruising, blooding and wounding, stabbing, mutilation,
> demembration, and some others. But although the injury do not come under
> any of those terms of style, nor be such as can be announced in a single
> phrase . . . [l]et the libel . . . give an intelligible account of it in terms at
> large; and, if it amount to a real injury, it shall be sustained to infer
> punishment . . .".

Despite its undoubted width, assault at common law in modern Scots law is a
more specific crime than the foregoing quotation would tend to imply, and, in
particular, can be distinguished from other forms of "real injury."

DEFINITION OF ASSAULT

9–05 Until fairly recently, criminal courts in Scotland have tended to favour the account
of assault given by Macdonald at pp.115–119.[14] The following working definition
is, therefore, based on Macdonald's central concept of an "attack": thus, an assault
is committed when one person makes an attack upon another with the intention of
effecting the immediate bodily injury of that other person or producing the fear of
immediate bodily injury in his mind. The details of this definition will be explained
in the following paragraphs.

The actus reus: an attack

9–06 Use of the term "attack" may seem strange in view of the great variety of
conduct which the common law has accepted as sufficient for assault (see below,
paras 9–07 to 9–12). But it is submitted that the sense of an unjustified, hostile,
direct approach to the victim, which the word carries, is apt to describe the vast
majority of assault situations encountered in practice. Whilst it is true that spitting
on someone has been described as an assault,[15] as has the cutting-off of a woman's

---

Court of Human Rights thereon, see, e.g. D. Harris, M. O'Boyle, E. Bates and C. Warbrick, *Law
of the European Convention on Human Rights*, 2nd edn (Oxford: Oxford University Press,
2009), Ch. 4.
[12] *Kennedy v Young* (1854) 1 Irv. 533 at 539.
[13] Hume, *Commentaries*, i, 327–328.
[14] See, e.g. *Smart v HM Advocate*, 1975 J.C. 30 at 33; cf. *Lord Advocate's Reference (No.2 of 1992)*
1993 J.C. 43.
[15] *James Cairns* (1837) 1 Swin. 597, per Lord Justice-Clerk Boyle at 610.

hair whilst she was asleep,[16] and the forcible stopping of a man's horse,[17] and that arguably some of these situations may not amount to "attacks" in any usual sense of that term, it is also clear that the law's acceptance of them as criminal assaults is highly exceptional, if not remarkable. It is also remarkable that a "verbal attack" on another seems not to amount to an assault. "[M]ere words cannot constitute an assault", says Macdonald at p.115; and this seems to be tacitly accepted. There is, however, no authority to vouch that rule, other than a passage in Alison[18] where that author appears to be expounding English rather than Scots law.

Attacks producing injury

Although Macdonald[19] emphasises that the conduct sufficient for an assault **9–07** need not injure the victim at all, bodily harm is very often the result of an attack. Such harm may be slight or serious. Examples of the former have included the marks produced by compressing the victim's arm[20] or seizing him by the throat in order to march him rapidly to a police interview-room,[21] or even the disfigurement effected by cutting off some of his hair.[22] But examples of trivial injuries are seldom included in the law reports, which tend to feature more serious matters. Thus, at the other end of the scale, are found the results of holding someone's head under water,[23] blocking the air supply to a critically-ill patient in intensive care,[24] and pouring petrol over someone whose clothing then caught fire.[25] It will be plain, therefore, that it matters not whether an injury is serious or utterly trivial, so long as it was produced by a deliberate attack upon the victim; and it will also be plain that it matters not whether the victim was conscious or not at the time of the attack made upon him. Thus, it made no difference at all that a man, who had part of his nose bitten off, had been insensible through drink at the time[26] or that a person had been asleep when paper was stuffed into his hand and ignited.[27]

Those entitled to use reasonable force

"It happens from time to time that charges of assault are made against **9–08** officials and others who are entitled, in virtue of their office, to exercise in certain circumstances physical force. I may cite as examples police

---

[16] *Charles Sweenie* (1858) 3 Irv. 109, per Lord Cowan at 145. (It should be noted that the *ratio* of this case was overruled by a majority of the seven judges who sat in *Lord Advocate's Reference (No.1 of 2001)*, 2002 S.L.T. 466.) cf. *DPP v Smith* [2006] EWHC 94; [2006] 1 W.L.R. 1571 (interpreting the words "actual bodily harm" in English legislation).

[17] *Kennedy v Young* (1854) 1 Irv. 533.

[18] Alison, *Principles*, i, 176.

[19] Macdonald, *A Practical Treatise on the Criminal Law of Scotland*, 5th edn (1948), p.115.

[20] *Aitken v Wood*, 1921 J.C. 84.

[21] *Bonar v McLeod*, 1983 S.C.C.R. 161.

[22] See above, para.9–06.

[23] *Kepple v HM Advocate*, 1936 S.L.T. 294.

[24] *Atkins v London Weekend Television Ltd*, 1978 J.C. 48.

[25] *Williamson v HM Advocate*, 1984 S.L.T. 200.

[26] *Charles McEwan* (1824) in Hume, *Commentaries*, i, 331 fn.a.

[27] *Lachlan Brown* (1842) 1 Broun 230.

officers, prison warders, asylum attendants, railway servants and ships' officers."[28]

This is undoubtedly true; but such persons will not be seen as carrying out attacks, provided the force they use is no more than is necessary, for example, to arrest a suspect.[29] They will thus escape conviction for assault since there is no hostile use of force, although it can also be said, of course, that they lack the necessary mens rea for the crime (see below, paras 9–13 to 9–17).[30] In a similar way, parents (or those *in loco parentis*)[31] might at common law have disciplined their young children by slapping or smacking, and would not have been seen to be "attacking" them unless tempers were lost and reasonable chastisement became excessive punishment. That, of course, would have been a matter of degree in all the circumstances of each case.[32] Under statute, however, those who physically punish a child (i.e. a person under the age of 16) and who claim in answer to a charge of assault to have been justified in so doing (on the basis of the exercise of a parental right or a right derived from their having charge of that child) will have the grounds of that claim particularly scrutinised according to (*a*) the nature of what was done, the reason for it and the circumstances in which it took place; (*b*) the duration and frequency of what was done; (*c*) any mental or physical effect on the child; (*d*) the child's age; and (*e*) the child's personal characteristics—including (but not limited to) the child's sex and state of health at the time, and such other factors as the court in question considers appropriate: further, it is now the law that if the punishment included or consisted of a blow to the head, shaking or the use of an implement, a court must find that such an assault was *not* justifiable.[33]

Members of staff at Scottish schools (whether public or private) were at common law permitted to keep discipline by imposing reasonable corporal punishment on pupils[34]; but their power to do so has been abrogated by statute.[35] Although any physical conduct which is intended to *punish* has thus been declared unjustifiable, the use of physical force to *control* misbehaving pupils may be legitimate if it is moderate and reasonable in the circumstances.[36]

Those who play sports, such as rugby or ice-hockey, which allow physical tackling of opponents in the course of play, will, however, escape conviction for criminal assault, provided that they confine themselves to what the rules of the

---

[28] *Brown v Hilson*, 1924 J.C. 1, per Lord Sands at 6. The list may now include stewards or "bouncers" whose responsibilities extend to the maintaining of order at events attended by large numbers of people—see, e.g. *HM Advocate v Harris*, 1993 J.C. 150.

[29] Cf. *Marchbank v Annan*, 1987 S.C.C.R. 718; *Codona v Cardle*, 1989 S.L.T. 791; *Norman v Smith*, 1983 S.C.C.R. 100.

[30] See, e.g. *HM Advocate v Harris*, 1993 J.C. 150, Lord McCluskey (diss.) at 161 B–C.

[31] See, e.g. *Stewart v Thain*, 1981 J.C. 13.

[32] Contrast *Guest v Annan*, 1988 S.C.C.R. 275, and *Peebles v MacPhail*, 1990 S.L.T. 245. See also *Kennedy v A*, 1993 S.L.T. 1134.

[33] See the Criminal Justice (Scotland) Act 2003 (asp 7) s.51.

[34] See, e.g. *McShane v Paton*, 1922 J.C. 26; cf. *Gray v Hawthorn*, 1964 J.C. 69.

[35] See Standards in Scotland's Schools etc. Act 2000 (asp 6) s.16. "Pupil" and "school" for the purposes of the 2000 Act (see s.58(2)) have the same meanings as they have in the Education (Scotland) Act 1980 s.135 (as amended, *quoad* relevant, by the Registered Establishments (Scotland) Act 1987 s.2(2); the 2000 Act (asp 6) Sch.2 para.3, and Sch.3; the Education (Additional Support for Learning) (Scotland) Act 2004 (asp 4) Sch.3 para.3; and the School Education (Ministerial Powers and Independent Schools) (Scotland) Act 2004 (asp 12) s.3).

[36] See, e.g. *Barile v Griffiths* [2009] HCJAC 88; 2010 S.L.T. 164.

game allow by way of physical contact with members of the opposing team. There will then be no question of there being any "attack."[37]

Attacks aroducing fear

> "Gestures threatening violence so great as to put another in bodily fear, **9–09** whether accompanied by words of menace or not, constitute assault."[38]

This statement was impliedly approved by Lord Justice-Clerk Ross in *Atkinson v HM Advocate*[39] where the masked accused burst into a shop and vaulted a counter, thus placing a cashier in a state of fear and alarm for his safety. This was considered quite sufficient by itself for conviction, and confirms the conclusion derivable from earlier authorities that actual injury is not required. All that is necessary is that the accused should have made some unjustified, hostile, direct approach to the victim which led him to fear that he was about to be injured. Thus, if a weapon such as a firearm is directed threateningly towards another, that will be enough, even if the accused himself knows that no injury can actually be caused by it.[40] Similarly, where the victim is menaced with a cutting, striking or stabbing instrument, assault may well be made out at that stage.[41] It would be a mistake, however, to imagine that presenting a weapon at another is always sufficient for assault; it has been held, for example, that producing a knife during an interlude in a fight, and holding it out towards one's opponent whilst saying "fuck off", could be a legitimate method of trying to avoid the resumption of hostilities rather than a hostile act itself.[42] No weapons, however, are necessarily required for this form of assault. In *John Irving*,[43] for example, the accused had repeatedly shaken his fist in the face of his victim; and that, accompanied by threatening words, was clearly sufficient.

The question arises in relation to attacks which produce fear rather than actual **9–10** injury whether the victim has to be conscious of the attack made upon him. Must he have been personally aware of the menaces and threats to his safety? Although the matter is not free from difficulty, it is suggested that it should be unnecessary to show that he was so aware. On any other view, it would be no assault to brandish an axe in anger at a person who was asleep or intoxicated, which surely cannot be right. There is no authority on the point, however. Where the victim has actually been alarmed, it is equally unclear whether his alarm must be considered

---

[37] See, e.g. *Lord Advocate's Reference (No.2 of 1992)* 1993 J.C. 43, per Lord Justice-Clerk Ross at 48E. cf. *Dobbs and Macdonald v Neilson* (1899) 3 Adam 10, where an inferior criminal court quite unaccountably convicted two professional boxers for what they did to each other during the course of a friendly contest, fought according to that sport's normal rules. Cf also the law in England relative to "common assault" and the organised-sport analogy in *H v CPS* [2010] EWHC 1374 (Admin); [2012] 2 W.L.R. 296, where criteria laid down in *R. v Barnes* [2004] EWCA Crim 3246; [2005] 1 W.L.R. 910 were considered.

[38] Macdonald, *Criminal Law*, 5th edn (1948), p.115.

[39] *Atkinson v HM Advocate*, 1987 S.C.C.R. 534 at 535.

[40] *Gilmour v McGlennan*, 1993 S.C.C.R. 837; *Lord Advocate's Reference (No.2 of 1992)* 1993 J.C. 43.

[41] See *Norval v HM Advocate*, 1978 J.C. 70, where a sword, hammer and knife were presented; *Bryson v HM Advocate*, 1961 S.L.T. 289, where a candlestick was brandished at a policeman and a threat made to strike him with it. See also *Strachan v HM Advocate*, 1995 S.L.T. 178 (where the charge was actually one of attempted murder).

[42] *Mackenzie v HM Advocate*, 1983 S.L.T. 220, per Lord Justice-Clerk Wheatley at 223.

[43] *John Irving* (1833) Bell's Notes 88.

reasonable in the circumstances. The point was raised, but not decided, in *Gilmour v McGlennan*.[44]

Indirect attacks

9–11   The classic example of an indirect attack is the setting of some animal upon one's victim. Naturally, the animal would have to be one generally regarded as amenable to human control, such as a dog. In *Kay v Allan*[45] it was indeed said that encouraging a boxer-dog to attack two young boys trespassing in the accused's garden was an assault; but the decision of the Appeal Court proceeded on a concession by the Crown to the effect that it had to be shown in such a case

> "that the person accused caused the dog in some way to move at the alleged victim with the intention that the dog in so moving would at least frighten him."[46]

It appears, then, that it is not necessary for the dog (or similar animal) to attack and injure the victim. An unusual instance of an indirect attack occurred in *David Keay*,[47] where the accused, who was riding in a carriage, whipped a pony as he overtook it. This caused the frightened animal to bolt and throw its young rider, who was seriously injured. The court seemed to entertain no doubt that this was an assault on the person who was hurt. It has been held to be no answer to a charge relating to an instruction to a dog that it should "fetch" another person that the instruction was intended as a joke, since a dog cannot distinguish between a jocular command and a hostile one.[48]

The immediacy of the attack

9–12   It would seem that an attack, as described above, should be followed, or be capable of being followed, by immediate injury if assault is to be made out. If a significant temporal gap exists between the conduct of the accused and some resultant injury, then the crime (if any) is probably not one of assault. So, in *Charles Costello*[49] a separate, innominate offence was significantly charged (and upheld) where the accused had sent the victim a box of gunpowder, so ordered as to explode in his face when the package was delivered and opened. On the other hand, in *Smith v Paton*[50] the accused was charged with attempted assault, in that he had sent to his victim a postal packet so designed that concealed razor blades would lacerate the fingers of anyone opening it. He pled guilty, however, and thus no matter of principle was discussed.[51]

---

[44] *Gilmour v McGlennan*, 1993 S.C.C.R. 837.
[45] *Kay v Allan* (1978) S.C.C.R. Supp. 188.
[46] *Kay v Allan* (1978) S.C.C.R. Supp. 188 at 190.
[47] *David Keay* (1837) 1 Swin. 543.
[48] *Quinn v Lees*, 1994 S.C.C.R. 159.
[49] *Charles Costello* (1882) 4 Coup. 602.
[50] *Smith v Paton* Unreported, June, 1986, Dundee Sheriff Court.
[51] Paton's case is doubly curious in that it is often stated that in view of the width of the concept of "attack", there is no such thing in practice as attempted assault—see P. W. Ferguson, *Crimes Against the Person,* 2nd edn (Edinburgh: Butterworths, 1998), para.1–03; Gordon, *Criminal Law,* 3rd edn (2000/2001), para.29.02. See also above, para.6–08.

The mens rea of assault

The overwhelming preponderance of authority points to assault being a crime **9–13** of intention.[52] Although Hume's treatment of assault is somewhat superficial, he does refer to intent being required—in particular the intent to hurt and wound[53]; and in the case of *John Roy*[54] it is plain that the prosecutor gave up the case because he could not show any intention to injure. It had been suggested by him that assault covered all injuries causally connected to a criminal act of the accused (in this case, the kicking-in of a house window—malicious mischief) but the court would have none of that. Again, in the later case of *HM Advocate v Phipps*[55] Lord Ardwall told the jury that they could not convict of assault unless they found that the accused had had evil intent or an intention to do bodily injury. This was a curious way to present the matter in the context of that case, since the accused (the two sons of the shooting tenant on a Scottish estate) conceded that they intended to frighten the victims by the device of firing off loaded shotguns. They had heard voices from the far banks of a river, and had assumed that they were having to contend with poachers. At the pitch-black of midnight, therefore, they fired off their weapons in the direction of the voices they had heard, their object being to scare off the men in question and secure their poaching gear. It did not occur to them that anyone on the far bank would be within range; but such was the case. Two of the "poachers" were injured. Clearly the accused had no intention of injuring anyone but they did intend to frighten off the men concerned, by causing them to be alarmed for their personal safety. As actions on the part of one person which cause another to feel alarm for his safety are undoubtedly sufficient for the actus reus of assault, an intention to produce such alarm must certainly form the correlative mens rea. Lord Ardwall's virtual direction to the jury to acquit the accused must, therefore, be based on his belief that it was lawful to frighten off persons supposed to be engaged in poaching.[56]

It must follow, therefore, that two forms of mens rea are sufficient for assault. **9–14** The first relates to an intention to do bodily harm,[57] and the second to an intention to place someone in a state of fear and alarm for his personal safety.

Must the intent be evil?

According to Macdonald,[58] "Evil intention [is] of the essence of assault." A **9–15** similar remark was made by Lord Ardwall in the case of *HM Advocate v Phipps*,[59]

---

[52] See *Lord Advocate's Reference (No.2 of 1992)*, 1993 J.C. 43, per Lord Justice-Clerk Ross at 48C–D, Lord Cowie at 51B–C, and Lord Sutherland at 52I to 53A; *HM Advocate v Harris*, 1993 J.C. 150, per Lord Justice-Clerk Ross at 154D–E (quoting Gordon, *Criminal Law*, 2nd edn (1978), para.29–30), and Lord Murray 156C; *Drury v HM Advocate*, 2001 S.L.T. 1013, Lord Mackay of Drumadoon at 1033I–J, para.10, where his Lordship refers, inter alia, to the "standard definition of assault".

[53] Hume, *Commentaries*, i, 328.

[54] *John Roy* (1839) Bell's Notes 88.

[55] *HM Advocate v Phipps* (1905) 4 Adam 616 at 630.

[56] *HM Advocate v Phipps* (1905) 4 Adam 616 at 634.

[57] In *Scott v HM Advocate* [2011] HCJAC 110; 2012 S.C.C.R. 45, opinion of the court at 49D, para.13, this was rendered as "intent to cause harm"; but the court in *McDonald v HM Advocate*, 2004 S.C.C.R. 161, at 170E–F, para.23, reserved its opinion "as to whether . . . notwithstanding consent to the infliction of pain in a sexual context, an intention to cause pain could justify a conviction for assault in the absence of an intention to cause actual physical injury."

[58] Macdonald, *Criminal Law*, 5th edn (1948), p.115.

[59] *HM Advocate v Phipps* (1905) 4 Adam 616 at 630.

although he seemed to explain there that "evil" intent meant "an intention to do bodily injury." In the leading case of *Smart v HM Advocate*[60] the Appeal Court said:

> "If there is an *attack* on the other person *and it is done with evil intent*, that is, intent to injure and do bodily harm, then . . . the fact that the person attacked was willing to undergo the risk of that attack does not prevent it from being the crime of assault."[61]

Discounting for the present what the court said about the role of consent (see below, para.9–19), it seems that the relevant form of the mens rea here is really a straightforward "intent to do bodily injury" rather than an "evil intent" to do so. And this, with some degree of hesitation, appears to be the present law. In the leading modern authority on this precise issue,[62] the trial judge directed the jury that whether or not there was evil intent was at the heart of the case.[63] The accused had burst into a shop, held out a handgun in front of him, and given the startled assistants a command to hand over the contents of the till. The assistants were alarmed for their own safety. The accused's story was, however, that he had then begun laughing, announced it was all a joke, and left the premises. At his trial for (inter alia) assault, he submitted that he had had no evil intent, the whole episode having been an essay in the art of the practical joke. The trial judge told the jury that if they believed the accused's story, they should acquit since there would indeed be no *evil* intent. The accused was duly acquitted (on a not proven verdict) and in the course of a subsequent Lord Advocate's Reference,[64] Lord Justice-Clerk Ross opined as follows:

> "It has often been said that evil intention is of the essence of assault (Macdonald's *Criminal Law*, p. 115). But what that means is that assault cannot be committed accidentally or recklessly or negligently (Gordon's *Criminal Law* (2nd ed.), para. 29–30). In the present case, it is plain that when the accused entered the shop, presented the handgun at Mrs Daly and uttered the words which he did, he was acting deliberately. That being so, in my opinion, he had the necessary intent for his actions to amount to assault . . . ".[65]

It appears to follow, therefore, that the epithet "evil" is an unnecessary, if not misleading, one, and that the proper recension of the mens rea is indeed what is stated above, at para.9–14. A difficulty with this view, however, is that it was not necessarily shared by the other two judges in the case. Lord Cowie, for example, was of the opinion that "evil intent" *was* an essential element in the crime,[66] and

---

[60] *Smart v HM Advocate*, 1975 J.C. 30 at 33.
[61] This passage was quoted, with evident approval, in the homicide case of *McDonald v HM Advocate*, 2004 S.C.C.R. 161; see the opinion of the court at 170D–E, para.23.
[62] *Lord Advocate's Reference (No.2 of 1992)*, 1993 J.C. 43.
[63] *Lord Advocate's Reference (No.2 of 1992)*, 1993 J.C. 43 quoted by Lord Justice-Clerk Ross at 46D.
[64] For a "lord Advocate's Reference", see above, para.2–65.
[65] *Lord Advocate's Reference (No.2 of 1992)*, 1993 J.C. 43 at 48C–D.
[66] *Lord Advocate's Reference (No.2 of 1992)*, 1993 J.C. 43 at 51B.

that it was necessary to establish that the act of the accused had indeed been evil. As he put it:

> "Having established that the act is an evil one [based on its quality], all that is then required to constitute the crime of assault is that that act was done deliberately and not carelessly, recklessly or negligently."[67]

Equally, Lord Sutherland in his opinion indicated that "[t]he words 'evil intent' have an eminently respectable pedigree."[68] It is true too in other modern cases that some judges continue to favour "evil intention" as the proper description of the mens rea of assault.[69] The conclusion is that one cannot entirely be certain whether "evil intent" is simply an outmoded way of referring to "intent" or whether (for some judges at least) "evil intent" has a meaning distinct from simple intent. It is suggested that the former is the better view.

There may be some advantage, nevertheless, in requiring an intention to be **9–16** "evil". Sportsmen playing a physical contact sport where heavy tackling, or even punching is permitted within the rules; police arresting unwilling suspects; nurses subduing violent patients; and parents and others disciplining unruly children (on all which, see above, para.9–08), may all be said in a quite literal sense to intend the force they use. But, provided that the force used is no more than permitted within the rules of the sport or than necessary for the legitimate aim pursued, there is no evil intention in respect of it. If only bare intent is required for the crime, rather than evil intent, then a game of, say, rugby must inevitably be analysed as a continuous sequence of assaults, which will then require justification or excuse. Even more telling is the effect upon surgical or dental treatment. It is very odd somehow to have to regard a surgical operation, say, for the amputation of a limb, as a theoretical assault requiring justification by way of "necessity" or "the ultimate good of the patient"; and yet it is certainly arguable that the surgeon involved intends to do what he does, and that that involves bodily harm. But a surgeon (or indeed any other professionally trained medical operative) will not lightly be assumed to have any *evil* intent. Insistence on an *evil* intention will thus avoid the awkward notion of a prima facie, but justifiable assault in relation to medical treatment. As against all this, of course, is the inherent vagueness of the moral concept "evil". Vague concepts within a criminal justice system are perfectly capable of giving rise to unexpected, and even unwanted submissions— such as, that practical joke scenarios do not qualify as assaults since they cannot be thought of as "evil". There may, however, be *something* to be said in favour of terms which allow discretion to the court to deal with awkward situations sensibly.

---

[67] *Lord Advocate's Reference (No.2 of 1992)*, 1993 J.C. 43 at 51C–D.

[68] *Lord Advocate's Reference (No.2 of 1992)*, 1993 J.C. 43 at 52H.

[69] See, e.g. *Boyle v HM Advocate*, 1993 S.L.T. 577, Lord McCluskey's charge to the jury at 579K to 580C; *HM Advocate v Harris*, 1993 J.C. 150, Lord Justice-Clerk Ross at 154D–E (quoting directly from Macdonald, *Criminal Law,* 5th edn (1948), p.115), Lord McCluskey (dissenting) at 158I to 159A, 159B; *Kennedy v A*, 1993 S.L.T. 1134, opinion of the court at 1137A: *Drury v HM Advocate*, 2001 S.L.T. 1013, Lord Mackay of Drumadoon at 1033I, para.10, where his Lordship states: "The standard direction on assault refers to the fact that 'evil intention' is of the essence of the crime"; *McDonald v HM Advocate*, 2004 S.C.C.R. 161, opinion of the court at 170D, para.23. Cf. *Clark v Service* [2011] HCJAC 65; 2011 S.C.C.R. 457, opinion of Lord Bonomy (dissenting), at 467G, para.29: "evil intent requires quite simply that [the accused person] acts deliberately meaning to harm the victim".

It cannot always be wise to rely solely on the exercise of restraint on the part of the prosecutor.[70]

Is recklessness sufficient for assault?

9–17 There is no evidence in favour of recklessness, still less negligence, being a sufficient form of mens rea for assault, and indeed a considerable body of evidence against. Quite apart from the authorities referred to above at para.9–13, the court in *David Keay*[71] was at some pains to avoid concluding that an assault might have been recklessly committed. Where the accused had whipped a pony because it was apparently in the path of his carriage, thus causing it to throw and injure its rider, Lord Moncreiff said: "I cannot see what purpose the pannel could have, except either to do him a direct injury, or to put him in alarm."[72] His Lordship also remarked there that it would not amount to an assault if a person were to throw a stone heedlessly out of a window and thus injure some innocent passer-by.[73] Further evidence is provided by the decision of the Appeal Court in *Roberts v Hamilton*.[74] There, the accused was charged with assault in that she had aimed a blow with a stout pole at A but had in fact missed and hit B, who happened to be within range. The accused had had no intention to injure B at all; and, in fact, it would seem to have been an act of recklessness or carelessness that had resulted in the injury. But the court held[75] that as long as there was intent to hit someone, then that intent was transferred to the person actually struck. Thus assault has been zealously preserved as a crime of intention in Scots law.[76]

AGGRAVATED ASSAULTS

9–18 An assault charge may be aggravated, or made more serious in various ways. Prime amongst these are statements in the indictment (or, as the case may be, complaint) of ultimate intentions which the accused is alleged to have had. Hume[77] mentions particularly in this context the intent to kill,[78] the intent to ravish,[79] and the intent to rob. The mode of perpetration of the assault is also often encountered as an aggravation, particularly if a weapon such as a firearm was used.[80] It is also

---

[70] See *Lord Advocate's Reference (No.2 of 1992)*, 1993 J.C. 43, Lord Justice-Clerk Ross at 48E–F.
[71] *David Keay* (1837) 1 Swin. 543.
[72] *David Keay* (1837) 1 Swin. 543 at 545.
[73] It could, however, amount to some crime involving culpable and reckless behaviour—as in *W v HM Advocate*, 1982 S.L.T. 420; sub nom. *RHW v HM Advocate*, 1982 S.C.C.R. 152. Such crimes are dealt with separately in this chapter (see paras 9–31 to 9–40, below); and their very existence underlines the fact that recklessly caused injuries are not assaults.
[74] *Roberts v Hamilton*, 1989 S.L.T. 399.
[75] *Roberts v Hamilton*, 1989 S.L.T. 399 at 401F–H.
[76] Compare the position in England, as shown in *R. v Venna* [1976] Q.B. 421.
[77] Hume, *Commentaries*, i, 328–329.
[78] See, e.g. *Mysie or Marion Brown or Graham* (1827) Syme 152; cf. P. Ferguson, *Crimes Against the Person*, 2nd edn (Hayward's Heath: Bloomsbury Professional, 1998), para.1–17.
[79] See, e.g. *James Gibbs* (1836) 1 Swin. 263; *HM Advocate v Stopper*, 2002 S.C.C.R. 668. cf. *Rodgers v Hamilton*, 1994 S.L.T. 822, where the outcome of the appeal would now have been different, *stante* the decision in *Lord Advocate's Reference (No.1 of 2001)*, 2002 S.L.T. 466: see below, paras 9–83 and 9–90; cf. *Spendiff v HM Advocate*, 2005 S.C.C.R. 522.
[80] Macdonald, *Criminal Law*, 5th edn (1948), p.118. Assault, and other offences may also be aggravated by racism, religious prejudice or a connection with serious organised crime: see the Crime and Disorder Act 1998 s.96 (as amended by the Criminal Justice and Licensing (Scotland) Act 2010

common, even up to the present day, to find the results of the attack specified as aggravations—for example, that they were "to the danger of life",[81] "to severe injury, permanent disability and permanent disfigurement",[82] or even "to severe internal injury".[83] The place of the assault may be taken as an aggravation. It has always been regarded as more heinous, for example, to attack a person violently in his own home—and especially so if his home had been entered by the accused for that very purpose. (This used to be regarded as the separate offence known as "hamesucken"[84]; but that is not the present practice.[85]) An assault may also be aggravated by indecencies[86]: thus, punching (or threatening) a woman and then fondling her breasts is clearly an aggravated assault[87]; but such fondling unaccompanied by such violence or intimidation[88] seems to be either an "indecent" assault[89] or no crime at all, depending upon whether such familiarities are consented to (see para.9–20, below).

CONSENT AS A DEFENCE

No current version of the definition of assault at common law in Scotland includes **9–19** the phrase "without his consent" among its terms.[90] "Lack of consent" is not, therefore, a definitional element. "Consent of the victim" might nevertheless be considered as a defence to an assault charge. But in the few cases where consent has been tendered as a defence, the courts have generally reacted unenthusiastically. Where, for example, what is involved is the deliberate physical injury of another, in pursuance of a quarrel at least, it is no defence that that other person agreed to accept the risk of injury, as in *Smart v HM Advocate*[91] where both parties to a consensual, "no holds barred" fight stood to be successfully prosecuted for assault. It may be too that where a person agrees to be injured for his own (perhaps sexual) gratification, his consent will not prevent his injurer's conviction for assault. If that is so, then Scots and English law would be at one in this matter, namely, that for reasons of public policy, persons cannot be permitted to consent

---

(asp 13) s.25(1)), the Criminal Justice (Scotland) Act 2003 (asp 7) s.74 (as amended by the Criminal Justice and Licensing (Scotland) Act 2010 (asp 13) s.25(2)) and the Criminal Justice and Licensing (Scotland) Act (asp 13) s.29 (as also s.28(3))).

[81] Which can be added whether or not there were actual injuries. See *Peter Leys* (1839) 2 Swin. 337; cf. *Jane Smith or Thom* (1876) 3 Coup. 332, *Kerr v HM Advocate*, 1986 S.C.C.R. 91. cf. also *Gaffney v HM Advocate*, 2007 S.C.C.R. 296 (not possible to dispose of a case on the basis that it had been "to the danger of life" when such an aggravation had not been included in the indictment).

[82] Which may appear separately, or together as in *Williamson v HM Advocate*, 1984 S.L.T. 200.

[83] As in *Kirkwood v HM Advocate*, 1939 J.C. 36, where the shaft of a hammer was thrust into the victim's private parts.

[84] See Hume, *Commentaries,* i, pp.312–333; Alison, *Principles*, pp.199–208; cf. Macdonald, *Criminal Law*, 5th edn (1948), p.118.

[85] See *HM Advocate v Forbes*, 1994 S.L.T. 861, per Lord Justice-General Hope at 862J–L.

[86] Macdonald, *Criminal Law,* 5th edn (1948), p.119.

[87] Cf., charge (2) in *Grainger v HM Advocate* [2005] HCJAC 11; 2005 S.C.C.R. 175, quoted in the opinion of the court at 177B–C, para.1.

[88] Cf. the charges in, e.g. *Turner v Scott*, 1996 S.L.T. 200.

[89] In *Grainger v HM Advocate* [2005] HCJAC 11; 2005 S.C.C.R. 175, at 179F–180A, para.17, the Appeal Court rejected the submission that "indecent assault" was an offence separate from assault: it was "essentially an assault aggravated by indecency in the manner of its commission."

[90] Cf. the definition of theft below, para.10–02.

[91] *Smart v HM Advocate*, 1975 J.C. 30 at 33. Cf. *Scott v HM Advocate* [2011] HCJAC 110; 2012 S.C.C.R. 45 opinion of the court at 49D–50B, paras 14–15.

to their own injury.[92] It remains uncertain whether or not consent would be a defence where the victim agreed to be placed in a state of fear and alarm for his personal safety.

Consent and indecent assault

9–20 "If A touches B in a sexual manner and B consents to him doing so (and there is nothing else involved which would constitute a crime under statute or at common law) there is no assault because there is no evil intention to attack the person of B."[93]

But perhaps what truly elides assault in that sort of situation is the consent of the person being touched, or rather, A's knowledge of that. Indeed, if that person consents to straightforward fondlings, touchings, embracings and the like, there is probably no need to consider the intent of the other person at all. If there was in fact no consent on the part of the victim, an honest belief in consent on the part of the accused should be sufficient to secure his acquittal of a "pure" indecent assault, on analogy with the decision in *Meek v HM Advocate*[94] relating to common law rape. But in one case which raised this issue,[95] the advocate-depute maintained that such a belief might secure an acquittal if based on reasonable grounds.[96] At the end of the day, however, the Appeal Court was content to declare that the victim had not consented, that the appellant had gone further than had been justi-fied by the general conviviality of the occasion, and that he had taken advantage of the victim by "touching her in a sexual manner deliberately and without her consent . . .".[97] Whether an honest belief *not* based on reasonable grounds would have been sufficient was not commented upon. If consent is obtained by fraud, then that probably precludes conviction for indecent assault[98]; but a medical prac-titioner cannot claim that a patient's consent to medical examination for a specific complaint permits him to explore the patient's body entirely as he wishes until the patient expressly demurs.[99] For their greater protection, it appears to be accepted that girls under the age of 12 can give no valid consent to sexual "indecencies".[100]

---

[92] *R. v Brown* [1994] 1 A.C. 212 HL; *Laskey, Jaggard and Brown v United* Kingdom (1997) 24 E.H.R.R. 39: cf. *Re Attorney General's Reference (No.6 of 1980)* [1981] Q.B. 715, which appears to preserve consent as a "defence" in relation to minor injuries—a distinction which the court in *Smart v HM Advocate*, 1975 J.C. 30, considered wrong. (The Scottish Law Commission, in its *Report on Rape and Other Sexual Offences* (The Stationery Office, 2007), Scot. Law Com. No.209, recommended a change to the common law position here: see p.171 of the Report, Draft Bill cl.37, and relative text at paras 5.19 to 5.27; but the Sexual Offences (Scotland) Act 2009 (asp 9), contains no such specific provision.)

[93] *Smart v HM Advocate*, 1975 J.C. 30, at 33.

[94] *Meek v HM Advocate*, 1983 S.L.T. 280, confirmed in *Jamieson v HM Advocate*, 1994 S.L.T. 537; see also *Lord Advocate's Reference (No.1 of 2001)*, 2002 S.L.T. 466, Lord Justice-General Cullen at 473C–H, paras 28–29.

[95] *Young v McGlennan*, 1991 S.C.C.R. 738. Cf., *Peace v HM Advocate*, 2003 S.L.T. 419, where the existence of a "genuine belief in consent" defence was simply assumed.

[96] *Young v McGlennan*, 1991 S.C.C.R. 738 at 742F (as précised by Lord Justice-General Hope).

[97] *Young v McGlennan*, 1991 S.C.C.R. 738 at 743F.

[98] See the civil case of *Gray v Criminal Injuries Compensation Board*, 1993 S.L.T. 28, where the "victim" was the innocent partner in a bigamous marriage. Fraud itself would remain a legitimate charge, however.

[99] *Hussain v Houston*, 1995 S.L.T. 1060.

[100] See *C v HM Advocate*, 1987 S.C.C.R. 104, where the point was strongly urged by the Crown and conceded by the appellant.

That safeguard for girls under puberty is presumably derived from the correlative common law offence of "lewd, indecent and libidinous practices and behaviour".[101]

LEWD, INDECENT OR LIBIDINOUS PRACTICES

"In the modern law, where indecent conduct is directed against a specific **9–21** victim who is within the class of persons whom the law protects, the crime is that of lewd, indecent or libidinous practices."[102]

Children under the age of puberty (that is, under 14 for boys, and under 12 for girls) are certainly within that class, and may be exclusively so. In *McLaughlan v Boyd*,[103] it was decided that the common law did not support the contention that such lewd practices could be committed only where the victim had been proved to be below the age of puberty at the time; and in *Bratty v HM Advocate*,[104] an appeal against conviction on charges of lewd practices, on the ground that each of the female victims had been over the age 12 at the relevant time, was refused: but much of the former decision has subsequently been disapproved,[105] whilst much of the latter has been described as "confused".[106] Consent of the child is irrelevant. It seems that the essence of the crime lies in "the tendency of the conduct to corrupt the innocence"[107] of the victim; and the conduct thus may take many forms, as, for example, indecent exposure,[108] indecent contact,[109] the taking of indecent photographs,[110] the showing of indecent materials,[111] sending sexually suggestive text messages,[112] and "other forms of indecent conduct carried out in the presence of the victim."[113]

---

[101] See below, para.9–21.

[102] *Webster v Dominick*, 2005 J.C. 65, per Lord Justice-Clerk Gill at 79, para.49.

[103] *McLaughlan v Boyd*, 1934 J.C. 19.

[104] *Batty v HM Advocate*, 1995 J.C. 160, as properly understood: see *Webster v Dominick*, 2005 J.C. 65, opinion of Lord Justice-Clerk Gill at 76–77, paras 35–36.

[105] *Webster v Dominick*, 2005 J.C. 65, opinion of Lord Justice-Clerk Gill at 78, para.46.

[106] *Webster v Dominick*, 2005 J.C. 65 at 76, para.35. Both cases mentioned in the text were contaminated by the discussion they contain of the now discredited offence of "shamelessly indecent conduct". See also *Sneddon v HM Advocate* [2005] HCJAC 41; 2005 S.L.T. 651, where in charge (1), concerning the appellant "P", although the victim had been aged 15 at the relevant time, it was not suggested that a verdict of lewd practices could be substituted for that of the now discredited offence mentioned above.

[107] *Webster v Dominick*, 2005 J.C. 65, per Lord Justice-Clerk Gill at 79, para.49; *Moynagh v Spiers*, 2003 S.L.T. 1377, opinion of the court at 1378I–J, para.2; *Sommerville v HM Advocate* [2010] HCJAC 14; 2010 S.L.T. 616; and *Casey v HM Advocate* [2010] HCJAC 40; 2010 S.L.T. 1020 per Lord Justice-Clerk Gill at 1022F–H, paras 11–13.

[108] See, e.g. the charge in *Hogg v Normand*, 1992 S.L.T. 736; cf. *Anderson v HM Advocate*, 2001 S.C.C.R. 738.

[109] See, e.g. the charges in *RL v HM Advocate*, 1969 J.C. 40; *Moynagh v Spiers*, 2003 S.L.T. 1377; *NKS v HM Advocate* [2006] HCJAC 01; 2006 S.C.C.R. 70; *Dunnigan v HM Advocate* [2006] HCJAC 50; 2006 S.C.C.R. 398.

[110] Cf. the charges in *HM Advocate v Millbank*, 2002 S.L.T. 1116.

[111] Cf. the charge, framed as one of "shameless indecency", in *Webster v Dominick*, 2005 J.C. 65, and the Lord Justice-Clerk's comments upon it as possibly being one of lewd practices, at 81, para.61.

[112] See, e.g. the sending of same, charged as part of a course of indecent conduct, in *Stephen v HM Advocate* [2006] HCJAC 78; 2006 S.C.C.R. 667; and cf. Lord Justice-Clerk Gill's opinion in *Webster v Dominick*, 2005 J.C. 65 at 79, para.49, that the crime may be committed "by means of a lewd conversation with the victim, whether face to face or by a telephone call or through an internet chat room."

[113] *Webster v Dominick*, 2005 J.C. 65, per Lord Justice-Clerk Gill at 79, para.49.

PROVOCATION

9–22 The treatment of provocation by both Hume[114] and Macdonald[115] strongly suggests that it is available as a complete defence. This may be correct relative to intentional murder,[116] due to the way in which that crime has been redefined[117]; but, unless the "wicked intent" of murder is to be equated with assault's "evil intent",[118] it seems reasonable to endorse the accepted view[119] that the function of provocation in assault[120] is to "have a very considerable bearing upon the penalty which ought to be imposed in respect of [a] finding of guilt."[121] In short, the expectation is that it will lessen the sentence which might otherwise be imposed.

9–23 It seems that a wide variety of matters may be raised as provocation at a trial for assault. These obviously include a violent attack made on the accused to which he responds there and then in the heat of the moment[122]; but there the response must keep some sort of proportion to the original violence offered. As Hume put it:

"The general rule being once announced, that the person assaulted must keep within the bounds of an allowable resentment, the application is matter of common sense; and little aid is to be derived from any thing that books can teach on the subject."[123]

But finding one's spouse in the throes of homosexual passion has also been considered sufficiently provoking,[124] as have insulting words and behaviour. Thus, in the old case of *Ensign Andrew Monro*[125] the accused was understandably moved to violence on being called a "bougar" and "son of a whore"; and in *James*

---

[114] Hume, *Commentaries*, i, 333–337.

[115] Macdonald, *Criminal Law,* 5th edn (1948), pp.116–117.

[116] But not to culpable homicide: see below, paras.9–51 and 9–66.

[117] See *Drury v HM Advocate*, 2001 S.L.T. 1013, and below, para.9–49.

[118] See above, paras 9–15 to 9–17, as to the meaning of "evil intent" in assault; and see *Drury v HM Advocate*, 2001 S.L.T. 1013, Lord Mackay of Drumadoon at 1033I, para.10, where it is opined that the wickedness which murder requires is different from "evil intent" in assault.

[119] See Gordon, *Criminal Law,* 3rd edn (2000/2001), para.29.44; *Lennon v HM Advocate*, 1991 S.C.C.R. 611, opinion of the court at 614F.

[120] As also in appropriate cases of breach of the peace: *MacNeill v McTaggart* (1976) S.C.C.R. Supp. 150 at 151.

[121] *MacNeill v McTaggart* (1976) S.C.C.R. Supp. 150 at 151. See, e.g. *Barile v Griffiths* [2009] HCJAC 88; 2010 S.L.T. 164.

[122] See Hume, *Commentaries*, i, 334–335.

[123] Hume, *Commentaries*, i, 335; and see *Lennon v HM Advocate*, 1991 S.C.C.R. 611, although what was said there relative to homicide must now be read subject to the opinions of the court in *Drury v HM Advocate*, 2001 S.L.T. 1013. It should be noted that in *Gillon v HM Advocate* [2006] HCJAC 61; 2006 S.L.T. 799 (court of five judges) at 806D, para.19, the court upheld the proportionality test, where the provocation consists of violence, "as expounded particularly by Lord Justice Clerk Ross in *Robertson v HM Advocate*", 1994 J.C. 245, at 249E–F, viz: ". . . the principle has been expressed in different ways but it has been made clear that the retaliation used by the accused must not be grossly disproportionate to the violence which has constituted the provocation." Thus the phrase "no gross disproportion" has been authoritatively preferred to the alternative "no cruel excess" (cf. *Lennon v HM Advocate*, 1991 S.C.C.R. 611).

[124] *HM Advocate v Callander*, 1958 S.L.T. 24.

[125] *Ensign Andrew Monro* (1700) Hume, *Commentaries,* i, 334 fn.2.

McEwen[126] provocation was found in a newspaper article which was libellous of the accused's mother. In cases such as these, however, where there is no physical assault on the accused, it is unrealistic to require some degree of proportion to be shown between the provoking event and the accused's reaction to it, and it would be better to follow the lead set by the full bench in the homicide case of *Drury v HM Advocate*[127]: there the test laid down for cases of provocation by discovery of sexual infidelity was one of loss of self-control on the part of the accused, provided that an ordinary man or woman (as the case may be) would have reacted in a similar way to the accused in the same circumstances.[128]

In all cases, however, the assault must follow soon after the provocation, whatever it be. The intention is to make suitable allowance for incidents and events which excite the accused to a state of retaliatory passion, and not to cater in any way for a long-nurtured thirst for vengeance. Hume[129] mentions the 1746 case of *Alexander Lockhart* who was permitted to adduce evidence of provocation by insulting words given him by the victim in the morning of May 4, in alleviation of an assault perpetrated by him on the evening of the same day; but that must surely be the limit of the law's toleration. It is probable, however, that this rule and other rules for provocation are less strictly applied in assault than they are in homicide cases.[130]

2. (B) "ASSAULTS" UNDER THE SEXUAL OFFENCES (SCOTLAND) ACT 2009

Introduction

The Sexual Offences (Scotland) Act 2009 (asp 9)—hereafter referred to as "the 2009 Act"—was enacted to provide a new code of sexual or sexually-related offences for Scots law.[131] When the Act is fully in force,[132] certain common law **9–24**

---

[126] James McEwen (1838) Bell's Notes 91; cf. the case of *Patrick Murray Kay* (same citation) decided on the same day, where the article in question was directed against the accused's father—but in respect of his "public character as provost of Dundee."

[127] *Drury v HM Advocate*, 2001 S.L.T. 1013.

[128] See, in particular, the opinion of Lord Justice-General Rodger in *Drury v HM Advocate*, 2001 S.L.T. 1013 at 1021I to 1022F, paras 27–30. This means that there are two types of rule—depending on the nature of the provocation: in the homicide case of *Gillon v HM Advocate* [2006] HCJAC 61; 2006 S.L.T. 799, it was argued (inter alia) that there should be but one type—viz the one currently employed in cases of sexual infidelity—irrespective of the provocation; but the court (of five judges) affirmed that there should be no change (other than by legislation) to the present law: cf. Chalmers and Leverick, *Criminal Defences and Pleas in Bar of Trial* (2006), Ch.10, especially para.10–09 (written prior to the decision in *Gillon*). [It should be noted that of the two English cases (*R. v Smith (Morgan)* [2001] 1 A.C. 146 HL, and *Attorney General for Jersey v Holley* [2005] UKPC 23; [2005] 2 A.C. 580) particularly referred to in *Gillon*, the English Court of Appeal has subsequently preferred the approach adopted in *Attorney General for Jersey v Holley*: see *R. v James* [2006] EWCA Crim 14; [2006] 2 W.L.R. 887.]

[129] Hume, *Commentaries*, i, 334, 336 and 337.

[130] See below, paras 9–67 to 9–68.

[131] This code follows upon recommendations by the Scottish Law Commission: see *Report on Rape and other Sexual Offences* (The Stationery Office, 2007), Scot. Law Com. No.209.

[132] Under the Sexual Offences (Scotland) Act 2009 (Commencement No.1) and the Criminal Justice and Licensing (Scotland) Act 2010 (Commencement No.4) Order 2010 (SSI 2010/357) art.2(a), the provisions of the 2009 Act were brought fully into force on December 1, 2010, *save for* those in ss.52 and 53(2)(a)–(d).

offences will be abolished,[133] whilst other such offences[134] will be reduced in scope to the extent that their original ambit is subsumed by any of the new statutory provisions. These provisions are not always easy to classify; but where they resemble (to any degree), or bear alternative verdicts of "assault at common law"[135] (or purport to be "assaults"), it will be convenient to deal with them at this point in the text. It should be noted, however, that the offences created by the 2009 Act are not necessarily mutually exclusive.

Administering a substance for sexual purposes

9–25   Under s.11 of the 2009 Act, an offence is committed if a person[136] intentionally administers a substance[137] to, or causes a substance to be taken by, another person[138] for the purpose of "stupefying or overpowering" the victim, so as to enable "any person to engage in a sexual activity which involves" the victim. The administration (or causing) must be without the victim's knowledge—but this is extended to cover the situation where the accused (by act or omission) induces a reasonable belief in the victim that the substance in question is of a substantially lesser strength or quantity than it actually is; the accused must also be without any reasonable belief[139] that the victim has the appropriate knowledge. An activity is sexual "if a reasonable person would, in all the circumstances of the case, consider it to be sexual."[140] This offence is gender neutral.

Sexual assault

9–26   Under s.3 of the 2009 Act, it is an offence for a person[141] to do any of a number of things to another person,[142] without the victim's consent[143] and where the

---

[133] Under s.52 of the 2009 Act, the common law offences of rape; clandestine injury to woman; lewd, indecent or libidinous practices or behaviour; and sodomy are to be abolished "[f]or all purposes not relating to offences committed before the coming into force" of the section. In addition, "in so far as the provisions of [the 2009 Act] regulate any conduct they replace any rule of law regulating that conduct." These specific common law offences are also referred to in s.53(2)(a)–(d) for reasons which will be apparent when that section is read as a whole.

[134] Such offences will include assault where it is aggravated by circumstances of indecency: see above, para.9–20.

[135] See the 2009 Act Sch.3 for alternative verdicts; see also s.50.

[136] Hereafter referred to, for convenience, as "the accused". The 2009 Act itself uses alphabetic letters to denote the parties to the offence.

[137] "Substance" is not defined in the 2009 Act.

[138] Hereafter referred to, for convenience, as "the victim". The 2009 Act itself uses alphabetic letters to denote the parties to the offence.

[139] In determining whether the accused's belief is reasonable here, regard is to had "to whether [he or she] took any steps to ascertain whether there was . . . knowledge; and if so, to what those steps were": see the 2009 Act s.16. (It seems that this provision may also apply to the determination of whether a belief induced in, and thus held by, the victim was reasonable—since that belief is also one as to knowledge of a substance's "strength or quantity".)

[140] See the 2009 Act s.60(2)(a).

[141] Hereafter referred to, for convenience, as "the accused". The 2009 Act itself uses alphabetic letters to denote the parties to the offence.

[142] Hereafter referred to, for convenience, as "the victim". The 2009 Act itself uses alphabetic letters to denote the parties to the offence.

[143] In terms of the 2009 Act s.12, "consent" means "free agreement". Such agreement is declared to be absent (see s.13) in a situation where the conduct occurs when the victim is incapable of consenting to it due to the effect of alcohol "or any other substance"; when the victim submits or "agrees" to it because of violence (or threats of same) used (or made) against that victim "or any other person";

accused is without any reasonable belief[144] in such consent. The things, any of which engage the offence, are as follows: sexual penetration (by any means[145] and to any extent) of the victim's vagina,[146] anus or mouth—either intending to do so or being reckless as to whether such penetration will occur; sexual touching of the victim—intentionally or recklessly; engagement

> "in any other form of sexual activity in which [the accused], intentionally or recklessly, has physical contact (whether bodily contact or contact by means of an implement and whether or not through clothing) with"

the victim; ejaculation of semen onto the victim—intentionally or recklessly; and, emission of urine or saliva onto the victim—intentionally or recklessly, and provided the same is done "sexually".[147] The 2009 Act creates similar offences (which, however, *exclude* any "consent" or "belief in consent" provisions) of "sexual assault on a young child"[148] and "engaging in sexual activity with or towards an older child".[149] All these offences are intended (so far as possible) to be gender neutral.

Sexual assault by penetration

Under s.2 of the 2009 Act, it is an offence for a person[150] to penetrate sexu- **9–27** ally[151] to any extent with any part of his[152] or her body (or indeed with anything

---

when the victim submits or agrees to it because he or she is "unlawfully detained" by the accused; when the victim submits or agrees to it because he or she is mistaken due to deception by the accused as to its nature or purpose; when the victim is induced to submit or agree to it because of impersonation by the accused of a person "known personally" to the victim; or, when the sole "expression or indication of agreement to [it] is from a person other than" the victim. The foregoing list is effectively extended by s.14, which declares that a "person is incapable, while asleep or unconscious, of consenting to any conduct." And, under s.15(2)–(3), it is further declared that consent to one type of conduct does not (per se) imply consent to any other, and that consent, once given, may be withdrawn at any time before, or during, the conduct in question: see also s.15(4) which deals generally with withdrawal of consent. Where the victim suffers from "mental disorder" (as defined in the Mental Health (Care and Treatment) (Scotland) Act 2003 (asp 13) s.328(1)), he or she is deemed incapable of consenting to particular conduct if, by reason of such disorder, he or she is unable to understand it, decide whether to engage in it, or communicate a decision relative to it: see the 2009 Act s.17.

[144] In determining whether an accused's belief is reasonable here, regard is to be had "to whether [he or she] took any steps to ascertain whether there was consent . . . and if so, to what those steps were": see the 2009 Act s.16. See also the 2009 Act Sch.2 (for penalties relative to the offences) and Sch.3 (for a list of alternative verdicts to most, but not all, of the offences).

[145] This includes penetration by the accused's "penis"—as that is defined broadly in the 2009 Act s.1(4).

[146] "Vagina" is defined broadly in the 2009 Act s.1(4).

[147] "Sexual", or any of its correlatives, is declared to apply as a description (of penetration, touching, emission, or an activity) "if a reasonable person would, in all the circumstances of the case, consider it to be" so: see the 2009 Act s.60(2)(a).

[148] See the 2009 Act s.20—a "young child" being defined as one who "has not attained the age of 13 years".

[149] See the 2009 Act s.30—an "older child" being defined as one who (a) has attained the age of 13 years, and (b) has not attained the age of 16 years; this offence can only be committed by an accused who "has attained the age of 16 years" himself or herself, but there is a defence under the 2009 Act s.39(1)(a) (that the accused reasonably believed that the victim had attained the age of 16 years, provided that s.39(2)(a)(i) does not apply to him or her).

[150] Hereafter referred to, for convenience, as "the accused". The 2009 Act itself uses alphabetic letters to denote the parties to the offence.

[151] See above, para.9–26, fn.147.

[152] This includes penetration with his "penis" (as defined in s.1(4) of the 2009 Act): see s.2(4).

else) the vagina[153] or anus of another person,[154] either intending to do so or being reckless as to whether penetration will occur, without the victim's consent[155] and where the accused is without any reasonable belief[156] in such consent. The Act creates similar offences (which *exclude* any "consent" or "belief in consent" provisions) of "sexual assault on a young child by penetration"[157] and "engaging in penetrative sexual activity with or towards an older child".[158] These offences are intended (so far as possible) to be gender neutral.

Sexual coercion

9–28   Under s.4 of the 2009 Act, it is an offence for a person[159] intentionally to cause another person[160] to participate in a sexual[161] activity if the victim does not consent[162] to so participate and the accused is without any reasonable belief[163] that the victim so consents. It is to be noted that the operative word used is "cause" rather than "compel" (which the *nomen iuris* would seem to anticipate). The Act also creates similar offences (which *exclude* the "consent" and "reasonable belief in consent" provisions) of "causing a young child to participate in a sexual activity"[164] and "causing an older child to participate in [such an] activity".[165] These offences are intended to be gender neutral.

Coercing a person into being present during a sexual activity

9–29   Under s.5 of the 2009 Act, it is an offence for a person[166] (a) intentionally to engage in a sexual activity[167] in the presence of another person[168] and that for the purpose of obtaining sexual gratification[169] or humiliating, distressing or alarming

---

[153] "Vagina" is defined in s.1(4) of the 2009 Act.

[154] Hereafter referred to, for convenience, as "the victim". The 2009 Act itself uses alphabetic letters to denote the parties to the offence.

[155] See above, para.9–26, fn.143.

[156] See above, para.9–26, fn.144.

[157] See the 2009 Act s.19—a "young child" being one "who has not attained the age of 13 years".

[158] See the 2009 Act s.29—an "older child" being one "who (a) has attained the age of 13 years, but (b) has not attained the age of 16 years"; this offence must be committed by an accused who "has attained the age of 16 years", but there is a defence under s.39(1)(a) of the Act (that the accused reasonably believed that the victim had attained the age of 16 years, provided that s.39(2)(a)(i) does not apply to him or her).

[159] Hereafter referred to, for convenience, as "the accused". The 2009 Act itself uses alphabetic letters to denote the parties to the offence.

[160] Hereafter referred to, for convenience, as "the victim". The 2009 Act itself uses alphabetic letters to denote the parties to the offence.

[161] See above, para.9–26, fn.147.

[162] See above, para.9–26, fn.143.

[163] See above, para.9–26,fn.144.

[164] See the 2009 Act s.21—a "young child" being one who has not attained the age of 13 years.

[165] See the 2009 Act s.31—an "older child" being one "who (a) has attained the age of 13 years, but (b) has not attained the age of 16 years"; this offence must be committed by an accused who "has attained the age of 16 years", but there is a defence under s.39(1)(a) of the Act (that the accused reasonably believed that the victim had attained the age of 16 years, provided that s.39(2)(a)(i) does not apply to him or her).

[166] Hereafter referred to, for convenience, as "the accused". The 2009 Act itself uses alphabetic letters to denote the parties to the offence.

[167] See above, para.9–26, fn.147.

[168] Hereafter referred to, for convenience, as "the victim". The 2009 Act itself uses alphabetic letters to denote the parties to the offence.

[169] I.e. for the accused himself or herself.

the victim[170] (or for both those purposes), or (b), again intentionally (and also for such a purpose), to cause the victim to be present "while a third person engages in such an activity"—all without the victim's consent[171] and where the accused is without any reasonable belief[172] that the victim consents. Lest this should not be clear, s.5(3) specifically declares that the offence includes a case where the accused engages in the relevant sexual activity in a place where he or she can be observed by the victim, and also a case where, relative to a third person's engaging in such an activity, the victim is in a place from which he or she can observe that third person—in both cases, the victim being in a position to observe "other than by . . . looking at an image". The Act also creates similar offences (which *exclude* the "consent" and "reasonable belief in consent" provisions) of "causing a young child to be present during a sexual activity"[173] and "causing an older child to be present during a sexual activity".[174] These offences are gender neutral.

Coercing a person into looking at a sexual image

Under s.6 of the 2009 Act, it is an offence for a person[175] intentionally (and for **9–30** the purpose of obtaining sexual gratification,[176] or of humiliating, distressing or alarming[177] another person[178]—or both theses purposes) to cause the victim to look at a "sexual image" if the victim does not consent[179] to look at it and the accused is without any reasonable belief[180] that the victim so consents. "Sexual image" here means an image (produced by any means and whether moving or not) of the accused (or a third, or even an imaginary, person) engaging in a sexual activity[181] or of the genitals of the accused (or such third or imaginary person). The Act also creates similar offences (which *exclude* the "consent" or "reasonable belief in consent" provisions) of "causing a young child to look at a sexual image"[182] and "causing an older child to look at a sexual image".[183] These offences are gender neutral.

---

[170] Whether or not the victim was actually humiliated, distressed or alarmed: see the 2009 Act s.49(1),(2).

[171] See above, para.9–26, fn.143.

[172] See above, para.9–26, fn.144.

[173] See the 2009 Act s.22—a "young child" being one "who has not attained the age of 13 years".

[174] See the 2009 Act s.32 an "older child" being one "who (a) has attained the age of 13 years, but (b) has not attained the age of 16 years"; this offence must be committed by an accused who "has attained the age of 16 years", but there is a defence under s.39(1)(a) of the Act (that the accused reasonably believed that the victim had attained the age of 16 years, provided that s.39(2)(a)(i) does not apply to him or her).

[175] Hereafter referred to, for convenience, as "the accused". The 2009 Act itself uses alphabetic letters to denote the parties to the offence.

[176] I.e. for the accused himself or herself.

[177] Whether or not the other person was actually humiliated, distressed or alarmed: see the 2009 Act s.49(1),(2).

[178] Hereafter referred to, for convenience, as "the victim". The 2009 Act itself uses alphabetic letters to denote the parties to the offence.

[179] See above, para.9–26, fn.143.

[180] See above, para.9–26, fn.144.

[181] See above, para.9–26, fn.147.

[182] See the 2009 Act s.23—a "young child" being one "who has not attained the age of 13 years".

[183] See the 2009 Act s.33—an "older child" being one "who (a) has attained the age of 13 years, but (b) has not attained the age of 16 years"; this offence must be committed by an accused who "has attained the age of 16 years", but there is a defence under s.39(1)(a) of the Act (that the accused reasonably believed that the victim had attained the age of 16 years, provided that s.39(2)(a)(i) does not apply to him or her).

3. NON-INTENTIONAL INJURY

Introduction

9–31   Using Hume's concept of "real injury" (see para.9–04, above) as an established general principle[184] the Scottish courts have developed a series of related crimes. These differ from common law assault in that injuries suffered by the victim are not caused intentionally by the accused. Rather they are the product of recklessness on his behalf. It has been said frequently by the judiciary that non-intentionally caused injuries are not criminal at common law unless the conduct of the accused went well beyond carelessness. A very significant derogation from the standard of care expected of a person of ordinary understanding and competence has to be shown. In the leading case of *HM Advocate v Harris*,[185] three of the five judges emphasised this point,[186] and indeed considered that the standard referred to in *Quinn v Cunningham*[187] was essentially correct. That standard was itself derived from an earlier culpable homicide case[188] where the requirement was stated to be "gross, or wicked, or criminal negligence, something amounting, or at any rate analogous, to a criminal indifference to consequences . . .". A high standard of recklessness[189] of this nature is, therefore, essential, and forms the mens rea of each such crime. It was also held to be correct in *Harris* that actual injury was not always necessary—that there was a crime, or class of crimes, of which the essence was causing danger to the "lieges" by the recklessness of one's conduct.[190] Although criticised by Lord McCluskey,[191] Lord Prosser was surely correct when he opined that recklessness (in this context at least) consists of a failure in one's duty to so conduct oneself that foreseeable danger of significant injury to others as a consequence of one's actions is set at an absolute minimum.[192] Clearly the nature of the activity and the degree of risk involved are important considerations in the assessment of conduct as "reckless"; but Lord Prosser

---

[184] See *Khaliq v HM Advocate*, 1984 J.C. 23, per Lord Justice-General Emslie at 31–32.

[185] *HM Advocate v Harris*, 1993 J.C. 150.

[186] *HM Advocate v Harris*, 1993 J.C. 150, Lord Murray at 155H–I, Lord Morison at 162A–C, and Lord Prosser at 168E and 169B (where he sought to distinguish between recklessness of the required high standard, and "mere" recklessness).

[187] *Quinn v Cunningham*, 1956 J.C. 22—overruled in other respects by *HM Advocate v Harris*. See also *Cameron v Maguire*, 1999 S.C.C.R. 44, opinion of the court at 46F–47A.

[188] *Paton v HM Advocate*, 1936 J.C. 19, Lord Justice-Clerk Aitchison at 22.

[189] It has to be noted, however, that in some cases, the Appeal Court has criticised judges who directed juries that a *high degree* of recklessness was required. The criticism was based on the view that such directions introduced unnecessary complications where the simple distinction to be made was between negligent or accidental conduct (which was not criminal) and reckless behaviour (which was): see, e.g. *Carr v HM Advocate*, 1995 S.L.T. 800, Lord Justice-General Hope at 803K–L and 804A (a case involving reckless fire-raising).

[190] This was conceded by counsel for the respondent in the case, a concession which all five judges considered to have been correctly made. Notice that Lord Prosser sensibly objected to the use of the archaic expression "lieges": as he put it, at 166C, ". . . danger to others can be referred to as danger to others without obsolete terms which need explaining." Evidence of actual danger to others is not always necessary, since the quality of the conduct may be sufficient to "satisfy the test of being described as culpable and reckless": *Robertson v Klos* [2005] HCJAC 136; 2006 S.C.C.R. 52, opinion of the court at 60D, para.21; see also 61B, para.24.

[191] *HM Advocate v Harris*, 1993 J.C. 150, at 159H–I. The basis of his criticism was that complex accounts of the *mentes reae* appropriate to particular crimes will simply create difficulties for judges and confusion for juries.

[192] *HM Advocate v Harris*, 1993 J.C. 150 at 165C–D.

appears to emphasise that recklessness and danger to others are interdependent in crimes of this nature—and that it makes sense to consider whether there had been danger to others even where injury *is* actually caused.[193] Certainly, where unintentional injury does result from the conduct of the accused, it is plainly necessary to categorise that injury as accidentally, negligently or recklessly caused—only the last of the three being relevant from the point of view of the criminal law. Equally, if significant unintentional injury has been caused by one's conduct, a strong inference arises that one's conduct probably was dangerous to others. It may be sufficient in fact that the conduct was dangerous in respect of the victim alone. The existence of danger to others, due to one's conduct, is thus a useful (if not essential) guide to separating the relevant from the irrelevant in crimes of this sort. Of course, "conduct" in this context will generally be something positive on the part of the accused—including, for example, the denial of the existence of some factor which creates danger for the potential victim[194]; where the conduct is said to be a mere failure to declare the existence of such a factor, the sufficiency of such conduct will depend on the exact circumstances of each case.[195] The essential elements of the best known of these offences are discussed in the paragraphs which follow.

OFFENCES INVOLVING A RELATIONSHIP BETWEEN ACCUSED AND VICTIM

Cruel and barbarous treatment

Indictments for offences of this description were found frequently in the nineteenth century. Very often such a charge would be combined with an allegation of "Wilful and Culpable Neglect"[196]; but a composite charge of that nature was regarded as containing one offence only.[197] It seems, since it is difficult to be certain about this, that the offence is aimed at those who are close relatives or guardians of the victim, or at any person who can be said to have undertaken his care and custody.[198] Thus, in *John McRae*, the accused was alleged to have confined his weak-minded wife in a space no longer than three and a half feet, and no higher than two and a half feet for almost four months. This was further alleged to have caused the unfortunate woman serious injury to her mind and body. He was convicted—as was his co-accused, a female servant within the household. It is to be noted that a close, personal relationship existed between victim and accused, and that the injurious consequences of their actions featured prominently

9–32

---

[193] *HM Advocate v Harris*, 1993 J.C. 150 at 165E–F.

[194] See, e.g. *Kimmins v Normand*, 1993 S.L.T. 1260 (false denial by a man about to be searched under s.23 of the Misuse of Drugs Act 1971 that he had an unguarded hypodermic needle about his person).

[195] *Mallin v Clark*, 2002 S.L.T. 1202, opinion of the court at 1205F–G, para.10 and J–K, para.12: in this case, *Kimmins v Normand*, 1993 S.L.T. 1260, was distinguished—see opinion of the court at 1205H, para.11.

[196] The epithets "culpable" and "wilful" although often found in indictments and complaints for these offences are possibly mere surplusage—see, e.g. *HM Advocate v Harris*, 1993 J.C. 150, Lord Justice-Clerk Ross at 154C–D, Lord McCluskey (dissenting) at 158A–C, Lord Prosser at 165H to 166A–B.

[197] *John McRae* (1842) 1 Broun 395, per Lord Cockburn at 399.

[198] See the form of indictment in *John McRae* (1842) 1 Broun 395.

in the charge. Where these features were found to be absent from an apparently similar indictment, the High Court found the charge to be irrelevant.[199]

Cruel and unnatural treatment

9–33   Nineteenth-century indictments[200] often alleged cruel and unnatural, or just cruel treatment; but it is difficult to see how that varied (if at all) from the "cruel and barbarous" variety. In *William Fairweather*,[201] for example, a father was accused of confining his weak-minded daughter in a small hutch in an outhouse for about a month, whereby her life was endangered and she was reduced to a state of almost total idiocy. He pled guilty to the charge, which factually looked identical to that in *John McRae* (see above, para.9–32). In both cases, it is very likely that the accused meant the victims no harm. They probably thought, given nineteenth-century standards, that what they did was as good a method as any of coping with mental illness. But they all exhibited utter disregard for the health and safety of the persons concerned. Very much the same might be said of the innkeeper and his assistant in *McManimy and Higgans*.[202] Those two accused evicted a man suspected of typhoid from an inn in Stirling, and carried him by rail (on the outside part of a carriage) to a Glasgow station where he was abandoned for the police to discover. Although the unfortunate victim died shortly thereafter in hospital, the accused pled guilty to reckless, cruel and culpable removal of a sick person from his bed whilst he was helpless, to his injury and the danger of his life, and to reckless and cruel treatment involving desertion of a sick person. Their pleas were accepted; and it is to be noted that they were designed as persons *entrusted* with the care of a sick person, or who had *assumed custody and charge* of him. Such ascriptions would be unnecessary, of course, where the accused was a parent of the victim. Thus, in *Rachel Gibson*[203] a mother was alleged, amongst other things, to have treated her new born child cruelly and unnaturally by putting it in a basket and sending it, suitably labelled, by rail as an ordinary parcel. It was her clear intention to desert the child in that somewhat novel way, by which it "was seriously injured in its health." (She pled guilty after the indictment had been held relevant.)

OFFENCES INVOLVING INJURY, OR DANGER OF INJURY TO ONE OR
MORE OF THE LIEGES

Reckless Injury

9–34   It has been made clear in modern times that there is a discrete offence of unintentionally but recklessly causing injury to another. In *HM Advocate v Harris*,[204] a steward at a night club was charged with recklessly seizing hold of the victim, pushing her on the body and causing her to fall down a flight of steps onto the

---

[199] See *Robert Watt and James Kerr* (1868) 1 Coup. 123, where the accused was alleged to have forced young, ill-clad stowaways to leave his ship and find their way as best they could across ice floes towards land, which was many miles distant.

[200] For a more modern example, see *Lambert v HM Advocate*, 1993 S.L.T. 339.

[201] *William Fairweather* (1842) 1 Broun 309.

[202] *McManimy and Higgans* (1847) Ark. 321, which also involved homicide.

[203] *Rachel Gibson* (1845) 2 Broun 366.

[204] *HM Advocate v Harris*, 1993 J.C. 150.

roadway outside the premises, where she was run over by a vehicle to her severe injury and permanent disfigurement. This was one of two alternative charges in the indictment, the other being one of assault. It was objected firstly that the non-assault charge was not a crime known to the law of Scotland since it had not been specifically stated that what the steward had done was also "to the danger of the lieges". It was held on this point that such an addendum was unnecessary, and, in so far as prior authority[205] had required such an additional formula, that prior authority would be overruled. Secondly, it was claimed that since the facts were identically stated in both alternative charges, there was no difference between those charges, and that both, therefore, amounted to assault. (No doubt since it was possible that the accused had not intended to do more than carry out his duty of ejecting the complainer from the premises, using no more than reasonable force, it was also possible that the prosecutor would not succeed in proving that the accused had intended to injure her. It was thus to the accused's possible advantage to have the "recklessness" charge removed, since he might remain vulnerable to that.) Four of the five judges supported the prosecution's view that recklessly causing injury was a distinct type of crime, and that it was properly posited here as an alternative to assault.[206] It was emphasised that although a steward may be entitled intentionally to manhandle persons attending a night club and to eject them using reasonable force without being criminally liable for assault, yet

"if reasonable force is not exceeded, ejection may . . . be culpably reckless . . . if insisted upon in face of danger to the person being ejected or to that person's actual severe injury."[207]

As a result of the clarification of the law in *Harris*, this particular crime probably now embraces former cases relating to injuries caused by the reckless driving of a horse and cart[208] or a locomotive,[209] the reckless navigation of a ship,[210] the reckless disposal of a glass bottle,[211] and the like. There must, of course, be a causal link established between the accused's reckless conduct and the injury to the complainer, but that link seems easily drawn. In *Kimmins v Normand*,[212] for example, a person being legitimately searched for drugs by the police was asked if he had about his person any needles or similar sharp instruments. It was held on appeal that his denial of having any such object, when he well knew that he had an unprotected hypodermic needle in his pocket, provided the necessary causal link to the injury of a policeman who subsequently placed his hand in that pocket in the course of the search.[213] The charge was thus fully relevant as one of "recklessly causing injury". (That charge also alleged that the unfortunate policeman had been "exposed to the risk of infection" when the needle entered his

---

[205] *Quinn v Cunningham*, 1956 J.C. 22.
[206] See *HM Advocate v Harris*, 1993 J.C. 150, Lord Justice-Clerk Ross at 154D–E, Lord Murray at 156E, Lord Morison at 162G, and Lord Prosser at 167H–I. (Lord McCluskey dissented on this point.)
[207] *HM Advocate v Harris*, 1993 J.C. 150, Lord Murray at 156E.
[208] *Alexander Lawson* (1829) Bell's Notes 76.
[209] *Thomas Smith* (1853) 1 Irv. 271.
[210] *Archibald Grassom* (1884) 5 Coup. 483.
[211] *W v HM Advocate*, 1982 S.L.T. 420; sub nom. *RHW v HM Advocate*, 1982 S.C.C.R. 152.
[212] *Kimmins v Normand*, 1993 S.L.T. 1260.
[213] *Kimmins v Normand*, 1993 S.L.T. 1260, per Lord Justice-General Hope at 1261H.

hand; but this is probably a matter of aggravation rather than any necessary element in the description of the crime.[214])

Reckless endangerment of the lieges

9–35   Where no injury is caused by reckless behaviour, but that behaviour is objectively dangerous to others, a distinct offence of recklessly causing such danger is available.[215] Modern examples may be seen in *Normand v Robinson*,[216] where the accused organised a mass entertainment known as "a rave" in derelict premises which were completely unsafe for the holding of such an event, and in *Normand v Morrison*,[217] where the accused allegedly denied to police officers who were about to search her that she had an unprotected hypodermic needle in her handbag—thus exposing those officers (or any one of them who undertook the search) to the risk of infection. It does not seem essential to the relevancy of such a charge that the words "to the danger of the lieges [or others]" should actually appear on it, provided that such danger can readily be inferred[218]: and it does not seem to be (nor could be) an objection to such a charge that injuries were actually caused. In *MacPhail v Clark*,[219] for example, the accused set fire to stubble in a field in such a reckless manner that smoke in great quantity drifted over the carriageway of a nearby road thus causing acute problems of visibility for drivers of vehicles there. Whilst the accused unconcernedly continued with other tasks in the same field, road accidents occurred because of the smoke. There were injuries as a result of those accidents; but the charge appears to have been one of reckless endangerment to which the accounts of accident and injury were added by way of aggravation. In a case where the causal link between the accused's reckless conduct and actual injury to another is weak or difficult to prove, treating the injury as an aggravation is obviously a sensible course of action for the Crown to adopt.

Administration of noxious substances

9–36   It has been clear since the early nineteenth century that the deliberate and reckless (in the sense of having complete disregard for the consequences) administration of deleterious substances to anyone, to his injury, is criminal.[220] Thus Hume makes mention that the administration of a powerful aphrodisiac (cantharides) to three women, such that they were injured in their health, was considered a relevant crime.[221] Nor did it matter that the motive was merely one of sport or jest. In *Henry Inglis, Andrew and Robert Colvilles*,[222] for example, the administration of

---

[214] Cf., the charge in *Mallin v Clark*, 2002 S.L.T. 1202.
[215] *HM Advocate v Harris*, 1993 J.C. 150.
[216] *Normand v Robinson*, 1994 S.L.T. 558.
[217] *Normand v Morrison*, 1993 S.C.C.R. 207 Sh. Ct.
[218] See the complaint in *Normand v Morrison*, 1993 S.C.C.R. 207. See also *Donaldson v Normand*, 1997 S.C.C.R. 351, and *Robertson v Klos* [2005] HCJAC 136; 2006 S.C.C.R. 52.
[219] *MacPhail v Clark*, 1983 S.L.T. (Sh. Ct.) 37.
[220] *Alexander Mitchell* (1833) Bell's Notes 90.
[221] Hume, *Commentaries*, i, 237 at note "b"—the case of *John Ferguson and John Eadie* (1822). The mention of "aphrodisiac" in this case probably would now result in a charge of "administering a substance for sexual purposes" under the Sexual Offences (Scotland) Act 2009 (asp 9) s.11, rather than of the broader common-law offence being considered here: cf. above, para.9–25.
[222] *Henry Inglis, Andrew and Robert Colvilles* (1784) Hume, *Commentaries*, i, 237.

snuff in a draught of liquor to the victim as something of a joke was clearly criminal (although charged as culpable homicide, since the person who drank it died
in consequence). It will be plain, therefore, that it is not necessary to show that the
accused forced the noxious substance into the mouth or body of the victim. It is
quite enough that he caused the victim to take it, the self-administration, so to
speak, not representing any *novus actus interveniens* (see paras 5–17 and
following, above). In *Robert Brown and John Lawson*[223] it seems to have been
quite sufficient that the accused gave a quarter of a pint of whisky to a seven year
old child, who then, as far as one can determine, proceeded to drink it off by
himself. (The child suffered from epileptic fits thereafter.) Naturally, whether a
substance is truly noxious or not will depend on the age and disposition of the
victim[224]; but substances prescribed by a doctor, or having apparent medicinal
properties, are unlikely to be regarded as "deleterious", unless the circumstances
are special.[225] It is possible too that consent might be a defence to a charge of
administration of things having such medicinal properties.[226]

Supplying of potentially noxious substances

A state of intoxication has always held a considerable fascination for human **9–37**
beings of all ages, and the obtaining of substances which will effect such a state
has been seen at all times as a desirable goal. Those who are excluded by virtue of
youth or lack of means from having ready access to "normal" and reasonably safe
intoxicants have proved peculiarly inventive in exploiting substances really
intended for some harmless, household purpose. Boot-polish, lighter fuel, paint
thinners, and various glues, for example, can be turned to use as highly dangerous
intoxicants when inhaled or ingested instead of being utilised for their intended
purposes. It was indeed the desire to control abuse of such substances which led
the Appeal Court in *Khaliq v HM Advocate*[227] to invent or perhaps "discover" the
crime referred to here as "supplying potentially noxious substances." The offence
itself is rather more complex, however, than that somewhat simple title would
suggest.

The charge in *Khaliq*[228] contained at least five elements: (1) that the accused **9–38**
shopkeepers wilfully and recklessly supplied (i.e. sold, or perhaps bartered)
substances capable of giving off toxic fumes (e.g. "Evo-stik" glue); (2) that they
did so to customers who were children, aged between eight and 15 years; (3) that
the substances were specially supplied in, or with, containers (e.g. otherwise
empty plastic bags) to facilitate the inhalation of those toxic fumes; (4) that the
accused did so, well knowing that those customers intended to inhale the fumes
and that such inhalation would or could be injurious to their health and a threat to
their lives; and (5) that by virtue of their conduct, the accused caused those

---

[223] *Robert Brown and John Lawson* (1842) 1 Broun 415.
[224] Cf., *Borwick v Urquhart*, 2003 S.C.C.R. 243, where the accused supplied the complainer (a 13 year
old girl) with a half-bottle of vodka for which she provided the purchase price; she then proceeded
to consume the contents at a rapid rate, with the inevitable consequence of acute intoxication: the
complaint, however, followed the type of charge favoured in *Khaliq v HM Advocate*, 1984 J.C. 23
(see paras 9–37 to 9–39, below).
[225] *Peter Milne and John Barry* (1868) 1 Coup. 28, per Lord Cowan at 31.
[226] *Peter Milne and John Barry* (1969) 1 Coup. 28.
[227] *Khaliq v HM Advocate*, 1984 J.C. 23.
[228] *Khaliq v HM Advocate*, 1984 J.C. 23, quoted at 24 (charge (1)).

customers to inhale the fumes to the danger of their health and lives (on which, see above, para.5–18). That complex indictment was found relevant before the trial court, and the accused were convicted. Both findings were upheld on appeal. Although Lord Justice-General Emslie said[229]: "That the persons supplied were children is not . . . essential to the relevancy of the charge", it was widely felt that his remarks were mere obiter, since public concern at the time had centred on glue-sniffing *by children*. Indeed, when Parliament eventually placed a virtual embargo on sales of such substances to children[230] it did not extend the legislation to Scotland, since it apparently was of the persuasion that that was already the law in this country due to the decision in *Khaliq*. It was also widely felt that it had been very significant that the substances had been supplied in "user-friendly" kits. These "feelings" thus enabled the decision in *Khaliq* to be limited in a sensible way, so that it would not be seen as extending to the supply of whisky to a known alcoholic or cigarettes to a known sufferer from lung cancer.[231] But the subsequent decision in *Ulhaq*[232] (see below, para.9–39) has demonstrated that such perceived limitations were wrong.

9–39   In *Ulhaq v HM Advocate*[233] a shopkeeper was again charged with the same type of offence first seen in *Khaliq*. Significant differences existed, however, between the two fact situations. In *Ulhaq*, the customers were not children. They were all between 20 and 29 years of age, and could thus be described accurately as adults. What they had bought from the store in question were vast quantities of lighter fuel and glue—but all in their original cartons, tins and tubes. No inhalation-assisting "kits" were supplied at all. It was argued in vain, however, that those issues made any significant difference. It was enough that the store-keeper knew that his customers intended to use the substances for no proper purposes, that he supplied them on that basis, and that he thus caused them to abuse the substances in question to their injury and danger. This decision then resurrects the spectre of criminality surrounding, for example, the sale of significant quantities of alcohol to a known alcoholic. It may be that the case depends solely on its own facts, and is confined to volatile substances such as lighter fuel and glues. If that, however, is felt to be an essentially naïve view, then the decision may only be rescued from uncontrolled expansion by reference to this: that the crime ought to be limited to the kind of substances which are potentially noxious if used in a way that their manufacturers never intended as proper (e.g. by being inhaled or swallowed) and which are not otherwise regulated in terms of sale, purchase or possession by Parliament.[234] (The signs are, however, that the courts are not persuaded that such limitations upon the offence would be justified.[235]) It might be thought, of course,

---

[229] *Khaliq v HM Advocate*, 1984 J.C. 23 at 33.

[230] See the Intoxicating Substances (Supply) Act 1985. See also the indictments in *Khalid v HM Advocate*, 1990 J.C. 37, and *Borwick v Urquhart*, 2003 S.C.C.R. 243.

[231] See *Skeen v Malik* Unreported, 1977, in C.H.W. Gane, C.N. Stoddart and J. Chalmers, *A Casebook on Scottish Criminal Law*, 4th edn (Edinburgh: W. Green, 2009), para.4–12 at note 2.

[232] *Ulhaq v HM Advocate*, 1991 S.L.T. 614.

[233] *Ulhaq v HM Advocate*, 1991 S.L.T. 614.

[234] cf. tobacco and ethyl alcohols. See, e.g. the Tobacco and Primary Medical Services (Scotland) Act 2010 (asp 3) ss.4–7 and 35(1); and the Licensing (Scotland) Act 2005 (asp 16) ss.102–109 (ss.103, 106 and 107 as amended by the Criminal Justice and Licensing (Scotland) Act 2010 (asp 13) s.195(2)(b)–(d)) and 147(1).

[235] See *Lord Advocate's Reference (No.1 of 1994)*, 1995 S.L.T. 248, where the "supplying" of drugs (controlled under the Misuse of Drugs Act 1971) was considered equivalent to the offence

that there is a problem with establishing a causal link in such cases since the person supplied must choose to use the substance in a way that its manufacturer did not intend. It might be thought, therefore, that the exercise of such choice amounts to a novus actus interveniens[236] which thus breaks the chain of inter-linking events between the supplying and the abuse. In *Khaliq*,[237] however, such an argument was dismissed by the Appeal Court. The view was taken that the abuse of the substances was the "known, intended and expected purpose"[238] of their being supplied at all, and that there was such a close connection between supplying and administration in such circumstances that it was legitimate to treat the supply as analogous to administration (and thus criminal) "even in the absence of words of instigation on the part of the suppliers."[239]

Discharge of firearms

It is certainly criminal to discharge firearms recklessly to the danger or actual **9–40** injury of the lieges.[240] That no one need actually be injured is understandable given the lethal nature of such weapons; but in the absence of real injury, it seems necessary that there were likely to be people within range at the time, as in *David Smith and William McNeil*[241] where much emphasis was placed on the fact that the accused shot through the glass window of an inhabited house, to the imminent danger of those living there. There seems little to be gained by treating this as an offence separate from "reckless injury" (see above, para.9–34) or "reckless endan-germent of the lieges" "(see above, para.9–35), although an especially dangerous modus, of course, is involved in this instance of those crimes.

---

fashioned in *Khaliq* and *Ulhaq* for the purposes of culpable homicide where the person supplied died after ingesting those drugs. The "rules" pertaining to the "reckless supply of potentially noxious substances" were thus made available against the supplier in a culpable homicide prosecu-tion, and enabled objections to the establishing of a causal link there to be swept aside: cf. *HM Advocate v C* [2007] HCJ 10; 2007 S.L.T. 963 (opinion of Lord McEwan on a preliminary plea). See also *Borwick v Urquhart*, 2003 S.C.C.R. 243, where the court held (at 247C–D, para.7) that the circumstances fell "very directly within the decision in *Khaliq*", in that the appellant had (at his suggestion) bought alcohol (a half-bottle of vodka) for a 13 year old female complainer, who had supplied the money for same and who had proceeded to drink all of the bottle's contents "very quickly": she became very drunk, if not unconscious, as a result. It was argued that *Borwick's* conviction of the relevant offence had represented an extension of the crime set out in *Khaliq*; but the appeal court rejected that submission and declined to refer in any detail to the "crime of culpable and reckless conduct in *Khaliq*, or [any] other case" (opinion of the court at 247C, para.7). Cf. the House of Lords' decision in *R. v Kennedy (No.2)* [2007] UKHL 38; [2007] 3 W.L.R. 612, where it appears that English law differs from the law in Scotland—as is confirmed by the five judge decision in *MacAngus v HM Advocate* [2009] HCJAC 8; 2009 S.L.T. 137, where the deci-sion in the Scottish case (*Lord Advocate's Reference (No.1 of 1994)*) was considered and approved.

[236] See above, paras 5–17 to 5–23.
[237] *Khaliq v HM Advocate*, 1984 J.C. 23.
[238] *Khaliq v HM Advocate*, 1984 J.C. 23, per Lord Justice-General Emslie, at 33.
[239] *Khaliq v HM Advocate*, 1984 J.C. 23. This method of establishing a causal connection was used a fortiori in *Lord Advocate's Reference (No.1 of 1994)*, 1995 S.L.T. 248 (see above, fn.235, above) where prohibited (and thus dangerous per se) drugs were supplied to a person who had voluntarily sought them, voluntarily selected a particular dose of them, voluntarily taken that dose, and then died from the effects.
[240] See, e.g. *Robert Anderson* (1832) Bell's Notes 73; *Gizzi v Tudhope*, 1983 S.L.T. 214; *Cameron v Maguire*, 1999 S.C.C.R. 44.
[241] *David Smith and William McNeil* (1842) 1 Broun 240.

4.(A) COMMON LAW HOMICIDES

Introduction

9–41   There are two forms of criminal homicide recognised by Scots common law —murder and culpable homicide. The actus reus of both of those crimes is identical. It consists of positive conduct by the accused, or a failure by him to act where he had a legal duty to do so, which causes the death of another human being.[242] "Failures to act" have already been explored in Ch.3,[243] and "causation" issues in Ch.5. But the question of when a person is dead raises some nice issues of its own. Before a "person" can be killed, he must have been alive. In a sense (and for some, a very real sense), a human foetus is alive from the moment of its conception onwards. If that were so for the purposes of the criminal law, then it would be homicide to end a foetus's "life" by destroying it in its mother's womb. That is not, however, the approach taken. Hume makes it plain that the destruction of life in the womb is not homicide but the separate crime of abortion.[244] The criterion for homicide thus appears to be that the victim had been a "self-existent human life."[245] At the very least, the victim must have been born alive at one point in time, and killed at another, because of some action or inaction on the accused's part. As Hume colourfully indicates,[246] until a foetus is born alive, it is merely "pars viscerum matris" (i.e. part of its mother's viscera).[247] It seems, however, that the Appeal Court has accepted that a child born alive can be subsequently killed by some injury which was caused to it in the womb.[248]

Abortion

9–42   The crime of abortion at common law consists of intentionally causing or procuring the termination of pregnancy and consequently the destruction of a developing foetus.[249] The method of achieving such an end is probably of little moment, but the cases on the subject generally refer to the use of instruments or the administration of drugs.[250] It is also essential that there had been a criminal purpose, since it may have been necessary to cause the abortion[251]—to save the life of the mother, for example. Since the Abortion Act 1967, however, the

---

[242] Gordon, *Criminal Law,* 3rd edn (2000/2001), paras 23.04 to 23.08. If, of course, there is sufficient evidence that the deceased was seen alive after the date and time when he is alleged to have been killed by the accused, it may be impossible to sustain a conviction for homicide: see *Johnston v HM Advocate* [2006] HCJAC 30; 2006 S.C.C.R. 236.

[243] See above, paras 3–09 to 3–14.

[244] Hume, *Commentaries,* i, 186; see below, para.9–42.

[245] As Macdonald puts it, *Criminal Law,* 5th edn (1948), p.87, although this has to be seen simply as a useful way of referring to the demarcation line between a foetus and a child born alive. A newly born infant, and indeed a person in a coma or persistent vegetative state (see below, para.9–77) can hardly be said to be "self-existent", yet are clearly not beyond the protection of the law of homicide.

[246] Hume, *Commentaries,* i, 186.

[247] Cf. the view in English law: see *Attorney General's Reference (No.3 of 1994)* [1998] A.C. 245 HL, especially the opinion of Lord Hope of Craighead at 267D–G. See also *Smith and Hogan Criminal Law,* edited by David Ormerod, 12th edn (Oxford: Oxford University Press, 2008), pp.474–476.

[248] *McCluskey v HM Advocate,* 1988 S.C.C.R. 629 at 632.

[249] *Macdonald, Criminal Law,* 5th edn (1948), p.114.

[250] See *Minnie Graham* (1897) 2 Adam 412.

[251] Macdonald, *Criminal law,* 5th edn (1948), p.114.

common law crime has ceased to be of any real significance. The import of the Act[252] is that an abortion carried out by a qualified doctor will not be criminal, provided that two independent doctors certify that there would be greater risk to the physical or mental health of the mother or any of her existing children in carrying the foetus to term than in terminating the pregnancy (which may be done on these grounds until the end of the 24th week of the pregnancy only), or (and the following are without time limit) that there would be grave permanent injury (mental or physical) to the mother (or risk to her life) if the pregnancy were allowed to continue, or that there would be substantial risk of serious handicap to the child if the foetus were allowed to be born.

Death

There is no particular legal definition of death. In modern times, it is clear that **9–43** the cessation of breathing or heart-beat does not conclusively show that a person is dead. Medical science has in any event invented the technological means of sustaining breath and pulse in situations where a person has lost the means of sustaining them for himself.[253] It is thought, therefore, that an appropriate legal test for death must now involve the permanent cessation of brain activity. But the courts have not commented on the matter, although at least one reported case presented the opportunity for them to do so.[254]

Double Jeopardy

Homicides are often caused by actions which are crimes in their own right, for **9–44** example, by assaults or by administration of noxious substances such as active poisons. Since Scots law never had any rule equivalent to that of the now repealed English "year and a day" rule[255] it can happen that an accused is convicted and sentenced for an assault upon a person who later, much later, dies of his injuries. The view taken at common law, however, was that the original conviction for any such crime less than homicide did not prevent a new trial for homicide, if the victim subsequently died[256]; and essentially the same approach is now taken under the Double Jeopardy (Scotland) Act 2011 (asp 16) s.16. From this point of view, homicide is not just an aggravated form of assault or other offence of real injury, but a separate class of crime.

Casual Homicide

The older text writers[257] emphasise that some killings are not criminal, and that **9–45** in particular some may be described as "casual." Hume indicates that such a killing occurs

---

[252] See Abortion Act 1967 s.1(1), as amended by the Human Fertilisation and Embryology Act 1990 s.37.
[253] See e.g. below, para.9–77 (Persistent Vegetative State).
[254] See *Finlayson v HM Advocate*, 1979 J.C. 33; see para.5–23, above.
[255] See *R. v Dyson* [1908] 2 K.B. 454; Law Reform (Year and a Day Rule) Act 1996.
[256] *Tees v HM Advocate*, 1994 S.L.T. 701.
[257] See e.g. Hume, *Commentaries*, i, 194.

"when a person kills unintentionally, who is lawfully employed, and neither means bodily harm to any one, nor has failed in the due degree of care for preventing danger to his neighbour."

What he seems to mean by this is simply that accidental homicides are not criminal (as in the case of *John Leper*,[258] where a prisoner insisted on running ahead of his guard, despite warnings that the castle which they were traversing was in part ruinous and dangerous; the prisoner having become lost and fallen 20 feet to his death, it was held that no blame for the death could be attached to his escort).

Justifiable homicide

9–46 Other killings which are not criminal are those which are justifiable. Hume,[259] for example, mentions homicides effected by soldiers with good cause (in war, perhaps, or in the quelling of a riot), or police officers. It is thought, however, that police officers would only be justified in killing where it was necessary to do so in self-defence—a broad category open to anyone (see above, paras 8–17 to 8–35), and also, at common law it seems, to women in particular in avoidance of rape (see above, para.8–35). Despite some dicta to the contrary,[260] it is not thought that homicide in defence of property alone can ever be justifiable.

Excusable homicide

9–47 It is not clear whether there is any such class as that of "excusable homicide"[261] but it remains possible that the Scottish courts will not follow English authority, and will not rule out a defence of coercion to a homicide charge (see above, para.8–76).[262]) If that happens then, as coercion is an excuse personal to the accused, this class would have at least one member.

Penalties for homicide

9–48 The two forms of criminal homicide are distinguishable from one another by reference to their mens rea requirements and also according to the penalty which follows conviction. For murder there is a mandatory life sentence, with appropriate provision for those who are under 18 and those who are under 21.[263] The trial judge must, however, state the length of the "punishment part" of the sentence which he thinks appropriate to be served in order to "satisfy the requirements for retribution and deterrence".[264] Culpable homicide, on the other hand, has no

---

[258] *John Leper* (1682) Hume, *Commentaries*, i, 194.
[259] See Hume, *Commentaries*, i, 195–222, especially from p.205 at "5".
[260] *Edward Lane* (1830) Bell's Notes 77, per Lord Moncreiff, that a servant might be justified in killing an intruder found in his master's house "[if he] had reasonable grounds to think . . . that he could not otherwise protect his master's property."
[261] See above, paras 8–03 and 8–04, for the difference between an excuse and a justification.
[262] Which refers to Lord Allanbridge's direction to the jury in *Collins v HM Advocate*, 1991 S.C.C.R. 898 at 902C. See the detailed consideration given to this matter in Chalmers and Leverick, *Criminal Defences and Pleas in Bar of Trial* (2006), pp.113–118, paras 5.27 to 5.31.
[263] Criminal Procedure (Scotland) Act 1995 s.205, as amended by the Convention Rights (Compliance) (Scotland) Act 2001 (asp 7) s.2.
[264] Custodial Sentences and Weapons (Scotland) Act 2007 (asp 17) s.20. For further details, see *Sentencing Practice* (Edinburgh: W. Green, 2002), C 10.0001 et seq.

mandatory penalty, and carries a sentencing range no different from that which a trial court has for any common law crime (see Appendix D). It follows then that wide sentencing options exist for those convicted of culpable homicide, and instances can easily be found of very lenient disposals which reflect the circumstances involved. In *Robert Bruce*,[265] for example, where the death was something of a mischance occasioned during the course of a consensual fight, the accused was convicted and fined one shilling (although he was also required to find caution to keep the peace for one year); and in the controversial case of *HM Advocate v Sherman*[266] the accused was admonished after having been convicted of the culpable homicide of his wife and child by shooting. The implication of the penalty differences between the two crimes is that in essence all murders are taken to be equally morally bad,[267] whereas culpable homicide cases vary enormously in moral culpability. It is also implied, of course, by reference to sentence that only a High Court can deal with a case of murder; and it is a matter of law that a J.P. Court can never deal with a case of murder or culpable homicide.[268]

MURDER

Definition of murder

In the homicide case of *Drury v HM Advocate*,[269] the majority of the five-judge **9–49** Appeal Court was of the view that Macdonald's oft-quoted account of murder was incomplete.[270] In terms of that account, murder was

> "constituted by any wilful act causing the destruction of life, whether intended to kill, or displaying such wicked recklessness as to imply a disposition depraved enough to be regardless of consequences."[271]

The case was chiefly concerned with the plea of provocation; but the majority of the court was of the view that Macdonald's account did not explain why, for example, a person who killed intentionally while defending himself or while responding to provocation was either not guilty of anything (in the case of self-defence) or guilty only of culpable homicide (in the case of provocation): if he intended to kill, why was he not guilty of murder, since he appeared to fall within the first limb of Macdonald's account of that crime? The court's answer was that although the Macdonald account would suffice "in many cases—as, for instance, where the only real issue in dispute is the identity of the killer . . .",[272] that account

---

[265] *Robert Bruce* (1855) 2 Irv. 65.

[266] *HM v Sherman* Unreported February 27, 1990, High Court at Aberdeen.

[267] It should be noted that this proposition is tempered by the concept of the "punishment part" referred to in the text above.

[268] Criminal Procedure (Scotland) Act 1995 s.7(8)(b)(i), as amended by the Criminal Proceedings etc. (Reform) (Scotland) Act 2007 (asp 6), Sch. para.9(4).

[269] *Drury v HM Advocate*, 2001 S.L.T. 1013.

[270] *Drury v HM Advocate*, 2001 S.L.T. 1013, Lord Justice-General Rodger at 1016H–I, para.10; Lord Johnston at 1029F–G, para.18; Lord Nimmo Smith at 1030I–K, para.2; and Lord Mackay of Drumadoon at 1033F, para.8.

[271] Macdonald, *Criminal Law*, 5th edn (1948), p.89.

[272] *Drury v HM Advocate*, 2001 S.L.T. 1013, Lord Justice-General Rodger at 1016I, para.10; cf., Lord Nimmo Smith at 1030I–J, para.2.

was not an appropriate jury direction where provocation or self-defence was in issue, since (in the words of the Lord Justice-General) "it does not describe the relevant intention."[273] To remedy this defect, the Lord Justice-General stated:

"In truth, just as the recklessness has to be wicked so also must the intention be wicked. Therefore, perhaps the most obvious way of completing the definition is by saying that murder is constituted by any wilful act causing the destruction of life, by which the perpetrator either wickedly intends to kill or displays wicked recklessness as to whether the victim lives or dies. Saying that the perpetrator 'wickedly' intends to kill is just a shorthand way of referring to what Hume (vol. i, p. 254) describes as the murderer's 'wicked and mischievous purpose' in contradistinction to 'those motives of necessity, duty, or allowable infirmity, which may serve to justify or excuse' the deliberate taking of life".[274]

In consequence, the definition of murder became a little uncertain—given that the court in *Drury* seemed to consider Macdonald's account of the crime to be satisfactory where, for example, self-defence or provocation was not in issue at a trial. Also it was a little uncertain what the term "wickedly" should mean when allied to Macdonald's "intention to kill", since Lord Justice-General Rodger's opinion in particular could be read restrictively[275] (in the sense that "wickedly" was but an abbreviation for the absence of a limited range of applicable "defences" such as self-defence, provocation and diminished responsibility[276]) or rather more widely (in the sense that "wickedly" referred to the absence of any acceptable factor which could excuse, justify or provide mitigation for the killing[277]). Further uncertainty too was created in that the opinions in *Drury* could be read as if the element of wickedness carried the same meaning across both branches of the mens rea of the crime.[278] It would have been awkward, however, to have to conclude that there were two different definitions of murder depending upon the circumstances of an individual trial; it would also have placed too much discretion in the hands of a jury if a wide interpretation of "wickedly" were to have been preferred in relation to intentional killings; and, it would perhaps have been too bold to conclude that in *Drury's* case the Appeal Court had swept away the

---

[273] *Drury v HM Advocate*, 2001 S.L.T. 1013, Lord Justice-General Rodger at p.1016J, para.11.

[274] *Drury v HM Advocate*, 2001 S.L.T. 1013, Lord Justice-General Rodger at 1016J–K, para.11. See also Lord Johnston at 1029E–F, para.18; Lord Nimmo Smith at 1030L–1031A, para.3; Lord Mackay of Drumadoon at 1033G–H, para.9. For criticism of this "completion" of Macdonald's account of murder, see James Chalmer, "Collapsing the Structure of Criminal Law" (2001) S.L.T. (News) 241; Fiona Leverick, "Mistake in Self-defence after *Drury*" 2002 J.R. 35. That the intention to kill is usually now qualified by "wickedness" is referred to by the court in *HM Advocate v Purcell* [2007] HCJ 13; 2007 S.C.C.R. 520, at 526, para.9.

[275] See *Drury v HM Advocate*, 2001 S.LT. 1013, at 1018F–H, para.18, and 1019I–J, para.20.

[276] See Chalmers, "Collapsing the Structure of Criminal Law" (2001) S.L.T. (News) 241, 242; Leverick, "Mistake in Self-Defence after *Drury*" 2002 J.R. 35, 41; Sir Gerald H. Gordon, "Commentary" to *Drury v HM Advocate*, 2001 S.C.C.R. 583, at 618G–619A, 619F.

[277] Cf., Gordon, "Commentary" to *Drury v HM Advocate*, 2001 S.C.C.R. 583, at 619G to 620C.

[278] See *Drury v HM Advocate*, 2001 S.L.T. 1013, Lord Justice-General Rodger at 1016J, para.11: "In truth, just as the recklessness has to be wicked so also must the intention be wicked."

accepted view of the meaning of "wicked recklessness" without detailed consideration of the relevant cases and text-writings.[279]

It is now clear, however, that in a murder case

"where intention to kill is either admitted or proved . . . in the absence of any legally relevant factor capable of justifying or mitigating the accused's actions, the jury should be directed that they must convict of murder."[280]

If a killing then is admitted as, or shown to be, deliberate on the part of the accused, that killing will fulfil the definition of murder in the sense that there will be "wicked" intention to kill (in so far as the law requires to refer to "wickedness" in relation to intention at all)—provided that there is no evidence to support "any legally relevant factors capable of justifying or mitigating the accused's actions." Although the court in question declined to provide a definitive list of such "legally relevant" factors,[281] it is plain that self-defence, provocation and diminished responsibility are certainly included,[282] whilst self-induced intoxication is not.[283] There remains, however, continuing uncertainty as to the mens rea element of this crime, and corresponding unease amongst at least some of the judiciary.[284]

Actus reus

Murder is a result crime (see para.2–36, above). From this point of view, it is **9–50** certainly correct to say that the type of conduct which causes death is of little consequence (see above, para.3–05). But the conduct in question must be capable of raising an inference that mens rea of either type existed. What might reasonably be said at present, therefore, is that the range of conduct capable of raising such an inference is vast. It extends, for example, to the use of severe physical violence, as in *Charles McDonald*[285]—fists, stones and bottles; the employment of weapons, as in *Cawthorne v HM Advocate*[286]—rifle firing high-velocity bullets; the administration of poisons, as in *Christian Gilmour*[287] and *Madeleine Smith*[288]; setting fire to the victim's clothing, as in *HM Advocate v Kennedy*[289]; boring holes in a ship's bottom, as in *HM Advocate v Monson*[290]; throwing the victim twice from a

---

[279] It was also the express or implied view of the commentators mentioned in fn.276, above, that the re-definition of murder undertaken in *Drury* applied only to intentional killings; and indeed the judge's direction at *Drury*'s first trial was considered by the Appeal Court to have been defective in relation to intentional rather than "wickedly reckless" killings.

[280] *Elsherkisi v HM Advocate* [2011] HCJAC 100; 2011 S.C.C.R. 735, opinion of the court (per Lord Hardie) at 743D, para.12.

[281] *Elsherkisi v HM Advocate* [2011] HCJAC 100; 2011 S.C.C.R. 735, at 741D, para.10.

[282] *Elsherkisi v HM Advocate* [2011] HCJAC 100; 2011 S.C.C.R. 735, at 742B-C, para.11.

[283] *Elsherkisi v HM Advocate* [2011] HCJAC 100; 2011 S.C.C.R. 735, at 743A-B, para.12. It should be noted too that the court (at 742G, para.12) expressly rejected "any suggestion that the question of the wickedness of an intention to kill is at large for the jury in every case, or that the determination of that question is not constrained by any legal limits."

[284] See, e.g. *Petto v HM Advocate* [2011] HCJAC 80; 2011 S.L.T. 1043, opinions of Lord Justice-Clerk Gill at 1046L, para.22, and Lord Carloway at 1047J, para.32.

[285] *Charles McDonald* (1867) 5 Irv. 525.

[286] *Cawthorne v HM Advocate*, 1968 J.C. 32.

[287] *Christian Gilmour* (1844) 2 Broun 23.

[288] *Madeleine Smith* (1857) 2 Irv. 641.

[289] *HM Advocate v Kennedy* (1907) 5 Adam 347.

[290] *HM Advocate v Monson* (1893) 1 Adam 114.

fourth floor window, as in *McGuire v HM Advocate*[291]; and deserting a young child as in *Elizabeth Kerr*[292] or a seriously injured adult, as in *HM Advocate v McPhee*.[293]

Mens rea: wicked intent

9–51   As discussed above (see para.9–49), a "wicked" intent to kill is a sufficient form of mens rea for murder, provided it is understood that "wicked" means deliberate killing (on the part of the accused) "in the absence of any legally relevant factors capable of justifying or mitigating the accused's actions."[294] These factors certainly extend to self-defence,[295] provocation[296] and diminished responsibility.[297] It follows that intentional killings (where no such factor arises) based on "good" ulterior motives, such as mercy killings, are prima facie murders.[298] How prosecutors in the exercise of their discretion deal with such "good motive" intentional killings is, of course, beside the point, as far as the mens rea of murder is concerned.

It also follows that the notion of "wicked" in "wicked intent" is not of the same order as the "wickedness" in relation to that recklessness which is sufficient as the alternative mens rea for murder.[299]

Mens rea: wicked recklessness

9–52   The alternative form of mens rea is "wicked recklessness", and it is thought that this means a form of recklessness which transcends "simple" recklessness. More is required than the usual "utter disregard of what the consequences of the act in question may be, so far as the public are concerned." That may be enough for some instances of culpable homicide; but it clearly cannot also be sufficient for murder, if the two crimes are to be distinguished successfully. The difference, of course, may simply be one of degree; that recklessness for murder is morally a more reprehensible form than normal. It is thought, however, that it is possible to be more specific than that. In particular, from the accounts of this alternative form of mens rea given by Hume,[300] three issues seem to be involved: first, that the accused should have meant to perpetrate some great and outrageous bodily harm; second, that that harm was such as might well have resulted in death; and third, that that harm showed an absolute or utter indifference as to whether the victim lived or died. Hume requires, then, an assault (or something close to it) of such seriousness that it might easily have resulted in death and which shows in the circumstances a complete indifference to the life of the victim. That sort of approach will certainly suit most of the reported cases,[301] though not all of the judicial dicta on the matter.

---

[291] *McGuire v HM Advocate*, 1995 S.C.C.R. 776.
[292] *Elizabeth Kerr* (1860) 3 Irv. 645, though she pled guilty to culpable homicide.
[293] *HM Advocate v McPhee*, 1935 J.C. 46.
[294] *Elsherkisi v HM Advocate* [2011] HCJAC 100; 2011 S.C.C.R. 735, 743 D, para.12.
[295] See above, paras 8–17 to 8–35.
[296] See below, paras 9–66 to 9–72.
[297] See below, paras 9–73–9–76.
[298] This would simply confirm the view of some commentators: see Gordon, *Criminal Law,* 3rd edn (2000/2001), paras 25.02 and 25.03; Ferguson, *Crimes Against the Person,* 2nd edn (1998), para.3.02.
[299] See below, para.9–52.
[300] Hume, *Commentaries*, i, 191, 238, 256.
[301] See, in particular, *Arthur v HM Advocate*, 2002 S.C.C.R. 796. It probably also suits the opinion of the court (on a certified issue) in *HM Advocate v Purcell*, 2007 S.C.C.R. 520: see in particular

Intent to do outrageous or excessive bodily harm

It must be remembered, of course, that "wicked recklessness" is an alternative **9–53** form of mens rea, and that it applies where the accused is assumed not to have had a "wicked" intent to kill. Hume's initial requirement of an intent to "do him an excessive and outrageous bodily harm"[302] will itself, however, be objectively assessed, such that it can be deduced not only from actual physical violence[303] but also, for example (and more controversially), from setting fire to a house, *known to be inhabited*.[304] It is more difficult to make such a deduction in some cases, such as that of *Cawthorne v H.M. Advocate*.[305] There, the accused fired several rounds of high-velocity bullets into a room where, as he well knew, a number of people had taken refuge from him. No attempt was made to avoid hitting anyone there by, for example, firing towards the ceiling. On the assumption that this intent was merely to frighten those people and not to injure or kill them at all, the Appeal Court still determined that he had shown the wicked recklessness necessary for murder. It may be that this is a maverick decision; or it may be that Hume's initial requirement would be better phrased as "an intent to do the victim any great and outrageous *harm*", so as to accommodate frightening persons in such a way. It is difficult, however, to see that *Cawthorne's* case was one of wicked recklessness at all. Anyone doing what he did might reasonably be supposed to have ("wickedly") intended to kill.

Hume, of course, made an intent to do outrageous bodily harm only one of **9–54** three necessary requirements if murder was to be brought home to a person who did not have an intent to kill. An intent to do serious bodily harm is not by itself, therefore, a sufficient form of mens rea for murder. Unfortunately, it is clear that some judges have taken the view that it was. This must be a clear misreading of what Hume intended. Certainly Hume did write the following: "[O]ur practice . . . does not distinguish between an absolute purpose to kill, and a purpose to do any excessive and grievous injury to the person."[306] But, after quoting some illustrations, he continued:

> "Because in committing any such desperate outrage on the body [i.e. any one of the examples he had just quoted], the pannel shows an utter contempt of the safety and the life of his neighbour, and if not a determination to kill him, at least an absolute indifference whether he live or die."[307]

His illustrations (hamstringing the victim, cutting out his tongue, beating him to within an inch of his life) clearly support the three-fold approach detailed

---

526E–527D, paras 10–11. (Commentators differ on the significance of *Purcell*: cf. Michael Plaxton, "Foreseeing the consequences of *Purcell*" (2008) S.L.T. (News) 21, and Gordon's commentary to the case at 2007 S.C.C.R. 520 at 530.) See also *Petto v HM Advocate* [2011] HCJAC 80; 2011 S.L.T. 1043.

[302] Hume, *Commentaries*, i, 238.

[303] As in *HM Advocate v Fraser and Rollins*, 1920 J.C. 60, or *Brennan v HM Advocate*, 1977 J.C. 38.

[304] See *Petto v HM Advocate* [2011] HCJAC 80; 2011 S.L.T. 1043 (court of five judges). Cf. the facts in the English cases of *R. v Nedrick* [1986] 1 W.L.R. 1025; *Hyam v DPP* [1975] A.C. 55.

[305] *Cawthorne v HM Advocate*, 1968 J.C. 32.

[306] Hume, *Commentaries*, i, 256.

[307] Hume, *Commentaries*, i, 257.

above (see para.9–52), and thus give no support for the view that death following *any* deliberate infliction of grievous bodily harm is automatically murder.

9–55   In any event, a mens rea for murder in terms of "an intent to do serious bodily injury" is part of the English account of this crime[308]; and the Appeal Court has soundly rejected the view that the Scots and English definitions of murder are the same.[309] Beyond that, the vagueness of the phrase "serious bodily injury" makes for uncertain and possibly unfair decisions. In the event of someone dying, for example, after having had his arm deliberately broken by the accused, it would have to follow that the crime was murder,[310] notwithstanding that death was not reasonably to be anticipated from such an injury, and that the actions of the accused might not have shown utter indifference whether the victim lived or died. It is submitted, therefore, that Scots cases, where judges have opined that an intent to do serious injury is an independent form of mens rea for murder, are wrong.[311] Such a submission can be supported by reference to the House of Lords Select Committee on Murder and Life Imprisonment.[312] Not only did many prestigious contributions from advocates, solicitors and academics in Scotland deny the existence of such a form of mens rea, but so also did evidence from the Lord Justice-Clerk, Lord Ross and the then Lord Justice-General, Lord Emslie. Lord Emslie in particular[313] implied that Lord Sutherland in *HM Advocate v Hartley*[314] had been incorrect to tell the jury that an intent to do serious bodily harm was enough by itself to constitute the mens rea of murder; and he also said[315] in relation to the opinion of the court in *Brennan v HM Advocate*, which was apparently compiled by him, that he had merely been careless in expressing himself there, when he had written: "Our definition of murder includes the taking of human life by a person who has an intent to kill or to do serious injury or whose act is shown to have been wickedly reckless as to the consequences."[316] Alternatively, he thought that perhaps the second "or" in the quotation should have appeared as "and".

Lethal weapons and particular crimes

9–56   Some judicial dicta, and Hume,[317] appear to support the view that death causally connected to the use of certain weapons or the perpetration of certain crimes, will automatically be classed as murder. The authority for this is sparse, however.

---

[308] See, for example, *R. v Moloney* [1985] A.C. 905, per Lord Bridge of Harwich at 927H; *Attorney General's Reference (No.3 of 1994)* [1998] A.C. 245, Lord Mustill at 250D–F.

[309] *Brennan v HM Advocate*, 1977 J.C. 38.

[310] *R. v Cunningham* [1982] A.C. 566, per Lord Edmund Davies at 582H–583A.

[311] See, e.g. *Margaret Robertson or Brown* (1886) 1 White 93, per Lord McLaren at 104; *William Marshall* (1897) 4 S.L.T. 217, per Lord Young at 217; *George Paterson* (1897) 5 S.L.T. 13, per Lord Young at 13; *Kennedy v HM Advocate*, 1944 J.C. 171, per Lord Justice-General Normand at 177; *HM Advocate v Kidd*, 1960 J.C. 61, per Lord Strachan at 74; *Cawthorne v HM Advocate*, 1968 S.L.T. 330, per Lord Avonside at 330 and Lord Guthrie at 332; *Brennan v HM Advocate*, 1977 J.C. 38 at 47; and *HM Advocate v Hartley*, 1989 S.L.T. 135, per Lord Sutherland at 135.

[312] HL 78–I to III, session 1988–89.

[313] HL 78–III, Q.2017.

[314] *HM Advocate v Hartley*, 1989 S.L.T. 135 at 135.

[315] HL 78-III, Q.2020.

[316] *Brennan v HM Advocate*, 1977 J.C. 38 at 47.

[317] Hume, *Commentaries*, i, 24, 25.

Lord Sands in *HM Advocate v Fraser and Rollins*[318] certainly told the jury that if there was an attempt at a crime of serious violence, then any resultant death of the victim was murder. He further gave as examples an abortion involving the use of instruments which ended with the death of the woman concerned,[319] and any rape or robbery in which the victim was killed.[320] His conclusion then followed

> "if a man uses reckless violence that may cause death, and uses that violence in perpetrating a crime, it is murder. You do not require the deliberate intention to kill, but you must have reckless use of force without any consideration of what the result of that use of force may be."[321]

It is submitted that this is either a rather loose form of Hume's tripartite requirement (see above, para.9–52) or is simply wrong.[322] Similarly, it would be wrong to imagine that murder is automatically relevant if death follows upon a crime in which a certain type of weapon was employed. In *HM Advocate v McGuinness*,[323] for example, Lord Justice-Clerk Aitchison told the jury:

> "If people resort to the use of deadly weapons of this kind [knives, pokers, hatchets], they are guilty of murder whether or not they intended to kill."

That, however, is not really the point. The true issue is that the more dangerous to life a particular weapon is, the more likely its deployment will show that the accused meant to perpetrate some outrageous bodily harm, that his actions were very likely to result in death, and that those actions showed an absolute indifference as to whether his victim lived or died. In other words, dangerous or lethal weapons will often make it simpler to fulfil Hume's requirements for non-intentional murder.[324]

Examples of "wicked recklessness"

Cases of murder founded on "wicked recklessness" are easily found amongst **9–57** the law reports. Amongst the clearest of these must figure the ancient case of *Patrick Stewart*.[325] In the belief that the victim had had sexual intercourse with his daughter, the accused had him bound with cords, his penis cut off, his scrotum filled with ashes, his leg broken with a blow from an axe, and his person then carried off to a close confinement—where death ensued. An equally clear

---

[318] *HM Advocate v Fraser and Rollins*, 1920 J.C. 60 at 62.
[319] *HM Advocate v Fraser and Rollins*, 1920 J.C. 60 at 62.
[320] *HM Advocate v Fraser and Rollins*, 1920 J.C. 60 at 62.
[321] *HM Advocate v Fraser and Rollins*, 1920 J.C. 60 at 63.
[322] Cf., Gordon, *Criminal Law*, 3rd edn (2000/2001), paras 23.26 to 23.28; Ferguson, *Crimes Against the Person* (1998), paras 2.18, 2.19.
[323] *HM Advocate v McGuinness*, 1937 J.C. 37 at 40.
[324] See above, para.9–52; *Parr v HM Advocate*, 1991 J.C. 39, Lord Justice-General Hope at 47; *Broadley v HM Advocate*, 1991 J.C. 108; *Arthur v HM Advocate*, 2002 S.C.C.R. 796; *Anderson v HM Advocate* [2010] HCJAC 9, 2010 S.C.C.R. 270; cf., Gordon, *Criminal Law*, 3rd edn (2000/2001), paras 23.26 to 23.28, for the support which exists for the view that a death caused in the course of a robbery is always to be treated as murder.
[325] *Patrick Stewart* (1602) Hume, *Commentaries*, i, 260; R. Pitcairn, *Ancient Criminal Trials in Scotland* (Edinburgh: William Tait, 1833), Vol.II, p.392.

application of the "wicked recklessness" test can be found in *George Paterson*[326] where the drunken accused not only violently struck the unfortunate female victim, but also thrust a red-hot poker into her rectum and private parts. The test was also considered to be fulfilled in the case of *John McCallum and William Corner*.[327] These two accused partially severed the cable which lowered men in a bucket to the bottom of a pit. Their intention was to cause some injury to the victim, who they knew would be next to be lowered on that particular cable. He fell violently to the bottom of the mine shaft when the cable broke under the strain—just as the accused had intended. They had not intended his death, however. On their own admissions, they had simply intended to injure him to a certain degree, to the extent of a broken leg, for example. In the whole circumstances of the case, there could be little doubt that wicked recklessness was displayed there.[328]

It has been held too that, in an appropriate case, evidence of the accused's utter indifference as to whether his victim lived or died may be sought from his conduct during, before and after the fatal attack.[329]

Consent and murder

9–58   In *HM Advocate v Rutherford*,[330] where the accused had strangled a woman, part of the defence case involved the plea that the victim had desired him to do so—that she had wanted to be killed. Lord Justice-Clerk Cooper simply told the jury that consent was not a defence to murder, apparently as a matter of law. He made no attempt to justify his ruling, although the accused in that case would have faced almost insuperable difficulties in establishing that the woman had indeed consented. Even if cast-iron proof had been available, however, it seems unlikely in the extreme that it would have been treated as having any relevance to the outcome of the trial.

CULPABLE HOMICIDE

Definition of culpable homicide

9–59   There is no single, simple definition of culpable homicide. Essentially (and admittedly unhelpfully) it covers any killing of a human being brought about by another in circumstances where that other should be accounted criminally responsible for it.[331] It clearly excludes murder, and both casual and justifiable homicides (see above, paras 9–45, 9–46, and 9–49 to 9–58); and it is common enough for juries to be told that culpable homicide "means unlawful killing of a human being in circumstances which don't amount to murder."[332] The actus reus

---

[326] *George Paterson* (1897) 5 S.L.T. 13.
[327] *John McCallum and William Corner* (1853) 1 Irv. 259.
[328] See also *Andrew Ewart* (1828) Syme 315, and *Miller and Denovan v HM Advocate*, 1960, noted at 1991 S.L.T. 211; cf. the fact situation in *John Campbell* (1836) 1 Swin. 309, where at the end of the day the jury convicted of culpable homicide.
[329] *Halliday v HM Advocate*, 1998 S.C.C.R. 509.
[330] *HM Advocate v Rutherford*, 1947 J.C. 1 at 5–6; cf. *McDonald v HM Advocate*, 2004 S.C.C.R. 161, where the accused was convicted of culpable homicide on a charge of murder.
[331] In *Drury v HM Advocate*, 2001 S.L.T. 1013, Lord Justice-General Rodger said at 1017B, para.13: "[Culpable homicide] covers the killing of human beings in all circumstances, short of murder, where the criminal law attaches a relevant measure of blame to the person who kills."
[332] *Berry v HM Advocate* (1976) S.C.C.R. Supp. 156, per Lord Keith at 156.

of the crime is plainly the same as that for murder, although the conduct would presumably be less than that capable of raising an inference of murderous mens rea, except perhaps where there is virtually murder (in the sense that wicked recklessness has been established) but for the existence of provocation or diminished responsibility (see below, paras 9–66 to 9–72, and 9–73 to 9–76). The mens rea of culpable homicide depends on the category of the crime.

Hume deals with four categories of culpable homicide. The first of these **9–60** clearly relates to an assault which results in death, yet does not display either an intent to kill or the excessive violence, the great likelihood of death, and the utter indifference to the life of the victim that are the hallmarks of murder (see above, paras 9–51 and 9–52 to 9–57). As he puts it:

> "[W]here there is a wrongful purpose to do any bodily harm, though not outrageous or excessive, yet still if death unfortunately ensue, the invader is not free of guilt ... He is so far blameable, as he did a thing which was wrong and unlawful in itself, and which might [in the sense of 'did'(?)] end in the death of his neighbour."[333]

The second covers a situation "where the homicide is done in prosecution, generally, of any wrong and unlawful act, though without malice to any individual",[334] and seems to involve offences of recklessly caused real injury. Thirdly, Hume mentions that

> "some punishment is due, though the slaughter happen in the performance even of a lawful act, if there be great heedlessness and indiscretion, or a want of due caution and circumspection, in the way of doing the thing."[335]

This may be termed "recklessly-performed, lawful-act" culpable homicide. Fourthly, and finally, Hume considers cases where the killing is preceded by provocation[336] to be culpable homicide. To that fourth category must now be added killings where the accused was suffering from diminished responsibility at the time.[337] All these categories are illustrated in the paragraphs which follow.

Assault type

Where death is causally related to an assault, but is not the readily foreseeable **9–61** result of it, it will not generally be possible to infer the mens rea for murder; but

---

[333] Hume, *Commentaries*, i, 191; see also i, 234 at "3."

[334] Hume, *Commentaries*, i, 192; see also i, 234 at "2."

[335] Hume, *Commentaries*, i, 192; see also i, 233 at "1."

[336] Hume, *Commentaries*, i, 239–254.

[337] See the Criminal Procedure (Scotland) Act 1995 s.51B, as inserted by the Criminal Justice and Licensing (Scotland) Act 2010 (asp 13) s.168; see also the 2010 Act s.171 (which inter alia abolishes the common law rules relative to diminished responsibility). It is also possible for the Crown to take the view that killings which fulfil the requirements for murder (e.g. mercy killings) should be indicted ab initio as cases of culpable homicide: but that is a matter of prosecutorial policy and not of law: see Gordon, *Criminal Law*, 3rd edn (2000/2001), paras 25.02 to 25.07: the last of these paragraphs concerns death caused by omission—in respect of which see *Bone v HM Advocate* [2005] HCJAC 124; 2005 S.C.C.R. 829, where the appellant appears initially to have been charged with murder.

the perpetrator of the assault is not guiltless, nor is he guilty only of assault. He is taken as a matter of law to be guilty of culpable homicide, irrespective of how trivial the assault may have been.[338] Of course, the more serious the assault is in real terms, the more likely that the mens rea for murder may be inferred, as in the border-line case of *Patrick Slaven and Others*,[339] where the victim was twice assaulted by men who were intent on ravishing her, and, having made her escape, was chased by them until she fell over a precipice to her death. As it was put in *John McCallum and William Corner*[340]:

> "If one purposes to inflict a very slight injury, which he has no right to inflict, and death unexpectedly and out of all reasonable calculation ensues, that is culpable homicide; if a more serious injury was intended, the case may be one of murder."

This is clearly capable of being a very harsh rule, bearing in mind the great width of the crime of assault (see above, paras 9–04 to 9–12, above). In *Robert Vance*,[341] for example, the accused who was fighting another, threw back his arm and struck the victim, causing him to fall over and hit his head. The victim died from the resultant injury. It was not even clear from the facts that the accused knew the victim had been standing behind him; but as Lord Moncreiff[342] was reported to have said:

> "[I]n so far as the misfortune which befell Deans [the victim] was concerned, it was clear that it was undesigned on the part of the pannel, yet . . . it could not be said that the pannel was free from blame, inasmuch as he was engaged in an illegal act at the time, and the blow was given in the course of the fight . . . [and] it must be held to be culpable homicide."

The jury, however, found the accused not guilty (as is always their privilege).

Unlawful act type

9–62   What is thought to be involved here is the perpetration of a crime other than assault which might reasonably involve personal injury, and in fact ends in death.

---

[338] See, e.g. *HM Advocate v Delaney*, 1945 J.C. 138; *Bird v HM Advocate*, 1952 J.C. 23; *McDermott v HM Advocate*, 1973 J.C. 8; *Gardiner v HM Advocate* [2007] HCJAC 14; 2007 S.C.C.R. 379. Cf. *HM Advocate v McGinlay*, 1983 S.L.T. 562; *Drury v HM Advocate*, 2001 S.L.T. 1013, Lord Cameron of Lochbroom at 1025I, para.6.

[339] *Patrick Slaven* (1885) 5 Coup. 694; cf. the unusual situation in *McDonald v HM Advocate* [2006] HCJAC 89; 2007 S.C.C.R. 10, where culpable homicide was charged ab initio, and the main issue concerned the causal link between the assault and the death. See also the case of *McDonald v HM Advocate*, 2004 S.C.C.R. 161, where it was accepted by the Crown that an intention to cause pain (in the context of an allegedly consensual sexual encounter) would have been insufficient to justify a conviction for culpable homicide (see the opinion of the court at167D, para.15, and 168B, para.18: the court, however, reserved its opinion as to whether in an appropriate case such an intention, in such a context, would be insufficient to meet the requirements of assault (opinion of the court at 170F, para.23).

[340] *John McCallum and William Corner* (1853) 1 Irv. 259, per Lord Justice-General McNeill at 270–271.

[341] *Robert Vance* (1849) J. Shaw 211.

[342] *Robert Vance* (1849) J. Shaw 211 at 214.

Crimes of real injury, where the mens rea requirement is recklessness, are prime candidates.[343] The causal connection between the crime itself and the death must, of course, be established; but once it is established, the result is culpable homicide, even though there was no question of there being any intent to kill. There are many reported cases which support this type. For example, in *James Niven*[344] the accused discharged a firearm in a public street. An innocent passer-by was killed due to, according to the accused's story, a piece of metal having by accident been included with the gunpowder. The court had no doubt that this was culpable homicide (although the jury acquitted Niven of the charge). The offence involved there was clearly the reckless discharge of firearms to the danger of the lieges (see above, para.9–40). A very similar offence is involved in the hypothetical situation spoken of by Lord Moncreiff in *David Keay*.[345] There, his Lordship said that if a person threw a stone out of a window, and the stone happened to hit someone causing his death, then that would be culpable homicide. Similarly again, in *Mathieson v HM Advocate*[346] the accused committed the crime of reckless fire-raising by setting some cans of paint alight. The paint was stored at the rear entrance of a building which itself caught fire, thus resulting in the deaths of four persons. And in *Sutherland v HM Advocate*,[347] even wilful fire-raising of the accused's own property with intent to defraud insurers was considered appropriate since the way in which the operation had been carried out exhibited the necessary recklessness in relation to the death which occurred. There have also been cases of culpable homicide where the unlawful activity consisted of the administration of noxious substances to the victim in a reckless fashion. Thus, in *Elizabeth Hamilton*[348] the accused nursery maid gave ten drops of laudanum to her 10 month-old charge to quieten him, even though she had been distinctly told by the child's mother to administer nothing of that nature to him at all; and again in *Adam Philip*[349] the accused gave 10 full glasses of whisky to a 10 year old boy, thus occasioning his death. It has also been held that recklessly supplying a controlled drug (amphetamine) to a person who died after ingesting it provided a proper basis for culpable homicide.[350] Equally, therefore, the reckless supply of potentially noxious substances (see above, paras 9–37 to 9–39) should merit a charge of culpable homicide, where death resulted.

    The mens rea element for culpable homicide of this sort is presumably the reck- **9–63** lessness generated by, or associated with, the primary crime, which recklessness is carried forward as it were to the death itself. If that is so, then it may be possible to charge culpable homicide in relation to primary crimes (unlawful acts) which would not normally be expected to cause personal injuries at all, but where the

---

[343] See in particular the opinion of the court in *HM Advocate v Purcell*, 2007 S.C.C.R. 520 at 527A–D, para.11.
[344] *James Niven* (1795) Hume, *Commentaries*, i, 192.
[345] *David Keay* (1837) 1 Swin. 543 at 545.
[346] *Mathieson v HM Advocate*, 1981 S.C.C.R. 196.
[347] *Sutherland v HM Advocate*, 1994 S.L.T. 634.
[348] *Elizabeth Hamilton* (1857) 2 Irv. 738.
[349] *Adam Philip* (1818) Hume, *Commentaries*, i, 237, fn.a.
[350] *Lord Advocate's Reference (No.1 of 1994)*, 1995 S.L.T. 248, subsequently approved by a court of five judges in *MacAngus v HM Advocate; Kane v HM Advocate* [2009] HCJAC; 2009 S.L.T. 137, where it was also held that the voluntary act of the deceased was not necessarily fatal to the conviction of the supplier (see, e.g. the opinion of the court at 151, para.48). See also *HM Advocate v C* [2007] HCJ 10; 2007 S.L.T. 963.

crime itself was carried through in such a reckless manner as to make a resulting death not entirely unforeseeable. An example of such a crime would be theft. Unlike robbery (for which see Ch.10), theft would seldom be linked with injury, let alone death; but Gordon refers to the unreported case of *Finnigan*[351] where the accused was convicted of culpable homicide for having stolen a gas meter by wrenching it away from its supply pipe, thus causing the death of a person who occupied another part of the same building. A more modern version of the same thinking may be found in *Lourie v HM Advocate*[352] where two youths, who were alleged to have pushed their way into an elderly woman's house and there stolen her handbag in her presence, were convicted of culpable homicide, on the basis that their behaviour had caused her fatal shock. (Their convictions were quashed on appeal on the ground of insufficiency of evidence.)

Recklessly-performed, lawful-act type

9–64   The essence of this form of culpable homicide is that the accused in fact caused the death of another because of the grossly careless way in which he performed some otherwise not-unlawful (i.e. not-criminal at common law) activity. Hume[353] gives the example of building-work being carried out in such a fashion that debris is carelessly cast into the street below, to the fatal injury of some passer-by. He also mentions the careless felling of a tree,[354] the careless driving of a coach[355] and also the presenting of a gun at another, not knowing it was loaded[356]: in each case a fatality had resulted. The lack of care which must be shown, however, is high. In the "driving" case of *Paton v HM Advocate*[357] Lord Justice-Clerk Aitchison remarked:

> "[I]t is now necessary to show gross, or wicked, or criminal negligence, something amounting, or at any rate analogous, to a criminal indifference to consequences."

It used to be assumed that gross negligence or simple recklessness[358] (as opposed to the "wicked" variety which suffices for murder) was all that was required for conviction of this type of culpable homicide[359]: indeed in *Transco Plc v HM Advocate*,[360] the Crown argued at the trial stage "that *mens rea* played no part in culpable homicide of the kind with which the present case is concerned."[361] It is

---

[351] *Finnigan* Unreported 1958, High Court at Glasgow, at Gordon, *Criminal Law*, 3rd edn (2000/2001), para.26.27.
[352] *Lourie v HM Advocate*,1988 S.C.C.R. 634.
[353] Hume, *Commentaries*, i, 192–193.
[354] *Mathew Graham* (1813) Hume, *Commentaries*, i, 192, fn.2.
[355] *Thomas Clerk* (1805) Hume, *Commentaries*, i, 192, fn.2.
[356] *David Buchanan* (1817) Hume, *Commentaries*, i, 192, fn.2.
[357] *Paton v HM Advocate*, 1936 J.C. 19 at 22.
[358] As described in *Allan v Patterson*, 1980 J.C. 57: and indeed the test there was applied in *Sutherland v HM Advocate*, 1994 S.L.T. 634, and also in effect by the trial judge in *McDowall v HM Advocate*, 1998 S.C.C.R. 343, although that test was not considered appropriate for all crimes where recklessness was sufficient as the mens rea—see, e.g. *Thomson v HM Advocate*, 1995 S.L.T. 827 (involving reckless fire-raising).
[359] See above, para.9–52. It seems that "gross negligence" is all that is required in English law for "lawful act" type manslaughter: see *R. v Adomako* [1995] 1 A.C. 171 HL.
[360] *Transco Plc v HM Advocate*, 2004 J.C. 29.
[361] *Transco Plc v HM Advocate*, 2004 J.C. 29, Lord Hamilton (with whose opinion Lord MacLean agreed) at 50, para.41.

now clear from *Transco*, however, that mens rea or dole is an essential element in all common law offences,[362]although the nature of it varies "as between one crime and another."[363] What is not particularly clear is the form which mens rea takes in this type of culpable homicide, save that it is "the state of mind of the particular accused."[364] and that "the state of knowledge of the accused is clearly critical."[365] Inferences may be drawn from the lack of care exhibited by the accused—in the sense of setting what he did "against standards of conduct to be expected of persons carrying on operations of the relevant kind"[366]: but such inferences may be offset, it seems, by explanations offered by the accused.[367]

Reported cases involving this form of culpable homicide are legion. They **9–65** include deaths caused by the grossly careless navigation of a boat,[368] dangerous driving of a motor vehicle,[369] folding up of a bed which had a child in it at the time,[370] and preparation of a headache remedy.[371] The unreported case of *Ross Fontana*[372] is also not without interest. He was convicted of culpable homicide because of the grossly improper way in which he had installed a gas fire. He had recklessly failed to provide flues for the removal of fumes, with the result that two people were poisoned by carbon monoxide when the fire was turned on.

Killings following upon provocation

It is a common human failing to lose one's self-control if one is suddenly **9–66** attacked or insulted or taunted by another; and that loss of control often manifests itself in violence, sometimes with fatal consequences for the victim. Such a victim is hardly blameless himself, of course, and may be said to have played some part in his own demise. For that reason, it may be thought that the law should make some concession to

---

[362] *Transco Plc v HM Advocate*, 2004 J.C. 29 at 50–51, para.42.

[363] *Transco Plc v HM Advocate*, 2004 J.C. 29 at 51, para.43.

[364] *Transco Plc v HM Advocate*, 2004 J.C. 29 at 51, para.44.

[365] *Transco Plc v HM Advocate*, 2004 J.C. 29 at 51, para.45.

[366] *Transco Plc v HM Advocate*, 2004 J.C. 29 at 51, para.44.

[367] This follows from Macdonald, *Criminal Law*, 5th edn (1948), p.1—to which Lord Hamilton makes reference in *Transco Plc v HM Advocate*, 2004 J.C. 29, at 51, para.42: see also the opinion of Lord Osborne there at 31, para.3 (where he quotes from Macdonald), and at 34, para.4, where his Lordship seems to identify (by quoting from prior authorities) the mental element in this type of culpable homicide as "a complete disregard of potential dangers", or as "an utter disregard of what the consequences of the act in question may be so far as the public are concerned . . . [or as] recklessness so high as to involve an indifference to the consequences for the public generally." Lord Osborne's remarks probably do not form part of the *ratio* of the case—although both he and Lord Hamilton (with whom Lord MacLean agreed) criticise the circularity of Lord Justice-Clerk Aitchison's remarks (quoted in the text, above) as well as his use of the term "negligence": see *Transco Plc*, at 33, para.4, 48–49, para.37.

[368] *Angus MacPherson and John Stewart* (1861) 4 Irv. 85.

[369] See, e.g. *McDowall v HM Advocate*, 1998 S.C.C.R. 343; also see *HM Advocate v Purcell* [2007] HCJ 13; 2007 S.C.C.R. 520.

[370] *Williamina Sutherland* (1856) 2 Irv. 455.

[371] *Edmund Wheatley* (1853) 1 Irv. 225, where a medical student who was learning the art of dispensing medicines in a chemist's shop, and who had no authority to do what he did, prepared a potion for a friend, thus causing his death. His actions were treated as having gone well beyond a mere careless error in dispensing; cf. *George Armitage* (1885) 5 Coup. 675 and *HM Advocate v Wood* (1903) 4 Adam 150.

[372] *Ross Fontana* Unreported March 1990, High Court at Kirkcaldy.

"human infirmity in those difficult and agitating situations, which require a more than ordinary strength of mind, and command of temper to withstand them."[373]

Indeed as Lord Cowie once put it to a jury:

"If . . . you find that all the factors were present for a verdict of murder, but . . . you take the view . . . that he was provoked . . . then for that reason . . . you could reduce the offence of murder to culpable homicide."[374]

Much the same was said by Lord Cullen to a jury in *Graham v HM Advocate*.[375] This commonly expressed view, however, that provocation reduces murder to culpable homicide, was considered to be unsound (or at least in relation to intentional killings) in *Drury v HM Advocate*.[376] As Lord Justice-General Rodger said of the trial judge's directions to the jury in that case:

"By saying that, if provocation were established, this would reduce the crime from murder to culpable homicide, the judge could be thought to give the impression that provocation acts as some kind of laissez-passer by virtue of which an accused, who displays the hallmarks of a murderer and would otherwise find himself convicted of murder, is entitled to escape from that predicament to the somewhat less serious predicament of a conviction of culpable homicide. While the terminology of 'reducing murder to culpable homicide' is frequently encountered, it is essentially misleading . . . [since] it suggests that the jury would first conclude that, absent provocation, the accused would have been guilty of murder, and only at that stage would they consider provocation. In reality, however, evidence relating to provocation is simply one of the factors which the jury should take into account in performing their general task of determining the accused's state of mind at the time when he killed his victim."[377]

The tenor of the decision in *Drury* seems to be that a person who intentionally kills another because he was provoked into doing so lacks murderous intent: he does not have "wicked" intent, and thus cannot be shown to have had the necessary mens rea for murder. He will, however, be convicted of culpable homicide. (The same reasoning should probably have applied in relation to diminished responsibility,[378] although in *Galbraith v HM Advocate*,[379] which was decided after *Drury*, the Appeal Court appeared to favour the formerly held view that that plea was a mitigatory one, in which murder gave way to culpable homicide in

---

[373] Hume, *Commentaries*, i, 249.
[374] *Stobbs v HM Advocate*, 1983 S.C.C.R. 190 at 199.
[375] *Graham v HM Advocate*,1987 S.C.C.R. 20 at 22.
[376] *Drury v HM Advocate*, 2001 S.L.T. 1013.
[377] *Drury v HM Advocate*, 2001 S.L.T. 1013 at 1018D–F, para.17.
[378] The past tense has to be used here since the common law rules relating to diminished responsibility have been abolished: see the Criminal Justice and Licensing (Scotland) Act 2010 (asp 13) s.71(b). For diminished responsibility after the 2010 Act, see below, para.9–74.
[379] *Galbraith v HM Advocate*, 2002 J.C. 1.

order to reflect the lower level of responsibility involved.[380]) This leaves unclear how provocation operates when the evidence in a homicide case reveals wicked recklessness on the part of the accused[381]: it seems that there, the mens rea for murder will have been established, and that the former theory—that provocation reduces murder to culpable homicide—will probably continue to apply. If this is so, there then arises a theoretical awkwardness which is not easy to defend. Irrespective of whether this is truly the theoretical position, and, if so, what further implications it may have, no one doubts that the outcome of a successful plea of provocation will be a conviction for culpable homicide and not one for murder.[382] There are, however, various criteria to be met if a plea of provocation is to be attended with success.

Immediacy of retaliation

Hume[383] requires there to be a "sudden impulse of resentment" in retaliation of **9–67** provocation "suffered upon the spot." Macdonald puts the same point even more forcefully: "Provocation, although great, will not palliate [sic] guilt if any interval have elapsed between the provocation and the retaliation."[384] The point is that provocation is still at basis a concession to human infirmity and not an excuse for cold-blooded vengeance-taking. Once passions have been allowed to cool, provocation no longer applies.[385] Thus, in *Walter Redpath*[386] the accused was attacked by his eventual victim, and made efforts there and then to lift a stone in order to retaliate. He thought better of it, however, and instead went indoors to look out a firearm. Not long after, he returned to the scene of the initial attack with a gun and shot the victim. Although afterwards convicted of culpable homicide only, he should have been convicted of murder, according to Hume, since an interval for "cooling-off" had been allowed to elapse prior to the fatal conduct. It seems, then, that instant retaliation to a provoking incident is to be taken quite literally. Although the courts have not been quite as strict as Hume might have wanted them to be, any significant gap between provocation and retaliation is certainly such as to elide the plea.[387]

Cumulative provocation

Linked to the requirement of immediacy of retaliation is the rule that there must **9–68** be a specific, provoking incident. There must be such an incident, sufficiently provoking in itself in the eyes of the law, just before the fatal violence was delivered by the accused. If there had been a course of incidents of a provocative nature over a series of days, weeks or even years, but no final incident to which the accused responded then no provocation exists in law, and the crime will be murder.

---

[380] *Galbraith v HM Advocate*, 2002 J.C. 1, opinion of the court at 18A–B, para.45; cf. Gordon's "Commentary" to the case, at 2001 S.C.C.R. 551, at 575, at "1" and "2."
[381] *Pace*, Lord Justice-General Rodger in *Drury v HM Advocate*, 2001 S.LT. 1013 at 1018F–G, para.18, since what is said there appears to ignore what has come to be understood as "wicked recklessness".
[382] *Drury v HM Advocate*, 2001 S.L.T. 1013, Lord Justice-General Rodger at 1017I, para.16.
[383] Hume, *Commentaries*, i, 239.
[384] Macdonald, *Criminal Law*, 5th edn (1948), p.94.
[385] See *Drury v HM Advocate*, 2001 S.L.T. 1013, Lord Justice-General Rodger at 1019L, para.21.
[386] *Walter Redpath* (1810) Hume, *Commentaries*, i, 252, n.1.
[387] See *Parr v HM Advocate*, 1991 J.C. 39.

This has consistently been upheld by the courts.[388] In particular, this means that a woman, who for years has been subjected to violence by her partner, and who one day "snaps" at the end of her tether and kills him as he lies sleeping in a chair, must be convicted of murder, although she may be able to show that she was acting under diminished responsibility: see below, para.9–73. In practice, of course, it may be possible for particular judges to direct juries in appropriate cases involving provocation to ignore this rather harsh rule,[389] or for the Crown to accept a plea of guilty to culpable homicide.[390]

Recognised Provocation

9–69   *Violence.* According to Macdonald,[391] the usual form of acceptable provocation is violence.

"The defence of provocation is of this sort—'Being agitated and excited, and alarmed by violence, I lost control over myself, and took life, when my presence of mind had left me, and without thought of what I was doing'."

This statement has been specifically approved on several occasions.[392] However, the degree of violence visited upon the accused is of considerable importance. As Lord Cooper once said:

"It takes a tremendous amount of provocation to palliate stabbing a man to death . . . A blow with the fist is no justification for the use of a lethal weapon. Provocation, in short, must bear a reasonable retaliation to the resentment which it excites."[393]

It is now clear that there must indeed be a reasonable or proportionate relationship between the accused's reaction and the victim's provocative attack.[394] There must

---

[388] See *Thomson v HM Advocate*, 1986 S.L.T. 281; *Graham v HM Advocate*, 1987 S.C.C.R. 20; *Parr v HM Advocate*, 1991 J.C. 39.

[389] See, e.g. *Crawford v HM Advocate*, 1950 J.C. 67; but cf. *HM Advocate v Greig*, 1979, noted in Gane, Stoddart and Chalmers, *A Casebook on Scottish Criminal Law*, 4th edn (2009), p.444, para.10–40.

[390] See, e.g. *Walker v HM Advocate*, 1996 S.C.C.R. 818, at 822A, where in an appeal against sentence for culpable homicide, the court opined: "Considerable leniency was shown already to the appellant in the decision to reduce the charge from one of murder to culpable homicide . . . ". See also Clare Connelly, "Women who kill violent men" (1996) J.R. 215.

[391] Macdonald, *Criminal Law*, 5th edn (1948), p.94.

[392] See, e.g. *Cosgrove v HM Advocate*, 1990 J.C. 333, at 339; *Low v HM Advocate*, 1994 S.L.T. 277, Lord Justice-Clerk Ross at 285L.

[393] *Smith v HM Advocate* Unreported 1952, High Court at Glasgow, at Gordon, *Criminal Law*, 3rd edn (2000/2001), para.25.19. Notice that in *Robertson v HM Advocate*, 1994 J.C. 245, Lord Justice-Clerk Ross (at 247F) thought that "retaliation" in the quotation should read "relation".

[394] *Gillon v HM Advocate* [2006] HCJAC 61; 2006 S.L.T. 799, opinion of the court (of five judges) at 811C–D, para.39; *McCormack v HM Advocate*, 1993 J.C. 170; *Robertson v HM Advocate*, 1994 S.L.T. 1004. The decision in *Gillon* brings to an end the suggestion that the "ordinary person" test, adopted by the Appeal Court in relation to "sexual infidelity" type provocation (see below, para.9–70), might be applied to provocation by violence too: see Chalmers and Leverick, *Criminal Defences and Pleas in Bar of Trial* (2006), paras.10.09 and 10.18–10.20 (written prior to the decision in *Gillon*). There are thus two separate conditions to be met for the plea of provocation to succeed, the one to be used depending upon the nature of the provocation itself.

not be a gross disproportion between that reaction and the attack,[395] for it is accepted that an equality or fine balance between the two cannot be looked for in such situations where there is loss of control.[396] Thus, in *Thomson v HM Advocate*[397] the accused stabbed his victim repeatedly with a knife (which he had taken the precaution of bringing with him to a meeting) after a trivial assault, which consisted in no more than the victim's physically attempting to stop him leaving the room where they both were. There was a gross disproportion between the violence and the retaliation, and the plea of provocation was ruled out. In the same way, it was ruled out in *Fenning v HM Advocate*[398] since it was a gross over-reaction to counter a drunken man's random gesticulations with a knife by beating his brains out with a stone or rifle butt. *Ensign Hardie*[399] was on firmer ground, however, since he had been struck with a "tree" (i.e. a baulk of wood) and beaten by the eventual victim, who had been on horseback at the time.

Sexual infidelity. Since well before the time of Hume, it has been recognised that **9–70** a man who found his wife in the very act of adultery with another man might be convicted of culpable homicide rather than murder if he killed him, her or them on the spot.[400] Presumably, this would apply to a wife who had found her husband in similar adulterous circumstances. The basis was (and is) that such a spouse had been sorely provoked. The issue has not been confined, however, to cases where the adultery was discovered as it actually took place. In *HM Advocate v Gilmour*[401] Lord Justice-Clerk Aitchison told the jury:

> "If you are satisfied that the accused found his wife in the act of adultery, or in circumstances that reasonably conveyed to his mind that his wife had just committed adultery, or was just about to commit adultery when discovered, you are entitled . . . to acquit the accused of murder and to find him guilty of culpable homicide only."

And further, in *HM Advocate v Hill*[402] it was accepted that provocation could be made out where a man's wife and her lover confessed to having committed adultery. This was all the more surprising since "words" are not generally accepted as sufficient for the plea of provocation to be upheld; and, of course, a confession refers to some incident which has taken place in the past. Still further, however, it has been decided that this form of provocation is open to a person merely

---

[395] *Gillon v HM Advocate* [2006] HCJAC 61; 2006 S.L.T. 799, opinion of the court (of five judges) at 811C–D, para.39, where the formulation of the proportionality test favoured by Lord Justice-Clerk Ross in *Robertson v HM Advocate*, 1994 J.C. 245, at 249E–G, is preferred. See also *Low v HM Advocate*, 1994 S.L.T. 277, per Lord Justice-Clerk Ross at 286D–G (where it is stated that the self-defence threshold of "no cruel excess" should be confined to that defence, and not applied also to provocation).

[396] *Robertson v HM Advocate*, 1994 J.C. 245. See also *Gillon v HM Advocate* [2006] HCJAC 61; 2006 S.L.T. 799, opinion of the court (of five judges) at 807B–D, para.22, where the fallacy of arguing that there never can be a reasonably proportionate retaliation, where death is caused by that retaliation, is exposed.

[397] *Thomson v HM Advocate*, 1986 S.L.T. 281.

[398] *Fenning v HM Advocate*, 1985 S.C.C.R. 219.

[399] *Ensign Hardy* (1701) Hume, *Commentaries*, i, 244, fn.2.

[400] *James Christie* (1731) Hume, *Commentaries*, i, 245–246.

[401] *HM Advocate v Gilmour*, 1938 J.C. 1 at 2–3.

[402] *HM Advocate v Hill*, 1941 J.C. 59.

cohabiting with another, provided that there can be shown to have been a bond of sexual fidelity between them at the material time.[403] There is no requirement, therefore, that sexual infidelity should be confined to those who are married or are civil partners.[404] But the Appeal Court has made very plain that the words used must go beyond mere insults in the course of a quarrel: they must "disclose in clear and unequivocal terms that the deceased had been committing adultery . . .".[405] Immediacy of reaction to the disclosure or discovery is, of course, crucial; but it has been held that a subsequent disclosure (to which the accused immediately reacted) was sufficient since it had been substantially different from a previous disclosure (to which the accused had not reacted).[406]

There is not, nor could be, any requirement in law for a degree of proportionality between the discovery (or disclosure) of the infidelity and the accused's violent reaction to it,[407] since the two are plainly not commensurable. It is not, however, sufficient (although necessary) for provocation to exist in law that the accused should have lost his self-control immediately on making the discovery or receiving the disclosure, unless an ordinary man (or woman) "having been thus provoked, would have been liable to react as he [or she] did."[408] The test relates to whether the ordinary man or woman's response would have been as extreme as that of the accused; and thus the jury in question will have to consider the "nature and degree"[409] of the accused's actual response and relate that to the presumed response of an ordinary individual in the same circumstances. It is not clear whether, or to what extent, the individual characteristics of the accused are relevant to the jury's determination[410]; but the opinion of the court (of five judges) in *Gillon v HM Advocate*[411] suggests that Scots law should be slow to saddle itself with the difficulties evident in other jurisdictions which have adopted an "individual characteristics" approach to provocation.

Words not sufficient

9–71   The general consensus has always been that words however "foul or abusive or . . . signs or gestures, how contemptuous or derisive so ever" cannot operate as provocation in relation to a murder charge.[412] This represents a conspicuous difference between the application of provocation in homicide and in assault (see

---

[403] See *McKay v HM Advocate*, 1991 J.C. 91; *Rutherford v HM Advocate*, 1997 S.C.C.R. 711.

[404] See the Civil Partnership Act 2004. In *HM Advocate v McKean*, 1996 S.C.C.R. 402, the trial judge, Lord MacLean, directed the jury (at 403A) that he saw "no reason why, in the modern context, the plea should not also be available to homosexual couples who live together and are regarded in the community as partners bound together by ties of love, affection and faithfulness . . . ".

[405] *McKay v HM Advocate*, 1991 J.C. 91, per Lord Justice-General Hope at 96; see also *McCormack v HM Advocate*, 1993 J.C. 170, Lord Justice-General Hope at 179G–I.

[406] *Rutherford v HM Advocate*, 1997 S.C.C.R. 711.

[407] *Drury v HM Advocate*, 2001 S.L.T. 1013 (court of five judges).

[408] *Drury v HM Advocate*, 2001 S.L.T. Lord Justice-General Rodger at 1023F, para.34.

[409] *Drury v HM Advocate*, 2001 S.L.T. 1013.

[410] The court in *Drury v HM Advocate*, 2001 S.L.T. 1013, reserved its opinion on this matter: see Lord Justice-General Rodger's opinion at 1022D–E, para.29; cf. the law in England, as set out in *R. v James* [2006] 2 W.L.R. 887 CA (Crim Div), upholding the decision in *Attorney General for Jersey v Holley* [2005] 2 A.C. 280 PC rather than that of the House of Lords in *R. v Smith (Morgan)* [2001] 1 A.C.146 HL.

[411] *Gillon v HM Advocate* [2006] HCJAC 61; 2006 S.L.T. 799; see especially the opinion of the court at 809D to 811C, paras 31–38.

[412] Hume, *Commentaries*, i, 247; Macdonald, *Criminal Law* (1948), p.93.

above, para.9–23). In *William Aird*[413] the accused was denied provocation in relation to his killing of a woman who had thrown the contents of a chamber pot in his face; and that being so, abusive words and taunts could scarcely hope to fare any better. The Appeal Court, therefore, continues to uphold the orthodox view,[414] whilst recognising that there may be occasions when that view should yield.[415] It is not clear when that might legitimately happen, however, since each case appears to turn on its own facts and circumstances; but sexual insults and taunts were left to the jury as provocation in *Berry v HM Advocate*,[416] as were (alleged) threats to tell the accused's wife of an adulterous association clandestinely enjoyed by the accused in *Stobbs v HM Advocate*.[417]

Effect on attempted murder

If a successful plea of provocation on a murder charge results in a conviction **9–72** for culpable homicide, then provocation relative to a charge of attempted murder should logically result in a conviction for attempted culpable homicide. But the courts appear to have taken the view that attempted culpable homicide does not exist. The appropriate verdict, therefore, appears to be assault to severe injury under provocation.[418]

Diminished responsibility

The previous common law position

At common law, diminished responsibility was re-explained in the full bench **9–73** decision of *Galbraith v HM Advocate*.[419] Although the concept of diminished responsibility had been recognised in Scots law since the second-half of the nineteenth century as a means of reducing murder to culpable homicide,[420] the opinion of the court in *Galbraith* showed that both the terminology by which it was known and the content of that concept remained largely unsettled and confused.[421] The prior jurisprudence, for example, had insisted that a plea of diminished responsibility could not succeed unless there was "mental disease" or a state of mind virtually "bordering on insanity".[422] Following *Galbraith,* it became clear that

---

[413] *William Aird* (1693) Hume, *Commentaries*, i, 248.
[414] See *Thomson v HM Advocate*, 1986 S.L.T. 281; *Cosgrove v HM Advocate*, 1990 J.C. 333; *McCormack v HM Advocate*, 1993 J.C. 170, Lord Justice-General Hope at 179D–E.
[415] See *Thomson v HM Advocate*, 1986 S.L.T. 281 per Lord Hunter at 286D; *Cosgrove v HM Advocate*, 1990 J.C. 333, per Lord Cowie at 339.
[416] *Berry v HM Advocate* (1976) S.C.C.R. Supp. 156.
[417] *Stobbs v HM Advocate*, 1983 S.C.C.R. 190.
[418] *Brady v HM Advocate*, 1986 S.L.T. 686; *Salmond v HM Advocate*, 1992 S.L.T. 156; *Drury v HM Advocate*, 2001 S.L.T. 1013, Lord Cameron of Lochbroom at 1025H, para.6. See also the remarks of Lord McEwan in *HM Advocate v C*, 2007 S.L.T. 963, at 965D, para.14. Cf. *HM Advocate v Kerr* [2011] HCJAC 17; 2011 S.L.T. 430, on the close equivalence between the common law plea of provocation and diminished responsibility, and their respective effects on charges of attempted murder.
[419] *Galbraith v HM Advocate*, 2002 J.C. 1 (court of five judges).
[420] See, e.g. *Alexander Dingwall* (1867) 5 Irv. 466.
[421] See *Galbraith v HM Advocate*, 2002 J.C. 1, opinion of the court at 10I to 16D, paras 23–40.
[422] See, e.g. *HM Advocate v Savage*, 1923 J.C. 49; *Connelly v HM Advocate*, 1991 S.L.T. 397; *Williamson v HM Advocate*, 1994 S.L.T. 1000; *Martindale v HM Advocate*, 1994 S.L.T. 1093. *Galbraith* re-interpreted *Savage*, overruled *Connelly*, and, by implication, disapproved of much of what was said by the courts in *Williamson* and *Martindale*.

diminished responsibility referred to substantial mental impairment of an accused's ability to determine and control his acts and omissions due to mental abnormality.

"Because the individual is [thus] not fully responsible in law for what he does when his mental state is substantially impaired, the law mitigates the punishment which it deems appropriate for his criminal acts"[423];

it followed that to give effect to whatever mitigation was appropriate in an individual case, the accused had to be convicted not of murder (which carried a mandatory life sentence) but of culpable homicide (where the sentence was (and is) generally at the discretion of the trial judge).

The statutory re-formulation

9–74   Since the coming into force of the Criminal Justice and Licensing (Scotland) Act 2010 (asp 13), the common law plea of diminished responsibility has been abolished,[424] but has been replaced by a statutory re-formulation[425] which is based to a considerable degree on what was decided in *Galbraith*.[426] The law now stands, therefore, as follows:

"A person who would otherwise be convicted of murder is instead to be convicted of culpable homicide on grounds of diminished responsibility if the person's ability to determine or control conduct for which the person would otherwise be convicted of murder was, at the time of the conduct, substantially impaired by reason of abnormality of mind."[427]

It will be appreciated that the plea is restricted to murder charges (something which the common law failed to make clear), and should be noted that the conduct in question includes acts and omissions.[428] "Abnormality of mind" is deliberately, it seems, left unrestricted, save that it includes "mental disorder".[429]

Onus

9–75   As had been the case at common law,[430] an accused, who wishes to submit a plea of diminished responsibility in answer to a charge of murder, must "establish

---

[423] *Galbraith v HM Advocate*, 2002 J.C. 1, opinion of the court at 18A, para.45.
[424] See the Criminal Justice and Licensing (Scotland) Act 2010 (asp 13) s.171(b).
[425] See the Criminal Procedure (Scotland) Act 1995 s.51B, as inserted by the Criminal Justice and Licensing (Scotland) Act 2010 (asp 13) s.168.
[426] *Galbraith v HM Advocate*, 2002 J.C. 1; the impetus for change originated in recommendations made by the Scottish Law Commission: see *Report on Insanity and Diminished Responsibility* (The Stationery Office, 2004), Pt 3, Scot. Law Com. No.195.
[427] Criminal Procedure (Scotland) Act 1995 s.51B(1).
[428] Criminal Procedure (Scotland) Act 1995 s.51B(5).
[429] See the Criminal Procedure (Scotland) Act 1995 s.51B(3). In terms of s.307(1) of that 1995 Act, "mental disorder" is given the meaning it has in the Mental Health (Care and Treatment) (Scotland) Act 2003 (asp 13) s.328(1), i.e. "(a) mental illness; (b) personality disorder; or (c) learning disability." (Section 307(1) of the 1995 Act was amended to that extent by the said 2003 Act Sch.4 para.8(16)(d).)
[430] See *Lindsay v HM Advocate*, 1996 S.C.C.R. 870.

on a balance of probabilities" that his (or her) ability to determine or control the relevant conduct at the material time was substantially impaired by reason of abnormality of mind.[431] It must be noted in this connection, however, that:

> "The fact a person was under the influence of alcohol, drugs or any other substance at the time of the conduct in question does not of itself—
>
> (a) constitute abnormality of mind for the purposes of [the statutory re-formulation of diminished responsibility], or
> (b) prevent such abnormality from being established for those purposes."[432]

Effect on attempted murder

In a similar way to provocation (see above, para.9–72), diminished responsi- **9–76** bility at common law did not effect a conviction for attempted culpable homicide on an attempted murder charge—the appropriate verdict in such a case being one of assault.[433] It perhaps remains to be seen what the position will be in an attempted murder case vis à vis the statutory re-formulation of the diminished responsibility plea and the abolition of existing common law rules. To the extent that the Scottish Law Commission's recommendations and deliberations may be used as an aid to interpretation of legislative provisions, it seems that a rejuvinated common law solution here would not be the preferred approach.[434]

Persistent vegetative state

It has been declared by the Lord Advocate[435] that doctors who withdraw life- **9–77** sustaining "treatment" (in its widest sense, to include feeding and hydration) from patients who are in a "persistent vegetative state" will be immune from prosecution for homicide (murder or culpable homicide) in respect of such a patient provided that the Court of Session has first agreed to such withdrawal. The procedure to be employed before that Court was laid down in *Law Hospital NHS Trust v The Lord Advocate*,[436] where Lord President Hope described such a state as follows:

> "This is the result of irreversible damage to the cerebral cortex. The function of consciousness has been lost completely and for ever. The patient is wholly unaware of her surroundings. She cannot see, hear, feel pain or pleasure, communicate by words or movement or make voluntary movements of any kind. The brain stem structures are preserved, and so long as this continues she remains clinically alive. The vegetative reflexes which control such functions as breathing, cardiac action and digestion are maintained. Involuntary movements of the eyes and the ability to make sounds give the impression of apparent wakefulness . . . [S]he remains alive only because

---

[431] Criminal Procedure (Scotland) Act 1995 s.51B(4).
[432] Criminal Procedure (Scotland) Act 1995, s.51B(3).
[433] *HM Advocate v Blake*, 1986 S.L.T. 661, per Lord Brand at 663. In *Galbraith v HM Advocate*, 2002 J.C. 1, at 18C, para.45, the court reserved its opinion on this issue; but *Blake* was approved in *HM Advocate v Kerr* [2011] HCJAC 17; 2011 S.L.T. 430.
[434] See Scottish Law Commission, *Report on Insanity and Diminished Responsibility* (The Stationery Office, 2004), paras 3.49 and 3.50, Scot. Law Com. No.195.
[435] Policy statement, made on April 11, 1996.
[436] *Law Hospital NHS Trust v Lord Advocate*, 1996 S.C. 301.

feeding and hydration are provided to her artificially and because of the nursing care which she continues to receive in the hospital."[437]

4.(B) CORPORATE HOMICIDE

9–78 There is a statutory offence known in Scotland as "Corporate Homicide".[438] This offence is complex, and reference must be made to the appropriate legislation (the Corporate Manslaughter and Corporate Homicide Act 2007) for a detailed account of it.[439] In general, an organisation[440] commits this offence if the way in which its activities are managed or organised causes a person's death and amounts to a gross breach[441] of a relevant duty of care owed by it to that person. (An individual cannot be prosecuted for this offence by, for example, being allegedly art and part in its commission.[442]) An organisation is not liable unless the way in which its activities are managed or organised *by its senior management* is a substantial element in the breach of the relevant duty of care[443]: and a "relevant duty of care" means any of the duties, owed under the law of negligence,[444] as these are set out in s.2 of the Act.[445] These duties are qualified, however, by the exceptions detailed in ss.3–7, which cover certain issues relating, for example, to public policy decisions, military activities, policing and law enforcement, emergencies, and child protection.[446] The offence can be tried only on indictment and

---

[437] *Law Hospital NHS Trust v Lord Advocate*, 1996 S.C. 301 at 305.
[438] See the Corporate Manslaughter and Corporate Homicide Act 2007 s.1(5)(b).
[439] See also Peter Ferguson QC, "Corporate Manslaughter and Corporate Homicide Act 2007" (2007) S.L.T. (News) 251, for a detailed and helpful critique of the Act.
[440] "Organisation" means a corporation, a police force, a partnership (see s.25 of the Act), certain trade unions or employers' associations, and the government departments and other bodies set out in Sch.1 (which inter alia lists the Crown Office, the Procurator Fiscal Service, the National Records of Scotland, and the Scottish Executive) as amended by (inter alia) the Serious Crime Act 2007 Sch.8 para.178; the Corporate Manslaughter and Corporate Homicide Act 2007 (Amendment of Schedule 1) Order 2008 (SI 2008/396) art.2(2); and the Budget Responsibility and National Audit Act 2011 Sch.5 para.32.
[441] A breach is "gross" if the conduct in question "falls far below what can reasonably be expected of the organisation in the circumstances": see s.1(4)(b) of the Corporate Manslaughter and Corporate Homicide Act 2007.
[442] See s.18(2) of the Corporate Manslaughter and Corporate Homicide Act 2007.
[443] See s.1(3) of the Corporate Manslaughter and Corporate Homicide Act 2007. "Senior management" is defined in s.1(4)(c).
[444] Certain rules of the common law of negligence, which would have defeated a relevant duty of care from being owed by an organisation, are to be disregarded in the context of this offence: see s.2(6) of the Corporate Manslaughter and Corporate Homicide Act 2007.
[445] These duties include those owed to employees or other persons working for the organisation or performing services for it, those owed by it as an occupier of premises (or as a supplier of goods or services, as a "person" carrying on construction or maintenance operations, or as a user or keeper of plant, vehicles or "other thing"), or those owed to anyone held in custody: note that s.2 is amended by the Corporate Manslaughter and Corporate Homicide Act 2007 (Amendment) Order 2011 (SI 2011/1868) art.2. Whether an organisation owes such a duty of care to any particular individual is a question of law: see s.2(5); but whether or not a breach of a duty is sufficiently "gross" for conviction is a matter for a jury to consider: see s.8—all sections being those of the Corporate Manslaughter and Corporate Homicide Act 2007.
[446] See also ss.11–14 of the Corporate Manslaughter and Corporate Homicide Act 2007 (noting that s.7 is amended by the Offender Management Act 2007 (Consequential Amendments) Order 2008 (SI 2008/912) Sch.1 para.25; and that s.13 is amended by the Police Reform and Social Responsibility Act 2011 Sch.16 para.365).

only in a High Court.[447] If an organisation is convicted of such an offence, the maximum penalty is "a fine"[448]; but the court can also make a "remedial order", under which that organisation must remedy the breach of duty (as also any identified health and safety deficiency) which led to the death, and/or a "publicity order", under which that organisation must publicise the fact and detail of the conviction, the amount of the fine imposed, and the terms of any remedial order passed.[449]

5. SPECIFIC SEXUAL OFFENCES

Introduction

The Sexual Offences (Scotland) Act 2009 (asp 9)[450] was enacted to provide a **9–79** modern "code" of specific sexual offences for Scots law. Most, but not all, of those offences have counterparts at common law; and the intention is that those offences should either stand in place of their particular common law counterparts or limit the ambit of such relevant common law offences as continue to survive.[451] It is not always easy to classify the 2009 Act offences, especially as they are generally not mutually exclusive[452]; some of those offences have already been summarised above,[453] others will be considered in this part of this chapter, and a further selection will be dealt with below, in Ch.12. At the time of writing, most of the 2009 Act is in force,[454] but the provisions abolishing certain common law crimes[455] (as also those provisions which limit the ambit of other common law offences[456]) have not, as yet, been given legal effect. As it may be some time before those provisions are given such effect, it remains necessary to consider the common law offences discussed in the following paragraphs. It must be borne in mind, however, that the rules evolved by the common law for any such crime provide no necessary guide to the interpretation of any 2009 Act offence—even where the *nomen iuris* should happen to be the same.

---

[447] See s.1(7) of the Corporate Manslaughter and Corporate Homicide Act 2007. Under s.19, an organisation can also be charged, cumulatively or sequentially, with an appropriate "health and safety" offence.

[448] See s.1(6) of the Corporate Manslaughter and Corporate Homicide Act 2007.

[449] See ss.9 and 10 of the Corporate Manslaughter and Corporate Homicide Act 2007.

[450] Hereafter referred to as "the 2009 Act".

[451] See the 2009 Act ss.52(a),(b).

[452] The 2009 Act is largely based on recommendations of the Scottish Law Commission in its *Report on Rape and other Sexual Offences* (The Stationery Office, 2007), Scot. Law Com. No.209; it was not the intention of the Commission that the (then) proposed new offences should necessarily be discreet—thus providing maximum room for alternative verdicts in individual cases in an area of law where it is not always possible to be certain of the evidence prior to trial—and the 2009 Act follows the Commission in this respect.

[453] See above, paras 9–24 to 9–30.

[454] See the Sexual Offences (Scotland) Act 2009 (Commencement No.1) and the Criminal Justice and Licensing (Scotland) Act 2010 (Commencement No. 4) Order 2010 (SSI 2010/ 357) art.2(a).

[455] See the 2009 Act ss.52(a) and 53(2)(a)–(c).

[456] See the 2009 Act ss.52(b) and 53(2)(d).

(1) Rape at common law

9–80   The actus reus of rape[457] consists of a male person having vaginal sexual intercourse with a female person[458] without the "active" consent of that female person.[459] The mens rea of the crime "includes the intention to have intercourse with the woman without her consent"[460] or recklessness as to the matter of consent.[461] The elements of the offence are considered in the paragraphs which follow.

Gender specific

9–81   Rape is a gender-specific crime. In Scotland, it can only be committed by males upon females, which appears to mean by persons biologically male at birth upon persons born biologically female[462]; but this is not necessarily so in modern times. Under the Gender Recognition Act 2004, a person who fulfils the statutory requirements may be issued with a "full gender recognition certificate", under which a person who had been male acquires "for all purposes"[463] the female gender, or a person who had been female—the male gender. If such a person acquires such a gender, and has also had full gender reassignment surgery, the law of rape operates as expected—as a gender specific crime. Since the issue of a full gender recognition certificate is not, however, dependent upon the completion of such surgery,[464] the 2004 Act makes provision for those in possession of such certificates (but who have not had such surgery) to be treated for the purposes of any gender specific offence as if they had not acquired their new gender.[465]

In historical times, the crime was thought to be an off-shoot of abduction.[466] The view then taken was that the carrying off and defiling of a female was of greater offence to her husband or father than to the female herself, a view which would now be regarded as outrageous. Echoes of it could still be heard in the nineteenth century, however, as in the case of *Charles Sweenie*[467] where Lord

---

[457] Settled as recently as March, 2002: see *Lord Advocate's Reference (No.1 of 2001)*, 2002 S.L.T. 466 (court of seven judges).

[458] Sometimes referred to archaically as having "carnal knowledge" of her.

[459] *Lord Advocate's Reference (No.1 of 2001)*, 2002 S.L.T. 466, Lord Justice-General Cullen at 475F, para.39; cf. his Lordship's opinion at 476A, para.44.

[460] *Jamieson v HM Advocate*, 1994 S.L.T. 537, per Lord Justice-General Hope at 541C (presumably now meaning knowledge on the male's part that the female had not given her consent): see *Lord Advocate's Reference (No.1 of 2001)*, 2002 S.L.T. 466, Lord Justice-General Cullen at 476B, para.44, where this interpretation is accepted without discussion.

[461] *Jamieson v HM Advocate*, 1994 S.L.T. 537 at 541K (presumably meaning utter indifference on the part of the accused whether the female had consented or not). The account of the mens rea (mutatis mutandis) given in *Jamieson* was accepted by the majority of the court in *Lord Advocate's Reference (No.1 of 2001)*, 2002 S.L.T. 466—see in particular the opinion of Lord Justice-General Cullen at 473B—H, para.28–29, and at 476B, para.44.

[462] Cf. current English law, as contained in the Sexual Offences Act 2003 s.1 (with which must be read in particular ss. 74, 75 and 76); cf., s.2.

[463] See s.9 of the Gender Recognition Act 2004.

[464] See s.1 of the Gender Recognition Act 2004.

[465] See s.20 of the Gender Recognition Act 2004.

[466] See above, para.9–02; Sir George Mackenzie, *The Laws and Customs of Scotland in Matters Criminal*, 2nd edn (Edinburgh: 1699), Vol.I, p.16.

[467] *Charles Sweenie* (1853) 3 Irv. 109 at 142: the decision in *Sweenie* was overruled by a seven judge court in *Lord Advocate's Reference (No.1 of 2001)*, 2002 S.L.T. 466.

Ivory listed the evil consequences of rape as: "the danger of impregnation—the loss of status,—the taint to her family."

Vaginal sexual intercourse

Abduction is now totally unnecessary in relation to rape; and the old rule that **9–82** the victim must register her complaint within 24 hours of the act has long ceased to apply.[468] Long delay in making a complaint is, however, unlikely to be propitious for a successful prosecution. But the act must consist of penetration of the victim's vagina by the accused's penis. Penetration need not be more than slight[469] but it must occur. Most authorities correctly say that ejaculation is unnecessary[470] but prosecutions are likely to be difficult without ejaculate to examine and submit to DNA profiling. Unlike the previous law in England, in this country there has never been any set age below which male sexual potency is presumed impossible. If a youngster in fact proves himself capable of penile penetration, then he can be prosecuted (all other things being equal).[471] What have come to be known graphically as "oral-sex" and "anal-sex" do not qualify as rape, however astonishing this may appear.[472] The essence of rape may well be considered popularly as the unwanted, violent invasion of any body orifice by any means, but nothing short of, or different from, penile penetration of the vagina will suffice at common law; sexual activity short of, or different from, that amounts to indecent assault.[473]

Without her consent

The Appeal Court (organised as a court of seven judges) has determined by a **9–83** majority of five to two that the essence of the actus reus of rape consists in the accused male's having vaginal intercourse with a female without that female's consent.[474] Consequently, the former requirement espoused by Hume,[475] in terms that there had to be evidence of resistance on the part of the female and corresponding force on the part of the male, was considered to be incorrect.

Hume was an avid reader of contemporary English legal works, and was especially impressed it seems by the writings of William Blackstone. Blackstone's *Commentaries on the Laws of England* were first published in 1769, and rape is described therein as: "the carnal knowledge of a woman forcibly and against her will."[476] Unsurprisingly, Hume uses much the same description,[477] Alison follows suit[478] and Burnett treads the same well-worn path.[479] Macdonald, whether he

---

[468] *Captain Charles Douglas* (1697) Maclaurin's Cases 13, No.12.

[469] *Alexander Macra or Macrae* (1841) Bell's Notes 83.

[470] *Duncan Macmillan* (1833) Bell's Notes 82; *Archibald Robertson* (1836) Bell's Notes 82–83.

[471] See *Robert Fulton Jnr* (1841) 2 Swin. 564.

[472] *Barbour v HM Advocate*, 1982 S.C.C.R. 195.

[473] *Barbour v HM Advocate*, 1982 S.C.C.R. 195.

[474] *Lord Advocate's Reference (No.1 of 2001)*, 2002 S.L.T. 466.

[475] See below. cf. Chalmers, "How (Not) to Reform the Law of Rape" (2002) 6 Edin. L.R. 388, 391, where the author argues that Hume had been misconstrued.

[476] William Blackstone, *Commentaries on the Laws of England* (Oxford: Clarendon Press, 1769), Vol.IV, Ch.15, p.210.

[477] Hume, *Commentaries*, i, 302.

[478] Alison, *Principles*, i, 209.

[479] Burnett, *A Treatise on Various Branches of the Criminal Law of Scotland* (1811), p.101.

realised it or not, reproduced Blackstone's words exactly.[480] The courts too had been unusually conservative in their description of rape, mainly, it appears, preferring a definition which featured the formula "forcibly and against her will."[481]

9–84   But in *Lord Advocate's Reference (No.1 of 2001)*,[482] the Appeal Court by a majority declined to follow Hume, declared that an earlier court in *Charles Sweenie*[483] had been in error in following Hume, and corrected that error by laying down that neither resistance nor force is an essential requirement of rape. Henceforth, therefore, any male who, with the required mens rea, has vaginal intercourse with a female without her consent will prima facie be guilty of rape. It is highly possible that "without her consent" means here "without her *active* consent"[484]: and this will mean that a female who is asleep or intoxicated or unconscious at the time of the act may well be in a state of neutrality in relation to consent, but plainly is not in any condition in which she can *actively* give consent, and thus may be a victim of rape if taken advantage of whilst she is so asleep, intoxicated or unconscious.[485] It must also be the case that the intercourse must be without her *valid*[486] consent, in the sense at least that a female under the age of 12 and (perhaps) a female who is suffering from a sufficient degree of mental abnormality are considered not to have consented as a matter of law[487]; and this may be extended to the victim who is coerced by violence or threats into permitting the intercourse to take place—for there, there is no valid consent, but mere submission.[488] Although resistance and force are not now required elements of the actus reus of rape, evidence of such things will continue to be important, of course, in supporting the Crown's contention that the act of intercourse was without the victim's consent.[489]

---

[480]   Macdonald, *Criminal Law*, 5th edn (1948), p.119.

[481]   See, e.g. amongst the more modern cases, *Stobbs v HM Advocate*, 1983 S.C.C.R. 190, per Lord Cowie at 200; *C v HM Advocate*, 1987 S.C.C.R. 104, per Lord Mayfield at 105; and *S v HM Advocate*, 1989 S.L.T. 469 at 471L–472E; *Jamieson v HM Advocate*, 1994 S.L.T. 537, per Lord Justice-General Hope at 541C. Cf. *W v HM Advocate*, 1995 S.L.T. 685, Lord Penrose's charge to the jury at 686B–C.

[482]   *Lord Advocate's Reference (No.1 of 2001)*, 2002 S.L.T. 466 (court of seven judges).

[483]   *Charles Sweenie* (1858) 3 Irv. 109. The decision in *Sweenie* was overruled.

[484]   See *Lord Advocate's Reference (No.1 of 2001)*, 2002 S.L.T. 466, Lord Justice-General Cullen at 475F, para.39.

[485]   The court in *Charles Sweenie* (1858) 3 Irv. 109, where the victim was alleged to have been asleep when she was violated, decided that she had not been raped, either because no force had had to be used or because it could not be determined that she had been "unwilling" in the sense of having withheld her consent: but *Sweenie* is overruled by *Lord Advocate's Reference (No.1 of 2001)*, 2002 S.L.T. 466, and such a victim may now be viewed as having given no consent to the act of intercourse. Similarly, where the female has been intoxicated to the point of insensibility prior to the intercourse, there may have been no consent on her part: cf., e.g. *HM Advocate v Logan*, 1936 J.C. 100, in which Lord Justice-Clerk Aitchison's charge to the jury, in so far as inconsistent with the decision in *Lord Advocate's Reference (No.1 of 2001)*, must be considered as wrong. Cf. also *HM Advocate v Grainger and Rae*, 1932 J.C. 40, where Lord Anderson's opinion on the relevancy of the indictment is now impliedly overruled.

[486]   But see below, para.9–87 on the matter of consent obtained by fraud.

[487]   See *Lord Advocate's Reference (No.1 of 2001)*, 2002 S.L.T. 466, Lord Justice-General Cullen at 473J, para.31, and again at 476A, para.44 where he states: ". . . in the case of females who are under the age of 12 or who for any other reason are incapable of giving . . . consent, the absence of consent should, as at present, be presumed." See also Hume, *Commentaries*, i, 303, and below, para.9–89.

[488]   See *Lord Advocate's Reference (No.1 of 2001)*, 2002 S.L.T. 466, Lord Justice-General Cullen at 475F, para.39; see also, e.g. the situation in *Barbour v HM Advocate*, 1982 S.C.C.R. 195.

[489]   They would also help to establish that the accused had the requisite mens rea: see *Lord Advocate's Reference (No.1 of 2001)*, 2002 S.L.T. 466, Lord Justice-General Cullen at 474K–L, para.35: mens rea is considered below at para.9–85. Cf. *Burzala v HM Advocate* [2007] HCJAC 67; 2008 S.L.T. 61.

The mens rea of rape

The mens rea of rape was effectively settled in *Jamieson v HM Advocate*,[490] **9–85** where the trial judge told the jury that the accused's "defence" of error as to the victim's consent was not sustainable unless based on reasonable grounds. The Appeal Court held that this was a clear misdirection, since the trial judge had been wrong not to follow a prior ruling by the Court in 1982.[491] But the Court also took the opportunity of explaining why reasonable grounds were *not* required in such cases. This was due to the form of the mens rea in rape. As Lord Justice-General Hope put it:

> "[T]he *mens rea* of this crime includes the intention to have intercourse with the woman without her consent. The absence of a belief that she was consenting is an essential element in it. If a man has intercourse with a woman in the belief that she is consenting to this he cannot be guilty of rape."[492]

It is to be noted that the Lord Justice-General referred to the mens rea of rape as *including* such intention. There is, therefore, an alternative form, viz: where there is recklessness on the part of the male as to the female's consent.[493] If a man had intercourse with a woman who in fact had not consented, but he had failed to think about whether she was consenting or was utterly indifferent as to whether she consented or not, then he could be said to have a sufficient form of mens rea for the crime of rape. The two (known)[494] alternate forms of mens rea are thus intention (involving knowledge of her lack of consent) or recklessness (involving failure to think about, or complete indifference as to the issue of, her consent).[495] It had to follow, then, that an honest belief in the consent of the victim would, if believed by the jury, be sufficient to acquit, since it would negative both recognised forms of the mens rea of the crime at common law.[496]

---

[490] *Jamieson v HM Advocate*, 1994 J.C. 88; what is stated there about rape in general is now modified, however, by the decision of the court in *Lord Advocate's Reference (No.1 of 2001)*, 2002 S.L.T. 466.

[491] *Meek v HM Advocate*, 1983 S.L.T. 280, which had apparently been followed in many similar (unreported) cases, such as that of *HM Advocate v Stevenson* Unreported July 5, 1985 Appeal Court.

[492] *Jamieson v HM Advocate*, 1994 J.C. 88, at 92E.

[493] *Jamieson v HM Advocate*, 1994 J.C. 88, at 93F–G.

[494] Since it seems that the *Jamieson* account of the mens rea of rape was simply adopted without discussion in the leading case of *Lord Advocate's Reference (No.1 of 2001)*, 2002 S.L.T. 466—see the opinion of Lord Justice-General Cullen at 473B–H, paras.28–29, and his conclusion at 476B, para.44. All subsequent reported rape cases have accepted these two alternative forms of the applicable mens rea: see, e.g. *Gordon v HM Advocate*, 2004 S.C.C.R. 641, opinion of the court at 645B, para.6; *Blyth v HM Advocate* [2005] HCJAC 110; 2005 S.C.C.R. 710, opinion of the court at 714C, para.10. Where there is no evidence of force having been used by the accused, a jury must be told of the need for sufficient evidence not only that the victim did not consent, but also that the accused knew of her lack of consent or was reckless as to whether she consented or not: see, e.g. *Cinci v HM Advocate*, 2004 S.C.C.R. 267 (where the trial judge's general account of the mens rea for rape is considered to have been correct—see opinion of Lord McCluskey, at 273G–274C, para.18); *McKearney v HM Advocate*, 2004 S.C.C.R. 251, Lord Justice Clerk Gill at 254A–C, paras 8–9, and Lord McCluskey at 256C–F, para.23, and 263E–264A, para.34.

[495] In *Lord Advocate's Reference (No.1 of 2001)*, 2002 S.L.T. 466, Lord Justice-General Cullen referred to recklessness as thus being understood in its subjective form: see 476B, para.44, which refers to what his Lordship had said earlier, at 473G–H, para.29.

[496] In so laying down the mens rea of rape, the Court in *Jamieson* (as in *Meek*) followed the earlier English decision of the House of Lords in *DPP v Morgan* [1976] A.C. 182—even though the account of rape given by English law was not then identical to that accepted in Scotland.

Marital rape

9–86 Hume hinted, rather than advanced as a definite rule, that a married man could not be convicted of raping his wife, if he had sexual intercourse with her without her consent.[497] What this was based on is hard to imagine, other than totally unacceptable views such as that a man had some "right" of property in his wife's body, or a "right" to expect that she would not deny him the means of acquiring legitimate heirs. In any event, if there ever was a soundly based "rule" of that nature in Scots law, it was laid to rest in *S v HM Advocate*.[498] The Appeal Court decided there that a married man was in no better position than any other man vis à vis the rape of his wife, thus culminating a process of attrition in respect of the "rule" begun by *HM Advocate v Duffy*[499] and *HM Advocate v Paxton*.[500] English common law soon followed the Scottish lead here.[501]

Fraud and rape

9–87 Since consent to sexual intercourse now clearly elides rape at common law, the question arises: "What is the law if consent is obtained by deception?" Relevant pretences here might include promises of marriage, promotion or other reward. If these promises were never intended to be fulfilled, then fraud could certainly be made out.[502] In a slightly different way, fraud would also be relevant if a man deceived a woman into thinking that he was someone with whom she would have been happy to have intercourse, as where he pretended to be her husband[503] or lover. Such a case of "husband impersonation" arose in *William Fraser*.[504] Fraser was alleged to have inserted himself into the bed of a married woman, and there, by behaving familiarly with her, made her believe that he was her husband. It was on that basis that she allowed him to have intercourse with her. Three offences were charged as alternatives in the indictment against him, namely—rape; assault with intent to ravish; and the innominate crime of "fraudulently obtaining access to a married woman." The main debate centred on whether rape or the innominate offence was relevant in the circumstances. Four of the six judges observed that the proper definition of rape was the having of sexual intercourse without the woman's consent (see the opinions of Lord Justice-Clerk Hope, and Lords Mackenzie, Moncreiff and Cockburn). If that observation was correct (and later authorities did not accept that it was correct until the decision in *Lord Advocate's Reference (No.1 of 2001)*[505]), it seemed irrefutable that the victim had consented. Therefore, there could be no rape. Only Lord Cockburn, however, accepted the logic of that. The other three all maintained that Fraser was guilty of rape, apparently since the victim's consent had not been a proper one. There was no "informed" consent on her part owing to the element of deception. This interesting, if not bold, view was

---

[497] Hume, *Commentaries*, i, 306.
[498] *S v HM Advocate*, 1989 S.L.T. 469.
[499] *HM Advocate v Duffy*, 1983 S.L.T. 7.
[500] *HM Advocate v Paxton*, 1984 J.C. 105.
[501] See *R. v R* [1991] 3 W.L.R. 767. The alteration of the law achieved in *R. v R.* was considered not to be in breach of art.7(1) of the European Convention on Human Rights: *SW v United Kingdom* (1996) 21 E.H.R.R. 363.
[502] See below, paras 10–68 to 10–71.
[503] Cf., *Gray v Criminal Injuries Compensation Board*, 1993 S.L.T. 28 (Court of Session, Lord Weir).
[504] *William Fraser* (1847) Ark. 280.
[505] *Lord Advocate's Reference (No.1 of 2001)*, 2002 S.L.T. 466.

regrettably not shared by the remaining three judges, who sided with Lord Cockburn in deciding that consent obtained by fraud was nevertheless consent. In the final analysis, then, there was no rape here.

Disquiet over the decision in *William Fraser's* case (and similar cases in **9–88** England[506] led in 1885 to a change in the law. Under the Criminal Law Amendment Act of that year, it was declared to be common law rape in both Scotland and England to pretend to be a married woman's husband and thus obtain intercourse with her. That rule was subsequently re-enacted in s.7(3) of the Criminal Law (Consolidation) (Scotland) Act 1995; but s.7 was repealed by the Sexual Offences (Scotland) Act 2009—thus leaving the matter of such deceptions to be regulated by the statutory law.[507]

Mentally disordered complainers

It was possible to argue that females suffering from certain mental illnesses or **9–89** defects should be treated in the same way as young children. It would then be the case that intercourse with them could be assumed to be rape. Any consent apparently given could be ignored (although this could be harsh indeed where the victim exhibited no outward signs of mental illness). Despite some isolated dicta, however, such as that by Lord Cockburn in *William Fraser*,[508] there was no firm authority for treating mentally ill females any differently from females of normal mental capacities and abilities.[509] There were statutory offences which might have been used as alternatives to common law rape where the complainer was mentally disordered—but these have been repealed by the Sexual Offences (Scotland) Act 2009 (asp 9) Sch.6; see the mention there of the Mental Health (Care and Treatment) (Scotland) Act 2003 ss.311 to 313. As the relevant provision of the 2009 Act (s.17) applies only to ss.1 to 9 of the 2009 Act itself, the position at common law remains uncertain.[510]

(2) Clandestine injury to women

In *Charles Sweenie*,[511] as an alternative to common law rape, the indictment **9–90** contained the innominate offence of "wickedly and feloniously having carnal knowledge of a woman whilst asleep, and without her consent." Four of the six judges eventually decided that the accused was guilty of the innominate offence, in that he had climbed into bed with a sleeping woman and had intercourse with her. She did not wake until he was withdrawing, it appears. Rape was out of the question in terms of the law at that time, since a sleeping victim could not be shown to have been "actively" unwilling.[512] Gordon, following Macdonald,

---

[506] *R. v Clarke* (1854) 6 Cox C.C. 412; *R. v Barrow* (1868) 11 Cox C.C. 191.
[507] See below, paras.9–91 to 9–94.
[508] *Wlliam Fraser* (1847) Ark. 280 at 308.
[509] See Gordon, *Criminal Law,* 3rd edn (2000/2001), paras 33.09 to 33.11 (as substituted by the *Supplement* of 2005).
[510] This problem will be resolved, of course, once common law rape is abolished by the Sexual Offences (Scotland) Act 2009 (asp 9).
[511] *Charles Sweenie* (1858) 3 Irv. 109: any authority which *Sweenie* represented (as to the requirements of rape) has been set aside by *Lord Advocate's Reference (No.1 of 2001)*, 2002 S.L.T. 466 (court of seven judges).
[512] The then law required "resistance" on the part of the victim, that resistance having to be overcome by force on the part of the accused: see now *Lord Advocate's Reference (No.1 of 2001)*, 2002 S.L.T. 466.

referred to that innominate offence as "clandestine injury to women"[513]; but the changes effected to the definition of common law rape by the majority decision in *Lord Advocate's Reference (No.1 of 2001)*[514] made it difficult to understand what future the offence of "clandestine injury" could then have.[515] The circumstances which led to its recognition as an independent offence, i.e. the vaginal penetration of a female when she is unconscious and unable to show her unwillingness, would not now be inconsistent with common law rape.[516] Yet, the offence was not condemned as obsolete in *Lord Advocate's Reference (No.1 of 2001)*.[517]

(3) Offences under the Sexual Offences (Scotland) Act 2009 (asp 9)[518]

Rape (s.1 of the 2009 Act)

9–91 Many of the anomalies and difficulties experienced in defining the crime of rape at common law[519] will be set aside or resolved when the 2009 Act comes fully into force.[520] Thus, under that Act, a crime is created whose *nomen iuris* is "Rape" but which differs considerably from its namesake at common law; in particular (and there are many other points of distinction) it is, so far as possible, non gender-specific. In essence, it is now a statutory offence[521] for an accused person with that person's penis[522] to penetrate[523] (to any extent, and either intending to do so or being reckless as to whether penetration occurs) the vagina,[524] anus or mouth of another person where that other person does not consent[525] to

---

[513] Gordon, *Criminal Law*, 3rd edn (2000/2001), para.33.19, following Macdonald, *Criminal Law*, 5th edn (1948), p.120. The *Supplement* to Gordon, of 2005, replaces the whole of the original Ch.33, and downgrades "clandestine injury" in view of the decision in *Lord Advocate's Reference (No.1 of 2001)*, 2002 S.L.T. 466; see the *Supplement* at p.146.

[514] *Lord Advocate's Reference (No.1 of 2001)*, 2002 S.L.T. 466.

[515] Indeed, of course, it will have no future at all when the Sexual Offences (Scotland) Act 2009 (asp 9) ss.52(a)(ii) and 53 come fully into force.

[516] See, e.g. *Wiles v HM Advocate* [2007] HCJAC 26; 2007 S.C.C.R. 191; *HM Advocate v L* [2007] HCJ 16; 2008 S.C.C.R. 51.

[517] *Lord Advocate's Reference (No.1 of 2001)*, 2002 S.L.T. 466; see Lord Justice-General Cullen's opinion at 474C–D, para.32.

[518] Hereafter referred to as "the 2009 Act".

[519] See above, paras 9–80 to 9–89.

[520] Inevitably, however, problems of interpretation concerning the relevant statutory provisions will require resolution by the courts in particular cases.

[521] See the 2009 Act s.1 ("Rape").

[522] "Penis" is defined in the 2009 Act s.1(4) to include a surgically constructed penis "if it forms part of" the accused person.

[523] "Penetration" is interpreted to mean a continuing act "from entry until withdrawal of the penis" or, where consent of the other person was initially given but is countermanded "at some point of time", such an act "from that point of time" until such withdrawal: see the 2009 Act s.1(2),(3).

[524] "Vagina" is defined in the 2009 Act s.1(4) to include the vulva, as also a surgically constructed vagina (together with similarly constructed vulva) "if it forms part of "the person concerned.

[525] In terms of the 2009 Act s.12, "consent" means "free agreement". Such agreement is declared to be absent (see s.13) in a situation where the conduct occurs when the victim is incapable of consenting to it due to the effect of alcohol "or any other substance"; when the victim submits or "agrees" to it because of violence (or threats of same) used (or made) against that victim "or any other person"; when the victim submits or agrees to it because he or she is "unlawfully detained" by the accused; when the victim submits or agrees to it because he or she is mistaken due to deception by the accused as to its nature or purpose; when the victim is induced to submit or agree to it because of impersonation by the accused of a person "known personally" to the victim; or, when the sole

such and the accused is without any reasonable belief[526] that that other person does so consent.[527]

Rape of a young child (s.18 of the 2009 Act)

This offence makes the complainer's consent (or any belief in such by the **9–92** accused) an entirely irrelevant issue—thus distancing itself, to that extent, from rape under s.1 of the 2009 Act.[528] In essence, it is committed if a person, with that person's penis,[529] penetrates (to any extent, and either intending to do so or being reckless as to whether it occurs) the vagina,[530] anus or mouth of a young child (that is to say, a child who has not attained the age of 13 years). This is, as far as possible, a gender neutral offence; and it is not a defence that the person accused believed, however honestly or reasonably, that the said child had attained 13 years of age.[531]

Having intercourse with an older child (s.28 of the 2009 Act)

This offence makes the complainer's consent (or any belief in such by the **9–93** accused) an entirely irrelevant issue. In essence, it is committed if a person (who must have attained the age of 16 years), with that person's penis,[532] penetrates (to any extent, and either intending to do so or being reckless as to whether it occurs) the vagina,[533] anus or mouth of an older child (that is to say, a child who has attained the age of 13, but not that of 16, years). This is, as far as possible, a gender neutral offence; but there is a defence to it[534]: if the accused reasonably believed that such a child had attained the age of 16 years at the material time, then acquittal will follow unless that accused had previously been charged by the police with a "relevant sexual offence"[535] or there was in force in respect of that

---

"expression or indication of agreement to [it] is from a person other than" the victim. The foregoing list is effectively extended by s.14, which declares that a "person is incapable, while asleep or unconscious, of consenting to any conduct." And, under s.15(2)–(3), it is further declared that consent to one type of conduct does not (per se) imply consent to any other, and that consent, once given, may be withdrawn at any time before, or during, the conduct in question: see also s.15(4) which deals generally with withdrawal of consent. Where the victim suffers from "mental disorder" (as defined in the Mental Health (Care and Treatment) (Scotland) Act 2003 (asp 13) s.328(1)), he or she is deemed incapable of consenting to particular conduct if, by reason of such disorder, he or she is unable to understand it, decide whether to engage in it, or communicate a decision relative to it: see the 2009 Act s.17.

[526] In determining whether an accused's belief is reasonable here, regard is to be had "to whether [he or she] took any steps to ascertain whether there was consent . . . and if so, to what those steps were": see the 2009 Act s.16.

[527] See also the 2009 Act Sch.2 (for penalties relative to this, and other, offences created by the Act) and Sch.3 (for a list of alternative verdicts to this offence, and most other, but not all, of the offences so created).

[528] See above, para.9–91.

[529] "Penis" is defined in s.1(4) of the 2009 Act.

[530] "Vagina" is defined in s.1(4) of the 2009 Act.

[531] See the 2009 Act s.27, which applies to all the relevant offences in that Act (i.e. those to be found in ss.18 to 26); see also the important exceptions detailed in the 2009 Act s.51, relative to guilt by incitement or art and part.

[532] "Penis" is defined in s.1(4) of the 2009 Act.

[533] "Vagina" is defined in s.1(4) of the 2009 Act.

[534] See the 2009 Act s.39 (which also applies to offences under ss.29 to 37 of that Act). See also the important exceptions detailed in the 2009 Act s.51, relative to guilt by incitement or art and part.

[535] "Relevant sexual offences" are listed in the 2009 Act Sch.1.

accused a "risk of sexual harm order".[536] It is not, for the avoidance of doubt (perhaps), any defence that the accused believed that the child in question had not attained the age of 13 years; and "deeming provisions" apply where the child in question has not been proved to have attained 13 years of age at the relevant time, but the court or jury is satisfied that that child had not attained the age of 16 years at that time.[537]

Engaging while an older child in sexual conduct with or towards another older child; engaging while an older child in consensual sexual conduct with another older child (s.37(1) and (4) of the 2009 Act)

9–94   The first of these two offences is in essence committed if a child (who has attained the age of 13, but not that of 16, years) either penetrates[538] sexually[539] with that child's penis[540] (to any extent, and either intending to do so or being reckless as to whether it occurs) the vagina,[541] anus or mouth of another child (with similar age attainments) or (intentionally or recklessly) touches sexually (with his or her mouth[542]) the vagina, anus or penis of such another child. The second of these offences is in essence committed by the other child who is so penetrated or touched (that is to say, the "complainer" in the first offence) if he or she consents[543] to such conduct. Thus consent is irrelevant to criminal liability in respect of the first offence, but relevant to such liability in the second.[544] These offences are essentially gender-neutral; but to both offences there is a defence[545]: if the accused reasonably believed that the other child had attained the age of 16 years, then acquittal will follow unless the accused had previously been charged by the police with a "relevant sexual offence",[546] or if there was in force in respect of that accused a "risk of sexual harm order".[547] It is not a defence at all, however, relative to either offence, that the accused believed that the other child had not attained the age of 13 years; and "deeming provisions" apply where the child in question has not been proved to have attained the age of 13 years (or, as the case may be, it has not been proved that he or she had *not* attained the age of 16 years) at the relevant time, but the court or jury is satisfied that that

---

[536] A "risk of sexual harm order" is an order made under the Protection of Children and Prevention of Sexual Offences (Scotland) Act 2005 (asp 9) s.2 (as amended by the Criminal Justice and Licensing (Scotland) Act 2010 (asp 13) s.103(2)) or under the (English) Sexual Offences Act 2003 s.123.

[537] See the 2009 Act ss.40(1) and 41.

[538] Under the 2009 Act s.38(2), "penetration" for the purposes of s.37 is a "continuing act from entry until withdrawal of whatever is intruded", although it should be noted that only penetration with a penis is mentioned in s.37(3)(a).

[539] Under the 2009 Act s.60(2)(a), "penetration, touching or any other activity is sexual if a reasonable person would, in all the circumstances of the case, consider it to be sexual".

[540] "Penis" is defined in the 2009 Act s.1(4).

[541] "Vagina" is defined in the 2009 Act s.1(4).

[542] "Mouth" includes the "tongue or teeth": see the 2009 Act s.37(5).

[543] What is meant here by "consent" is detailed in the 2009 Act s.38(3)–(8).

[544] It follows that only the first of these two offences (i.e. the one under s.37(1)) has any pretensions to be analogous to "rape"; the second offence (under s.37(4)) is thus "sui generis", but is included here for the sake of completeness.

[545] See the 2009 Act s.39(1)(a),(b); (2)(a),(b). See also the important exceptions in the 2009 Act s.51, relative to guilt by incitement or art and part.

[546] "Relevant sexual offences" are listed in the 2009 Act Sch.1.

[547] See above, para.9–93, fn.536.

child had not attained 16 years (or, as the case may be, had attained the age of 13 years) at that time.[548]

6. THREATS AND EXTORTION

Introduction

Since it is accepted that words cannot amount to an assault (see para.9–06, **9–95** above), it still seems necessary to deter in some other way the using of words in such a manner as to cause fear and alarm. The method adopted by the common law is to recognise that it is sometimes criminal to threaten to do things to the detriment of the person threatened. Depending on what is said, some threats are criminal as soon as they are communicated, irrespective of why they were said, as long as the accused meant to communicate them to the victim. With respect to other threats, they are not reckoned as criminal at common law[549] at all, unless they are made with the object of forcing the victim to do something he otherwise would not have been willing to do. In both cases, the mens rea element appears to be intention.

Threats criminal by themselves at common law

Hume[550] made a distinction between verbal threats and written ones. On the **9–96** apparent view that what is said is usually as transient as hot-air, verbal threats were only criminal if they related to burning down the victim's house or the like.[551] If they related only to "personal mischief", then the most that could be hoped for was an action for caution to keep the peace. This was apparently so even where there had been a threat to kill.[552] Written threats, however, were more serious—possibly since they could be read and re-read. If they related to personal violence or property damage, *and* demanded something as the price of non-implementation of the threat, then there was proper criminality.[553] As can be seen, however, all Hume's authorities are old and the law on this matter did not fully develop until much later in the nineteenth century.

The leading case on criminal threats at common law is still that of *James* **9–97** *Miller*.[554] It is important not for its facts, but for the light thrown on the whole subject by Lord Justice-Clerk Inglis.[555] His view was that it was wrong to make any distinction between what had been spoken and what had been written. (This is clearly correct. The effect on the victim is what really matters, rather than the method of communication.) He also opined that certain threats, however made, were criminal by themselves. He listed those as threats to burn down a house, to

---

[548] See the 2009 Act ss.40 and 41.
[549] Cf. below, para.9–98.
[550] Hume, *Commentaries*, i, 135, 442.
[551] *Grizzel Sommerville* (1686) Hume, *Commentaries*, i, 135; *Laird and Lady Grant* (1712) Hume, *Commentaries*, i, 135.
[552] *Captain Andrew Nairne* (1712) Hume, *Commentaries*, i, 442.
[553] See *John Fraser* (1759) Hume, *Commentaries*, i, 439; *James Gray* (1737) Hume, *Commentaries*, i, 441.
[554] *James Miller* (1862) 4 Irv. 238.
[555] *James Miller* (1862) 4 Irv. 238 at 244–245.

put someone to death, to do someone serious bodily harm, and (perhaps less understandably) to do someone serious injury as to his property, fortune, or reputation. With all of those, it did not matter whether the accused ever intended to carry out what he threatened; nor did it matter that he had no particular purpose to serve in making the threat at all. Thus, in the later case of *Elizabeth Edmiston*[556] the accused tried in vain to show that written threats to blow out the victim's brains and burn his house about his ears were at worst a thoughtless frolic. The court, following *James Miller*, ruled that it was of no consequence whether or not the accused really intended to cause serious alarm. It was enough that threats of that description had been communicated at all. Also in the still later case of *Margaret McDaniel*[557] there was a verbal threat to tear the victim in pieces and "do for her". Although there was an ulterior purpose of discouraging the victim from giving evidence at a criminal trial, it is significant that that purpose was libelled as an aggravation of the threat—strongly suggesting that the threat was criminal by itself. A less usual, but still criminal, threat consisted of part words, part conduct in *HM Advocate v Hayes*.[558] There, the accused sent a package containing explosives to the victim along with a letter. The note indicated that an electric detonator would be sent next time, thus threatening that the next package would blow up as soon as it was opened. Lord Cameron had no doubt at all that a threat criminal by itself was there involved, and that such a threat constituted a crime as soon as it was uttered, or placed with the postal authorities for onward transmission to the victim. There can be little doubt then that *James Miller* has been followed in subsequent cases, and must be taken to represent the modern common law.

Threatening behaviour under statute

9–98   It is now a statutory offence[559] for a person to behave in a threatening (or abusive) manner if that behaviour would "be likely to cause a reasonable person to suffer fear or alarm" and if he or she intends thereby to cause fear or alarm or is reckless as to whether it would do so. Behaviour of any kind will suffice—but it specifically includes things said (or otherwise communicated) or done—whether as a "single act" or as a course of conduct. It is a defence for a person charged with such an offence to show that the behaviour was, "in the particular circumstances, reasonable".[560]

Extortion at common law

9–99   In *James Miller*,[561] Lord Justice-Clerk Inglis intimated that threats, insufficient to be then thought criminal by themselves, could become criminal at common law if "used for an unlawful purpose such as extorting money."[562] Here, both the

---

[556] *Elizabeth Edmiston* (1866) 5 Irv. 219, approved (*quoad* the principle it espouses) in *Lord Advocate's Reference (No.2 of 1992)*, 1993 J.C. 43.
[557] *Margaret McDaniel* (1876) 3 Coup. 271.
[558] *HM Advocate v Hayes*, 1973 S.L.T. 202.
[559] See the Criminal Justice and Licensing (Scotland) Act 2010 (asp 13) (hereafter referred to as "the 2010 Act") s.38.
[560] For current maximum penalties, whether on indictment or complaint, see the 2010 Act s.38(4).
[561] *James Miller* (1862) 4 Irv. 238.
[562] *James Miller* (1862) 4 Irv. 238 at 246.

nature of the threat and the demand must be considered. In *Marion Macdonald*,[563] for example, the accused undertook to expose the alleged sexual improprieties of the victim upon her to his whole family, unless he agreed to pay her £10. The court had no doubt that a relevant charge had been made out when that sort of threat was allied to that sort of demand; and it was also opined that any offer by such an accused to show the truth of what she threatened to expose would be entirely irrelevant.[564] A similar type of decision can also be seen in *Hogg v HM Advocate*.[565]

There must, of course, be an actual threat—express or implied—for extortion **9–100** to be made out. In *HM Advocate v Donoghue*[566] the accused told an agent for the owner of five stolen paintings that for £1200 he would probably be in a position to secure their return. This was charged as attempted extortion; but clearly it could not succeed, since no threat (such as to destroy the paintings) had been made. It did constitute a suitable threat, however, for the accused to affix a notice to a car which had been parked on private property without permission, where that notice indicated that a wheel clamp had been secured to the vehicle, and that it would not be removed until a "levy on trespass parking" of £45 had been paid.[567] The threat, of course, must be accompanied by a demand. That demand generally is for the payment of money[568] but it is not necessarily restricted to that. Thus, in *George Jeffrey*,[569] the demands made were sometimes for goods; and in *Rae v Donnelly*[570] the price demanded for silence as to alleged sexual impropriety was the giving up of a claim for unfair dismissal on the part of one victim, and the tendering of his resignation on the part of the other.

Status of the threat and the demand

The crime of extortion must obviously not be so widely drawn that it prevents, **9–101** say, a creditor from threatening to sue his debtor as a means of obtaining repayment of what is lawfully due. There, the demand for money would be quite legitimate, assuming that the due date for payment had come, as would the threat employed to pressurise the debtor. In the same way, it might be thought wrong for the law to penalise as extortion some matter which was ultimately for the victim's own benefit. If, for example, an employee had been "caught with his hand in the till", it would clearly be to his benefit to take advantage of an offer from his employer to accept his resignation, even if pressurised into that by the threat of bringing in the police.[571] It was possibly to cater for situations such as these that Lord Justice-Clerk Thomson said of the type of threat made:

---

[563] *Marion Macdonald* (1879) 4 Coup. 268.
[564] *Marion Macdonald* (1979) 4 Coup. 268, per Lord Deas at 273.
[565] *Hogg v HM Advocate*, 1954 S.L.T. (Notes) 82.
[566] *HM Advocate v Donoghue*, 1971 S.L.T. 2.
[567] *Carmichael v Black; Black v Carmichael*, 1992 S.L.T. 897.
[568] See *Priteca v HM Advocate* (1906) 5 Adam 79; *Carmichael v Black; Black v Carmichael*, 1992 S.L.T. 897.
[569] *George Jeffrey* (1840) 2 Swin. 479.
[570] *Rae v Donnelly*, 1982 S.C.C.R. 148.
[571] See *Hill v McGrogan*, 1945 S.L.T. (Sh.Ct.) 18.

"When the pressure consists in creating in the victim fear that, unless he yields, his position will be altered for the worse, it is criminal unless the pressure sought to be exerted is regarded by the law as legitimate."[572]

He then continued:

"Legal process is such a form of pressure. So too . . . is the pressure exerted by one contracting party on another contracting party. I need not consider whether these are exhaustive of legitimate forms of pressure."

But more modern authority has emphasised that to enforce payment of a debt by any means other than those the law regards as legitimate is extortion, and that the only legally acceptable methods of enforcement are due process in a court of law, or lien (or retention) in relation to specific contracts.[573] Thus, irrespective of whether what is demanded is lawfully due or not (and that, of course, may be a matter which can only be resolved in court), a threat (for example) to detain (or injure) the "debtor's" person or property[574] would lead to a relevant charge of extortion.

---

[572] *Silverstein v HM Advocate*, 1949 J.C. 160 at 163.
[573] *Carmichael v Black; Black v Carmichael*, 1992 S.L.T. 897, per Lord Justice-General Hope at 900D–E.
[574] *Carmichael v Black; Black v Carmichael*, 1992 S.L.T. 897 at 900E.

CHAPTER 10

CRIMES OF DISHONESTY

1. THEFT

Introduction

Scots law recognises a right of property or ownership in many different things. **10–01** It subsists, for example, in relation to land, buildings, jewellery, farm and domestic animals, vehicles, foodstuffs, crops, money, debts, stocks and shares, copyright, patents and so on. A right of property is a complex one, under which owners, depending on the precise nature of what they own, may normally use, consume, destroy, keep, conceal from public gaze, transfer to another (for a price or by way of gift), pawn, mortgage or otherwise deal with the subject of the right. At any one time, owners may or may not have possession; they may indeed be temporarily debarred from possession, as where, for example, they have pawned or hired out the thing that is owned. Ownership, however, will normally continue to exist notwithstanding the loss of possession. Theft is designed to help protect the right of property in things. It protects more than the mere possession, but less than the whole gamut of things in which ownership is legally recognised.

GENERAL DEFINITION OF THEFT

In the modern law, it is theft to appropriate moveable, corporeal things belonging **10–02** to another person, without the consent of that person, where the accused knows that those things belong to another and intends to deprive the owner of them or their use permanently, indefinitely, or (in certain circumstances) temporarily. No Scottish authority conclusively shows that any additional requirement of "dishonesty" (despite the title of this chapter) has to be shown or inferred[1]—unlike the situation in current English law under the Theft Act 1968 s.1(1): but honesty, or rather the lack of it, cannot entirely be divorced from any meaningful discussion of theft. It is unnecessary to show that the accused made any material gain from the appropriation. "[I]t is the owner's loss and not the other's gain which is important."[2]

---

[1] Cf. *Kane v Friel*, 1997 S.C.C.R. 207, a case of alleged theft by finding where the Appeal Court proceeded on the basis of the advocate-depute's concession that the Crown had to prove that any appropriation by the appellant of the goods in question had been dishonest: see 209G. See also *Mackenzie v MacLean*, 1981 S.L.T. (Sh.Ct.) 40, Sheriff Scott Robinson at 41, final text paragraph.

[2] *Carmichael v Black; Black v Carmichael*, 1992 S.L.T. 897, per Lord Justice-General Hope at 902F, quoting with approval from Gordon, *Criminal Law*, 2nd edn (1978), para.14–63.

The *Actus Reus* of Theft

Appropriation

10–03   It is thought[3] that this term now more accurately represents the essential element in the actus reus than the "taking" referred to by Hume. His views[4] were somewhat eccentric and can be seen clearly in the following extract:

> "All the necessary characters seem to be set forth in that short description of it, given in the civil law [*i.e.* Roman law], . . . the felonious taking and carrying away of the property of another, for lucre.
>
> I. The fundamental circumstance here . . . is this of the *taking* . . . In which it is implied, that the thing has not been previously in the possession of the thief, but in that of the owner, or some person for him, out of which the thief, without the consent of the owner, removes it."

For Hume, then, it was necessary to show that the accused had deprived the owner of the possession of the thing, provided that the accused had the necessary mens rea at the very moment of deprivation. If the accused had been given possession of the thing with the consent of the owner, and only later formed the intention of keeping it for himself and treating himself as if he were its owner, that was not theft. If a person hired a horse, took a watch on loan, or agreed to carry goods to a certain destination, then as a matter of fact he would have had possession with the owner's consent and it would be assumed that he had originally meant to act honestly, unless the contrary was clearly proved. If that was not proved and he subsequently converted the horse, watch or goods to his own purpose (for example, by selling it or them), "he only breaks his contract, and abuses his powers as possessor."[5] In brief, a person already in possession of the thing with the consent of the owner would (somewhat generously) be presumed to be in honest possession of it. A later manifestation of dishonest intention might result in a wrong being committed, but it did not amount to theft.[6]

10–04   That Hume was strongly of the persuasion that theft protected the owner's possession is further illustrated by his treatment of a finder of things which had been lost.[7] The person who lifts a wallet from the street where its owner has accidentally dropped it is plainly from that moment onwards in possession of it. In Hume's estimation, it could not be theft for him subsequently to "keep it to himself" since

> "there is no felonious intention, nor even a *trespass* in the first occupying of the thing, which is lying vacant, and inaccessible to the owner, and may lawfully be taken possession of for the sake of custody, or till offer of a reward. So much is this the case, that though caught in the very act of laying hold of the thing, the man could not be punished or found fault with."[8]

---

3 *Carmichael v Black; Black v Carmichael*, 1992 S.L.T. 897 at 901H.
4 Hume, *Commentaries*, i, 57.
5 Hume, *Commentaries*, i, 58–9.
6 Hume, *Commentaries*, i, 58 at "2."
7 Hume, *Commentaries*, i, 62.
8 Hume, *Commentaries*, i, 62.

The assumption of initial honesty in such a case[9] seemed, indeed, to be decisive; on the premise that theft required a dishonest taking of possession, no subsequent dishonesty could count since no-one could again take what he had already taken.

Attractively logical though Hume's views were, the premise on which they **10–05** were founded was openly doubted by the judiciary even before his death on August 30, 1838. The leading reported case in this respect is that of *John Smith*,[10] although earlier cases in which Hume was not followed are referred to in the pleadings and opinions. Smith was alleged to have found a pocket book, £112 in bank notes and a bill of exchange—all of which having been accidentally dropped by the owner on or near a public road. The name of the owner appears to have been contained in the pocket book, and thus Smith could have had no doubt to whom the items belonged. He was charged with theft since, having found these things, he "did then and there, or at some other time and place . . . appropriate the same to his own uses and purposes." The words "at some other time and place" plainly covered a situation which Hume would not have counted as theft; but the court of six judges unanimously found the whole indictment relevant. As Lord Meadowbank trenchantly remarked[11]:

> "It is of no consequence of what character the original possession of the property is. The moment the intention of appropriating the property of another is formed, then the theft is committed."

Lord Mackenzie was equally forthright in that he stated[12]:

> "We have determined that in the case of carriers, servants, clerks, shopmen, the appropriation of goods held on a limited title for behoof of the owner is theft; and of course all these decisions apply with greater force to the case of a finder, who took the goods honestly, and subsequently formed the felonious intention of appropriating them."

The words of Lord Cockburn[13] are also worthy of notice:

> "The definition which our law gives of theft, is, that it is . . . fraudulent taking of the property of another for the sake of lucre. Now what is meant by this word *taking*? I know no authority, and no principle, for confining it to the act of first possessing . . . I don't conceive that there can be any taking, in the sense of this definition, without an intention to take. It means appropriation."

If "appropriation" is what is required, and it is submitted that it is, then it covers a **10–06** number of different situations. Certainly it includes Hume's dishonest taking

---

[9] Cf. Burnett, *A Treatise on Various Branches of the Criminal Law of Scotland* (1811), p.123, where the assumption is put the other way.

[10] *John Smith* (1838) 2 Swin. 28, decided on March 12, 1838. For a more modern example of a charge of theft by finding, see *MacMillan v Lowe*, 1991 J.C. 13, where in the special circumstances of the case, possession of the goods a mere four hours after they were found was sufficient to justify the conclusion that the finder had appropriated them.

[11] *John Smith* (1838) 2 Swin. 28 at 52.

[12] *John Smith* (1838) 2 Swin. 28 at 53–54.

[13] *John Smith* (1938) 2 Swin. 28 at 56.

possession of a thing and carrying it away. It has also been held to apply where a car found on private land without permission to be parked there was "wheelclamped", thus immobilising it and depriving the owner of its use and enjoyment as a vehicle.[14] This would not be the case, however, if property had been incidentally (as opposed to deliberately) immobilised—for example, "as a result of some legitimate act such as the closing or locking of a gate for security."[15] Appropriation also extends more widely to a manifest change in attitude towards things that the thief originally possessed lawfully and honestly, as where he subsequently applies or converts those things to his own use,[16] or claims them as his own.[17] That "appropriation" is indeed what is required is the only plausible explanation of the judiciary's rejection of Hume's view that a footman could not steal his livery[18] in cases such as *Elizabeth Anderson*,[19] where a discharged poorhouse inmate committed theft by purporting to sell the petticoat, shawl and shift given into her temporary possession by the relevant parochial board, and *John Martin*,[20] where again an inmate committed theft by purportedly selling his poorhouse "uniform." It also explains Lord Mackenzie's remarks in *George Brown*[21] that

"in the case of a horse hired without any felonious purpose, and afterwards carried off by the hirer, we have decided that a theft is committed [see Alison, i, at pages 259–260 for possible authorities]. But that decision is contrary to the opinion of Baron Hume."

Thus Hume had become "greatly qualified"[22] or "seriously modified."[23] No doubt, the courts felt less need than usual to follow that authoritative writer since he himself had admitted[24]:

"Thus much of the taking which is essential to the crime of theft. Upon the whole of which inquiry . . . it may be proper to remark, that our practice has not yet attained to sufficient maturity in these matters."

Moveable, corporeal things

10–07   Things can be stolen if they can be physically possessed and can be moved from place to place. As Alison[25] narrates:

---

[14] *Carmichael v Black; Black v Carmichael*, 1992 S.L.T. 897, per Lord Justice-General Hope at 902B-C. Notice, however, that Lord Allanbridge considered that the facts amounted to a case of theft by finding (at 903B-C). (For wider discussion of the issues raised by this case, see Robin M. White, "Parking Fine: The Enforceability of 'Private' Parking Schemes" (2007) J.R. 1.)

[15] *Carmichael v Black; Black v Carmichael*, 1992 S.L.T. 897 per Lord Justice-General Hope at 902D.

[16] *John Smith* (1838) 2 Swin. 28, per Lord Cockburn at 56–57.

[17] *John Waugh* (1873) 2 Coup. 424, per Lord Ardmillan at 427.

[18] Hume, *Commentaries*, i, 60.

[19] *Elizabeth Anderson* (1858) 3 Irv. 65.

[20] *John Martin* (1873) 2 Coup. 501.

[21] *George Brown* (1839) 2 Swin. 394 at 428.

[22] *John Smith* (1838) 2 Swin. 28, per Lord Moncreiff at 54.

[23] *Elizabeth Anderson* (1858) 3 Irv. 65, per Lord Ardmillan at 68.

[24] Hume, *Commentaries*, i, 69–70.

[25] Alison, *Principles*, i, 278.

"Theft may be committed of every inanimate thing, which is either moveable or capable of being severed from that which is naturally or artificially attached to it."

It follows then that a growing crop becomes moveable property when cut from the field or dug up from the earth, and thus at that stage can be possessed and stolen.[26] Even a piece of land might gradually be stolen (all things being equal) by excavating its substance[27]; that could not, however, exhaust the right of property involved in land ownership, since that is a metaphysical entity said to extend *a coelo usque ad centrum*.[28] Such a right of property in land is, of course, created and evidenced by title deeds or land certificates. Once again, whilst it is possible to steal such deeds or certificates,[29] what is stolen is not the right of property in the land itself but the documents themselves, considered as miscellaneous collections of paper and parchment. The right to the land cannot in fact be stolen because it is the incorporeal (i.e. intangible, non-possessable) property of a particular individual.

Corporeal moveables are referred to by Bell[30] as including   **10–08**

"all things which, being themselves capable of motion or of being moved, may be perceived by the senses—seen, touched, taken possession of: as ships, household furniture; goods and effects of all kinds; farm stock and implements; horses, cattle and other animals; corn, money, jewels, wearing apparel."

Such moveables, it is said,[31] are the only things which can be stolen, since they are the only things capable of being physically possessed and carried away in accordance with Hume's account of theft (see para.10–03, above). Since his account has been departed from somewhat in modern law,[32] the need to confine theft to moveable, corporeal property is questionable. An extension of the crime to cover the appropriation of at least some types of incorporeal (i.e. intangible) property would, therefore, seem worth considering. No reported case has endorsed such an extension, however, and so called "intellectual property" (e.g. copyrights, patents and designs) is protected either by civil law remedies or by particular statutory offences.[33] On the other hand, no reported case has ruled out such an extension, such authorities as there are having been concerned with innominate offences rather than theft.[34]

---

[26] See, e.g. *James Miln* (1758) Hume, Commentaries, i, 79 grain; and *Andrew Young* (1800) Hume, *Commentaries*, i, 79–80 potatoes.

[27] Hume, *Commentaries*, i, 80.

[28] I.e. "from the heavens right to the centre of the earth", see Bell, *Principles of the Law of Scotland*, 10th edn (1899), s.940.

[29] See *Patrick Eviot* (1614) Hume, *Commentaries*, i, 80.

[30] Bell, *Principles of the Law of Scotland*, 10th edn (1899), s.1285.

[31] Gordon, *Criminal Law*, 3rd edn (2000/2001), para.14.20.

[32] See above, paras 10–05 to 10–06.

[33] See, for example, the Copyright, Designs and Patents Act 1988 s.107 (as amended by the Copyright, etc. and Trade Marks (Offences etc.) Act 2002 s.1(2); the Copyright and Related Rights Regulations 2003 (SI 2003/2498) reg.26(1) and Sch.1 para.9(2); the Digital Economy Act 2010 s.42(2), and the Copyright, Designs and Patents Act 1988 (Amendment) Regulations 2010 (SI 2010/2694) reg. 5).

[34] See *John Dewar*, Burnett, 115; N.R.S., J.C.13/21, October 3, 1777 (erroneously, it seems, referred to as a case of theft in Macdonald, *Criminal Law*, 5th edn (1948), p.20); *HM Advocate v Mackenzie*, 1913 S.C. (J.) 107; *Grant v Allan*, 1988 S.L.T. 11.

10–09   As is obvious from the passage quoted from Bell, animate things can also meet the test of being moveable and corporeal. Thus animals may be stolen,[35] as also "infant" children.[36] The conventional view is that an "infant" child is one below the age of puberty,[37] which means a boy under 14 or a girl under 12,[38] and the authorities certainly support the view that a young child must be involved.[39] The Scottish Law Commission, however, has recommended that such children should cease to be considered as "stealable", and that an appropriate statutory offence should be substituted.[40] Adults (i.e. apparently anyone beyond the age of pupillarity) cannot be stolen; but the crime of abduction substitutes for theft where such persons are forcibly taken away.[41]

10–10   Some things are difficult to perceive as moveable and corporeal in the required sense. Currency, for example, in the form of banknotes can certainly be stolen, although the notes themselves appear to represent some ill defined, intangible right. Prosecutions for thefts of money assume, however, that the face value of what has been appropriated is involved, and not just such value as mere pieces of paper attract.[42] The reason for this is that such promise (an incorporeal matter) as is contained in a banknote is made to the bearer, and not to any particular person. Electricity is also thought to pose conceptual difficulties,[43] but it is clearly moveable and corporeal. The fact that it cannot as easily be possessed and taken away as many other forms of stealable property is probably not of great importance once it is recalled that appropriation is what is required in the modern law.

Belonging to another person

10–11   Since theft protects an owner's right of property, stealable things must be owned—and owned by someone other than the accused. As Macdonald puts the matter[44]:

> "[A] person is not guilty of theft for irregularly taking that which is his own, although he may thereby commit some offence other than theft."

It is not possible in Scotland, therefore, for a person to steal his own car, by driving it off clandestinely from a repair-garage in order to avoid paying for work done on it.[45] Although the garage proprietor would have had a lien over such a car until the work had been paid for, such a lien (i.e. a right to retain possession) does not amount to any right of ownership. It has been declared that a pawnbroker has

---

[35] Hume, *Commentaries*, i, 81.
[36] Hume, *Commentaries*, i, 84. See below, para.10–15.
[37] Macdonald, *Criminal Law*, 5th edn (1948), p.21; Gordon, *Criminal Law*, 3rd edn (2000/2001), para.14.26.
[38] See The Scottish Law Commission, *Child Abduction* (HMSO, 1987), Pt III, para.3.3, Scot. Law Com. No.102.
[39] *Rachel Wright* (1808–9), Hume, *Commentaries*, i, 84, n.2 child aged between two and three; *Mary Millar or Oates* (1861) 4 Irv. 74 child aged nine years nine months.
[40] Scottish Law Commission, *Child Abduction* (1987), Pts III and IV, Scot. Law Com. No.102.
[41] *Barbour v HM Advocate*, 1982 S.C.C.R. 195.
[42] *John Mooney* (1851) J. Shaw 496.
[43] Gordon, *Criminal Law*, 3rd edn (2000/2001), para.14.16.
[44] Macdonald, *Criminal Law*, 5th edn (1948), p.16.
[45] Cf. *R. v Turner (No.2)* [1971] 1 W.L.R. 901, which depended on the extended meaning given to "belonging to another" by the (English) Theft Act 1968 s.5(1).

some form of ownership in relation to things which are pawned—certainly a form sufficient to save him from conviction for theft if he disposes of such things before the conclusion of the redemption period,[46]—but this is at odds with the tenor of the present legislation[47] and Gordon[48] is surely correct to say that the view taken in the case must be wrong.

In contracts of sale involving "stealable property", ownership passes to the buyer **10–12** according to the rules contained in the Sale of Goods Act 1979[49] ss.17, 18, 19, 20A and 21; but in lesser contracts than sale, such as loan, where the subject of the loan is money, or anything else which is consumed by use and is intended to be so consumed (e.g. a jar of coffee), ownership must pass on delivery by the lender. As Bell remarks[50]: "Possession in this, as in the case of ordinary moveables, presumes property." The obligation of the recipient is thus to return an equivalent sum of money, together with any interest charged, or an equivalent amount of the thing consumed. It is difficult to see that failure to do so could be more than a breach of contract. Theft must be negatived by his ownership of the thing lent. In a similar way, if a banknote is tendered for change into coin or notes of smaller denomination, or is tendered in payment for a purchased item, it seems that ownership of the note must pass on delivery. Failure either to give change at all or to give the correct change would, therefore, seem to be a breach of contract rather than theft. The original note and the pool of cash from which change might be had are both in the possession, and thus ownership of the defaulting party. Yet in *John Mooney*,[51] where a banknote was indeed tendered in payment for goods of considerably less value, and no change given, Lord Justice-Clerk Hope directed the jury that: "If there was theft at all, it was theft of the one-pound note." Although that direction might have had the merit of granting relief to the "innocent" party from having to pursue a claim according to the vagaries and expense of the civil law, his Lordship advanced no justification for considering that theft could be relevant there at all. Nevertheless, Mooney was convicted of the theft of the banknote and transported for seven years. If that was a "just" result, it was certainly not arrived at by any principled argument.

Almost all moveable, corporeal property in Scotland is owned by someone— **10–13** either by a particular person or, by way of fiction, by the Crown. If such property is truly abandoned by its modern-day owner, then the Crown fills any hiatus in ownership between abandonment and, say, its collection as waste by a local authority.[52] It thus remains theoretically stealable at every step.[53] It is also the case

---

[46] *Catherine Crossgrove or Bradley* (1850) J. Shaw 301, per Lord Moncreiff at 305.

[47] Consumer Credit Act 1974 especially ss.116(3), 117(2), 118(1), 119(2) (though not applicable to Scotland), s.120 (as amended by the Consumer Credit (EU Directive) Regulations 2010 (SI 2010/1010) reg.35), ss.121 and 122.

[48] Gordon, *Criminal Law*, 3rd edn (2000/2001), para.14.30.

[49] As amended by the Sale of Goods (Amendment) Act 1995 s.1.

[50] Bell, *Principles of the Law of Scotland* (1899), s.1333.

[51] *John Mooney* (1851) J. Shaw 496 at 497.

[52] *Mackenzie v Maclean*, 1981 S.L.T. (Sh.Ct.) 40; see also Environmental Protection Act 1990 s.45(9), noting that "waste" is defined by s.75(2) as substituted by the Environment Act 1995 Sch.22 para.88, and as amended by the Waste (Scotland) Regulations 2005 (SSI 2005/22) reg.3(4), and by the Manufacture and Storage of Explosives Regulations 2005 (SI 2005/1082) Sch.5 para.19(2); cf. the offence under s.60(1).

[53] In *Kane v Friel*, 1997 S.C.C.R. 207 at 209A, Lord Justice-General Rodger (giving the opinion of the Court) said: "It is true that at common law most abandoned moveable property belongs to the Crown. The Advocate-depute did not seek, however, to found on that somewhat technical doctrine when arguing that the appellant had had the necessary mens rea for conviction of [theft]."

under feudal theory that treasure hidden or abandoned in antiquity belongs to the Crown[54] and can, therefore, be stolen by its finder. As Bell puts it[55]: "The rule is, 'Quod nullius est fit domini regis'." No doubt, neither that maxim nor its import is widely known to the general public, and it may be that a non-lawyer accused of stealing abandoned property could not be shown to have had sufficient dishonesty for an inference of theftuous intent to be drawn[56]; but where a crematorium manager espoused an honest belief that coffins delivered to his premises to be burnt were ownerless scrap, lawfully able to be appropriated by anyone including himself, the Appeal Court rejected his defence of error on the grounds that it did not rest on reasonable grounds.[57] Temporarily-lost property is, of course, not abandoned by its owner; and its finder is not even entitled to claim ownership where the original owner remains untraced.[58]

10–14 The case of indigenous animals living naturally in the wild is special, although the rule is one of considerable antiquity. They form a conspicuous exception to what was stated at the beginning of the preceding paragraph. According to Hume[59]:

"Our practice acknowledges, of course, the exception of those animals which are wild, and in no degree *sub domino* [*i.e.* within anyone's ownership], such as game in the fields, or fish in a lake or river: There may be a trespass in taking these without leave of the owner of the grounds, but they are not his property, to be stolen."

In fact they are no one's property until killed or taken into captivity. Then ownership follows possession[60] and they may then be stolen. The Theft Act 1607,[61] as it has come to be known,[62] is the sole survivor of a number of pieces of legislation passed by the Scots Parliament to clarify doubtful cases relating to wild animals.[63] It states (as amended[64] and using modern orthography): "Whosoever steals bees shall be called and convened therefor as a breaker of the law." Since the penalty was (and is) a small fine, it is difficult to be confident that this offence is "raised to the rank of theft."[65]

10–15 Since "infant" children are stealable property (see para.10–09, above), they would apparently require to be owned by their parent(s) or guardian, if the usual rules for theft are applicable. This would involve a very odd conception of

---

[54] *Lord Advocate v University of Aberdeen and Budge*, 1963 S.C. 533.
[55] Bell, *Principles of the Law of Scotland* (1899), s.1291.
[56] See *Kane v Friel*, 1997 S.C.C.R. 207.
[57] *Dewar v HM Advocate*, 1945 J.C. 5; see paras 8–46 and 8–47, above. There is, however, a considerable difference between sinks and metal *abandoned* as scrap (see Kane v Friel, 1997 S.C.C.R. 207), and a coffin (containing a human corpse) *delivered* to a crematorium for reduction to ashes.
[58] See the Civic Government (Scotland) Act 1982 s.73.
[59] Hume, *Commentaries*, i, 81.
[60] Bell, *Principles of the Law of Scotland* (1899), s.1290.
[61] A.P.S. IV, c.6, p.373.
[62] Statute Law Revision (Scotland) Act 1964 Sch.2.
[63] Hume, *Commentaries*, i, 82.
[64] See the Salmon and Freshwater Fisheries (Consolidation) (Scotland) Act 2003 (asp 15) Sch.4 Pt 2.
[65] Hume, *Commentaries*, i, 82. There is also a modern statutory offence (based on repealed parts of the 1607 Act) under which a person is guilty if, without legal right or without permission, he fishes "in a proper stank or loch". See the Salmon and Freshwater Fisheries (Consolidation) (Scotland) Act 2003 (asp 15) s.11(1): "stank" and "proper stank or loch" are defined in s.11(2).

ownership since it clearly could not involve the usual property rights of, for example, destruction or sale. The essence of this sort of theft has, however, been described as the

> "deliberate taking of a child from the custody of a parent or other person who has for the time being the parental right of custody in terms of the statute[66] or under an order made by the court. The matter does not depend on the natural relationship which exists between a father and his child. It depends entirely upon interference with the parental right of custody, by virtue of which the child is in the care and possession of the person from whom it has been taken."[67]

Consequently, a parent may be excluded from having lawful custody, and may be able to steal his own child simply because he is excluded from possession.[68] It might be advantageous, therefore, to treat child stealing as a special crime of its own kind—as is more or less admitted by the authoritative writers in their description of it as "Plagium."[69] A similar problem is encountered with the "theft" of human corpses. This is partly solved by the existence of the special crime of violation of sepulchres. It is committed by raising the body of a deceased person from its grave; but ceases to apply once the process of dissolution of the corpse has reached a rather ill defined stage.[70] That crime does not depend, however, on the recognition of any person's ownership of the remains. Between death and burial (or cremation), it is presumed that theft may still apply to the corpse[71]; but the early case of *Mackenzie* (1733), mentioned in the report of *HM Advocate v Coutts*,[72] does not seem to provide authority for this, since the charge was not one of theft.[73] In the case of *Dewar v HM Advocate*[74] a conviction for stealing coffins (or at least their lids), which had been delivered to a crematorium to be burnt, was upheld on appeal. There was no discussion which addressed the question of who owned these items at the time. But ownership here may be clearer than in the other situations outlined above. For the executors in each case must have authorised payment for the coffin and lid out of funds in respect to which they stood as

---

[66] See now the Children (Scotland) Act 1995 ss.1–4A, and 11 (noting that ss.3 and 11 are amended by the Family Law (Scotland) Act 2006 (asp 2) ss.23 and 24; that ss.1–3 are amended, and s.4A inserted, by the Human Fertilisation and Embryology Act 2008 Sch.6 paras 45–51; that s.3 is further amended by the Welfare Reform Act 2009 Sch.6 para.25; and that s.11 is further amended by the Adoption and Children (Scotland) Act 2007 (asp 4) s.107 Sch.2 para.9(2), and Sch. 3, and by the Human Fertilisation and Embryology Act 2008 Sch.6 para.52): under these provisions, the appropriate right would now be one of regulating the child's residence; cf. *Orr v K*, 2003 S.L.T. (Sh.Ct.) 70.

[67] *Hamilton v Wilson*, 1994 S.L.T. 431 (father of illegitimate child convicted of theft of the child from its mother), per Lord Justice-General Hope at 433E.

[68] *Hamilton v Wilson*, 1994 S.L.T. 431. See also *Downie v HM Advocate*, 1984 S.C.C.R. 365 Sh.Ct.; *Hamilton v Mooney*, 1990 S.L.T. (Sh.Ct.) 105.

[69] *Hume, Commentaries*, i, 82; Alison, *Principles*, i, 280 and see *Brouillard v HM Advocate*, 2004 S.C.C.R. 410, opinion of the court at p.416B, para.19; J.M. Fotheringham, "Plagium: The Sins of the Father v. The Rights of the Parent" (1990) J.L.S.S. 506.

[70] *HM Advocate v Coutts* (1899) 3 Adam 50.

[71] Hume, *Commentaries*, i, 85, n.1.

[72] *HM Advocate v Coutts* (1899) 3 Adam 50 at 57, fn.1.

[73] Gordon, *Criminal Law*, 3rd edn (2000/2001), para.14.27.

[74] *Dewar v HM Advocate*, 1945 J.C. 5.

trustees.[75] They were, therefore, the true owners[76] until such time as the whole coffin (along with its contents) was reduced to ashes in the crematorium's furnace.[77]

10–16   "[T]he charge of theft is competent . . . though the case should be such in which it is difficult precisely to describe the owner, or the quality of the immediate interest in the thing . . . We are . . . content with such a description of the thing, as makes the title of possession or management clear, and excludes all pretence of right in the pannel."[78]

It is, thus, sufficient in a charge of theft to allege that the property is owned by someone unknown, as long as it is made clear that that someone could not have been the accused.[79]

10–17   Where the alleged thief asserts a belief that the property in question was his own, or at least was available for him to deal with as he pleased, this is an admissible defence.[80]

"[T]he person must however be excusable for believing, that the thing which he has taken is his own. For as to that sort of belief . . . which is directly in the face of law, and is grounded only in the violent passions of the man, or his blind prejudices in his own favour, it is what the Judge can have no regard to, and what none of the lieges can be allowed to entertain."[81]

Such a belief must, therefore, be more than honestly held; it must be based on reasonable grounds, as in *Dewar v HM Advocate*,[82] and the evidential burden of establishing that appears to lie with the accused.[83] This may or may not amount to what Gordon refers to as a "Claim of Right"[84] or the defence of "Entitlement."[85]

Without the consent of the owner

10–18   What was done must have been done without the consent of the owner or his authorised agent or representative. This is usually obvious from the facts and circumstances. Plainly there is appropriation without the owner's consent if foodstuffs or beverages given to the accused for safekeeping are consumed or destroyed by him. Similarly, a person entrusted with valuables whilst the owner travels abroad has no authority to sell or pawn them, or indeed to devote them to some worthy charity. To do so is to arrogate to himself the rights of the owner and that

---

[75] See Gordon, *Criminal Law*, 3rd edn (2000/2001), para.14.33, for authority that trustees own trust property.

[76] See the Succession (Scotland) Act 1964 s.14(1).

[77] See also *Herron v Diack and Newlands*, 1973 S.L.T. (Sh.Ct.) 27, a macabre case where it was assumed that an American funeral casket was stealable until committed with its contents to the waters of the River Clyde.

[78] Hume, *Commentaries*, i, 78.

[79] See the statutory styles in the Criminal Procedure (Scotland) Act 1995 Schs 2 and 5.

[80] Hume, *Commentaries*, i, 73.

[81] Hume, *Commentaries*, i, 74.

[82] *Dewar v HM Advocate*, 1945 J.C. 5, per Lord Justice-Clerk Cooper at 9.

[83] *Dewar v HM Advocate*, 1945 J.C. 5, per Lord Justice-General Normand at 12.

[84] Gordon, *Criminal Law*, 3rd edn (2000/2001), para.14.55; see also para.8–45, above.

[85] Gordon, *Criminal Law*, 3rd edn (2000/2001), para.14.57.

amounts to appropriation in the absence of error as to consent or a contract allowing him such rights (e.g. sale or gift). It probably also amounts to appropriation to sell such a valuable opportunistically for a far greater price than would normally have been commanded, even if the accused believed in good faith that he was thus benefiting the owner.[86] Retrospective consent might, of course, be given in such a case.

Whether appropriation within Hume's category of "taking and carrying away" **10–19** is without the owner's consent is also usually obvious from the facts. Indeed, very little is required to satisfy the notion of "taking and carrying away"[87] and thus it may be crucial to discover what consent, if any, the owner actually gave. According to Hume[88]:

> "In general, the law intends that the thing must be removed from the place and state of keeping in which it had been,"

but that slight removal will suffice if the owner must then search to find it. An illustration he gives (translated into modern terms) concerns a hotel guest who places an item of hotel property in his own case. Plainly, hotel managements intend that towels, televisions, kettles and the like should be used by guests; but they give no consent to their being removed from their possession and control in such a manner. In a similar way, there is probably appropriation where a person removes goods from a supermarket shelf (to which the management does presumably consent) but places them at once in his own bag or coat-pocket instead of the receptacle provided by the store.[89] Whether such appropriations amount to theft will, of course, depend on whether the mens rea element is satisfied (see below, paras 10–21 to 10–28).

Error as to consent

According to Alison[90]: **10–20**

> "If the taker believed on rational grounds, that the owner would not object to his taking the goods, the crime will not be theft. This presumed consent may be inferred from the near relationship of the parties, or their intimate connexion, in the way of friendship, partnership, or business."

Although Alison provides no examples, it must be plain that a house guest might well consider that he would have the consent of his host to assuage nocturnal pangs of hunger or thirst by visiting the larder, fridge or wine cellar. It is to be noted that Alison requires such a belief to be based on reasonable grounds; and it

---

[86] Gordon, *Criminal Law*, 2nd edn (1978), para.14–64.
[87] See, e.g. *John Paterson and Alexander Glasgow* (1827) Syme 174—bed clothes removed from beds and rolled in a counterpane to await later collection; *Cornelius O'Neill* (1845) 2 Broun 394— accused arrested as he drew a pile of clothes with a stick towards an open window outside which he was standing.
[88] Hume, *Commentaries*, i, 70 and 71.
[89] See *R. v McPherson* [1973]Crim. L.R. 191—a case under the (English) Theft Act 1968, wherein "appropriation" is given an interpretation at s.3(1) probably similar to that now favoured in Scotland; see also *Barr v O'Brien*, 1991 S.C.C.R. 67.
[90] Alison, *Principles*, i, 273.

may be thought that an honest but unreasonable belief would not be sufficient here (despite the decision to the contrary effect, so far as rape at common law is concerned, in *Jamieson v HM Advocate*[91]).

THE MENS REA OF THEFT

Knowledge and intention

10–21   Hume's view of the mens rea of theft is encapsulated in the following quotation[92]

"[The appropriation] must be with a felonious purpose; by one who knows that the thing belongs to another, and who means to deprive him of his property."

It follows that if the accused does not know that the property is owned by another, then he ought to be acquitted provided (most probably) that the court takes the view that his lack of knowledge is reasonably understandable.[93] Thus in *Fraser v Anderson*,[94] by a majority of two to one, the High Court decided that where a person who had sold cattle to another, on a promise to pay at a fixed future date (a promise that appeared not to have been honoured), he might well not have understood that a breach of contract did not retransfer the right of property in them to himself. Consequently, where he had retained possession of the animals throughout, it was not theft for him to have purported to resell them to a third party.

10–22   Hume did not expressly say whether an intent to deprive the owner of his property *permanently* was required, but since he gave examples where only temporary deprivation was involved and plainly stated that these did not suffice for theft, it is highly probable that permanency was indeed what he had in mind.[95] Even as late as 1976, the conventional view remained that

"the essential feature of the *mens rea* of theft is an intention to appropriate and that appropriation involves an intention to deprive the owner permanently of his goods."[96]

10–23   That view had been given added veracity by the decision in *Strathern v Seaforth*.[97] In that case, the accused had taken a car from where it had been parked in a Glasgow street in order to have the pleasure of driving it for a limited period. He

---

[91]   *Jamieson v HM Advocate*, 1994 S.L.T. 537, following *Meek v HM Advocate*, 1983 S.L.T. 280. Cf. the definition of statutory rape in the Sexual Offences (Scotland) Act 2009 (asp 9) s.1(1) as also the further explanation (of what is meant there by the requirement of "reasonable belief") given in s.16. At the time of writing, the provisions of the 2009 Act are all in force—save for those in s.52 (abolition of relevant common law offences, including rape) and s.53(2)(a) to (d): see the Sexual Offences (Scotland) Act 2009 (Commencement No. 1) and the Criminal Justice and Licensing (Scotland) Act 2010 (Commencement No. 4) Order 2010 (SSI 2010/357) art.2(a).

[92]   Hume, *Commentaries*, i, 73.

[93]   Cf. *Kane v Friel*, 1997 S.C.C.R. 207.

[94]   *Fraser v Anderson* (1899) 2 Adam 705.

[95]   Hume's examples (*Commentaries*, i, 73) include a servant riding his master's horse at night without permission, and a farmer finding his neighbour's plough and putting it to his own, unauthorised, temporary use.

[96]   *Herron v Best*, 1976 S.L.T. (Sh.Ct.) 80, per Sheriff Macphail at 81.

[97]   *Strathern v Seaforth*, 1926 J.C. 100.

was charged with clandestinely taking the vehicle where he knew that he did not have, nor could have expected to have the permission of the owner. The charge did not libel theft; nor did the court consider it as a case of stealing. It was a separate crime of its own kind. Macdonald[98] considers the case to illustrate that a kind of theft—*furtum usus*—had been accepted in Scotland. But *furtum usus* (theft of use) involves unauthorised use of what one possesses by consent of the owner,[99] which is clearly rather different from the true situation in the case.In the following year, the same crime featured in the case of *Murray v Robertson*,[100] where an acquittal was entered on appeal since the taking of fish boxes for unauthorised use had been openly rather than clandestinely done. A description of the essentials of the offence, therefore, in terms of clandestine "taking and using" (for a limited period) seems peculiarly apt[101]—and distances the crime from the conventional view of theft that there must be intent to deprive permanently.

Of course, at the precise moment when a car is taken away without authority, it **10–24** is impossible to say what the exact intention of the taker is. Indeed, it might well be inferred from his actions that his intent was to deprive the owner of it permanently. In any event, where any "taking and carrying away" is involved it is sufficient for inferring the mens rea of theft if the thing is left in a place where the owner would not be liable to find it by his own investigative efforts. For these reasons, then, in *Kivlin v Milne*[102] it was decided that theft was legitimately charged where a "joy-rider" of a motor vehicle had abandoned it in such a place that the owner would not have found it. As "joy-riders" may be assumed seldom to return the vehicle to the precise spot from which it was taken, *Kivlin v Milne*[103] substantially undermines the need for a separate crime of "taking and using" in such cases. In any event, such cases now fall under the terms of the statutory offence presently contained in s.178 of the Road Traffic Act 1988. More recently, the Appeal Court has decided that an intention to deprive someone of his property "indefinitely" would be sufficient in an appropriate case. In *Fowler v O'Brien*,[104] the accused had been refused permission to have a "shot" of the victim's bicycle, but decided to take the bike away in any event. This was *not* done clandestinely but quite openly. The accused gave no indication when it would be returned, nor did he state any conditions which would have to be fulfilled before its return. The victim did eventually recover his cycle—several days later. In upholding the conviction for theft, Lord Justice-General Hope concluded that this was not a case where an intent to deprive permanently might be inferred, since the victim had been able to recover the bike through his own efforts. Equally, however, it was not one of those cases where an intent to deprive temporarily might be sufficient— since the accused had not laid down any conditions relative to the return of the goods. There was thus no clear "nefarious purpose".[105] Instead he said this:

---

[98] Macdonald, *Criminal Law,* 5th edn (1948), pp19–20.
[99] See A. Matthaeus, *De Criminibus: Text and Translations*, edited by M. L. Hewett and B. C. Stoop (Cape Town: Juta, 1987), Vol.1, p.50, para.8.
[100] *Murray v Robertson*, 1927 J.C. 1.
[101] Cf. Gordon, *Criminal Law*, 3rd edn (2000/2001), paras 15.29 to 15.32.
[102] *Kivlin v Milne*, 1979 S.L.T. (Notes) 2.
[103] *Kivlin v Mine*, 1979 S.L.T. (Notes) 2, in which no formal opinion was delivered by the Appeal Court.
[104] *Fowler v O'Brien*, 1994 S.C.C.R. 112.
[105] See below, paras 10–25 to 10–27.

"It appears to us that it would be more accurate to say that the owner was deprived of his bicycle indefinitely, since it was not made clear to him whether and, if so, when it would ever be returned to him."[106]

On the assumption then that an intent to deprive indefinitely can be distinguished from an intent to do so permanently, and can be applied generally, there must be at least two forms of the mens rea for theft.

10–25 There is, however, yet another possibility for the mens rea of theft. This was pointed out by Lord Justice-Clerk Macdonald, but lay dormant for many decades. In *HM Advocate v Mackenzie*,[107] the male accused was charged with the theft of a book of secret chemical formulae. He had apparently "borrowed" the book just for the limited purpose of making copies of its contents. Was this truly theft? Lord Justice-Clerk Macdonald had no doubt that it was.

"That such a taking, although there is no intention to retain the article, may be theft is, I think, clear. The article is taken from its owner for the serious purpose of obtaining something of value through the possession of it . . . In this case . . . if he [the prosecutor] can make out by his evidence that the book was taken, and taken for a nefarious purpose, he may be able to obtain a direction in law from the Judge at the trial that what was done constituted a theft of the book."[108]

In the current edition of Macdonald it is declared that temporary deprivation for an "illegitimate" purpose can constitute theft.[109] It seemed, therefore, that the intent required for this crime might be either an intention to deprive the owner permanently or an intention to deprive him temporarily provided that a nefarious or illegitimate purpose lay behind it.

10–26 But what was a nefarious or illegitimate purpose? The temporary removal of a car to drive around in it did not seem to qualify[110]; nor did the unauthorised but temporary taking and using of fish boxes.[111] Removal of a book to copy out its secret and valuable contents was, however, sufficient, provided that the thief had no authority to have the book in his possession.[112]

10–27 The Appeal Court eventually seems to have endorsed Macdonald's view. In *Milne v Tudhope*[113] the accused had been paid in advance for certain house improvements. When these were completed, the owner of the house expressed dissatisfaction, and required further work to be done. The accused was unwilling to do so unless he obtained a promise of further payment. In the absence of such a promise, he removed a significant number of fittings from the house in order to force the owner to allow him to carry out the further work and to agree to pay him for it. The fittings were thus taken and held hostage temporarily to force the owner's hand. At the appeal against conviction for theft, counsel for the appellant

---

[106] *Fowler v O'Brien*, 1994 S.C.C.R. 112 at 115B.
[107] *HM Advocate v Mackenzie*, 1913 S.C. (J.) 107.
[108] *HM Advocate v Mackenzie*, 1913 S.C. (J.) 107 at 110—a view in which Lord Dundas concurred.
[109] Macdonald, *Criminal Law*, 5th edn (1948), p.20.
[110] *Strathearn v Seaforth*, 1926 J.C. 100.
[111] *Murray v Robertson*, 1927 J.C. 1.
[112] *HM Advocate v Mackenzie*, 1913 S.C. (J.) per Lord Salvesen at 113.
[113] *Milne v Tudhope*, 1981 J.C. 53.

seems to have conceded that intent to deprive temporarily for a nefarious purpose was sufficient. The main part of the debate thus focused on whether there had been a nefarious purpose in this case. The court held that there had been.

"The appellant was trying to achieve something by a scheme which he must have known was unlawful. Whether 'nefarious' means 'criminal' in this context or unlawful does not matter for present purposes."[114]

Additionally, in *Kidston v Annan*[115] the Appeal Court determined that where the accused was in possession of a television set with the consent of the owner, it was "nefarious" for him to refuse to return it until an unagreed-to repair was paid for. Once again, there was no argument as to whether this alternative form of intent was valid or not; in the absence of contrary authority, therefore, its validity must be accepted. In *Sandlan v HM Advocate*[116] Lord Stewart seems to have accepted just that, in that he informed the jury that there were now two types of theft—the ordinary sort where there was intention to acquire things for personal benefit or profit, and the more unusual sort where things were taken

"not for the enjoyment or profit of the accused, but [as in this case] simply taken to give verisimilitude to the pretence of a robbery. The intention would not be to deprive Hamilton Laidlaw permanently of their property in the jewellery, but simply to take it for a time as a manoeuvre to save Sandlan's face so that the true stock position could be concealed ... The law is that such a taking of the goods of another, aimed at achieving a nefarious purpose, constitutes theft even if the taker intends all along to return the thing taken when his purpose has been achieved."

Intention may be inferred

Two fairly modern cases of theft have emphasised that although theftuous **10–28** intent will normally be inferred from the facts and circumstances (in the usual Scottish manner, see above, paras 3–27 and 3–28), such an inference need not always be drawn, and sometimes is not to be drawn where evidence to the contrary is believed; as in *Petrovich v Jessop*[117] where a law student and alleged shoplifter had maintained that he had simply forgotten to pay for two books, on the basis that he had not slept for two nights and had been under examination and business stress; and, *Mason v Jessop*[118] where it was held that an intent to steal could not be inferred from the mere breaking of panes of glass in a church window by a drunken person looking for a place to consume a can of beer.

For lucre

Despite the inclusion of these words in Hume's definition of theft it is **10–29** obviously unnecessary for the thief to make any economic gain from his crime. What matters is the owner's loss. Indeed, Hume concedes as much when he states

---

[114] *Milne v Tudhope*, 1981 J.C. 53 at 57. This point remains unsettled.
[115] *Kidston v Annan*, 1984 S.L.T. 279.
[116] *Sandlan v HM Advocate*,1983 S.C.C.R. 71 at 82–83.
[117] *Petrovich v Jessop*, 1990 S.L.T. 594, as explained in *Ivers v Normand*, 1994 S.L.T. 317.
[118] *Mason v Jessop*, 1990 S.C.C.R. 387.

that the phrase "for lucre" simply implies detention from its owner, or destruction of the thing taken.[119] For this reason, it cannot matter what actual value the thing appropriated has[120]; and prosecutions for thefts of items of minimal value are not uncommon.[121] It might be noted, however, that the value of items stolen does have a bearing on the jurisdiction of the JP Courts.[122] The fact that the de minimis rule (see above, para.2–54) plays an especially small part in this crime may reflect the lasting feeling that theft is a peculiarly heinous offence—having once, of course, been punished by hanging.[123] It is also obviously of no benefit to the thief for him to change his mind and return what he had taken. Provided that he had at one time appropriated the property with the required sort of mens rea, the crime has been committed and cannot thereafter be uncommitted. In this connection, Hume quotes the case of *Finlay Macgibbon* (1669),[124] where the accused stole six horses, and was prosecuted for their theft notwithstanding that he ultimately had returned them to their owner along with 200 merks by way of "compensation."

AGGRAVATIONS

10–30 Since theft ceased to be in any way a capital crime,[125] aggravations have ceased to be of great importance; but two still figure prominently in charges, namely "housebreaking" and "opening lockfast places." According to Lord Justice-General Hope in *Peter Alston and Alexander Forrest*,[126] the old custom was to charge housebreaking as a separate crime. If that was ever so, however, it had certainly been abandoned by the time of Hume.[127]

Housebreaking

10–31 This aggravation applies where a theft was committed after the thief entered any "shut and fast building,"[128] provided he effected entry by forcing a way past some obstacle placed there by the owner or occupier to deny access to those not entitled or invited to enter.[129] Despite its title, "housebreaking" is applicable to any building, whether a dwelling-house (occupied or not) or a commercial estab-lishment (such as an office or shop). In the case of *John Fraser*[130] it was held that a hen house was a sufficient building for this purpose; and the statutory styles for

---

[119] Hume, *Commentaries*, i, 75. See above, para.10–03.

[120] Hume, *Commentaries*, i, 76.

[121] See, e.g. *Walker v MacGillivray* (1980) S.C.C.R. Supp. 244, where newspapers valued at 38p were allegedly stolen.

[122] Criminal Procedure (Scotland) Act 1995 s.7(4), as amended by the Criminal Proceedings etc. (Reform) (Scotland) Act 2007 (asp 6) Sch. para.9(4).

[123] See *James Joss* (1821) Shaw 29; cf. the Criminal Procedure (Scotland) Act 1887 s.56 (now repealed).

[124] *Finlay Macgibbon* (1669), Hume, *Commentaries*, i, 79.

[125] Criminal Procedure (Scotland) Act 1887 s.56 (now repealed).

[126] *Peter Alston and Alexander Forrest* (1837) 1 Swin. 433 at 473.

[127] Hume, *Commentaries*, i, 98 et seq. That there is no separate crime of housebreaking is well established: see, e.g. *Cochrane v HM Advocate*, 2002 S.C.C.R. 1051.

[128] Hume, *Commentaries*, i, 103.

[129] Hume, *Commentaries*, i, 98.

[130] *John Fraser* (1831) Bell's Notes 41.

theft mirror that exactly.[131] Of course, the most obvious instance of housebreaking occurs where a door or window has been broken or smashed by the prospective thief. The concept extends, however, rather more widely than that.

It seems to be well established that the security of a building can be overcome **10–32** in a variety of ways which do not involve destructive measures at all. Thus, if a key to a door is stolen, or a skeleton key carried and used to obtain unauthorised entry, that will be quite sufficient.[132] There is a suggestion in some cases that such housebreakings can be taken to the ultimate degree. So in *John Maclean*,[133] and also in *Crown v Devin and Polin*,[134] placing one's hand through a hole in a door and sliding back a bolt on the other side was considered sufficient; and in *John Dewar*[135] it seems that the court was prepared to accept that pressing a key out of a lock and winkling it out from a gap under the door in question constituted housebreaking. The more extreme decisions of this sort, however, have been put in doubt since the case of *Peter Alston and Alexander Forrest*.[136] There, by a narrow majority of four to three, the High Court decided that it was not housebreaking to obtain entry by turning a key left in a door-lock. As Lord Gillies put it[137]:

> "The object of the law is to protect the property of those who show due regard to their own property. The law cannot protect the careless and negligent."

Still less, then, can it be housebreaking to enter a building through an unlocked door or an open (or unfastened) window.[138]

Unusual routes of entry may also be described as housebreaking, even where **10–33** the owner or occupier has taken no steps at all to make such routes secure. The view taken is that there is no need to secure chimney vents and sewer pipes since access to a building via them is hardly to be anticipated, or, in modern times, thought to be possible.[139]

Opening lockfast places

Once a thief has gained entry to a building, he may be confronted by further **10–34** obstacles to his theftuous progress. Individual rooms may themselves be locked, and it is then moot whether "breaking" into them constitutes housebreaking[140] or the opening of lockfast places.[141] Since it will certainly constitute either one aggravation or the other, the issue is probably academic. But it is certainly not housebreaking to force open chests, safes, cupboards or vehicles. These do not

---

[131] See the Criminal Procedure (Scotland) Act 1995 Sch.5—"You did break into a poultry house and steal three fowls."

[132] Hume, *Commentaries*, i, 98 and the case of *Colin Fraser and Daniel Gunn* (1827) there at fn.a.

[133] *John Maclean* (1828) Bell's Notes 36.

[134] *Crown v Devin and Polin* (1829) 5 Deas & Anderson 145.

[135] *John Dewar* (1777) Burnett 115; N.R.S. J.C. 13/21, loose papers Box 213.

[136] *Peter Alston and Alexander Forrest* (1837) 1 Swin. 433.

[137] *Peter Alston and Alexander Forrest* (1837) 1 Swin. 433. at 466.

[138] Hume, *Commentaries*, i, 98; *Lafferty v Wilson*, 1990 S.C.C.R. 30.

[139] But see *Rendal Courtney* (1743) Hume, *Commentaries*, i, 99 and *John Hunter* (1801) Hume, *Commentaries*, i, 99 n.5.

[140] Hume, *Commentaries*, i, 101.

[141] See *Mary Young or Gilchrist and Cecilia Hislop* (undated) Bell's Notes 34.

constitute "buildings" of any sort, and the appropriate aggravation will be the opening of lockfast places.[142]

Housebreaking with intent to steal

10–35　According to Hume[143] this was recognised as a crime separate from, and of a lower order than theft in *Charles Macqueen and Alexander Baillie*.[144] This is still the case today.[145] The Appeal Court has determined that disconnecting a burglar-alarm system can amount to attempted housebreaking with intent to steal.[146] The view taken was that the alarm system was an integral part of the security of the building. It has also been decided that such an attempt could (depending upon the precise circumstances) be shown by smashing a security light.[147] Logically too, the separate crime of "opening lockfast places with intent to steal" might be anticipated; and it certainly exists.[148]

THEFT IN OTHER PARTS OF THE UNITED KINGDOM

10–36　If property is stolen in another part of the United Kingdom and brought to Scotland by the thief, he may be dealt with as if the theft had been effected in Scotland.[149] This represents an extension of the normal, geographically limited jurisdiction of the Scottish Courts (see above, para.2–38).

2. EMBEZZLEMENT

Introduction

10–37　The *Oxford English Dictionary*[150] gives the following as the only modern definition of "embezzlement": "the fraudulent appropriation of entrusted property." This is not at all at odds with the meaning of "embezzlement" as a crime, despite the curious way in which nineteenth-century indictments were framed. In *John McLeod*,[151] for example, the accused was charged in terms that he did "embezzle and fraudulently appropriate to [his] own uses and purposes" one pound sterling entrusted to him. Such tautology, however, was not unusual in the florid styles employed at that time, and does not imply that embezzlement had some meaning radically different from the accepted dictionary definition.

---

[142] See Hume, *Commentaries*, i, 98 and the statutory styles for theft in the Criminal Procedure (Scotland) Act 1995 Sch.2.
[143] Hume, Commentaries, i, 102.
[144] *Charles Macqueen and Alexander Baillie* (1810) Hume, Commentaries, i, 102 fn.2.
[145] See, e.g. *Mason v Jessop*, 1990 S.C.C.R. 387.
[146] *Burns v Allan*, 1987 S.C.C.R. 449.
[147] *Heywood v Reid*, 1996 S.L.T. 378.
[148] See, e.g. *Thompson v Carmichael*, 1990 S.C.C.R. 51.
[149] See the Criminal Procedure (Scotland) Act 1995 s.11(4)(a). This also appears to apply if the accused has simply received property stolen in any other part of the United Kingdom–s.11(4)(b) (noting that s.11(4) is amended by the Criminal Justice and Licensing (Scotland) Act 2010 (asp 13) Sch.7 para.28(b)); see also s.11(5), as inserted by the Postal Services Act 2000 Sch.8 para.24.
[150] Oxford English Dictionary (1989).
[151] *John McLeod* (1858) 3 Irv. 79.

In the time of Hume and Alison, an important distinction lay between "theft" **10–38** on the one hand and "breach of trust and embezzlement" (as embezzlement was then known) on the other. Theft was a capital offence, whereas the other crime was not.[152] Because of this important practical difference, fine lines often required to be drawn and "many nice cases require[d] to be distinguished."[153] This did not lead to a clear contrast being drawn between the two crimes. Today, neither offence being capital, it may seem unnecessary to distinguish between them at all; and the very real difficulty of attempting to do so is revealed in the Criminal Procedure (Scotland) Act 1995[154] which allows a conviction for theft to be returned on a breach of trust and embezzlement charge, and vice versa. From this point of view, then, it would not seem to matter which of the two was in fact charged. There are also very few modern, reported cases which comment on the essential features of embezzlement; and some modern texts on criminal law have omitted any reference to this crime at all.[155] But there is a definite role for it—separate from theft. Indeed, it covers dishonest appropriations where theft cannot operate, as where, say, a trustee or executor appropriates the trust or executry funds. He cannot steal these, since he stands as owner towards them[156]; but he can certainly embezzle them. It may also be possible to embezzle property which is incorporeal and, therefore, cannot be the subject of theft.[157]

General definition

A general definition in terms of Hume's[158] and Alison's[159] accounts is made **10–39** difficult by their view that theft only applied to a dishonest taking-possession of goods from the owner, or other person legally entitled to such possession. For them, appropriation where there was no such taking was at best a breach of trust. Thus the appropriation by a servant of his uniform, by a watchmaker of the watch given him to repair, or by the finder of lost property was a breach of trust[160]; but such appropriations are now clearly thefts (see above, paras 10–05 and 10–06). In modern times, therefore, it would be better to regard embezzlement as the deliberate appropriation to one's own use and purpose of property entrusted to one by the owner (or person otherwise entitled) in such a way as to confer the status of a quasi-owner, for the purposes of dealing with that property and accounting for one's dealings with it to that owner (or person otherwise entitled). The various facets of this definition are developed below.

---

[152] Hume, *Commentaries*, i, 61.

[153] Alison, *Principles*, i, 354.

[154] Criminal Procedure (Scotland) Act 1995 Sch.3 para.8(3),(4); see also (3A) and (3B) (as inserted by the Criminal Justice and Licensing (Scotland) Act 2010 (asp 13) s.48) which allow an alternative verdict of fraud (see below, paras 10–66 to 10–79) to be returned on an embezzlement charge, and vice versa.

[155] See, e.g. P. Hamilton and J.R. Harper, *A Fingertip Guide to Criminal Law*, 5th edn (Edinburgh: Tottel, 2008).

[156] Gordon, *Criminal Law*, 3rd edn (2000/2001), paras 14.33 and 17.28.

[157] Cf. Gordon, *Criminal Law*, 3rd edn (2000/2001), para.17.01; see also *Grant v Allan*, 1988 S.L.T. 11; and Guild v Lees, 1995 S.L.T. 68 (Note).

[158] Hume, *Commentaries*, Ch.II.

[159] Alison, *Principles*, Ch.XII.

[160] Alison, *Principles*, i, 354, 359 and 360.

ACTUS REUS

Entrusted by the owner to the accused

10–40   The "owner" may be an individual, or the partners of a firm,[161] or a co-executor or trustee[162]; and he (or they) must have given the accused authority to deal with the property in question on a quasi-owner basis.[163] Naturally, that authority must not have been rescinded before the act of appropriation. If it had been, then such appropriation would be theft (all other things being equal).[164] The range of persons entrusted with quasi-ownership status might include trustees, executors, factors, agents, managers, administrators, distributors and collectors, according to J. W. Angus[165]; but much depends on what persons answering to such descriptions are entitled to do with the property in question.[166] They should be authorised to avail themselves of some of the powers which an owner might have—such as the selling of the property, or its investment (speculatively or otherwise) or the using of it to raise money—all subject to an obligation to account to the owner for what has been done. A stock-broker, for example, may be given wide-ranging powers to "play the market" with a specific sum of money; in the course of his dealings with that money, he may in fact reduce the value of the capital sum to naught (since all investors are on notice that the value of investments may go down as well as up). And yet, provided he honestly discloses to the owner all that he has done (however incompetently) in the way of dealing, and has not pocketed any of the proceeds thereof without authority, there will be no question of embezzlement. Bad management or incompetence is not criminal; pocketing or otherwise appropriating the results of authorised dealings may well be.

10–41   If the accused lacked the powers which could be described as those of a quasi-owner, if he had been handed the property for a specific purpose and for a limited time (say, a broken watch to be repaired), then his appropriation of that property may well be theft rather than embezzlement.[167] If a painting or a book, for example, is loaned by its owner to another, it is plainly theft for that other person to sell it or destroy it or give it away.[168]

10–42   On the other hand, if an accused person had powers of dealing with the property, and had indeed dealt with it, the appropriation to his own use and purpose of any of the proceeds of that dealing would almost certainly identify him as an embezzler. The fact that his obligation was to account for those proceeds to the owner, and that he had failed to do so, might provide sufficient proof of his appropriation of them.[169] Were he to have had such "dealing" powers, but appropriated the property in the form in which it was received, or at least before any

---

[161] See *Peter A. Sumner* Unreported November 1983, Appeal Court, but see Gordon, *Criminal Law*, 3rd edn (2000/2001), paras 14.34 (at fn.25) and 17.28.

[162] *John Lawrence* (1872) 2 Coup. 168.

[163] Cf. *Kent v HM Advocate*, 1950 J.C. 38, where there was no evidence that such authority had ever been given and thus no prospect of a claimed appropriation being one of embezzlement.

[164] See *Alexander Mitchell* (1874) 3 Coup. 77.

[165] J.W. Angus and R.B. Shearer, *A Dictionary of Crimes and Offences According to the Law of Scotland* (Edinburgh: W. Green and Sons, 1895), under "Embezzlement."

[166] See, e.g. Hume's account of the powers of a farm steward at *Commentaries*, i, 60.

[167] Cf. *William Keith* (1875) 3 Coup. 125, especially Lord Ardmillan at 133.

[168] See the statutory styles for theft in the Criminal Procedure (Scotland) Act 1995 Sch.5.

[169] See, e.g. *Edgar v Mackay*, 1926 J.C. 94.

authorised "dealing" with it was entered into at all, there is precedent for the resulting crime being one of theft.[170] From this point of view also, the accused in *Catherine Crossgrove or Bradley*[171] should have been convicted of theft. Thus, if a stock-broker is given a sum of money by a client, with instructions to invest it as he sees fit for the best profit of that client, it would probably be theft for the broker to use the money to pay off his most pressing, personal creditors. It would certainly not amount to embezzlement since he had never begun the dealing he had been authorised to do.

THE MENS REA OF EMBEZZLEMENT

It is difficult to deduce from the case authorities what is the precise mens rea **10–43** element of embezzlement. In *Edgar v Mackay*[172] what seemed to be looked for was evidence from which "the inference of dishonesty" might be drawn, so that it could be concluded "that the money in question was fraudulently appropriated." This is not very helpful; but what may have been meant is that a deliberate intent to appropriate has to be proved or inferred. This would involve forms of mens rea similar to those required in theft (see above, paras 10–21 to 10–27). Nevertheless, whereas "dishonesty" may not be particularly relevant to theft, it was made almost the rationale of embezzlement in the decision in *Allenby v HM Advocate*.[173] There, a fish salesman sold the catches brought to port by several different trawler skippers, and placed the proceeds in one undivided account, as was his known, normal practice. He then advanced money from the pooled account to trawler skippers other than those entitled to it, and was charged with embezzlement. But since this was all done openly, and according to the custom pertaining at that port (Aberdeen), the Appeal Court felt that there was a basic lack of dishonesty and acquitted him. It is also noteworthy that in *HM Advocate v Wishart*[174] an intent to place clients' money at risk, or perhaps just a reckless course of action involving funds owing to them, was considered sufficient for conviction.[175] Whether a reckless course of action would per se provide sufficient evidence of "dishonest intent" was considered, but expressly not settled, in *Moore v HM Advocate*.[176] There, the Appeal Court had to consider whether mens rea had been sufficiently established where the sole director of a company had been convicted of embezzlement in these circumstances: he had withdrawn from the company's bank account significant sums of money as "loans", although these were well in excess of what could legitimately be granted as such to a director; these sums had been used by him for gambling and stock-market speculation, and were habitually repaid to the company's bank just before an accounting period—only to be withdrawn again by him just after the accounting was completed (all apparently without

---

[170] *J. D. Wormald* (1876) 3 Coup. 246.

[171] *Catherine Crossgrove or Bradley* (1850) J. Shaw 301; see above, para.10–11.

[172] *Edgar v Mackay*, 1926 J.C. 94, per Lord Justice-Clerk Alness at 97.

[173] *Allenby v HM Advocate*, 1938 J.C. 55. See also *Moore v HM Advocate* [2010] HCJAC 26; 2010 S.C.C.R. 451, which is discussed in more detail below.

[174] *HM Advocate v Wishart* (1975) S.C.C.R. Supp. 78.

[175] It might also have involved an intent to deprive the true owners temporarily for a nefarious purpos- esee above, paras 10–25 to 10–27.

[176] *Moore v HM Advocate* [2010] HCJAC 26; 2010 S.C.C.R. 451. See in particular the opinion of the court at paras 6–8, where dicta expressed in *HM Advocate v City of Glasgow Bank Directors* (1879) 4 Couper 161 were followed.

objection by the company's accountants); he and his estranged wife each held fifty per cent of the company's issued shares, and he was found to have declared to a third party that his intention in acting as he had done was to ensure that she should receive nothing—"not a penny from him". On such evidence, the Appeal Court considered that the appellant had been correctly convicted since he had acted with a "corrupt motive" and in "bad faith", so that there was sufficient evidence of a "dishonest intent—"the reckless purpose for which the funds were withdrawn [being] an additional pointer to dishonesty".

DIFFICULT CASES

10–44 Since the Criminal Procedure (Scotland) Act 1995 (see above, para.10–38) virtually allows charges of theft and embezzlement to be interchanged, it will be obvious that in some cases there is uncertainty as to which of the two would be the more appropriate. Indeed, some offences which clearly fit the definition of theft have been prosecuted to conviction as embezzlement—and vice versa. For example, in *Edgar v Mackay*[177] a solicitor was instructed to obtain payment of a debt for one of his clients. He apparently did succeed in obtaining the money; but did not forward it to the client or indeed communicate with him on the subject at all. After months of fruitless inquiries, that client instructed a second solicitor to pursue the matter. It was then discovered that the original solicitor had indeed secured possession of the moneys in question, but had unaccountably refused to hand them over. Eventually, the arrest of the first solicitor was effected on a charge of embezzlement. On appeal against conviction, it was held that conviction for embezzlement was justified in the circumstances. But since the lawyer in question had no authority to deal with the money, the conviction should probably have been one for theft. It may be said that a lawyer collecting such a debt is entitled to deduct his expenses and fees from the money received. But it is highly questionable whether such deductions would amount to "dealing by a quasi-owner." It may be, however, as Gordon aptly states, that professional persons embezzle rather than steal, theft being reserved for non-professional appropriators of property.[178]

3. ROBBERY

Introduction

10–45 This crime might loosely be described as "theft achieved by violence."[179] On that sort of description, robbery would appear to be no more than an aggravated theft. However, the tradition has always been to treat it as a crime separate from theft.[180] It is, however, often difficult to make such a distinction in an individual case.[181] Because of such difficulty, it is permissible to convict of theft on a robbery

---

[177] *Edgar v Mackay*, 1926 J.C. 94.
[178] See Gordon, *Criminal Law*, 3rd edn (2000/2001), paras 17.06, 17.16 and 17.17.
[179] Or as "forcible theft"—Hume, *Commentaries*, i, 104.
[180] See Alison, *Principles*, i, 227 and 236.
[181] See *O'Neill v HM Advocate*, 1934 J.C. 98, per Lord Justice-Clerk Aitchison at 101.

charge.[182] Nevertheless, one significant difference between the two offences is that a later appropriation of property already in one's possession can never be robbery (since a taking of possession is of the essence of robbery). It may also be true that violent efforts to retain what has already been snatched without force are not such as to convert a simple instance of theft to one of robbery.[183]

The force or violence involved in robbery tends to associate it with the crime of **10–46** assault but the violence used need not amount to an assault at all and robbery is regarded as independent of it.[184] In *O'Neill v HM Advocate*,[185] where assault and robbery were both apparently charged, the accused was found guilty of robbery only, the assault having been found "not proven." The Appeal Court affirmed that that verdict had been competent and correct; but two of the Appeal Judges (Lords Hunter and Anderson) were of the persuasion that the "assault" mentioned in the indictment had been libelled as a mere aggravation of the robbery rather than as a separate crime.[186] Where specific acts of violence (or threats of violence) are narrated in the indictment or (less likely) complaint, and those acts (or threats) are not proved, there may be no other evidence from which it can be established that there was any violence associated with the taking of the property at all: and without violence, there can be no robbery.[187] If, however, there is sufficient evidence of force or violence (in fact or established by inference) apart from what had been so narrated, then a conviction for robbery may be justifiable.[188]

DEFINITION OF ROBBERY

Robbery may be considered as the deliberate taking of moveable and corporeal **10–47** property from another by force and against his will. The "taking" referred to means the seizing of physical possession of the article in question. All other things being equal, "as soon as any article has fully passed into the hands of the invader,"[189] the crime is complete. It is even considered a "taking" for the purposes of this crime if the victim is so intimidated that he hands the things over himself, or stands passively by whilst the accused helps himself to what might be had.[190] Equally, if there is a struggle and the victim drops some article, there is a sufficient "taking" if the accused immediately picks it up.[191] There is little need to show that the things taken were then actually carried away; for even if the accused is arrested as soon as he has taken possession of them, or hands them back almost at once, the actus reus of the crime is still considered complete.[192]

---

[182] Criminal Procedure (Scotland) Act 1995 Sch.3 para.8(3).

[183] See *Thomas Innes and Ann Blair* (1834) Bell's Notes 42; *Daniel or Donald Stuart* (1829) Bell's Notes 42–43.

[184] See, e.g. *James Campbell* (1824) Hume, *Commentaries*, i, 107 fn.a; *James Fegen* (1838) 2 Swin. 25.

[185] *O'Neill v HM Advocate*, 1934 J.C. 98.

[186] *O'Neill v HM Advocate*, 1934 J.C. 98 at 102, 103.

[187] See, e.g. *Flynn v HM Advocate*, 1995 S.L.T. 1267.

[188] See *Morrison v HM Advocate* [2010] HCJAC 16; 2010 J.C. 174, in which *Flynn v HM Advocate*, 1995 S.L.T. 1267 was distinguished.

[189] Hume, *Commentaries*, i, 105.

[190] Hume, *Commentaries*, i, 105.

[191] *Anderson, Paul and Bannatyne* (1791) Hume, *Commentaries*, i, 105.

[192] Hume, *Commentaries*, i, 105; Alison, *Principles*, i, 235.

10–48   It is probably popularly supposed that robbery involves the taking of things which were about the victim's person or being carried by him at the time. Whilst that is often the case, it is not necessary that it should be so. As Hume puts it[193]

> "[robbery is applicable to] any thing which is under the immediate care and protection of the person invaded; so that unless by force or terror applied to him, it cannot be taken away."

A fair example of this point occurs in the case of *Thomas Kelly*[194] where a girl left in charge of a house was compelled to rush from it because of the accused's swearing and abusive, threatening words. Thus, the coast was left clear for the accused to take what he desired from the building. That, however, was no less a crime than robbery.[195]

The taking must be by force and against the victim's will

10–49   The important consideration is that the seizing or snatching should be contrary to the wishes of the victim. This can be exhibited in various ways. There might, for example, have been the application of real, physical force. The accused might have struggled with the victim for mastery of some article that he had, or might have beaten him senseless in order to overcome his resistance.[196] Alternatively, "constructive" force or intimidation might be applied; and that would usually be quite sufficient. In *Samuel Riccards*,[197] for example, the accused made verbal threats of violence to a woman who at once handed over money and other goods. Again in *William Macmillan and Spence Gordon*,[198] repeatedly shaking a stick over a woman's head eventually achieved the desired result—i.e. she opened her lock-fast repositories from which the robbers could then help themselves. Even aggressive demands for money, coupled to "gripping" the victim, have been held sufficient.[199] Hume[200] is at pains to point out, however, that such intimidation has to make the victim fear reasonably for his immediate, personal safety and thus overcome his will to prevent the property being taken. What will reasonably achieve that is obviously a question of fact, but the number of persons involved, the weapons that they display, their demeanour and language are all of some significance. In one modern case, where two employees were told by an agent for an alleged creditor of their employer that they would not be allowed to leave their employer's premises until they had handed over the contents of the till (to help repay an alleged debt), their proven alarm was considered sufficient for robbery in relation to what they consequently handed over.[201] If the threat is other than one of immediate, personal violence—for example, to set fire to a building, or to make false accusations of crime—Hume doubts its effectiveness to render the crime one

---

[193] Hume, *Commentaries*, i, 106.
[194] *Thomas Kelly* (1837) Bell's Notes 44.
[195] Or "stouthrief," as that form of robbery was then known.
[196] See, e.g. *William Adams or Reid* (1829) Bell's Notes 43.
[197] *Samuel Riccards* (1710) Hume, *Commentaries*, i, 107.
[198] *William Macmillan and Spence Gordon* (1829) Alison, *Principles*, i, 231.
[199] *Hugh Lundie* (1754) Hume, *Commentaries*, i, 107.
[200] Hume, *Commentaries*, i, 108.
[201] *Harrison v Jessop*, 1992 S.L.T. 465.

of robbery; but Alison[202] is surely correct to point out that much will depend on the precise circumstances of each case. Who or what is liable to be consumed by a blazing building must obviously figure in the analysis. The evidential presumption applicable to theft and to reset that very recent possession of stolen property may, if there are other criminative circumstances, point to the possessor's being guilty of theft or reset (as the case may be),[203] would seem to be applicable also to robbery.[204] This is somewhat surprising, however, for the mere possession of property—no matter how recently taken from the owner or custodier—can raise no reasonable presumption as to the use or threat of violence, which is an essential feature of the crime of robbery.

Moveable and corporeal property

Robbery probably extends to the same sort of property as can be stolen (see **10–50** above, paras 10–07 to 10–10), the value of what is taken being of little importance.[205] It is unclear if one can commit robbery in respect of property one owns but is not entitled at the material time to possess. The close links with theft would suggest, however, that a negative answer should be given.[206] It must be the case, however, that the property in question has to be owned by someone at the material time. This might pose problems if the accused intended to kill his victim, and only after he had succeeded in that purpose decided to make off with property from the body. Since no force would then have had to be applied, the subsequent taking would probably be theft rather than robbery; but to whom would the property then have belonged? Benjamin Bell, the author of the notes to the 1844 edition of Hume, points up this very problem and makes reference to the case of *James Blair*.[207] There no objection was apparently made to a charge of robbery from a dead body, where it was asserted that what was taken was "the property or in the lawful possession . . . of his [i.e. the deceased's] heirs and executors."

THE MENS REA OF ROBBERY

This is uncertain, but appears to encompass the intent to use force and the intent **10–51** to devote things taken by force to one's own uses and purposes. Hume unhelpfully refers to the mens rea as felonious intent—that is, "a purpose to appropriate the thing."[208] Presumably, there must also be knowledge that the thing taken by force is not one's own. If that is so, then the position (apart from the matter of force) must be analogous to that which pertains in theft (see above, paras 10–21 to 10–28). It seems, however, that an assault, which in fact results in the accused's coming into possession of some property that the victim then had about his person, will raise the presumption that the mens rea for robbery exists—although that presumption may be rebutted.[209] It has also been recently affirmed that the intent

---

[202] Alison, *Principles*, i, 231–33.
[203] See, e.g. *Steele v HM Advocate*, 1992 J.C. 1.
[204] See *L v Wilson*, 1995 S.L.T. 673.
[205] See *James Brodie* (1842) 1 Broun 341, where a conviction for robbery was obtained in respect of coin worth two pence.
[206] Cf. Alison, *Principles*, i, 239.
[207] *James Blair* (1830) Bell's Notes 43, 44.
[208] Hume, *Commentaries*, i, 108.
[209] See Hume, *Commentaries*, i, 108 and the case of *Edgar Wright* (1788) mentioned there.

"to steal" need not have preceded the violence used; it is sufficient, it seems, if such an intent "developed in the course of the attack and was present at the time" of appropriation.[210]

4. RESET

Introduction

10–52   The crime of reset in its traditional form is straightforward and easy to understand. It exists to provide a strong disincentive to theft[211] by providing that those who knowingly receive stolen property will themselves be guilty of an offence. Since reset applies to property obtained by robbery, fraud or embezzlement too,[212] it provides a disincentive to those crimes also. Unfortunately, the traditional form of the crime has been thrown into confusion by Lord Justice-Clerk Macdonald. As will be seen below, he added to its scope in a way which might be regarded as "unjustified" or even "unauthorised", but which certainly detracted from its clarity. For that reason, the text below discusses "traditional" and "Macdonald" resets separately.

Traditional reset

10–53   The definition of the traditional form is succinctly given out by Hume[213] as follows:

"Reset of theft, is the receiving and keeping of stolen goods, knowing them to be such, and with an intention to conceal and withhold them from the owner."

Alison[214] reproduces that formula, and indeed it admirably encapsulates the essence of the crime. The only addition is necessitated by the fact that reset is not now confined to the fruits of theft or robbery. It extends in modern times to property obtained by embezzlement and fraud as well.[215] The identification, let alone conviction, of the thief, robber, fraudster or embezzler is not a prerequisite for prosecution[216]; nor is it now necessary[217] to give details of the original theft, robbery, embezzlement or fraud in the complaint or indictment.[218] The crime, moreover, appears to apply to *plagium*.[219]

---

[210] *Coubrough v HM Advocate* [2008] HCJAC 13; 2008 S.C.C.R. 317, opinion of the court at 348B–D, para.88, which approved a statement to similar effect in Gordon, *Criminal Law*, 3rd edn (2000/2001), para.16.08.

[211] Hume, *Commentaries*, i, 113.

[212] See Criminal Law (Consolidation) (Scotland) Act 1995 s.51; Criminal Procedure (Scotland) Act 1995 Sch.3 para.8(1).

[213] Hume, *Commentaries*, i, 113.

[214] Alison, *Principles*, i, 328.

[215] See above, para.10–52.

[216] Hume, *Commentaries*, i, 119, 120.

[217] Cf. Alison, *Principles*, i, 335.

[218] Criminal Procedure (Scotland) Act 1995 Sch.3 para.8(1).

[219] See above, para.10–15, and *Margaret Cook* (1897) 2 Adam 471 at 474, which concerned an eight year old child.

THE ACTUS REUS OF RESET

"It is the fundamental circumstance in the description of this crime, that the **10–54** stolen goods are *received into the offender's possession* . . . [There must be] *a handling* of the things themselves, for the purpose of detention and concealment."[220]

There is little doubt, then, that the traditional form of the crime requires the accused to have received possession of the property in question. It does not seem to matter greatly how that possession is acquired—Hume mentioning pledge, barter, safe-keeping (for the thief) and purchase (even for a fair price). It has to be noted, however, that the fairer the price, the more difficult it will be to show that the accused possessed the required mens rea. Possession, of course, is not confined to personal handling. Goods delivered by others to one's house and placed somewhere within its rooms are as much possessed as if one had done the carrying and locating oneself—always provided that one knew they were to be so delivered and placed. It is within this context that Hume[221] refers to the "privity and connivance" of the house owner. If he permits the property to be so deposited, then he possesses it.[222] It is not, however, necessary for the accused to have received possession directly from the original thief, robber or whoever; but, naturally, the greater the number of hands through which it has passed en route to the accused, the greater will be his chances of casting doubt on his ever having known that it had been dishonestly come by in the first place.[223] It is, for example, clearly not unknown for stolen goods to find their way back eventually to legitimate retail outlets.

THE MENS REA OF RESET: KNOWLEDGE

There are two parts to the mens rea of reset. The first concerns "knowledge of the **10–55** vicious quality of the thing."[224] Presumably this should mean knowledge that the goods one receives were originally obtained from their true owner by theft, robbery, fraud or embezzlement. But strict adherence to that would often make the crime impossible to substantiate; and it is thought that knowledge that the goods were not honestly come by would suffice, provided that they were in fact stolen, or obtained by robbery, fraud or embezzlement. The requisite knowledge need not exist when possession is first taken. Macdonald[225] is surely correct to point out that knowledge can arise at a later point than that, and indeed this is borne out by case law, as in the case of *Latta v Herron*[226] where it was held that the accused, a lawyer, must have come to realise that two antique guns were stolen property when he reflected later on the suspicious circumstances of their sale to him.

Hume is adamant that anything less than "knowledge" will not do. Thus, **10–56** he rules out "bare suspicion" or "indiscretion."[227] Negligent inattention to the

---

[220] Hume, *Commentaries*, i, 113, emphasis added; see also Alison, *Principles*, i, 328.
[221] Hume, *Commentaries*, i, 114.
[222] Cf. *John and Elizabeth Bell* (1736) Hume, *Commentaries*, i, 114.
[223] See Alison, *Principles*, i, 329.
[224] Hume, *Commentaries*, i. 114.
[225] Macdonald, *Criminal Law*, 5th edn (1948), p.68.
[226] *Latta v Herron* (1967) S.C.C.R. Supp. 18.
[227] Hume, *Commentaries*, i, 114.

possibility that the goods are tainted by a dishonest mode of acquisition is, therefore, insufficient; but the Appeal Court has, in recent times, accepted that deliberately shutting one's eyes to the obvious is equivalent to knowing the true position.[228] It will be clear, then, that knowledge can be inferred from the circumstances. If that were not so, then again it would be difficult to substantiate the offence in the absence of the theft, robbery, fraud or embezzlement having been observed by the accused, or the person from whom possession was obtained having confessed to the dishonest mode of acquisition. Such an inference will not, however, inevitably be drawn[229] since otherwise the whole notion of mens rea would be very substantially defeated.

10–57 Circumstances which Hume[230] considered valid in relation to the inference of knowledge are still in use today. They may be enumerated as follows (though most seem plain applications of common sense):

1. Concealment of the property in hidden places, which would include "under a seat"—for example, see *MacLennan v Mackenzie*[231] where this was held not to be a usual place for the location of a car radio-cassette player—but not, in respect of carpet-laying tools, a bathroom cupboard[232];
2. False denial of having the goods at all[233];
3. Attempts to disguise or efface identification marks on the property, as, for example, the scraping-off of the serial number on a piece of electrical equipment[234];
4. Payment of a low price for the property—less than half the true value, for example, in *Latta v Herron*[235]—provided that the accused would or ought to have been aware of their true worth[236];
5. "Awkward" (as Hume puts it) stories of how the goods had been acquired, as in *MacLennan v Mackenzie*,[237] where the accused told the police that a stolen radio-cassette player had been taken by him from a car being repaired in his boss's premises, and that with the full permission of his boss; as in *Watt v Annan*,[238] where the accused claimed to have bought a valuable saw two and a half years earlier from one "Doddy Boyle" who had subsequently, and conveniently, died; as in *McKellar v Normand*,[239] where it seems that the accused implied that it would be quite usual to buy a bed and a blanket at the door of one's house; or as in *Forbes v HM Advocate*,[240] where the accused, in respect of a substantial package partially concealing a valuable art-work, in an obvious position in the back of his vehicle, denied knowing that it was

---

[228] See, e.g. *Latta v Herron* (1967) S.C.C.R. Supp. 18 and *Friel v Docherty*, 1990 S.C.C.R. 351.
[229] See, e.g. *Shannon v HM Advocate*, 1985 S.C.C.R. 14.
[230] Hume, *Commentaries*, i, 114.
[231] *MacLennan v Mackenzie*, 1987 S.C.C.R. 473.
[232] See *Craigie v HM Advocate*, 1989 S.L.T. 631.
[233] See, e.g. *Davidson v Brown*, 1990 S.C.C.R. 304; cf. *Girdwood v Houston*, 1989 S.C.C.R. 578, where knowledge was more or less admitted.
[234] *MacLennan v Mackenzie*, 1987 S.C.C.R. 473.
[235] *Latta v Herron* (1967) S.C.C.R. Supp. 18.
[236] See *Latta v Herron* (1967) S.C.C.R. Supp. 18, where the accused was a knowledgeable collector of antique firearms; cf. *Murray v O'Brien*, 1993 S.C.C.R. 90.
[237] *MacLennan v Mackenzie*, 1987 S.C.C.R. 473.
[238] *Watt v Annan*, 1990 S.C.C.R. 55.
[239] *McKellar v Normand*, 1992 S.C.C.R. 393.
[240] *Forbes v HM Advocate*, 1995 S.L.T. 627.

there at all, because he never checked the vehicle (which was normally left unlocked) for strange objects that might have been left there by persons unknown[241];

6. Where the quality of the property, in view of the circumstances and station in life of the accused, suggests that it could not have been come by honestly— a matter raised by the prosecutor, but not accepted by the Appeal Court, in *Craigie v HM Advocate*[242] in relation to two holdalls of expensive carpet fitter's tools found in the bathroom cupboard of a house where no one followed the profession of carpet-fitting, as was evident from the way in which the only carpet in that house had been laid; and

7. Where the pannel or his "author"[243] is a reputed thief or resetter.

To Hume's list, it may be prudent to add that it is a suspicious circumstance if the property found in the accused's possession has been very recently stolen, as in *Davidson v Brown*,[244] where garments and toiletries had been stolen just a few hours before they were found by the police in a plastic swing-bin balanced on the accused's knees as she sat in the back seat of a car.

Knowledge that the property in question was stolen or otherwise dishonestly **10–58** come by is, of course, insufficient by itself as the mens rea of reset. The second part of the mental element here is that the accused must have intended to detain the property from its true owner,[245] though he need not propose to do so by keeping it permanently himself.[246] If this second requirement were not to be insisted upon, then police and court clerks, who happened to have known stolen property in their possession for legitimate reasons connected with the administration of justice, would be guilty of reset. Such an intention to detain may be established by confession, or by inference from the same sorts of circumstances as figure in the establishing of knowledge. Where such an inference can be drawn from the circumstances, the accused will have to provide some evidence to the contrary if it is not then to be drawn.[247] That does not imply, however, that some burden lies on the accused to show his innocence.[248]

TRADITIONAL RESET AND THEFT

Statute has permitted a conviction for reset to be returned on a theft charge.[249] **10–59** This is because of the close connection that there can be between the two crimes. In *O'Brien v Strathern*,[250] for example, a serving soldier sold his regimental kilt (his uniform) to a shopkeeper who knew perfectly well that that amounted to theft on his customer's part. The shopkeeper was convicted of reset. But considering

---

[241] See also *Mearns v McFadyen*, 2001 S.C.C.R. 25, where a series of "awkward", and inconsistent, stories was given out by the accused.

[242] *Craigie v HM Advocate*, 1989 S.L.T. 631.

[243] Or now, apparently, the company that he keeps—*Davidson v Brown*, 1990 S.C.C.R. 304.

[244] *Davidson v Brown*, 1990 S.C.C.R. 304.

[245] Hume, *Commentaries*, i, 115.

[246] Alison, *Principles*, i, 333.

[247] Hume, *Commentaries*, i, 115.

[248] See *McDonald v HM Advocate*, 1989 S.C.C.R. 559.

[249] The Criminal Procedure (Scotland) Act 1995 Sch.3 para.8(2); see, e.g. *Gillespie v Brown*, 1999 S.L.T. 1115; and, *Mearns v McFadyen*, 2001 S.C.C.R. 25.

[250] *O'Brien v Strathern*, 1922 J.C. 55.

that the soldier's appropriation could be evidenced in no other way than by the sale itself, to which the shopkeeper was a party, the purchaser might as well have been convicted of theft, art and part, as of reset. (It would not be possible, of course, for the same person to be convicted of both theft *and* reset in respect of the same property.[251]) The instances which Hume[252] gives in illustration of the close connection between theft and reset tend to be ones where the "resetter" could well have been art and part guilty of theft in the circumstances. But conviction of reset on a theft charge does not require any suspicion of complicity in the original stealing.[253] It has also been held that although the original theft charge must specify with some precision when the alleged theft took place, this does not bind the Crown to establish that the implied alternative of reset occurred within the same stated time period (although, of course, no other time period will appear in the complaint or indictment).[254]

10–60   There is no provision, however, for a conviction for theft to be returned on a complaint or indictment which specifies reset.[255] This is probably because reset was seen historically as the lesser of the two crimes, and it would have been unfair to convict of an offence more serious than the one actually charged. Nevertheless, where the prosecutor has evidence which supports reset rather than theft, he may still charge theft, where there is evidence of possession of recently stolen property and of other "material" circumstances, and where the accused is reckoned as being unable to show a fair way of coming by that property.[256] It is impossible to be certain what will be acceptable as "recent" in this connection but possibly a matter of hours or days is the limit.[257]

Obviously, the shorter the time period involved, the more likely it is that the person found in possession of the property is also the person who stole it. But there must be more to it than that. There must be "other material circumstances" leading to the inference that the possessor is the thief. What are material circumstances or, as they now tend to be called, "criminative circumstances,"[258] will depend on the facts of the individual case. In *Cassidy v McLeod*,[259] for example, the accused were found in possession of beer (cans and bottles) and plastic crates in a house not far from an inn where a theft of such things had occurred the night before. The fact that the bottles and cans were similar to those stolen, and of such a mixed variety and type as to suggest that it was unlikely that they had been purchased, made it easy to infer that the accused were in possession of the very property that had been recently stolen, and indeed that was conceded when the case was argued before the Appeal Court. It was further established that the crates were not generally sold to the public, that one of the accused had telephoned the

---

[251] See, e.g. *Druce v Friel*, 1994 S.L.T. 1209.
[252] Hume, *Commentaries*, i, 115–116.
[253] See, e.g. *MacLennan v Mackenzie*, 1987 S.C.C.R. 473; *Watt v Annan*, 1990 S.C.C.R. 55.
[254] *MacLennan v Mackenzie*, 1987 S.C.C.R. 473.
[255] cf. Criminal Procedure (Scotland) Act 1995 Sch.3, para.8(2),(3),(4).
[256] See, e.g. *Young v Webster*, 1993 S.L.T. 349; *Druce v Friel*, 1994 S.L.T. 1209.
[257] See *Watt v Annan*, 1990 S.C.C.R. 55—six months too long after the theft; *MacLennan v Mackenzie*, 1987 S.C.C.R. 473—two and a half months too long; *Craigie v HM Advocate*, 1989 S.L.T. 631— where a sheriff directed a jury that six weeks was too long; *Tudhope v Smellie* (1977) S.C.C.R. Supp. 186—where 19 to 20 days was held sufficient, although it was emphasised that it depends ultimately on the circumstances of each case.
[258] See, e.g. *Fox v Patterson*, 1948 J.C. 104.
[259] *Cassidy v McLeod*, 1981 S.C.C.R. 270.

inn the previous evening and had asked for a "carry-out" on credit (which had been refused), and that a trail of cans and crates led across some waste-ground from the scene of the theft towards the very house occupied by the accused. The Appeal Court, therefore, considered that other criminative circumstances had indeed been established, that the accused had been unable to show an honest way of coming by the beer, and that therefore the charge of theft in the complaint had been fully substantiated.

MACDONALD RESET

Macdonald[260] narrates that there is another form of reset, namely: "being privy to **10–61** the retaining of property that has been dishonestly come by." No attempt, however, is made to explain what is meant by "being privy." The Oxford English Dictionary[261] definitions of "privy" suggest that it might mean "participating in the knowledge of something secret" or "being an accessory to some secret transaction." If these suggestions are taken to be what Macdonald had in mind, then he surely refers to nothing more than a form of art and part guilt in relation to traditional reset. There would be nothing objectionable in that, save perhaps the undue widening of the offence to property that had been "dishonestly come by." Although that would include property obtained by theft, robbery, embezzlement or fraud, it might also cover property acquired in some non-criminal way which could nevertheless be stigmatised as "dishonest."[262] But it is thought that there is no warrant for such an extension to traditional reset. In any event, Macdonald gives out this alternative form of the crime without reference to authority of any kind. In 1968, however, the Appeal Court decided that it represented a correct statement of the law,[263] although it remains unclear what the alternative form is supposed to mean. It is plain, however, from Macdonald's own example of its use, that it is by no means confined to art and part guilt of traditional reset.

The example that is given in Macdonald's text runs as follows: **10–62**

> "It is reset for a person to connive at a third party possessing or retaining the stolen goods, even if the person charged never laid a finger on the property stolen."

Again, this might refer to a form of art and part guilt. If so, it would be wholly acceptable and unexceptionable. But the example is derived, and obtains whatever authority it possesses, from a direction to a jury made by Lord Justice-Clerk Macdonald himself in 1903 in *HM Advocate v Browne*.[264] In the course of that direction, he said:

> "If a man steals a bundle of notes out of a man's pocket, and after that informs another man that he has got these notes, that he has stolen them, or if the other man saw him stealing them and knew that they were stolen, then if the

---

[260] Macdonald, *Criminal Law*, 5th edn (1948), p.67.

[261] *Oxford English Dictionary* (1931).

[262] Cf. the situation in *Grant v Allan*, 1988 S.L.T. 11.

[263] See *McNeil v HM Advocate*, 1968 J.C. 29, following *McCawley v HM Advocate* (1959) S.C.C.R. Supp. 3.

[264] *HM Advocate v Browne* (1903) 6 F. (J.) 24 at 26.

other man connived at it remaining in the possession of the thief or being put in any place for safe custody, such as hiding it in a cupboard, he is guilty of receiving feloniously even although he never puts his fingers on the notes at all. Reset consists of being privy to the retaining of property that has been dishonestly come by."

This must be taken along with a later passage in Macdonald's text book[265] which reads: "If the first offender with his knowledge hide the property, even in a hole in a wall, and he connive at this, he is guilty." There are a number of objections to this.

10–63   Firstly, Macdonald thus makes dispensable what both Hume and Alison[266] state is essential, that is, that the resetter should have received (handled, taken possession of) the property in question. This point was well taken by both Lord Justice-Clerk Grant and Lord Strachan in *Clark v HM Advocate*[267] and made them doubt that Macdonald could possibly have been correct. Their doubts were dismissed, however, by the Appeal Court in *McNeil v HM Advocate*,[268] apparently on the basis that the Macdonald alternative had appeared in his text book without objection for a very long time. Secondly, it is clear from his examples that Macdonald did not have in mind any mere "art and part" form of guilt. The person who sees or knows of the thief's concealment of the property and "connives at" that is simply guilty of reset as actor. There is no other person, by hypothesis, who is guilty of reset and in respect of whose crime he might be art and part guilty; and Macdonald does not suggest that the accused might be art and part guilty of the theft itself. Thirdly, Macdonald makes no attempt to explain what is meant by "connive at", and this caused great difficulty to the trial judge and jury in *Clark v HM Advocate*.[269] The sheriff there, in fact, directed that the accused would be guilty if he knew that stolen property was being disposed of, yet did nothing to inform the police; but there had to be more to it than proof that the accused was merely in the company of the thief when the property happened to be disposed of. This somewhat inconsistent direction was clearly enough to confuse any jury, as the Appeal Court conceded when quashing the conviction for reset. But their Lordships did little to clarify the meaning of "connive at" other than to agree with both counsel that acts of a positive nature would have to be shown. No doubt this better accords with the philosophy that a person should not be convicted of a crime because of his mental attitude alone[270] but it gives little guidance as to the scope of Macdonald's examples. For these reasons alone, it can be suggested that the Macdonald form of reset should be abandoned by Scots law. His examples are also probably contrary to principle, in that they seem to require a person who knows of, or observes a crime to inform the authorities,[271] in the absence of any of the accepted legal duties discussed in Ch.3.

---

[265] Macdonald, *Criminal Law,* 5th edn (1948), p.68.
[266] Hume, *Commentaries*, i, 113; Alison, *Principles*, 328.
[267] *Clark v HM Advocate*, 1965 S.L.T. 250 at 252, 253.
[268] *McNeil v HM Advocate*, 1968 J.C. 29.
[269] *Clark v HM Advocate*, 1965 S.L.T. 250.
[270] Cf. *Girdwood v Houston*, 1989 S.C.C.R. 578.
[271] *Pace* the view taken in *McNeil v HM Advocate*, 1968 J.C. 29.

MISCELLANEOUS MATTERS

If property was stolen in any part of the United Kingdom other than Scotland, **10–64** receiving of that property in this country can still be dealt with by the Scottish courts.[272] This privilege does not extend, however, to property obtained outwith Scotland by fraud or embezzlement. It is also the case that a JP Court can deal with a case of reset, theft, fraud or embezzlement on complaint provided that the value of the property in question does not exceed level four on the standard scale.[273] Such a court cannot try cases of robbery at all, however. It may follow then that the reset of the proceeds of a robbery must be tried in a sheriff or High Court.

Any exposition of common law reset must acknowledge the existence of **10–65** similar, but often wider, statutory offences which add somewhat to the complexity of the subject. For example, under the Proceeds of Crime Act 2002, a person commits an offence if he acquires, uses or has possession of criminal property.[274] "Property" for the purposes of this offence is construed very widely[275] and amounts to "criminal property" if it

"(a) constitutes a person's benefit[276] from criminal conduct or it represents such a benefit (in whole or part and whether directly or indirectly), and (b) the alleged offender knows or suspects that it constitutes such a benefit."[277]

This in turn requires "criminal conduct" to be defined—as it is in s.340(2).[278]

5. FRAUD

Introduction

The common law crime of fraud helps protect persons from their own gulli- **10–66** bility. Modern advertising techniques exploit the psychological fact that most persons can be imposed upon and influenced in ways they might hardly suspect.

---

[272] Criminal Procedure (Scotland) Act 1995 s.11(4)(b), as amended by the Criminal Justice and Licensing (Scotland) Act 2010 (asp 13) Sch.7 para.28(b); cf. the now replaced original wording in the Criminal Procedure (Scotland) Act 1975 ss.7(2), 292(2).

[273] Criminal Procedure (Scotland) Act 1995 Act s.7(8)(b)(iii), as amended by the Criminal Proceedings etc. (Reform) (Scotland) Act 2007 (asp 6) Sch. para.9(4).

[274] Proceeds of Crime Act 2002 s.329(1). "Defences" are explained in s.329(2), and these include that the person in question "acquired, or used or had possession of the property for adequate consideration" (s.329(2)(c)); "inadequate consideration" is defined in s.329(3): see on this *Hogan v DPP* [2007] EWHC 978 (Admin); [2007] 1 W.L.R. 2944 DC.

[275] See the Proceeds of Crime Act 2002 s.340(9)—where "property" includes money, things heritable or moveable, and intangible or incorporeal property.

[276] Under the Proceeds of Crime Act 2002 s.340(5), a "person benefits from conduct if he obtains property as a result of or in connection with the conduct".

[277] Proceeds of Crime Act 2002 s.340(3).

[278] "Criminal conduct is conduct which—(a) constitutes an offence in any part of the United Kingdom, or (b) would constitute an offence in any part of the United Kingdom if it occurred there." (It should be noted that ss.329 and 340 of the Proceeds of Crime Act 2002 Act are amended by the Serious Organised Crime and Police Act 2005 s.102(4); s.103(4), (6); and Sch.4 para.174: s.340 is further amended by the Serious Crime Act 2007 Sch.8 para.130—"SOCA" there being defined by s.74(4) of the 2007 Act.)

But the common law, knowing nothing of the advertising agent's skills, generally does not seek to prevent "bad bargains" or decisions taken on misleading information. Rather it seeks to proscribe deliberate falsehood, and not "legitimate" persuasion techniques, in interpersonal and business dealings. Such protection as the law gives to consumers short of deliberate falsehood is a modern development under statutory law.[279] Fraud is archaically called "falsehood, fraud and wilful imposition" in the Criminal Procedure (Scotland) Act 1995,[280] and "swindling" in Hume.[281] It is also an alternative verdict where theft has been charged,[282] presumably to cater for cases where consent to the appropriation is discovered in the course of the evidence.[283] It is further the case that a conviction for theft or reset can be returned on a fraud charge[284]; and, for good measure, it is now possible that a conviction for fraud can be returned on[285] a charge of embezzlement (and vice versa). All of these alternative verdicts serve, of course, to demonstrate the close relationship amongst these various offences.

Working definition

10–67 Currently, a working definition of the crime might run as follows: that fraud consists of a false pretence made to another person in the knowledge of its falsity and with the intention that that other person should be deceived by it into acting in a way in which he would not otherwise have acted, provided that that other person *is* so deceived and *does* so act on account of it. It will be noted that the proviso reveals fraud to be a result crime (see above, para.2–36); a false pretence is of no avail for the completed crime unless it causes the specified result. More detailed consideration of this definition will be found in the following paragraphs.

ACTUS REUS: FALSE PRETENCE

10–68 What may be pretended falsely, and what may be the methods of conveying falsehoods to another are matters difficult to generalise. As Hume puts it[286]:

"It would be a vain, and a tedious attempt, to enumerate all the manifold shapes of cheating or fraud, in which falsehood is one of the chief ingredients of the guilt."

Yet, whatever it be that is expressed or implied, it has to be verifiably false there and then. If it happens to be true, then there can be no question of fraud. Of course,

---

[279] See, e.g. the Trade Descriptions Act 1968.
[280] See e.g. Criminal Procedure (Scotland) Act 1995 Sch.3 para.8.
[281] Hume, *Commentaries*, i, 172.
[282] Criminal Procedure (Scotland) Act 1995 Sch.3 para.8(4).
[283] Consent obtained by falsehood is regularly taken at common law in Scotland to be a proper consent—*William Fraser* (1847) Ark. 280—although this would seem to be objectionable on moral grounds. In *Lord Advocate's Reference (No.1 of 2001)*, 2002 S.L.T. 466, opinion was reserved on this issue: see Lord Justice-General Cullen's opinion at 475B, para.36.
[284] Criminal Procedure (Scotland) Act 1995 Sch.3 para.8(2), (3).
[285] Criminal Procedure (Scotland) Act 1995 Sch.3 para.8(3A) and (3B)—both as inserted by the Criminal Justice and Licensing (Scotland) Act 2010 (asp 13) s.48.
[286] Hume, *Commentaries*, i, 177.

what is true or false is generally easy to establish. Whether a person is really who he says he is, whether the goods he has for sale are truly as he describes them, or whether he is really entitled to claim what he presently seeks, can be proved one way or the other with more or less difficulty. But if a person is, for example, induced to buy or to sell by reason of some future intention expressed by another, how can fraud ever be a relevant charge? It stands to reason that a person's future intentions relate to things that he would wish or hope to be able to undertake. But the best-intentioned hopes or wishes may never be fulfilled. They may turn out to have been over ambitious, or to be frustrated by events; and it is their very uncertainty that leads to the conclusion that future intentions cannot form part of the province of fraud. A person's intentions cannot generally be described as false when they are made. But it does not follow that express or implied statements of intent can never be false.

Scots law takes the view that a statement of intention which its maker *never* **10–69** plans to fulfil is false when it is made. Thus, where goods are obtained on credit by one who secretly plans not to pay for them at all, and indeed does not pay for them, there is a false pretence, since he has allowed the person delivering the goods to believe that the normally implied intent to pay at a future date applies in this case *comme toujours*.[287] In the same way, one who orders a meal in a restaurant implies that his intention is to pay for it after it has been consumed; but if he plans all along to walk out without paying and eventually does so walk out, the impression he creates in relation to his intentions is plainly false throughout. Similarly, booking a room in a hotel for a few days' stay does not normally involve payment in advance, but does involve the implied undertaking that the guest in question will pay in the future when his account is presented. If he plans from the moment of booking onwards not to pay at all, then he impliedly makes a false pretence, as has been recognised in the statutory styles of charge.[288]

In the case of *John Hall*[289] Lord Young rejected the view that future intentions **10–70** or promises could ever amount to false pretences for the purposes of fraud. As he put it:

> "A purchaser without intention to pay may afterwards think better of it and pay, or his creditor may succeed in compelling payment. Again a purchaser intending to pay may subsequently change his mind and dishonestly refuse. Shall the former (who in fact pays) be punished as a criminal, and the latter (who does not) go free? A crime committed cannot thereafter be uncommitted."

This interesting dilemma ignores, however, the practicalities—and Scots law is a very practical system. A crime cannot be committed by intention alone; the person who initially intends not to pay, but thereafter does pay, will be guilty of nothing since his secret intentions are ultimately unfulfilled. The law does not usually concern itself with unfulfilled intentions. Although there may well be a theoretical fraud in such a case, it is unlikely to be discovered, there are no outward signs of

---

[287] See, e.g. charge 2 in the indictment in *Drew v HM Advocate*, 1995 S.C.C.R. 647.
[288] See the Criminal Procedure (Scotland) Act 1995 Sch.5—"You did obtain from A.N. board and lodging to the value of £16 without paying and intending not to pay therefor."
[289] *John Hall* (1881) 4 Coup. 438 at 447.

criminality, and no harm or prejudice has been caused.[290] On the other hand, the person who initially intends to pay but ultimately changes his mind may well be charged with fraud, for it is impossible to see into a person's mind and detect such subtle changes in intent. If no payment is ever tendered, it may well be justifiably assumed that that person never intended to do so. That would not prevent, of course, the acceptance of some plausible excuse tendered on his part, for example, that he entered a restaurant and ordered a meal in good faith, thinking erroneously that he had his wallet or credit card in his pocket.

10–71   In any event, Lord Young's views were rejected in the more modern case of *Richards v HM Advocate*[291] where the sale of a mansion house and ornamental grounds was induced by the accused's (or rather his nominee's) professed intention to live in it with his family and retain it entirely in its then current state. The seller's desire was that the property should not be built upon and should therefore not be bought by any entrepreneur attracted by the lure of its development potential. The prosecutor's case was that the professed intention of the purchaser was false from the beginning; and on that basis, the Appeal Court affirmed the correctness of the conviction for fraud. What matters then is a person's present intent as to his future conduct. It is his present intent which can be described as false for the purposes of fraud.

Examples of false pretences

10–72   Pretences may be express or implied. Under the "express" banner, examples would include the written or spoken assumption of a false name or address, provided that gave the impression of wealth, status or just credit-worthiness[292]; assumption of a false status[293]; assertion that goods for sale were of much greater merit than was actually the case[294]; assertion that services rendered were of much greater value than was in fact true (provided, of course, that their true value is also stated in the charge)[295]; assertion that a named person was guilty of a crime[296]; making of false claims to be owed money and raising court actions to recover what was said to be due[297]; or, making of false insurance claims.[298]

---

[290] Lord Young's example, where payment is compelled by civil process, may, however, be different.

[291] *Richards v HM Advocate*, 1971 J.C. 29.

[292] See, e.g. *Thomas Macgregor and George Inglis* (1846) Ark. 49, where the first-named accused passed himself off as "Captain" Macgregor and managed to obtain on credit a carriage, two gold watches, cattle and a grand piano.

[293] See, for example, *Tapsell v Prentice* (1910) 6 Adam 354, where a woman gave a false name and address but also passed herself off as the manageress of a group of travelling people and thus able to purchase large quantities of groceries on the group's behalf.

[294] See, for example, *Hood v Young* (1853) 1 Irv. 236, where two knackery-ready horses were glowingly described as "good workers" at an auction sale, the only reason for sale being given (falsely) that the seller was going abroad.

[295] See, e.g. *HM Advocate v McAllister*, 1996 S.L.T. 220, where the accused pretended to an 87 year old woman that roof repairs (actually worth no more than £50—the cost of replacing one slate) had been done to the value of £2,000; cf. *Bennett v Houston*, 1993 S.L.T. 1182, where the actual value of the work done was omitted from the charges—which were, therefore, dismissed as irrelevant charges of fraud.

[296] See, e.g. *Elliot Millar* (1847) Ark. 355, where the accused misinformed the police that his wife was trying to murder him—even providing a cup of poisoned coffee and a bowl of his "own" vomit as real evidence.

[297] See, e.g. *George Kippen* (1849) J. Shaw 276; *McKenzie v HM Advocate*, 1988 S.L.T. 487.

[298] See, e.g *Maciver and Macallum* (1784) Hume, *Commentaries*, i, 176.

Pretences may be implied by what the accused does without any words being **10–73** spoken or written at all. In *James Paton*,[299] for example, bulls to be displayed at a prize show were made more attractive for the judges by having their skins inflated with air and their horns enhanced with false extensions; and in the English case of *R. v Morris*[300] the accused switched price labels on goods displayed on a super-market shelf so that the goods intended to be purchased then displayed a lower price than that originally attached by the store. Note might also be taken of *William Fraser*[301] where the accused was alleged to have tricked a married woman into believing that he was her husband. His behaviour towards her was said to have had that effect and, on that basis, she was said to have permitted him to have sexual intercourse with her. The majority of the court held that if the prosecutor's case could be substantiated, then the crime committed would be one of fraud rather than common law rape. Also, in *Strathern v Fogal*[302] the accused's failure to disclose on a rates return to the local assessor that he had obtained substantial premiums from tenants as a condition of his renewing their leases was considered to be sufficient for common law fraud. A failure to reveal what there is a legal duty to disclose can, therefore, be a sufficient false pretence.[303]

Cheque and "plastic money" transactions

It is probably clear (bearing in mind the relative dearth of Scottish authority) **10–74** that false pretences can be involved in transactions where cheques or credit cards are tendered in payment for goods or services. Since no one generally makes any statement concerning his relationship with the bank or credit card company where the account in question is held, what is in fact being asserted when a cheque or "plastic money" is tendered must be a matter of implication. In the nineteenth-century case of *Rae v Linton*[304] it was held that handing over a cheque in payment involves the following implied statements—that the person drawing the cheque has an account with the bank or other financial institution in question (which will not be true if, for example, that person has stolen the cheque book); that he has authority from that bank to draw a cheque for such an amount; and that there is good reason to believe that that cheque will be met when presented to that bank. It is not implied necessarily that the account holder has currently a credit balance in his account of at least the amount for which the cheque has been drawn; for it has to be accepted that in modern times, banks and similar institutions have a distinct interest in allowing customers to overdraw on their accounts—even where no special arrangements have been made. For that reason, it may be better to conclude that the important implied assertion is that

> "the present state of affairs is such that, in the ordinary course of events, the cheque will on its future presentment be duly honoured."[305]

---

[299] *James Paton* (1858) 3 Irv. 208.
[300] *R v Morris* [1983] Q.B. 587.
[301] *William Fraser* (1847) Ark. 280 and 329.
[302] *Strathern v Fogal*, 1922 J.C. 73.
[303] Cf. *Buchmann v Normand*, 1994 S.C.C.R. 929, where, although the charge was brought under s.7(4) of the Civic Government Act 1982, the failure to reveal previous convictions by leaving blank the space intended for them in a licence application form, had clear affinities with common law fraud.
[304] *Rae v Linton* (1874) 3 Coup. 67.
[305] *R. v Page* [1971] 2 Q.B. 330, per Phillimore, L.J. at 333, quoting from an English textbook.

This is better since it takes into account the normal delay in clearing a cheque which is presented for payment in the ordinary way. Special presentations apart, a person with no funds in his account may thus still draw a cheque without making any (implied) false pretence. The normal delay in clearance would provide a period of grace during which to make overdraft arrangements with his bank, or to pay money into his account.

10–75   Most retail stores do not now accept cheques in face-to-face payment transactions. In any event, debit cards (or credit cards) can generally no longer be used to guarantee cheques; but in former times where (say) a cheque guarantee card was tendered along with a cheque, it would appear that "the main implicit assertion"[306] would always have been true. Provided that the conditions for the use of such a card were observed[307] then the bank or other issuing institution was obliged to honour the cheque in question, as a matter of commercial reality, if nothing else. However, it was held in England that there was in such cases an extra implied assertion, namely, that the person tendering the card had authority from the issuing bank or other institution to use it and had not had that authority cancelled.[308] The rationale of this was that if the person accepting a cheque backed by such a card had known that the person tendering it was not authorised to use it, the former person would still have been paid by (say) the bank in question if he nevertheless proceeded with the transaction; but he would then have been (in Scottish terminology) art and part guilty of that former person's fraudulent scheme. He could not, therefore, be taken to have treated such a consideration as irrelevant. The same implied assertion of "authority to use it" was applied in England to credit card transactions[309]; and it is thought that the same sort of reasoning would find favour with Scottish courts in relation to the use of both credit and debit cards in appropriate transactions.

Result of the false pretence

10–76   According to Macdonald[310]: "Fraud involves a false pretence made dishonestly in order to bring about some definite practical result." That the addressee of the pretence must be deceived by it in such a way that there is a "definite practical result" has received support in the cases of *Adcock v Archibald*[311] and *HM Advocate v Wishart*[312]; but those words provide little guidance as to what is in fact a sufficient result. For that reason, the working definition preferred above (at para.10–67) draws on part of the opinion of Lord Hunter in *Adcock v Archibald*[313] to the extent that the person deceived must be induced to do what he otherwise would not have done. It is thought that this provides a reasonable guide to what is required, provided that it is borne in mind that "doing what one otherwise would

---

[306] See above, para.10–74.
[307] See *R. v Charles* [1977] A.C. 177.
[308] *R. v Charles* [1977] A.C. 177.
[309] *R. v Lambie* [1982] A.C. 449; regard in English law must now be had, however, to the provisions of the Fraud Act 2006. For a succinct explanation of the modern legal complexities in credit card transactions, see *OFT v Lloyds TSB Plc* [2007] UKHL 48; [2007] 3 W.L.R. 733, per Lord Mance at 740D–H, para.23.
[310] Macdonald, *Criminal Law*, 5th edn (1948), p.52.
[311] *Adcock v Archibald*, 1925 J.C. 58, per Lord Justice-General Clyde at 61.
[312] *HM Advocate v Wishart* (1975) S.C.C.R. Supp.78, per Lord McDonald at 85.
[313] *Adcock v Archibald*, 1925 J.C. 58 at 61.

not have done" includes doing nothing at all, that is, "taking no steps to do what one otherwise would have done." It is also important to bear in mind that a conviction for fraud does not depend on the accused having gained anything as a result of his deception,[314] nor upon anyone having made any economic loss.[315] It is further important to note that where prejudice is suffered as a result of a false pretence, it may be so suffered by a person other than the very person deceived.[316]

Examples of results

Illustrations of "results" are numerous in the law reports and include a court **10–77** ordering the arrestment of sums in the accused's hands and owing to his own creditors, the accused having initiated completely false actions for debt in fictitious names against those creditors "to delay payment of a debt which was due from him"[317]; a mining company being induced to credit 1s 3½d to a team of miners who had not worked the load of coal it represented at all[318]; police being forced to investigate a false accusation of murder[319]; a purchaser being induced to purchase, and thus come under an obligation to take and pay for, a misdescribed horse[320]; a woman refraining from preventing sexual intercourse since she had been induced to think her assailant was her husband[321]; a person sending a money order for £2, having been induced to do so by a forged letter, even though the accused never obtained possession of the order[322]; a prize being awarded to a bull, the meritorious condition of which being the result of cheating[323]; a firm of stock-brokers having been able to demonstrate substantial credit balances to the auditors appointed to inspect their accounts, after a solicitor had drawn cheques on his clients' account payable to the stock-brokers for that purpose alone—the understanding being that the stock-brokers would return the moneys to the solicitor as soon as the auditors had been deceived[324]; and solicitors being induced to raise actions for debt based on fabricated documents and false information.[325] Of course, the result must be caused by the false pretence, otherwise there can be no completed fraud.[326] If the person in receipt of the deception would have acted as he did in any event, then again there can be no fraud, although attempted fraud might then be considered.

---

[314] *Alexander Bannatyne* (1847) Ark. 361, per Lord Justice-Clerk Hope (in his charge to the jury) at 380.

[315] See *Adcock v Archibald*, 1925 J.C. 58, where, because of a minimum wage agreement, neither the mining company nor any of its employees made any loss as a result of the accused's successful deceit.

[316] See, e.g. above, the subject matter of para.10–75, since there a retailer may be held to be deceived by any cheque or credit card fraud but only the bank or other institution will be prejudiced by having to pay out on the transaction.

[317] *George Kippen* (1849) J. Shaw 276, per Lord Justice-Clerk Hope at 286.

[318] *Adcock v Archibald*, 1925 J.C. 58.

[319] *Elliot Millar* (1847) Ark. 355.

[320] *Hood v Young* (1853) 1 Irv. 236—see in particular the reply to counsel by Lord Justice-Clerk Hope at 239.

[321] *William Fraser* (1847) Ark. 280 (a decision made with reference to rape at common law).

[322] *Daniel Taylor* (1853) 1 Irv. 230.

[323] *James Paton* (1858) 3 Irv. 208.

[324] *HM Advocate v Wishart* (1975) S.C.C.R. Supp. 78.

[325] *McKenzie v HM Advocate*, 1988 S.L.T. 487—though charged as attempt to defraud the alleged debtors.

[326] See, e.g. *Mather v HM Advocate* (1914) 7 Adam 525; *Tapsell v Prentice* (1910) 6 Adam 354.

THE MENS REA OF FRAUD

10–78 The accused must know that what he says or writes or implies is false, and must intend thereby to deceive. It seems unlikely that recklessness as to the truth of statements made to another would be sufficient, as is apparently borne out by the decision of the Appeal Court in *Mackenzie v Skeen*.[327] There the accused showed the utmost carelessness in weighing offal intended to be sold to a pet-food manufacturer by weight, but was nevertheless acquitted of fraud. Of course, it could not be shown in the circumstances that he had any intention to deceive either his own employers or the pet-food company—obviously a matter of some importance to this crime.[328]

JURISDICTION

10–79 In a country as small as the United Kingdom, it is inevitable that fraudulent schemes will not always be respecters of borders. This may pose nice problems of jurisdiction. For example, if letters containing false pretences and orders for goods on credit are sent from Scotland to suppliers in England, as in *Thomas Macgregor and George Inglis*,[329] and these suppliers are induced to send the goods in question, there is an immediate problem. Fraud, as was stated above at para.10–67, is a result crime and is not complete until someone is made to do what he otherwise would not have done (see above, para.10–76). No crime, therefore, would seem to have been completed in Scotland. Do Scottish courts, then, have jurisdiction over the whole crime? And what of the converse situation, as in *William Bradbury*[330] where goods were sent from Scotland in response to "false pretence" letters originating in England. If some definite rule was operated in Scots law, then one might be able to conclude that the Scottish courts had jurisdiction where, for example, the fraud was actually completed in Scotland, but not otherwise. In fact, in the two cases referred to above, the High Court affirmed that jurisdiction existed in Scotland over both situations as completed frauds; and it now seems clear that provided a material part of any fraudulent scheme can be said to have a Scottish domicile, the whole crime can competently be dealt with in Scotland, irrespective of whether the courts of any other country might also have had jurisdiction.[331] This is curious but is wholly in keeping with Scots law's intensely pragmatic approach to crime. If the courts of this country were to shackle themselves to a particular jurisdictional rule in such cases, then clear criminality might well go unpunished.

ARTICLES FOR USE IN FRAUD

10–80 It is now a statutory offence[332] for a person to possess or have under his control an article (which includes, but is in no sense limited to, a computer program or "data held in electronic form"[333]) for use in, or in connection with, the commission of

---

[327] *Mackenzie v Skeen*, 1971 J.C. 43.
[328] See, e.g. *Paterson v Ritchie*, 1934 J.C. 42.
[329] *Thomas Macgregor and George Inglis* (1846) Ark. 49.
[330] *William Bradbury* (1872) 2 Coup. 311.
[331] *Laird v HM Advocate*, 1985 S.L.T. 298.
[332] Criminal Justice and Licensing (Scotland) Act 2010 (asp 13) s.49(1).
[333] See the Criminal Justice and Licensing (Scotland) Act 2010 (asp 13) s.49(5).

fraud[334]; it is also a statutory offence[335] for a person to make, adapt, supply or offer to supply such an article if he knows that it is "designed or adapted for use in, or in connection with, the commission of fraud", or if he intends it "to be used in, or in connection with" such commission.

6. UTTERING AS GENUINE

DEFINITION OF THE CRIME

Uttering as genuine is a specialised type of fraud. It is closer to attempted fraud **10–81** than to fraud itself, since no result of the false pretence is required. The false pretence is also very specific. It has to amount to a forged document (or instrument, as the older authorities tend to call it). In the words of Lord Neaves in *Michael Hinchy*[336]:

> "Forgery, in order to satisfy the full meaning of the word as technically used, must be an overt act. The document must have gone forth to the world; the forgery is not committed unless this is done . . . [T]here is no doubt that the wicked and felonious using and uttering of a forged instrument is a completed crime. Whether the party succeeds is of no consequence; the essence of the crime is not the success but the perpetration of the act, of giving it forth from the party to another."

The mens rea element is probably very similar to that of fraud. Drawing the various facets of the crime together, an acceptable definition might read: a person is guilty of uttering as genuine if he deliberately exposes a forged document to another person, as if it was genuine, where he knows that it is forged and intends that that other person should be deceived by it.

A forged document

The classic example of such a document is one which bears a forged signature. **10–82** However, it is not necessary that the forgery should amount to a passable imitation of the signature of the person in question, nor is it necessary for the document even to purport to be signed by that person.[337] In *Daniel Taylor*,[338] the accused claimed to be the brother of the person to be deceived. He sent her a note in which he requested her to send money "poste restante" since he was in some kind of unexplained trouble. There was also an assertion that he had injured his hand. The note, he explained, had therefore been written at his request by another who had also had to adhibit his signature for him. It concluded with the words: "your

---

[334] Maximum penalty on summary conviction is 12 months and/or a fine of the statutory maximum (see below, Appendix C), and on conviction on indictment five years and/or a fine: see the Criminal Justice and Licensing (Scotland) Act 2010 (asp 13) s.49(2).
[335] Criminal Justice and Licensing (Scotland) Act 2010 (asp 13) s.49(3). Maximum penalty on summary conviction is 12 months and/or a fine of the statutory maximum (see below, Appendix C), and on conviction on indictment 10 years and/or a fine: see the 2010 Act (asp 13) s.49(4).
[336] *Michael Hinchy* (1864) 4 Irv. 561 at 565–566.
[337] Compare with Hume's definition of this crime at *Commentaries*, i, 140 at para.2.
[338] *Daniel Taylor* (1853) 1 Irv. 230.

afflicted brother Andrew Muir, signed for me—I cannot." The note was neverthe-less held to be a forgery, Lord Justice-General McNeill stating[339]:

"I do not think it necessary that the signature of Muir should be there. It is enough that the letter professes to be signed by a person authorised to sign Muir's name."

It would, of course, have been monstrous if so crafty a ruse had been successful in removing the finished article from the ranks of forgeries.

10-83 A document with a genuine signature on it may, however, also be a forgery. The point here concerns the authority given or intended by the person who signed it. If one party gives a cheque to another in payment of an account for £6, careless drawing of that cheque might well give scope for the recipient to alter "six" to "sixty" and 6 to 60, as in the case of *William Mann*.[340] But the altered cheque then does not have the authority of the person who signed it, and must be regarded in total as a forgery. The same conclusion follows if a person, for example, were to sign a cheque in blank, leaving the recipient on trust to fill in the name of the payee and the amount. If the recipient, say a business-employee, were to enter his own name on that cheque, instead of the business-name, as intended, or deliberately to double the agreed-on amount, there would certainly be a forgery.[341]

Deliberate exposure to another

10-84 The essence of this crime is not the forging of the document itself, but the delib-erate communication of that document to another as if it was genuine. As Lord Neaves aptly put it in *Michael Hinchy*[342]:

"A man may . . . fabricate a series of the most nefarious documents, but if he keeps them in his desk and never uses them, he has committed no crime . . .".

Were a thief, therefore, to break open such a desk and discover the forgeries, there would obviously be no crime of uttering as genuine; but if that thief were to take them and try to pass them off as genuine himself, the crime of uttering would then be committed thus far by him, and not by the original forger. It will be obvious, then, that the "utterer" need not himself be the manufacturer of the forgery[343] but that the actus reus is complete when the document is deliberately placed in the hands of a third party as genuine.[344] If the forgery is sent by post to another, it seems that the uttering might be complete when the packet containing it is deliv-ered to the postal authorities.[345] This would entail, however, completion of the crime before such a packet was ever opened and scrutinised by any third party. This odd rule, however, may simply represent a blurring of the edges of the crime

---

[339] *Daniel Taylor* (1953) 1 Irv. 230 at 234.
[340] *William Mann* (1877) 3 Coup. 376.
[341] Cf. *Simon Fraser* (1859) 3 Irv. 467, where there could be no such forgery since the accused had written above a signature on an originally blank sheet of paper only that which the person signing it had expected would appear.
[342] *Michael Hinchy* (1864) 4 Irv. 561 at 564–565.
[343] See *John Smith* (1871) 2 Coup. 1, per Lord Ardmillan at 12.
[344] *John Smith* (1871) 2 Coup. 1, per Lord Justice-General Inglis at 8.
[345] See *William Jeffrey* (1842) 1 Broun 337, in particular Lord Mackenzie at 341.

to enable the Scottish courts to retain jurisdiction in cases where the addressee is domiciled outwith Scotland.[346] Such blurring is not unusual in fraud cases, however.[347] If a forged document were to be handed to another as forged, then the present crime cannot possibly be committed; but, depending on the facts, there might be evidence of attempted fraud or a criminal conspiracy.[348]

MENS REA

The accused must, of course, be aware that the document he communicates to **10–85** another is forged.[349] He must also intend to deceive that other person[350] and, possibly, to prejudice the person whose name was forged.[351] But he need have no success in his intentions.

"It is sufficient, therefore, to complete the crime, if the forged instrument has been uttered . . . though it was challenged immediately as a forgery, and returned to the prisoner."[352]

In *John Smith*,[353] for example, a forged cheque crudely signed in the name of "Frankie Yewls" was sent by the accused to a "friend" to encash. The recipient, however, immediately reckoned it a forgery and handed it to the police. The fact that he was not himself deceived was held to be entirely irrelevant. A good or even understandable motive will also not suffice to acquit the accused. If, for example, goods were purchased and a receipt forgotten to be obtained from the seller, it might be understandable for the purchaser to write out an appropriate receipt so as not to trouble the seller—but use of such a receipt would certainly amount to uttering as genuine according to Hume.[354] Whether such a case would ever actually be prosecuted would, of course, depend on the whole circumstances.

7. BRIBERY

Introduction

Whether there was a distinct crime of bribery at common law in Scotland is **10–86** somewhat uncertain. Mackenzie[355] devotes a short title to "The Bribery, Partiality and Negligence of Judges" which he properly regards as "three distinct species forbidden by the common law [by which he means the civil or Roman law] and ours." In terms of bribery *per se*, however, he discusses the law relating to the

---

[346] As in *William Jeffrey* (1842) 1 Broun 337 itself.

[347] See above, para.10–79.

[348] Or even an entirely separate, common law crime—see *John Horne* (1814) Hume, *Commentaries*, i, 150, fn.1.

[349] See *John Smith* (1871) 2 Coup. 1, per Lord Justice-General Inglis at 9; *Barr v HM Advocate*, 1927 J.C. 51, per Lord Justice-General Clyde at 53.

[350] Hume, *Commentaries*, i, 154; *John Smith* (1871) 2 Coup. 1, per Lord Justice-General Inglis at 9–10.

[351] Hume, *Commentaries*, i, 154; *John Smith* (1871) 2 Coup. 1, at 10.

[352] Alison, *Principles*, i, 402.

[353] *John Smith* (1871) 2 Coup. 1.

[354] Hume, *Commentaries*, i, 154-155.

[355] Mackenzie, *Matters Criminal* (1678), Pt 1, tit xxv, pp.248–254.

taking of bribes by judges as it is set out in various early statutes; he further considers that a person who thus corrupts a judge (or attempts to do so) is also punishable (although this may again be a tenet of the "civil law" rather than of native Scots law). Bribery for him "is the taking of money, or other good deed, either for doing of justice, or committing injustice." Hume[356] repeats much of what Mackenzie writes, but adds that the taking of bribes by persons who are not judges—"such as clerks, fiscals, macers, and the like"—"is cognisable at common law, as a species of falsehood and breach of trust"; so too, apparently, is the giving or offering of a bribe to a judge or officer of court, or indeed to any person "whose station gives him a concern in the administration of justice". That such conduct (including attempts) must be offences at common law is justified by him on the basis that "the turpitude is undeniable of seducing any servant of the public to betray his trust, of what kind soever it be".

10–87   Alison[357] and Burnett[358] do not seem to mention any relevant offence at common law; but Macdonald[359] states that there is such an offence—that of "[b]ribe taking by, and attempting to bribe, judges or magistrates or members of a licensing court" or "[i]nferior officials"—for which he provides some authority.[360] Gordon,[361] by way of contrast, discusses this matter mainly in terms of the relevant statutory law (in particular the Prevention of Corruption Acts 1889 to 1916[362]), although he does mention in passing that "[c]orruption of public officials is an offence at common law",[363] and corruption of this sort must surely include bribery. Whatever the state, or indeed content, of a common law "bribery" offence, the Bribery Act 2010 makes plain that[364]

> "The following common law offences are abolished— . . . (b) the offences under the law of Scotland of bribery and accepting a bribe."

The same Act also repeals[365] the extant, relevant statutory laws, and substitutes a new, and complex, set of offences.[366]

---

[356] Hume, *Commentaries*, i, pp.407–408.

[357] Alison, *Principles*, i (1832).

[358] Burnett, *A Treatise on Various Branches of the Criminal Law of Scotland* (1811).

[359] Macdonald, *Criminal Law*, 5th edn (1948), p.163.

[360] See Macdonald, *Criminal Law*, 5th edn (1948), p.163 at fn.6, where he refers to *Logue v HM Advocate*, 1932 J.C. 1, as support for the existence of a common law crime of bribery. In that case, however, the opinion of Lord Justice-General Clyde (at pp.3–4) is based solidly on Hume, *Commentaries*, i, 408, and concludes that members of a licensing court are charged to act judicially (just as judges of any other type of court); but Lord Clyde reserves judgement in relation to the criminality (at common law) of "the case in which the consideration is offered or paid to a person acting in a public capacity for showing favour in the administration of a department of public concern which is connected neither with the functions of a Court nor with the enforcement of the law or of some system of legal regulation."

[361] Gordon, *Criminal Law*, 3rd edn (2001), Vol.2, paras 21.23–21.29 and 44.04–44.08.

[362] The Acts included in that general title are: the Public Bodies Corrupt Practices Act 1889, the Prevention of Corruption Act 1906, and the Prevention of Corruption Act 1916.

[363] Gordon, *Criminal Law*, 3rd edn (2001), Vol.2, para.21.23.

[364] Bribery Act 2010 s.17(1), which either indicates a strong belief in the existence of such offences or has been included *ex abundantia cautelam*.

[365] Bribery Act 2010 Sch.2.

[366] The Bribery Act 2010 was brought fully into force on July 1, 2011: see the Bribery Act 2010 (Commencement) Order 2011 (SI 2011/1418) art.2. There are, however, transitional arrangements: see the 2010 Act s.19(5), (6).

THE BRIBERY ACT 2010

(A) GENERAL BRIBERY OFFENCES

(1) Bribing another person

Under the heading "General bribery offences" the 2010 Act first specifies an offence of "bribing another person."[367] This offence is committed by a person[368] who offers, promises or gives a financial or other advantage[369] to another person, intending by that to induce "a" person to perform improperly some relevant function or activity or to reward "a" person for his having done so,[370] or knowing (or believing) that the acceptance of such advantage would per se constitute improper performance of such a function or activity.[371] Some phrases in the foregoing description require, of course, explanation. **10–88**

"Relevant function or activity." The definition offered applies wherever that phrase is encountered in the 2010 Act.[372] Any function is a relevant one if it is of a public nature; and, any activity is a relevant one if it is connected with a business,[373] is performed in the course of a person's employment or is performed by or on behalf of a body of persons (whether corporate or unincorporate)— provided that such a function or activity also meets one or more of three stated conditions. These conditions are that the person performing the function or activity is expected to do so in good faith (condition A), or is expected to do so impartially (condition B), or is in a position of trust by virtue of performing it (condition C). It is no objection to the relevance of a function or activity that it has no connection with, and is performed in a country or territory outside, the United Kingdom.[374] **10–89**

"Improper performance". The definition offered of "improper performance" also applies wherever that phrase occurs in the 2010 Act.[375] Any function or activity is performed improperly if it is performed in breach of a relevant expectation[376]; and it will be deemed to be so performed "if there is a failure to perform [it] and that failure is itself a breach of a relevant expectation."[377] This, of course, leaves "relevant expectation" in want of an explanation, and that is supplied in ss.4 and 5 of **10–90**

---

[367] Bribery Act 2010 (hereinafter referred to as "the 2010 Act") s.1. Notwithstanding the offence title, neither the word "bribe" nor any of its correlatives is used in the description of the offence; cf. the wording of s.6 of the 2010 Act.

[368] "Person" includes an individual, a body corporate, and a Scottish partnership: see, e.g. the 2010 Act ss.11(1), (2) and 14.

[369] "Financial or other advantage" is not defined in the 2010 Act; it would seem, therefore, that triviality is not an issue.

[370] Up to this point in the description of the offence, it does not matter whether the other person is the same person as the one who is to perform, or has performed, the function or activity: see the 2010 Act s.1(4).

[371] It does not matter whether the advantage is offered (etc.) directly or via a third party: see the 2010 Act s.1(5).

[372] See the 2010 Act s.3.

[373] "Business" includes a trade or profession: see the 2010 Act s.3(7).

[374] Jurisdictional issues are dealt with in the 2010 Act at s.12.

[375] See the 2010 Act s.4.

[376] See the 2010 Act s.4(1)(a).

[377] See the 2010 Act s.4(1)(b).

the 2010 Act. These sections provide that such an expectation is the expectation actually expressed in conditions A and B,[378] or (*quoad* condition C) any expectation (arising from the position of trust mentioned therein) as to the way in which a function or activity will be performed or as to the reasons for which it will be so performed. The test for what can be expected here is that of a reasonable person in the United Kingdom—namely, what such a person would expect "in relation to the performance of the type of function or activity concerned."[379]

10–91 *Defences and penalties.* It is a specific defence[380] to "bribing another person" that the conduct in question was necessary for the proper exercise of any function of an "intelligence service" (as defined), or for the proper exercise of any function of the "armed forces" when engaged on "active service" (as also defined). Presumably other defences at common law (for example, coercion) would also be available where appropriate. Section 11 of the 2010 Act details the maximum penalties which may be imposed for a contravention of this offence.

(2) Accepting (etc.) a bribe

10–92   Under the heading "General bribery offences" the 2010 Act secondly specifies an offence (or rather a series of offences) "relating to being bribed".[381] The offences (referred to as various "cases", 3 to 5)[382] all concern the criminal liability of a person[383] who (or which, as the case may be) requests, agrees to receive or accepts a financial or other advantage[384] (presumably from another person) and who does so (1) intending, as a result, that a "relevant function or activity"[385] should be "improperly preformed"[386] ("case 3"), or (2) where the request, agreement or acceptance is per se the improper performance by him (or it, as the case may be) of such a function or activity ("case 4"), or (3) as a reward for improper performance by him or another person of such a function or activity ("case 5"). The remaining offence here ("case 6") is rather different; it describes a situation where, in anticipation (or in consequence) of a person's requesting, agreeing to receive or accepting a financial or other advantage, that person (or, at that person's request or with his assent or acquiescence, another person) improperly performs a relevant function or activity. For these offences, it is of no matter whether the

---

[378] The expectation anent condition A is performance in good faith, and that for condition B is impartial performance: conditions A–C are set out more fully above, in para.10–89.

[379] See the 2010 Act s.5(1); see also s.5(2) and (3) relative to situations which are not subject to the law of any part of the United Kingdom.

[380] See the 2010 Act s.13 especially (1) and (6). Under s.13(6), the defence is not available relative to a s.1 offence ("bribing another person") where the circumstances would also amount to an offence under s.6 ("bribery of foreign public officials").

[381] See the 2010 Act s.2. Notwithstanding the section title, neither the word "bribe" nor any of its correlatives is used in the description of these offences; cf. the wording of s.6.

[382] Section 1 of the 2010 Act contains "cases" 1 and 2, although such nomenclature was omitted from the exposition of that section (see above, para.10–88) in the interests of simplicity and clarity.

[383] "Person" includes an individual, a body corporate, and a Scottish partnership: see, e.g. the 2010 Act ss.11(1), (2) and 14.

[384] "Financial or other advantage" is not defined in the 2010 Act; it would seem, therefore, that triviality of the advantage is not an issue—which may be justifiable in an offence impliedly founded upon dishonesty.

[385] For the meaning of "relevant function or activity" see above, para.10–89.

[386] For the meaning of "improper performance" see above, para.10–90.

person (who so requests, agrees to receive or accepts) does so directly or through a third party, or whether the advantage in question is for his benefit or for that of another person[387]; also (but excluding a "case 3" offence) it is of no matter whether the said person knows or believes that the performance of the function or activity is improper; and, further, anent a "case 6" offence alone, it is of no matter (where a person other than the said person performs the function or activity) whether the performer knows or believes that his performance is improper. It would seem, therefore, that the offences (known in the 2010 Act as cases 4 to 6) are of strict liability.[388]

Defences and penalties. It is a specific defence to offences "relating to being **10–93** bribed"[389] that the conduct in question was necessary for the proper exercise of any function of an "intelligence service" (as defined), or for the performance of any function of the "armed forces" when engaged on "active service" (also as defined). Since, it seems that the offences known in the 2010 Act as cases 4 to 6 are of strict liability,[390] it is uncertain which other defences (if any) would be available. Section 11 details the maximum penalties which may be imposed for a contravention of s.2.[391]

(3) Bribery of foreign public officials

There is but one offence under the above heading in the 2010 Act.[392] It is **10–94** committed when a person[393] "bribes"[394] a "foreign public official"[395] if that person intends thereby (1) "to influence [that official] in his capacity [as such]"[396] and (2) "to obtain or retain (a) business or (b) an advantage in the conduct of business."[397] Maximum penalties for this offence are contained in s.11.[398]

---

[387] See the 2010 Act s.2(6).

[388] For "strict liability", see below at paras 13–08 to 13–22.

[389] See the 2010 Act s.13 especially (1) and (6).

[390] For "strict liability", see below at paras 13–08 to 13–22.

[391] In respect of any individual prosecuted on indictment, the maximum prison sentence is 10 years; this may, perhaps, suggest to the courts that the imposition of strict liability is not justifiable here.

[392] See the 2010 Act s.6(1),(2).

[393] "Person" includes an individual, a body corporate and Scottish partnership: see, e.g. ss.11(1),(2) and 14; cf. s.6(5).

[394] The word "bribe" was not used in ss.1 and 2 of the 2010 Act; here, however, a person bribes a "foreign public official" if (and only if) that person (directly or through a third party) offers, promises or gives any financial or other advantage to that official (or to another person at the request, or with the assent or acquiescence of that official), and that official is neither permitted nor required by the "written law applicable" (which is itself defined in s.6(7) of the 2010 Act) to him to be so influenced in his capacity as such an official: see s.6(3) of the 2010 Act.

[395] Under s.6(5) of the 2010 Act, a "foreign public official" is an individual who holds a legislative, administrative or judicial position "of any kind" (whether appointed or elected thereto) of a country or territory (or subdivision thereof) outside the United Kingdom, or who exercises a "public function" [this being undefined] for or on behalf (or for any public agency or public enterprise) of such a country or territory, or who is an official or agent of a "public international organisation" (as defined in s.6(6) of the 2010 Act).

[396] Influencing a foreign public official, in his capacity as such, means influencing him in the performance of his functions, and includes (a) any omission to exercise those functions and (b) "any use of [his] position as such an official, even if not within [his] authority": see the 2010 Act s.6(4).

[397] In s.6(8) of the 2010 Act, it is declared (for the purposes of that section) that a trade or profession is a business.

[398] For jurisdictional issues, see s.12(1)–(4) of the 2010 Act.

(B) FAILURE OF COMMERCIAL ORGANISATIONS
TO PREVENT BRIBERY

10–95 It is an offence under s.7 (in terms of which the relevant commercial organisation is solely guilty) of the 2010 Act if a person associated with that organisation bribes another person,[399] and does so intending to obtain (or retain) business, or an advantage in the conduct of business,[400] for that organisation. Certain expressions used here obviously require clarification. Thus "relevant commercial organisation" is defined[401] widely as a body incorporated under the law of any part of the United Kingdom (provided it carries on a business there or elsewhere); any other "body corporate" (wherever incorporated) provided it carries on a business (or part of such) in any part of the United Kingdom; a partnership[402] formed under the law of any part of the United Kingdom (provided it carries on a business in the United Kingdom or elsewhere); or any other partnership (wherever formed) if it carries on a business (or part of it) in the United Kingdom. What is meant here by "bribery" is stated in s.7(3); thus, a person bribes another (for the purposes of this offence, at least) if, but only if, that person "is, or would be, guilty of an offence under sections 1 or 6" (whether or not actually prosecuted for such), or that person would be so guilty "if section 12(2)(c) and (4) were omitted" from the 2010 Act.[403] That person also must be "associated with" the relevant commercial organisation; and, under s.8 of the 2010 Act, such a person is one who (or which), in any capacity[404] performs services[405] for or on behalf of the organisation—as determined "by reference to all the relevant circumstances and not merely by reference to the nature of the relationship" between that person and the organisation.[406] There is, however, a rebuttable presumption that a person who is an employee of the organisation in question is a person who performs such services.

10–96 It would appear that the offence set out in s.7 of the 2010 Act is one of strict liability.[407] There is, however, a specific defence[408]; a relevant commercial organisation may be acquitted if it proves that it "had in place adequate procedures

---

[399] It must be assumed that "a person" in the context of s.7 might be an individual, a body corporate or a partnership—although, of course, the offence under that section is not committed by any of them: see s.7(1) and also s.8(3).

[400] For the purposes of this offence, a trade or profession is a business: see s.7(5); "advantage" is undefined.

[401] See the 2010 Act s.7(5).

[402] "Partnership" is itself defined in s.7(5) as a partnership within the meaning of the Partnership Act 1890 or registered under the Limited Partnerships Act 1907, or as something of a similar character to a partnership—but formed under the law of a country or territory outside the United Kingdom.

[403] Section 12 should be referred to for its precise terms; but, in précis, s.12(2) (read with (3)) allows proceedings to be taken in this country under ss.1, 2 or 6 of the 2010 Act notwithstanding that no act or omission relative thereto took place in the United Kingdom—provided that (inter alia) the person in question has a "close connection" (as defined in (4)) with the United Kingdom. It is not, therefore, essential for conviction of the relevant commercial organisation under s.7(1) that the "bribing person" should have any connection with the United Kingdom, other than (of course) the intention to benefit the commercial organisation in question.

[404] See the 2010 Act s.8(2). The 2010 Act nevertheless provides examples of capacities which will suffice—namely, as employee, agent or subsidiary of the organisation: see s.8(3).

[405] Such services are exclusive of any bribe "under consideration": see s.8(1).

[406] See the 2010 Act s.8(4).

[407] For "strict liability", see below, paras 13–08 to 13–22.

[408] See the 2010 Act s.7(2).

designed to prevent persons associated with [it] from undertaking" the bribery referred to in the section. It is unclear which procedures might be accepted as "adequate"; but the Secretary of State is obliged under s.9 of the 2010 Act to

"publish guidance about procedures that relevant commercial organisations can put in place to prevent persons associated with them from bribing as mentioned in section 7(1)."[409]

Whilst adherence to such guidelines cannot be (and is not stated to be) an absolute guarantee of having "adequate procedures" in place, such adherence must be a material consideration in establishing the defence.[410]

---

[409] See the 2010 Act ss.7(4) and 9(1). Current guidance is to be found on the web site of the Ministry of Justice, at the address: *http://www.justice.gov.uk/legislation* [Accessed June 1, 2012]; under the entry for "Bribery Act guidance", both full-text guidance and a "quick start" guide will be found.

[410] The maximum penalty for a s.7(1) offence is to be found in s.11(3), which specifies a fine of any amount; that would not per se, however, be a decisive issue militating against a finding that a particular offence was one of strict liability: see below, para.13–20.

CHAPTER 11

CRIMES AGAINST PROPERTY

11–01   The crimes in this chapter are mostly common law ones relating to the protection of property, other than incorporeal property, from encroachment, damage or destruction.

1. TRESPASSING ON HERITABLE PROPERTY

Introduction

11–02   "Unless by virtue of some special statutory provision . . . prosecution does not lie under Scottish law merely for unauthorised entry on another's land."[1]

This is undoubtedly true; and as far as the common law of crime is concerned, a trespasser "may indeed jeer at the time-honoured placard, which threatens him with rigorous prosecution, as *brutum fulmen* [a harmless thunderbolt]."[2] As long as he does no harm to property,[3] no common law accusation will lie. The status of "trespasser" in Scotland has, however, been considerably affected by the provisions of the Land Reform (Scotland) Act 2003 (asp 2). Under that Act, everyone is entitled to exercise "access rights" in respect of land in general, provided that this is done responsibly in relation to particular purposes: the exercise of such rights does not of itself amount to trespass. Existing statutory offences which give some protection against "trespassers" have, therefore, had to be modified to take account of such access rights.[4] A selection of these statutory offences is dealt with below.

(1) THE TRESPASS (SCOTLAND) ACT 1865

11–03   The offences contained in the Trespass (Scotland) Act 1865 as amended, most recently by the Roads (Scotland) Act 1984 and the Land Reform (Scotland) Act 2003 (asp 2), are contained in s.3(1) and currently stand as follows:

"Every person who lodges in any premises [as defined—see below], or occupies or encamps on any land, being private property, without the consent

---

[1] T. B. Smith, *A Short Commentary on the Law of Scotland* (Edinburgh: W. Green, 1962), p.526.
[2] J. Rankine, *The Law of Land-Ownership in Scotland*, 4th edn (Edinburgh: W. Green, 1909), p.140.
[3] Cf. malicious mischief below at paras 11–08 to 11–25.
[4] See the Land Reform (Scotland) Act 2003 (asp 2) Pt 1 (for a detailed account of "access rights"), and Sch.2 (for amendments to inter alia existing trespassory offences).

and permission of the owner or legal occupier of such premises or land, and every person who encamps or lights a fire on or near any road [as defined in s.2] or enclosed or cultivated land, or in or near any plantation, without the consent and permission of the owner or legal occupier of such road, land or plantation, shall be . . . punishable as herein-after provided."[5]

According to Rankine[6] this Act

"was passed for the purpose chiefly of preventing strolling tinkers, gypsies, and others from squatting without permission on private property or private roads."

But the offences are certainly not confined to such persons, the most significant limitation being concerned rather with the type of premises involved. In terms of s.2, premises "shall mean and include any house, barn, stable, shed, loft, granary, outhouse, garden, stackyard, court, close, or inclosed space." It must, therefore, be doubted whether this Act can appropriately be invoked where strikers occupy their employer's factory or students stage a "sit-in" protest within the administration block of their college or university. This may be a matter for regret in some quarters, since those found committing an offence under the Act may be "apprehended and detained" by the police under s.4—patently a more rapid and effective way of restoring possession of the premises to the owner or legal occupier than can be provided by the civil law. On the other hand, it may be said that such powers of arrest are remarkable, given that the maximum penalty for those convicted of such offences is a mere fine of level 1 on the standard scale (see Appendix C).

Rankine[7] believed that the Trespass (Scotland) Act 1865 had been "found very **11–04** useful in putting a stop to much petty pilfering and wanton destruction of woods and fences in country districts." That may well be so; but there are very few reported cases on such offences. Indeed, searches in the usual repositories suggest that *Paterson v Robertson*[8] is probably the only reported case. There, subtenants of a furnished house had been given appropriate notice to quit. Whilst they were absent from the premises, the furniture was removed, the house securely locked, and the keys returned by the tenant to the house factors who acted as agents for the owners. Nevertheless, the subtenants returned to the property and gained access by obtaining a key from a neighbour. According to Lord Justice-General Normand, from that time on,

"they were doing what they knew was wrong, and from that moment they were no better than squatters who had effected a lodgment in the house at their own hands."[9]

---

5 Under s.3(2), which is inserted by para.1 of Sch.2 of the Land Reform (Scotland) Act 2003 (asp 2), these offences do not apply to anything done by a person in the exercise of "access rights" as provided for under Pt 1 of the 2003 Act.
6 Rankine, *The Law of Land-Ownership in Scotland*, 4th edn (1909), p.144.
7 Rankine, *The Law of Land-Ownership in Scotland*, 4th edn (1909), p.145.
8 *Paterson v Robertson*, 1944 J.C. 166.
9 *Paterson v Robertson*, 1944 J.C. 166 at 170.

It would seem from this opinion that the mens rea of the crime might be knowledge on the accused's part that he had no entitlement whatsoever to lodge in the premises or encamp on the land; and, if that is so, then Gordon is possibly correct to say that a person who believed himself entitled, at least on reasonable grounds, would have a good defence.[10]

(2) The Criminal Justice and Public Order Act 1994

1. Trespasser failing to obey a police direction to leave

11–05 The complex offence contained in s.61 of the Criminal Justice and Public Order Act 1994 is applicable to Scotland.[11] In essence, it applies where at least two people "trespass" on land (where trespassing is defined[12] as entering or remaining upon land—which does not include buildings, other than agricultural ones or scheduled monuments, or roads, other than footpaths, cycle tracks and bridleways[13]—without lawful authority and without the occupier's[14] consent) and where they have the common purpose of residing[15] on that land for any period of time. That, however, is nowhere near sufficient for the offence to be committed. Not only must the occupier of the land have taken reasonable steps to ask them to leave, but he must also (apparently) have summoned the police. The senior police officer attending the locus must then reasonably believe that the people concerned are trespassers and that the occupier has indeed taken reasonable steps to persuade them to depart from his land; he must also reasonably believe that one at least of the following is satisfied, viz—that the trespassers (or any of them) have caused damage to the land or to property (defined as heritable property other than land, or corporeal moveable property[16]) on it; that the trespassers (or any of them) have used threatening, abusive or insulting words or behaviour to the occupier, any member of his family, his employee or his agent; or, that the trespassers have brought six or more vehicles[17] on to the land. If he is so satisfied as to these points, the police officer may then direct the trespassers, all or some of them, to leave and to remove their vehicles and other property. The offence is committed where such a trespasser, in the knowledge of the police direction, fails to leave as soon as reasonably practicable, or, having once left in obedience to the direction, returns to the same land as a trespasser within a period of three months from the day when the direction was first given.[18] (Failure to remove vehicles or other property seems to be excluded from the offence; but the police may seize such property in terms of s.62.) There is also a statutory defence available. A person accused of a contravention of this section may try to show that he was not in fact trespassing at the relevant time, or, he may

---

[10] Gordon, *Criminal Law*, 3rd edn (2000/2001), para.15.44.
[11] See the Criminal Justice and Public Order Act 1994 s.172(8).
[12] See s.61(9) of the 1994 Act, s.v. "trespass" at (b).
[13] See Criminal Justice and Public Order Act 1994 s.61(9).
[14] Occupier is defined in s.61(9), as the person in Scotland entitled to natural possession of the land.
[15] It is not a bar to being considered as having a purpose of "residing" there that one has a home elsewhere: Criminal Justice and Public Order Act 1994 s.61(9).
[16] See Criminal Justice and Public Order Act 1994 s.61(9).
[17] Vehicles need not be roadworthy, and the term includes a chassis, a caravan, or a load carried in, by or attached to such a conveyance: Criminal Justice and Public Order Act 1994 s.61(9).
[18] See Criminal Justice and Public Order Act 1994 s.61(4). See also s.61(4A) and (4B) as inserted by the Land Reform (Scotland) Act 2003 (asp 2) Sch.2 para.11. (Note that s.61(5) was repealed by the Serious Organised Crime and Police Act 2005 Sch.17 Part 2.)

try to show that he had a reasonable excuse either for not leaving as soon as reasonably practicable or for returning as a trespasser within the specified period.[19] In the one case so far reported on the operation of this offence in Scotland,[20] it appeared that the land in question was subject to a dispute. There were two possible occupiers. That being so, the sheriff who heard the case took the view that it was necessary for the police to make enquiry as to which of the competing parties was the true occupier, since only that person could give instructions (or, possibly, have instructions given on his behalf) to the trespassers to depart. This might have been a question of some difficulty if only one of the two claimants had been prepared to ask the trespassers to leave: but that was not the case. The contending occupiers were entirely at one in wishing and instructing the departure of the persons in question, and consequently the Appeal Court had no difficulty in rejecting the sheriff's view. (This offence is obviously one of fairly limited scope, since it does not apply in general to buildings and is hedged about with qualifying conditions.)

2. *Aggravated Trespass*

The offence of "aggravated trespass"[21] requires that a person should trespass[22] **11–06** on land[23] and deliberately conduct himself there so that those engaged (or about to be engaged) there (or on adjoining land) in "lawful activities"[24] will be intimidated and thus deterred from engaging in those lawful activities. It is also sufficient if he so conducts himself as to obstruct or disrupt those activities. This offence was originally aimed at those who set out to disrupt activities such as "field sports", and who did so (or attempted to do so) by trespassing on land; but since it probably now applies to buildings (since the original restriction to "in the open air" has been removed[25]), the offence has become much wider. There is clearly a "public order" dimension to this offence; but the device of linking the crime to trespassing secures its place in this section of the text.[26]

---

[19] See Criminal Justice and Public Order Act 1994 s.61(6).

[20] *Neizer v Rhodes*, 1995 S.C.C.R. 799.

[21] See s.68 of the 1994 Act, as that section is amended by the Anti-social Behaviour Act 2003 Sch.3. [Note that s.68(4) is repealed by the Serious Organised Crime and Police Act 2005 Sch.17 Pt 2.] For an example of a prosecution under s.68, see *McAdam v Urquhart*, 2004 S.C.C.R. 506.

[22] Under s.68(1A), as inserted by the Land Reform (Scotland) Act 2003 (asp 2) Sch.2 para.13, "trespassing" here includes the exercise of "access rights" (within the meaning of Pt 1 of the 2003 Act) up to the point when they cease to be exercisable by virtue of the commission of the offence under s.68(1).

[23] Land does not include highways or roads: see s.68(5)(*a*), which adopts the exclusion of such in the definition of "land" given out in s.61(9) at (b); there is no adoption, however, of the exclusion of buildings as that was expressly applied to the definition of "land" for s.61 by virtue of s.61(9)—s.v. "land" there, at (a). In England, it has been held that the definition of "land" for the purposes of s.68 must, therefore, include buildings: see *DPP v Chivers* [2010] EWHC 1814 (Admin); [2011] 1 W.L.R. 2324, where the judicial reasoning seems compelling—given that s.68 originally contained the words "in the open air", and that these words were subsequently deleted by virtue of the Anti-social Behaviour Act 2003 Sch.3 (which applies to Scotland by virtue of ss.92 and 96 thereof).

[24] As defined in s.68(2).

[25] See the Anti-social Behaviour Act 2003 Sch.3; *DPP v Chivers* [2010] EWHC 1814 (Admin); [2011] 1 W.L.R. 2324.

[26] Where a person is committing, intends to commit, or has committed an offence under s.68, or where two or more persons are trespassing with the common purpose of disrupting (etc.) lawful activities there, it is also an offence for him or them to refuse to leave the land when directed to do so by a police officer—see s.69, as amended by the Anti-social Behaviour Act 2003 Sch.3. A statutory defence is provided at s.69(4). (Note that s.69(5) is repealed by the Serious Organised Crime and Police Act 2005 Sch.17 Pt 2.)

3. Trespassory Assembly Offences

11-07   Equally, the "Trespassory Assemblies" offences[27] have public order connotations; but they too entail the protection of land from trespass. For such offences to exist, there are a number of qualifying conditions. First the chief officer of police must reasonably believe that an assembly of 20 or more persons[28] is intended to be held in a particular local authority area, at a place in the open air on land to which the public either has no right of access, or a very limited right of access.[29] He must also believe that that assembly is to be held there without the permission of the occupier,[30] or in excess of such permission as had been granted, or beyond the limited right of public access which exists. If he has such beliefs, he must also be of the reasonable persuasion that that assembly will effect "serious disruption to the life of the community" or significant damage to the land itself or to a building (or monument) erected on it—where that land or building is of historical, architectural, archaeological or scientific importance.[31] Provided that he has been satisfied in these ways, he may then apply to the council of the relevant local authority for an order to prohibit the holding of all trespassory assemblies within a specified area for a specific period.[32] Provided further that the relevant council sees fit to make such an order, the holding of any such assembly will be forbidden— i.e. one which

> "(a) is held on land to which the public has no right of access or only a limited right of access, and (b) takes place in the prohibited circumstances, that is to say, without the permission of the occupier of the land or so as to exceed the limits of any permission of his or the limits of the public's right of access."[33]

Once such an order has been made, it will be an offence to organise or take part in an assembly which contravenes the terms of the order—provided the organiser or the participant is aware of that order.[34] It will also be an offence under certain conditions to disobey a direction from a police officer that a particular person, reasonably believed to be *en route* to such an assembly, should not continue in a direction which would lead him there.[35]

---

[27] Public Order Act 1986 ss.14A to 14C, added thereto by ss.70 and 71 of the 1994 Act. (Note that s.14B(4) and s.14C(4) are repealed by the Serious Organised Crime and Police Act 2005 Sch.17 Pt 2.)

[28] See s.14A(9) of the Public Order Act 1986.

[29] The Public Order Act 1986 s.14A(9) suggests that a limited right of access would apply to a highway or a roadway. Under s.14A(9A), as inserted by the Land Reform (Scotland) Act 2003 (asp 2) Sch.2 para.9, the references in s.14A to the public's right (or limited right) of access does not include any right which the public or any member of the public may have by way of "access rights" within the meaning of Pt 1 of the 2003 Act.

[30] I.e the person in Scotland lawfully entitled to natural possession of that land—s.14A(9), s.v. "occupier", at (b).

[31] See The Public Order Act 1986 s.14A(1)(*b*).

[32] See The Public Order Act 1986 s.14A(6) for the maximum area and time-period allowed to such an order.

[33] See The Public Order Act 1986 s.14A(5)(*a*),(*b*).

[34] The offences are contained in s.14B.

[35] See The Public Order Act 1986 s.14C.

2. MALICIOUS MISCHIEF

Introduction

Malicious mischief might well be taken to be a result crime (see above, para.2– **11–08** 36) since the actions of the accused must normally be shown to have destroyed or damaged property belonging to another.[36] However, there are up to four different versions of the crime, and one of these appears to require no result at all (see below, para.11–23). Hume's account of malicious mischief[37] is particularly confusing and perplexing, and lends itself to misconstruction, as is evident in the case of *HM Advocate v Wilson*.[38] In an attempt to allay further confusion, four accounts of this crime are set out separately below, namely: Riotous and Wilful Mischief; Traditional Malicious Mischief; "Wilson" Type Malicious Mischief; and "Stewart" Malicious Mischief.

RIOTOUS AND WILFUL MISCHIEF

Hume[39] deals with a variety of cases which seem characterised by a form of **11–09** mobbing.[40] Certainly the essence of these appears to be "violent or tumultuous molestation, intrusion, or invasion of property",[41] in the course of which damage may be very slight, or even non-existent as in *Mungo Grant*.[42] There, the rightful possessor was simply denied access to his house by the intrusion of the accused with an armed force. In other examples in this series, the damage that did occur was predicated upon the vindication of some alleged civil wrong, such as the raising of turf for a bowling green from a disputed piece of land[43] or the encroachment upon the accused's loft in the parish church.[44] Further in *Glass of Sauchie v Monro of Auchinbowie*,[45] although the accused was alleged to have broken down dam-dykes and thus stopped the machinery at a mill, it was claimed that he enjoyed at least the privilege of doing so in order to draw water for mills on his own property. That all of these cases were essentially civil matters is clearly admitted by Hume,[46] when he writes:

> "These judgments may serve as a specimen of the course of practice in former times, (for of late years the Civil Courts have more commonly been resorted to for the redress of such injuries)."

Their rationale as criminal causes was consequently not dependent on the damage done but rather on "the due regard to the order and tranquillity of society." Of

---

[36] See, e.g. *Lord Advocate's Reference (No.1 of 2000)*, 2001 S.C.C.R. 296, at 309C, para.30.
[37] Hume, *Commentaries*, i, 122–125.
[38] *HM Advocate v Wilson*, 1984 S.L.T. 117; see particularly the opinions of Lord Justice-Clerk Wheatley and Lord McDonald.
[39] Hume, *Commentaries*, i, 122–123; see Alison, *Principles*, i, 448–449.
[40] See below, paras 12–02 to 12–09.
[41] Hume, *Commentaries*, i, 124.
[42] *Mungo Grant* (1712) Hume, *Commentaries*, i, 122.
[43] *Trotter of Mortonhall* (1714) Hume, *Commentaries*, i, 123.
[44] *Henry Trotter of Mortonhall* (1730) Hume, *Commentaries*, i, 123.
[45] *Glass of Sauchie v Monro of Auchinbowie* (1713) Hume, *Commentaries*, i, 122.
[46] Hume, *Commentaries*, i, 124.

course, it is correct that Hume thought true (or "traditional") malicious mischief depended upon significant damage, in the absence of violence or tumult; but these strange, civil-dispute, insignificant-damage cases are really of their own kind, and Hume's "grounds of relevancy in such cases" must be employed with caution in other types of malicious mischief.[47]

11–10   That they have not been employed with caution[48] means that Hume's "grounds of relevancy" and other comments cannot entirely be ignored. In particular he comments that:

> "It does not serve to acquit the pannel . . . that he proceeded in the belief of a civil wrong, previously committed by the pursuer [sic] against him: He is not excusable when he forgets that the courts of law are open to his complaint."[49]

Further, he notes that in this type of case

> "the pannel shall equally be convicted, whether he interferes with the property of another, or with his state only of peaceable and lawful possession."[50]

But that his comments here are confined to a special form of the crime is revealed in his final remark, namely:

> "That which the law chiefly regards in such debates, is not so much the patrimonial damage, which in most of these instances was but trifling, as the insult to the public and the individual, by the violence and tumult attending the execution."[51]

Actus reus and mens rea

11–11   So far as it can be determined, the actus reus of this type of the crime depends upon unauthorised interference with, and not necessarily physical damage to, the property of another, in circumstances of violence, tumult and public disturbance.[52] The mens rea appears to be "wilfulness"[53]; and it is not a defence that the accused acted out of a misapprehension of his civil law rights.[54]

TRADITIONAL MALICIOUS MISCHIEF

11–12   Traditional malicious mischief consists in the intentional or reckless damaging of property belonging to another, without that other's consent or permission.[55] Hume

---

[47] Hume, *Commentaries*, i, 124.
[48] See, e.g. *HM Advocate v Wilson*, 1984 S.L.T. 117.
[49] Hume, *Commentaries*, i, 124. In practice the courts have vacillated between giving effect to, and ignoring this remark in relation to examples of "traditional" malicious mischief; see below, paras 11–15 to 11–17.
[50] Reliance on these words has produced a novel type of malicious mischief in recent years; see above *Wilson*, 1984 S.L.T. 117 per Lord Justice-Clerk Wheatley at 119 and Lord McDonald at 120 to 121.
[51] Hume, *Commentaries*, i, 124.
[52] See, e.g. *Archibald Bar* (1834) Bell's Notes 47.
[53] Hume, *Commentaries*, i, 122.
[54] Hume, *Commentaries*, i, 124.
[55] Gordon, *Criminal Law*, 3rd edn (2000/2001), paras 22.01, 22.03.

clearly recognised this form of the crime[56] but required the damage to be "great" or considerable if conviction was to follow in the absence of violence and tumult. The modern law, however, does not appear to insist on any such restriction, since even the "injury" done to grass by walking over it has been held sufficient for this form of the crime.[57]

Actus reus

It has been said that "an omission could never be an act of malicious mischief"[58] **11–13** and this is probably correct in this form of the crime. The accused must, therefore, bring about the damage or destruction by positive acts on his part. Certainly, all of the reported cases are of that description. In relation to inanimate things, these include the cutting of leather hosepipes[59]; or a horse's harness[60]; the breaking of window panes[61]; the burning of a "chariot" by pouring acid on it[62]; the tearing down of a fence[63]; the knocking away of pit-props such that the roof of a mine fell in[64]; the ruination of several thousand gallons of oil by opening containers and letting the liquid run to waste[65]; damaging a ship, its fittings and equipment[66]; and the setting fire to growing trees and plants.[67] The injury or killing of animals is also relevant. Thus in *Thomas Bellie*[68] poisoned feed-stuffs were thrown into a neighbour's yard where they killed some of her hens; and in *Archibald Thomson*[69] the accused killed a cow in calf by inserting the handle of a pitch-fork into the animal's vagina. Likewise, trampling plants or pulling them out by the roots must be sufficient for this form of malicious mischief.[70] If, however, property is not destroyed or damaged where it is found, but first taken away from where the owner or legal possessor left it, that would normally be theft rather than the present crime.[71] It is, therefore, surprising that one of the three charges of malicious mischief in *Samuel Wallace and Thomas Ferguson*[72] referred to the removal of a gate and the dumping of it in a canal, unless, of course, the time interval involved had been so slight as to be considered irrelevant.[73]

---

[56] Hume, *Commentaries*, i, 122, 124.
[57] *Ward v Robertson*, 1938 J.C. 32.
[58] *HM Advocate v Wilson*, 1984 S.L.T. 117, per Lord Stewart (dissenting) at 122, commenting on a Crown concession there.
[59] *Robert Hall* (1837) 1 Swin. 420.
[60] *Speid v Whyte* (1864) 4 Irv. 584; though this was later thought to be too trivial by Lord Justice-General Clyde in *Clark v Syme*, 1957 J.C. 1 at 6.
[61] *Ann Duthie* (1849) J. Shaw 227.
[62] *Colin Campbell* (1823) Alison, *Principles*, i, 450.
[63] *John and William Black v Laing* (1879) 4 Coup. 276.
[64] *Nicolson Muir* (1825) Alison, *Principles*, i, 450.
[65] *David Munro* (1831) Bell's Notes 48.
[66] *Lord Advocate's Reference (No.1 of 2000)*, 2001 S.C.C.R. 296.
[67] *Archibald Phaup* (1846) Ark. 176, although the charge there might more appropriately have been one of reckless fire-raising.
[68] *Thomas Bellie* (1600) Hume, *Commentaries*, i, 124.
[69] *Archibald Thomson* (1874) 2 Coup. 551.
[70] See, e.g. *Samuel Wallace and Thomas Ferguson* (1839) Bell's Notes 47.
[71] See Alison, *Principles*, i, 273–274.
[72] *Samuel Wallace and Thomas Ferguson* (1839) Bell's Notes 47.
[73] See Burnett, *A Treatise on Various Branches of the Criminal Law of Scotland* (1811), p.116.

Mens rea

11–14   The title of the crime here is, of course, malicious mischief, which suggests that the mens rea required is "malice." Malice, indeed, was said by Lord Justice-Clerk Wheatley[74] to connote "the evil intent deliberately to do injury or damage to the property", though no authority was advanced to justify such a view. Nevertheless, that interpretation allied to Hume's insistence[75] that the damage or destruction be "wilful" suggests that the appropriate mens rea is intention.[76] If intention to damage or destroy can be shown or inferred from the circumstances, then that is certainly sufficient for conviction, and there is no need to show any further intent to spite the owner.[77] However, such intention is not necessary for conviction. As Lord Justice-Clerk Aitchison laid down in *Ward v Robertson*[78]:

> "It is not essential to the offence of malicious mischief that there should be a deliberate wicked intent to injure another in his property. I am prepared to take the case upon the footing, although it may involve some departure from the law as laid down by Hume, that it is enough if the damage is done by a person who shows a deliberate disregard of, or even indifference to, the property or possessory rights of others."

This strongly suggests that simple recklessness is an alternative form of mens rea for the crime[79]; and indeed Lord Justice-Clerk Aitchison's above quoted remarks were specifically approved by Lord Justice-General Clyde in *Clark v Syme*.[80] Consequently, if the damage or destruction can be shown to have been the product of the accused's recklessness (see above, paras 3–30 to 3–33), then conviction must follow. Such recklessness cannot always be inferred, however. Thus, in *Ward v Robertson*[81] mens rea could not be inferred from the mere fact that the appellant had walked in a straight line through a field of ordinary grass, causing some trivial damage thereto. No reasonable person would have considered any real or lasting harm to have been so caused. But the matter would have been different, as Lord Justice-Clerk Aitchison emphasised,[82] if a stroll had been taken through a more obvious crop (the grass here having been intended merely for sheep grazing), or, as Lord Mackay put it,[83] if the appellant had deliberately trampled the grass by taking many more steps than were necessary to traverse the field

---

74 *HM Advocate v Wilson*, 1984 S.L.T. 117 at 119, col.2.
75 Hume, *Commentaries*, i, 122.
76 Cf. Alison, *Principles*, i, 448, where mention is made of "the wanton or reckless destruction of property." See also *Lord Advocate's Reference (No.1 of 2000)*, 2001 S.C.C.R. 296, opinion of the court at 309C, para.30: "The *mens rea* of the crime in the case of intentional damage . . . consists in the knowledge that the destructive conduct complained of was carried out with complete disregard for, or indifference to the property or possessory rights of another." (The court there then referred to *Ward*, 1938 J.C. 32.)
77 *Archibald Thomson* (1874) 2 Coup. 551, per Lord Deas at 553; *Lord Advocate's Reference (No.1 of 2000)*, 2001 S.C.C.R. 296, opinion of the court at 309E, para.31.
78 *Ward v Robertson*, 1938 J.C. 32 at 36.
79 See Gordon, *Criminal Law*, 3rd edn (2000/2001), para.22.03.
80 *Clark v Syme*, 1957 J.C. 1 at 5.
81 *Ward v Robertson*, 1938 J.C. 32.
82 *Ward v Robertson*, 1938 J.C. 32 at 36.
83 *Ward v Robertson*, 1938 J.C. 32, at 37–38.

or by walking round and round in circles. It is also clear, however, that careless-ness will not be sufficient, even apparently if gross.[84]

Vindication of rights

Hume appears to remark generally that if damage or destruction is done **11–15** under a "misapprehension of right", that will not secure an acquittal.[85] This was undoubtedly upheld in *Clark v Syme*[86] where a farmer shot a sheep belonging to a neighbour on the basis that that neighbour had refused to prevent his animals straying into the farmer's fields and consuming turnips there. He shot the sheep in the belief that he was entitled to do so to protect his own property. His acquittal on a charge of malicious mischief was reversed on appeal, however, Lord Justice-General Clyde[87] holding:

"The respondent in this case acted deliberately. He knew what he was doing and he displayed in his actings a complete disregard of the rights of others."

The fact that the respondent had acted under a mistake of law did not afford him a defence.[88] The approach of the courts to this defence in relation to malicious mischief has not, however, been entirely consistent.

In *Speid v Whyte*[89] the condition on which timber was to be auctioned was that **11–16** the price should be paid before removal. Because some of the timber was located too far from a road to make extraction of it economic, the auctioneer purported to sell it to a neighbouring farmer who insisted that he be allowed to remove it forth-with. When the owner of the timber realised that this particular lot of wood was being removed without the price having been first paid, he remonstrated with the farmer's men who were even then loading it up, and eventually he cut the harness securing a horse to a cart. For this he was convicted of malicious mischief—but acquitted on appeal. As Lord Neaves put the matter[90]:

"[The appellant] was undoubtedly the proprietor of the wood till the condi-tions of sale were implemented, which they had not been; and although he may not have acted judiciously, or even legally, in the course he adopted to vindicate his property, still he did act in vindication of his supposed rights, and not merely from a desire to injure or destroy the property of another."

Whether the essence of this case can be distinguished from that in *Clark v Syme* must be doubted[91] but Lord Neaves also said

"[the acts done] do not amount to that reckless and wilful destruction of property which is essential to the constitution of malicious mischief."

---

[84] See *Archibald Phaup* (1846) Ark. 176, per Lord Justice-Clerk Hope's charge to the jury at 177.
[85] Hume, *Commentaries*, i, 122.
[86] *Clark v Syme*, 1957 J.C. 1.
[87] *Clark v Syme*, 1957 J.C. 1 at 5.
[88] See *Lord Advocate's Reference (No.1 of 2000)*, 2001 S.C.C.R. 296, opinion of the court at 335E, para.109. See also above, paras 8–40 to 8–44.
[89] *Speid v Whyte* (1864) 4 Irv. 584.
[90] *Speid v Whyte* (1864) 4 Irv. 584 at 586.
[91] See Gordon, *Criminal Law*, 3rd edn (2000/2001), para.22.10.

These words can be construed such as to rest the acquittal on the de minimis principle (see above, para.2–54); and indeed Lord Justice-General Clyde in a much later case considered that the acquittal there had been right on that basis, namely, that the trivial nature of what had been done was not consistent with the correct degree of recklessness or wilfulness required by the crime.[92] Significantly, it was not considered to have been correct on the grounds that a proprietor is entitled to damage the property of another in order to safeguard his own.[93]

11–17   Again, in *John and William Black v Laing*[94] a father and son were eventually acquitted of malicious mischief on appeal. They had torn down a fence, recently erected by another along the boundary of a piece of land they possessed, on the basis that it had blocked the only access to their land. Although no formal opinion was delivered by the court, it does appear that the appellants were felt to be justified in destroying the fence in these circumstances.[95] In a later case with not dissimilar facts, however, the accused was convicted and his appeal dismissed.[96] Either, as Gordon suggests,[97] these cases cannot be relied upon and there is no defence of acting in vindication of supposed rights, or each such case must be dealt with individually and decided according to its own facts and circumstances, a not uncommon way for Scots criminal courts to deal with awkward issues. It seems, however, that the matter may have been placed beyond doubt by the *Lord Advocate's Reference (No.1 of 2000)*,[98] since in that case one of the questions specifically referred to the High Court was this: "(3) Does the belief of an accused person that his or her actions are justified in law constitute a defence to a charge of malicious mischief . . . ?"[99] The Court's response was as follows:

> "The unequivocal answer to the question . . . is provided in the opinion of Lord Justice-General Clyde in *Clark v Syme* at p. 5. The mere fact that a person carried out acts which constituted a crime under a mistaken conception of legal rights is not a defence."[100]

Although the pre-*Clark v Syme* cases were not considered, it must be assumed that they are now of little or no authority. It is still possible, however, that vindication of supposed rights might be pled in mitigation of sentence.[101]

Provocation

11–18   It would seem on principle that provocation should be able to be pled in mitigation in a malicious mischief case (involving damage to property) just as it may be in a case of assault (involving injury to the person). In practice, this appears to be true. In *Andrew Steuart*[102] the accused, who had had his gun with him for sporting

---

[92] *Clark v Syme*, 1957 J.C. 1 at 6.
[93] Cf. *Lord Advocate's Reference (No.1 of 2000)*, 2001 S.C.C.R. 296.
[94] *John and William Black v Laing* (1879) 4 Coup. 276.
[95] *John and William Black v Laing* (1879) 4 Coup. 276 at 278.
[96] See *Forbes v Ross* (1898) 2 Adam 513.
[97] Gordon, *Criminal Law*, 3rd edn (2000/2001), paras 22.09, 22.11.
[98] *Lord Advocate's Reference (No.1 of 2000)*, 2001 S.C.C.R. 296.
[99] *Lord Advocate's Reference (No.1 of 2000)*, 2001 S.C.C.R. 296, quoted at 297.
[100] *Lord Advocate's Reference (No.1 of 2000)*, 2001 S.C.C.R. 296, at 335E, para.109.
[101] See *McDonald v Mackay* (1842) 1 Broun 435.
[102] *Andrew Steuart* (1874) 2 Coup. 554.

purposes on the day in question, shot a horse belonging to a tenant farmer of his who had provoked him by removing most of the crops before the rent due for his property had been met. As Lord Deas remarked[103]:

> "It is not in the least surprising that you were much offended and angry at what was going on. That, however, only goes to mitigate the offence. It does not take it away."

"WILSON" TYPE MALICIOUS MISCHIEF

This type of malicious mischief was recognised in the case of *HM Advocate v* **11–19** *Wilson*[104] and may generally be described as the unauthorised interference with another's property such as to cause deliberate consequential loss to the owner or lawful possessor. In this form of the crime, no physical damage need be caused to existing property at all.

In *Wilson* the accused was charged with malicious mischief in that he had **11–20** pressed the emergency stop-button of a turbine at a power station

> "whereby the full generation and feeding of electricity into the national electricity grid was brought to a halt for 28 hours or thereby and 12,113,800 kilowatt hour units of electricity . . . were lost and had to be replaced and fed into the national grid from other sources at a cost of £147,000 or thereby."[105]

The accused objected to the relevancy of this charge in that no physical damage had been caused either to the stop-button or to the turbine itself. This argument succeeded before Sheriff D.B. Smith but was rejected by a majority of the Appeal Court. Lord Justice-Clerk Wheatley[106] considered that physical damage was not essential to this type of charge, either because it accorded with Hume's views or because there was "a wider cover to be given to the earlier view of the nature of the offence." However, his Lordship could only achieve congruity with Hume by importing from "Riotous and Wilful Mischief" the conclusion that

> "the pannel shall equally be convicted, whether he interfere with the property of another, or with his state only of peaceable and lawful possession."[107]

It will be recalled, however, that mere interference with, as opposed to damage to, property was only to be considered criminal where there was also violence and tumult. As no violence or tumult was adverted to in the indictment, then it must follow that Lord Justice-Clerk Wheatley and Lord McDonald were really here extending the notion of traditional malicious mischief so as to create a novel form of the crime. It is thus criminal to interfere deliberately with the property of another with the intention of causing its owner or legal possessor financial loss,

---

[103] *Andrew Steuart* (1874) 2 Coup. 554 at 555.
[104] *HM Advocate v Wilson*, 1984 S.L.T. 117.
[105] *HM Advocate v Wilson*, 1984 S.L.T. 117, quoted in the opinion of Lord Justice-Clerk Weatley at 118.
[106] *HM Advocate v Wilson*, 1984 S.L.T. 117 at 120.
[107] Hume, *Commentaries*, i, 124; *HM Advocate v Wilson*, 1984 S.L.T. 117, per Lord McDonald at 120.

where such loss is actually incurred and where the property interfered with remains itself entirely undamaged. Loss, however, *must* be actual: in a case where the alleged conduct of the accused consisted in the redirecting of a surveillance camera so that it no longer cast its protective gaze over the front and entrance of bank premises, it was held that there was no loss since the running costs of the device would have been incurred in any event, and the "loss" of the security and deterrent effects normally provided by the camera were not quantifiable losses for the purposes of malicious mischief.[108]

11–21   Extending the ambit of a crime by judicial decision is not, of course, entirely illegitimate or unknown in a common law based system; and there is indeed something illogical in concluding that had the stop-button in *Wilson* been operated by being hit with a hammer then malicious mischief would have been a relevant charge, whereas that would not have been so if an "undamaging" finger had been used to operate it instead. That type of illogicality clearly weighed heavily with Lord Justice-Clerk Wheatley[109] and Lord McDonald.[110] But, as Lord Stewart[111] pointed out in his dissenting judgment

"if the infliction of damage is an essential element of the crime then the absence of such damage takes the actings, however reprehensible, out of the category of criminality . . . The distinction may seem narrow and artificial but it is nevertheless a distinction which in my opinion the law has made."

A dissenting judgment, however, can have no bearing on the outcome of the case—which is that a new form of malicious mischief has been conceived by the majority in *Wilson*. It differs from "Riotous and Wilful Mischief" in that no violence or tumult need be shown; and it differs from "Traditional Malicious Mischief" in that no physical damage to property need be caused.

Mens rea

11–22   It is as yet not entirely clear whether this new form of the crime can be committed recklessly. Although the indictment certainly referred to "wilfully, recklessly and maliciously" activating the emergency stop-button, Lord Justice-Clerk Wheatley's opinion[112] refers to the deliberate nature of the initial act, and to the Crown's proper concession that "consequential injury has to be intended", as also elsewhere to the libel's being

"habile to carry the inference that the initial positive, wilful, reckless and malicious act was intended to harm the employer by causing patrimonial injury."

This is admittedly rather confusing[113] and scarcely settles the matter.

---

[108] *Bett v Hamilton*, 1997 S.C.C.R. 621.
[109] *HM Advocate v Wilson*, 1984 S.L.T. 117 at 119, col.2.
[110] *HM Advocate v Wilson*, 1984 S.L.T. 117 at 121, col.1.
[111] *HM Advocate v Wilson*, 1984 S.L.T. 117 at 122, col.1.
[112] *HM Advocate v Wilson*, 1984 S.L.T. 117 at 119, col.2.
[113] See also Lord McDonald's opinion at 120, col.2, to 121, col.1.

"STEWART" MALICIOUS MISCHIEF

Lord Stewart's interesting dissenting opinion in *HM Advocate v Wilson*[114] contains **11–23** the following passage:

> "The term [i.e. malicious mischief] also includes maliciously placing any obstruction on a railway or wilfully and recklessly doing so in a manner calculated to obstruct [this being a quotation from Macdonald, *Criminal Law*, 5th edn (1948), p.84] (see *Miller* and *Murdoch*). Actual damage to property may not be necessary if the malicious act is clearly intended to cause such damage."[115]

As stated above at para.11–21, the content of a dissenting judgment can hardly be taken as a statement of law; but since Lord Stewart here envisages a form of malicious mischief without physical damage (apparently contrary to his own view of the crime) and refers for support to two nineteenth-century cases, his views merit some consideration.

Of the two cases to which Lord Stewart referred, only that of *David Miller*[116] is **11–24** truly relevant. There the accused placed a stone on the rails of a railway line at a time when he knew a train carrying passengers was due. In fact, the danger of damage to the train and of injury to passengers was averted, since some unknown third party removed the stone before the train could make contact with it.[117] Miller pled guilty to a charge at common law of:

> "Wilfully, maliciously and unlawfully placing [that stone] . . . in a manner calculated and intended to obstruct such train and carriages and to endanger the lives and safety of the passengers and others travelling thereby."

If this was genuinely an instance of malicious mischief, then, since the case has never been overruled or questioned, it was understandable that Lord Stewart should wish to consider it along with his account of the crime. But the case contains no discussion of malicious mischief at all. Nor does the reporter (Arkley) refer to it, or index it as an example of such a crime. Indeed, it seems closer to the crime of endangering the lieges[118] than to malicious mischief.

In short, it is submitted that *Miller* does not disclose an exceptional form of **11–25** malicious mischief at all. Rather at best it is, or would now be treated as, an example of attempted "traditional malicious mischief"—distinguishable from the completed crime by the very fact that no damage transpired. It seems to follow then that conduct which does not result in actual damage and which is not accompanied by violence and tumult or consequential loss cannot amount to the completed crime of malicious mischief, no matter how clear the intention to cause physical damage may appear to be. If this is correct, then the statutory form of charge in Sch.5 of the Criminal Procedure (Scotland) Act 1995—"You did

---

[114] *HM Advocate v Wilson*, 1984 S.L.T. 117 at 121–122.
[115] *HM Advocate v Wilson*, 1984 S.L.T. 117 at 122, col.1.
[116] *David Miller* (1848) Ark. 525.
[117] Cf. *John E. Murdoch* (1849) J. Shaw 229, where a similarly placed stone was not removed and much actual damage ensued.
[118] See above, para.9–35.

maliciously place a block of wood on the railway line and attempt to obstruct a train"—may simply be an example of attempted malicious mischief, or, if not that, then an example of an attempt to commit a distinct crime of obstruction.

3. Vandalism

11–26   A statutory crime with a specification similar to that of "traditional malicious mischief" was created in 1980,[119] but now appears in s.52 of the Criminal Law (Consolidation) (Scotland) Act 1995. In terms of that section

"any person who, without reasonable excuse, wilfully or recklessly destroys or damages any property belonging to another shall be guilty of the crime of vandalism."

This offence is plainly close to "traditional malicious mischief" in that it insists that there be actual damage caused to property and specifies that the mens rea required may be either wilfulness or recklessness. But there are some differences too. The Appeal Court, for example, in *Black v Allan*[120] emphasised that the statutory offence was not a mere echo of malicious mischief, but a separate crime in its own right. In particular, where recklessness is advanced as the appropriate form of mens rea, *Black v Allan* holds that part (at least) of the test for that in *Allan v Patterson*[121] is to be applied. Consequently, where one youth jumped on another's back in the course of horseplay in a public street and was somehow thrown or shrugged-off into a nearby glass window-pane (which broke), it was wrong for justices of the peace in a district court to conclude that there had been recklessness simply because there was always some danger of breakage when youths "fooled around" in such ways. What the justices should have asked themselves was whether the actions of the accused created such an obvious and material risk of damage to the window as to be considered reckless.[122]

11–27   Vandalism also differs from its common law equivalent in that the damage or destruction must be "without reasonable excuse." It will be necessary, therefore, for the Crown to show that what the accused did was without such excuse—not something which can be affirmatively stated in relation to traditional malicious mischief. What amounts to a reasonable excuse will depend on the facts and circumstances of each case.[123] In *MacDougall v Yuk-Sun Ho*,[124] for example, in immediate response to the breaking of a shop window by an unknown passer-by, the shop proprietor rushed into the street and damaged the windscreen of a car in which he erroneously supposed the culprit to be about to effect his escape: this was held to be a reasonable excuse in the given circumstances.[125] On the other

---

[119] Criminal Justice (Scotland) Act 1980 s.78(1).
[120] *Black v Allan*, 1985 S.C.C.R. 11 at 12–13.
[121] *Allan v Patterson*, 1980 J.C. 57; see above, para.3–31.
[122] It has, of course, not been determined whether the *Allan v Patterson* notion of recklessness (or any part of it) is applicable to "traditional malicious mischief."
[123] See *John v Donnelly*, 1999 S.C.C.R. 802 at 805C.
[124] *MacDougall v Yuk-Sun Ho*, 1985 S.C.C.R. 199.
[125] Cf. *Murray v O'Brien*, 1994 S.L.T. 1051, where the court held that a district court had not been wrong to decide that there was no reasonable excuse in circumstances which *ex facie* were not too dissimilar to those in *MacDougall v Yuk-Sun Ho*, 1985 S.C.C.R. 199.

hand, it has been decided that a sincerely held "belief in the illegality of nuclear weapons" and anxiety "at their potential appalling effects" did not amount to a reasonable excuse, where the accused had "quite deliberately and without any immediate stimulus" damaged the perimeter fence at a naval depot where submarines capable of carrying such weapons were based.[126]

Maximum penalties, as between malicious mischief and vandalism, are also different. As usual, conviction of the common law crime exposes the accused to the maximum range which the trial court possesses (see Appendix D); but the statutory offence[127] carries a maximum fine of level 3 on the standard scale (see Appendix C) or a maximum prison sentence of 60 days, or both of these, in a JP court, and maxima of the "prescribed sum" (see Appendix C) and/or three months (six months for a second or subsequent conviction) in a sheriff court. In addition, summary procedure is mandatory for vandalism whereas malicious mischief in its common law manifestations can be, and often is, taken on indictment.

4. FIRE-RAISING

Introduction

In essence, the crime of fire-raising involves the intentional or reckless **11–28** damaging or destroying of corporeal property belonging to another without his consent or permission. As such, it is simply a serious form of "traditional malicious mischief" where the damage or destruction is achieved in a specific way.[128] In modern times, therefore, there is probably little justification for treating fire-raising as a separate common law crime; but it does continue to be so treated.[129] In fact, however, there are two *separate* fire-raising offences. These are referred to as "wilful fire-raising" and "culpable and reckless fire-raising",[130] and are distinguished by their differing mens rea requirements—of "intention" in the former and "recklessness" in the latter. As there is no statutory or common law rule permitting a conviction for culpable and reckless fire-raising to be returned on a charge which libelled only wilful fire-raising, it follows that prosecutors often charge both offences in the alternative, so that, in effect and depending on the evidence, both forms of mens rea can be considered by the court or jury.[131] The rationale advanced in *Byrne v HM Advocate*[132] for having two separate offences is that "the degree of blameworthiness will be relevant to penalty"—thus confirming that prima facie intentionally caused harm is more deserving of punishment than harm effected by recklessness. For the avoidance of doubt, it must be noted that, whatever may have been the law in the past, the

---

[126] *John v Donnelly*, 1999 S.C.C.R. 802 at 805B–D.
[127] See the Criminal Law (Consolidation) (Scotland) Act 1995 s.52(3).
[128] See *John Mackirdy* (1856) 2 Irv. 474, per Lord Justice-Clerk Hope at 475.
[129] See, e.g. *Carr v HM Advocate*, 1995 S.L.T. 800; *Byrne v HM Advocate*, 2000 S.C.C.R. 77.
[130] *Byrne v HM Advocate*, 2000 S.C.C.R. 77 (court of five judges), opinion of the court, at 91G.
[131] *Byrne v HM Advocate*, 2000 S.C.C.R. 77, opinion of the court at 92B–C. Cf. malicious mischief, which is *one* offence with two alternative forms of mens rea.
[132] *Byrne v HM Advocate (No.2)*, 2000 S.C.C.R. 77 at 92B.

two fire-raising offences apply to the setting of fire to *any* type of corporeal property.[133]

WILFUL FIRE-RAISING

11–29 This may be defined as the intentional setting fire to corporeal property owned by another without his permission. Under s.5(4) of the Criminal Procedure (Scotland) Act 1995, it is competent to try wilful fire-raisings summarily—but not in a JP court.[134] Consequently, perhaps, under s.52(2) of the Criminal Law (Consolidation) (Scotland) Act 1995, it is declared incompetent "to charge acts which constitute the offence of wilful fire-raising as vandalism."[135]

Actus reus

11–30 It is sufficient if the property has been burnt to any degree, no matter how small.[136] Provided the fire has "taken effect", as nineteenth-century indictments put it,[137] then the actus reus of the crime is complete, even if the fire is extinguished by a "well disposed person" or of its own accord before any great damage has been done.[138] The property set on fire must, however, belong to another[139]; and in one nineteenth-century case, it was declared that an indictment was defective in that it failed to state that the shop set on fire was the property of someone other than the accused, notwithstanding that he had been designed as a mere tenant of the premises.[140] It is clear, therefore, that a tenant who sets fire to premises let to him has fulfilled the actus reus of the crime.[141] Curiously, the older text-writers state that although it is generally not criminal for an owner of property to set fire to it, since, of course, it is his own, it may be "wilful fire-raising" for him to do so if that property has been let to a tenant or is subject to a liferent interest at the time.[142] It is, thus, not sufficiently his own, if subject to a tenancy; yet not sufficiently the tenant's own, if the tenant sets fire to it. According to Alison[143] it is not the existence of the tenancy or liferent right that matters, but rather whether the tenant or liferenter has taken occupancy or possession. This may be a just way of looking at these complex cases since it focuses attention on

---

[133] *Byrne v HM Advocate (No.2)*, 2000 S.C.C.R. 77 at 92A, B. For an account of the complexities of the law prior to the decision in the leading case of *Byrne v HM Advocate*, see (e.g.) the second edition of this book (Edinburgh: W. Green, 1996), paras 11–28 to 11–42. See also J. Chalmers, "Fireraising: From the Ashes?" (2000) S.L.T. (News) 57, which contains a critique of *Byrne*.

[134] Criminal Procedure (Scotland) Act 1995 s.7(8)(b)(i), as modified by the Criminal Proceedings etc. (Reform) Scotland Act 2007 (asp 6) Sch. para.9(4). The exclusion extends to attempted wilful fire-raising.

[135] This rule also applies, however, to the sheriff court.

[136] Alison, *Principles*, i, 429; *John Arthur* (1836) 1 Swin. 124, per Lord Justice-Clerk Boyle at 152.

[137] See Hume, *Commentaries*, i, 127–128.

[138] See, e.g. *John Arthur* (1836) 1 Swin. 124, where due to the prompt action of a passer-by, a door was burnt only to the extent of one twentieth of an inch, according at least to the accused's counsel at 149; see also *Peter Grieve* (1866) 5 Irv. 263.

[139] Hume, *Commentaries*, i, 132–133.

[140] *John Mackirdy* (1856) 2 Irv. 474.

[141] Hume, *Commentaries*, i, 132; *Margaret Drysdale* (1826) Alison, *Principles*, i, 435.

[142] Hume, *Commentaries*, i, 133; Alison, *Principles*, i, 437; *Walter Buchanan* (1728) Hume, *Commentaries*, i, 133.

[143] Alison, *Principles*, i, 437.

the danger to property or persons rather than on ownership; but there is no other warrant for it[144] and it strays rather far from the concept of "belonging to another."

Mens rea

The fire must be raised "wilfully", and Hume[145] leaves his reader in no doubt **11–31** that that means "with a purpose to destroy the thing to which it is applied." Provided that there is such a purpose, then setting fire to something other than the property meant to be burned, in the knowledge that the fire will naturally and inescapably spread to that property, is probably sufficient.[146] Thus, for example, to set fire to a pile of furnishings (moveable property) within a house, meaning and expecting it to take effect on the fabric of the house itself, will be enough for wilful fire-raising of that house (as well as of the original moveables) if the house or any of its fixtures is actually burnt to any degree. Even setting fire to one's own property will suffice if the fire spreads to a neighbour's property—provided that the spreading of fire to his property had been one's intention all along.

The *mens rea* of "wilful fire-raising" is thus intention—actual intention to **11–32** damage or destroy the property burned.[147] Hume,[148] however, went further than that and considered a form of transferred mens rea to be applicable. If a person, for example, set fire to property A owned by another, intending to destroy or damage A only, but the fire spread to property B also owned by that other, then that person would be guilty of wilful fire-raising in respect of B, all other things being equal, provided that the spread of the fire to B was

> "not of quite a fortuitous and extraordinary nature, but such as might natu-rally and not improbably ensue ... What has ensued is a mischief, though higher, of the very same sort as that which he intended, and so likely to happen, that when he did the one, he must have been utterly indifferent whether this damage also should or should not ensue".[149]

Gordon[150] was of the opinion that Scots law did not accept the concept of trans-ferred mens rea, at all; but, since the airing of that opinion in 1978, the Appeal Court accepted that that concept does apply to assault (see above, para.3–37). It was possible, therefore, that it might also apply to "wilful fire-raising." The Appeal Court has subsequently determined, however, that that is not so. In *Blane v HM Advocate*,[151] the accused set fire to a quilt in the room he occupied in a hostel. His intention was to create smoke so that he could inhale the same and thus commit suicide. He did not intend that flames should be caused, and did not intend, or apparently even foresee, that any fire so created should, or might, spread to the hostel building itself. In the event, fire did take hold on the building—some £15,000 worth of damage being caused. The accused was charged with wilful

---

[144] Cf. Hume, *Commentaries*, i, 133.
[145] Hume, *Commentaries*, i, 128.
[146] Hume, *Commentaries*, i, 129–130.
[147] *Byrne v HM Advocate*, 2000 S.C.C.R. 77, opinion of the court at 92A.
[148] Hume, *Commentaries*, i, 130.
[149] Hume, *Commentaries*, i, 130.
[150] Gordon, *Criminal Law*, 2nd edn (1978), para.22–26.
[151] *Blane v HM Advocate*, 1991 S.C.C.R. 576; see also *Byrne v HM Advocate*, 2000 S.C.C.R. 77, opinion of the court at 90A.

fire-raising in relation to the bedding *and* the premises and was convicted (the sheriff having directed the jury in accordance with Hume's notion of transferred intent). On appeal, the court considered that an intention, directly or indirectly, to set fire to the hostel building was essential for conviction in respect of the building itself, and that a fulfilled intention to set fire only to moveable property which just happened in turn to set fire to the building was insufficient.

11–33 Intention to set fire to the property described in the complaint or indictment may, of course, be inferred from the evidence and in particular from the accused's conduct.[152] In *Blane v HM Advocate*,[153] however, it was suggested that the necessary intention for wilful fire-raising of a hostel building might be inferred if the accused had deliberately set fire to the furnishings in his room in such a way as to demonstrate his utter indifference whether the fire might spread to the building itself or not. This suggestion, that intention might be inferred from recklessness,[154] is unsound in principle and was emphatically rejected by a full bench in *Byrne v HM Advocate*.[155] Consequently, the law is that no form of recklessness can be treated as equivalent to, or provide a basis for inferring, the necessary intent.[156]

11–34 Motive is, as usual, of no moment in ascertaining the mens rea for the crime.[157] If one intended to burn part of a house, such as a door, in order to obtain unauthorised entrance or exit, then the mens rea for wilful fire-raising would be present whatever was the ulterior reason for so intending. In *Jean Gordon or Bryan*[158] Lord Mackenzie expressed great doubt as to whether escapees from a prison at Banff could be guilty of wilful fire-raising by burning a hole in the prison door to gain their liberty. His view appears to have been that their intention was to escape and not to harm the prison itself. But if they could not effect their escape other than by burning the prison door, then surely they must have intended to damage that part of the prison by fire? In any event, Lord Mackenzie's views are obiter, since the charge was one of prison-breaking aggravated by setting fire to the doors and other parts of Banff Prison, and further are contrary to Hume's opinion, namely that

> "it does not mend the case for the pannels, that this act [burning doors and other parts of a gaol] has been subservient to the other, and also felonious offence of mobbing, breaking gaol, and setting prisoners at large."[159]

CULPABLE AND RECKLESS FIRE-RAISING

11–35 Both Hume and Alison[160] clearly advert to such a crime. Alison in particular states[161] that

---

[152] *Byrne v HM Advocate*, 2000 S.C.C.R. 77, opinion of the court at 90G–91A.
[153] *Blane v HM Advocate*, 1991 S.C.C.R. 576.
[154] See also *Carr v HM Advocate*, 1995 S.L.T. 800.
[155] *Byrne v HM Advocate*, 2000 S.C.C.R. 77, opinion of the court at 90C–91D.
[156] *Byrne v HM Advocate*, 2000 S.C.C.R. 77 at 92A.
[157] See *Robert Smillie* (1883) 5 Coup. 287, per Lord Young at 290.
[158] *Jean Gordon or Bryan* (1841) 2 Swin. 545 at 546–547.
[159] Hume, *Commentaries*, i, 131.
[160] Hume, *Commentaries*, i, 128 and Alison, *Principles*, 433.
[161] Alison, *Principles*, i, 438.

"if the burning the pannel's own house be attended with obvious risk to adjoining tenements, and one of them be actually burned in consequence, the guilty party, as for *culpable and reckless fire-raising*, is amenable to a severe punishment."

And the existence of this crime—as one separate from wilful fire-raising—has been affirmed by a full bench in *Byrne v HM Advocate*.[162] The actus reus is similar to that of wilful fire-raising.[163] If fire in fact takes effect on the property of another, and it is causally related to an act on the part of the accused, then that is sufficient.

Mens rea

This offence is readily distinguishable from wilful fire-raising in terms of the **11–36** mens rea requirement. Wilful fire-raising cannot be committed recklessly; and the sole issue here is what recklessly means in this context. In *Robert Smillie*[164] Lord Young opined:

"If a man, while engaged in some illegal act, raises a fire, he is guilty of the crime of wicked, culpable, and reckless fire-raisings."

The truth of that statement was, however, questionable at the time of its utterance; if it had correctly reflected the law, it would have meant, for example, that a careless or unlucky thief would automatically have been guilty of reckless fire-raising if he had happened to cause a fire whilst engaged in the act of stealing property. That such automatic guilt was (and is) frowned upon in Scots law seemed apparent from the case of *James Stewart and John Walsh*.[165] There, the accused were stealing whisky from a cask on a railway waggon, and one of them "allowed" his lamp to come into contact with the spirit (or the fumes emanating from it), and thus caused a fire which destroyed the whisky, two casks, a chest of tea, six chairs and the railway waggon itself. There was no question of his having intentionally set fire to those items of property, of course; but because of grave doubts voiced by the court that he had scarcely done so recklessly either (in spite of having been engaged in an "illegal act" at the time) the Solicitor-General was compelled to withdraw the charge of reckless fire-raising. Any lingering doubts as to what was determined in that case have been resolved, however, by the more modern decision in *McCue v Currie*.[166] There, the appellant had been convicted of culpable and reckless fire-raising in circumstances where he had broken into a caravan in order to commit theft. He had been using a cigarette lighter to facilitate his search for goods to remove; that lighter had "burst in his hand", been dropped, and thus caused the caravan to catch fire. The appellant knew that a conflagration had been begun; nevertheless, he left the scene without making any attempt to extinguish the blaze or summon assistance to that end. His conviction was quashed by the High Court on appeal—the court's opinion including the observation that what

---

[162] *Byrne v HM Advocate*, 2000 S.C.C.R. 77.
[163] See above, para.11–30.
[164] *Robert Smillie* (1883) 5 Coup. 287 at 291.
[165] *James Stewart and John Walsh* (1856) 2 Irv. 359.
[166] *McCue v Currie*, 2004 S.C.C.R. 200.

Lord Young had said in *Smillie* (quoted above) had not been followed, had been subject to criticism, and (inferentially) should not be applied or taken to represent the law.[167] The question remained, of course, whether, apart from that consideration, the appellant had shown the necessary "recklessness" to be convicted of the crime charged: but on the version of the facts accepted by the lower court, it was clear that the conflagration had occurred as a result of the accidental dropping of the lighter. The court was, therefore, of the opinion

> "that fire raising which is merely accidental does not demonstrate the necessary mens rea and is not a crime, and cannot become so on account of subsequent behaviour on the part of the person concerned."[168]

11–37 There have, until recently, been few judicial pronouncements on the meaning of recklessness in this form of fire-raising. In *George MacBean* Lord Justice-Clerk Hope said[169] that it would be sufficient if a person set a house on fire

> "in such a state of reckless excitement, as not to know or care what he was doing, but who had no deliberate intention of setting fire to the house."

It now seems that that is the correct approach, and that, for example, directing a jury that the test for recklessness in such a crime can be taken from the road traffic case of *Allan v Patterson*[170] would be wrong. In *Thomson v HM Advocate*[171] therefore, Lord Justice-Clerk Ross said this:

> "[I]n a case of fire raising it is not the manner of doing an act which would otherwise be lawful which is in issue [as in *reckless* driving], but the question whether the accused had the mens rea for the commission of the crime. It would have been appropriate for the sheriff therefore to confine his definition to the question whether the accused's actions showed a complete disregard for any dangers which might result from what he was doing and in particular of the fire taking effect on the premises."[172]

In so quoting, Lord Ross was agreeing entirely with the view expressed by Lord Justice-General Hope in *Carr v HM Advocate*[173]; and the correctness of these

---

[167] *McCue v Currie*, 2004 S.C.C.R. 200 at 206F, para.22.
[168] *McCue v Currie*, 2004 S.C.C.R. 200 at 207D, para.25. The court did opine, however, at 207E, para.26, that there might be a case for "enacting a new crime . . . of culpably failing to take appropriate steps after a situation of danger to persons or property has arisen as a result of a person's actings."
[169] *George MacBean* (1847) Ark. 262 at 263.
[170] *Allan v Patterson*, 1980 J.C. 57 (a case of "reckless" driving in terms of the law then current).
[171] *Thomson v HM Advocate*, 1995 S.L.T. 827 at 829E (quoting from the opinion of the Lord Justice General in *Carr v HM Advocate*, 1995 S.L.T. 800).
[172] This accords (mutatis mutandis) only with the last part of the test for recklessness given in *Allan v Patterson*, 1980 J.C. 57, per Lord Justice-General Emslie at 60.
[173] *Carr v HM Advocate*, 1995 S.L.T. 800, at 803K–L. See also 803L to 804A, where Lord Hope opined that it was wrong for the sheriff in that case to have told the jury that a *high degree* of recklessness was what was required. As in other crimes where recklessness was sufficient for the mens rea element, the true contrast was a simple one—between carelessness on the one hand and recklessness on the other.

views has been underlined in the opinion of the full bench in *Byrne v HM Advocate*.[174] It must be borne in mind, however, that the required recklessness must be "determined by reference to the act of starting the fire and not by reference to something which took place thereafter."[175]

---

[174] *Byrne v HM Advocate*, 2000 S.C.C.R. 77, at 91B.

[175] *McCue v Currie*, 2004 S.C.C.R. 200, opinion of the court at 207A, para.23. It might be noted that the court observed at 206C, para.20, "that a distinction can be drawn between [the carrying of] a lit, scrunched up, roll of paper [as in *Carr v HM Advocate*, 1994 S.C.C.R. 521] which must be inherently dangerous and a lit cigarette lighter [as in *McCue*] which, barring an accident, is reasonably safe and easily extinguishable."

CHAPTER 12

CRIMES RELATING TO PUBLIC
ORDER AND MORALITY

General introduction

12–01   This chapter introduces crimes which attempt either to prevent disorder in the community or to uphold current notions of acceptability in individual behaviour. It must be noted at the outset that it has never been easy to justify all of the offences which presently fall within such parameters. Whilst public disorder can fairly easily be seen as a "harm" which requires discouragement (although it may sometimes be a somewhat vague "harm" against the community in general rather than particular individuals), it is much more difficult to justify the compelling of persons to behave, or not to behave, in specified ways because of the annoyance, nuisance or distress otherwise caused to other persons. One difficulty here is that individuals vary enormously in their sensitivity to the behaviour of others. It is far from easy, therefore, to establish what is acceptable and what is not acceptable, in the sense of being offensive, to the community in general. This is particularly so in sexual or quasi-sexual matters, where (for example) the identification of what is indecent or obscene is a difficult issue. In Scotland hitherto, such identification has usually been left to the good sense of the judge or jury, and little attempt has been made to specify in advance what is indecent or obscene as a matter of law. Arguably such appeal to good sense is the best method of resolving moral dilemmas affecting the common law, and of reflecting sufficient standards of acceptability.[1] Also of importance, of course, is the extent to which some of the crimes dealt with below comply with the rights and fundamental freedoms under the European Convention on Human Rights as these have been brought into the law by the Human Rights Act 1998.[2] Breach of the peace, for example, has been found to comply with art.7(1) of the Convention, provided that that offence is constrained in ways set out in certain authoritative dicta.[3]

Where the moral issue at stake is a much more "public" one involving, for example, one's duty to tell the truth (perjury) or to refrain from betraying the security of one's country (treason), then some form of identifiable "harm" is more readily apparent.

---

[1] Cf., however, statutory offences such as "Extreme Pornography". See below, para.12–35.
[2] See Human Rights Act 1998 Sch.1.
[3] See below, paras 12–11 to 12–16.

1. CRIMES RELATIVE TO PUBLIC ORDER

MOBBING

Definition of mobbing

The common law crime of mobbing is committed when persons combine **12–02** together to achieve a commonly–shared purpose by violence or intimidation (that is, by unlawful or criminal means), where their combined conduct causes alarm to the community and disturbance of the public peace. Everyone in a crowd or mob who, by his presence and behaviour, adopts and seeks to promote such a common purpose is guilty of this crime. In the very full indictments found in nineteenth-century case reports, accused persons (usually a mere fraction of the total mob) were always charged as having been part of a riotous and disorderly crowd which, acting of common purpose, did various alarming and disorderly things in implementation of that purpose. Thus was their guilt to be brought home; they had been part of a larger design—assisting, aiding and abetting it by their culpable presence.[4] This indeed is essentially still the way in which the crime is charged.[5] In addition to their being guilty of mobbing, the accused could also (and still can) be guilty of particular crimes, if such had been committed by individual members of the mob other than themselves—provided that such particular crimes were genuinely foreseeable, given the commonly-shared purpose and its method of implementation.[6] This, however, might be a very serious business if, say, someone had been killed as a result of the mob's conduct. Whereas mobbing in the nineteenth century was not itself a capital crime,[7] murder certainly was, even for one found guilty art and part.[8] Although murder is no longer, of course, a capital-punishment offence it is still today a serious matter for those accused of mobbing to face the prospect of conviction for murder or other offences which they did not personally commit; but that is certainly still the law.[9] Modern charges tend to be so drawn that particular offences can be brought home to the accused either as members of the mob or as individuals (if evidence exists that they were individually responsible for committing them).[10]

Actus reus of mobbing

There must be a number of persons present before a "mob" can be constituted. **12–03** It is uncertain, however, what the minimum acceptable number might be. Hume[11] unhelpfully refers to the necessity of there being "a great host or multitude",

---

4 See, e.g. *James Cairns* (1837) 1 Swin. 597 at 597–600; *Daniel Blair* (1868) 1 Coup. 168 at 169–171.
5 See the Criminal Procedure (Scotland) Act 1995 Sch.2 and below, para.12–06, fn.26; see also the indictments in (a) *Kilpatrick v HM Advocate*, 1992 J.C. 120, as quoted by Lord Justice-General Hope at 122, (b) *Coleman v HM Advocate*, 1999 S.C.C.R. 87, and *Weir v HM Advocate* [2007] HCJAC 2; 2007 S.C.C.R. 59, as quoted by Lord Osborne at 62D–E, para.1.
6 See, e.g. *Myles Martin* (1886) 1 White 297, per Lord Mure's charge to the jury at 304–306.
7 Hume, *Commentaries*, i, 426.
8 See, e.g. *William Gibson* (1842) 1 Broun 485.
9 See, e.g. *Hancock v HM Advocate*, 1981 J.C. 74; *Coleman v HM Advocate*, 1999 S.C.C.R. 87.
10 See *Kilpatrick v HM Advocate*, 1992 J.C. 120, Lord Justice-General Hope at 125–126; *Coleman v HM Advocate*, 1999 S.C.C.R. 87.
11 Hume, *Commentaries*, i, 416.

whereas Alison[12] adopts the number "12" from the Riot Act 1714.[13] In terms of reported cases, the size (often estimated) of a mob has varied from some 1,300[14] to eight[15]; and in *Sloan v MacMillan* Lord Salvesen hinted[16] that five might be too few. Clearly, however, the fewer the number involved, the more likely it is that all can be identified and charged directly with their individual offences, thus rendering resort to "mobbing" unnecessary.[17] It may be of interest here that the analogous English offence called "Riot" requires a minimum of 12 persons.[18]

Commonly-shared purpose

12–04   There must be a common purpose. That, however, is hardly the most important issue in rendering a crowd's activities criminal, since a common purpose may well be a quite lawful one, as where persons gather to greet the return of a successful sporting team or to protest in a silent and peaceful manner over the imposition of some disliked fiscal measure. The crux of the matter is, therefore, that the common purpose itself should be a violent and mischievous one[19] or, if more peaceful in concept, should be implemented in a violent or intimidatory way.[20] It certainly does not matter that the crowd considered that it was acting in vindication of some supposed public or legal right in, say, preventing fish being landed on a Sunday[21] or pulling down a wall thought to have been erected over a public footpath.[22] If there is believed to be infringement of a legal right, then the remedy of those disaffected is clear. They must resort to the civil courts. If they choose not to do so, but resort to main force and violence, that will certainly be construed as an appropriate common purpose for mobbing.[23]

12–05   Although it is natural to think of a common purpose as something planned and known well in advance of the actual incidents constituting mobbing, this need not be so. Provided that such a purpose can be shown, then it is of no moment whether it was conceived in advance or arose spontaneously at the relevant time.[24] In *George Smith*,[25] for example, a large crowd assembled to communicate to the

---

[12]   Alison, *Principles*, i, 510.
[13]   Now repealed; see the Statute Law (Repeals) Act 1973 s.1(1) and Sch.1 Pt V.
[14]   *John G Robertson* (1842) 1 Broun 152.
[15]   *Hancock v HM Advocate*, 1981 J.C. 74.
[16]   *Sloan v MacMillan*, 1922 J.C. 1 at 7.
[17]   It has been held competent for the Crown, where there are large numbers involved, to raise separate indictments against groups of the accused: see *Weir v HM Advocate* [2007] HCJAC 2; 2007 S.C.C.R. 59 (29 accused in all): it was also opined there (at 68F, para.21) that the court had no power to conjoin separate indictments.
[18]   Public Order Act 1986 s.1.
[19]   See, e.g. the violent obstruction of officers of law in the execution of their duty in *Alexander McLean* (1886) 1 White 232.
[20]   See, e.g. the fraudulent intimidation used by the "mob" to persuade voluntary workers in a coal mine to cease pumping operations during an industrial dispute—*Sloan v MacMillan*, 1922 J.C. 1; the violence used by those intent on upholding the Sabbath as a day of rest in *Alexander Gollan* (1883) 5 Coup. 317.
[21]   *Alexander Gollan* (1883) 5 Coup. 317.
[22]   *Alexander Macphie* (1823) Alison, *Principles*, i, 512, where the crowd's belief that such a wall had been erected in obstruction of a public right of way was later affirmed as correct by the jury court (civil) and the House of Lords.
[23]   See, e.g. *Thomas Wild* (1854) 1 Irv. 552, per Lord Cowan's charge to the jury at 558.
[24]   Alison, *Principles*, i, 513.
[25]   *George Smith* (1848) Ark. 473.

magistrates of Glasgow their demands for food, money and work. There seemed to be no pre-arranged plan to do anything beyond that but, following dissatisfaction with the magistrates' response to their demands, the crowd instantly became a mob by forming, and implementing, there and then a purpose to steal and rob.

Modern indictments and complaints are not, it seems, statutorily required to **12–06** specify the exact common purpose.[26] But failure by the Crown to show a specific common purpose or to prove facts from which one might be inferred will inevitably spell the end of any prosecution for mobbing.[27] Certainly, proof of a series of random acts of violence and depredation, carried out by varying sets of persons who alighted from time to time from a transit van at different locations in a Scottish town, was held insufficient to raise an inference as to any common purpose at all.[28]

Alarm and disturbance

It also seems essential to this crime that the conduct of the mob should cause **12–07** public alarm and disturbance.[29] Hume suggests too[30] that the level of such disturbance should be "significant", which, it is thought must be correct. In *John G. Robertson*, Lord Justice-Clerk Hope stated[31]:

> "If, as in this case, a crowd collect and act together, with intent to oppose the entrance of a Presbytery into a church where duty is to be performed, and oppose such entry by dense numbers, and by refusing to move, though there were no noise nor other acts,—that would be Mobbing . . .".

Were this dictum to be received as law, then peaceful protestors, who sit down in a road in order to block the entrance of traffic to some premises or other, would be guilty of mobbing for doing no more than that—which seems wholly inappropriate.[32] Indeed, in *Robertson*, there was substantial violence, damage and disturbance, such that Lord Justice-Clerk Hope's remarks are no more than obiter dicta. As such, they should not be followed. That is not to suggest, of course, that a crowd of persons could not cause alarm by intimidatory behaviour. But if that were claimed, much would depend on what was done or said.[33]

---

[26] See the Criminal Procedure (Scotland) Act 1995, where the appropriate style in Sch.2 is: "You formed part of a riotous mob, which, acting of common purpose, obstructed A.B., C.D., and E.F., constables of the Northern constabulary on duty, and assaulted them, and forcibly took two persons whom they had arrested from their custody." It falls to be decided whether it accords with Convention rights not to be more specific than the foregoing style requires: cf. *Smith v Donnelly*, 2001 S.C.C.R. 800, at 808D, para.20—where the court commented on the statutory style for breach of the peace.

[27] *Francis Docherty* (1841) 2 Swin. 635; *Hancock v HM Advocate*, 1981 J.C. 74; *Kilpatrick v HM Advocate*, 1992 J.C. 120.

[28] *Hancock v HM Advocate*, 1981 J.C. 74.

[29] Hume, *Commentaries*, i, 416.

[30] Hume, *Commentaries*, i, 419–420.

[31] *John G. Robertson* (1842) 1 Broun 152 at 192.

[32] It may also conflict with the "Right of freedom of expression" and the "Right of freedom of assembly and association", as set out in arts 10 and 11 of the European Convention on Human Rights. (See the Human Rights Act 1998 Sch.1.)

[33] See, e.g. *Sloan v MacMillan*, 1922 J.C. 1, where the mob claimed (falsely) that there were hundreds of disaffected, striking miners outside the pit, whose anger it would be difficult to contain if those working in the mine itself did not instantly cease their labours.

Mere presence in a mob

12–08   It is possible to find some judicial opinions which suggest that those who follow a crowd out of idle curiosity may be considered part of that crowd by their very presence there. Such persons might then become guilty of mobbing, and of anything else the crowd cares to do in pursuance of its common design, by presence alone, or rather by failing to remove themselves from that crowd once its common purpose of violence or intimidation had become clear.[34] The overwhelming preponderance of authority, however, shows that such fears are groundless; and it is thought that Lord Young was correct in *John Nicolson*,[35] when he said to the jury:

> "If the prisoners, or any of them, were there from idle curiosity, that would not make him or them one of the mob. He would have to take the consequences, and when violence is used to disperse a mob, it frequently happens that those present out of curiosity suffer from that violence. But if in point of fact the prisoners were there not as participants in the conflict, not assenting to it, and not aiding it, they would not be guilty of mobbing . . . although they were physically present."[36]

Even where there is evidence that a person was present in a mob, his presence there has to be shown to be a "consenting or a supporting" one[37] (in the sense that he countenances and encourages the common purpose of the mob) before he can be eligible for conviction of mobbing. And, where it is proved that some specific crime (such as murder) was committed by the mob or specific members of it, it will have to be shown not only that that common purpose included a murderous purpose and that that particular purpose had been appreciated and espoused by a particular accused (who did not himself kill the deceased but was a member of the mob) but also that such an accused had remained a "subscribing" member of the mob whilst the killing was executed: if the Crown is unable to establish these matters in respect of any such accused, that accused may be convicted of mobbing, but not of murder via his membership of the mob.[38] He might be guilty of the murder if there was sufficient evidence that he had actually participated in the killing (with the necessary mens rea) as an individual or by art and part,[39] quite apart from his being a member of the mob in question.

Mens rea

12–09   None of the reported cases seems to deal with the issue of mens rea in mobbing; but the clear implication is that no one can be convicted of this crime unless he

---

[34] See *James Farquhar* (1861) 4 Irv. 28, per Lord Ardmillan at 40–41; *John G. Robertson* (1842) 1 Broun 152, per Lord Justice-Clerk Hope at 194–195.

[35] *John Nicolson* (1887) 1 White 307 at 314–315.

[36] See also Hume, *Commentaries*, i, 422; *John Urquhart* (1844) 2 Broun 13, per Lord Justice-Clerk Hope at 15; *Hancock v HM Advocate*, 1981 J.C. 74, per Lord Cameron at 83–84 and Lord Justice-General Emslie at 86; and the similar directions given to the jury by Lord McCluskey in a case of breach of the peace by a crowd of persons in *Boyle v HM Advocate*, 1993 S.L.T. 577, at 579I.

[37] See *Coleman v HM Advocate*, 1999 S.C.C.R. 87, Lord Coulsfield at 110D.

[38] This seems to be what was decided (or observed) in *Coleman v HM Advocate*, 1999 S.C.C.R. 87.

[39] See above, Ch.7, paras 7–03 to 7–36.

knew what the common purpose of the mob was, and intended to aid and abet it by whatever means he could.

Rioting

Many of the older cases refer to this crime as mobbing and rioting. But "rioting" **12–10** was the general description of fighting between two or more persons[40] in breach of the public peace, and featured commonly before the inferior courts in Scotland from the seventeenth century onwards.[41] Although rioting was still being described as a viable offence in its own right as late as 1838,[42] it is now thought to be in desuetude. Particular examples of it today would be dealt with as assaults or breaches of the peace. In any event, it would be inaccurate to describe the crime currently being explored as mobbing and rioting, since fighting is very far from being an indispensable feature of it.

BREACH OF THE PEACE

Definition

The ambit of breach of the peace as a common law crime was clarified and **12–11** indeed somewhat narrowed by the decision of the Appeal Court in *Smith v Donnelly*.[43] Prior to that case, the offence had been very generally regarded as one applying to virtually any conduct which caused (or was reasonably likely to cause) alarm, annoyance, upset or embarrassment to another person or persons.[44] In *Smith v Donnelly*, however, the appellant argued that the offence had become so vaguely defined as to be in breach of art.7(1) of the European Convention on Human Rights.[45] That Article, which *ex facie* makes it unlawful for a person

> "to be held guilty of any criminal offence on account of an act or omission which did not constitute a criminal offence under national law . . . at the time when it was committed",[46]

---

[40] *Pace* Alison, *Principles*, i, 510.

[41] See especially the Baron Court and Justice of the Peace Court records of the 17th and 18th centuries.

[42] See *John McCabe* (1838) 2 Swin. 20.

[43] *Smith v Donnelly*, 2001 S.C.C.R. 800. The essence of the offence, as clarified in *Smith*, was applied by a bench of five judges in *Jones v Carnegie; Tallents v Gallacher; Barrett v Carnegie; Carberry v Currie; Park v Frame*, 2004 S.C.C.R. 361 (see, especially, the opinion of the court at 366B–D, para.2), where one of the conjoined appeals had been concerned with an attempt (unsuccessful) to challenge the ruling in *Smith*—see the opinion of the court in *Jones* at 367C, para.5. That ruling has been upheld as compliant with arts 5, 10 and 11 of the European Convention on Human Rights (on the matter of the admissibility of the application) by the European Court of Human Rights in *Lucas v United Kingdom* (2003) 37 E.H.R.R. CD 86, app. no.39013/02 (the decision there being conveniently set out at 2004 S.C.C.R. at 377F–383C).

[44] See, e.g. *Dougall v Dykes* (1860) 4 Irv. 101; *Whitchurch v Millar* (1895) 2 Adam 9; *Turner v Kennedy* (1972) S.C.C.R. Supp. 30; *Montgomery v McLeod* (1977) S.C.C.R. Supp. 164; *Sinclair v Annan*, 1980 S.L.T. (Notes) 55; *Alexander v Smith*, 1984 S.L.T. 176; *Derrett v Lockhart*, 1991 S.C.C.R. 109; *Stewart v Lockhart*, 1991 S.L.T. 835; *MacDougall v Dochree*, 1992 J.C. 154; *Wyness v Lockhart*, 1992 S.C.C.R. 808; *Cameron v Normand*, 1992 S.C.C.R. 866: cf., now, *McMillan v Higson*, 2003 S.C.C.R. 125, where *Smith v Donnelly* was applied.

[45] See the Human Rights Act 1998 Sch.1.

[46] This is plainly not applicable to breach of the peace, which has been a known crime since at least the eighteenth century: see Hume, *Commentaries*, i, 439.

has been construed by the European Court of Human Rights to include the rule "that an offence must be clearly defined in law." Further, that rule will be complied with

> "where the individual can know from the wording of the relevant provision and, if need be, with the assistance of the courts' interpretation of it, what acts and omissions will make him liable."[47]

The Appeal Court in *Smith v Donnelly* determined that breach of the peace was capable of being defined so as to comply with art.7(1), as so interpreted by the European Court of Human Rights. The decision of the Appeal Court concentrates, however, on the actus reus of the offence.

Actus reus—the tests

12–12   In *Smith v Donnelly*,[48] the Appeal Court agreed with counsel that the essence of breach of the peace was to be discovered not from a "close analysis of the facts of particular marginal decisions"[49] but from dicta in authoritative cases.[50] When properly understood, these dicta generated a clear general test for conduct alleged to be sufficient for the offence: to suffice, that conduct had to be "severe enough to cause alarm to ordinary people *and* threaten serious disturbance to the community."[51] That this was a conjunctive, two-part test was soon affirmed; so that where a trial sheriff had substituted the word "or" for the conjunctive "and" in setting out the *Smith v Donnelly* test, the Appeal Court found that there had been a misdirection and a miscarriage of justice.[52]

12–13   *(1) severe enough to cause alarm and threaten serious disturbance*

It is plain from *Smith v Donnelly*[53] (and other cases[54]) that no evidence of actual alarm or disturbance is required; should there be such evidence, that may not in itself be conclusive,[55] since the conduct in question must still meet the test set out above, in para.12–12.[56] And that test is an objective one, since individual

---

[47] *Kokkinakis v Greece* (1994) 17 E.H.R.R. 397 at 423, para.52.
[48] *Smith v Donnelly*, 2001 S.C.C.R. 800.
[49] *Smith v Donnelly*, 2001 S.C.C.R. 800 at 808B, para.19.
[50] The principal authoritative cases and dicta were *Ferguson v Carnochan* (1889) 16 R (J) 93, especially the opinion of Lord Justice-Clerk Macdonald at 94, and *Raffaelli v Heatly*, 1949 J.C. 101, the opinion of Lord Justice-Clerk Thomson at 104. Although mention was also made (see *Smith v Donnelly*, 2001 S.C.C.R. 800 at 806C–E, para.15; 807D, para.18; and 808A, para.19) of *Young v Heatly*, 1959 J.C. 101, and in particular the opinion of Lord Justice-General Clyde there at 70, there is no overt approval of that decision or of the reasoning in the case; and indeed *Young v Heatly* has now been overruled by a court of five judges in *Harris v HM Advocate* [2009] HCJAC 80; 2010 S.C.C.R. 15.
[51] *Smith v Donnelly*, 2001 S.C.C.R. at 807A, para.17 (emphasis added).
[52] See *Paterson v HM Advocate* [2008] HCJAC 18; 2008 J.C. 327 at 336–337, para.23, which was in turn confirmed by the five judge Appeal Court in *Harris v HM Advocate* [2009] HCJAC 80; 2010 S.C.C.R. 15 at 20B–E, paras 13–15.
[53] *Smith v Donnelly*, 2001 S.C.C.R. 800.
[54] See in particular *Jones v Carnegie; Tallents v Gallacher; Barrett v Carnegie; Carberry v Currie; Park v Frame*, 2004 S.C.C.R. 361 (court of five judges), at 368D–369E, paras 10–13, and *Dyer v Hutchison; Dyer v Bell; Dyer v Johnstone* [2006] HCJAC 45; 2006 S.C.C.R. 377.
[55] Cf. *Gifford v HM Advocate* [2011] HCJAC 101; 2011 S.C.C.R. 751, especially the opinion of the court at 755F, para.10, and 756C–D, para.12.
[56] See, e.g. *Farrell v Normand*, 1993 S.L.T. 793, where the accused's conduct, in beckoning a 10 year old girl and asking her if she would like a drink, was held not to be sufficient for breach of the

reactions to the behaviour of others can be highly subjective.[57] What seems to matter is the view the court takes of the ordinary (if not the reasonable) person's reaction to the conduct of the accused: should that estimated (or actual) reaction be one of annoyance, upset or mere irritation, or should the conduct be viewed as no more than inappropriate or a "breach of decorum",[58] it would be insufficient for breach of the peace.[59] The court in *Smith v Donnelly* realised that, of the many prior decisions relative to breach of the peace which existed, some would probably not have met the "conduct test" now represented as necessary for that offence to comply with art.7(1) of the Convention; but no attempt was made to review these decisions,[60] and the impression was given that this case was intended to mark a new beginning for the offence. Thereafter, therefore, "[W]hat is required . . . is conduct which does present as genuinely alarming and disturbing, in its context,[61] to any reasonable person."[62] Thus, if two men begin fighting in public, it might reasonably be supposed that such conduct is serious enough to cause

---

peace, notwithstanding that the girl was alarmed and upset. It follows, of course, that even where there is evidence of actual alarm, that alarm must have been caused by the accused's conduct: cf. *Jones v Carnegie; Tallents v Gallacher; Barrett v Carnegie; Carberry v Currie; Park v Frame,* 2004 S.C.C.R. 361(court of five judges), opinion of the court at 376E–F, paras 47–48.

[57] See *Donaldson v Vannet,* 1998 S.C.C.R. 422 at 424B.

[58] See *Raffaelli v Heatly,* 1949 J.C. 101, Lord Justice-Clerk Thomson at 104. Cf. *Allison v Higson,* 2004 S.C.C.R. 720, *HM Advocate v Greig,* 2005 S.C.C.R. 465 (Sh.Ct.), and *Dyer v Hutchison; Dyer v Bell; Dyer v Johnstone* [2006] HCJAC 45; 2006 S.C.C.R. 377.

[59] See, e.g. *Angus v Nisbet* [2010] HCJAC 76; 2011 S.L.T. 98 (adult male speaking to a 15 year old girl in a public place, handing her a piece of paper on which was written his mobile-phone number, and inviting her to keep in touch—held not to be sufficient for breach of the peace, notwithstanding that the conduct caused the girl to be worried and "scared"; test of the notional reasonable person, appraised of all the facts, applied); *Miller v Thomson* [2009] HCJAC 64; 2009 S.L.T. 59 (swearing at police officers in public in circumstances where but one of the officers, yet none of a number of bystanders, was alarmed or disturbed—held insufficient for breach of the peace). Cf. *Bowes v McGowan* [2010] HCJAC 55; 2010 S.C.C.R. 657, especially the opinion of the court at 665B–C, para.21 (inappropriate, "sexual" remarks made by an older man to a 14 year old schoolgirl in a taxi during a journey on public roads—held sufficient to meet the test for breach of the peace); *Russell v Thomson* [2010] HCJAC 138; 2011 S.C.C.R. 77, especially the opinion of the court at 85G–86A, para.26 (person who sent a threatening letter to a teacher via that teacher's solicitor, and who had been interdicted from (inter alia) approaching that teacher at her place of work, nevertheless approaching the complainer in a "forbidden" part of the relevant school playground—held properly convicted of conduct sufficient for breach of the peace).

[60] As a bench of three judges, it would not in any event have been possible for the Appeal Court in *Smith v Donnelly,* 2001 S.C.C.R. 800, to overrule prior decisions of the Appeal Court itself: 807F, para.19. The full bench in *Jones v Carnegie; Tallents v Gallacher; Barrett v Carnegie; Carberry v Currie; Park v Frame,* 2004 S.C.C.R. 361, did not attempt to review earlier decisions either. (That full bench did, at 376A–B, para.43, overrule *Cochrane v HM Advocate,* 2002 S.C.C.R. 1051; but *Cochrane* was not concerned with breach of the peace.)

[61] The importance of "the context" of the conduct in question is stressed particularly by the court in *Dyer v Hutchison; Dyer v Bell; Dyer v Johnstone* [2006] HCJAC 45; 2006 S.C.C.R. 377, at 387C–D, para.25—a case which also takes the view that any (even short lived) provocative (and/or racist) behaviour at a premier league football match (especially in sight of the opposing team's supporters) is likely to be taken as meeting the required test: see the opinion of the court at 387E–388D, paras 26–28; cf. *Owens v Donaldson* (unreported 2005, but in respect of which the court's opinion is conveniently set out at 2006 S.C.C.R. 389G–390F)—but see also the explanation for that decision offered by the court in *Dyer v Hutchison; Dyer v Bell; Dyer v Johnstone* [2006] HCJAC 45; 2006 S.C.C.R. 377, at 389A–B, para.31.

[62] *Smith v Donnelly,* 2001 S.C.C.R. 800, at 807C, para.17.

alarm to others and threaten "severe disturbance" to the community.[63] At the opposite extreme, behaviour amounting to remarks addressed to a person which merely cause her embarrassment must fail the test.[64] Between these two extremes, however, lie many situations of a borderline nature. The court in *Smith v Donnelly* recognised this, and whilst they suggested that such borderline cases must simply be determined by the courts on their facts as such cases arise,[65] they did provide some general guidance.

12–14   The Appeal Court in *Smith v Donnelly*[66] clearly favoured a "robust" approach to be taken in cases of swearing, on the basis that for many individuals, swearing can amount to part of their normal mode of communication.[67] It follows that prior decisions which had upheld convictions for breach of the peace where complainers were merely "upset" by swearing—especially where the complainers were police constables—may have been wrongly decided.[68] The Court also noted that conduct which amounted to no more than a refusal to co-operate with the police "even if forcefully or even truculently stated, is not likely to be sufficient in itself to justify a conviction."[69] On the other hand, the Court stressed the need to consider art.10[70] of the European Convention on Human Rights relative to certain cases of alleged breach of the peace—although art.10, of course, refers both to rights and responsibilities.[71] A situation such as was disclosed in *Alexander v Smith*[72] might be of particular concern here, since the accused was convicted of breach of the peace for insisting on attempting to sell right-wing newspapers to a crowd of persons, notwithstanding that some members of that crowd had announced their intention of stopping him from doing so—by force, if necessary.

(2) The "public element"

12–15   The conjunctive test in *Smith v Donnelly*[73] requires that the conduct (which reaches the required standard of severity) must also "threaten serious disturbance

---

[63] See, e.g. *Derrett v Lockhart*, 1991 S.C.C.R. 109, and *Butcher v Jessop*, 1989 S.L.T. 593; see also *Monson v Higson*, 2000 S.C.C.R. 751 (a case of "road rage"), and *McAlpine v Friel*, 1997 S.C.C.R. 453 (a case of "stalking" the complainer over an extended period, although the appeal is solely concerned with sentence).

[64] See *Sinclair v Annan*, 1980 S.L.T. (Notes) 55, and *Borwick v Urquhart*, 2003 S.C.C.R. 243 (in so far as concerns the charge of breach of the peace); cf. *Bryce v Normand*, 1997 S.L.T. 1351, and *Donaldson v Vannet*, 1998 S.C.C.R. 422.

[65] See, e.g. *Dyer v Bradley* [2006] HCJAC 72; 2006 S.C.C.R. 629 (low-key, peaceful protest held not to qualify as a breach of the peace).

[66] *Smith v Donnelly*, 2001 S.C.C.R. 800; see the opinion of the court at 808B–D, para.20.

[67] See, e.g. *Kinnaird v Higson*, 2001 S.C.C.R. 427; *Logan v Jessop*, 1987 S.C.C.R. 604: cf. *Grogan v Heywood*, 1999 S.C.C.R. 705.

[68] See, e.g. *Mackay v Heywood*, 1998 S.C.C.R. 210.

[69] *Smith v Donnelly*, 2001 S.C.C.R. 800, at 808B, para.20. As illustrations, see, e.g. *McDonald v Heywood*, 2002 S.C.C.R. 92; *Cardle v Murray*, 1993 S.L.T. 525.

[70] Article 10 refers to the right of freedom of expression: see the Human Rights Act 1998 Sch.1. See e.g. *Quinan v Carnegie* [2005] HCJAC 24; 2005 S.C.C.R. 267.

[71] See art.10(2). Since the issue of the effect of art.10 was not debated in *Smith v Donnelly*, 2001 S.C.C.R. 800, the court made no more than the observation mentioned in the text above. Cf. the facts in the case of *Smith v Donnelly* itself with those in *Colhoun v Friel*, 1996 S.C.C.R. 497; and see *Gifford v HM Advocate* [2011] HCJAC 101; 2011 S.C.C.R. 751, especially the opinion of the court at 756F–757D, paras 14–17.

[72] *Alexander v Smith*, 1984 S.L.T. 176. See also *Duffield v Skeen*, 1981 S.C.C.R. 66.

[73] *Smith v Donnelly*, 2001 S.C.C.R. 800.

to the community"—which is referred to in the full bench decision of *Harris (M) v HM Advocate* as the "public element" and as reflective of the "the true nature of breach of the peace as a crime".[74] It must be noted, of course, that there need not be any actual disturbance of the community, so long as such disturbance is threatened and is sufficiently "serious"; but it must also be noted that a sufficient threat to "public safety" has been judicially approved as a legitimate alternative.[75] It must further be appreciated that the "public element" does not require the conduct in question to have occurred in a public place, let alone to have been actually witnessed by members of the public; indeed the relevant conduct can take place in private if it was either detected by members of the "public" in a public place (such as in the street outside a building[76]) or realistically capable of being discovered by members of the "public" wherever such members happen (or might reasonably be expected) to be.[77] It might well be said, however, that these noteworthy points make it difficult to give accurate content to the "public element", and present difficulties in drawing any general conclusions from the growing list of appeals in which the presence or absence of that element has been at issue. Particular points of difficulty (arising from statements in leading decisions) have subsequently been disposed of by the Appeal Court in terms that they were obiter,[78] and refuge has had to be had to the comforting (and infinitely flexible) adage that all ultimately "depends on the circumstances in which the conduct occurs."[79] It has been decided, however, that conduct ("completely inappropriate conversations about intimate sexual matters") which occurred in a publicly-licensed taxi whilst it was on a journey on public roads, satisfied the element here, although the fact that the conduct was relayed to third parties by the 14 year old complainer (and thus was always at a realistic risk of discovery in the circumstances) was also a significant issue.[80] And it has also

---

[74] *Harris (M) v HM Advocate* [2009] HCJAC 80; 2010 S.C.C.R. 15, opinion of the court at 23A, para.22.

[75] See, e.g. *Gifford v HM Advocate* [2011] HCJAC 101; 2011 S.C.C.R. 751, opinion of the court at 756C–D, para.12. That case concerned conduct (by protestors) which, although invisible to members of the public, had the effect of disrupting operations at an airport, including "disruption to an air ambulance, and potential disruption of helicopter search and rescue operations" which by themselves would have entitled the jury "to convict on the basis of the threat to public safety even in the absence of serious disturbance to the community": see opinion of the court at 756D, para.12.

[76] See *Ferguson v Carnochan* (1889) 16R(J) 93, where police constables, passing in the street outside, were the sole witnesses to a disturbance taking place inside the accused's own premises.

[77] See, e.g. *MacDougall v Dochree*, 1992 J.C. 154.

[78] See, e.g. *Harris (M) v HM Advocate* [2009] HCJAC 80; 2010 S.C.C.R. 15, at 23F, para.25, "Disturbance or potential disturbance of even a small group of individuals in a private house . . . may suffice" (for the public element)—dismissed as obiter in *Hatcher v Harrower* [2010] HCJAC 92; 2010 S.C.C.R. 903 at 906E, para.6, in deciding that two children (of 12 and 15 years of age) in their own bedrooms at the time of heated conduct by their father towards their mother (described, at 905D, para.2, as "plainly sufficient . . . to satisfy the first part of the test for breach of the peace") did not qualify as "members of the public" for the purposes of the "public element"—whilst accepting that two parents, in a room adjacent to a kitchen (where their young daughter was being subjected to conduct of a sufficient nature for breach of the peace), did qualify to satisfy the element as decided in *Paterson v HM Advocate* [2008] HCJAC 18; 2008 J.C. 327: both *Hatcher* and *Paterson* were, of course, decided on the "realistic risk of discovery" aspect, relative to the second part of the conjunctive test.

[79] *Hatcher v Harrower* [2010] HCJAC 92; 2010 S.C.C.R. 903 at 908A, para.10.

[80] See *Bowes v McGowan* [2010] HCJAC 55; 2010 S.C.C.R. 657.

been decided that a "realistic risk of the conduct being discovered should be understood as referring to the risk of the conduct of the accused being come upon, that is to say being seen or heard, by a third party (or parties) or being brought to their attention, whilst that conduct continues or in the immediate aftermath of the conduct having come to an end."[81]

Statutory styles

12–16   The Appeal Court in *Smith v Donnelly*[82] notes that one of the statutory styles of charge for breach of the peace, viz "You did conduct yourself in a disorderly manner and commit a breach of the peace",[83] is so lacking in specification that it probably falls foul of art.6(3)(a) of the European Convention on Human Rights. That part of the Article narrates that:

> "Everyone charged with a criminal offence has the following minimum rights: *(a)* to be informed promptly, in a language which he understands *and in detail*, of the nature and cause of the accusation against him."[84]

Consequently, prior Scottish decisions,[85] which have upheld charges couched in the bare statutory style as adequate for the purposes of notice to the accused, may be considered to have been disapproved.[86]

Mens rea

12–17   The mens rea of breach of the peace has never been determined in any reported case. It is, therefore, uncertain what the mens rea might be. As breach of the peace is a common law crime, it must be assumed that strict liability (see Ch.13) is not applicable, since "[t]here is a presumption that all common law crimes require *mens rea*."[87] Probably if the accused's conduct, whatever it be, is deliberate or even reckless, and is causally connected, or reasonably could be so connected to the requisite alarm and disturbance, then that will suffice. It does not seem to be necessary for the accused to intend or even appreciate the effect (actual or likely) of his conduct on others. This seems to be borne out by *Hughes v Crowe*,[88] where the claim was made that the accused had had no mens rea at the relevant time. What had happened was that the occupants of the lower flat in a building were "entertained" to banging sounds and the playing of loud music from the flat above—all at 7.15 on a Saturday morning. The noises (all exceedingly loud) continued for about one hour, until put a stop to by the police. It was claimed that the accused had had no knowledge that there was anyone in the lower flat at

---

[81] See *WM v HM Advocate* [2010] HCJAC 75, opinion of the court at para.15.
[82] *Smith v Donnelly*, 2001 S.C.C.R. 800 at 808D, para.20.
[83] Criminal Procedure (Scotland) Act 1995 Sch.5.
[84] See the Human Rights Act 1998 Sch.1 (emphasis added).
[85] See, e.g. *Butcher v Jessop*, 1989 S.C.C.R. 119; *Anderson v Allan*, 1985 S.C.C.R. 399.
[86] Cf. *Jones v Carnegie; Tallents v Gallacher; Barrett v Carnegie; Carberry v Currie; Park v Frame*, 2004 S.C.C.R. 361 (five judges), opinion of the court at 375B–376C, paras 39–45, and *McGraw v HM Advocate*, 2004 S.C.C.R. 637, opinion of the court at 639C–D.
[87] Gordon, *Criminal Law*, 3rd edn (2000/2001), para.7.12.
[88] *Hughes v Crowe*, 1993 S.C.C.R. 320.

the time, and that he had not been warned about his conduct before being charged. The Appeal Court, however, took the view that although mens rea was required for breach of the peace, it was to be inferred from the nature and quality of the actings. Here, it would have been obvious in a four-flatted building that persons were likely to be at home at that hour on a Saturday, and that the acts of the appellant, persisted in for a considerable period, thus showed a "gross lack of consideration for others who might be present in the other flats in the block at the time."[89] This does not exactly settle what the precise mens rea element for the crime might be; but certainly a "good" or understandable motive for one's deliberate conduct seems to be of no moment at all, as in *Ralston v HM Advocate*[90] where a prisoner's deliberate roof-top protest caused complete disruption to the running of the prison, and was thus a breach of the peace—irrespective of the merits of his desire to publicise alleged poor prison conditions. On the other hand, in *MacDougall v Dochree*,[91] it appeared to be accepted by all three judges in the Appeal Court that it would not be breach of the peace for persons, who were suspicious that "peeping-tom" activities might be taking place in a locked toilet cubicle (which by exercise of ingenuity provided viewing access to a next-door solarium), to test their suspicions by peering under a gap at the bottom of the cubicle door whilst the toilet was occupied by the suspect. This suggests that a "good" motive (for example, crime detection by persons other than the police) may provide a defence.

Particular defences

It is apparently not a good defence that the accused committed a breach of the   **12–18** peace in order to bring to an end an existing breach, even one being committed outside his own house by some troublesome youths,[92] presumably on the basis that two wrongs do not make a right. But self-defence is definitely applicable to a "fighting" or assault type of the crime.[93] It may be a defence that only the police heard or saw the accused's conduct, unless the police, inured as they must be to reprehensible behaviour, were entitled to be (and, possibly, actually were) alarmed thereby.[94]

Analogous Statutory Offences

There are a number of statutory offences covering ground similar to   **12–19** some situations which would have been prosecuted in the past as breaches of

---

[89] *Hughes v Crowe*, 1993 S.C.C.R. 320, Lord Justice-General Hope at 323 F.
[90] *Ralston v HM Advocate*, 1989 S.L.T. 474; and see above, para.3–21.
[91] *MacDougall v Dochree*, 1992 J.C. 154; cf. *Woods v Normand*, 1992 S.C.C.R. 805 (attempting to end what was mistakenly thought of as an assault on a friend by use of threatening words and behaviour, where the Appeal Court opined that even if there had been a "good motive", the tactics adopted went far beyond what was justified): the decision, however, could also be explained as an example of self-defence (see below, para.12–18).
[92] *Palazzo v Copeland*, 1976 J.C. 52.
[93] *Derrett v Lockhart*, 1991 S.C.C.R. 109.
[94] See *Cavanagh v Wilson*, 1995 S.C.C.R. 693, applying the decision in *Logan v Jessop*, 1987 S.C.C.R. 604; but cf. *Norris v McLeod*, 1988 S.C.C.R. 572; *Saltman v Allan*, 1989 S.L.T. 262, and *Lochrie v Jessop*, 1992 S.L.T. 556, which all seemed to discredit *Logan v Jessop*, as having any value as a precedent.

the peace.[95] In most cases, these statutory offences may be charged (all things being equal) instead of, *or* as alternatives to, common law breach of the peace; but in relation to relevant offences created by the Sexual Offences (Scotland) Act 2009 (asp 9) these offences must (where the conduct could result in a charge of breach of the peace) be charged instead of that common law crime.[96] Some examples of such statutory offences will be found in the paragraphs which follow.

Failing to leave (etc.) a Rave after police direction

12–20 This statutory offence is to be found in s.63 of the Criminal Justice and Public Order Act 1994. The marginal note to that section refers to a "rave"; but the substance of the offence explains that the crime relates to an actual or planned gathering of more than 100 persons (whether trespassers or not[97]) on land in the open air[98], where amplified music[99] is played at night (whether with intermissions or not) and is of such duration and loudness as to be likely to cause serious distress to inhabitants of the locality.[100] If a police officer of at least the rank of superintendent reasonably believes that two or more persons are on any land[101] making preparations for such a "rave", and/or that ten or more persons are there attending it or waiting for it to begin, he can give direction that all such persons[102] are to leave the land and remove whatever vehicles or other property they may have brought to it. The offence is committed by failing to leave that land as soon as reasonably practicable, or returning to it within seven days of the direction's having been given[103]—both without reasonable excuse.[104] Before there can be a

---

[95] See, e.g. the Civic Government (Scotland) Act 1982 ss.46 (inter alia, prostitute soliciting in a public place), 49(1) (inter alia permitting any creature to give any other person reasonable cause for alarm or annoyance), 54(1) (inter alia failing to desist from playing a musical instrument so as to give any other person reasonable cause for annoyance), and 55(1) (touting for trade so as to give any other person reasonable cause for annoyance). See also the Criminal Law (Consolidation) (Scotland) Act 1995 s.50A, as inserted by the Crime and Disorder Act 1998 s.33 (racially aggravated harassment), the Antisocial Behaviour etc. (Scotland) Act 2004 (asp 8) s.45 (noise emitted from relevant property and exceeding the permitted level after service of a warning notice etc.), and the Prostitution (Public Places) (Scotland) Act 2007 (asp 11) s.1 (soliciting in a relevant place for the purpose of obtaining the services of a person engaged in prostitution).

[96] See the Sexual Offences (Scotland) Act 2009 (asp 9) s.52(b): it should be noted, however, that this provision has not yet been given legal effect—see the Sexual Offences (Scotland) Act 2009 (Commencement No.1) and the Criminal Justice and Licensing (Scotland) Act 2010 (Commencement No.4) Order 2010 (SSI 2010/357) art.2(a).

[97] This is not, therefore, predominantly a trespassory offence (see above, paras 11–05 to 11–07). "Trespasser" is defined as in s.61(9), see s.63(10).

[98] This includes a place partly open to the air, such as a sports stadium (s.63(10)), but not in Scotland a place which has been licensed, under the Civic Government (Scotland) Act 1982 s.41 (as amended by the Criminal Justice and Licensing (Scotland) Act 2010 (asp 13) ss.172(5) and 176) as a place of public entertainment (s.63(9)(b)).

[99] This includes "sounds wholly or predominantly characterised by emission of a succession of repetitive beats", s.63(1)(b).

[100] See Criminal Justice and Public Order Act 1994 s.63(1).

[101] The land here need not be in the open air: see Criminal Justice and Public Order Act 1994 s.63(2), as amended by the Anti-social Behaviour Act 2003 Sch.3.

[102] Under s.63(2), this is not applicable to exempt persons, i.e. the occupier of the land, members of his family, or his employee or agent, as also those who have homes situated there (see s.63(6) and (10)). "Occupier" is defined as in s.61(9), see s.63(10).

[103] See Criminal Justice and Public Order Act 1994 s.63(6). "Vehicle" is defined as in s.61(9)—see s.63(10).

[104] The onus of showing such an excuse is on the accused (s.63(7)).

conviction, it must be shown that the accused was aware of the direction; but the direction is deemed to have been properly communicated if reasonable steps have been taken to bring it to the attention of those concerned.[105] Within a defined distance of such a "rave", a police officer can stop persons he reasonably believes are on their way to it and require that they should proceed in a "non-rave" direction; it is also an offence to fail to comply with such a requirement.[106]

Stalking

The relatively new offence of stalking[107] is committed when a person (A) **12–21** engages in a course of conduct either with the intention of causing fear or alarm to another person (B) or where he knows (or ought to have known in all the circumstances) that that course of conduct would be likely to cause fear or alarm to B, *and* where B does suffer fear or alarm thereby. Conduct (which must occur on at least two occasions in order to qualify as a "course" thereof) relevant to the crime is defined as— following B or "any other person"[108]; contacting or attempting to contact B by any means; publishing any statement or material relating to or purporting to relate to B "and/or" purporting to originate from B; monitoring the use by B of the internet, email or any other form of electronic communication; entering any premises; loitering in any place (whether public or private); interfering with any property in the possession of B; giving something to B or leaving anything where it may be found by, given to or brought to the attention of B; watching or spying on B; acting in any other way that a reasonable person would expect would cause B (but not, in this case, "any other person") to suffer fear or alarm. The striking breadth of this offence (some of the specified conduct surely having been included *ex abundantia cautelam*) is tempered by the existence of a defence—namely, that A may show that the conduct in question was authorised by virtue of any enactment or rule of law, was for the prevention or detection of crime, or "was, in the particular circumstances, reasonable"; this is in turn, however, tempered by the existence of a specific alternative verdict—namely, conviction of the statutory offence of "threatening or abusive behaviour".[109]

Threatening or abusive behaviour

This statutory offence[110] is committed if a person (A) behaves in a threatening **12–22** or abusive manner, if such behaviour "would be likely to cause a reasonable person to suffer fear or alarm", and if A by such behaviour intends it to (or is reckless as to whether it would) cause fear of alarm.[111] It does not matter whether

---

[105] See Criminal Justice and Public Order Act 1994 s.63(4).
[106] See Criminal Justice and Public Order Act 1994 s.65.
[107] See the Criminal Justice and Licensing (Scotland) Act 2010 (asp 13) (hereafter in this paragraph referred to as "the 2010 Act") s.39.
[108] See the 2010 Act s.39(6). The phrase "Any other person" is left vague—whether as to relationship with B or as to overall rationale—but is insisted upon as an alternative to "B" in every instance of relevant conduct for the offence; references to "or any other person" is therefore to be understood in the entire catalogue of relevant conduct which ensues above in this paragraph.
[109] See the 2010 Act s.39(8),(9).
[110] See the Criminal Justice and Licensing (Scotland) Act 2010 (asp 13) (hereafter referred to in this paragraph as "the 2010 Act") s.38.
[111] See the 2010 Act s.38(1)(a)–(c).

333

the relevant behaviour was a "single act" or comprised "a course of conduct"[112]; and such behaviour can be "of any kind including, in particular, things said or otherwise communicated as well as things done".[113] There is, however, no requirement that there be any public element to the behaviour (as would be necessary relative to the common law offence of breach of the peace); but there is a specific defence—namely, that A may show "that the behaviour was, in the particular circumstances, reasonable."[114]

Threatening communications[115]

12–23   This statutory offence[116] is committed if a person communicates[117] material[118] to another person where either of two conditions is satisfied. The first of these conditions[119] requires that the material consists of (or contains or implies) a threat or incitement to carry out "a seriously violent act against a person or persons of a particular description",[120] where that material (or its communication) would be likely to cause a reasonable person to suffer fear or alarm and its communicator intends thus to (or is reckless as to whether it would) cause such fear or alarm. The alternative condition is that the material is threatening, and its communicator intends by so communicating it "to stir up hatred on religious grounds."[121] There is a defence to this offence—namely, that a person charged with committing it shows that "the communication of the material was, in the particular circumstances, reasonable."[122]

---

[112] "Course of conduct" is not defined; cf. the way in which the same phrase is to be construed for the purposes of the offence of "stalking": see the 2010 Act s.39(6), and above, para.12–21.

[113] See the 2010 Act s.38(3).

[114] See the 2010 Act s.38(2).

[115] Cf. threats at common law: see above, paras 9–95 to 9–97.

[116] See the Offensive Behaviour at Football and Threatening Communications (Scotland) Act 2012 (asp 1) (hereafter in this paragraph referred to as "the 2012 Act") s.6.

[117] "Communicates" entails communication by any means *other than* unrecorded speech: see the 2012 Act s.8(2). See also s.7, which contains express provisions to protect freedom of speech.

[118] "Material" means "anything that is capable of being read, looked at, watched or listened to, either directly or after conversion from data stored in another form": see the 2012 Act s.8(3).

[119] See the 2012 Act s.6(2)(a)–(c).

[120] If the relevant material consists of an image (still or moving), that image will be presumed to imply such threat or incitement if it "depicts or implies the carrying out of a seriously violent act (whether actual or fictitious) against a person or persons of a particular description" whether such person or persons are "living or dead or actual or fictitious" *and* a reasonable person would "be likely to consider that the image implies the carrying out of a seriously violent act against an actual person or against actual persons of a particular description." See the 2012 Act s.6(3); see also s.8(5) where a "seriously violent act" is defined as an act which would cause serious injury to, or the death of a person.

[121] See the 2012 Act s.6(5); see also s.8(4) where "hatred on religious grounds" is defined.

[122] See the 2012 Act s.6(6).

Offensive behaviour at regulated football matches

This complex statutory offence[123] is committed if a person, in relation to[124] a **12–24** regulated football match,[125] engages in particular behaviour which is likely, or would be likely, to incite public disorder.[126] The particular behaviour which engages the offence is that of "expressing hatred of, or stirring up hatred against"[127] either a group of persons or an individual based on their (or his or her) membership[128] (actual or presumed[129]) of a "religious group",[130] a "social or cultural

---

[123] See the Offensive Behaviour at Football and Threatening Communications (Scotland) Act 2012 (asp 1) (hereafter in this paragraph referred to as "the 2012 Act") s.1.

[124] Behaviour sufficiently relates to a "regulated football match" (see the immediately following footnote) if it occurs "in the ground where [that type of] match is being held on the day on which it is being held", while the person in question "is entering or leaving (or trying to enter or leave)" that ground, or "on a journey to or from" that type of match; it is also so sufficient (*pace* the "Explanatory Note" accompanying the 2012 Act at para.14, and reading the text of s.2 as if the "or" after (2)(a)(iii) postulated (2)(a) and (b) as proper alternatives —a reading which is somewhat uncertain) if "directed towards, or is engaged in together with, another person who is (i) in the ground where the regulated football match is being held on the day on which it is being held, (ii) entering or leaving (or trying to enter or leave) the ground where [such a match] is being held, or (iii) on a journey to or from [such a match]": see the 2012 Act s.2(2). Under s.2(3) of that Act, it should be noted that in essence behaviour also relates sufficiently to such a match if it so occurs, or is so directed (etc.), in or relative to any place (other than domestic premises) where that match is "televised"—i.e. (under s.4(4) of the 2012 Act) when it is "shown (on a screen or by projection onto any surface) whether by means of the broadcast transmission of pictures or otherwise." It is further to be noted that a person may be regarded as having been "on a journey" to or from a regulated football match (including a place where it is televised) whether or not he (or she) attended or intended to attend that match; and that a journey for these purposes includes "breaks", whether overnight or otherwise: see the 2012 Act s.2(4).

[125] "Regulated football match" is defined as in the Police, Public Order and Criminal Justice (Scotland) Act 2006 (asp 10) (hereafter in this paragraph referred to as "the 2006 Act") s.55(2): see the 2012 Act s.2(1)(a)—noting, for the purposes of the 2012 Act, that that definition in the 2006 Act is modified by the 2012 Act s.2(1)(b), *quoad* such matches outside Scotland. In essence, then, a "regulated football match" (for the purposes of this offence) is a football match in Scotland "where one or both of the participating teams (i) represents a country or territory; (ii) represents a club which is for the time being a member of the Scottish Premier League or the Scottish Football League; (iii) represents a club which is for the time being a member (whether a full or associate member) of the Football League, the Football Association Premier League, the Football Conference or the League of Wales"; a football match, in so far as not included amongst those already mentioned, in Scotland which is "part of a competition or tournament organised by or under the authority of the Federation internationale de Football Associations ("FIFA") or the Union of European Football Associations ("UEFA") and . . . where one or both of the participating teams represents a club which is for the time being a member (whether a full or associate member) of, or affiliated to, a national football association which is a member of FIFA: see the 2006 Act s.55(2),(3) as amended by the Football Banning Orders (Regulated Football Matches) (Scotland) Order 2007 (SSI 2007/125) art.2; or such a football match outside Scotland if it involves (i) a national team appointed to represent Scotland, or (ii) a team representing a club that is a member of a football association or league based in Scotland.

[126] The 2012 Act s.1(5) makes plain that behaviour would be so likely "if public disorder would be likely to occur but for the fact that—(a) measures are in place to prevent [such] disorder, or (b) persons likely to be incited to [such] disorder are not present or are not present in sufficient numbers."

[127] See the 2012 Act s.1(2)(a) and (b)—with respect to which it is made "irrelevant whether the hatred is also based (to any extent) on any other factor": see s.1(3).

[128] "Membership" relative to a group of persons "includes association with members of that group": see the 2012 Act s.4(2)(a).

[129] "Presumed" means by the person charged with the crime: see the 2012 Act s.4(2)(b).

[130] "Religious group" is given the broad meaning it has in the Criminal Justice (Scotland) Act 2003 (asp 7) s.74(7), i.e. "a group of persons defined by reference to their—(a) religious belief or lack

group with a perceived religious affiliation" or a group "defined by reference to certain" things[131]—namely, colour, race, nationality (including citizenship), ethnic or national origins, sexual orientation, transgender identity,[132] or disability[133]; also included is behaviour[134] motivated (wholly or partly) by hatred of such a group as is mentioned above, behaviour which is threatening, or such other behaviour as "a reasonable person would be likely to consider offensive."

2. CRIMES RELATIVE TO MORALITY

General introduction

12–25   The crimes dealt with under the above heading are those which generally cannot be justified on the basis of direct harm done to another. Certainly no harm in any conventional sense need be caused by them. Rather the badge of criminality is borne because what is done offends against the currently accepted standards of moral behaviour or against the tenets of the "honour-code" which all upstanding citizens are presently expected to observe. Examples of the former kind consist of various sorts of "indecent conduct" (including incest, which is usually dealt with separately), and examples of the latter are the crimes of treason, perjury, giving false information to the criminal authorities, and various "attempts" to pervert or hinder the course of justice.

2.(A)   PUBLIC INDECENCY

Introduction

12–26   From 1978 onwards,[135] the Scottish courts developed a crime of "shamelessly indecent conduct" which covered acts of indecent exposure,[136] the showing of indecent images (even to willing viewers in private),[137] selling or exposing for sale indecent things,[138] and various sorts of sexual behaviour.[139] The width of that crime and its amorphous nature made it very difficult to describe[140] or justify[141]; and in a case of 2003, Lord Justice-Clerk Gill concluded that that crime rested on an unsound theory, had an uncertain ambit of liability, and laid open

---

of religious belief; (b) membership or adherence to a church or religious organisation; (c) support for the culture and traditions of a church or religious organisation; or (d) participation in activities associated with such a culture or such traditions."

[131]   The "things" are specified in the 2012 Act s.1(4).

[132]   "Transgender identity" is defined in the 2012 Act s.4(3)(b), as any of "(i) transvestism, (ii) transsexualism, (iii) intersexuality, (iv) having by virtue of the Gender Recognition Act 2004 changed gender, (v) any other gender identity that is not standard male or female gender identity".

[133]   "Disability" means "physical or mental impairment of any kind": see the 2012 Act s.4(3)(a).

[134]   See the 2012 Act s.1(2)(c)–(e). Cf. this statutory offence with the situation (prosecuted as breach of the peace at common law) in *Walls v Brown* [2009] HCJAC 59; 2009 S.L.T. 774.

[135]   See *Watt v Annan*, 1978 J.C. 84.

[136]   See, e.g. *Usai v Russell*, 2000 S.C.C.R. 57.

[137]   As in *Watt v Annan*, 1978 J.C. 84, itself.

[138]   See, e.g. *Robertson v Smith*, 1980 J.C. 1.

[139]   See, e.g. *R v HM Advocate*, 1988 S.L.T. 623; *HM Advocate v K*, 1994 S.C.C.R. 499.

[140]   See editions (prior to the 4th) of this book, under the heading: "shamelessly indecent conduct".

[141]   It was especially difficult to justify in terms of art.7(1) of the European Convention on Human Rights: see the Human Rights Act 1998 Sch.1.

to prosecution some forms of private conduct the legality of which should have been a matter for parliament.[142] As a result of the decision of the Appeal Court in that 2003 case, "shamelessly indecent conduct" ceased to be an available criminal charge under Scots common law, and *Watt v Annan*,[143] the case which had begun its development, was overruled: also overruled was any case in which the *ratio* of *Watt v Annan* had been followed.[144] This did not necessarily mean that conduct formerly charged as "shamelessly indecent" would cease to be criminal at all[145]: what henceforward mattered (at common law) was whether such conduct could be brought within "lewd, indecent or libidinous practices"[146] or the crime (based on nineteenth century authority[147]) now known as "public indecency".[148]

Public Indecency

This should be seen as a crime which "fulfills an appropriate role in the main- **12–27** tenance of public order."[149] The actus reus of this common law offence has (or perhaps more accurately, had[150]) two elements: (1) indecent conduct, and (2) the effect of that conduct on the minds of the public.[151] As far as the first of these is concerned, the description certainly applies to sexual "improprieties" such as exposure of the "person" (usually the penis[152]), sexual intercourse in public view, and the making of sexual actions or gestures in a stage performance[153]: it is not yet decided whether "indecent conduct" can apply to non-sexual matters.[154] Whether or not relevant conduct can be described as "indecent" depends on the circumstances (including time and place) of each case, judged by the toleration standards of contemporary society—standards which will obviously be subject to change with the passage of time and alteration of tastes.[155] The "public" element is fulfilled if the indecent conduct occurs in public, or in private—if it is nevertheless visible to the public or takes place before unwilling witnesses[156]—and causes

---

[142] *Webster v Dominick*, 2005 J.C. 65 (a five judge decision of July 22, 2003), at 78, para.43.

[143] *Watt v Annan*, 1978 J.C. 84.

[144] *Webster v Dominick*, 2005 J.C. 65, Lord Justice-Clerk Gill at 78, para.46: the other four judges agreed with his opinion.

[145] See *Webster v Dominick*, 2005 J.C. 65, Lord Justice-Clerk Gill at 81, para.59.

[146] See above, para.9–21. Lewd, indecent or libidinous practices at common law will eventually be abolished under the Sexual Offences (Scotland) Act 2009 (asp 9) s.52(a): see in this connection The Sexual Offences (Scotland) Act 2009 (Commencement No. 1) and The Criminal Justice and Licensing (Scotland) Act 2010 (Commencement No. 4) Order 2010 (SSI 2010/357) art.2(a).

[147] See, in particular, *dicta* in *McKenzie v Whyte* (1864) 4 Irv. 570.

[148] *Webster v Dominick*, 2005 J.C. 65, Lord Justice-Clerk Gill at 79, para.51.

[149] *Webster v Dominick*, 2005 J.C. 65, Lord Justice-Clerk Gill (with whose opinion the other four judges agreed) at 80, para.58: see also 79, para.52.

[150] It must be borne in mind that under the Sexual Offences (Scotland) Act 2009 (asp 9) s.52(b) "in so far as the provisions of this Act regulate any conduct they replace any rule of law regulating that conduct." The effect of this *quoad* public indecency (that common law offence not being one to be abolished by the 2009 Act) is that the ambit of that offence is thus to be restricted by certain statutory offences created under the Act: see, e.g. below paras 12–28 to 12–30.

[151] *Webster v Dominick*, 2005 J.C. 65 at 79–80, para.53.

[152] See, e.g. the charge in *Nelson v Barbour*, 2007 S.C.C.R. 283, as set out by Lord Johnston at 284B, para.1, and to which the appellant had pled guilty.

[153] *Webster v Dominick*, 2005 J.C. 65, Lord Justice-Clerk Gill at 80, para.53.

[154] *Webster v Dominick*, 2005 J.C. 65 at 80, para.54.

[155] *Webster v Dominick*, 2005 J.C. 65 at 80, para.58.

[156] *Webster v Dominick*, 2005 J.C. 65 at 80, para.55.

(on an objective basis, it seems[157]) public offence[158] or "affronts public sensibility".[159] This offence is not committed if the conduct occurs in private but would cause offence to certain persons, were they to hear about it[160]; and it is not committed if there is a private showing of indecent images to willing viewers, or if indecent things are sold or exposed for sale. The one possible exception to such conduct which occurs in private before willing observers is said to be "where the conduct is such as to offend even members of a consenting audience."[161] Whether or not an accused person indulged in the conduct for sexual gratification is irrelevant (since that is a matter of motive—relevant only to sentence)[162]; and questions as to the conduct's depraving or corrupting effects[163] are "at most of indirect relevance".[164] The mens rea of the offence was not specifically explored in the leading case of *Webster v Dominick*[165]; but mens rea must form an essential element given the common law nature of the crime.[166] Indeed it now seems clear that proof of acts of indecent conduct in a public place, or in a private place where members of the public actually observe them,[167] or are likely to do so, is not sufficient for conviction without evidence of the mental attitude of the accused to those acts.[168] It is unlikely in the extreme, of course, that direct evidence of such attitudes will be available, but inference from the facts established will suffice[169]; and what should be inferred here on an objective basis is, at the very least, that the accused was recklessly indifferent as to whether or not his (or her) indecent conduct might be observed by the public.[170]

---

[157] *Webster v Dominick*, 2005 J.C. 65 at 79, para.52.

[158] *Webster v Dominick*, 2005 J.C. 65.

[159] *Webster v Dominick*, 2005 J.C. 65 at 79, para.50.

[160] Cf. what was alleged in *Bott v MacLean*, 2005 J.C. 83.

[161] *Webster v Dominick*, 2005 J.C. 65 at 80, para.56: reference is made by Lord Justice-Clerk Gill to *Geddes v Dickson*, 2001 J.C. 69, as an example of conduct which could be offensive to "willing" observers: in that case, persons had been encouraged (by promise of reward) to expose their breasts or penises at a "fun" night held on licensed premises.

[162] *Webster v Dominik*, 2005 J.C. 65 at 80, para.53.

[163] These were relevant considerations for the now discredited crime of "shamelessly indecent conduct".

[164] *Webster v Dominick*, 2005 J.C. 65, Lord Justice-Clerk Gill at 79, para.52, where it is emphasised that, as in the English offence of "outraging public decency" (see, e.g. *Rose v DPP* [2006] EWHC 852 (Admin); [2006] 1 W.L.R. 2626 oral sex in the foyer of a bank held to be insufficiently public, since witnessed only by one person), what really matters is whether the conduct objectively causes *public* offence; see also, however, *R. v Hamilton* [2007] EWCA Crim 2062; [2008] 2 W.L.R, 107 and the English authorities discussed there.

[165] *Webster v Dominick*, 2005 J.C. 65.

[166] See above, para.3–16.

[167] Opinion was reserved as to the necessity for actual observation in *F v Griffiths* [2010] HCJAC 108; 2011 S.L.T. 192, opinion of the court at 195E–G, para.11.

[168] See *F v Griffiths* [2010] HCJAC 108; 2011 S.L.T. 192, opinion of the court at 195E–L, paras 11–12.

[169] *F v Griffiths* [2010] HCJAC 108; 2011 S.L.T. 192, opinion of the court at195K–L, 196A and D, paras 12, 13 and 15.

[170] *F v Griffiths* [2010] HCJAC 108; 2011 S.L.T. 192, opinion of the court at 195H–L, para.12— quoting from *Usai v Russell*, 2000 J.C. 144 at 147, which case involved the now abandoned crime of shameless indecency. (It is to be noted that, as in *F v Griffiths*—see the opinion of the court at 194A, para.5, both (or all) parties to indecent conduct may be prosecuted for public indecency.)

2.(B) ANALOGOUS STATUTORY
OFFENCES

Sexual exposure

This statutory offence[171] is committed if a person intentionally and for the **12–28** purpose[172] of obtaining sexual gratification (or of humiliating, distressing or alarming another person) exposes his or her genitals in a sexual[173] manner to that other person with the further intention that that other person will see them—all without the consent,[174] and without any reasonable belief[175] in the consent, of that other person. This offence is gender neutral. Where the "other person" is a child who has not attained the age of 13 years, or is a child who has attained the age of 13 (but not that of 16) years, separate (similarly worded) offences are committed by the exposer[176]; but in neither case is consent of the child (or belief in the child's consent) a relevant consideration at all. These offences restrict, of course, the ambit of breach of the peace and public indecency at common law.

---

[171] See the Sexual Offences (Scotland) Act 2009 (asp 9) (hereafter, in this paragraph and paras 12–29 to 12–30, referred to as "the 2009 Act") s.8.

[172] See the 2009 Act s.49(1), under which such a purpose is presumed if "in all the circumstances of the case it may reasonably be inferred" that the relevant conduct was done for that purpose. Under s.49(2), it is not relevant to the determination of a person's purpose whether or not the other person "was in fact humiliated, distressed or alarmed by" what was done.

[173] A "manner of exposure" is "sexual" if a reasonable person, in all the circumstances of the case, would consider it to be sexual: see the 2009 Act s.60(2)(c).

[174] In terms of the 2009 Act s.12, "consent" means "free agreement". Such agreement is declared to be absent (see s.13) in a situation where the conduct occurs when the victim is incapable of consenting to it due to the effect of alcohol "or any other substance"; when the victim submits or "agrees" to it because of violence (or threats of same) used (or made) against that victim "or any other person"; when the victim submits or agrees to it because he or she is "unlawfully detained" by the accused; when the victim submits or agrees to it because he or she is mistaken due to deception by the accused as to its nature or purpose; when the victim is induced to submit or agree to it because of impersonation by the accused of a person "known personally" to the victim; or, when the sole "expression or indication of agreement to [it] is from a person other than" the victim. The foregoing list is effectively extended by s.14, which declares that a "person is incapable, while asleep or unconscious, of consenting to any conduct." And, under s.15(2)–(3), it is further declared that consent to one type of conduct does not (per se) imply consent to any other, and that consent, once given, may be withdrawn at any time before, or during, the conduct in question: see also s.15(4) which deals generally with withdrawal of consent. Where the victim suffers from "mental disorder" (as defined in the Mental Health (Care and Treatment) (Scotland) Act 2003 (asp 13) s.328(1)), he or she is deemed incapable of consenting to particular conduct if, by reason of such disorder, he or she is unable to understand what it is, decide whether to engage in it, or communicate a decision relative to it: see the 2009 Act s.17.

[175] In determining whether an accused's belief is reasonable here, regard is to be had "to whether [he or she] took any steps to ascertain whether there was consent . . . and if so, to what those steps were": see the 2009 Act s.16.

[176] See the 2009 Act, ss.25 and 35 respectively. It is to be noted that under s.35, the offence must be committed by a person "who has attained the age of 16 years"; see also ss.27, 39, 40 and 41.

Voyeurism

12–29   This statutory offence[177] is committed if a person[178] does any one of five specified "things" relative to another person[179] without the complainer's consent[180]
(and without any reasonable belief[181] that that complainer consents); in every
case, it is essential that the thing be done for a particular purpose—*either* that of
obtaining sexual gratification for the accused (or of humiliating, distressing or
alarming the complainer)[182] *or* that of obtaining sexual gratification for
the accused or a third party (or of humiliating, distressing or alarming the
complainer)[183]. The specific "things" are as follows: (first) observing the
complainer doing a private act[184]; (second) operating equipment[185] with the intention of enabling the accused or a third party to observe the complainer doing a
private act[186]; (third) recording the complainer doing a private act with the intention that the accused or a third party will look at an image of the complainer doing
a private act[187]; (fourth) operating equipment beneath the complainer's clothing
with the intention of enabling the accused or a third party to observe the complainer's genitals or buttocks "whether exposed or covered with underwear" or to
observe the complainer's underwear (covering his or her genitals or buttocks)—
both in circumstances where the genitals, buttocks or underwear "would not
otherwise be visible"[188]; and (fifth) recording an image beneath the complainer's
clothing of his or her genitals or buttocks "whether exposed or covered with
underwear" *or* of the complainer's underwear (covering the genitals or buttocks)
"in circumstances where the genitals, buttocks or underwear would not otherwise
be visible"—and in either case with the intention that the accused or a third party
"will look at the image".[189] There is also a sixth and more general "thing" which
an accused may do to incur guilt of this crime[190]; it involves installing equipment,

---

[177] See the 2009 Act s.9 (as amended by the Criminal Justice and Licensing (Scotland) Act 2010 (asp
13) s.43(2)).

[178] Hereafter referred to as "the accused" for convenience; the 2009 Act uses alphabetic letters to refer
to the various parties to the offence.

[179] Hereafter referred to as "the complainer" for convenience; the 2009 Act uses alphabetic letters to
refer to the various parties to the offence.

[180] For the meaning of "consent", see above fn.174.

[181] For the meaning of "reasonable belief", see above fn.175.

[182] See the 2009 Act s.9(6); this initial set of purposes apply solely to the first of the five "things".

[183] See the 2009 Act s.9(7), as amended by the Criminal Justice and Licensing (Scotland) Act 2010
(asp 13) s.43(2)(c); this second set of purposes apply to all of the "things" other than the first.

[184] See the 2009 Act s.9(2). "Private act" is defined in s.10(1) of that Act as one done in a place "which in
the circumstances would reasonably be expected to provide privacy" and in respect of which (a) the
"genitals, buttocks or breasts are exposed or covered only with underwear, (b) [the complainer] is using
a lavatory, or (c) [the complainer] is doing a sexual act that is not of a kind ordinarily done in public."

[185] "Operating equipment" includes (see the 2009 Act s.10(2), as amended by the Criminal Justice and
Licensing (Scotland) Act 2010 (asp 13) s.43(3)) enabling or securing the activation of equipment
by a person without his or her knowledge.

[186] See the 2009 Act s.9(3).

[187] See the 2009 Act s.9(4).

[188] See the 2009 Act s.9(4A), as inserted by the Criminal Justice and Licensing (Scotland) Act 2010
(asp 13) s.43(2)(a).

[189] See the 2009 Act s.9(4B), as inserted by the Criminal Justice and Licensing (Scotland) Act 2010
(asp 13) s.43(2)(a).

[190] See the 2009 Act s.9(5), as amended by the Criminal Justice and Licensing (Scotland) Act 2010
(asp 13) s.43(2)(b).

or constructing (or adapting) a structure[191] (or part of it) with the intention in either case of enabling the accused or a third party to do an act referred to in subss. (2), (3), (4), (4A) or (4B) (i.e. to do any of the five "things" referred to above). This offence (or perhaps series of offences) is (or are) intended to be gender neutral; it (or they) is (or are) also intended to limit the ambit of breach of the peace and public indecency at common law. Where the complainer is a child who has not attained the age of 13 years, or is a child who has attained the age of 13 (but not that of 16) years, separate (similarly worded) offences of voyeurism are committed by the accused[192]; in neither case, however, is consent of the child (or belief in the child's consent) a relevant issue at all.

Communicating indecently; Causing a person to see or hear an indecent communication

These two statutory offences are to be found in the 2009 Act s.7, and have **12–30** certain factors in common. "Communicating indecently" is committed if a person[193] intentionally and for a specific purpose sends by any means a sexual[194] written communication[195] to "or directs, by whatever means, a sexual verbal communication[196] at" another person,[197] without the complainer's consent[198] (and without any reasonable belief[199] in the complainer's consent). "Causing a person to see or hear an indecent communication" is committed if, in circumstances other than those which apply to "communicating indecently", the accused intentionally and for a specific purpose causes the complainer to see or hear by any means a sexual written communication or a sexual verbal communication, without the complainer's consent (and without any reasonable belief in the complainer's consent). The "specific purpose" for either offence means a purpose of obtaining sexual gratification, or a purpose of humiliating, distressing or alarming the complainer. If the complainer is a child who has not attained the age of 13 years, or is a child who has attained the age of 13 (but not that of 16) years, separate similarly worded offences are committed by the accused[200]; but in such offences, consent of the child, or reasonable belief in that child's consent, is not a relevant issue at all.

---

[191] "Structure" includes a tent, vehicle or vessel "or other temporary or moveable structure": see the 2009 Act s.10(3).

[192] See the 2009 Act ss.26 and 36 (as amended by the Criminal Justice and Licensing (Scotland) Act 2010 (asp 13) s.43(4) and (5) respectively). It is to be noted that under s.36, the offence must be committed by a person "who has attained the age of 16 years"; see also ss.27, 39, 40 and 41.

[193] Hereafter for convenience referred to as "the accused"; the 2009 Act uses alphabetic letters to denote the various parties involved in the offence.

[194] A communication is sexual if "a reasonable person would, in all the circumstances of the case, consider it to be sexual": see the 2009 Act s.60(2)(b).

[195] A "written communication" is defined in the 2009 Act s.7(4) as a communication in any written form and includes writings "of a person other than [the accused] (as for example a passage in a book or magazine)".

[196] A "verbal communication" is defined in the 2009 Act s.7(4) as a communication in any verbal form and includes "(a) a communication which comprises sounds of sexual activity (whether actual or simulated) and (b) a communication by means of sign language."

[197] Hereafter for convenience referred to as "the complainer".

[198] For the meaning of "consent", see above fn.174.

[199] For the meaning of "reasonable belief", see above fn.175.

[200] See the 2009 Act ss.24 and 34 respectively. It is to be noted that under s.34, the offences must be committed by a person "who has attained the age of 16 years"; see also ss.37, 39, 40 and 41.

2.(C) INCEST

12–31 The crime of incest has been largely statutory since the Reformation; but references in the standard texts[201] to the Incest Act 1567 must now be replaced by references to the Criminal Law (Consolidation) (Scotland) Act 1995.[202] In terms of the modern law, it is incest for a person to have sexual intercourse with a close relative of the opposite sex, where he knew of the relationship at the time.[203] It is of no moment what age the closely related sexual partner is at the time; but if the sexual partner consents to the intercourse, and he or she also knew of the close relationship, then both parties will be guilty.[204]

12–32 The crime is confined to sexual intercourse, which, although not defined in the Act, must be taken to mean penetration of the vagina by the penis. It follows then that any lesser or different form of sexual behaviour cannot be incest. The close relatives of the opposite sex with whom one is not permitted to have sexual intercourse are clearly set out in a table in the Act.[205] Most are blood relatives, but it is to be noted that half-blood relationships are included. Thus, it would be incest for a brother to have sexual intercourse with his half-sister, e.g. where they were both born of the same mother but had been sired by different fathers. Legitimacy or illegitimacy is of no consequence in assessing relationships in the table. It is also to be noted that two adoptive relationships are within the ambit of the crime. It is, therefore, incest for a man to have sexual intercourse with his adoptive mother (or former adoptive mother) or with his adopted daughter (or former adopted daughter); and vice versa for a female, of course. Adoption is the process by which a person's ties with his natural parents are legally terminated. But for the purposes of incest, his relationship with his natural parents is deemed to continue.[206] It is a defence if the accused proves that he did not know of the close relationship and had no reason to suspect it, or that he did not consent to the sexual intercourse, or that he was married to the other person at the time.[207] Such a marriage would have had to have been contracted outwith Scotland, since the

---

[201] See, e.g. Hume, *Commentaries*, i, 447 et seq.; Alison, *Principles*, i, 563 et seq.

[202] The modern statutory law dates from the coming into force of the Incest and Related Offences (Scotland) Act 1986 on November 1, 1986, when the 1567 Act was repealed: see the Incest and Related Offences (Scotland) Act 1986 (Commencement) Order 1986 (SI 1986/1803) art.2. For appropriate cases where the conduct took place prior to that date, the Incest Act 1567 remains as the relevant law—and such cases occasionally do come before the courts: see, e.g. *HM Advocate v L* [2008] HCJAC 77; 2009 S.L.T. 127, which concerned relevant conduct alleged to have taken place between "2 February 1976 and 1 February 1982" and between a man and his step daughter. In that case, the trial judge took the view that the 1567 Act did not apply to a relationship of that nature, especially since that Act was a penal statute and should therefore be construed strictly; the Appeal Court, however, disagreed.

[203] Criminal Law (Consolidation) (Scotland) Act 1995 Act s.1, as amended by the Human Fertilisation and Embryology Act 2008 Sch.6 para.55.

[204] See, e.g. *P v HM Advocate* 2011 S.C.C.R. 36.

[205] Criminal Law (Consolidation) (Scotland) Act 1995 Act s.1(1), Table. Note that the Table is enlarged by virtue of the Human Fertilisation and Embryology Act 2008 Sch.6 para.55: see the fairly complex purposes of Pt 2 of that Act, and in particular ss.33, 35, 41, 42, 43, 44, 45, 47, 48, 56, 58 and 67.

[206] Adoption (Scotland) Act 1978 s.41(1), as amended by the Incest and Related Offences (Scotland) Act 1986 Sch.1 para.5, and by the Civil Partnership Act 2004 s.86(10); Adoption and Children (Scotland) Act 2007 (asp 4) s.41(1)(b).

[207] Criminal Law (Consolidation) (Scotland) Act 1995 s.1(1)(a)-(c).

marriage and incest laws have been harmonised in this country, but be recognised as valid under Scots law.[208]

Rationale and related offences

The present formulation of incest is founded on a Scottish Law Commission **12–33** Report[209] which considered several reasons for maintaining it as a crime. These included protection and maintenance of the family unit,[210] genetic fault (in that the offspring of intercourse between persons closely related are more likely to suffer from mental or physical abnormalities than the children of non-closely related unions),[211] and moral repugnancy.[212] In modern society, however, where traditional family units are not as conspicuous as they once were, contraceptive measures are well understood and practised, techniques for the prediction and detection of foetal abnormalities are highly advanced, and abortions available widely, it is suggested that the only convincing rationale for the retention of incest in the criminal law is moral repugnancy. The crime is limited, however, in the sense that it does not extend to step-relationships, although moral repugnancy might well be thought to apply there also. If a man marries a woman who already has a daughter by a prior partner, it is not incest under the Act for him to have sexual intercourse with his wife's daughter—now his stepdaughter. For that reason, the 1995 Act contains the separate offence of "intercourse with step-child."[213]

2.(D) BREACH OF TRUST OFFENCES

Under Part 5 of the Sexual Offences (Scotland) Act 2009 (asp 9),[214] two statutory **12–34** offences are created. The first of these ("sexual abuse of trust") is committed[215] if a person (who has attained the age of 18 years) intentionally engages in sexual activity[216] with (or directed towards) another person (aged under 18) to whom he or she stands in a position of trust[217]; but a person charged with such an offence may have a defence—as specified in s.45 of the 2009 Act. The second such offence ("sexual abuse of trust of a mentally disordered person") is committed[218] if a person intentionally engages in sexual activity with (or directed towards) a

---

[208] On which, see P. R. Beaumont and P.E. McEleavy, *Anton's Private International Law*, 3rd edn (Edinburgh: W. Green, 2011), Ch.15.

[209] Scottish Law Commission, *Report on the Law of Incest in Scotland* (HMSO, 1981), Scot. Law Com. No.69, Cmnd.8422.

[210] *Report on the Law of Incest in Scotland* (HMSO, 1981), paras 3.10 to 3.16, Scot. Law Com. No.69.

[211] *Report on the Law of Incest in Scotland* (HMSO, 1981), paras 3.19 to 3.23, Scot. Law Com. No.69.

[212] *Report on the Law of Incest in Scotland* (HMSO, 1981), paras 3.17 to 3.18, Scot. Law Com. No.69.

[213] Criminal Law (Consolidation) (Scotland) Act 1995 s.2.

[214] Hereafter referred to in this paragraph as "the 2009 Act".

[215] See the 2009 Act s.42.

[216] Under the 2009 Act s.60(2)(a), an activity is sexual "if a reasonable person would, in all the circumstances of the case, consider it to be sexual."

[217] A person is in a "position of trust" in relation to another person if any of the five conditions in s.43(2)–(6) are fulfilled—as amplified in s.43(7) and explained (as necessary) in s.44. These complex provisions should carefully be consulted with reference to any particular case.

[218] See the 2009 Act s.46.

mentally disordered[219] person, and that person provides care services[220] to the mentally disordered person or is employed (or contracted) to provide services in or to (or is a manager of) "a hospital, independent health care service or state hospital in which [the mentally disordered person] is being given medical treatment"[221]; a person charged with such an offence may have a defence—as specified in s.47 of the 2009 Act. These offences are gender neutral.

2.(E) EXTREME PORNOGRAPHY

12–35 This statutory offence was created in 2010.[222] It is committed (in essence) if a person is in possession of an "extreme pornographic image"—i.e. an image[223] which is obscene,[224] pornographic a (meaning that the image "is of such a nature that it must reasonably be assumed to have been made solely or principally for the purpose of sexual arousal"[225]) and extreme. An image is to be taken as extreme[226]

"if it depicts, in an explicit and realistic way one of the following:—(a) an act which takes or threatens a person's life, (b) an act which results, or is likely to result, in a person's severe injury, (c) rape or other non-consensual penetrative sexual activity, (d) sexual activity involving (directly or indirectly) a human corpse,[227] or (e) an act which involves sexual activity between a person and an animal (or the carcase of an animal)."[228]

An "image" can be a "moving" or "still" image "made by any means", or it can mean "data" (however stored) which can be converted into an image.[229] Following the above complex narration of the offence, there are exceptions and defences;

---

[219] The 2009 Act s.17(3), defines "mental disorder" (and correlative expressions) throughout the Act as having the meaning it is (or they are in effect) given in the Mental Health (Care and Treatment) (Scotland) Act 2003 (asp 13) s.328(1).

[220] The 2009 Act s.46(3),(4), explains what is meant by "provision of care services" and "care services" respectively.

[221] See the 2009 Act s.46(2) as also (3) and (4).

[222] See the Civic Government (Scotland) Act 1982 (hereafter in this paragraph referred to as "the 1982 Act"), ss.51A–51C, as inserted by the Criminal Justice and Licensing (Scotland) Act 2010 (asp 13) s.42(2). The "model" for this offence can be found in the Criminal Justice and Immigration Act 2008 ss.63–67 which was not made applicable to Scotland: see s.152(1),(2); there are, however, significant differences between the Scottish and English versions of the offence. For criticism of the English version, see C. McGlynn and E. Rackley, "Criminalising Extreme Pornography: A Lost Opportunity" [2009] Crim. L.R. 245.

[223] See the 1982 Act s.51A(4), and (5) which (unusually) provides an example of when an image, forming part of a series of images, may be considered not "pornographic" on the basis of the offending image's context.

[224] The word "obscene" is left undefined.

[225] See the 1982 Act s.51A(3).

[226] See the 1982 Act s.51A(6).

[227] This is perhaps the only member of this group which would not hitherto have amounted to an offence in Scotland; cf. Scottish Law Commission, *Report on Rape and Other Sexual Offences* (HMSO, 2007), paras 5.28 and 5.29, Scot. Law Com. No.209.

[228] Whether an image depicts any of the acts, mentioned above in the text, may be determined by reference to that image's description, any sounds accompanying it, or ("where the image forms an integral part of a narrative constituted by a series of images") any sounds accompanying that series or the context of that narrative: see the 1982 Act s.51A(7).

[229] See the 1982 Act s.51A(9).

these are plainly necessary given (for example) that some images which are parts of properly "certificated" cinematic films may nevertheless fall within the offence's wide parameters. Excluded from those parameters are, therefore, "excluded images".[230] These are images which form all or part of a "classified work"—meaning "a video work in respect of which a classification certificate has been issued by a designated authority."[231] But these exclusions are not all that they seem: an image is excepted from those excluded if that image

"(a) has been extracted from a classified work and (b) it must reasonably be assumed to have been extracted (whether with or without other images) from the [video] work solely or principally for the purpose of sexual arousal"[232]

—assistance with making the assumption in (b) being provided by consideration of (inter alia) the description of the image, any sounds accompanying it, and how it was stored.[233] And there is more: a person charged with this offence will have a defence if he proves[234] one (or more) of the following—namely, that he had a legitimate reason for his possession of the image in question; that he had not seen the said image "and did not know, nor had any cause to suspect, it to be an extreme pornographic image"; that he had been sent the said image without his (or any person on his behalf) having made any prior request for it, and had then not kept it for an unreasonable time.[235] Such a person will also have a defence if he proves that he "directly participated in the act depicted" (in the image in question) *and* that that act "did not actually take or threaten a person's life", "did not actually result in (nor was it actually likely to result in) a person's serious injury", "did not actually involve non consensual activity", did not in fact involve a human corpse or an animal (or its carcase)—provided that he had not shown, given or offered for sale "the image to any person who was not also a direct participant in the act depicted."[236]

---

[230] See the 1982 Act s.51B.
[231] See the 1982 Act s.51B(1), (2) and (5). "Video work", "classification certificate" and "designated authority" are as defined in the Video Recordings Act 1984 s.1 (as amended by the Criminal Justice and Public Order Act 1994 Sch.9 para.22; see also the Digital Economy Act 2010 Sch.1 para.3), s.7 (as amended by the Video Recordings Act 1993 s.1(3); the Criminal Justice and Public Order Act 1994 s.90(2); and the Digital Economy Act 2010 Sch.1 para.3—and see also para.4, which adds s.7A to the 1984 Act), and s.4 (as amended by the Video Recordings Act 1993 s.1(1),(2) and the Digital Economy Act 2010 Sch.1 para.2)—and see also s.4ZA ("designated authority" for video games), as inserted by the Digital Economy Act 2010 s.41. [The curious repeal, and re-enactment of (inter alia) ss.1, 4 and 7 of the 1984 Act by the Video Recordings Act 2010 may here be ignored.]
[232] See the 1982 Act s.51B(3) para.(b) of which being somewhat inelegantly expressed.
[233] See the 1982 Act s.51B(4).
[234] This, of course, would be "on the balance of probabilities", rather than the "prosecutorial standard" of "beyond reasonable doubt". See generally on such statutory burdens placed on the accused *Glancy v HM Advocate* [2011] HCJAC 104; 2012 S.C.C.R. 52, and note that in that case (opinion of the court at 58, paras 11–13) it is confirmed that no elucidation of the phrase "balance of probabilities" is required of a trial judge in his charge to the jury.
[235] See the 1982 Act s.51B(1), (2).
[236] See the 1982 Act s.51C(3), (4) and (5).

2.(F) "HONOUR-CODE" OFFENCES

Introduction

12–36   The crimes, briefly dealt with below, can be classified as "honour-code" offences, meaning those where the accused was in breach of his plain duty to behave as an upright citizen of his country should. They can also, of course, be classified in other ways—for example, as "offences against the state," "offences against public welfare," or "offences against the course of justice."[237] But none of these classifications has any official status; and, in the interests of economy, the one title which appears to cover all of those selected here has been preferred.

Treason

12–37   Since the Union with England, the Scots law of treason has been replaced by that which pertains in England.[238] There is consequently nothing particularly Scottish about it. Hume[239] and Gordon[240] both more than adequately describe the law; and reference to these standard texts should be made when details of the crime are needed. It must be seldom, however, that such details will be required. The crime of treason is of importance only in wartime, or in time of rebellion, when the aspect of it known as "adhering to the Queen's enemies" may assume importance. At basis, as Hume narrates, treason includes

> "all such offences as are more immediately directed against the person and Government of the [Queen]; and amount to a violation of that fidelity and allegiance which is due to [Her] Majesty from all [her] subjects . . .".[241]

Offences against state security in peace time are generally not regarded as treasons, but as specific statutory offences where the requirements of the statutes in question can be met.[242]

Perjury

12–38   This common law crime consists of "the judicial affirmation of falsehood upon oath."[243] When a witness is called upon to give evidence under oath (or affirmation) in any judicial proceedings, then he promises to tell the truth, and clearly is on honour to do just that. If he gives evidence which he knows is not true, then he is in breach of the faith reposed in him and can be prosecuted for perjury if the evidence he gave was "pertinent to the point at issue."[244] The actus reus of the offence is thus complete when the false evidence is uttered; and the mens rea is

---

[237] See Gordon, *Criminal Law*, 3rd edn (2000/2001), Vol.II, Pts VI, VII and VIII.
[238] See the Treason Act 1708.
[239] Hume, *Commentaries*, i, 512 et seq.
[240] Gordon, *Criminal Law*, 3rd edn (2000/2001), paras 37.01 to 37.25.
[241] Hume, *Commentaries*, i, 512.
[242] See, e.g. the "Official Secrets Acts 1911 to 1989" as they are now referred to under the Official Secrets Act 1989 s.16(2). See also the Terrorism Prevention and Investigation Measures Act 2011— which is merely the latest in a series of anti-terrorism related enactments, such as the Counter-Terrorism Act 2008.
[243] Hume, *Commentaries*, i, 366.
[244] Hume, *Commentaries*, i, 369.

satisfied if the accused can be shown to have known that that evidence was false at the time he gave it. It has been held to be perjury where the accused gave evidence that he had been with A at the relevant time, when in truth he knew he could not recall whether he had been with A or with B.[245] As far as the "pertinence" of the evidence to the proceedings in which it was given is concerned, the following statements by Alison have been approved by the High Court:

> "The falsehood must be in a matter pertinent to the issue, and competent to be asked of the witness; but if this be the case, it matters not in how trivial a matter the falsehood may consist, or how far from the original relevant matter the witness may have been led before he makes the false [statement]."[246]

It has also been held to be perjury for an accused person to give false evidence denying his guilt at his own trial.[247] There also exists the related offence of "Subornation of Perjury," which consists in the deliberate "seducing" of someone to commit perjury by, for example, promises of reward, actual bribery or threats of violence, provided that false evidence is eventually given by the "victim."[248]

Attempt to pervert or defeat or hinder the course of justice

It is thought that "attempt to pervert the course of justice" is not a distinct **12–39** common law offence, but is either a general principle used to generate a variety of related, specific offences,[249] or a convenient description for a series of innominate crimes.[250] As a principle or a description, it can take a number of different formulations, such as "attempt to defeat the course of justice,"[251] "hindering the course of justice,"[252] or "hinder and frustrate the course of justice and attempt to defeat the course of justice."[253] Where a complaint or indictment of such a nature uses a form which includes the word "attempt," this is generally not to be understood as a reference to an attempt to commit the crime. "Attempt" is used in this context as a mere word of style, as must be obvious from cases of "escaping from lawful custody" where the prisoner did indeed escape,[254] and of "hiding oneself away to avoid giving evidence for the Crown" where the accused did successfully spirit himself away.[255] These are completed crimes, and not attempts in the normal sense. Indeed it is equally common in such circumstances for the word "attempt" to be dropped altogether such that the charge simply narrates the perversion of the

---

[245] *Simpson v Tudhope*, 1988 S.L.T. 297.
[246] Alison, *Principles*, i, 469 at "4"; approved in *Lord Advocate's Reference (No.1 of 1985)*, 1987 S.L.T. 187 at 192J.
[247] See *HM Advocate v Cairns*, 1967 J.C. 37, where Cairns had been acquitted of murder on a verdict of not proven, at a trial where he himself had given evidence denying that he had stabbed the victim; cf. *R. v Miell* [2007] EWCA Crim 3130; [2008] 1 W.L.R. 627.
[248] See Hume, *Commentaries*, i, Chap.XII, p.381 et seq.
[249] See *Bernard Greenhuff* (1838) 2 Swin. 236, per Lord Cockburn at 274.
[250] See *HM Advocate v Martin*, 1956 J.C. 1, per Lord Cameron at 3, where both views appear to have been advanced, the former ultimately being favoured.
[251] See, e.g. the charge in *HM Advocate v Martin*, 1956 J.C. 1.
[252] See, e.g. the charge in *Turnbull v HM Advocate*, 1953 J.C. 59.
[253] See *HM Advocate v Mannion*, 1961 J.C. 79.
[254] See, e.g. *HM Advocate v Martin*, 1956 J.C. 1.
[255] See *HM Advocate v Mannion*, 1961 J.C. 79.

course of justice.[256] The course of justice must, of course, have been running in order to have been perverted; but not much seems necessary to satisfy this element, since in one case it was held sufficient that police officers, having been shown an arrest warrant for a particular person, had set off to find him.[257] The mens rea element of these offences appears to be behaviour deliberately aimed at perverting the course of justice.[258] It is suggested that what unites cases classifiable under the heading of this paragraph is the accused's failure to obtemper his public, moral duty to allow the criminal justice system to run its appointed course, once set in motion. Witnesses should thus recognise their duty to give evidence when called upon to do so, or, at least, to make themselves available to give evidence when they suspect that that will be required of them; persons in lawful custody should seek only lawful methods of securing their liberty; witnesses should tell the truth when under oath to do so in judicial proceedings; and so on.[259] Where a specific named crime exists, however, it is customary to charge that rather than an "attempt to defeat the course of justice," as happens plainly in the case of perjury.[260]

Giving false information to the criminal athorities

12–40   The crime of giving false information to the criminal authorities could be seen as an example of "attempting to defeat the ends of justice." But since the giving of such false information usually applies to the setting in motion of an investigation rather than contributing something negative to one already in train, the tendency is to charge it as a crime of its own kind. There are two distinct aspects. The first relates to the making of a false accusation of crime against a particular, named individual, where the accusation is, of course, known by its maker to be false. This is recognised as criminal by Hume[261]; and the case of *Simpkins v HM Advocate*[262] provides a modern example (although reported only on sentence). Hume[263] requires that there be special malice shown by the accused, although it is probably now sufficient that he plainly knew the story to be untrue when he uttered it. Negligence or perhaps even recklessness in assembling the facts on which such an accusation is based would probably not be enough, since there is clearly a public need not to discourage the reporting of crimes to the police or fiscal.

12–41   The second aspect relates to the giving of false information to the police (or perhaps the local prosecutors) which makes them commence an investigation. This is certainly criminal, and is sometimes referred to as "wasting police time."[264]

---

[256] See, e.g. *McElhinney v Normand*, 1996 S.L.T. 238.
[257] *McElhinney v Normand*, 1996 S.L.T. 238, opinion of Lord Sutherland at 242D. The police had in fact spotted the person named in the warrant and were chasing him down the street when the accused in this case intervened by picking up the wanted man in a car and carrying him "safely" away.
[258] See, e.g. *Carney v HM Advocate*, 1995 S.L.T. 1208; *Johnstone v Lees*, 1995 S.L.T. 1174.
[259] It has been held insufficient, however, for an accused person to say that he will not co-operate with a warrant for him to be medically examined—unless his stated refusal is first put to the test: see *Vaughan v HM Advocate*, 2004 S.C.C.R. 537.
[260] See above, para.12–38; but cf. *Waddell v MacPhail*, 1986 S.C.C.R. 593, where lies told to the police were dealt with under the present general principle.
[261] Hume, *Commentaries*, i, 341 to 343.
[262] *Simpkins v HM Advocate*, 1985 S.C.C.R. 30.
[263] Hume, *Commentaries*, i, 342.
[264] See, e.g. Gane, Stoddart and Chalmers, *A Casebook on Scottish Criminal Law*, 4th edn (2009), paras 17–02 to 17–05.

Whilst the information must be known to be false,[265] there is no need here for any person to be named as a culprit or for any suggestion to be made that a crime has been committed at all. In *Kerr v Hill*,[266] for example, the accused merely told the police that he had seen a collision between a bus and a cyclist, and left it entirely open as to whether a crime had been involved. As Lord Justice-General Normand put it[267]:

> "The point is that the criminal authorities were deliberately set in motion by a malicious person by means of an invented story. That is the essence of the crime . . .".

This appears to be confirmed by the decision in *Bowers v Tudhope*[268] where a false allegation was made to the police that a giro cheque had been lost (not stolen). Once again, it seems sufficient that the accused knew that the information was false. In practice, malice on his part does not seem to be required.[269]

---

[265] See *Walkingshaw v Coid*, 1988 S.C.C.R. 454 Sh.Ct.
[266] *Kerr v Hill*, 1936 J.C. 71.
[267] *Kerr v Hill*, 1936 J.C. 71 at 75.
[268] *Bowers v Tudhope*, 1987 S.L.T. 748.
[269] See, e.g. *Gray v Morrison*, 1954 J.C. 31.

CHAPTER 13

STATUTORY OFFENCES

Introduction

13–01　Most of this book has been concerned with non-statutory offences, since Scotland still places reliance upon the common law to generate and define its criminal law. But it is not possible to ignore or underestimate the considerable importance and impact of statutory crimes. Much of the time of the criminal courts is taken up, for example, in dealing with a wide range of particular offences set out in the Road Traffic Act 1988 and in the Misuse of Drugs Act 1971. It can hardly be expected, of course, that an introductory text on criminal law would deal in detail with all of the crimes to be found within those two Acts, let alone the many offences set out in literally hundreds of statutes currently in force.[1] Indeed, adequate consideration of road traffic and of drugs offences would require the construction of individual volumes of some length devoted entirely to those subjects. It must also be borne in mind that there has never been a period since its inception when the United Kingdom Parliament has not been active in the promulgation of new crimes; and the Scottish Parliament now has similar powers in relation to non-reserved criminal matters.[2] The range of statutory offences is, therefore, constantly expanding, and now includes areas of law at one time dominated by the common law.[3] As far as the Scottish courts are concerned, the United Kingdom Parliament may do as it pleases. If a new offence has been created in an enactment which has passed both Houses and received the Royal Assent, then it is formally valid and cannot be questioned on the basis that it is otherwise unconstitutional.[4]

INTERPRETATION I

13–02　Although a statutory crime cannot in general be struck down on the basis of its unconstitutionality[5] (unlike, say, the position in the United States), the criminal courts may still make a substantial contribution to the way in which that crime is received. This is achieved by the device of interpretation. A court has a duty to interpret the bare words used by Parliament.[6] In theory, anyone with a reasonable

---

[1] Indeed, every piece of legislation should be closely examined for the presence of offences; for example, even the innocuous sounding Christmas Day and New Year's Day Trading (Scotland) Act 2007 (asp 13) contains an offence which carries a maximum penalty on summary conviction of £50,000: see s.4.

[2] See above, para.2–11 to 2–13.

[3] See, e.g. the Sexual Offences (Scotland) Act 2009 (asp 9).

[4] For the position relative to the Scottish Parliament, see above, para.2–12.

[5] Cf. above, paras 2–11–2–13.

[6] This includes the correction of an obvious drafting error: see, e.g. *Johnstone v HM Advocate* [2011] HCJAC 66A; 2011 S.C.C.R. 470.

350

command of English should be able to understand the import of any statutory crime. It will after all have been laid out in a particular provision of the statute in question in plain English words. But initial appearances can be deceptive. A particular word may be found to have no plain, simple significance at all. Again, the plain meaning of a particular word may not have been intended. If that was not intended, then one would expect Parliament to have made that clear; and generally it does, by allocating a particular meaning in an "Interpretation Section"—which may be far removed from the very section which contains the word in focus. In s.28(1) of the Road Traffic Act 1988 (as substituted by the Road Traffic Act 1991 s.7), for example, it is stated: "A person who rides a cycle on a road dangerously is guilty of an offence." Relative to that, the United Kingdom Parliament has seen fit to give particular meanings to "dangerously" (in s.28(2) and (3)), and to "cycle" and "road" (both defined in s.192(1) of the Road Traffic Act 1988, as amended by the Road Traffic Act 1991 Sch.4 para.78(2)). It will be noted that with respect to "road", the inquirer is directed to a completely different Act—namely, the Roads (Scotland) Act 1984[7]—for part of the desired definition. Such definitions, however, may themselves require more particular interpretation when they are considered in relation to an actual case.[8] Where given definitions require more particular interpretation, or where statutory words have not been defined at all, it is judges in courts, in actual criminal cases before them, who must so interpret or assign meanings.[9] When they do so, their decisions may be considered authoritative,[10] in which event the interpretations and assigned meanings become part of the statutory law itself. In relation to statutory road traffic offences, for example, what it means to "drive" a mechanically propelled vehicle is often crucial; but the Road Traffic Acts have never defined "driving" at all. The courts have, therefore, had to decide the meaning of that word, and its correlatives.[11] Clearly these interpretations and meanings do not appear in the bare text of the statutory crime. They will have to be searched for by the inquirer, using, for example, the *Current Law Statute and Legislation Citator* volumes.[12]

Decisions by English courts

When the precise meaning of a particular word or phrase in a statutory crime is **13–03** an issue in criminal proceedings, a court will look for interpretation sections within the Act itself, and also for interpretations laid down in authoritative decisions in the past. It is to be noted here that decisions by English criminal

---

[7] See, in particular, the Roads (Scotland) Act 1984 s.151(1), as amended by the New Roads and Street Works Act 1991 Sch.8 para.94(b), and the Local Government etc. (Scotland) Act 1994 s.146.

[8] See, e.g. *Beattie (John M) v Scott*, 1990 S.C.C.R. 435; *Young v Carmichael*, 1991 S.C.C.R. 332; and *Aird v Vannet*, 1999 S.C.C.R. 322, in relation to the definition of "road" under the Roads (Scotland) Act 1984. See also *Dick v Walkingshaw*, 1995 S.L.T. 1254 (as to whether and in what circumstances the deck of a ferry can be considered as a "road") and *Teale v MacLeod*, 2008 S.C.C.R. 12.

[9] Cf. the English case of *R. v Da Silva* [2006] EWCA Crim 1654; [2007] 1 W.L.R. 303, where the meaning of "suspecting" in the Criminal Justice Act 1988 s.93A(1)(a) (as inserted by the Criminal Justice Act 1993 s.29) was at issue: the modern equivalent of the now repealed s.93A(1)(a) is to be found in s.328(1) of the Proceeds of Crime Act 2002, which applies to Scotland: see the 2002 Act s.461.

[10] See above, para.2–10.

[11] See, e.g. *Ames v MacLeod*, 1969 J.C. 1; *McArthur v Valentine*, 1990 S.L.T. 732; *Guthrie v Friel*, 1993 S.L.T. 899 (attempt to drive); and the unusual case of *Hoy v McFadyen*, 2000 S.C.C.R. 875. See also below, para.13–03.

[12] Covering 1948 to date: see the prefaces to each volume for full instructions on use.

courts (or those elsewhere in the United Kingdom), no matter how eminent, are never more than "persuasive" in Scotland[13]; they are never required to be followed in this country, where judges may take an entirely different view. This certainly does happen—however regrettable it may be in relation to statutory offences which the United Kingdom Parliament intended to be applied uniformly on both sides of the border. In many offences under the Road Traffic Act 1988, for example, that the accused was "driving" a motor vehicle at the time is of some importance. But, where a person is standing outside a broken-down car, pushing it along a road by muscle power and making occasional adjustments to its direction by reaching for the steering-wheel, he is definitely "driving" that car under Scots law[14] but probably would not be doing so under English law.[15] Again, in *Kelly v MacKinnon*[16] Lord Justice-General Emslie refused to entertain the view of the Lord Chief Justice of England in *Cafferata v Wilson*[17] that, for the purposes of s.57(1)(b) of the Firearms Act 1968, a starting-pistol or similar "gun" was a component part of a lethal weapon and thus a "firearm" since it could, by boring out the barrel and carrying out certain other operations, be made capable of firing live ammunition; and indeed the Lord Justice-General described the views expressed in the English case as "manifestly absurd" and "not only unsound but patently unsound."[18]

Repealed versions of the same crime

13-04   In *Kiely v Lunn*[19] a boy of 15 had had many absences from school. Consequently his father was charged with an offence under s.35(1) of the Education (Scotland) Act 1980,[20] namely:

> "Where a child of school age . . . fails without reasonable excuse to attend regularly at . . . school, his parent shall be guilty of an offence."

The reason for the boy's protracted absence was that he was chronically addicted to glue sniffing, and showed no willingness to accept help in breaking the habit. In terms of s.42(1)(b) of the same Act, there would be deemed to be a reasonable excuse if "the child had been prevented by sickness from attending school." The question which arose for decision was, therefore, whether a self-inflicted and self-perpetuated disability could be construed as "sickness." Since no interpretation was offered by the Act itself, and no previous cases could be found to shed light

---

[13] They may, of course, be regarded as "highly persuasive", usually meaning that they are well worth following—see, e.g. *Davies v Smith*, 1983 S.L.T. 644 (which adopts the reasoning given in *Federal Steam Navigation Company Ltd v Department of Trade & Industry* [1974] 1 W.L.R. 505); see also the general remarks of Lord Justice-General Hamilton (on the interpretation of the Human Rights Act 1998) in the full-bench decision of *Dickson v HM Advocate* [2007] HCJAC 65; 2008 S.L.T. 12 at 18–19, para.27.
[14] *Ames v MacLeod*, 1969 J.C. 1; *McArthur v Valentine*, 1990 S.L.T. 732.
[15] See, e.g. *R. v MacDonagh* [1974] Q.B. 448.
[16] *Kelly v MacKinnon*, 1982 J.C. 94, at 98, 99.
[17] *Cafferata v Wilson* [1936] 3 All E.R. 149.
[18] In one case it was said: "The result may be that different constructions are placed upon the Act of 1988 [Road Traffic Act] in Scotland and England, but this is the result of different police procedures in the two countries"—*Simpson v McClory*, 1993 J.C. 110, per Lord Justice-Clerk Ross at 119D.
[19] *Kiely v Lunn*, 1983 J.C. 4.
[20] Education (Scotland) Act 1980 (c.44), but given erroneously as (c.20) in the report.

on the matter, the Appeal Court looked at previous versions of the same crime. In particular, they looked at the Education (Scotland) Act 1883 s.11, which held out as a reasonable excuse: that "the child had been prevented from attending school by sickness or any other unavoidable cause." Although the last five words had been dropped from s.42(1)(b) of the 1980 Act, the Appeal Court took the view that these words still provided an excellent guide as to how "sickness" was to be interpreted, namely that it meant

> "an unavoidable cause of absence, at least in the sense that it cannot be construed to include a state of ill health brought about by the deliberate actings of the child concerned."[21]

The conclusion is, then, that it is legitimate to use the original wording of repealed but re-enacted statutory crimes as an aid to the construction of the latest re-enacted form, provided, of course, that it was not the legislature's clear intention to alter the substance of the original crime.

Use of dictionaries

Where all else fails, and the meaning to be assigned to a particular word in a **13–05** statutory offence is crucial to the determination of a case, the courts will often turn to dictionary definitions. If several meanings are proffered by a dictionary, the court will generally adopt the one that best accords with the word in its statutory context. In *Patchett v MacDougall*,[22] for example, the accused had shot a collie dog in the head and killed it. There was no evidence that it had survived the shooting for any significant length of time, or at all. Nevertheless, the accused was charged with causing "unnecessary suffering to [the] animal" by wanton or unreasonable conduct, in terms of s.1(1)(a) of the Protection of Animals (Scotland) Act 1912. As he had shot the dog deliberately and without reason, his guilt or innocence plainly depended upon whether he had caused it to "suffer" or not. To determine this issue, Lord Justice-Clerk Wheatley examined the definition of "suffering" as given in the Shorter Oxford English Dictionary (a favoured work amongst the judiciary, presumably because of its convenient, two-volume size). He chose the second of the meanings offered there, namely "the bearing or undergoing of pain", and concluded that there was no evidence that the unfortunate animal had undergone any such thing. The accused, therefore, had his conviction quashed, the Lord Justice-Clerk dismissing the argument that the dog had suffered by losing its life as metaphysical, and not what the Act envisaged at all.[23]

Similarly, in *White v Allan*[24] a woman was convicted of the offence specified in **13–06** s.46(1) of the Civic Government (Scotland) Act 1982, which states that:

---

[21] *Kiely v Lunn*, 1983 J.C. 4 at 7.

[22] *Patchett v MacDougall*, 1983 J.C. 63.

[23] *Patchett v MacDougall*, 1983 J.C. 63 at 64. Most (and in particular s.1) of the 1912 Act is now repealed by the Animal Health and Welfare (Scotland) Act 2006 (asp 11) Sch.2 para.5: s.19 of the 2006 Act now frames the appropriate offence of causing unnecessary suffering to a "protected animal" (as defined in s.17)—but "suffering" now receives a statutory definition in s.48 of that Act. (The 2006 Act in fact contains many interesting offences which will repay close study.)

[24] *White v Allan*, 1985 S.C.C.R. 85.

"A prostitute (whether male or female) who for the purposes of prostitution
. . . (c) importunes any person who is in a public place, shall be guilty [of an
offence] . . .".

She was charged, then, as a person possessing a certain qualification, i.e. that she
was a prostitute. She challenged the applicability of that special capacity to her.[25]
It thus became necessary for the Crown to demonstrate that she had possessed that
qualification at the time of the alleged importuning. The main thrust of the argument was that this offence had originally been enacted in 1892[26] and was then
committed only if the accused was a "common prostitute." Since Parliament had
changed the wording of the offence in 1982 by dropping the adjective "common",
this was claimed to have opened the way for a different interpretation, namely that
if a person, such as the accused, behaved on the occasion in question as a prostitute might (as indeed the accused had), then she fell within the qualification and
thus within the ambit of the offence. The Appeal Court, however, rejected that
contention. It considered that the elision of the word "common" in the re-enacted
offence made no difference, and that the standard meaning of "prostitute" in the
Concise Oxford Dictionary ("a woman who offers her body to promiscuous
sexual intercourse, especially for payment") still applied. Further, the court
interpreted the statutory offence such that the accused had to possess the title of
"prostitute", with that dictionary meaning, prior to the incidents which had led
to the prosecution. Since the Crown had been quite unable to show that, then the
conviction had to be quashed.[27]

Common law alternatives

13–07   If by way of interpretation (or otherwise) it is decided that the statutory offence
charged cannot be established on the facts admitted or proved, all is not necessarily lost for the Crown. In terms of para.14(b) of Sch.3 to the Criminal Procedure
(Scotland) Act 1995

> "where the facts proved under the indictment or complaint do not amount to
> a contravention of the enactment but do amount to an offence at common
> law, it shall be lawful to convict of the common law offence."

This rather useful provision was taken advantage of by the sheriff in *Buchanan v
Hamilton*[28] where he decided that vandalism had not been proved but that breach
of the peace had. Although his decision to convict of the common law crime was
overturned on appeal, this was simply on the basis that it was not for the sheriff to
do so on his own, in the absence of a specific submission to invoke the provision

---

[25] See now the Criminal Procedure (Scotland) Act 1995 s.255, as amended by the Criminal Procedure
(Amendment) (Scotland) Act 2004 (asp 5) Sch. para.38.
[26] Burgh Police (Scotland) Act 1892 s.381(22).
[27] Where the meaning of legislation is ambiguous or obscure, it may be possible to use material from
Hansard, or other reports of Parliamentary debates (or committee proceedings) to assist in interpretation—*Pepper v Hart* [1993] A.C. 593 HL. It has been held that a court may correct obvious
drafting errors in a statutory provision: see *Johnstone v HM Advocate* [2011] HCJAC 66A; 2011
S.C.C.R. 470.
[28] *Buchanan v Hamilton*, 1990 S.L.T. 244.

from the Crown. The Appeal Court did not decide that it was incompetent to convict of breach of the peace in such circumstances.[29]

INTERPRETATION II

There is also a wider dimension to a court's interpretative powers. This relates **13–08** to a court's ability to decide whether mens rea will have to be proved, or facts from which it can be inferred will have to be established, by the Crown in relation to a particular statutory crime. It is usually taken that mens rea must be proved, or facts from which it can be inferred must be established in relation to all common law crimes as a matter of principle[30]; but it is accepted in modern criminal law that some statutory offences do not, and need not, conform to that principle. These form the class of "strict liability" crimes[31] within the general field of statutory offences. These "strict" offences and the courts' role in identifying them are considered in the paragraphs which follow.[32] Also briefly considered below is the subject of "vicarious liability." This sort of liability—where one person is deemed liable for the criminal act or omission of another—is again thought to be peculiar to statutory offences. It is peculiar to those Acts of Parliament which expressly allow it, or to those where the courts, by dint of interpretation, deem it to apply. Careful note must be taken, however, that in the totality of statutory offences, strict liability or vicarious liability is unusual, and certainly does not represent the norm.

How strict liability arises

Offences created by the United Kingdom or Scottish Parliament have **13–09** precisely worded definitions. Every word which appears in a statutory crime must, therefore, be taken to be meaningful. Equally, it can be argued that what does not appear is also meaningful (see below, para.13–10). As far as mens rea is concerned, many statutory offences expressly refer to some form of that concept. Thus, in the Criminal Law (Consolidation) (Scotland) Act 1995, it is stated in s.48(2)(a) that:

"Any person who intentionally obstructs a constable in the exercise of the constable's powers under sub-section (1) [i.e. powers to search suspects for offensive weapons] . . . shall be guilty of an offence . . .".

---

[29] Cf. *Anderson v Griffiths*, 2005 J.C. 169, where the Appeal Court considered it to be within its powers to substitute a "breach of the peace" verdict at an appeal, even though such a verdict had not been sought by the Crown at the original trial for a statutory offence. See also *Horsburgh v Russell*, 1994 S.L.T. 942.

[30] See, e.g. Gordon, *Criminal Law*, 3rd edn (2000/2001), para.7.12.

[31] For some comment on the justifications for the existence of these crimes, and an introduction to relevant (modern) academic literature on the subject, see John Stanton-Ife, "Strict Liability: Stigma and Regret" (2007) 27 O.J.L.S. 151.

[32] If a statutory offence expressly announces that it is to be taken as one of "strict liability", that must be accepted, and no "identification" criteria need then be applied: that would be rather unusual, but see, e.g. s.6 (relative to the offence created by s.4) of the Christmas Day and New Year's Day Trading (Scotland) Act 2007 (asp 13)—which nevertheless provides for a defence of "due diligence". Thus, s.6 of that Act provides an illustration of an offence which is of "strict", but not "absolute", liability: see para.13–13, below.

355

There, the central element of the actus reus of the offence is "obstruction", and clearly it will have to be shown by the Crown that the obstruction was "intentional" on the accused's part. A similar conclusion follows from the way in which the statutory offence of vandalism has been defined.[33] The central element of that crime relates to the destruction or damaging of property, and it is expressly stated that that must be shown to have been wilful or reckless on the part of the accused. The Misuse of Drugs Act 1971 also contains a further instance of the same idea. Section 8,[34] for example, indicates that:

> "A person commits an offence if, being the occupier or concerned in the management of any premises, he knowingly permits or suffers any of the following activities to take place on those premises. . .".

It will there not be sufficient if any of the forbidden activities (which include producing or using a controlled drug) happens to take place on the premises concerned. To be convicted, an accused person must be shown to have *known* that they were taking place, and allowed them to do so in that state of knowledge.

13–10 Relative to crucial (or central) elements of the offences in question, the express use of words such as "intentionally", "recklessly", "wilfully", or "knowingly" demonstrates that these statutory crimes are to be treated similarly to common law ones—namely, that the specified form of mens rea must be proved by the Crown. If it cannot be proved, or if facts from which it might be inferred[35] cannot be established, then the prosecution's case will founder. But what is to be made of offences where Parliament has not made specific provision for any mens rea concepts? In s.47(1) of the Criminal Law (Consolidation) (Scotland) Act 1995, for example, it is laid down[36] that:

> "Any person who has with him in any public place any offensive weapon shall be guilty of an offence . . .".

Quite apart from the oddity of the definition of "public place"[37] and the difficulty of construing "offensive weapon"[38] it would seem that conviction could follow on mere proof that the accused *had* an offensive weapon about his person, whether he knew it was there or not. That would appear to be a fair reading of the subsection, taking the words used in a completely literal sense; but whether it would be

---

[33] See above, para.11–26.

[34] As amended by the Criminal Justice and Police Act 2001 s.38.

[35] See e.g. *Lees v Haig*, 1993 S.L.T. (Sh.Ct.) 76, where the inference was drawn that a concealed, rusty meat cleaver was intended by the accused for use by him for causing personal injury (relative to what is now s.47(4) of the Criminal Law (Consolidation) (Scotland) Act 1995—noting that s.47(4) now reads as it appears in the Criminal Justice and Licensing (Scotland) Act 2010 (asp 13) s.37(2) (c); see also the terms of s.49C of the 1995 Act—offence of having an offensive weapon etc. in a prison—as inserted by the Custodial Sentences and Weapons (Scotland) Act 2007 (asp 17) s.63, and as amended by the Criminal Justice and Licensing (Scotland) Act 2010 (asp 13) s.37(5)).

[36] As amended by the Criminal Justice and Licensing (Scotland) Act 2010 (asp 13) s.37(2)(a).

[37] See Criminal Law (Consolidation) (Scotland) Act 1995 s.47(4), as substituted by the Criminal Justice and Licensing (Scotland) Act 2010 (asp 13) s.37(2)(c), and, e.g. *Normand v Donnelly*, 1994 S.L.T. 62.

[38] See again s.47(4), as substituted by the Criminal Justice and Licensing (Scotland) Act 2010 (asp 13) s.37(2)(c); and see also, e.g. *McGlennan v Clark*, 1993 S.L.T. 1069; *McKee v MacDonald*, 1995 S.L.T. 1342; and *Lees v Haig*, 1993 S.L.T. (Sh.Ct.) 76.

a fair interpretation in relation to an accused person, who had had an offensive weapon slipped surreptitiously into his coat pocket by another, is a different matter; and that is where the difficulty lies. It certainly can be argued that if Parliament had wanted the courts to insist on mens rea being shown, then it would have made appropriate provision. It may, therefore, be meaningful that Parliament has chosen here to exclude any reference to intention, recklessness, knowledge or the like; and so the conclusion may well follow that mens rea is not required to be shown by the Crown. Thus, on this argument, if an offensive weapon had really been slipped into the accused's pocket without his having been aware of it, then he would still have "had it with him" as a matter of fact, and must be convicted—his lack of knowledge being an irrelevant consideration, since knowledge did not have to be shown. This is clearly a harsh, but tenable, interpretative argument. On the other hand, if there is some principle at work, even in statutory crimes, that mens rea is to be presumed to be part of the definition of all offences, then mens rea ought to be required even in the case of statutory offences which are silent on the matter. Were the courts to adopt that principle, then all statutory crimes would require some form of mens rea, unless the United Kingdom or Scottish Parliament had made it abundantly clear that that was exceptionally not to be so in relation to a particular offence. The question faced by courts which do espouse that view is, of course: "What form of *mens rea* is to be required in the absence of the legislature's having given any plain directions?"[39]

Presumption in favour of mens rea

It seems well established under English law that there is a presumption in **13–11** favour of mens rea being required even in the kind of statutory offences where the text is silent as to intention, recklessness, knowledge, wilfulness or the like.[40] That presumption yields, however, where a court is satisfied that Parliament really did not wish mens rea to be considered. Since Parliament seldom[41] makes that plain, the courts must look for signs and hints within, or even outwith, the Act itself in order to deduce Parliament's intention. As can be imagined, this is a somewhat arbitrary process. But it does result in some such statutory offences being considered as of mens rea quality and others acquiring "strict liability" status,[42] where "strict liability" means that no mens rea need be proved or inferred in respect of an issue crucial for conviction.[43]

In Scotland, it seems to be the case that that presumption in favour of mens rea **13–12** is fully accepted. Gordon[44] suggested that it was, although his authorities were mostly English; but acceptance of a sort can be shown in some twentieth century

---

[39] For the answer given by English courts in relation to what is now s.47(1) of the Criminal Law (Consolidation) (Scotland) Act 1995 Act, see *R. v Cugullere* [1961] 1 W.L.R. 858, per Salmon J. at 860.

[40] See *Sweet v Parsley* [1970] A.C. 132 HL, per Lord Reid at 148G–H; *Gammon (Hong Kong) Ltd v Attorney General of Hong Kong* [1985] A.C. 1 PC, per Lord Scarman at 14B–D; *B. (A Minor) v DPP* [2000] 2 A.C. 428 HL, Lord Nicholls of Birkenhead at 460F–G, Lord Steyn at 470H to 471E, Lord Hutton at 478D to 479E; and *R. v M(D)* [2009] EWCA Crim 2615, [2011] 1 W.L.R. 822.

[41] Unusually, the Scottish Parliament has made this plain in s.6 of the Christmas Day and New Year's Day Trading (Scotland) Act 2007 (asp 13) relative to the offence created by s.4 of that Act.

[42] See, e.g. *Strowger v John* [1974] R.T.R. 124.

[43] Cf. Scottish Law Commission, *Report on Rape and Other Sexual Offences* (HMSO, 2007), para.4.32, Scot. Law Com. No.209 (meaning of "strict liability"): see also below, para.13–13.

[44] Gordon, *Criminal Law*, 3rd edn (2000/2001), paras 8.01, 8.02, fn.10.

dicta, especially in the opinions of Lord Justice-General Normand and Lords Wark, Moncrieff and Mackay in *Mitchell v Morrison*.[45] Lord Cameron, in *Swan v MacNab*,[46] was also moved to consider it as "a general proposition." Now, however, the position established in English law[47] seems to have been accepted as also forming part of Scots criminal law.[48] But it must be remembered that that presumption is a rebuttable one, and that a particular statutory offence may nevertheless be considered as one of "strict liability".[49] It must also be remembered that, in both Scotland and England, the threshold for the identification of "strict liability" is the existence of a statutory offence which omits any of the usual references to mens rea, at least in relation to the central element of the crime.[50] The question therefore lies as to the sort of criteria which might then be invoked to displace the presumption and mark the statutory offence under scrutiny as being one of strict liability. These criteria are considered below at paras 13–14 to 13–20. The existence of a specific statutory defence is generally not, however, one of those criteria; a defence is usually reserved for a situation where the necessary elements of an offence have otherwise been established, and so "is at best a neutral factor."[51]

Strict or absolute liability

13–13   Two terms of art have been employed to denote criminal liability which does not depend upon proof of mens rea. "Absolute liability" is the older, and now less fashionable of the two. It was certainly used extensively in Scotland during the first half of the twentieth century[52] and may indeed be not yet dead.[53] With its connotation of criminal liability not only without proof of mens rea but also without benefit of any form of defence, the term is probably much too sweeping, and is best reserved perhaps for those peculiar, "states of affairs" statutory offences which are sometimes encountered.[54] Better, probably, is the term "strict liability." It means criminal liability where the central element of the actus reus of the offence does not require proof of mens rea on the part of the accused, but does not exclude the possibility of there being some form of defence or indeed the possibility of some form of mens rea being required in relation to subsidiary elements. It sounds fairer, in other words, to assert that liability is "strict" rather than "abso-

---

[45] *Michell v Morrison*, 1938 J.C. 64, at 71, 87, 72–73 and 81–82, respectively.
[46] *Swan v McNab*, 1977 J.C. 57 at 61.
[47] See above, para.13–11.
[48] See *Smart v HM Advocate* [2006] HCJAC 12; 2006 S.C.C.R. 120, opinion of the court at 127G–128E, para.22. It is to be noted that in considering what form the mens rea should take, after applying the presumption and concluding that the offence in question was not of strict liability, the court accepted that form favoured by the English Court of Appeal in *R. v Smith; R. v Jayson* [2003] 1 Cr. App. R. 212 (case 13), at 222, para.34, relative to the equivalent statutory offence under English law.
[49] See above, para.13–11.
[50] See *Wings Ltd v Ellis* [1985] A.C. 272, in relation to the Trade Descriptions Act 1968 s.14(1)(a).
[51] *R. v M(D)* [2009] EWCA Crim 2615; [2011] 1 W.L.R. 822, per Rix L.J. at 831, para.32.
[52] See, e.g. *Gordon v Shaw* (1908) 5 Adam 469, where Lord McLaren refers to "absolute prohibition" at 478; *Howman v Russell*, 1923 J.C. 32, per Lord Cullen at 36; *Mitchell v Morrison*, 1938 J.C. 64, per Lord Justice-General Normand at 71.
[53] See, e.g. *MacNeill v Wilson*, 1981 J.C. 87, opinion of the court at 91; see also the relatively modern English case of *R. v M(D)* [2009] EWCA Crim 2615; [2011] 1 W.L.R. 822, where the opinion of the court seems to treat "absolute liability" and "strict liability" as synonymous.
[54] See above, para.3–15, and *Strowger v John* [1974] R.T.R. 124.

lute", and indeed may more accurately reflect the true situation.[55] In *Alphacell Ltd v Woodward*,[56] for example, Viscount Dilhorne pointed out that the statutory offence of "causing" polluting matter to enter a stream was not absolute. If it had been absolute, then mere accidental pollution of a stream might result in conviction, which he did not think to have been Parliament's intention at all. Rather, if the accused had been intentionally carrying on some industrial process, in such a way that the natural consequence would have been the pollution of a stream, and such pollution had in fact occurred, then he could be convicted—even though he had neither intended nor known about such pollution at all.[57] *Alphacell Ltd v Woodward* is, of course, an English case, but was specifically approved in *Lockhart v National Coal Board.*[58]

Criteria for identifying strict liability

It is rare for Scottish courts to discuss, let alone follow, specific criteria for the   **13–14** identification of strict liability, statutory offences. The tendency in fact is to follow English precedents, if such exist[59] or to treat such problems of identification as meriting little more than the application of well-known interpretative techniques in a common-sense way.[60] There is the tendency also to treat each statute as a separate entity and to avoid laying down rules which might be generally applicable to other statutory offences. It would seem, therefore, fairly academic to attempt to consider what sort of criteria might carry weight with a Scottish court. But certain trends are discernible; and failure to consider these would make it impossible to predict when, in the case of new or untested statutory offences which made no express reference to mens rea, the accepted presumption in favour of mens rea could be displaced.[61] In any event, the sort of criteria to be borne in mind were hinted at by Lord McLaren in the early twentieth century case of *Gordon v Shaw.*[62]

Gordon v Shaw

In this case, the Sea Fisheries Regulation (Scotland) Act 1895,[63] by virtue of s.   **13–15** 10(4) and associated by-laws,[64] made it an offence for any person to use certain trawl-fishing methods in the Moray Firth (i.e. within a line drawn between Duncansby Head in Caithness and Rattray Point near Peterhead). The accused was not the master of the vessel concerned, but an ordinary member of the crew. The court was prepared to accept that he might have been quite unaware of the

---

[55] See the use of the term "strict liability" in s.6 of the Christmas Day and New Year's Day Trading (Scotland) Act 2007 (asp 13)—clearly a correct use, since that section provides a defence to the offence created under s.4 of the Act; cf. the "Explanatory Notes" (prepared by the "Non-Executive Bills Unit")—which are not, of course, part of the Act and do not have the authority of the Scottish Parliament—where no attempt is made to explain what "strict liability" means, and where the relevant offence is erroneously attributed to s.5.

[56] *Alphacell Ltd v Woodward* [1972] A.C. 824.

[57] *Alphacell Ltd v Woodward* [1972] A.C. 824 at 839F, 839H to 840C.

[58] *Lockhart v National Coal Board*, 1981 S.L.T. 161.

[59] See, e.g. *Lockhart v National Coal Board*, 1981 S.L.T. 161.

[60] See, e.g. *Smith of Maddiston Ltd v MacNab*, 1975 J.C. 48, where nine judges sat.

[61] See above, paras 13–11,13–12.

[62] *Gordon v Shaw* (1908) 5 Adam 469.

[63] Now repealed by the Inshore Fishing (Scotland) Act 1984 s.10 Sch.2.

[64] See above, para.2–15.

exact location of the boat when the prohibited fishing took place; and the question lay whether his lack of such knowledge would be of any moment, given the non-mens rea wording of the offence. In deciding that it would not, and that the accused should be convicted, Lord McLaren mentioned four possible criteria which might be used to decide if such statutory offences were "absolute". These consist of the "policy of the statute", its "language", whether or not a requirement for mens rea might make it "very difficult to get a conviction against anyone", and

> "the duty of those who engage in the fishing industry to inform themselves, and to take care that they do not fish where they are not entitled to fish."[65]

They are considered further in the paragraphs which follow.

Policy of the statute

13–16 This criterion involves a court deciding that the aim which a particular statutory offence sets out to achieve is of such importance that it ought to prevail over the maxim *actus non facit reum nisi mens sit rea*.[66] In other words, some statutory offences promote such things as the safety of the public[67] or the protection of the environment, and the securing of these aims may be considered to justify conviction without proof of mens rea. That this sort of thinking may figure in the deliberations of Scottish judges can be seen by considering such cases as *Mitchell v Morrison*,[68] where Lord Justice-General Normand referred to the "safety of the public" in the context of the statutory requirement to maintain records of truck-drivers' hours; *Anderson v Rose*,[69] where the prohibition against selling a heifer in calf for slaughter was clearly designed as a wartime measure to protect scarce food resources (as was hinted at by Lord Justice-Clerk Scott Dickson)[70]; *MacNeill v Wilson*,[71] where the prohibition against having an insecure load on a truck was obviously designed to prevent danger to the public; and *Lockhart v National Coal Board*,[72] where the protection of water supplies from pollution could be said to have taken precedence over the coal board's understandable claim to have done all that could reasonably have been expected of it in the circumstances.

Language used

13–17 Although it is unwise to rely too strongly on this, because of the very varied nature of expression found in statutory offences, some words do appear to carry a similar significance relative to criminal liability, irrespective of the statute in which they appear. Thus, where liability depends on "possession" of some article, it is usual to regard the offence as requiring mens rea in the form of knowledge, whether the statute specifically mentions knowledge or not. One cannot "possess"

---

[65] *Gordon v Shaw* (1908) 5 Adam 469 at 477–478.
[66] See above, para.3–01, for translation.
[67] See, e.g. *Gammon (Hong Kong) Ltd v Attorney General of Hong Kong* [1985] A.C. 1.
[68] *Mitchell v Morrison*, 1938 J.C. 64 at 71.
[69] *Anderson v Rose*, 1919 J.C. 20.
[70] *Anderson v Rose*, 1919 J.C. 20 at 22.
[71] *MacNeill v Wilson*, 1981 J.C. 87.
[72] *Lockhart v National Coal Board*, 1981 S.L.T. 161.

Statutory Offences

what one does not know one has; and further, as Lord Justice-Clerk Ross said in *Gill v Lockhart*[73]:

"Before there can be possession in terms of the Act [i.e. the Misuse of Drugs Act 1971 s.5(2)], it is well established that there must be, on the part of an accused, both knowledge and control."[74]

The word "use", however, seems to be given a "strict" interpretation. Thus, where it is criminal to "use" on a road a motor vehicle which does not comply with prescribed regulations, it is not necessary to show that the user knew that his vehicle did not so comply at the relevant time.[75] On the other hand, where a statute forbids someone to "cause or permit" the "use" of something whilst it does not comply with prescribed regulations, both "causing" and "permitting" appear to require knowledge on the part of the accused that the thing was being so used in contravention of those regulations.[76] The "knowledge" need not be actual, however, where the court is satisfied that the accused deliberately avoided informing himself of the obvious.[77] But, where a statute forbade "causing or knowingly permitting" the entry of pollutants into a stream, the "causing" alternative was considered to be "strict".[78] In that case, however, English authority existed, which was accepted by both counsel and eventually the Appeal Court as being correct. Presumably also, the deliberate attachment of "knowingly" to the "permitting" was seen as significant. With reservations, then, it would seem worthwhile to argue by way of analogy that the interpretation given to a particular word in one statute ought to be decisive of its meaning in another.

Prosecution difficulties

That the insistence upon proof of mens rea would lead to the ineffectiveness of **13–18** an offence is occasionally voiced as a reason for holding that offence to be of strict liability.[79] The argument is that such insistence would make things just too difficult for the Crown, and that that would be disastrous given the aim which the statute seeks to achieve. Under the Road Traffic Regulation Act 1984 s.89(1), for example:

"A person who drives a motor vehicle on a road at a speed exceeding a limit imposed by or under any [relevant] enactment . . . shall be guilty of an offence."

Clearly, if the prosecution were required to prove that a motorist knew he was exceeding a particular speed limit (the central element of the offence), there would be very few convictions and the purpose of the provision (presumably connected

---

[73] *Gill v Lockhart*, 1988 S.L.T. 189 at 190G.
[74] See also *Black v HM Advocate*, 1974 J.C. 43 (relative to s.3— as amended by the Terrorism Act 2006 s.17(5), (6)—and s.4 of the Explosive Substances Act 1883) and *Smith v HM Advocate*, 1996 S.C.C.R. 49 (which confirms that a person possesses a firearm for the purposes of s.1 of the Firearms Act 1968 if he knows he has, and has control over, an object which happens to be a firearm).
[75] This is assumed in, e.g. *Swan v MacNab*, 1977 J.C. 57; see opinion of Lord Cameron at 58–63.
[76] See *Smith of Maddiston Ltd v MacNab*, 1975 J.C. 48. Cf. *MacDonald v Howdle*, 1995 S.L.T. 779.
[77] *Brown v W Burns Tractors Ltd*, 1986 S.C.C.R. 146.
[78] *Lockhart v National Coal Board*, 1981 S.L.T. 161.
[79] See, e.g. the English case of *R. v M(D)* [2009] EWCA Crim 2615; [2011] 1 W.L.R. 822, and the opinion of the court at 831, para.33.

with road safety) would be substantially undermined. Similar thinking probably lies behind the view that offences of possessing or supplying controlled drugs do not require the Crown to show that the accused knew that some package or other actually contained controlled drugs. It is enough if an accused person can be shown to have had the knowledge (and control) necessary to establish his possession of the package—which happens to contain such drugs.[80] If he claims that he did not know what the contents of the package were, that is a matter for him to raise by way of defence.[81] "Prosecution Difficulty" seems, however, to be a somewhat specious way of arguing for the imposition of strict liability. No doubt the Crown can experience similar difficulty in relation to the proof of some common law crimes; but few would suggest that those common law crimes should accordingly be treated as "strict".

Trade regulation

13–19   It is often argued too that statutory offences which bear no express reference to mens rea and which are basically designed to impose standards for the carrying on of particular trades or activities should be prime candidates for strict liability. This is particularly so, apparently, where the offence can be regarded as dealing with acts which "are not criminal in any real sense, but are acts which in the public interest are prohibited under a penalty."[82] Such *mala prohibita*,[83] it might be argued, are the price which has to be paid for participating in that trade or activity. Those who do so must simply observe strictly the standards imposed. If they fail to do so, even unknowingly, then they should be convicted.[84] Much the same might be said of motorists, of course, in relation to many offences found in the Road Traffic Act 1988.[85]

---

[80]   See *Tudhope v McKee*, 1988 S.L.T. 153, in relation to the Misuse of Drugs Act 1971 s.4(3)(b). See also *Salmon v HM Advocate; Moore v HM Advocate*, 1998 S.C.C.R. 740; *Wali v HM Advocate* [2007] HCJAC 11; 2007 S.C.C.R. 106.

[81]   See Misuse of Drugs Act 1971 s.28, as interpreted in *Salmon v HM Advocate; Moore v HM Advocate*, 1998 S.C.C.R. 740 and *Henvey v HM Advocate* [2005] HCJAC 10; 2005 S.C.C.R. 282. This is not a book about evidence, of course; but (e.g.) s.28(2) of the above mentioned 1971 Act allows an accused to "prove" (by way of defence to certain offences under that Act) that he did not know or suspect or have reasonable cause to suspect that particular relevant items were the controlled drugs they turned out to be. To the extent that such a defence requires an accused person to assume the burden of proving his innocence (a "persuasive burden"), it runs contrary to the European Convention on Human Rights, art.6(2)—and thus in *R v Lambert* [2002] 2 A.C. 545, the House of Lords "wrote down" s.28(2) so that the words "to prove" were to be read as "to provide sufficient evidence" (an "evidential burden") which the Crown would then have the burden of negating. This approach was specifically endorsed (although on the basis of a Crown concession) by the five judge court in *Henvey*; and it is perhaps significant that, in modern statutes, Parliaments now tend to use the word "show" (instead of "prove") in relation to "s.28(2)"—type defences.

[82]   See Wright J. in *Sherras v De Rutzen* [1895] 1 Q.B. 918 at 922, quoted by Viscount Dilhorne in *Alphacell Ltd v Woodward* [1972] A.C. 824 at 839G, and by Lord Scarman in *Wings Ltd v Ellis* [1985] 1 A.C. 272 at 293D to 294E–F.

[83]   See, e.g. *Beattie v Waugh*, 1920 J.C. 64, and the opinion of Lord Justice-Clerk Scott Dickson at 69 that the offence there was "a clear case of *malum prohibitum*"; see also above, para.2–37.

[84]   See, e.g. *Dickson v Linton* (1888) 2 White 51; *Gordon v Shaw* (1908) 5 Adam 469, per Lord McLaren at 478.

[85]   See, e.g. *Howman v Russell*, 1923 J.C. 32—the present law pertaining to the situation in that case now being found in the Road Traffic Act 1988 s.42 (as substituted by the Road Traffic Act 1991 s.8, and as amended by the Road Safety Act 2006 ss.18(3) and 26(2)), and the Road Vehicles Lighting Regulations (SI 1989/1796) reg.24(1)(a).

Criteria in general

It would be wrong to imagine that the various criteria mentioned above form an **13–20** exhaustive list or are applied on any consistent basis. It is also far from clear whether Scottish courts apply them at all.[86] Of far greater importance, probably, is the court's "feeling" for the particular offence in question; if it seems trivial, from the point of view of its maximum penalty,[87] and regulatory, as measured from the point of view of its content, it will probably be taken as "strict". Otherwise, it is much more difficult to predict how a court will react. It may be safest to conclude that the only strict liability offences are those which have already been recognised as such by a competent court in Scotland. Although that gives little insight into the likely treatment by the courts of new statutory offences, it should be borne in mind that most genuinely new offences, as opposed to re-enacted former ones,[88] do specify some form of mens rea.[89]

Defences to "strict" offences

If a particular statutory offence has been recognised as "strict", this does not **13–21** preclude the possibility of a defence. This is obviously so in relation to statutes which themselves cater for such defences. In the Food Safety Act 1990, for example, s. 8(1) narrates that

"any person who (a) sells for human consumption . . . any food which fails to comply with food safety requirements shall be guilty of an offence."

There is nothing to suggest that this would not be considered as a crime of strict liability.[90] But the Act provides specific defences to that crime. In s.21, for example, it is stated that it shall

"be a defence for the person charged to prove that he took all reasonable precautions and exercised all due diligence to avoid the commission of the offence by himself or by a person under his control."

Where no specific defences are provided by an Act to a strict liability offence, it was **13–22** at one time thought that there might nevertheless be a defence of "excusable igno- rance" in relation to matters central to that offence. In particular, a defence of that nature seemed to be recognised by Lord McLaren in *Gordon v Shaw*[91] when he said

"where a person in the position of the respondent comes forward, and is able to satisfy the Sheriff that he was excusably ignorant of the position of the fishing vessel . . . his case will always receive indulgent consideration."

---

[86] Cf. the approach of English courts, as in *R. v Bradish* [1990] 1 Q.B. 981.
[87] Although the matter of maximum punishment is very far from being decisive, in England, at least— see *Gammon (Hong Kong) Ltd v Attorney General of Hong Kong* [1985] A.C. 1, Lord Scarman at 17F.
[88] See, e.g. the Food Safety Act 1990.
[89] See, e.g. the Computer Misuse Act 1990 ss.1 (as amended by the Police and Justice Act 2006 s.35), 2 (as amended by the 2006 Act Sch.14 para.17), 3 (as substituted by the 2006 Act s.36) and 3A (as inserted by the 2006 Act s.37).
[90] See, e.g. *Dickson v Linton* (1888) 2 White 51, per Lord McLaren at 58.
[91] *Gordon v Shaw* (1908) 5 Adam 469 at 479.

Lord Kinnear, however, reserved his opinion on the correctness of that view,[92] which was in turn doubted by Lord Justice-Clerk Scott Dickson in *Beattie v Waugh*,[93] and ignored in *Howman v Russell*.[94] On balance, it probably must be accepted that there is no such general defence to strict liability offences in this country; and that the concept of "excusable ignorance" can be given effect to, if at all, only as an aspect of prosecutorial discretion before commencement of proceedings[95] or in mitigation of sentence following conviction.

Vicarious liability

13–23   In the criminal law, vicarious liability means the responsibility which A might be considered to have for the criminal conduct of B in the absence of any question of complicity (see above, Ch.7). This is bound to be unusual, since it involves imposing punishment on A where the actus reus of the crime in question was not committed by him and where he personally had no mens rea. For it to arise at all, therefore, there requires to be some relationship between A and B. In terms of the case law, that relationship is usually that of employer (A) and employee (B), or principal (A) and agent (B); but other relationships could be involved, if these were expressly catered for in a particular Act of Parliament.[96] The criminal conduct of B, however, must occur within the scope of the employment or agency agreement concerned.[97] If it does not, then only the actor (B) is criminally liable for what was done or omitted. The basis for this unusual form of responsibility is thought to be that those who employ others about a particular trade or business are responsible for the way in which those others conduct themselves in relation to the regulations which apply to that trade or business. The employer or principal will certainly avail himself of the rewards of that business; so it is not totally unfair to make him stand the risks—including vicarious criminal liability, where that is considered to exist. In any event, it may well make him more vigilant in relation to the law's requirements.

Presumption against

13–24   It seems to be well accepted that this form of liability does not exist in relation to common law crimes.[98] Even in the field of statutory offences, there is a presumption against it[99]; and it is clearly for the Crown to show that it ought to exist in relation to a particular crime.[100]

---

[92] *Gordon v Shaw* (1908) 5 Adam 469 at 481.
[93] *Beattie v Waugh*, 1920 J.C. 64 at 68; cf. Lord Salvesen (dissenting) at 69.
[94] *Howman v Russell*, 1923 J.C. 32.
[95] *Howman v Russell*, 1923 J.C. 32 per Lord Sands at 36.
[96] For a modern example of express imposition of vicarious liability, see the Breastfeeding etc. (Scotland) Act 2005 (asp 1) s.2; see also below, para.13–25.
[97] See, e.g. *City and Suburban Dairies v Mackenna*, 1918 J.C. 105, per Lord Justice-Clerk Scott Dickson at 110.
[98] See, e.g. *Haig v Thompson*, 1931 J.C. 29, per Lord Ormidale at 33; *Dean v John Menzies (Holdings) Ltd*, 1981 J.C. 23, per Lord Cameron (dissenting) at 33 and 34, Lord Stott at 36 and Lord Maxwell at 39; and *Transco Plc v HM Advocate*, 2004 J.C. 29, per Lord Hamilton (with whom Lord MacLean agreed) at para.53.
[99] See, e.g. *Haig v Thompson*, 1931 J.C. 29, per Lord Anderson at 33: "the general rule is that an employer cannot be made constructively or vicariously liable for the criminal acts of an employee."
[100] See *City and Suburban Dairies v Mackenna*, 1918 J.C. 105, per Lord Dundas at 110; *Duguid v Fraser*, 1942 J.C. 1, per Lord Mackay at 6.

Ambit

Vicarious liability will certainly apply if the United Kingdom or Scottish 13–25
Parliament has expressly said that it should. In such cases, the prosecutor will
have no greater task than to point to the plain words of the statute. Thus, in terms
of the Breastfeeding etc. (Scotland) Act 2005 (asp 1) s.2(1):

> "Anything done by a person in the course of that person's employment shall
> in any proceedings brought under this Act [i.e. for the commission of an
> offence under section 1(1)—deliberately preventing or stopping a person in
> charge of a child (under 2 years of age) from feeding milk to that child in a
> public place[101] or on licensed premises[102]] be treated for the purposes of this
> Act as done also by that person's employer, whether or not it was done with
> the employer's knowledge or approval."

The heading to the section actually reads "Vicarious liability"—which puts the
matter beyond any semblance of doubt. Express imposition of that sort is, however,
unusual; and indeed an employer in such a situation is permitted a defence. He is
invited to prove that he

> "took such steps as were reasonably practicable to prevent the employee from
> committing such an offence in the course of the employer's employment."[103]

In the absence of express imposition, vicarious criminal liability has been recog- 13–26
nised in relation to regulatory offences concerned with various business transactions normally conducted by employees. Examples include selling things at prices
beyond what the law permits,[104] using motor vehicles which do not comply with
"construction and use" regulations,[105] and keeping records of hours worked by
drivers.[106] In each of these cases, of course, it may be said that the selling, or the
using or the keeping of records was something the employer could have done by
himself as well as by the hands of his employees, and that that demonstrates that
the employer was meant to "share" liability. It may be, therefore, that such liability
will not be recognised where the wording of the offence makes it difficult to show
that anyone other than the employee himself was intended to be responsible as, for
example, where an offence is expressly aimed at those "driving" as opposed to
"using" motor vehicles in contravention of regulations.[107]

---

[101] See Breastfeeding etc. (Scotland) Act 2005 (asp 1) s.1(4), as amended by the Licensing (Scotland)
Act 2005 (Consequential Provisions) Order 2009 (SSI 2009/248) Sch.1 para.11.
[102] See s.1(4), noting that the Licensing (Scotland) Act 1976 is repealed by the Licensing (Scotland)
Act 2005 (asp 16) Sch.7: such premises are now defined in s.147(1) of the 2005 Act; see the
Licensing (Scotland) Act 2005 (Consequential Provisions) Order 2009 (SSI 2009/248) Sch.1
para.11.
[103] See Breastfeeding (Scotland) Act 2005 (asp 1) s.2(3). Cf. the system to ensure compliance set up
by the employer in *Readers' Digest Association Ltd v Pirie*, 1973 J.C. 42, which was concerned
with the Unsolicited Goods and Services Act 1971.
[104] See *Duguid v Fraser*, 1942 J.C. 1.
[105] See *Swan v MacNab*, 1977 J.C. 57.
[106] See *Mitchell v Morrison*, 1938 J.C. 64.
[107] Cf. *Swan v MacNab*, 1977 J.C. 57; see also *Docherty v Stakis Hotels Ltd; Stakis Hotels Ltd v
Docherty*, 1991 S.C.C.R. 6, where the Appeal Court decided that certain food regulations were
aimed only at those who actually had management and control of the premises in question, and,
further, that a company could not have actual management and control.

Compared with corporate liability

13–27 Since employers may be not only sole traders but also public limited companies or partnerships, which have separate legal personality yet are incapable of doing or intending anything save through their management and employees, the whole subject of vicarious liability is easily confused with "corporate criminal responsibility." The topic of such corporate responsibility concerns a direct criminal liability. It is not concerned with the vicarious liability of a company for crimes actually committed by its employees or agents, but rather with the criminal liability of the company itself. There, the actions and mentes reae of particular managers or senior employees are imputed to the company (according to the prevailing "controlling mind" theory)[108]; these become the actions and mentes reae of the company. In vicarious liability, on the other hand, the company becomes liable for what individual employees have done. The conduct remains that of the employees involved, the only question then being whether the company, as employer, should also be criminally liable on a vicarious basis.

13–28 The above distinction must be borne in mind where a statutory offence imposes liability not only on the actor but also on any person who "caused or permitted" the offence to occur. If an employer, for example, is charged with "permitting" the contravention of a statutory rule by an employee, then that is a direct liability attaching to the employer. As Lord Justice-Clerk Grant put it in *Mackay Brothers v Gibb*[109]:

> "It is true that the general rule is that a person is not vicariously liable for the criminal acts of another. This, however, is not a case of vicarious liability and is not so charged. [It was in fact a "permitting" case.] The appellants, being a firm, act by the hands of their partners and employees . . . Like a limited liability company, they are a separate legal *persona* and have no mind. The question accordingly is not whether they are vicariously liable for what their garage controller did [i.e. hire out a car which had an insufficient depth of tread on one of its tyres], but whether through him, knowledge of the defect is brought home to them."

Whether or not knowledge is required to be imputed to a company or partnership in a true case of vicarious liability is a moot point. It can certainly be argued that it is not so required, even where the offence in question is not "strict". That, however, would tend to suggest that all vicarious liability was a form of "strict" liability, which probably goes further than present case law or thinking will allow.

---

[108] See *Purcell Meats (Scotland) Ltd v McLeod*, 1987 S.L.T. 528; *Transco Plc v HM Advocate*, 2004 J.C. 29. Cf., relative to homicide, the terms of the Corporate Manslaughter and Corporate Homicide Act 2007: see para.9–78, above.

[109] *Mackay Brothers v Gibb*, 1969 J.C. 26 at 31.

CHAPTER 14

CONCLUSION

Introduction

It is not common practice to include a conclusion in a work which aims to **14–01** describe and analyse the criminal law. In many ways, however, Scotland is not quite like any other jurisdiction. It is felt that some general observations are appropriate. First, as the preceding chapters have detailed, the broad sweep of the criminal law, including both general principles and specific offences, is governed by the common law. It is true that there is a myriad of statutory offences and that much of the time of the criminal courts is spent dealing with these, specifically under road traffic legislation. Nevertheless, the articulation of the criminal law continues to be a significant function of the Scottish judiciary. Rather than a criminal code or a collection of statutes, it is a body of case law which defines most of the more serious crimes, as well as the fundamental concepts, including attempt and complicity. Moreover, many of the statutory offences are not strictly necessary, since the conduct in question is already punishable at common law. Nor does the fact that Parliament has chosen not to treat a given kind of behaviour as a statutory offence preclude it being regarded as a common law offence,[1] although the courts could well disapprove of an attempt to circumvent a statutory prescription by prosecuting at common law.[2]

Secondly, for the better part of three centuries, the legal system in Scotland **14–02** bore the heavy burden of serving as an expression of nationhood. Following the Union of 1707 with England, the fact that Scotland possessed its own indigenous legal institutions and law (particularly criminal law) served as a foundation of national identity. On occasion, this may have led to support for aspects of the Scottish system purely because they were different from those elsewhere in the United Kingdom, and not because of a thorough examination of their appropriateness. It may also have led to a certain defensiveness and insularity in the face of the perceived threat of Anglicisation of the law. These might be seen as aspects of what has come to be known as "legal nationalism".[3] The unspoken counterpart must, of course, be "legal unionism". Writing from a unionist perspective, Dicey and Rait observed[4]:

---

[1] See *HM Advocate v K*, 1994 S.C.C.R. 499.
[2] See *Webster v Dominick*, 2003 S.C.C.R. 525 at 542G–543A, para.60, per Lord Justice-Clerk Gill. There may be an expectation that, where the common law crime also constitutes a statutory offence, the maximum sentence which can be imposed is that set by the statute: *Cartwright v HM Advocate*, 2001 S.C.C.R. 695.
[3] See L. Farmer, "Under the Shadow over Parliament House: The Strange Case of Legal Nationalism" in L. Farmer and S. Veitch (eds), *The State of Scots Law* (Edinburgh: Butterworths, 2001), Ch.9.
[4] A.V. Dicey and R.S. Rait, *Thoughts on the Union Between England and Scotland* (London: Macmillan, 1920), p.329.4

367

"Much less attempt than one would have expected has been made to assimilate the law of each country to one another, and even where the diversity has caused considerable evil."

Indeed, one of the more remarkable features of the Union has been the continuing existence of the divergent criminal justice system in Scotland. No doubt the absence of an appeal to the House of Lords in criminal cases helped to preserve the native law. A further part of the explanation undoubtedly lies in the recognition in the Acts of Union that "a union of nations did not require a union of laws."[5] Scots law has long been dangerous territory for English trespassers to enter. Nevertheless, for almost 300 years, the two legal systems were the responsibility of the same (predominantly English) Parliament. Following the Scotland Act 1998, and the establishment of the Scottish Parliament, that is no longer the case. For the first time in the modern era, Scotland has its own legislature able to give attention to the criminal justice system. It is surely not coincidental that the post-devolution period has seen an (unofficial) *Draft Criminal Code for Scotland with Commentary*, produced by a group of legal academics.[6]

THE SCOTTISH ORTHODOXY

14–03 The onus is on those who would wish to change the current system to convince that reform is necessary. It might require rather more than asserting that codification, "is a useful thing to do", on the basis that, "[a]n organised set of legal rules is better than a disorganised set."[7] This is the more so given the extent to which codification has in the past been regarded as distinctly counter to Scottish tradition.[8] From a historical perspective, there has been little evidence of any great pressure among Scots lawyers for more reliance on statute law or for codification. The orthodox view has been that the common law allows the courts a desirable flexibility in dealing with the cases that come before them. Lord Avonside commented in *Khaliq v HM Advocate*[9]:

"The great strength of our common law in criminal matters is that it can be invoked to fill a need. It is not static."

And indeed the law has on occasion been driven forward with considerable boldness in modern times. In particular, reference may be made to developments

---

[5] B.P. Levack, "The Proposed Union of English and Scots Law in the Seventeenth Century" (1975) J.R. 97, 115.

[6] This was published under the auspices of the Scottish Law Commission in 2003. For differing views on the document, compare P.R. Ferguson, "Codifying Criminal Law (1): A Critique of Scots Common Law" [2004] Crim. L.R. 49 and "Codifying Criminal Law (2): The Scots and English Draft Codes Compared" [2004] Crim. L.R. 105, with T.H. Jones, "Towards a Good and Complete Criminal Code for Scotland" (2005) 68 M.L.R. 448. For further, critical discussion, see L. Farmer, "Enigma: Unravelling the Draft Criminal Code" (2002) 7 S.L.P.Q. 68.

[7] E. Clive, "Law-Making in Scotland from APS to ASP" (1999) 3 Edin. Law Rev. 131 at 149

[8] See, e.g. J.A. Dixon, "The Codification of the Law" (1878) 18 *Journal of Jurisprudence* 305.

[9] *Khaliq v HM Advocate*, 1984 J.C. 23 at 26.

in the common law of rape[10] and the recognition of a defence of necessity.[11] With only occasional (but perhaps more frequent) exceptions,[12] there has been no question of a court's waiting for a Parliamentary solution when novel problems have been set before it.

This tradition owes much to the continuing influence of Hume, who was a **14–04** strong advocate of a flexible, common law system. He recognised that the criminal law had, "to be bent and accommodated to the temper and exigencies of the times".[13] Hume saw this as a judicial function. Not all have shared this perspective. A century before Hume, Mackenzie was arguing:

> "It were to be wisht, that nothing were a Cryme which is not declared to be so, by a Statute; for this would . . . prevent the arbitrariness of Judges".[14]

In a review of the 1844 edition of Hume, Lord Ardmillan commented[15]:

> "The proper function of judges is *jus dicere*, not *jus dare;* and nothing is more perilous to constitutional government and public liberty, than the confusion of the judicial and legislative departments of the State. The voice of the judge is but the voice of the existing law, statutory or common, which it is his part to declare and administer. New laws must proceed from the Legislature . . . in whom alone rests the power of enacting what all subjects are bound, as subjects, to obey."

Thus whilst the Humean approach may have prevailed, there has long been a competing tradition in Scots law. There has continued to be voiced dissatisfaction with the expanded role accorded to the judiciary in the development of the criminal law under what remains predominantly a common law system.[16] The (unofficial) *Draft Criminal Code*, with its proposal, "to convert the common law to statutory form",[17] can be seen as a continuation of this alternative tradition.

IS RELIANCE ON THE COMMON LAW DESIRABLE?

In other jurisdictions, particularly in England and Wales, it has increasingly been **14–05** felt that the defining of crimes is beyond the competence of the courts. In respect of English law, Ashworth identifies it as a, "constitutional principle . . . that the

---

[10] *S v HM Advocate*, 1989 S.L.T. 469 (abolition of marital rape exemption); *Lord Advocate's Reference (No.1 of 2001)*, 2002 S.L.T. 466 (redefinition of the actus reus of rape as non-consensual sexual intercourse). See now the Sexual Offences (Scotland) Act 2009 (asp 9), discussed, for example, in Ch.9, above.

[11] *Moss v Howdle*, 1997 J.C. 123.

[12] See, e.g. *Quinn v Cunningham*, 1956 J.C. 22; *Grant v Allan*, 1987 J.C. 71; *HM Advocate v Forbes*, 1994 S.L.T. 861; *Paterson v Lees*, 1999 J.C. 159; *Transco Plc v HM Advocate (No.1)*, 2004 J.C. 29; *Hatcher v Harrower* [2010] HCJAC 92; 2010 S.C.C.R. 903.

[13] Hume, *Commentaries*, i, 2.

[14] Mackenzie, *The Laws and Customs of Scotland in Matters Criminal* (Edinburgh: 1678), p.3.

[15] Lord Ardmillan, "Scottish Criminal Law" (1846) IV *North British Review* 313 ("*jus dicere*" means "to declare the law"; "*jus dare*" means to "to give the law").

[16] See, e.g. W.A. Elliott, "*Nulla Poena Sine Lege*" (1956) J.R. 22; G.H. Gordon, "Crimes Without Laws" (1966) J.R. 214.

[17] E. Clive and P. Ferguson, "Unravelling the Enigma: A Reply to Professor Farmer" (2002) 7 S.L.P.Q. 81 at 82.

reach of the criminal law should be declared by the legislature".[18] On this view, it is not felt to be appropriate for the judiciary to play a leading role in formulating the criminal law. Such formulation is generally thought to be the prerogative of the legislature, in view of the policy considerations inevitably involved. As Lord Kilbrandon (an eminent Scottish judge elevated to the House of Lords) stated in *DPP for Northern Ireland v Lynch*[19]:

> "It will not do to claim that judges have the duty-call it the privilege-of seeing to it that the common law expands and contracts to meet what the judges conceive to be the requirements of modern society. Modern society rightly prefers to exercise that function for itself, and this it conveniently does through those who represent it in Parliament."

Lord Kilbrandon's brethren sitting in the High Court of Justiciary, however, have not consistently taken this view. Indeed, it has been known for a Scottish judge to take a position quite opposed to this. In *Watt v Annan*[20] Lord Cameron wished to place the responsibility on Parliament not to create a crime, but to restrict the extent of the common law crime of shameless indecency:

> "It would be impracticable as well as undesirable to attempt to define precisely the limits and ambit of this particular offence . . . If it were considered desirable or necessary that this was a chapter of the criminal law in which precise boundaries or limits were to be set then the task is one which is more appropriate for the hand of the legislator."

14–06 It is perhaps just as well that contemporary Scottish judges have tended not to apply an unalloyed version of Lord Cameron's philosophy. They recognise that there are limits to their powers and that there are some issues best left to Parliament.[21] There is also an appreciation that it is the duty of the judiciary to clarify the limits of common law crimes.[22] The Human Rights Act 1998, and the associated impact of the European Convention on Human Rights, have no doubt had some influence in this regard.[23] The important decision in *Webster v Dominick*,[24] effectively replacing the common law crime of shameless indecency with one of public indecency, indicates the modern approach of the High Court to reducing the scope of vague common law crimes.[25] It has become evident that there is no ratchet effect in the common law of crimes. A similar exercise in

---

[18] A. Ashworth, *Principles of Criminal Law*, 6th edn (Oxford: Oxford University Press, 2009), p.48.

[19] *DPP for Northern Ireland v Lynch* [1975] A.C. 653 at 700.

[20] *Watt v Annan*, 1978 J.C. 84 at 89. This case was overruled in *Webster v Dominick*, 2003 S.C.C.R. 525.

[21] See, e.g. *Transco Plc v HM Advocate (No.1)*, 2004 J.C. 29; *Hatcher v Harrower* [2010] HCJAC 92; 2010 S.C.C.R. 903.

[22] As suggested in *Lindsay v HM Advocate*, 1997 J.C. 19 at 22A–B, it might be regarded as an occasion more appropriate for legislative reform, "[w]here the law has been stated so clearly and consistently by the judges."

[23] See T.H. Jones, "Common Law Crimes and the Human Rights Act 1998" (2000) S.L.T. (News) 95; Lord Reed and J. Murdoch, *A Guide to Human Rights Law in Scotland* (London; Edinburgh: Butterworths, 2001), paras 5–138 to 5–140.

[24] *Webster v Dominick*, 2003 S.C.C.R. 525.

[25] The approach typified by cases such as *Watt v Annan*, 1978 J.C. 84, and *McLaughlan v Boyd*, 1934 J.C. 19 (both now overruled), is a thing of the past.

Conclusion

delimitation has been conducted in respect of breach of the peace. In *Smith v Donnelly*[26]there was a clear attempt to identify with sufficient certainty the core elements of the actus reus of the most flexible of common law crimes. The result of this process received the endorsement of the European Court of Human Rights in *Lucas v United Kingdom*.[27] It considered

> "that the definition of the offence of breach of the peace as stipulated in *Smith v Donnelly* . . . is sufficiently precise to provide reasonable foreseeability of the actions which may fall within the remit of the offence."[28]

Decisions such as *Webster v Dominick* and *Smith v Donnelly* demonstrate great sensitivity to the principle of *nullum crimen sine lege*[29] and to the approach required to ensure compliance with the European Convention on Human Rights. The role of the High Court is to ensure that its decisions provide sufficient guidance as to the boundaries of conduct covered by the common law of crimes.

Between 1707 and 1999 there was no separate Scottish legislature; and, given **14–07** its generally unenthusiastic attention to matters of Scottish law reform, the Westminster Parliament tended to be viewed with a somewhat jaundiced eye north of the border. In itself, of course, this state of affairs could not justify an extended role for the judiciary in the articulation of the criminal law. It could equally have led to an argument for a reform of the legislative process in respect of Scots law.[30] This saw fruition in the Scotland Act 1998. That said, the prevailing tradition in Scotland has been that judges are to be intimately involved in the shaping and defining of crimes. It would, therefore, be no argument at all to assert that the traditional Scottish position ought to be discontinued just because the traditions are different elsewhere. There is, nevertheless, a constitutional and democratic dimension to Scottish criminal law. Since the criminal law is society's most important form of sanction, it can be argued that decisions on its scope should be taken by elected representatives, rather than by past and present judges. It should not be thought that this is a characteristically modern thesis. Writing extra-judicially a century-and-a-half ago, Lord Cockburn rejected with scorn the notion

> "that on the question, whether any action is held to be indictable or not, the *community is safer under the absolute wisdom of two or three individuals*, no matter how great their wisdom and virtue, *than under the wisdom of Parliament!*"[31]

---

[26] *Smith v Donnelly*, 2001 S.L.T. 1007; for detailed discussion, see above, paras 12–11 to 12–16.

[27] *Lucas v United Kingdom* (2003) 37 E.H.R.R. CD 86.

[28] *Lucas v United Kingdom* (2003) 37 E.H.R.R. CD 86 at CD89.

[29] "No crime without a law"; see above, para.2–20; L. Loucaides, *Essays on the Developing Law of Human Rights* (Netherlands: Martinus Nijhoff, 1995), Ch.2. Compare the decision of the House of Lords in *R. v Rimmington; R. v Goldstein* [2005] UKHL 63; [2006] 1 A.C. 459, where Lord Bingham said that conduct forbidden by law should be clearly indicated so that a person is capable of knowing that it is wrong before he does it and that no one should be punished for doing something which was not a criminal offence when it was done.

[30] See T.H. Jones, "Criminal Justice and Devolution" (1997) J.R. 201.

[31] Lord Cockburn, "Scottish Criminal Jurisprudence and Procedure" (1846) 83 Edin. Rev. 196, 198.

It is undeniable that there are policy considerations involved in formulating the criminal law. But a counter-argument to Lord Cockburn might have been that in a small, relatively homogeneous country such as Scotland, the judiciary is as much in touch with public opinion as the group of men and women elected to the Parliament. That argument, of course, might be thought to lack continuing validity in light of the existence of a distinctively Scottish Parliament. Nevertheless, the lack of public criticism of the inherent flexibility of Scots criminal law in the hands of the judiciary, and the apparent Parliamentary acquiescence in the role played by Scottish criminal judges, are not insignificant matters. The difficulty with this argument is that it is premised on the idea that judges are qualified to discern and represent societal values. Lord Cockburn was in no doubt that, on this issue, "Parliament is a better, and infinitely more extended representation of public sentiment."[32] The general principles of the criminal law, and almost all the crimes detailed in this book, come within the domain of the Scottish Parliament. The future will reveal whether the extended role assumed by the judiciary has been a response to legislative neglect, or whether it continues to be a supportable feature of the Scottish legal and political system.

JUDICIAL DEVELOPMENT OF THE LAW

14–08 It is well understood that the courts in any jurisdiction have an important role in the development of the law through their decisions. It is generally recognised, however, that the opportunities for doing so are much greater in a common law system than in one based on a code or on statutes. Of course, judges can effectively develop law through their interpretation of a statutory or code provision. But there they simply consider the detailed meaning of what has already been given clear shape by a distinct policy-making body. Scottish judges of the High Court of Justiciary, of course, may go much further than that. They may, in relation to non-statutory matters, act as a policy maker and give shape to the law in the very case before them. Objections to this judicial role can be based not so much on the usurpation of a parliamentary function as on the principles of prospectivity and certainty.

Prospectivity

14–09 The principle of prospectivity stands for the proposition that criminal liability should only attach to conduct which has previously been declared to be criminal. It is reflected in art.7 of the European Convention on Human Rights, which sets out the fundamental freedom from retroactive criminal offences and punishment. The European Court of Human Rights has interpreted this provision as not being confined to prohibiting the retrospective application of the criminal law to an accused's disadvantage. It has been taken to embody the more general principles that only the law can define a crime and that the criminal law should not be

---

[32] Lord Cockburn, "Scottish Criminal Jurisprudence and Procedure" (1846) 83 Edin. Rev. 196, 215. These extra-judicial observations lend perspective to Lord Cockburn's opinion in *Bernard Greenhuff* (1838) 2 Swin. 236, discussed above in paras 2–28 to 2–33. It is evident that the Scottish Parliament can take an active role in the criminal law; see, e.g. Pt 3 of the Criminal Justice and Licensing (Scotland) Act 2010 (asp 13).

extensively construed to an accused's detriment, for instance by analogy.[33] The freedom appears to have considerable significance for any common law system. The common law method appears to preclude the requisite degree of forewarning: a judicial decision will apply to the case immediately before the court, as well as forming a precedent for the future.[34] To some extent the same is true if the decision called for is the interpretation of a statutory provision; but the problem is raised in a crucial form by judicial creativity in the common law, where there is no legislative framework. The particular issue which will face a court is the fairness of deciding a case on the basis of a rule articulated after the conduct in question took place.

In a general sense all judicial decisions in the criminal law are retrospective, in **14–10** that "it is the subsequent decision which reaches back into time and places the authoritative stamp of criminality upon the prior conduct."[35] This is so whether the case is one of common law adjudication or statutory interpretation (although the task being attempted by the court will be different according to which category is involved). But, as Hall points out[36]

> "the inevitability of a slight, 'normal' degree of retroactivity in judicial decisions provides no ground for tolerating it in its obvious manifestations."

Thus, the issue is the "quality of the adjudication", rather than an absolute compliance with the principle of prospectivity. The crucial question to be asked is whether a particular decision is,

> "retroactive only in ... [an] unavoidable way or is it also unexpected and indefensible by reference to the law which had been expressed prior to the conduct in issue?"[37]

The European Court of Human Rights has adopted a similar approach. It has accepted that it is consistent with art.7 of the Convention for a court to clarify the existing elements of a common law offence and to adapt it, "to new circumstances which can reasonably be brought under the original conception of the offence."[38] The key issue is whether the judicial development of the common law is, "consistent with the essence of the offence and could reasonably be foreseen".[39] The fundamental freedom from retroactive criminal offences should, "not be read as outlawing the gradual clarification of the rules of criminal liability through judicial interpretation from case to case".[40]

---

[33] *Kokkinakis v Greece* (1994) 17 E.H.R.R. 397 at [52].

[34] This is not so if the law is developed in a Lord Advocate's Reference, where the decision of the court has no impact upon the immediate case. Compare the observations of Lord Maclean in *HM Advocate v H*, 2002 S.L.T. 1380 at 1381.

[35] J. Hall, *General Principles of Criminal Law*, 2nd edn (New Jersey: The Lawbook Exchange, 2005), p.61.

[36] Hall, *General Principles of Criminal Law*, 2nd edn (2005), p.61.

[37] Hall, *General Principles of Criminal Law*, 2nd edn (2005), p.61.

[38] *X Ltd and Y v United Kingdom* (1982) (Case no.8710/79), para.9. This was a decision of the now-defunct European Commission of Human Rights.

[39] *SW v United Kingdom; CR v United Kingdom* (1996) 21 E.H.R.R. 363, para36/34.

[40] *SW v United Kingdom; CR v United Kingdom* (1996) 21 E.H.R.R. 363, para.36/34. See *HM Advocate v H*, 2002 S.L.T. 1380 at 1381. The essence of these principles is restated in *Streletz v Germany* (2001) 33 E.H.R.R. 31.

14-11   On the face of things, the decisions in *S v HM Advocate*[41] (removal of the marital rape exemption) and *Khaliq v HM Advocate*[42] ("causing real injury" through supply of glue-sniffing kits) might appear to have been unexpected and thus indefensible in relation to the principle of prospectivity. On the law believed to have been current when each of the accused in these cases performed his deliberate actions, neither of them could have anticipated that his actions would have been criminal (according to the argument). That argument assumes that the prior law applicable to the case was itself precisely expressed. But the prior law applicable to marital rape, for example, was not in fact clearly expressed at all. It had been referred to obliquely by Hume[43] and eroded by the decisions in *HM Advocate v Duffy*[44] and *HM Advocate v Paxton*.[45] The European Court of Human Rights accepted an argument to this effect in deciding that the judicial abrogation of the exception in English law was compatible with art.7.[46] It is not in the nature of the common law of crimes that its individual proscriptions are expressed with particular precision. Rather, the common law proceeds from a set of principles of a plain, moral nature. From that point of view, it rings hollow for the accused husband in *S v HM Advocate*,[47] for example, to claim that he forced sexual intercourse on his wife because he knew that the criminal law of rape granted immunity to husbands who behaved in that way; or for the accused in *Khaliq v HM Advocate*[48] to claim that he knowingly supplied children with vast quantities of life-threatening substances since he knew the criminal law could not touch him for that sort of thing at all. Naturally, if the accuseds' views of the pre-existing law had been correct, then one would have concluded that the criminal law was grossly defective. Indeed, the European Court of Human Rights has observed that the marital rape exemption was itself inconsistent with fundamental objectives of the Convention, the very essence of which was respect for human dignity and human freedom.[49] The only question then concerns the *method* by which such defects should be rectified. Scots law has to date chosen a method which has sometimes entailed conviction of the person whose conduct highlights the need for change, or, in the language appropriate to common law, clarification or correction[50]; and the persons so convicted, at least in the two cases cited, could hardly claim to be outraged on any moral considerations.

Certainty

14-12   It would appear, then, that any failure on the part of Scots law to observe the principle of prospectivity is predicated on the basic uncertainty of common law rules. There can be no doubt that there is a degree of uncertainty in the common law. By definition, a common law system is less canonical and certain than one based on legislation. The courts have defined the actus rei of a number of offences,

---

[41] *S v HM Advocate*, 1989 S.L.T. 469.
[42] *Khaliq v HM Advocate*, 1984 J.C. 23.
[43] Hume, *Commentaries*, i, 306.
[44] *HM Advocate v Duffy*, 1983 S.L.T. 7.
[45] *HM Advocate v Paxton*, 1984 J.C. 105; see above, para.9–86.
[46] *SW v United Kingdom; CR v United Kingdom* (1996) 21 E.H.R.R. 363.
[47] *S v HM Advocate*, 1989 S.L.T. 469.
[48] *Khaliq v HM Advocate*, 1984 J.C. 23.
[49] *SW v United Kingdom; CR v United Kingdom* (1996) 21 E.H.R.R. 363, para.44/42.
[50] See *HM Advocate v H*, 2002 S.L.T. 1380, per Lord Maclean at 1381.

such as shameless indecency and breach of the peace, in very broad terms. The objection to uncertain rules of criminal law is, of course, the subsequent inability of persons to be wholly confident that their proposed conduct will not fall foul of the law; and that is an objection which a common law system may find it more difficult to meet. The European Court of Human Rights has held that the law has to be "adequately accessible", by which is meant that citizens,

> "must be able to have an indication that is adequate in the circumstances of the legal rules applicable to a given case".[51]

They must also be able, "to foresee, to a degree that is reasonable in the circumstances, the consequences which a given action may entail".[52] The need to satisfy these requirements could lead one to the conclusion that a common law based system is fundamentally flawed and must be replaced by a code or a collection of statutes. But this conclusion is not inevitable: much depends on the degree of uncertainty, and whether that degree of uncertainty can be tolerated. Much depends also on the extent to which uncertainty is absent from codified or statutory regimes.[53] There are limits to how much uncertainty can be legislated away.[54]

The common law of crimes in Scotland is by no means uncertain. If it were, it **14–13** would not have been possible for this book to be written, or for the courts to operate on a daily basis. But there may remain a degree of uncertainty as to the precise boundaries of murder, theft, malicious mischief and indeed any other such crime. It is the acceptability of that degree of uncertainty which is the true issue here. That is not to deny or ignore the very real problem posed in the past by the power of the High Court of Justiciary to declare new crimes[55]; but the exercise of that power would now be unlawful under the Human Rights Act 1998. The declaratory power will not therefore be used in modern circumstances, and it is, in any event, a separable issue. Certainly, in relation to crimes already recognised by the common law, there can be scant sympathy for those who attempt to exploit "blurred edges" for their own advantage—if that does, indeed, happen. In reality, it seems that few people ever take steps to ascertain whether or not their proposed conduct would definitely constitute a crime. Even if they did take such steps, they would still find a degree of uncertainty in a statute or code based system of criminal law. The argument that, because of its statutory basis, English criminal law is more predictable and stable than its Scottish counterpart would be difficult to sustain. The English Theft Act 1968, for example, has attracted a considerable body of interpretative case law, and, without access to those cases, the exact extent of what is forbidden cannot properly be appreciated. The English courts also seem on occasion to reach decisions which are difficult to reconcile with the intention of Parliament,[56] which rather undermines the claim of predictability of meaning for statute law. That body of case law is also constantly expanding. This is true

---

[51] *Sunday Times v United Kingdom* (1979) 2 E.H.R.R. 245 at [49].
[52] *Sunday Times v United Kingdom* (1979) 2 E.H.R.R. 245 at [49].
[53] See A. Cadoppi, *"Nulla Poena Sine Lege* and Scots Criminal Law" (1998) J.R. 73, 81.
[54] See, generally, W. Brugger, "Concretization of Law and Statutory Interpretation" (1996) 11 Tul. Eur. & Civ. L.F. 207.
[55] See, further, the account of the declaratory power of the High Court in Ch.2.
[56] See, e.g. the decisions of the House of Lords in *Lawrence v Metropolitan Police Commissioner* [1972] A.C. 626; *DPP v Gomez* [1993] A.C. 442; *R. v Hinks* [2001] 2 A.C. 241.

also of offences found within the Road Traffic Acts, and indeed any other enactments which flow from Parliament. What matters to individuals, it seems, is that they should be able to have a fairly good outline of what the law is and what is expected of them; and it is on that sort of basis that most people are able to avoid criminality fairly successfully in the course of their daily business. From that argument of pragmatism, rather than principle, then, it does not greatly matter on what basis (judicial or legislative) the criminal law rests. A code may make the criminal law more accessible to those who work within the criminal justice system, but this is not the same thing as making the law available to the general public. To that end, a much more radical approach would be necessary, with a code drafted in everyday language and with simple proscriptions.[57] If there is a need to make the criminal law more understandable to the public, the solution may not lie in a document written by lawyers for other lawyers.[58] Codification is far from being a guarantor of an accessible criminal law.

Effectiveness and fairness

14–14   The effectiveness of the criminal law is only partly determined by the way in which crimes are defined or brought into existence. It is rather a function of the whole of the criminal justice system in question. Thus, where flexible, common law methods define crimes and their extent, the system of criminal law can still be effective and fair provided that flexibility extends to the prosecutor and to the judge. In Scotland, prosecutors are trusted to proceed only where they perceive a need to do so in the public interest. Judges too are trusted in the same public interest to ensure that charges which come before them on complaint or indictment answer properly to the moral principles embedded in the common law. These public trusts reposed in prosecutors and judges amount to checks and balances to ensure that the Scottish criminal justice system operates fairly and effectively. That criminal justice system may not secure absolute compliance with all desirable principles of abstract criminal law, but, in the real world, compromises probably have to be made if the system is to function at all. And the Scottish system does seem to work, and to enjoy a high level of public confidence.

LAW REFORM

14–15   There is no system of criminal law, however, which could not benefit from frequent scrutiny and re-appraisal.[59] Whilst it is true that the Scottish system is gradually re-appraised by judges of the High Court, the weakness of that method lies in the random way in which that service is performed. It can only be done on a case by case basis, and is thus dependent to a large extent on matters of pure chance. Leaving to one side the judiciary's suitability to perform this function, an accusatorial criminal appeal court may not be the best forum in which to consider

---

[57]   See, generally, P.H. Robinson, *Structure and Function in Criminal Law* (Oxford: Clarendon Press, 1997).

[58]   There is an argument that this is to make the law more accessible to the public, via the indirect route of consultation with a lawyer. See J. Austin and R. Campbell, *Lectures on Jurisprudence or The Philosophy of Positive Law* (New Jersey: The Lawbook Exchange, 2004), p.327.

[59]   See, generally, C.H.W. Gane, "Criminal Law Reform in Scotland" (1998) 3 S.L.P.Q. 101 (noting that this article is rather more "reformist" than the current text).

the wider policy issues involved in the development of the criminal law. The provision of a systematic re-appraisal programme would be better, such as has been mounted, in effect, by the Scottish Law Commission in relation to the civil law. Whilst it is true that matters affecting the criminal law have from time to time been referred to that Commission, these have been ad hoc and rather limited in scope. There is, therefore, a good case to be made for more active appraisal. The Scottish Parliament should be prepared to play a key role. The Sexual Offences (Scotland) Act 2009, following the Commission's *Report on Rape and Other Sexual Offences*,[60] provides a good example of what a thorough review can achieve.

The desirability or otherwise of restating the common law in statutory form, as **14–16** proposed by the authors of the (unofficial) Draft Criminal Code, remains an open question. The common law can reflect the values of prospectivity and certainty.[61] Indeed, this is a requirement of the human rights regime prevailing under the Human Rights Act 1998 and the Scotland Act 1998. The European Court of Human Rights has accepted that "rules of common law or other customary law may provide a sufficient legal basis".[62] Provided that the common law meets the qualitative standards of accessibility and foreseeability,[63] it can be certain enough under the European Convention on Human Rights. What reliance upon the common law can never satisfy, of course, is the political argument that Parliament is the only legitimate institution to articulate and develop the criminal law. If that argument founded upon the separation of powers is felt to be decisive, the judiciary should certainly be participating much less in the development of legal doctrine.[64] This does not, however, provide a conclusive argument for codification. There is no reason why the Scottish Parliament could not pass statutes to reform or consolidate aspects of the criminal law, without seeking codification. This would be incremental change, in contrast to the disruptive change represented by codification.[65] It may be that reform by instalments is more realistic than comprehensive codification (given the constraints on the time of parliamentarians).[66]

---

[60] Scottish Law Commission: *Report on Rape and other Sexual Offences* (The Stationery Office, 2007), Scot. Law Com. No.209.
[61] See, e.g. *HM Advocate v Harris* [2010] HCJAC 102; 2010 S.C.C.R. 931.
[62] *Gay News Ltd v United Kingdom* (1983) 5 E.H.R.R. 123 at [6]. See to the same effect *Wingrove v United Kingdom* (1997) 24 E.H.R.R. 1; *Steel v United Kingdom* (1999) 28 E.H.R.R. 603.
[63] See *Sunday Times v United Kingdom* (1979) 2 E.H.R.R. 245 at [9].
[64] Compare also the argument to this effect made by the accused in *HM Advocate v H*, 2002 S.L.T. 1380.
[65] These terms are used in a descriptive sense. The outcome of disruptive change can be beneficial.
[66] A. Eser, "Major Stages of Criminal Law Reform in Germany" (1996) 30 Israel L.R. 28, 33. An example is the Sexual Offences (Scotland) Act 2009 (asp 9).

SELECT BIBLIOGRAPHY OF SCOTS CRIMINAL LAW

1. Works accorded authoritative status

Alison, Archibald J., *Principles and Practice of the Criminal Law of Scotland*, 2 Vols (Edinburgh: Wm Blackwood 1832–1833; Edinburgh: Law Society of Scotland/ Butterworths, reprinted 1989).

Hume, D., *Commentaries on the Law of Scotland Respecting Crimes*, edited by B.R. Bell, 4th edn, 2 Vols (Edinburgh: Bell & Bradfute, 1844 (with Bell's Notes); Edinburgh: Law Society of Scotland, reprinted 1986).

Macdonald, J.H.A., *A Practical Treatise on the Criminal Law of Scotland*, edited by J. Walker and D.J. Stevenson, 5th edn (Edinburgh: W. Green, 1948, reprinted 1986).

2. General Texts

Anderson, A.M., *The Criminal Law of Scotland*, 2nd edn (Edinburgh: Bell & Bradfute, 1904).

Burnett, J., *A Treatise on Various Branches of the Criminal Law of Scotland* (Edinburgh: printed by George Ramsay and Co for Archibald Constable and Co, 1811).

Cubie, Andrew M. (ed.), *Scots Criminal Law*, 3rd edn (Edinburgh: Tottel Publishing, 2009).

Ferguson, P.R. and McDiarmid, C., *Scots Criminal Law: A Critical Analysis* (Dundee: Dundee University Press, 2009).

Gordon, G.H., *The Criminal Law of Scotland*, 3rd edn, 2 Vols (Edinburgh: W. Green 2000–2001), together with the *Third Edition Supplement* (Edinburgh: W. Green, 2005), and *The New Law of Sexual Offences in Scotland, Supplement 1 to Vol II* (Edinburgh: SULI/W. Green, 2010) by James Chalmers.

Mackenzie, Sir George, *The Laws and Customs of Scotland in Matters Criminal*, 1st edn (Edinburgh: 1678; facs. ed., The Law Book Exchange Ltd: Clark, New Jersey, 2005), 2nd edn (Edinburgh: 1699).

Smith, T.B., *A Short Commentary on the Law of Scotland* (Edinburgh, W. Green, 1962), particularly Chs 5–7.

Stair Memorial Encyclopaedia, The Laws of Scotland (Edinburgh: Butterworths, 1995; reissue, LexisNexis, 2005), Vol. 7, s.v. "Criminal Law".

3. Texts on Particular Subjects

Chalmers, J. and Leverick, F., *Criminal Defences and Pleas in Bar of Trial* (Edinburgh: SULI/W. Green, 2006).

Davidson, F. P., *Evidence* (Edinburgh: SULI/ W. Green, 2007).

Farmer, L., *Criminal Law, Tradition and Legal Order: Crime and the Genius of Scots Law, 1747 to the Present* (Cambridge: Cambridge University Press, 1997).

Ferguson, P.W., *Crimes Against the Person*, 2nd edn (Edinburgh: Butterworths, 1998).

Gane, C.H.W., *Sexual Offences* (Edinburgh: Butterworths, 1992).

Sentencing Practice (Edinburgh: W. Green).

379

Raitt, F., *Evidence – Principles, Policy and Practice* (Edinburgh, W. Green, 2008).
Renton and Brown's Criminal Procedure According to the Law of Scotland, 6th edn (Edinburgh: W. Green).
Renton and Brown's Statutory Offences (Edinburgh: W. Green).
Ross, M.L. and Chalmers J., *Walker and Walker on Evidence*, 3rd edn (Edinburgh: Tottel Publishing, 2009).
Wheatley, J., *Road Traffic Law in Scotland*, 4th edn by Andrew Brown (Edinburgh: Tottel Publishing, 2007).

4. Case Books (Excluding standard case report volumes)

Gane, C.H.W., Stoddart, C.N. and Chalmers, J., *A Casebook on Scottish Criminal Law*, 4th edn (Edinburgh: W. Green, 2009).
Sheldon, D., *Evidence: Cases and Materials*, 2nd edn (Edinburgh: W. Green, 2002).

CRIMINAL LAW CASE REPORTS

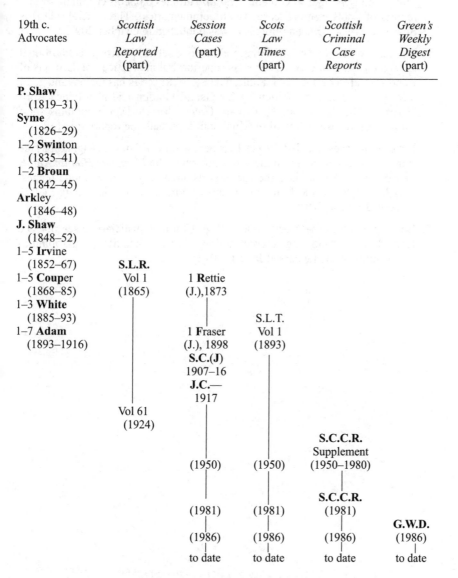

19th c. Advocates	Scottish Law Reported (part)	Session Cases (part)	Scots Law Times (part)	Scottish Criminal Case Reports	Green's Weekly Digest (part)
P. Shaw (1819–31)					
Syme (1826–29)					
1–2 **Swinton** (1835–41)					
1–2 **Broun** (1842–45)					
Arkley (1846–48)					
J. Shaw (1848–52)					
1–5 **Irvine** (1852–67)	**S.L.R.**				
1–5 **Couper** (1868–85)	Vol 1 (1865)	1 Rettie (J.),1873			
1–3 **White** (1885–93)			S.L.T.		
1–7 **Adam** (1893–1916)		1 Fraser (J.), 1898 **S.C.(J)** 1907–16 **J.C.—** 1917	Vol 1 (1893)		
	Vol 61 (1924)				
				S.C.C.R. Supplement	
	(1950)	(1950)	(1950–1980)		
				S.C.C.R.	
	(1981)	(1981)	(1981)		
					G.W.D.
	(1986)	(1986)	(1986)	(1986)	
	to date	to date	to date	to date	

Notes

1. *Session Cases* include (in the "P.C." section from 2000 to 2009) relevant cases on "devolution issues" decided by the Judicial Committee of the Privy Council and (in the "UKSC" section from 2010 onwards) such cases (including those on "compatibility issues") decided by the Supreme Court of the United Kingdom. *Scots Law Times* Reports and *Scottish Criminal Case Reports* carry such cases as part of their normal stock.

2. From January 2008, *Scottish Criminal Law* has been published by W. Green. This monthly periodical contains *inter alia* articles on Scots criminal law and reports of Scots criminal cases (with commentaries). The general editor is Sheriff T. Welsh. Q.C.; a pilot issue was published in October 2007.

3. The same case may be found in more than one set of Reports. It is traditional to regard a *Session Cases* version as superior; but in practice, modern sets of Reports tend to be equally reliable. The S.C.C.R. series has the advantage of having Commentaries written by Sir Gerald Gordon and also (since April 2010) by Sheriff Alastair N. Brown. *Greens Weekly Digest* contains short summaries of cases – not all of which will eventually be reported in full.

4. Reports of cases decided by the European Court of Human Rights may be found most conveniently in the series known as the *European Human Rights Reports* from 1979 to date: the bare reports, including the most modern ones, may be located at the following internet address: *www.echr.coe.int/ECHR/* [accessed June 1, 2012]

5. Bare opinions in the most modern High Court of Justiciary cases may be located at the following internet address: www.scotcourts.gov.uk/opinionsApp/supreme.asp [accessed June 1, 2012]

THE STANDARD SCALE OF FINES

Almost all statutory criminal offences triable by summary procedure refer for their maximum fines to the standard scale. This was introduced by the Criminal Justice Act 1982 (c.48) which, by virtue of s.54, added s.289G to the now repealed Criminal Procedure (Scotland) Act 1975 (c.21). That Act of 1982, by s.53(a), also amended s.289D of the 1975 Act such that by new subss.289D(1) and (1A), the Secretary of State for Scotland might alter the various sums appearing on the standard scale if a change in the value of money seemed to necessitate this. In fact, the present scale values were set by Parliament itself, under s.17(1) of the Criminal Justice Act 1991 (c.53) but now appear in the Criminal Procedure (Scotland) Act 1995 (c.46) at s.225(2) for offences triable only by summary procedure, and, of course, remain alterable by the Secretary of State or Scottish Ministers (see the Scotland Act 1998 (c.46) s.53) in terms of the 1995 Act s.225(4). (See also the more modern Interpretation and Legislative Reform (Scotland) Act 2010 (asp 10) Schedule 1 (definition of inter alia the "standard scale") which simply provides a further reference to the 1995 Act s.225.) The current standard scale values are as follows:

Level 1 .... £200
Level 2 .... £500
Level 3 .... £1000
Level 4 .... £2500
Level 5 .... £5000

Where, however, a statutory offence is triable either on indictment or summary complaint, *and* the maximum fine on summary conviction is specified as one of level 5 on the standard scale, this is now to be read as a reference to the "statutory maximum" (see the Criminal Proceedings etc. (Reform) (Scotland) Act 2007 (asp 6) s.47, and the "Statutory Maximum" below).

THE PRESCRIBED SUM

Many statutory criminal offences refer to the "prescribed sum" as their maximum available fine. That term was introduced by the Criminal Law Act 1977 (c.45) s.63, Sch.11, para.5 which inserted section 289B into the Criminal Procedure (Scotland) Act 1975 (c.21). That provision is now repealed; and the present value of the prescribed sum can be found in section 225(8) of the Criminal Procedure (Scotland) Act 1995 (c.46), as amended by s.48 of the Criminal Proceedings etc. (Reform) (Scotland) Act 2007 (asp 6). The value, shown below, is alterable by the Secretary of State or Scottish Ministers (see the Scotland Act 1998 (c.46), s.53) in the same way indicated above for levels on the standard scale.

Prescribed sum £10,000

THE STATUTORY MAXIMUM

The maximum fine for some statutory offences is expressed as "the statutory maximum". In Scotland this is to be taken as a reference to the "prescribed sum" (see above) by virtue of (1) the Interpretation Act 1978 (c.30), Sch.1 (definition of *inter alia* the statutory maximum, as inserted by the Criminal Justice Act 1988 (c.33), Sch.15, para.58(b)), as amended by the Criminal Procedure (Consequential Provisions) (Scotland) Act 1995 (c.40), Sch.4, para.17(b), and also (2) by virtue of the more modern Interpretation and Legislative Reform (Scotland) Act 2010 (asp 10) Sch.1 (definition of, inter alia, "the statutory maximum").

SCOTTISH CRIMINAL COURTS

1. JP Courts

In 1975 (under provisions of the now repealed District Courts (Scotland) Act 1975) the older Burgh, Justice of the Peace and other minor courts were replaced by "District Courts". These were (as were the courts they replaced) local criminal courts with limited jurisdiction — both territorially and by crime. Under particular provisions of Pt 4 of the Criminal Proceedings etc. (Reform) (Scotland) Act 2007 (asp 6), district courts were themselves replaced by "Justice of the Peace Courts" (known as "JP Courts") according to a timetable drawn up by the Scottish Ministers (see the 2007 Act ss.59 (as amended by the Judiciary and Courts (Scotland) Act 2008 (asp 6) s. 57(2)) and 64, and the Explanatory Notes relative thereto). It was intended that there would be a phased introduction of JP courts, and that both types of court would thus exist simultaneously, for a time at least (see the 2007 Act, s.64). That phased introduction is now complete.

The judges of these courts are called "Justices of the Peace", or JPs for short (see the 2007 Act, s.67). They are usually, although not necessarily (see, e.g. the 2007 Act s.72), non-legally qualified but are always assisted by legally qualified clerks (see the 2007 Act, s.63(3)–(5), noting that subs.(5) is amended by the Judiciary and Courts (Scotland) Act 2008 (asp 6), s.57(3)(b)). Procedure is always summary i.e., on complaint, and non-jury if matters proceed to trial.

In relation to such common law crimes as can be heard in these courts, maximum powers of punishment extend to imprisonment for 60 days or a fine not exceeding level 4 on the standard scale: see the Criminal Procedure (Scotland) Act 1995 s.7(4), (6), (8) (as amended by the 2007 Act, Sch., para.9(2)–(5)), and the Sexual Offences (Scotland) Act 2009 (asp 9), Sch.5, para.2(3); see also above, Appendix C. Statutory Offences, i.e. those which are triable by summary procedure, are punishable according to maxima similar to those which pertain to common law crimes, unless the enactment in question specifically allows a wider or different range (see the 1995 Act, s.7(3),(7), as also amended by the 2007 Act, Sch., para.9(2)(b), (4) and (5)).[1] JPs have important roles to perform in the granting of preliminary and incidental warrants. Where a Stipendiary Magistrate is appointed (see the 2007 Act, ss.74 (as amended by the Judiciary and Courts (Scotland) Act 2008 (asp 6), s.58(3) and the Criminal Justice and Licensing (Scotland) Act 2010 (asp 13), Sch.7, para.80) and 74A (as inserted by the Criminal Justice and Licensing (Scotland) Act 2010 (asp 13), Sch.7, para.81)) and he presides in a JP court, he has the enhanced jurisdiction and powers which a sheriff enjoys in a summary sheriff court (see below, "2." and see the 1995 Act, s.7(5), as amended by the 2007 Act, Sch., para.9 (2)(c), (4) and (5)). The proceedings of JP courts are never reported (except sometimes in the press). Appeal lies only to the Scottish Court of Criminal Appeal.

---

[1] It should be noted that the Scottish Ministers may, by Scottish statutory instrument, modify the maximum powers of JP courts relative to common law crimes or statutory offences, but not so as to exceed six months in prison or a fine of level five on the standard scale: 2007 Act, s.46.

2. Sheriff Courts

Founded probably in the twelfth century, these are local courts (with both civil and criminal law functions). They have limited territorial jurisdiction but extensive jurisdiction by crime. Of the commonly encountered common law crimes, only murders and rapes cannot be dealt with in these courts (see the Criminal Procedure (Scotland) Act 1995 (c. 46), s.3(6), as amended by the Sexual Offences (Scotland) Act 2009 (asp 9) Sch.5, para.2(2), which adds to the list of excluded offences the statutory offences under ss.1(1) and 18 of the 2009 Act). Judges are called sheriffs of various descriptions (*e.g.* sheriff principal, floating sheriff, honorary sheriff) but all are of equal authority in criminal proceedings. With the exception of honorary sheriffs, they must be legally qualified and experienced in practice as either advocates or solicitors. Procedure may be either summary or on indictment (*i.e.* non-jury or jury if matters proceed to trial). In relation to common law crimes, Scottish prosecutors decide whether an offence merits jury trial or not. The choice exercised determines the maximum punishment available, *i.e.* in a solemn or indictment case, five years in prison (or more if the sheriff chooses to remit for sentence to the High Court: see the Criminal Procedure (Scotland) Act 1995, ss.3(3),[2] 195,[3] 219(8)[4]) and/or a fine of any amount; in a summary case, twelve months (see the Criminal Procedure (Scotland) Act 1995, s.5(2)(a) and (d)[5] *or* a fine not exceeding the prescribed sum: see above, Appendix C. Statutory offences (triable summarily, either way, or on indictment only) may be punished according to the maximum laid down by the enactment in question (but if the maximum laid down is more than five years in prison, a sheriff's powers are restricted to five years (the Criminal Procedure (Scotland) Act 1995, s.3(4), (4A),[6] (5)); though, once again, he might choose to remit for sentence to the High Court. Proceedings before sheriff courts are occasionally reported (in S.C.C.R. or in the Sh.Ct. part of S.L.T.). Appeals of whatever nature may be taken only to the Scottish Court of Criminal Appeal.

3. High Courts of Justiciary

Founded as the court of the Justiciar in the twelfth century, a modern high court consists (normally) of one judge. Such a court has territorial jurisdiction throughout Scotland, and can deal with all common law offences (and indeed is the only court competent to conduct rape and murder trials (see the Criminal Procedure (Scotland) Act 1995 (c. 46), ss.1 and 3(2)) in addition to all statutory offences (other than those designated as "summary procedure" only). Judges (who are said to belong to the high court considered as a "college") are professional lawyers of great experience and are called "Lords Commissioners of Justiciary". (They are also the judges of the civil law court known as the Court of Session.) The effective president is titled "the Lord Justice-General", and the vice-president has the title of "Lord Justice-Clerk". Procedure is always solemn (*i.e.* involving a jury if matters proceed to trial). Maximum powers of punishment extend to life in prison and/or a fine of any amount (for common law crimes), or to the maximum laid down in the enactment in

---

[2] As amended by s. 13(1)(*a*) of the Crime and Punishment (Scotland) Act 1997; this amending provision was brought into force on May 1, 2004 by virtue of The Crime and Punishment (Scotland) Act 1997 (Commencement No. 6 and Savings) Order 2004 (SSI 2004/176), art.2: cf. *McGhee v HM Advocate* [2006] HCJAC 87; 2006 S.C.C.R. 712.

[3] As amended by the Crime and Punishment (Scotland) Act 1997, s.13(3), and the Criminal Justice (Scotland) Act 2003 (asp 7), Sch.1, para.2(5) — noting that s.210E of the Criminal Procedure (Scotland) Act 1995, referred to in para.2(5), was inserted by s.1 of the 2003 Act.

[4] As amended by the Proceeds of Crime Act 2002 Sch. 11, para. 29(4).

[5] S.5(2)(d) is amended by the Criminal Proceedings etc. (Reform) (Scotland) Act 2007 (asp 6), s.43.

[6] Subsection (4) is amended, and subsection (4A) is inserted, by virtue of s.13(1)(b) and (c) of the Crime and Punishment (Scotland) Act 1997; and s.13(1)(b) and (c) came into force on May 1, 2004: see The Crime and Punishment (Scotland) Act 1997 (Commencement No. 6 and Savings) Order 2004 (SSI 2004/176), art.2.

question (in the case of statutory crimes). Proceedings are quite regularly reported (in S.L.T., J.C., S.C.C.R. and G.W.D.: see above, Appendix B), and appeals of whatsoever nature lie to the Scottish Court of Criminal Appeal. Difficult matters arising during a trial may be referred (by a process called "certification") to a larger body of High Court judges.

4. The Appeal Court

The Scottish Court of Criminal Appeal (to give it a title which is increasingly in use) was founded in 1926 and consists of a minimum of two or three judges of the high court (considered as a "college" of all high court judges): see the Criminal Procedure (Scotland) Act 1995 (c. 46), ss.103,(1) to (4), and 173.[7] All appeals from all lower courts are dealt with by such a bench of judges (which is called a "full bench" if more than three are present— although the exact number comprising such a full bench has always in modern times been an uneven one). Decisions are by a simple majority (where that is possible) of those present, and such decisions are final unless a bench of two judges cannot agree (see the Criminal Procedure (Scotland) Act 1995, ss.103(3) and 173(2)[8]). There is *no* further appeal to any court sitting in England.[9] (Individual petition to the European Court of Human Rights is, however, recognised by the United Kingdom.)

5. Nobile Officium Court

This court consists of a minimum of three judges of the high court (considered as a "college" of all high court judges). It may provide a solution on an equitable basis where petitioned in relation to a matter of injustice which is truly unexpected and unforeseeable and where the law provides no alternative remedy. (See above, paras. 2–67 and 2–68 of the main text for further information on the *nobile officium*.)

---

[7] As amended by the Protection of Children (Scotland) Act 2003 (asp 5), s.16(6), the Protection of Vulnerable Groups (Scotland) Act 2007 (asp 14), Sch.4, para.20, and the Criminal Justice and Licensing (Scotland) Act 2010 (asp 13), Sch.2, para.11 (noting also para.12(a)(ii)).

[8] As amended by the Protection of Children (Scotland) Act 2003 (asp 5), s.16(6), and the Protection of Vulnerable Groups (Scotland) Act 2007 (asp 14), Sch.4, para.20.

[9] See above, para. 2.13 of the main text for "compatibility and devolution issues" and references or appeals to (formerly) the Judicial Committee of the Privy Council, or (now) to the Supreme Court of the United Kingdom.

INDEX

389

Index

Index